M000010268

CULTURE AND HUMAN SEXUALITY
A READER

EDITED BY

DAVID N. SUGGS

ANDREW W. MIRACLE

BROOKS/COLE PUBLISHING COMPANY
PACIFIC GROVE, CALIFORNIA

Brooks/Cole Publishing Company
A Division of Wadsworth, Inc.

© 1993 by Wadsworth, Inc., Belmont, California 94002.
All rights reserved. No part of this book may be reproduced,
stored in a retrieval system, or transcribed, in any form or
by any means—electronic, mechanical, photocopying, recording,
or otherwise—without the prior written permission of the
publisher, Brooks/Cole Publishing Company, Pacific Grove,
California 93950, a division of Wadsworth, Inc.

Printed in the United States of America

10   9   8   7   6   5   4   3   2   1

Library of Congress Cataloging in Publication Data

Culture and human sexuality / [edited] by David N. Suggs and Andrew W.
   Miracle.
        p.   cm.
      Includes bibliographical references.
      ISBN 0-534-16998-8
      1. Sex customs—Cross-cultural studies. 2. Sex role—Cross-
cultural studies.   I. Suggs, David N., [date].   II. Miracle,
Andrew W.
GN484.3.C83   1993
306.7—dc20   92-27565
                                                  CIP

Sponsoring Editor: *Vicki Knight*
Editorial Assistant: *Heather L. Graeve*
Production Editor: *Linda Loba*
Manuscript Editor: *Barbara Kimmel*
Permissions Editor: *Karen Wootten*
Interior Design: *Lisa Berman*
Cover Design: *Lisa Berman and Susan Haberkorn*
Cover Photo: *Susanne Klinke*
Art Coordinator: *Lisa Torri*
Interior Illustration: *Lisa Torri*
Photo Editor: *Larry Molmud*
Typesetting: *Shepard Poorman Communications Corp.*
Printing and Binding: *Malloy Lithographing, Inc.*

PREFACE

Some of the universal dimensions of human sexuality are readily apparent. *Homo sapiens* everywhere share common biological traits which in turn affect our sexual nature as individuals, and define the reproductive necessities and potentials of our species. Other universal dimensions of human sexuality are less easily recognized, and still others remain to be discovered and described.

The cultural dimension of our sexuality, however, is seldom apparent. The enculturation and socialization processes which help to define our sense of sexuality tend to limit our ability to perceive the role of culture in shaping our sexual selves.

Articulating the dynamics between the biological and the cultural, always a challenging task, is especially difficult with regard to human sexuality. Lacking much definitive research, one is often forced to resort to speculation.

We believe that research on these matters should be encouraged to test basic assumptions and hypotheses related to existing models of culture and human behavior. The perspectives in this volume, some voiced in the early decades of the 20th century and some only recently, provide a foundation for initiating such an examination.

In order to make the knowledge in this volume more accessible, we have organized the discussions around pertinent topics: evolution, life course, gender, family, incest, religion, sexual orientation, sexual variations, and disease-related issues. Each section is preceded by a brief introduction to the subjects and issues covered by the readings that follow. However, these introductions are not intended to summarize the articles that need to be read in full to appreciate the quality of the data, the logic of the argument, or the elegance of the presentation.

We designed this book with two goals in mind. One has been to provide a variety of ethnographic data to illustrate the range of human sexual beliefs and behaviors, and underscore the role of culture in the patterning of sexual ideas and activities. The second goal has been to provide a balance of theoretical positions, demonstrating how social scientists continue to struggle with explanations of human sexuality.

We have tried to include articles that: 1) are readable and not overly technical; 2) provide descriptions or points of view that most readers will find inherently interesting and worthy of discussion; and 3) are challenging intellectually.

In all possible ways we have attempted to provide a balanced set of readings. The volume includes both ethnographic descriptions and theoretical essays. Some articles examine exotic sexual practices among peoples living in faraway places, others examine more familiar North American sexual mores. Several of the articles describe practices that may seem bizarre, unbelievable, even disgusting, because they are in opposition to normative North American beliefs. However, our purpose for including such articles is not merely to titillate, but to stimulate intellectual consideration of the reader's own cultural suppositions.

Our intended purpose is to guide the reader through the variety of cross-cultural sexual expressions and simultaneously provide an appreciation for the cultural logic underlying particular sexual behaviors and beliefs. We also wish to promote an understanding of that which is universal and generalizable with regard to human sexuality. We hope that this collection of articles works toward these ends.

Finally, we wish to acknowledge our indebtedness to our many students and colleagues who have helped bring this work to fruition. The quality of any text depends on the quality of the prepublication reviews by experts around the country. The following individuals have assisted in the development of this book by providing extensive, constructive reviews and suggestions: Professor Ralph Bolton, Pomona College; Professor M. Michele Burnette, Western Michigan University; Professor Dona L. Davis, University of South Dakota; Professor Suzanne G. Frayser, University of Denver; Professor Robert Pollack, University of Georgia; Professor Lynn Stephen, Northeastern University; and Professor Linda D. Wolfe, East Carolina University. In addition, we wish to thank those who have provided comments on and citations for particular parts of the book. These would include our colleagues in the departments of anthropology and sociology at Texas Christian University and Kenyon College, especially Rita Kipp and Howard Sacks; the clerical assistance of Sharon Duchesne and Stacy Smiar; and the assistance of Fred Hay of the Tozzer Library at Harvard University for assistance in locating manuscripts and reference materials. Finally, we wish to thank Managing Editor Vicki Knight, and the other professionals at Brooks/Cole for their patience, courtesy, knowledge, and attention to detail—without their considerable help and expertise this volume would not have become a reality.

David N. Suggs
Andrew W. Miracle

CONTENTS

I

INTRODUCTION

1

ON THE ANTHROPOLOGY OF SEXUALITY

ANDREW W. MIRACLE / DAVID N. SUGGS

Given its commitment to cross-cultural research from a holistic perspective, anthropology has a great deal to offer the multidisciplinary study of human sexuality. Cross-cultural studies can provide a means for examining sexuality and related phenomena outside of the restricted perspectives of Western-based culture. This is essential if we want to understand what it means to be human. If we are limited to the study of North American and western European perspectives, there is little hope of distinguishing between the culturally specific and the universals of human behavior. Of course, anthropologists are not the only social scientists to conduct cross-cultural studies, and works by psychologists and sociologists have been included and listed in the suggested readings in this volume.

When we examine the context of variation in human sexual behavior, it becomes evident that it is largely coincident with the variation in cultures. Thus, it is important to look at human variety as expressed through culture. Too often, cross-cultural studies outside anthropology are based on comparison of "modern" and "traditional" societies (read "Western" versus "non-Western"). The articles in this volume demonstrate that such a distinction is no more useful than is a biological taxonomy of primates versus nonprimates, since there is greater variation within the second category than there is between the two.

By approaching the study of human sexuality holistically—that is, by integrating biological, cultural, historical, and psychological perspectives and methods of research—anthropologists hold forth the promise of gaining a fuller understanding of the subject than is possible through any one of these approaches alone. This seems especially important in the study of sexuality, where there are obvious interactions between genetic, psychological, and sociocultural factors. Recognizing this fact may be critical in our efforts to respond to contemporary social issues related to sexuality.

Most of the early cross-cultural reports on sexuality were ethnographic in nature and were usually incidental to the primary focus of study; that is, anthropologists who spent an extended period of time studying a particular culture would learn of the local customs and beliefs or would observe behaviors related to sexuality. These findings might then be reported in a section of a longer ethnographic account, or they might be published as a separate article. There were a few notable exceptions to this pattern, who deserve mention here.

Edward Westermarck (1891; 1917) devoted a great deal of attention to the cross-cultural study of issues of marriage and family. Today, he is perhaps best remembered for his study of the incest taboo—rules prohibiting an individual from marrying certain kinspeople. However, his writings covered a variety of related topics. His influence on many of the works included in this volume will be obvious to some readers.

After an extended period of participant observation, Bronislaw Malinowski (1927; 1929) reported on the sexual practices and mores of the Trobriand Islanders. Later, Margaret Mead (1930; 1932; 1935; 1949) gained considerable fame for her investigations of gender roles. Works such as those of Malinowski and Mead were controversial because they challenged basic cultural assumptions of Western societies. However, they were also widely read and discussed for decades, perhaps because they titillated, and perhaps because they were harbingers of chang-

ing attitudes in the West. The influence of these individuals also is plain in a number of readings in this volume, and we have included articles from each of them as well.

The single most important and provocative cross-cultural work on sexuality to date has been that of Clellan S. Ford and Frank A. Beach. *Patterns of Sexual Behavior* (1951) treated the subject with such detachment that it could juxtapose the study of human sexuality with that of other animals. This book appeared on the heels of the first Kinsey (1948) report on male sexuality in the United States, which may have affected its impact. It also provided the intellectual—if not the methodological—foundation for the subsequent work of Masters and Johnson (1966).

The cross-cultural study of human sexuality has become more serious and more legitimate during the past 15 years or so. Anthropologists are beginning to provide us with book-length ethnographic studies (see, for example, Gregor, 1985; Herdt, 1986) focused specifically on issues of sexuality. Moreover, there have been attempts to move beyond culture-specific descriptions and to focus more on theoretically-grounded universal models and explanations of human sexuality (see, for example, Reiss, 1986; Symons, 1979).

Given the increased scientific attention to sexuality and the marked increase in anthropological and cross-cultural studies of human sexuality, we may be witnessing the beginnings of a broad-based quest for such knowledge. If this is so, it undoubtedly has been fueled by the many changes in Western societies that have taken place since the 1960s: the pill; the women's movement; the gay and lesbian movement; baby boomers entering middle age; increased knowledge about genetics; new technology for affecting fertility; incidents of herpes and other sexually transmitted diseases, especially AIDS (or HIV). And, related to all of this, is a change in values and beliefs surrounding sexuality held by the majority of citizens in Western societies.

Anthropologists always have tended to respond to such societal concerns. Indeed, it would be naive to assume they have studied human sexuality without any cultural restraints or biases affecting their research. As members of a particular society, anthropologists are responsive to social pressures from within that society. Davis and Whitten (1987) noted this in their extensive review of the anthropological literature on human sexuality. "The specific nature of cross-cultural sex research has typically been a function of how the West views sexuality at a given time" (p. 70).

The research questions and concerns that anthropologists carry into their fieldwork usually have been a reflection of issues in vogue at home. Citing Rubin (1984), Davis and Whitten (1987) state, "Current popular Western concerns with such phenomena as premarital sex, prostitution, child molestation, or homosexuality influence the specific customs that become the focus of research" (p. 70). Even their own work reflects this. Davis and Whitten divide the entire scope of the literature on human sexuality into "Heterosexual Behavior" and "Homosexual Behavior," with the section on homosexual behavior receiving slightly more space in the text than the section on heterosexual behavior. Given that questions about homosexuality are currently a dominant concern in our society, such extensive coverage may seem reasonable.

Culturally biased concerns, however, may blind us to alternative conceptualizations. For example, dividing human sexual behavior into dichotomous realms of heterosexuality and homosexuality may prevent students of human sexuality from appreciating the full variety of sexual behaviors exhibited cross-culturally. Alfred Kinsey (1948) noted that dichotomizing heterosexuality and homosexuality provided an inadequate paradigm for dealing with white, middle-class, collegiate Americans. Thus, surely, it is inadequate for cross-cultural studies.

Our goal in selecting articles for this volume has been to provide a wide coverage of the cultural patterning of sexuality, utilizing early ethnographic studies as well as contemporary theoretical arguments. Although limited by pragmatic considerations, we have attempted to utilize articles that focus on an array of topics related to human sexuality. In addition, we have sought a broad cultural representation, with descriptions of sexual beliefs and practices from around the world (such as Africa, Asia, India, New Guinea, Melanesia, and North America). Finally, although we have a definite perspective to communicate in the concluding chapter, we have tried to provide articles from a variety of theoretical positions. We hope to stimulate discussion, not to stifle it.

We begin this volume with articles that attempt to define sexuality within the context of human nature. For instance, the articles of Part II focus on the evolution of human sexual behavior with the aim of establishing the common biological parameters of human sexual interaction. The authors raise such issues as the sociocultural significance of continuous receptivity among human females (Hrdy), the role of sexual interaction in generalized social bonding (Fox; Hrdy), the myth of female sexual passivity and male sexual aggressivity as biologically based determinants in the evolution of human social organization (Fausto-Sterling), and the evolutionary (that is, adaptive) role of human sexual response (Symons).

Each of the articles in Part III examines some aspect of sexual behavior relative to one's position in the life cycle. Topics covered are the extent to which children's sexual expression is allowed or encouraged (Malinowski), the cultural use of sexuality in distinguishing between child and adult status (Marshall), and the extent to which reproduction is tied to the status of adulthood (Suggs).

The articles in Part IV explore the nature of gender; that is, the extent to which particular and differential sexual behaviors are normatively defined in gender roles. Included are discussions of the differential socialization of men and women in matters sexual, and differential control over sexual access (Shostak; Mead; Margolis & Arnold).

Part V provides discussions on the nature of sexuality within the context of the family. Specifically, sexual behaviors and beliefs as they relate to marriage and family are examined: the impact of economic necessity and ideal family size on population growth and control (Freed & Freed); the relationship between beliefs about procreation and practices of contraception (Schapera); cultural variation in the concept of marriage (Gough); and factors affecting polygyny (White & Burton).

Few questions have engaged anthropologists as thoroughly as has that of the origins of the incest taboo. Why do all cultures define some kin (however these kin may be variously defined) as inappropriate marriage partners? Part VI includes readings that cover both biosocial (Fox) and cultural (Wolf; Lévi-Strauss) explanations for this universality.

The articles in Part VII examine some of the ways in which magico-religious beliefs control and/or promote sexual interaction. Ethnographic studies reveal a continuum of beliefs from cultures that hold only limited marital sexual interaction as valid (Messenger), to those that use sexuality—including intercourse—as a form of worship (Kehoe; Tuck; Nanda).

Part VIII examines the question of how cultures define appropriate sexual partners and sexual identities. All of the articles center on the extent to which homosexual interactions are defined as normative and demonstrate the extent of the need to distinguish homosexual and heterosexual behaviors from identities. The articles included in this section describe: a society in which all males are expected to participate in fellatio for a period in their lives prior to marriage and the subsequent development of sexual relationships with their wives (Herdt); societies in which lesbian relationships are neither devi-ant nor taboo (Blackwood; Gay); and the history of homosexuality in the West (Ariès).

The articles in Part IX explore the range of what is considered cross-culturally to be "normal" sexual behavior. In other words, behaviors normatively labeled unacceptable, weird, or perverted in one society may be tolerated or even positively valued in another. Included are discussions of transvestism and cross-gender behaviors (Callender & Kochems), and the cultural definition of what is considered erotic (Brown).

Part X looks at how cultures define some diseases as sexual, and also looks at how culture and the epidemiology of sexually transmitted diseases are interactive. The articles consider: the origins of syphilis (Baker & Armelagos), culture-bound syndromes and the construction of gender (Levine; Yap), and cultural factors affecting the conceptualization and transmission of AIDS (Ingstad).

We conclude with an attempt to initiate discussions and investigations of a nomothetic anthropology of sexuality. Situated within existing theories of culture, anthropological studies of sexuality primarily have been descriptive. There have been few attempts to explain the nature of human sexuality and its relationship to culture. As Davis and Whitten (1987) noted, "There is need for further open discussions of human sexuality and for the development of uniquely anthropological theories of the relevant phenomena" (p. 88). Part XI echoes this appeal. This concluding chapter is a review of anthropological theories and their implications for the study of sexuality and a call for an explanatory or nomothetic approach to the study of culture and human sexuality.

REFERENCES

Davis, D. L., and R. G. Whitten. (1987). The Cross-Cultural Study of Human Sexuality. *Annual Review of Anthropology, 16*:69–98.

Ford, Clellan S., and Frank A. Beach. (1951). *Patterns of Sexual Behavior.* New York: Harper & Brothers.

Gregor, Thomas. (1985). *Anxious Pleasures.* Chicago: University of Chicago Press.

HERDT, GILBERT H. (1986). *The Sambia: Ritual and Gender in New Guinea.* New York: Holt, Rinehart & Winston.

KINSEY, A. C., W. B. POMEROY, AND C. E. MARTIN. (1948). *Sexual Behavior in the Human Male.* Philadelphia: Saunders.

MALINOWSKI, BRONISLAW. (1927). *Sex and Repression in Savage Society.* Chicago: Meridian Books, New American Library.

MALINOWSKI, BRONISLAW. (1929). *The Sexual Life of Savages in North-Western Melanesia.* London: Routledge & Kegan Paul, Ltd.

MASTERS, WILLIAM H., AND VIRGINIA E. JOHNSON. (1966). *Human Sexual Response.* Boston: Little, Brown.

MEAD, MARGARET. (1930). *Growing Up in New Guinea.* London: Morrow.

MEAD, MARGARET. (1932). *Coming of Age in Samoa.* New York: Morrow.

MEAD, MARGARET. (1935). *Sex and Temperament in Three Primitive Societies.* New York: Morrow.

MEAD, MARGARET. (1949). *Male and Female: A Study of the Sexes in a Changing World.* New York: Morrow.

REISS, IRA L. (1986). *Journey into Sexuality.* Englewood Cliffs, NJ: Prentice-Hall.

RUBIN, G. (1984). Thinking Sex. In C. S. Vance (Ed.), *Pleasure and Danger* (pp. 267–319). Boston: Routledge & Kegan Paul.

SYMONS, DONALD. (1979). *The Evolution of Human Sexuality.* New York: Oxford University Press.

WESTERMARCK, E. (1891). *The History of Human Marriage.* New York: Macmillan.

WESTERMARCK, E. (1917). *Origin and Development of Moral Ideas* (2nd ed.). London: Macmillan.

II

SEX AND THE
NATURE OF HUMANITY

INTRODUCTION

There are many reasons for students of human behavior to begin their studies with an evolutionary perspective. Human beings are unique in a number of ways. For example, only humans utilize symbolic thought and complex language, and it behooves us to know something about how we acquired such obviously advantageous features that allow for the development of culture. Just as important as understanding our uniqueness, however, is the realization that we are not *wholly* or absolutely unique. Molecular biologists tell us that we share roughly 98% of our genetic material with chimpanzees. Those

who doubt whether we can learn anything about humans via the study of our primate relatives would do well to keep that figure in mind.

Furthermore, the general question of the relationship between biology and culture begs an evolutionary analysis. For many years, the academic community has been arguing over whether human behavior is predominantly biological or cultural in origin. The nature versus nurture debate, as it has come to be called, has found fertile ground in studies of human sexuality.

For the most part, anthropology has straddled the fence in this debate, even if the discipline has leaned somewhat toward the nurture side. Clearly, anthropological studies have shown us that biology predisposes us to behave in certain ways. Yet, our cultural heritage in turn limits our potential for physical expression in some ways while expanding it in others. For example, consider crying and smiling. Universally, crying is a sign of unhappiness. Yet, the Tapirapé of Brazil learn to express happiness over the return of long-absent friends by crying; thus, Charles Wagley's title for his excellent ethnography of the Tapirapé is *Welcome of Tears.* Smiling is a universal sign of happiness. Yet, a man approaching you with a smile on his face and a knife in his hand may mean many things other than happiness. So, although all peoples associate crying with sadness and smiling with happiness, each population constructs layers of cultural meaning on these biological predispositions of emotional expression.

Sexual interaction is no different. There are certainly some biological constants—those imposed on us by the anatomy and physiology of our evolutionary heritage—and these are not trivial. The physical aspects of the sexual response cycle are presumably universal. Such constants form the foundation upon which we build meaningful acts of sexuality. The readings in this section, then, consider the relationship between biology and culture, between physical evolution and behavioral expression in human sexuality.

Robin Fox suggests that, in any primate social order, there are three competing groups: (1) established, older breeding males; (2) females and dependent young; and (3) young adult, aspiring males. He argues that male hunting has been central to the evolution of humanity, as has the competition between males for control of the other groups. He further suggests that socially engineered changes to this basic evolutionary pattern may be quite dangerous, even genocidal.

Sarah Hrdy's chapter is an argument that suggests that it is culture, rather than sexual dimorphism, that is primarily responsible for the exploitation of women in human societies. Hrdy's data suggest that female primates are not, in fact, simply passive pawns in the power struggles of males. On the contrary, commonly females are socially competitive and sexually assertive. Hrdy then considers the connections between primate heritage and cultural heritage as they relate to female sexuality among humans.

Anne Fausto-Sterling examines the theoretical problems she finds associated with sociobiological arguments. She considers the theory in general, as well as applying it specifically to sexual studies. Of particular interest are her analyses of sociobiological studies of rape and of reproductive strategies. She argues that sociobiology is implicitly a political science that supports the status quo and an "inherently" nonprovable strategy in the realm of human sexuality research.

Donald Symons explores the relationship between biological evolution and cultural patterning in a discussion of such issues as differential socialization of men and women, women's sexual potential, and individual sexual self-interest. His argument leads to interesting questions about the relationship between data and theory, as well as between the "natural" and the "potential" in human behavior.

REFERENCES

WAGLEY, CHARLES. (1977). *Welcome of Tears: The Tapirapé Indians of Central Brazil.* New York: Oxford University Press.

SUGGESTED READINGS

Biology, Human Evolution, and Primate Sexuality

EMBER, CAROL R., AND MELVIN EMBER. (1984). The Evolution of Human Female Sexuality: A Cross-Cultural Perspective. *Journal of Anthropological Research, 40*:1:202–210.

GOODALL, JANE. (1986). *The Chimpanzees of Gombe: Patterns of Behavior.* Cambridge, MA: Belknap.

MITCHELL, G. (1981). *Human Sex Differences: A Primatologist's Perspective.* New York: Van Nostrand Reinhold.

SMUTS, BARBARA B. (1985). *Sex and Friendship in Baboons.* New York: Aldine.

Cross-Cultural and Ethnographic Studies

FOUCAULT, MICHEL. (1980). *The History of Sexuality.* New York: Vintage.

FRAYSER, SUZANNE G. (1985). *Varieties of Sexual Experience: An Anthropological Perspective on Human Sexuality.* New Haven, CT: HRAF Press.

GREGERSEN, EDGAR. (1991). *The World of Sex: Customs and Beliefs.* Manchester, NH: Irvington.

GREGOR, THOMAS. (1985). *Anxious Pleasures: The Sexual Lives of an Amazon People.* Chicago: University of Chicago Press.

MARSHALL, DONALD S., AND ROBERT C. SUGGS (EDS.). (1971). *Human Sexual Behavior: Variations in the Ethnographic Spectrum.* New York: Basic Books.

PARKER, RICHARD G. (1991). *Bodies, Pleasures, and Passions: Sexual Culture in Contemporary Brazil.* Boston: Beacon Press.

REISS, IRA L. (1986). *Journey into Sexuality: An Exploratory Voyage.* Englewood Cliffs, NJ: Prentice-Hall.

2

THE CONDITIONS OF SEXUAL EVOLUTION

ROBIN FOX

There are various levels of approach to the evolution of sexual behaviour, from that of all sexually reproducing organisms (including plants) to that of a particular species or sub-species. The problems of the latter cannot ignore the more general problems of sexual reproduction, in particular the problem of why there should be sexual reproduction at all. Theoretically, in any competitive situation, sexually reproducing organisms should lose in competition with asexual. Assuming the original situation to be asexual, it remains a constant theoretical problem how sexual reproduction can have arisen, since any favourable mutation in an asexually reproducing organism can be immediately and rapidly replicated, while its sexual competitor must dilute the next-generation effect through breeding. Even inbreeding will not help for sexual competitors, since it is bound to be slower than in the asexual, and also will produce lethal homozygotes.

The only conclusion is that the one advantage of sexual reproduction—increased genetic variation—must have been of such overwhelming advantage in some circumstances that it had a slight competitive edge and became the domi-

SOURCE: From "The Conditions of Sexual Evolution" by R. Fox in *Western Sexuality: Practice and Precept in Past and Present Times* by P. Ariès and A. Béjin (Eds.), pp. 1–13. Copyright © 1985 by Basil Blackwell. Reprinted by permission.

nant partner in an evolutionarily stable strategy. This still raises theoretical difficulties, but it can be seen that recombination might just win out over simple mutation and mitosis under marginal conditions. A "very rapidly changing environment" is often invoked (although this too is vague), as is sibling conflict in offspring.

However started, sexual reproduction, at whatever level, sets certain conditions. Some are minimal. The two sexes must have sufficient contact to exchange genetic material—this is perhaps the only basic requirement. The more complicated this exchange becomes, the more complicated the relations between the sexes. Hermaphroditic species solve the problem by having both sexes in the same organism. In some primitive organisms there is no definite sex distinction. The faster-moving organism of any two by definition becomes "male" because its slightly greater speed implants material in the slower one. But it is relative. In higher organisms this becomes fixed. But the basics are not lost: sperm is faster than ovum.

Exchange not only has to take place, but it then becomes the responsibility of one "sex" to undertake gestation. After that, one or both or neither undertake nurturance depending on the evolutionary path the organism has taken. Usually the "female" undertakes gestation, and either the female alone, the female in consort with other females, the female and the inseminating male, or groups of males and females—and other combinations—undertake a variety of forms of gestation and nurturance. There is no need here to elaborate the many forms this can take throughout sexually reproducing species—this would simply stress their variety.

When we come to the mammals, we also find much variety, but this is constricted by the very characteristics of mammalian adaptation: warm blood, live birth, suckled young, internal gestation, etc. A great deal that can be said about human sexuality can be disposed of as the sexual behaviour to be expected of a large-bodied, large-brained, slow-breeding, omnivorous mammal, with moderate sexual dimorphism and a lack of seasonal breeding. This does not mean

that only one pattern of sexual behaviour is to be expected: it simply sets the limits within which variation will occur. We can best understand this variation by asking what the variables are, and this is difficult since it is all too easy to beg the question by the way it is posed. Rather than take cultural categories of dubious universality like "nuclear family" and "marriage," it is better to take as a starting point an objective unit that is, by definition, universal in the mammals and thus not contaminated by cultural categories. The obvious unit is the mother and her dependent offspring.

It is basic to the definition of a mammal that the young are born live and suckled by the mother. What varies is (a) the amount of investment the mother herself puts into the offspring beyond the necessary minimum, and (b) the degree and nature of the attachment of a male or males to this basic unit (and the relations of the units to each other).

One interesting result of the human development of culture is that we reproduce within our own species almost all the variation found across the mammalian orders—but we shall return to that. For the moment let us consider some mammalian extremes by way of illustration. The hamster lives in solitary burrows, and the contact of males and females is limited to a brief encounter during a brief mating season when a male enters a female's burrow and copulates. The female has a short gestation period; suckles the young for a few weeks, after which they disperse and make their own burrows. This is about the lower limit of mating organization in mammals. Consider then certain ungulates such as gazelles, zebra, deer, etc. They differ considerably in their herd organization, but basically the permanent herd is one of females and young. The males are either solitary for most of the year or rove in all-male bands. During the breeding season (autumn) the males compete, and the winners mate with the herds of females, then depart. The females give birth (in the spring) to precocial young who are soon able to follow and suckle. After one year the males disperse. Take then a band of hunting dogs, or hyenas. The males and females are together all year round whether or not there is a breeding season. There is a complex hierarchy of mating. The females give birth to slow-maturing young and both males and females care for the off-spring in various ways, including the regurgitation of food from kills, etc.

Thus we move from virtually no male-female contact save for the necessary ninety seconds, through seasonal contact, to permanent year-round contact. We also move from absolutely minimal parental care, through care from the mother and the herd females, to care by all the males and females of a complexly organized pack. There are many variations on these themes including monogamous territorial pair-bonding (gibbons, for example) and large male-female troops (howler monkeys)—but the variables we are looking at are what are important. In each case, the crucial variables we have mentioned earlier are affected by circumstances of adaptation to involve the males more or less in the affairs of the females and young. Basically, the males are dispensable. If the female has no need of the male over and above his procreative function—then he is usually dispensed with. The more complex the life of the animal, however, the more likely it is that the male will serve some other function, largely that of defence, but in some carnivores also that of providing meat for the relatively slow-developing young, and even of "teaching" them (if only through imitation) the arts of hunting. The females will also differ in the degree to which they need each other. Female hamsters are solitary, female gibbons live only with their mates, ungulate females congregate in herds, and so on.

One thing is relatively certain: when females congregate to their mutual advantage, they are likely to be related. The same *may* be true of males, but is less likely. To understand this, and consequently to understand the human variant which we call "systems of kinship and marriage," it is necessary to look at the process Darwin christened "sexual selection," and its subsidiary process which has recently found a name as "kin selection."

Basically, sexual selection is a variant of natural selection but one where the struggle is not so much against what Darwin called "the hostile forces of nature," but is the struggle of the sexes for reproductive advantage. This involves the *competition* between animals of one sex—usually the males—for mates from the other, and the *choice* by the other sex—usually the females—of mates from the successful competitors.

We can see this arising from the adaptational exigencies discussed earlier: the females need the males for at least insemination, but also for protection and food perhaps, and therefore they select among them the most able as demonstrated by success in competition. This competition can take many forms, and Darwin was chiefly interested in it as a process which explained extraordinary anatomical developments such as the antlers of the stag, or the huge claw of the fiddler crab. But of course the developments can be purely behavioural and involve "ritualized" fighting displays, for example. What is demanded of the males will differ according to the species. In the ungulates and sea mammals, for example, where the male-female association is purely seasonal and for breeding, displays of superior strength are sufficient. Where the males and females are permanently together, other qualities may be more important—the ability to rise in the male hierarchy, for example, which may involve far more than just strength.

The point about sexual selection however is that *whatever* criterion is used (strength, speed, territory, display, etc.) the result is that only a minority of the males get to breed, while all the females usually succeed in breeding at least once. The reason why it should be this way is easy to see: a male can breed successfully with a large number of females, while a female, once pregnant, is committed to the foetus for anything up to a year, and in many cases well beyond that in suckling and rearing the infant. The "strategies" of the two sexes therefore are bound to differ markedly. It is to the male's reproductive advantage to mate with as many females as possible, while the female must try—since she has only one chance a year—to obtain the "best" genes for herself. The point about "kin selection" in this context is that she is often better off doing this in collaboration with related females—and we must explore why. But first we should note that the above "strategies" will be severely restricted once it is in the male's reproductive interest to invest in his offspring. Where there is no such advantage—as with most ungulates and sea mammals—then the out-and-out competition we have discussed seems to prevail. Where the males must invest in their offspring to ensure their survival, then competition still exists but becomes more subtle and complicated, and the male must pay more attention to fewer females. This becomes more important with the primates, the social carnivores, and in particular with man. It results, for example, in much less extreme sexual dimorphism and a lack of those highly specialized anatomical features that first led Darwin to enquire into this mode of selection.

But we must return to the question of relatedness or kinship since this concerns genes and this is where selection is in fact at work. And here, if I speak of the "strategies" of the genes, or of the animals, it should be needless to point out that conscious strategies are not implied. (Otherwise well-educated people, however, still seem to miss this point.) It is just sometimes easier to speak metaphorically of "intentions" rather than to spell out the whole argument in correct "selection" language. Strictly speaking, the only goal of the genes is to produce replicas of themselves. Organisms are their agents. However, identical genes are not confined to one organism, but are shared by related organisms in declining proportion as the degree of relatedness becomes more distant. There is always, therefore, a group of closely-related organisms sharing a large number of identical gene-replicas: a kind of small gene-pool. Parents and children are the closest in relatedness, together with groups of siblings. Now the "groups of females"

that we have been discussing above are almost always mother-daughter extended families; groups of female kin, closely related. If we view these, then, as a small pool of identical genes seeking to replicate themselves, we can see how, under certain evolutionary circumstances, they will do better if they act in concert than alone, and better still if they can choose "superior" male genes to combine with their own to produce a new generation.

In earlier studies of sexual selection, the emphasis was heavily on the male competition and indeed selection does seem to work most spectacularly here. But it has more recently been seen that *female choice* may well be the ultimate determinant of the route selection will take. The males, as it were, exhaust themselves on competition, then the female groups pick out the winners as studs. Once it is realized that there can thus be considerable difference in reproductive success between the different female groups, the full dynamics of the system can be understood.

The females' strategy has to be to pick the "best" male, whatever the criteria. If a group of females can become inseminated by superior male genes, not only do their female offspring get the immediate advantages, but the chance of their "sons" inseminating many groups of females itself increases. Thus the genes of the original female kin-group will spread in the total population more successfully than those of rival groups. If we paraphrase Samuel Butler's famous statement (that a chicken is the egg's way of making another egg) and say that a male is the females' way of making more females (or that a male is the female kin-group's way of making another female kin-group) then we are getting close to the heart of the sexual selection process. But we have to see it, ultimately, as the strategy of the genes to produce replicas of themselves.

We cannot here go into all the conditions that produce such "kin-coalition" behaviour and its consequent interesting mode of sexual selection—indeed they are not all known, although the most plausible candidate is advantages in foraging. It is enough that they *are* produced, and very important to us because the primates, our own order, show strong tendencies in this direction in many species including our own. The primates, however, unlike the ungulates we have been discussing, live in groups where there is year-round contact between males and females. This factor—shared for example by the social carnivores—exercises a profound influence. It does not stop the processes of either sexual selection or kin selection, but modifies them, and this modification is the first step on the road to human sexual behaviour.

It is as if the ungulate females, instead of meeting briefly with the successful males in the mating season, had decided to incorporate them permanently into the group, and what is more, to amalgamate several female kin-groups into a larger group. The reasons why this occurs in some species (like the primates) are variable, with foraging success, the need for the defence of the females, and, with the carnivores, the need for provisioning the relatively slow-maturing young by the males, as leading contenders. The higher primates are vegetarian (baboons and chimpanzees hunt only sporadically) and do *not* provision their young who must find their own food once weaned. Protection therefore seems the most likely reason. Now the number and combination of males incorporated, and the resulting modes of social organization are very varied across species, and we can only here give a highly summary sketch of some very general features. At one extreme, there will only be one male incorporated into one group of females: at the other there will be many males incorporated into an equally large number of female families. Monogamous pairs—as with the gibbon—can be seen as a limiting case where, for ecological reasons, a territory will only support one female and one male. With the orang-utan, females establish ranges, and males attempt to monopolize several of these females without staying permanently with any one. With chimpanzees, groups of males on the one hand, and groups of female families on the other, form a forest "band," thus

bringing the males more closely into the group—but still as a separate "block" of the social system. With common baboons and macaques, female families, hierarchically arranged, are arrayed against a hierarchy of individual males. With hamadryas baboons and geladas, herds are composed of "harems" each under the control of one male. Gorillas live in bands with one dominant male, some younger males and females with young.

The "law of the dispensable male" operates here. Under extreme conditions, for example, macaque groups "shed" males until there is only one, while under lush conditions there may be a large number. Those species characterized by "one-male groups" or harems are most like the ungulates: males compete in various ways and only some get harems. In the "multi-male groups" it is different: the competition between the males is there, but since they stay together, they must settle it by arranging themselves in a hierarchy. Similarly the female families are hierarchically organized, with the higher-ranking families tending to mate more frequently with high-ranked males. The "sons" of these families in turn, are more likely than others to become high-ranking and thus perpetuate the process. Thus we can see how the ungulate "seasonal" pattern has been, as it were, "collapsed" here into a hierarchically organized year-round collaboration of males and female families.

The major modification this produces in the sexual selection process is in the criteria for "best genes" in the male. The one-male group species are most like the ungulates, with, for example, greater sexual dimorphism and special anatomical features for the male (the mane and "cape" of the hamadryas for example). The multi-male species show less sexual dimorphism and specialization, and capacities for group-living and organization are obviously being selected for rather than mere strength or endurance or display. High-ranking female groups, for example, will often not tolerate males who are too aggressive and competitive, and these leave the group and become solitaries.

Is there, however, a basic primate pattern in this wide range of breeding/social systems? It is important to establish if there is, since it would be the pattern that characterized our own ancestors before the "transition to humanity" took place: it would be the raw material of hominid society: the breeding system that became the "social system." I think there is a pan-primate pattern in the group-living primates which involves the dynamics of relationship, or what we have called "strategies," that exist between the three major "blocks" or interest groups of the system: (a) the established males, (b) the females and young, and (c) the peripheral or aspirant males. The "established" males are those who have access to the breeding females by virtue of having obtained harems, moved up in the hierarchy, maintained territories—or whatever is demanded. Against them are arranged the—usually younger—males who aspire to breeding status. The females are between these two groups "supplying" young males to the peripheral groups, and seeking the "best genes" from the mature males. The possible combinations are large, but the basic pattern is there. It is not all that different from the basic pattern of the other group-living mammals, with the exception that the males are permanently incorporated, and we have seen that this itself strongly influences the criteria for "best male."

If this then is the basic pattern of the vegetarian primate, we have next to ask ourselves what the crucial change was that produced the hominid line and finally ourselves. Our ancestors would have been vegetarian primates following some variant of the pattern—most likely, given the close genetic relationship with the chimpanzee and the similarity of ecological adaptation to the common baboon/macaque, some version of the "multi-male group with female kin-group" system. What is incontestable now in view of the East African evidence is that somewhere between two and three million years ago this ancestor took up hunting and scavenging on a large scale. It was already bipedal, but the change from sporadic meat eating to a diet incorporating more than 50 per cent meat meant a radical change in the relations between the sexes and between the old and the young males. It is these changes that *created* man as we know him, for by the advent of *Homo erectus* the irreversible change had taken place—as measured by stature and brain size. And this is the crucial fact: the unprecedented rapidity of the evolution of the hominid brain (a threefold increase inside two million years) occurred exactly during the period when the scale of hunting increased—and increased in proportion. That is, exactly as the size and scale of prey increased, so did the size and complexity of the brain.

The causal factors are not too difficult to see here, but the consequences for the internal process of sexual selection are harder to spell out. Let us take it from the male point of view. In the "winner-take-all" type of competition sheer strength is what counts; in the primate "hierarchical" competition it is more control and timing; in the hunting situation it is obviously the ability to provide meat—to provision the females and children. But it is much more complex than this: strength, control, and hunting ability cumulate in importance, but many other qualities must accrue to a successful dominant male in a co-operative hunting society. Leadership, organizational ability, and even such burgeoning talents as eloquence, shamanistic skills, etc. eventually come to characterize "dominance" and hence breeding advantage. All this is of particular importance in hominid evolution since the evolving hominids did not have millions of years of carnivorous experience in their genes as do the social carnivores. They could not, for example, use their natural weapons in hunting but had to invent weapons; they could not regurgitate food for the young but had to carry it back to the home base—bipedalism and the freeing of the hands are of great importance here. But the major point for the males is that they had to develop intelligent solutions to the hunting challenge in all its facets; there was therefore a premium on intelligence over and above the other skills.

From the female point of view, the essential change lay in the division of labour forced on them by the new hunting way of life. Essentially, hominid females were the producers of vegetable food—for the omnivorous diet—for meat they depended on the males. Equally, the males depended on the females for two essential services that did not exist in the primate "baseline" situation: gathering and preparation of vegetable food, and care and provision for the more slowly maturing young. (The young were maturing more slowly because of progressive neoteny that was a consequence of bipedalism, foetal birth, and the requirements of the larger brain to grow outside the mother's body.)

The requirement that the males "invest" more heavily in their young is underlined here—as opposed to the primate situation where the weaned young fend for themselves. The strategy of the foraging female kin-groups therefore must have been not only to acquire the "best genes" (which now meant "best hunters"), but to hold on to the males in order to continue having the infants provisioned with the now necessary meat.

Overall what happened to the hominid breeding/social system in the period between two and a half and one million years ago, was that the relations between the three "blocks" of the system were revolutionized, although building on the old base. We *must* understand that a new creature was being forged here in the crucible of natural and sexual selection: a hunting ape-man. And in evolutionary terms it was a rapid change. The tensions therefore between the basic pattern and the new demands made upon it by the new creature are at the heart of the current human condition. The three blocks still had to accommodate each other and make demands on each other, but this was under ever changing conditions. The major change, as we have seen, was in the origin of the division of labour between the sexes, which revolutionized not only the relations between the two sexes, but also the relations within the sexual groups.

The burden of this clearly fell—as is always the case in sexual selection—on the young or peripheral males. The conditions whereby they could rise in the hierarchy and become effective breeders were constantly made more complex. In turn, the older, established males found themselves faced by well-armed and capable youngsters. Thus the struggle within the male sex between established and aspirant males must have been intensified at the same time as the females were making demands for permanent provisioning from the males.

The revolutionary response to this, judging from the end product—that is, the social/breeding system of *Homo sapiens*—was the dual invention of initiation and alliance. There was no way, once the status of *Homo* was achieved, that the free-for-all competition of the males could continue. On the other hand, the rapidity of brain evolution could not have occurred without a highly assortative mating system in which only selected male genes were transferred to successive generations. The consequence was the evolution of a system geared to the control of the young males' access to the breeding system and the control of the allocation of mates by the older males.

The role of systems of initiation is easy to see in this. They are direct systems of constraint and selection, and have the psychological function of "identification with the aggressor" (Freud) ensuring that the young males will identify with the older males. Since access to the breeding system is usually delayed until after initiation—and even service as a warrior—this ensures a "pool" of young females for the old polygynists. The young males will of course try to circumvent this with illicit sexual liaisons. The higher the age of marriage of males is driven, and the younger the age at which females are betrothed, the greater the chances of polygyny flourishing. The most widespread marriage pattern in human society is "the polygyny of the powerful" (75 per cent of human societies), and even in those either officially or "ecologically" monogamous, the powerful usually enjoy extended sexual access to young females or at least a monopoly of them for marriage purposes.

What is not so easily seen is that human kinship systems—again building on the already existing kin-selection tendencies—are equally a response to the control of younger males by the older and/or more powerful males. (Originally this would have been a pure gerontocracy. With the advent of rank and class society, it was power rather than *simply* age that counted, although within classes the young-old clash continued.) It was obviously impossible for the old "winner-take-all" system of mating to endure under the changed conditions of sexual division of labour and co-operative hunting. Freud's vision of a parricidal (and possibly fratricidal) primal horde is probably near the truth. Mitigation already existed in the selective influence of the female kin-groups, and this must have been further modified by the need of the males to form alliances both within and across bands, and of the females to enjoy some security of tenure with selected males. Among the primates both alliance, in the sense of permanent mating, and kinship, in the sense of groups based on common descent, existed—but not in the same system. The human innovation was to combine these in one system, by using the definition of relatedness to define the possibilities of alliance. (It was *not* the incest taboo. Humans, like most sexually reproducing species, avoid an excess of close inbreeding anyway. The taboo is simply confirmation of this, with certain uniquely human ingredients.)

Thus systems of "kinship and marriage" arose to re-define the relationships and strategies between the three blocks. The major innovation was that kinship not only *linked* the members of the three blocks together, but it was used to define the mode of *allocation* of spouses: that is, effectively, the distribution of young females among the males. It is then exogamy—rightly seen by Lévi-Strauss as a positive system of exchange—that is the truly human innovation. What is not usually perceived is that kinship systems do not simply ensure the exchange of

spouses, but that they are "rigged" to ensure that the choice of mates open to the younger generation of males is made dependent on choices made by the older generation, thus controlling their access to the mating system through the rules themselves. The onus of control is therefore thrown on to the collectivity, and collective representations assume their role as "constraints" on the behaviour of the young. Where the kinship system does not do this through its rules, the older (or more powerful) males have to intervene directly in the marriage choices and opportunities of the young. I have stressed the males, but of course the co-operative female kin-groups are not silent in this matter of with whom their members mate, and often exercise considerable influence—as the basic pattern would predict—although this is highly variable. Very rarely do the interests of these groups coincide, and the ensuing struggle is what lies behind the dynamics and high degree of variability of human mating and social systems. Many other factors—of ecology, economics, politics, class, power, ideology and technology (e.g., the pill)—intervene to present new challenges to the basic pattern. But as long as assortative mating must take place to ensure the production of future generations, the basic pattern must be respected and the new conditions have to come to terms with it. The much vaunted "nuclear family," for example, is simply one possible kind of accommodation that occurs, predictably, in certain societies. It is certainly not the basic pattern itself, as has often been stated by social scientists.

In this evolutionary perspective, therefore, we are able to take a new look at historical developments in the relations between the sexes, and one of the most important lessons is that we must view this always as a triangular relationship: established males; females and young; aspirant males. Young females currently are exercising more free choice than ever before; the old, as a result of the pill, have lost considerable control. It will be interesting to see to what extent the basic pattern can reassert itself. I believe it shows signs of doing so and that many things—such as teenage pregnancy rates, growing divorce rates, female solidarity movements, etc.—are probable signs of a reassertion of the pattern rather than either pathologies or results of raised consciousness. They are only one or other of these if one takes the "nuclear family" as a starting point, which it is not, but rather one possible outcome.

It will be interesting for historians and anthropologists to look again at their data which I believe can be reconciled in this framework. The work, for example, of Lévi-Strauss and Ariès makes good sense within this framework of analysis; both are dealing with aspects of the basic pattern. This is not to say that the basic scheme can never be sundered—but it is the cause of our present behaviour; it is what produced us and, as Freud saw, what we are fated to reproduce. Our brains, physiology, and behaviour are the living memory of its evolution; our societies the various outcomes of the possibilities it leaves open to us. We could depart totally from it—and we show great danger of so doing. But it would then be doubtful if what remained could still be considered "human society"—or whether it would last.[1]

[1]Full references for all the evidence behind the summary assertions made here can be found in my book *The Red Lamp of Incest* (University of Notre Dame Press, 1983).

3

A DISPUTED LEGACY

SARAH HRDY

I [Boswell] argued that the chastity of women was of much more consequence than that of men, as the property and rights of families depend upon it.
Surely [said Boswell's ladyfriend] that is easily answered if a woman does intrigue but when she is with child. [Boswell could not answer this, but it made him feel "uneasy."]

DIARY OF JAMES BOSWELL, 1774–1776

An assertive, temporarily insatiable female sexuality, epitomized by the seemingly nymphomaniac solicitations of a Barbary macaque in estrus—what earthly relevance does the conduct of this monkey have for understanding her culture-bearing cousin, whose solicitations are sedate, self-conscious, often elaborate in their subtlety and indirection? We can imagine sound evolutionary reasons for Nature to cultivate an assertive sexuality in her prehuman daughters— we examined some of these reasons in Chapter 7—but to trace natural selection's legacy to the present, through the intervening biological and historical vicissitudes, is even more difficult than making an after-the-fact inventory of the contents of an intricate estate which at different times has been owned by a variety of people. Some of its heirs might wish to know which are its initial assets and which were more recent acquisitions. Which assets were abandoned along the way as ill-suited to prevailing conditions? The heirs here, of course, are women, and the legacy is the biological infrastructure of their sexuality.

May it please the court, there are circumstances in this case which are unusual. Ownership of the legacy is not in question. Disputation

SOURCE: Reprinted by permission of the publishers from *The Woman That Never Evolved* by Sarah Hrdy, Cambridge, Mass.: Harvard University Press, Copyright © 1981 by the President and Fellows of Harvard College.

arises when we attempt to determine just exactly *what* is owned, and how it was acquired. A more awkward litigation can scarcely be imagined. First, the court will be asked to admit evidence for events which have no surviving witnesses or documentation. Surrogate depositions will be taken from witnesses who watched distant relatives. We are asked to regard living nonhuman primates as stand-ins for our common ancestors who lived twenty million years ago, and the perils of this assumption must be acknowledged. It is entirely feasible to examine clinical evidence for female sexual responsiveness in other primates, but when we extrapolate from these laboratory depositions to the lives of primates who lived in the forests and savannas where the relevant transactions actually took place, the record goes hazy. Halfway through the litigation, the court recorder is asked to skip across vast tracts of evolutionary time and to substitute for hard evidence about our surrogate ancestors a haphazard collection of ethnographic and historical hearsay about our actual ancestors and very near relations—accounts which describe the way woman's sexual proclivities have been perceived in various societies. But it has to be recognized that such accounts do not necessarily tell us anything about the legacy itself, woman's sexuality.

Then we close the depositions and turn to a title search through the fossil evidence. These proceedings are even more disappointing than makeshift testimony and hearsay: the record is mostly blank. The record for the longest and most critical period in the whole litigation, the period from twelve to five million years before the present, is absent entirely. Even when our genealogy becomes populated with some of the better known hominids, beginning about five million years ago, the most we can say about these owners of the legacy, the australopithecines, is that they walked on two feet but otherwise resembled chimpanzees: their brains were similar in size, they had large front teeth, and the disparity in size between the two sexes was at least as great—quite probably greater—than is the case in contemporary human populations.

Jurors, you may grumble at the poverty of such evidence and at the awkward transitions from monkey facts to human ideologies. But recognize that the alternative is to abandon hope altogether of establishing what the legacy consisted of. Above all, keep in mind, lest you leap to false conclusions, that no party in this litigation is suggesting that people are nothing but sophisticated monkeys. Culture-bearing monkeys maybe, but that seven letter word spells a world of difference.

"Sex," Bronislaw Malinowski wrote after he had traveled among Pacific Islanders, "is not a mere physiological transaction . . . it implies love and love-making; it becomes the nucleus of such venerable institutions as marriage and the family; it pervades art and it produces its spells and magic. It dominates in fact almost every aspect of culture."[1] Yet it stretches the fabric of culture beyond its true limits to assert, as another very eminent anthropologist, Clifford Geertz, has, that sexuality is merely "a cultural activity sustaining a biological process."[2]

For women, the physiology of sex is, to be sure, profoundly influenced by socially conditioned expectations, their attitudes toward men and marriage, and their self-image. Even responses such as sexual climax, which ought to be physiologically straightforward, are contingent in real life upon individual attitudes and cultural practices. Arapesh women, for example, rarely experience orgasm—no concept of a female's sexual climax even exists for them—whereas among the Mundugumor or Samoans the woman's orgasm is considered a routine part of sex.[3] A single culture—our own, for example—can change rapidly. Consider the pendulum swing in less than three decades between the women reported on by Alfred Kinsey in 1948 and those surveyed by *Cosmopolitan* magazine in the fall of 1980. In Kinsey's study, 3 percent

[1]Bronislaw Malinowski, *The Sexual Life of Savages* (New York: Harcourt, Brace and World, 1929), p. xxiii.
[2]Clifford Geertz, "Sociosexology," *New York Review of Books,* January 24, 1980, p. 4.
[3]Margaret Mead, *Male and Female* (New York: William Morrow, 1968), p. 219.

of girls had had intercourse by age 15. By age 24, 8 percent of young wives had engaged in extra-marital affairs; the incidence rose to 20 percent by age 35. Slightly less than half of the women surveyed reported that they usually had orgasms, 8 percent reported that they never did. Of the women who responded to the *Cosmopolitan* questionnaire in 1980, 20 percent had had intercourse by age 15. Among married women 18–34, 50 percent had been unfaithful, while among women older than 35 the rate of infidelity rose to nearly 70 percent. For those having intercourse on a regular basis, 60 percent responded that they usually or always achieved orgasms; only one percent responded that they never did. The most striking change in the last thirty years has been in the number of lovers a woman is likely to have. Some 30 percent of the *Cosmopolitan* sample have had 2 to 5 lovers; 10 percent have had more than 25.[4]

Few generalizations about sexuality apply cross-culturally. But one of the few that does hold is that couples engaged in sexual activity tend to seek privacy. To get their information, ethnographers and social scientists must rely mainly on interviews, often with self-selected volunteers or paid informants. Only very recently has anyone collected rigorous data amenable to verification by repeating the study in a laboratory. No one has undertaken a study in which women were followed for years and asked about their sexual experiences. Even the suggestion to participate in such a study would probably be shocking to a substantial portion of the very cross-section of humanity whose participation would be essential for validity of the study. In sum, we have no information about the sexual lives of women comparable in its validity to what is known about savanna baboons.

When a paucity of information is combined with poignant interest, controversy is the inevitable result. So it is scarcely surprising that the few authors writing in any detail about the evolution of women's sexuality have come to radically different verdicts. At one extreme, it has been argued that all women have inherited a strong, innate sexual drive from their primate forebears; the only reason this fact of life is not acknowledged is that male-dominated, patriarchal cultures suppress it to make their control of women more effective. At the other pole, it has been argued that sexual feeling in women has no evolutionary importance. Rather, male sexual drive has been critical in human evolution, and desire in females is merely vestigial, a by-product of the masculine phenomenon.

Mary Jane Sherfey, a feminist psychiatrist, addressed women's sexuality in attempting to bring a revised Freudian theory in line with more recent findings of sex research and biology. The cornerstone of her evolutionary argument was the assertion that "throughout primate evolution, selective pressure has always tended in the direction of favoring the development of the longer duration of the intense orgasmic contractions in the females" in order to "remove the largest amount of venous congestion in the most effective manner."[5] This emphasis on the medical value of the orgasm has a certain venerable provenance. It can be traced at least to Galen in the second century, and it has persisted, passing in and out of favor, since then. Catholic women in seventeenth-century France were permitted by medical opinion to masturbate to orgasm should the husband ejaculate and withdraw before she was satisfied—but not as a concession to pleasure. Rather, it was believed that her orgasm would contribute to producing strong, healthy children.[6]

Apart from this vague notion that orgasms are therapeutic, Sherfey offered no evolutionary

[4]A. C. Kinsey, W. B. Pomeroy, C. E. Martin, and P. H. Gebhard, *Sexual Behavior in the Human Female* (Philadelphia: W. B. Saunders, 1953). Linda Wolfe, "The sexual profile of that cosmopolitan girl," *Cosmopolitan,* September 1980, pp. 254–265.

[5]Mary Jane Sherfey, *The Nature and Evolution of Female Sexuality* (New York: Vintage Books, 1973). pp. 29, 80. A shorter version of this book appeared earlier in the *Journal of the American Psychoanalytic Association* 14:28–128 (1966).
[6]Changes through time in western attitudes toward female sexuality are examined in Lawrence Stone's monumental book, *The Family, Sex and Marriage in England 1500–1800* (New York: Harper and Row, 1977), esp. p. 489.

rationale for her proposition that "to all intents and purposes, the human female is sexually insatiable in the presence of the highest degree of sexual satiation."[7] Her ideas were enthusiastically endorsed by some feminists and social scientists, ignored or rejected by others.[8] Her reconstruction of human evolution, which was definitely idiosyncratic, fueled the criticisms. She accepted the radical feminist vision, adapted from nineteenth-century antecedents, of a matriarchal stage in human evolution. This brazen age was supposedly an era in which women engaged unrestrainedly in sexual activity. To maintain this hypothesis, however, it is necessary to brush aside the troubling fact that there is virtually no archaeological or ethnographic evidence for it.

Lacking support from either biology or the social sciences, Sherfey's evolutionary views have not caught on, and her belief in the fundamental sexual nature of women, though not necessarily wrong, has been neglected. One of her harshest critics (but also someone who has read her work carefully) is Donald Symons, an anthropologist-turned-sociobiologist, who has recently written:

It is difficult to see how expending time and energy pursuing the will-o'-the-wisp of sexual satiation, endlessly and fruitlessly attempting to make a bottomless cup run over, could conceivably contribute to a female's reproductive success. On the contrary, insatiability would markedly interfere with the adaptively significant activities of food gathering and preparing and child care. Moreover, to the extent that insatiability promoted random matings, it would further reduce female reproductive success by subverting female choice.

Symons' case rests on the conclusion that "in a natural habitat, females appear to vary relatively little in the number of children they produce during their lifetime" and that females cannot improve their statistics "by copulating with many males."[9] The strict measure of a woman's evolutionary success will be relatively constant in a given environment and not much affected by her sexual conduct. Therefore, her sexuality is immaterial to her evolutionary history.

Why then do women ever experience sexual desire, much less orgasm? Symons argues that women have sexual feelings for much the same reason that men have nipples: nature makes the two sexes as variations on the same basic model. From this perspective, female orgasms occur as "a by-product of mammalian bisexual potential: orgasm may be possible for female mammals because it is adaptive for males."[10]

If Sherfey's ideas smack of Galen and of France under Louis XIV, Symons' has antecedents not only in Aristotle but in the early nineteenth-century denial that women have any sexual drive whatever. The Victorian belief, which gained credence just as evolutionary thought was also taking hold, was a reversal of the view prevailing just a century earlier: that women had an "exuberant and inexhaustible appetite for all variety of sexual pleasure." By the second half of the nineteenth century, the popular medical authority William Acton could assert with confidence that "the majority of women (happily for them) are not much trou-

---

[7]Sherfey, *Evolution of Female Sexuality* (note 5), p. 112.

[8]The Harvard psychologist George Goethals was one who welcomed Sherfey's ideas. I first heard of her work in a lecture by him. In his article, "Factors affecting permissive and nonpermissive rules regarding premarital sex," in *Studies in the Sociology of Sex*, ed. J. M. Henslin (New York: Appleton-Century-Croft, 1971), pp. 9–26, Goethals referred to "the brilliant paper by Mary Jane Sherfey, which . . . abolishes once and for all the whole psychoanalytic interpretation of 'female sexuality.'" Sherfey's writing was similarly credited by Shere Hite in *The Hite Report* (New York: Macmillan, 1976). But Sherfey's ideas were not universally acclaimed. A later issue of the *Journal of the American Psychoanalytic Association,* which had originally published Sherfey's ideas, was devoted to papers refuting them. The major criticisms appeared in a paper by Marcel Heiman, "Discussion of Sherfey's paper on female sexuality," *Journal of the American Psychoanalytic Association,* July 1968. A highly critical book review by Irving Singer appeared in the *New York Review of Books* 19(9):29–31 (November 30, 1972). Similarly, there is more than a hint of sarcasm in Donald Symons' rejection of "Sherfeyian" females. "The sexually insatiable woman is to be found primarily, if not exclusively, in the ideology of feminism, the hopes of boys, and the fears of men." According to Symons, "Sherfey is a sexual radical for whom paradise is endless, orgiastic sexual indulgence." From *The Evolution of Human Sexuality* (Oxford: Oxford University Press, 1979), pp. 92, 94.

[9]Symons (note 8), pp. 89, 91, 192.
[10]Symons (note 8), p. 92.

bled with sexual feelings of any kind," and as late as 1906 the doctrine persisted that "in many [women] the appetite never asserts itself."[11]

The notion that woman's orgasm is "in an evolutionary sense a 'pseudo-male' response"[12] appears to be a vestige of Victorian thought on the subject. But it is buttressed by a kind of evolutionary utilitarianism that has a more modern flavor: female orgasm is unpredictable, unreliable. An organ—or in this case a physiological mechanism—that is important to fitness (or reproductive success) and properly adapted to its task should work better than that. As evidence in support of this argument, it is often argued that the orgasm in human females is an evolutionary oddity—a relatively new phenomenon arising from the heightened sexuality of human males and not a legacy from their remote maternal ancestors. Animal females, it is said, do without.

Physiologically detectable, psychologically impressive, the female orgasm has become the central issue in a long debate about the nature and evolution of female sexuality. We need to consider this psychophysiological response in some detail.

Nobody really denies that orgasm occurs sporadically among women. Margaret Mead pointed out the differences among both individuals and cultures in this regard. She referred to the climax as a "potentiality" not always realized.[13] Yet it is clear that the capacity for orgasm is universal. One of the insights gained from the research of Masters and Johnson is that virtually all women, sufficiently prepared and stimulated, do have orgasms, but not necessarily from intercourse or from intercourse alone.

Surveys conducted by Seymour Fisher, Shere Hite, and others indicate that for the majority of American women clitoral stimulation—manual, oral, or otherwise—is necessary for orgasm, and that intercourse does not suffice in the absence of clitoral stimulation. From these surveys, it

appears that only about a quarter of women regularly climax from intercourse alone.[14] Consequently, Hite characterizes "conventional" orgasms, achieved through indirect stimulation of the clitoris during intercourse, as, at best, a "Rube Goldberg scheme"—on the whole impractical.

In strictly anatomical terms, then, the human clitoris is the core of the problem. Evolution is virtually always a compromise between preexisting structures and selection favoring improvement. Yet even as a compromise, women's sexual machinery seems peculiarly inefficient. On the other hand, it is not a new invention; it is widespread among mammals and nearly universal among primates (though with widespread variation in size, design, and placement). It is inconspicuous in the tree shrew but clearly detectable in lemurs, lorises, and virtually all the higher primates. It may be somewhat more prominent in species such as baboons and macaques which tend to live in troops with many males, but otherwise the clitoris is surprisingly variable in species of Old World monkeys. Among some baboons, the fold of skin surrounding the clitoris expands into a pendulous lobe during estrus. In the apes, particularly the gibbon and chimpanzee, the clitoris is well developed; it is larger than the human organ, both absolutely and relative to body size.[15]

No function other than sexual stimulation of the female has ever been assigned to the clitoris,[16] and this is very likely the reason that it has been a subject either tabooed or ignored in

---

[11]Stone (note 6), p. 676.
[12]Desmond Morris, *The Naked Ape* (New York: McGraw-Hill, 1967), p. 66.
[13]Mead (note 3), p. 219.

[14]Twenty percent of 300 married women interviewed by Fisher, and some 30 percent of those responding to the Hite survey, said that they could regularly climax from intercourse alone, without additional clitoral stimulation. See review of these studies in Hite (note 8).
[15]Larry McFarland, "Comparative anatomy of the clitoris," in *The Clitoris,* eds. Thomas Lowry and Thea Snyder Lowry (St. Louis: Warren H. Green, Inc., 1976), pp. 24–34.
[16]"The clitoris is a unique organ in the total of human anatomy. Its express purpose is to serve both as a receptor and transformer of sensual stimuli. Thus, the human female has an organ system which is totally limited in physiological function to initiating or elevating levels of sexual tension. No such organ exists within the anatomic structure of the human male." William Masters and Virginia Johnson, *Human Sexual Response* (Boston: Little, Brown and Co., 1966), p. 45.

textbooks, even very recent accounts.[17] Are we to assume, then, that this organ is irrelevant—a pudendal equivalent of the intestinal appendix? It would be safer to suspect that, like most organs—including even the underrated appendix—it serves a purpose, or once did. But the purpose, as noted above, appears to be transmitting the pleasurable sexual stimulations that sometimes culminate in orgasm. And that brings us full circle: to rationalize the existence of a clitoris in evolutionary terms, we must show that female orgasms confer some reproductive advantage on the creatures experiencing them.

Orgasm was originally a general term for any intense excitement, or merely a dispassionate noun meaning inflammation or swelling, as in either a wound or a ripe fruit. Nowadays, when applied to American women, orgasm refers to a highly variable, typically pleasurable phenomenon. At its culmination, a local build-up of blood in the vessels is released, and muscular tension developed in response to sexual—most often clitoral—stimulation is relaxed. Most of what we know about female orgasms comes from rather recent research by Masters and Johnson and others, from interviews with articulate groups of Western women, and from somewhat sparse investigations in other societies.[18] Cross-cultural study of the subject is bedeviled by problems of translation; experienced anthropologists are often unsure what term connotes orgasm, or whether such a word even exists.

Whether nonhuman females experience something corresponding to orgasm is also difficult to ascertain—and there are no words with which to put the question directly—but at least animals can be directly observed in a way that human females rarely have been.

Both wild and captive female primates of many species experience "orgasms," if we accept the opinions of many of the researchers who have studied them in the wild. But what is the evidence? Certain responses to copulation—such as spasmodic arm movements, staccato grunts, and lipsmacks which could merely indicate general excitement—are routinely reported. "Trancelike expressions" sometimes follow self-manipulation (a phenomenon that may depend on the eye of the beholder). And specific physiological responses have been recorded: rhythmic contractions of the vagina and changes in heart rate, which correspond to similar observations in human females. Unfortunately, the data are precise only when the animals are removed from their natural surroundings and studied in white-walled laboratories. The experimental conditions themselves may be stressful and abnormally stimulating.

All in all, the straightforward question, "Do other primates experience orgasms?" yields a mixed bag of answers. A poll, probably not exhaustive, of published opinions on the subject turns up two groups of authors. One of them has written that female orgasms are uniquely or primarily a human experience. It includes Desmond Morris, David Barash, George Pugh, Frank Beach, Richard Alexander, Katharine Noonan, and Donald Symons. Another group (which, interestingly, contains more women) opines that nonhuman females do have such orgasms. Among its members are Frances Burton, Elaine Morgan, Suzanne Chevalier-Skolnikoff, Jane Lancaster, Doris Zumpe, Richard Michael, Donald Goldfoot, and myself.[19] This state of

---

[17]In Roger Short's detailed article, "Sexual selection and its component parts, somatic and genital selection, as illustrated by man and the great apes," *Advances in the Study of Behavior* 9 (1978), twenty sections of the paper deal with sexual dimorphism, the testes, the penis, seminal vesicles, and semen in gorillas, orangutans, chimpanzees, and humans. The female genitalia are scarcely mentioned and are covered in four summary statements at the end of each long section on male anatomy.

[18]Useful reviews of this literature can be found in Symons (note 8). *The Hite Report* (note 8) provides concise summaries of the clinical studies but references to the anthropological literature in that book are not well balanced. Authoritative reviews of human sexuality from a cross-cultural perspective can be found in W. H. Davenport, "Sex in cross-cultural perspective," in *Human Sexuality in Four Perspectives,* ed. F. Beach (Baltimore: Johns Hopkins, 1977), and in *Human Sexual Behavior,* eds. D. S. Marshall and R. C. Suggs (New York: Basic Books, 1971).

[19]See references to Barash, Beach, Pugh, Alexander and Noonan, and myself in Chapter 7, and references to Burton, Lancaster, Chevalier-Skolnikoff, Zumpe, Michael, and Goldfoot in notes 20, 21, 25, and 26 for this chapter. Elaine Morgan's ideas on female orgasms can be

affairs should caution us to pay close attention to the evidence and its limitations, and to distinguish between what is known, what is experienced, and what is believed.

Among rhesus macaques, a female at the time of her partner's ejaculation turns her head and looks back toward the mounted male; she reaches toward him with spasmodic arm movements known as a "clutch reflex." In 1968 the psychiatrists Doris Zumpe and Richard Michael tentatively suggested that this reaction might be "an external expression of consummatory sexual behavior in the female rhesus monkey."[20] Zumpe and Michael monitored the copulations of three non-pregnant rhesus females. Of 389 copulations that culminated in ejaculation, 97 percent were associated with a clutch response. Frame-by-frame analysis of films taken during the copulations shows that the clutch reflex begins while the male is still thrusting. This sequence suggests that the female's clutch response itself may trigger ejaculation. The clutch response depends on normal levels of estrogen, the female hormone; it is suppressed by ovariectomy and restored when estrogen is administered.

More physiological evidence for orgasm in nonhuman primates was collected several years later in experiments undertaken by the anthropologist Frances Burton. In her experimental trials, Burton subjected three rhesus females to five minutes of grooming, five minutes of clitoral stimulation mechanically applied by the experimenter, four minutes of rest, and five more minutes of vaginal stimulation.[21] Each of the

monkeys clearly exhibited three of Masters and Johnson's four copulatory phases: the excitement phase characterized by vaginal dilation, mucous secretion, and labial engorgement; a plateau phase with clitoral tumescence; and the resolution phase involving detumescence of the clitoris. As with the human subjects, specific signs of the third "orgasmic phase" could not be detected because the clitoral glans is obscured during this phase.[22] Burton concluded from her experiments that rhesus do indeed possess orgasmic capacity, but she acknowledged a major difficulty in interpreting her results: the actual duration of each copulatory bout among rhesus monkeys under natural conditions is very short, about three or four seconds. Levels of stimulation comparable to those which induced orgasm in the laboratory would occur in the wild only if there were multiple copulatory bouts and sexual stimulation was cumulative from bout to bout.

At least the first set of circumstances—repeated copulations with partners in a very short time—are observed among macaques, baboons, and chimpanzees living under natural conditions. Yet, no one can say what levels of sexual stimulation are achieved in the wild, or how the animals experience them. In the human female, orgasm may be greatly facilitated by high arousal prior to intromission; arousal may accumulate over a period of hours,[23] and women, unlike men, do not return to a physiologically unaroused state after orgasm but to the preorgasmic level. In short, although there is no way to measure the level of sexual arousal these wild primates experienced during hours and days of sexual activity, there exists a distinct possibility that stimulation sufficient for orgasm occurs in the wild.

The occurrence of orgasm in wild primates even seems probable if we allow ourselves to accept less rigorous specifications than those set forth by Masters and Johnson. Behaviors readily apparent to a fieldworker, who cannot assess specific physiological responses, are suggestive

found in chapter five of *The Descent of Woman* (London: Souvenir Press, 1972).

[20]Doris Zumpe and Richard Michael, "The clutching reaction and orgasms in the female rhesus monkey (*Macaca mulatta*)," *Journal of Endocrinology* 40:117–123 (1968). For competent reviews of the literature on female orgasm in primates, see also Symons' book (note 8) and Jane Lancaster, "Sex and gender in evolutionary perspective," in *Human Sexuality: A Comparative and Developmental Perspective,* ed. Herant Katchadourian (Berkeley: University of California Press, 1979).

[21]Frances Burton, "Sexual climax in female *Macaca mulatta*," *Proceedings of the Third International Congress of Primatology* 3:180–191 (1971).

[22]Masters and Johnson (note 16), p. 52.

[23]Hite (note 8), pp. 190–192

indeed. "Copulation calls,'" that is, the series of staccato grunts given by a wild baboon or macaque female at about the moment her partner ejaculates,[24] involuntary muscle spasms affecting the whole body or portions of it,[25] or a pause after sexual activity which is accompanied by particular facial expressions and panting[26] have all been construed as signs of the female's climax. Such signals may accompany heterosexual or homosexual interactions. Homosexual activity involving two females has been reported for a variety of wild and captive primates.[27]

While observing a captive group of stumptail macaques, Suzanne Chevalier-Skolnikoff saw one female mount another on 23 occasions. Although female monkeys may mount others as an expression of dominance (just as males mount males), sexual stimulation can be a prominent feature in such interactions. Chevalier-Skolnikoff detailed the course of events of such

mountings. Typically, the soliciting female approaches another with a teeth-chattering expression, then the approached female presents her rump: "Soliciting female mounts presenting female and, over a period of about one minute, executes a series of pelvic thrusting movements, thereby rubbing her genitals on the back of her mountee. [The mounter is stimulated, but the mountee is not.] Both females make puckered-lips, lip-smacking, or square-mouthed expression." Then, in what Chevalier-Skolnikoff refers to as the "orgasmic phase," the "mounter pauses, and for about ten seconds, manifests muscular spasms, accompanied by the frowning round-mouth look and the rhythmic expiration vocalization."[28]

Stumptail macaques observed in a laboratory by D. A. Goldfoot and his colleagues confirm the impression that females engaged in either homosexual or heterosexual activities experience some sort of sexual climax. These experimenters were able to establish that the female's round-mouthed face (which in a male signals ejaculation) coincided with intense uterine contractions and a sudden increase in heart rate. Four of ten females observed during heterosexual copulations displayed the round-mouthed response during at least one copulatory episode; on average the female would

[24]G. Saayman, "The menstrual cycle and sexual behaviour in a troop of free-ranging chacma baboons (*Papio ursinus*) under free-ranging conditions." *Folia Primatologica* 12:81–100 (1970). W. J. Hamilton and P. C. Arrowood, "Copulatory vocalizations of chacma baboons (*Papio ursinus*), gibbons (*Hylobates hoolock*), and humans," *Science* 200:1405–1409 (1978).

[25]Richard Michael, M. I. Wilson, and D. Zumpe, "The bisexual behavior of female rhesus monkeys," in *Sex Differences in Behavior*, eds. R. C. Friedman, R. M. Richart, and R. L. Vande Wiele (New York: Wiley, 1974); Suzanne Chevalier-Skolnikoff, "Male-female, female-female, and male-male sexual behavior in the stumptail monkey, with special attention to the female orgasm," *Archives of Sexual Behavior* 3:95–116 (1974).

[26]Chevalier-Skolnikoff (note 25), p. 109; J. K. Hampton, S. J. Hampton, and B. T. Landwehr, "Observations on a successful breeding colony of the marmoset *Oedipomidas* oedipus," *Folia Primatologica* 4:265–287 (1966). Philip Hershkovitz, *Living New World Primates (Platyrrhini)*, vol. I (Chicago: University of Chicago Press, 1977), p. 769. It is worth noting that some women experiencing orgasm pant and make a face similar to the round-mouthed expression given by macaques. The incidence of this response is not known, and I know of no research which describes in detail facial expressions during human orgasm nor attempts to examine the origins of such responses.

[27]Akers and Conaway, reviewing the literature on female homosexual mounting among rhesus, captive pigtailed, Japanese, and stumptail macaques and among chimpanzees, squirrel monkeys, and wild vervet monkeys, stress the effects of both hormonal factors (typically, the mounted female is in the ovulatory phase of her cycle) and close affiliative relationships between the females involved. J. H. Akers and Clinton Conaway, "Female homosexual behavior in *Macaca mulatta*," *Archives of Sexual Behavior* 8(I):63–80 (1979). Similar observations have been made for caged pygmy chimpanzees and wild gorillas.

[28]Chevalier-Skolnikoff indicates that female responses during heterosexual copulations are less intense and external manifestations of "orgasm" less obvious than they are in homosexual mounts. Some—for example Symons (note 8)—believe this finding contradicts the claim that stumptail macaque females experience orgasms during both homosexual and heterosexual interactions, since the clear pattern of orgasmic response observed during homosexual mounting are not seen during heterosexual copulations. It is worth noting, however, that Chevalier-Skolnikoff addresses this very problem by pointing out—through extrapolation from the human data—that intensity of female orgasm and its manifestations may vary with circumstances. "Masters and Johnson [1966]," she writes, "have found that the intensity of the human female orgasm is variable, mild orgasm being hardly distinguishable behaviorally or physiologically, while intense ones involve dramatic behavioral and physiological changes. They have also found that the more intense clitoral stimulation tends to produce a more intense orgasmic response than vaginal coitus. In view of this variability in the human female orgasm, it is conceivable that in stumptail females less intense and less easily identifiable orgasm than those observed during homosexual interactions might occur during heterosexual copulation." Chevalier-Skolnikoff (note 25), p. 113.

FIGURE 3-1   Stumptail macaques

make the face 10 times in the course of 52 tests, but females were very individual in their responsiveness. One of them made the "ejaculation face" in 40 percent of her sexual encounters.[29]

Free-ranging Japanese macaques living on a ranch near Laredo, Texas, resemble their stumptail cousins in their sexual behavior. (Their troop has been named Arashiyama West after the original primate colony of that name in Japan.) Because the monkeys are unrestrained, mechanical devices were not inserted to measure their internal physiological events. Even so, we can say that the females unambiguously seek the same sort of genital stimulation that led to orgasm in the laboratory. A third of all observed matings were preceded by the *female* mounting her partner several times to rub her perineal region against his back. As the observer, Linda Wolfe, points out: "Thigh pressure and rubbing would, of course, facilitate orgasm if these females possess the capacity for orgasm. That adult females who mounted males were more sexually motivated is borne out by the finding that those adult females who mounted males had a statistically significant

greater number of male partners . . . than those females . . . who did not."[30]

A conservative interpretation of all these findings would be that under some circumstances female primates find genital stimulation positively reinforcing. Orangutan and chimpanzee females living in the forest as well as captive monkeys and apes will, on occasion, provide it for themselves, although masturbation among females is observed far less commonly than it is among males.[31] Still and all, it seems unlikely that primate females "are not much troubled with sexual feelings of any kind." What, then, are we to make of this libidinous aspect of their nature?

Although evidence is increasing that orgasms do occur in other primates, no really plausible explanation for their purpose has been forthcoming. None of the various physiological or therapeutic rationalizations (relieving congestion of blood, promoting fertilization)[32] has

---

[29]D. A. Goldfoot, H. Westerborg-van Loon, W. Groeneveld, and A. Koos Slob, "Behavioral and physiological evidence of sexual climax in the female stump-tailed macaque (*Macaca arctoides*)," *Science* 208:1477–1479 (1980). See also Eric Phoebus, "Coital heart rate in the female rhesus monkey (*Macaca mulatta*)," Ph.D. thesis presented to University of California, Irvine (1977).

[30]Linda Wolfe, "Behavioral patterns of estrous females of the Arashiyama West Troop of Japanese macaques (*Macaca fuscata*)," *Primates* 20(4):525–534 (1979).

[31]The most detailed account concerns wild orangutans in Sumatra. "Several wild orang utans, especially youngsters, were observed to stimulate their own genitals, either manually or by means of inanimate objects. Female orang utans might masturbate by rubbing their fingers, their foot or an object along their clitoris . . . or they might insert their hallux or objects into their vagina. One adolescent female . . . was observed to suck and wet the finger she used during her masturbation," H. D. Rijksen, *A Field Study on Sumatran Orang utans (Pongo Pygmaeus Abelii Lesson 1827): Ecology, Behaviour and Conservation* (Wageningen: H. Veenman and B. V. Zonnen, 1978), pp. 262–263. Caroline Tutin reports similar behavior for a young female chimpanzee: "Gremlin showed a fascination with her own genitals during her fourth year, manipulating them directly with her hand and also rubbing objects, such as stones and leaves against them," C. E. G. Tutin, "Sexual behaviour and mating patterns in a community of wild chimpanzees (*Pan troglodytes schweinfurthii*)," Ph.D. thesis presented to University of Edinburgh (1975), p. 139. Comparable accounts for captive animals include several for the monogamous tamarins (*Saquinus oedipus*) in which hand-tamed females masturbate either with their tails or against soft surfaces in the environment until stopping in a "trancelike" state, or until "satisfied." See reports by Hampton et al. and Hershkovitz, cited in Hershkovitz (note 26), p. 769.

[32]Current hypotheses to explain the existence of female orgasms include: (1) Orgasms are therapeutic either because, as Sherfey suggested, they relieve "venous congestion," or because, as Margaret Hamilton has suggested (unpublished manuscript), uterine contractions during intercourse somehow prepare the female for childbirth. (2) Orgasm enhances the probability of insemination either by transporting the sperm, as suggested by Fox et al., or by stimulating the male to ejaculate. Among some primates (many macaques, for example) males must mount, intromit the penis, and thrust many times

received much support from clinical research. The lack of obvious purpose has left the way open for both orgasm, and female sexuality in general, to be dismissed as "nonadaptive," "incidental," "dysgenic," or adaptive only insofar as it provides a service to males.

Sherfey began her investigation from an equally plausible postulate: that genital pleasure is as adaptive in females as it is in males, that it creates an inclination to seek partners and persist in copulation until satisfaction is obtained. But adaptive for what?

The point of copulation, most biologists would hasten to point out, is insemination. Be-

before ejaculation is possible. This might be viewed as a reason for females to continue to be receptive and to solicit males for prolonged periods. This argument is by no means persuasive, however, since if it were the case that mechanical peculiarities of the male constituted the chief selection pressure for female sexual traits, any male capable of quick ejaculation would outbreed these slower suitors. Hence, the answer in this case must be the other way around: males in these species take longer to ejaculate because prolonged stimulation somehow increases the likelihood of ovulation by the female or else other responses by the female conducive to eventual fertilization by this male.

As for the sperm-transport theory, the relevant data are contradictory. In an experimental study of the effects of orgasm on sperm transport, Masters and Johnson made radiographic check plates of six subjects (all of whom were orgasmic during the experimental session) to determine the direction of transport of a radio-opaque facsimile of seminal fluid which had been placed over the cervix of each subject. In none of the six individuals was there evidence of "the slightest sucking effect" of the semen facsimile, leading Masters and Johnson to conclude that orgasmic uterine contractions are "expulsive, not sucking or ingestive in character." Similar results had been obtained in a study by Bardwick and Behrman in which balloons had been extruded during uterine contractions. However, the additional finding that ejection via uterine contractions was most characteristic of subjects who were "anxious" raises the possibility that there may be differences among women and that women may respond differentially under different circumstances, and in particular, highlights the general difficulties of interpreting findings on this particular point on the basis of clinical experiments. Whatever the results, it is obvious from the existence of viable populations in cultures where females rarely or never experience orgasms during intercourse that orgasms are scarcely essential in order for fertilization to take place. The same—and several other—objections can be raised for Desmond Morris's idea (3) that orgasms keep females flat on their backs after sex, lest the seminal fluid flow out. See C. A. Fox, H. S. Wolff, and J. A. Baker, "Measurement of intra-vaginal and intra-uterine pressures during human coitus with radiotelemetry," *Journal of Reproductive Fertility* 22:56–76 (1970). Masters and Johnson (note 16), pp. 122–123. J. M. Bardwick and S. J. Behrman, "Investigation into the effects of anxiety, sexual arousal, and menstrual cycle phase on uterine contractions," *Psychosomatic Medicine* 29(5):470–482 (1967).

cause a female need be inseminated only once to establish a pregnancy, it would seem that there could be little advantage to her from repeated copulations, and none whatever from copulation when she is not ovulating. This objection leads with apparent inevitability to the conclusion that female sexuality is an evolutionary vestige.

Yet only a failure to think seriously about females and to consider the evidence would allow someone to conclude that natural selection operates more powerfully on male sexuality than on female sexuality, or to believe that the female's reproductive character could be "invisible" to natural selection. When some variability occurs in the members of a species, natural selection has an opportunity to choose between them, no matter how slight the variation. And for females, faced with the doubly difficult adaptive task of gaining access to resources in the environment, converting them into offspring, and seeing that those offspring survive, the stakes are very high, every bit as high as for males. There is clear evidence that females of many species take advantage of numerous opportunities to augment their chances for reproductive success. For example, one female may forestall reproduction in another—what might be called the "Hagar phenomenon": a socially dominant female suppresses ovulation in her subordinates or excludes a rival from safe harbors and feeding sites, just as Abraham's wife, Sarah, drove her husband's concubine, Hagar, into the wilderness. For another example, females take advantage of high social rank, which entitles them and their offspring to nutritious food, caretaking, and protection—factors that matter a great deal in the survival of offspring. A female who lacks protection and support may fail to raise a single offspring to breeding age, even though she gives birth repeatedly. We now know that females are not breeding machines that automatically produce one offspring after another from menarche to menopause; in fact, only a portion, perhaps a small one, of females living in nature could even approach the theoretical maximum number of offspring (see Chapter 7). A mother's social circumstances have far-reaching consequences: the availability of food and helpers, protection from predation and from other members of her own species, all of these are critical for both her and her offspring. In such a world, selection could hardly be operating only on males, and it is exceedingly unlikely that the energy consumed by female sexual activity, or the risk it entails, could have persisted unless it somehow enhanced a female's reproductive success.

If we recognize that a female's reproductive success can depend in critical ways on the tolerance of nearby males, on male willingness to assist an infant, or at least to leave it alone, the selective importance of an active, promiscuous sexuality becomes readily apparent. Female primates influence males by consorting with them, thereby manipulating the information available to males about possible paternity. To the extent that her subsequent offspring benefit, the female has benefited from her seeming nymphomania.

Under some circumstances, of course, sharing the pleasure of intercourse with a particular male might reinforce her ties to him, but enjoyment of sex could also serve her interests at the expense of the male's. "Insatiability"— Sherfey's term—is probably too strong a word, but an inclination in the appropriate situation to solicit males could serve an important adaptive purpose in the lives of female primates. Sherfey's premise that the main features of woman's sexual anatomy evolved in a context where selection favored prolonged solicitations involving multiple partners no longer looks so far-fetched.

Mary Jane Sherfey, it should be remembered, was writing in the early sixties without benefit of the post-1965 explosion in knowledge about primate behavior. Although she is not explicit on this point, readers should be aware that she bases her model of primate sexuality on the behavior of only a few species—rhesus macaques, savanna baboons, and chimpanzees, all of which live in polygynous breeding systems. She did not consider, for example, nonhuman primates living in monogamous families. But Sherfey's main focus was on the human case, and as luck would have it, her errors of omission do not necessarily jeopardize her arguments. None of the great apes—indisputably our closest living relatives—are obligate monogamers, and evidence of pronounced sexual dimorphism in fossil anthropoids and hominids makes it unlikely that any of our immediate ancestors were either.

Rarely can paleontology provide insights into social structure, but on this particular point— whether or not a species possessed a monogamous breeding system—I think we are on fairly firm ground. Recall that most primates in which females are equal in status to males are monogamous, and virtually all monogamous species are characterized by monomorphic, or same-size, sexes. By contrast, polygynous species tend to be characterized by sexual dimorphism, with males substantially larger than females, owing to the fact that males in polygynous species fight among themselves for access to harems of females. In monogamous species there exist approximately equivalent levels of overt intrasexual competition in both sexes.

When we look at the fossil record in the hominid line, the degree of sexual dimorphism among our antecedents was at least as great as that in contemporary human populations, where men are 5 to 12 percent larger than females; recent fossil evidence from Hadar in Ethiopia and Laetoli in Tanzania provides grounds for believing that hominids four million years ago were even *more* dimorphic than humans are today. Certainly this was the case for Old World higher primates in the more distant past, at thirty million years before the present. When we compare our statistics to those for mammals generally, *Homo sapiens* falls into the range of a "mildly polygynous species." Among our highly polygynous hominoid relatives, the gorillas, chimpanzees, and orangutans, males tend to be 25 percent (or more) larger than females.

Despite these findings about sexual dimorphism, the old idea that early humans were monogamous continues to attract proponents. However, taking this position now necessitates a certain anthropocentrism and special pleading. For example, in his otherwise very innovative and comprehensive essay "The Origin of Man," Owen Lovejoy argues that pair-bonding and a monogamous breeding system were crucial to the emergence of modern man; but to do so he must first downplay the evidence for dimorphism in early humans by arguing that "human sexual dimorphism is clearly not typical." He stresses the fact that human canine teeth are not dimorphic, as is the case in other sexually dimorphic, polygynous animals. But this is a weak link in his argument, since it does not seem necessary to assume that early man used his teeth in fighting as other primates do. If a club better served his purposes, there would no longer be selection for male canines.[33]

The paradoxes of human sexuality—the mismatch between men, who are transiently impotent after an orgasm, and women, who are not only capable of multiple orgasms but may prefer them[34]—may not be so paradoxical after all, if we no longer assume that these traits evolved in a strictly monogamous context. The physiology of the clitoris, which does not typically generate orgasm after a single copulation, ceases to be mysterious if we put aside the idea that women's sexuality evolved in order to "serve" her mate, and examine instead the possibility that it evolved in order to increase the reproductive success of primate mothers through enhanced survival of their offspring.

But even so, the conundrums hardly disappear. If we assume that women have been biologically endowed with a lusty primate sexuality, how have cultural developments managed to alter or override this legacy? Has women's sexual behavior been permitted to drift from its biological moorings? Is it no longer subject to natural selection? Must we assume that behavior which was once adaptive is no longer adaptive? How has women's sexuality changed in the intervening five million or so years since we shared an ancestor in common with the chimpanzees?

How do we even approach such questions? Rarely does a human society permit women the sexual independence that, say, macaques have. If there were no such thing as a "compromising" situation, what would women do? Reports of women engaging in intercourse with a series of partners are few indeed, and it is hard to know how to interpret them.[35] What we know of primates suggests that prehominid females embarking upon the human enterprise were possessed of an aggressive readiness to engage in both reproductive and nonreproductive liaisons with multiple, but selected, males. What happened next is, and probably will always remain, shrouded in mystery. We can only document the attitudes prevalent in human cultures during historical times. There can be no doubt from

[33]Owen Lovejoy, "The Origin of Man," *Science* 211:341–350 (1981). On dimorphism in polygynous Old World primates, see T. Clutton-Brock, P. Harvey, and B. Rudder, "Sexual dimorphism, socionomic sex ratio and body weight in primates," *Nature* 269:797–800 (1970); R. D. Alexander, J. L. Hoogland, R. D. Howard, K. Noonan, and P. W. Sherman, "Sexual dimorphism and breeding systems in pinnipeds, ungulates, primates and humans," in *Evolutionary Biology and Human Social Behavior,* eds. N. A. Chagnon and W. Irons (North Scituate, Mass., Duxbury Press, 1979). M. W. Wolpoff provides evidence for sexual dimorphism among fossil hominids in "Sexual dimorphism in the australopithecines," in *Paleoanthropology: Morphology and Paleoecology,* ed. R. H. Tuttle (The Hague: Mouton, 1975). See also D. C. Johanson and T. D. White, "A systematic assessment of early African hominids," *Science* 203:321–329 (1979); J. G. Fleagle, R. F. Kay, and E. L. Simons, "Sexual dimorphism in early anthropoids," *Nature* 287:328–330 (1980).

[34]According to Kinsey et al. (note 4), pp. 375–376, 14 percent of females in their sample regularly responded with multiple orgasms. Some females had two, three, or as many as a dozen or more orgasms in a relationship in which their husbands ejaculated only once. See also Masters and Johnson (note 16), p. 65.

[35]In a recent survey of 106,000 readers of *Cosmopolitan* magazine, 23 percent of the respondents answered that they had had sex with more than one partner at a time; for most of these, sex with multiple partners meant two males. Of these respondents, 9 percent replied that they occasionally experimented with multiple partners; 14 percent replied that they had done so once. Linda Wolfe (note 4), p. 263. In the ethnographic literature, one of the very few known cases where women actually cite desire for multiple or sequential orgasms as a factor influencing the number of sexual partners is recorded for the aboriginal people of Western Arnhem Land, Australia. Women said to be dissatisfied by single male ejaculations may seek coitus with several different (marital and extramarital) partners within the same 12-hour period. R. M. Berndt and C. Berndt, "Sexual behavior in Western Arhem Land," *Viking Fund Publications in Anthropology,* vol. 16 (1951), p. 57.

such evidence that the *expectation* of female "promiscuity" has had a profound effect on human cultural institutions.

Two conflicting idealizations—woman as chaste, passive, sexually innocent, and woman as possessor of a dangerous sexuality—always have dominated historical assessments of female nature. Similar tensions characterize the beliefs in many preliterate, traditional societies.[36] Female sexuality is much on people's minds. Whether in village gossip or television soap operas, the affairs of women are a matter of compelling interest.

Almost universally, sexual sanctions are stricter for women than for men. As the anthropologist Alice Schlegel has pointed out, nearly twice as many human cultures forbid adultery by wives as those that proscribe it for husbands.[37] Even societies which appear to esteem women for their sexual purity and passivity nevertheless take extensive precautions to prevent them from breaching their chastity. On one point there is an extraordinary consensus: woman's readiness to engage in sexual activity is great enough that the majority of the world's cultures—most of which determine descent through the male line—have made some effort to control it. The reason for expending all this effort usually comes down to some variant of Samuel Johnson's conviction that otherwise there would be "confusion of progeny."

According to Engels, for example, the human family, developing "in the transitional period between the upper and middle stages of barbarism," was a harbinger of civilization. The family, he wrote,

is based upon the supremacy of the man, the express purpose being to produce children of undisputed paternity; such paternity is demanded because these children are later to come into their father's property as his natural heirs. It is distinguished from pairing marriage [an earlier stage] by the much greater strength of the marriage tie, which can no longer be dissolved at either partner's wish. As a rule it is now only the man who can dissolve it, and put away his wife. The right of conjugal infidelity also remains secured to him . . . and as social life develops he exercises his right more and more; should the wife recall the old form of sexual life and attempt to revive it, she is punished more severely than ever.[38]

These issues surfaced again in the 1960s as part of feminist doctrine. According to Mary Jane Sherfey, "One of the requisite cornerstones upon which all modern civilizations were founded was *coercive* suppression of woman's inordinate sexuality." This theme is summarized well by Nancy Marval, though I wonder whether she would not be a bit surprised to know that several sociobiologists, approaching the problem from a different angle, and (I suspect) completely independently, have ended up by concurring with her point by point. Marval writes:

> In a patriarchal culture . . . sexuality is a crucial issue . . . men have no direct access to reproduction and survival of the species. As individuals, their claim to any particular child can never be as clear as that of the mother who demonstrably gave birth to that child. . . . The only way a man can be absolutely sure that he is the one to have contributed that sperm is to control the sexuality of the woman. . . .
> He may keep her separate from any other man

---

[36]The belief that female sexuality and reproductive capacity is somehow "dangerous" is widespread in various cultures throughout the world, and is often manifested in the special sanctions surrounding menstruating women. See for example Paula Weideger, *Menstruation and Menopause: The Physiology and Psychology, the Myth and Reality* (New York: Alfred A. Knopf, 1976); and J. Delaney, M. J. Lupton, and E. Toth, *The Curse: A Cultural History of Menstruation* (New York: E. P. Dutton, 1977).

[37]Alice Schlegel, *Male Dominance and Female Autonomy* (New Haven: Human Relations Area Files Press, 1972), p. 88. See also Gwen Broude, "Extramarital sex norms in cross-cultural perspective," *Behavior Science Research* 15(3):181–218 (1980).

[38]Friedrich Engels, *The Origin of the Family, Private Property, and the State* (New York: International Publishers, 1942; English translation of the 1884 German original), pp. 54–55. At about the same time (1865) the anthropologist John McLennan was pursuing similar ideas: "The blood-ties through females being obvious and indisputable the idea of blood relationship, as soon as it was formed, must have begun to develop . . . into a system embracing them. . . . But blood-ties through fathers could not find a place in a system of kinship, unless circumstances usually allowed of some degree of certainty as to who the father of a child was." *Primitive Marriage: An Inquiry into the Form of Capture in Marriage Ceremonies,* ed. Peter Riviere (Chicago: University of Chicago Press, 1970, reprint).

as in a harem, he may devise a mechanical method of preventing intercourse like a chastity belt, he may remove her clitoris to decrease her erotic impulses, *or* he may convince her that sex is the same thing as love and if she has sexual relations with anyone else she is violating the sacred ethics of love.[39]

The only major difference between Marval's statement and those of some sociobiologists[40] would be identification of the enemy. Marval suggests it is "he" who is responsible for suppression of females. Sociobiologists, extending her arguments to creatures other than *Homo sapiens,* point out that natural selection—and not "men" *per se*—is responsible, and note that females as well as males are implicated.

Lest anyone doubt that women collude in the supposed "plot" to suppress them, consider the court ladies of ancient China, the *nu shih* whose job it was to supervise the wives and concubines of the emperor. As have mothers, fathers, in-laws of both sexes, neighbors, and nosy parkers through the ages, these women busied themselves with the sexual status and conduct of women—in this case, residents of the emperor's seraglio. Seldom has the scrutiny of women's sexual lives been raised to such a high level of professionalism. Modern scientists might well covet the detailed information available to the *nu shih.*

Elaborate protocol surrounded the hundreds of women housed in the harems of T'ang dynasty emperors; the ever increasing numbers made meticulous bookkeeping essential to the emperor's confidence in his paternity and to ensure that only his progeny received the benefits of imperial investment. In her records the *nu shih* entered the "date and hour of every successful sexual union, the dates of menstruation of every woman, and the first signs of pregnancy." In some cases, even more exacting measures

were deemed necessary. The "Notes of the Dressing Room" by Chang Pi, a scholar whose teachings flourished around A.D. 940, records that at the beginning of the K'ai-yuan era (713–741) every woman with whom the emperor had slept was stamped on her arm and the mark then rubbed with cinnamon to make it indelible.[41] In earlier times, and perhaps also as late as the T'ang, as another form of recordkeeping, a silver ring was transferred from the woman's right leg to her left to mark each sexual union with the emperor. If she conceived, she was given a golden ring to wear.

Whole chapters of human history could be read as an effort to contain the promiscuity of women and thus to establish, from circumstantial evidence, the paternity that could never be proved directly (before the advent of sophisticated laboratories). Whatever the biological component may be, the behavioral component is readily demonstrated.

Only an anthropologist could have undertaken this task with the richness of ethnographic detail that has characterized the work of Mildred Dickemann. In a brilliant series of three papers, she has reviewed human practices that serve to cloister women and expropriate their fecundity.[42] She has focused particularly on stratified human societies, in which women typically marry "up" into families of higher standing than their own. This practice, called "hypergyny" by anthropologists, is common throughout much of the world. Dickemann has drawn much of her material from accounts of ancient China, medieval Europe, and north In-

---

[39]Nancy Marval, "The case for feminist celibacy," 1971 pamphlet, cited in Hite (note 8), p. 152. Sherfey (note 5, 1966).

[40]See for example Jeffrey A. Kurland, "Paternity, mother's brother, and human sociality," in *Evolutionary Biology and Human Social Behavior* (note 33), p. 176.

[41]Robert van Gulik, *Sexual Life in Ancient China: A Preliminary Survey of Chinese Sex and Society from ca. 1500 B.C. till 1644 A.D.* (Leiden: E. J. Brill, 1974), p. 189.

[42]Mildred Dickemann, "Female infanticide and the reproductive strategies of stratified human societies: a preliminary model," in *Evolutionary Biology and Human Social Behavior* (note 33), pp. 321–367; "The ecology of mating systems in hypergynous societies," paper presented at the Maison des Sciences de l'Homme, Paris, at an International Conference on Kin Selection and Kinship Theory, October 1978; "Paternal confidence and dowry competition: a biocultural analysis of purdah," in *Natural Selection and Social Behavior,* eds. R. D. Alexander and D. Tinkle (in press).

dia just after its colonization by the British. She takes as given that higher status improves the reproductive success of men and women alike. Quantitative data in support of this point are hard to come by, but she points to the relationship throughout history between possession of property and the survival of family lines. She also cites the extreme vulnerability of the dispossessed, particularly during times of famine.

Dickemann's focus on stratified societies is important to her argument because it allows her to assume that a properly hypergynous marriage benefits not only the bride but her family. Her parents can look forward to grandchildren born into a world of improved opportunities; large dowries are understandable as the price paid for high-status grandsons, whose prospects include good health, longevity, perhaps multiple wives, and, crucially, many children of their own. The bride's family, then, as well as the groom's, has an interest in ensuring her virginity and future fidelity. Access through marriage or concubinage to a wealthy family is competitive, and the bride's family has a direct stake in her reputation and eligibility. Where these are connected to extreme standards of modesty, such as veiling women in purdah or strict seclusion, the bride's family forces her compliance, though in many cases special pressure is unnecessary because, as Dickemann points out, the woman herself is indoctrinated from infancy to value and manifest ideals of feminine modesty. Even without seraglios, the behavior of women is shaped through physical coercion (beatings or the threat of them) or, more commonly, superstition (the threat of "damnation" or rape by demons). In contemporary Maya-speaking communities throughout Central America, for example, female sexuality is considered extremely dangerous. Women thought to be careless or excessive in their sexuality—and "excessive" here includes any adoption by women of a copulatory position likely to increase clitoral stimulation—are publicly mocked or threatened with rape by a mythical demon so potent that the offending woman will give birth every night, night after night, until she swells up and dies.[43]

The more clearly stratified the society, and the higher the sights set by the family for a young girl's future, the easier it is to justify the time and expense (particularly in lost labor) of elaborate claustration. As Dickemann puts it, "Women's modesty and the investment of energy into its maintenance become marks of family pride, major indices of public reputation." By way of example, she cites the north Indian ethnographer Elizabeth Cooper:

> You can tell the degree of a family's aristocracy by the height of the windows in the home. The higher the rank, the smaller and higher are the windows and the more secluded the women. An ordinary lady may walk in the garden and hear the birds sing and see the flowers. The higher grade lady may only look at them from her windows, and if she is a very great lady indeed, this even is forbidden to her, as the windows are high up near the ceiling, merely slits in the wall for the lighting and ventilation of the room.[44]

At this higher grade of the social scale, it was common practice in north India to destroy daughters due to the impossibility for them to marry up and thereby improve the fortunes of the family. Better to invest entirely in sons and recruit wives from the lower ranks. Infanticide is widespread in traditional societies.[45] Unlike other animals, which are seldom inclined to kill their own young but rather only those belonging to competitors, humans dispatch their own infants for a variety of reasons, often due to economic constraints or inopportune timing of a birth, without regard to the infant's sex. But when a discrimination between offspring is made on the basis of sex, it is virtually always the female infant that is killed. Preferential

---

[43]Sarah C. Blaffer, *The Black-man of Zinacantan: A Central American Legend* (Austin: University of Texas Press, 1972), pp. 34–35; 118–119.

[44]From Dickemann, "Paternal confidence" (note 42).

[45]Mildred Dickeman, "Demographic consequences of infanticide in man," *Annual Review of Ecology and Systematics* 6:107–137 (1975). (Note that M. Dickeman and M. Dickemann are the same person; she changed the spelling of her name in 1978.)

FIGURE 3-2 Women in purdah

female infanticide occurs in both stratified societies such as the Rajputs and in more egalitarian societies such as the Yanomamo Indians of South America, where sons are greatly valued as warriors and where, if women are in short supply, wives are obtained by raiding women from other villages.

Influential members of cultures throughout north India, ancient China, medieval Europe, and the Arab world (to name only some of the best-documented cases) have subscribed to a "Sherfeyian" assessment of women's readiness to engage in sexual activity. Whatever the biological facts, female sexuality has been seen as a force sufficiently real as to be worth guarding against. The very sexual feelings that are often interpreted as bonding a woman to her mate can also be viewed as forces which would incite a woman to extramarital activity.

Myriad rationalizations are offered for forbidding women their freedom of movement, for sequestering them. Some Muslims and Rajputs that I know argue that claustration of women is undertaken for their own good, to protect them from kidnap or rape. No doubt it does. The feet of daughters in ancient China might have been bound not to incapacitate them, to tether them forever on tiptoes, but to show off the lady's status and advertise the fact that her family could afford to do without her labor. Killing daughters might be explained away as simply a logical response to poor marriage possibilities in societies where a spinster's life is not worth living. One need not accept the interpretation that in hypergynous mating systems the inclusive fitness of the entire family is diminished if the resources of a high-ranking family are diverted to a daughter. Yet taken together, the evidence falls again and again into a similar configuration, making Mildred Dickemann's sociobiological analysis of such practices a compelling one.

Furthermore, some practices, such as clitoridectomy, have no convincing alternative explanation and make sense in no other context. Efforts to explain away this practice by calling it "female circumcision"—a companion practice to removing the male foreskin as an initiation rite—are too obviously exercises in anthropological euphemism. They don't wash. Cultural beliefs can only be an overlay upon this straightforward effort to alter female anatomy through surgical removal of the clitoris or sewing together the lips of the vagina (infibulation). The consequences to male and female of the respective procedures are radically dissimilar. Male circumcision has little obvious consequence to sexuality. Clitoridectomy is an effective means of reducing sexual pleasure.

The earliest evidence for clitoridectomy dates from ancient Egypt, where both clitoral excision and labial fusions were practiced, as can be seen from female mummies. The Greek historian and geographer Agatharchides, who visited Ethiopia in the second century B.C., noted that the people there excised their women in the Egyptian tradition.[46] Perhaps the most remarkable aspect of female circumcision is that it continues to be practiced; one estimate holds that upward of 20

---

[46]Agatharchides' observations are cited by Diodorus and Strabo. These and other early observations are summarized in Carl Gosta Widstrand, "Female infibulation," *Studia Ethnographica Upsaliensia* 20 (varia I):95–122 (1964).

million women in the world today are affected,[47] despite the fact that it can cause serious medical complications, including septicemia, hemorrhage, and shock, as well as serious urinary and obstetrical problems and threats to female fertility. So extensive is the infibulation operation—the clitoris is excised and the surrounding tissue scarified so that the fusion of the labia will occur during healing—that approximately 9 percent of girls operated on under semimodern conditions (with some anesthesia) suffer hemorrhage or shock. Infibulated women are partially cut open at marriage, and must be fully opened at childbirth—after which they are sewn up again. Hence, the possibility of impaired fertility or death from the procedure persists throughout the woman's reproductive years. In a recent study of 4,024 women at Khartoum, in the Sudan, the percentage of infibulated women suffering from urinary infection was four times as great as noncircumcised women, the rate of chronic pelvic infection more than twice as high. Of 3,013 of these women who had been infibulated, 84 percent reported that they had never had an orgasm.[48] Far from finding intercourse pleasurable, many circumcised and infibulated women find it painful.

From a biological point of view, women can scarcely be said to benefit from this practice. Why, then, does the society subject women to an operation which both pains and endangers them? Why do men in some societies refuse to marry uncircumcised women? The obvious answer, recognized by feminists and sociobiologists alike, is that female circumcision increases the certainty of paternity and reduces the likelihood that a man will be cuckolded and thus tricked into supporting some other man's offspring. In fact, a commonly cited folk rationale for female circumcision is that the operation promotes chastity by reducing sexual desire.[49]

There is a certain irony that any feminist should ever have undertaken intellectual lobbying to exclude knowledge about other nonhuman primates from efforts to understand the human condition. No doubt there seemed good reason at the time. Primatologists, and those social scientists who relied upon their work, made much of the supposedly greater competitive potential of males, the importance of males in structuring the society, and the apparent inability of females to maintain stable social systems.[50] Such models were too obviously a projection of androcentric fantasy. It was not unreasonable to fear that such views might lead to policies contrary to the aspirations of women. As late as 1980, one can find it seriously suggested that differences in competitiveness between girl and boy athletes may be "adaptive for our species" and therefore "should not be erased."[51] Yet if more reliable information about the actual workings of primate social systems had been available, quite a different portrait of females would have been painted. The real irony, though, is that women in so many human societies occupy a position that is far worse than that of females in all but a few species of nonhuman primates.

[47]Fran P. Hosken, "Female circumcision and fertility in Africa," *Women and Health* I(6):I–II (1976). It should be noted that counted in this large estimate are operations varying greatly in severity. In some cultures the clitoris is clipped rather than excised, and there is some dispute over the extent to which clitoridectomy reduces orgasmic capacity.

[48]A. Abu-el-Futuh Shandall, "Circumcision and infibulation of females: a general consideration of the problem and a clinical study of the complications in Sudanese women," *Sudan Medical Journal* 5(4):178–212 (1967). Further consideration of the medical consequences of circumcision are discussed in J. A. Verzin, "Sequelae of female circumcision," *Tropical Doctor* 5:163–169 (1975); R. Cook, *Damage to Physical Health from Pharonic Circumcision (Infibulation) of Females: a Review of the Medical Literature,* report from regional advisor of World Health Organization to Division of Family Health (Geneva: WHO, 1976).

[49]For example, see John Hartung, "On natural selection and the inheritance of wealth," *Current Anthropology* 17(4):612–613 (1976), or Soheir Morsy, "Sex differences and folk illness in an Egyptian village," in *Women in the Muslim World,* eds. Lois Beck and Nikki Keddie (Cambridge: Harvard University Press, 1978). pp. 610–611. [50]Carol L. Cronin, "Dominance relations and females," in *Dominance Relations: An Ethological View of Human Conflict and Social Interaction,* eds. D. R. Omark, F. F. Strayer, and D. G. Freedman (New York: Garland Press, 1980), esp. pp. 299, 302–303, and 317. See also notes 40 and 41 in Chapter 6. [51]Cronin (note 50), pp. 317–318.

Incontestably, weaker individuals are often victimized by stronger ones. This can certainly be documented throughout the primates, but never on the scale with which it occurs among people, and never directed exclusively against a particular sex after the fashion of female infanticide, claustration of daughters and wives, infibulation, or the suttee—the immolation of widows which rather effectively preserves the chastity of the wife of a dead man. Only in human societies are females as a class systematically subjected to the sort of treatment that among other species would be rather randomly accorded to the more defenseless members of the group—the very young, the disabled, or the very old—regardless of sex. This is another way of saying that among people, the biological dimorphism of the sexes has become institutionalized. How did this come about?

Division of labor (and with it the potential for one person to benefit from another's work), the means to accumulate property and not just territory, and the organizational ability to allocate tasks—all of these altered a fundamental relationship between mates. Whereas among other mammals the most polygynous males are necessarily those which invested least in offspring, men could control both large numbers of women *and* the resources they needed to survive and reproduce.[52] Among other animals there is an inverse relationship between polygyny and male investment: males must sacrifice additional mates for the sake of rearing the offspring that they do sire by carrying, feeding, or protecting them. If high levels of male investment are required, male primates are monogamous. But this old relationship no longer necessarily holds in the human case. Polygyny coupled with substantial, albeit sometimes indirect, paternal investment is entirely possible. (*Vide* the three families of H. L. Hunt.) Polygyny can occur together with high levels of paternal investment and also—by virtue of either guards or gossips—surveillance.

The shift toward reckoning inheritance in the father's line and living near his birthplace has also had far-reaching consequences for women. Among all but a handful of other primates, females define a territory and occupy it from generation to generation. Only two of the three great apes and four apparently unusual species of monkeys ensure outbreeding through female transfer. But female transfer is the rule for most human societies. For women, the social consequences of joining the man's family have been well documented. The anthropologist Naomi Quinn sums up the straits of a bride moving in with her husband's people:

> Such a bride suffers the loneliness and the scrutiny of her affines which typifies the lot of all virilocally married women . . . ; in addition she may find herself under the authority of a hostile mother-in-law, whose interests are opposed to hers in competition for the affection and loyalty of her husband. Her only claim to status rests on her success in bearing and raising sons and her eventual position as a mother-in-law herself. Typically, women can only gain power in such households indirectly, through men, and their strategies for so doing may be characterized by gossip, persuasion, indirection and guile.[53]

Most importantly, except for those cases in which additional wives are typically close relatives of the first one (as in sororal polygyny), women exchanged in marriage with other villages are more or less cut off from the support of their relatives. Unrelated women marrying into the same families often have conflicts of interest which preclude either collective action or individual resistance.[54] For generations and genera-

---

[52]I am indebted to Mildred Dickemann, who pointed this out to me. Dickemann lays out the theoretical groundwork for this view in the series of three papers listed in note 42.

[53]Naomi Quinn, "Anthropological studies on women's status," *Annual Review of Anthropology* 6:181–225 (1977).

[54]Anthropologist Louise Lamphere writes that "ethnographic reports show that many kinds of domestic groups are ridden with conflict and competition between women. Accounts of jealousy among co-wives, of the dominance of mother-in-law over daughter-in-law, and of quarrels between sisters-in-law provide some of the most common examples." She reviews this material in her article "Strategies, cooperation, and conflict among women in domestic groups," in *Woman, Culture and Society*, eds. M. Z. Rosaldo and L. Lamphere (Stanford: Stanford University Press, 1974). Among the more remarkable findings in this area are those of Robert LeVine, who analyzed jealousy and hostility between co-wives in polygynous societies. LeVine found that polygynous societies where

tions, then, in populations where a woman moved away from her natal home, her freedom was severely constrained by the scrutiny of her husband's relatives.

Close observation of the sexual conduct of women is universal in human communities. Even in largely hunter-gatherer societies where property is not owned and women enjoy considerable freedom of action and movement—a freedom dictated by the community's reliance on food gathered by women—it is virtually impossible to keep sexual liaisons secret. As Lorna Marshall, who has recounted the lives of Kalahari desert foragers, puts it: "There is no privacy in a !Kung encampment, and the vast veld is not a cover. The very life of these people depends on their being trained from childhood to look sharply at things. . . . They register every person's footprints in their minds . . . and read in the sand who walked there and how long ago."[55] Worse, they talk about it among themselves.

Throughout much of evolutionary history, the uncertainty of paternity has been one of several advantages females retained in a game otherwise heavily weighted toward male muscle mass. Female primates evolved a variety of strategies to pursue this advantage—the shift to situation-dependent receptivity, concealed ovulation, an assertive sexuality. Such attributes improved the abilities of females to manipulate males and to elicit from them the care and tolerance needed to rear the infants they bore. Females were abetted in this by selection upon males themselves to promote the survival of infants which were likely, or even just possibly, their own. But such advantages were not granted to females in a vacuum; once again the ball was tossed back into the other court. To keep women (and their sexuality) in check, husbands and their relations (and perhaps especially property-owning families) devised cultural practices which emphasized the subordination of women and which permitted males authority over them. Presumably, females have adapted to these new constraints, becoming, among other things, more discreet and more subdued, but the fact is that little is known about the sexual life histories of women, and the matter of their legacy will not be soon resolved.

The human world is radically different from that of other primates. Human ingenuity, and with it the ability to build walls, to count, to tell tales, to transport food and store it, and particularly to allocate labor (to control not just the reproductive capacities but also the productive capacities of other individuals), all of these eroded age-old female advantages. Yet, by the same token, in areas of the Near and Far East, in ancient Greece, in pockets of civilization in South America and northern Europe, to take only those cases we have documentation for, the same ingenuity that permitted people to oversee and manipulate complex transactions gave rise to standards of morality which could be articulated and set down in the form of legal systems. In the Western world, the rights of "man" were gradually extended to both sexes. Women can now aspire to a degree of independence corresponding to that of men. In this respect people are in a class by themselves. Of all females, the potential for freedom and the chance to control their own destinies is greatest among women.

co-wives lived close to one another, in the same house or in adjacent households sharing a compound, were more liable to exhibit high levels of hostility between women as manifested by more frequent accusations of witchcraft. In a cross-cultural survey to test his hypothesis, he found a strong association between polygyny and sorcery, and this effect appeared to be magnified by having women live close by rather than in separate residences. "Witchcraft and co-wife proximity in southwestern Kenya," *Ethnology* 1(1):39–45 (1962).

[55]Lorna J. Marshall, *The !Kung of Nyae Nyae* (Cambridge: Harvard University Press, 1976), p. 280.

4

PUTTING WOMAN IN HER (EVOLUTIONARY) PLACE

ANNE FAUSTO-STERLING

The willy-nilly disposition of the female is as apparent in the butterfly as in the man, and must have been continually favored from the earliest stages of animal evolution. . . . Coyness and caprice have in consequence become a heritage of the sex.

SIR FRANCIS GALTON [Circa 1887]

It pays males to be aggressive, hasty, fickle and undiscriminating. In theory it is more profitable for females to be coy, to hold back until they can identify the male with the best genes. . . . Human beings obey this biological principle faithfully.

EDWARD O. WILSON, 1978

SOCIOBIOLOGISTS: WHO ARE THEY AND WHAT DO THEY SAY?

Imagine a look into the future. The headlines leap off the front pages of newspapers across the country. ADMITTED RAPIST FREED AS JURY BUYS BIOLOGICAL DEFENSE! A feature article says the following:

Admitted rapist Joe Smith was released today after a jury—in a landmark decision—bought the defense that sexual assault is biologically natural, and that some men—including Smith—have especially strong urges to rape. Since courts have not established procedures for confining "involuntary rapists" Smith was freed.

There are precedents for this decision. For some years now, women committing violent acts during their premenstruum have been absolved of legal responsibility after testimony that they suffered extremely from the Premenstrual Syndrome, a hormonal imbalance resulting in temporary insanity. In some courts convicted rapists have been offered the option of freedom conditional upon taking the female hormone D.E.S. Before freeing Smith the jury sifted through several volumes of highly technical testimony given by expert witnesses, all scientists trained in the

SOURCE: "Putting Woman in Her (Evolutionary) Place" from *Myths of Gender* by Anne Fausto-Sterling. Copyright © 1986 by Basic Books, Inc. Reprinted by permission of Basic Books, a division of HarperCollins Publishers Inc.

field of sociobiology. According to these biologists, three different theories—the "concealed ovulation" theory, the "unsuccessful competitor" theory, and the theory of "competition between the sexes"—all lead to similar conclusions.

Expert witness A attested that "Rape is common among birds and bees and is epidemic among mallard ducks. . . . When mallards pair up for breeding there often remain a number of unmated males. . . . These bachelors have been excluded from normal reproduction and so they engage in what is apparently the next best strategy: raping someone else's female. . . . Rape in humans is by no means so simple. . . . Nevertheless mallard rape . . . may have a degree of relevance to human behavior. Perhaps human rapists, in their own criminally misguided way, are doing the best they can to maximize their fitness."[1] "In human evolutionary history, larger males were favored because of the increased likelihood of successful rape if they failed to compete successfully for parental resources."[2]

Expert witness B offered a somewhat different viewpoint. Since unlike other apes and monkeys, human females do not have a visible estrus, that is they do not advertise the fact that they are about to ovulate, human males who want to increase their own reproductive fitness—in lay terms—to pass on their own genes, face special problems. "As females evolved to deny males the opportunity to compete at ovulation time, copulation with unwilling females became a feasible strategy for achieving reproduction."[3]

Finally, expert witness C testified that when it comes to reproduction, males and females have completely different interests, their sexual patterns having evolved in totally different directions. "With respect to sexuality there is a female human nature and a male human nature and these natures are extraordinarily different. . . . The evidence does appear to support the views—which are ultimately explicable by evolutionary theory—that human males tend to desire no-cost, impersonal copulations, that there is nothing natural about the Golden Rule, and hence that there is a possibility of rape wherever rape entails little or no risk."

When asked by the prosecuting attorney whether such sexual behavior could be controlled, witness C replied, "socialization toward a gentler, more humane sexuality entails inhibition of impulses . . . [that] are part of human nature because they proved adaptive over millions of years. . . . Given sufficient control over rearing conditions, no doubt males could be produced who would want only the kinds of sexual interactions that women want; but such rearing conditions," he warned, "might well entail a cure worse than the disease."[4]

The Joe Smith case is both fact and fiction. Although no man has yet beaten a rape rap by arguing that he carries "rapist genes," some have received light sentences after agreeing to take female sex hormones, and some women have escaped criminal prosecution altogether by claiming to be victims of PMS. And although all of the writers cited as "expert witnesses" explicitly condemn rape in contemporary societies, the quotes constituting their "testimony" nevertheless come verbatim from the writings—in both popular and scientific literature—of four different sociobiologists. The words of Dr. David Barash and Dr. Randy Thornhill form the composite testimony of witness A. Barash has published one scientific paper on rape in mallard ducks and expanded his views in a popular book entitled *The Whisperings Within,* while Thornhill has written several scientific articles on rape in the scorpionfly, an insect so named because its long curved abdomen resembles the tail of the scorpion. The quotations placed in the mouths of witnesses B and C come from two other well-known sociobiologists. Dr. Richard Alexander, a professor at the University of Michigan, and Dr. Donald Symons, an anthropologist who put forth his ideas about rape in a book called *The Evolution of Human Sexuality.*

Rape is but one among many human behaviors for which sociobiologists try to provide explanation. Harvard biologist Edward O. Wilson, whose weighty book, *Sociobiology: The New Synthesis,* initiated a rush of writing, arguing, hypotheses,

---

[1]David Barash, *The Whisperings Within: Evolution and the Origin of Human Nature* (New York: Harper & Row, 1979), 54.
[2]Randy Thornhill, "Rape in Panorpa Scorpionflies and a General Rape Hypothesis," *Animal Behavior* 28(1980):57.
[3]Richard D. Alexander and K. M. Noonan, "Concealment of Ovulation, Parental Care and Human Social Evolution," in *Evolutionary Biology and Human Social Behavior,* ed. N. Chagnon and William Irons (North Scituate, Mass.: Duxbury, 1979), 449.

[4]Donald Symons, *The Evolution of Human Sexuality* (New York: Oxford University Press, 1979), 284–85.

charges, and countercharges, begins simply. "Sociobiology is defined as the systematic study of the biological basis of all social behavior." Although apparently uncomplicated, Wilson's proposal is far from modest. Among the tasks he sets for the field are the reformulation of the disciplines of anthropology, psychology, and sociology in terms of biology to—as Wilson says—"biologicize" them. He suggests also that sociobiology will shed light on such matters as the origins of war and the development of the state and class conflict, as well as providing the basis for a natural system of human ethics.[5] Robert Trivers, professor of biology at the University of California at Santa Cruz, believes that sociobiology can tell us why parents and children fight with each other and help us understand the relationships between the sexes.[6] Richard Alexander applies sociobiological reasoning to the evolution of Western systems of legal justice,[7] while some anthropologists have joined these biologists in trying to explain the evolution of kinship systems,[8] the existence of female infanticide, the presence of social stratification,[9] and the possible biological origins of sex discrimination.[10] In short, in their enthusiasm for the vistas they believe were opened by what Wilson has named "the New Synthesis," sociobiologists seem willing to apply their approach to just about anything. As David Barash puts it, "we can safely go on our sociobiological way, confident that evolution has relevance to behavior—all behavior."[11]

Sociobiological theory is so fraught with difficulty that one is sometimes at a loss to know how to approach it. To begin with, it can purport to explain absolutely anything, a fact made clear by Wilson's broad vision of its future. Because it makes claims about matters as diverse as aggression, woman's place (in the home, of course), male and female sexuality, and so on, choosing which claims to analyze is in itself not an easy task. I chose to analyze in depth the sociobiological studies of rape because the myriad difficulties unearthed in this specific examination have general applicability to all sociobiological accounts of human behavior.

Using scorpionflies as his starting point, Randy Thornhill originally proposed a general theory of rape that predicts a more frequent occurrence of sexual assault in animal species in which the male offers some resource needed by the female for reproduction.[12] Under these circumstances a rapist could increase his evolutionary fitness by taking an unwilling female. In scorpionflies the male usually obtains and defends some food and attracts the female to partake of a nuptial meal, following which the two mate. Sometimes, however, a male without a food offering grabs a passing female and mates with her by holding on tightly to her wings and then positioning himself for copulation. Since the male incurs considerable risk in gathering food—sometimes even filching a dead insect from an active spiderweb—he may find it advantageous to mate without courting such danger. Not shy about drawing implications for human rape, Thornhill and Thornhill have recently written an extensive analysis of what they see as its evolutionary basis. They hypothesize that men rape when they "are unable to compete for resources and status necessary to attract and reproduce successfully with desirable mates."[13]

Barash's analysis is similar. He observed a population of mallard ducks living in the arboretum at the University of Washington. Mallards

[5]Edward O. Wilson, *Sociobiology: The New Synthesis* (Cambridge, Mass.: Harvard University Press, 1975), 4.
[6]Robert Trivers, "Sociobiology and Politics," in *Sociobiology and Human Politics,* ed. Elliott White (Lexington, Mass.: Heath, 1981).
[7]Richard D. Alexander, *Darwinism and Human Affairs* (Seattle: University of Washington Press, 1980).
[8]Robin Fox, "Kinship Categories as Natural Categories," in *Evolutionary Biology and Human Social Behavior,* ed. Chagnon and Irons.
[9]M. Dickerman, "Female Infanticide, Reproductive Strategies, and Social Stratification: A Preliminary Model," in *Evolutionary Biology and Human Social Behavior,* ed. Chagnon and Irons.
[10]Lionel Tiger, "The Possible Biological Origins of Sexual Discrimination," *Impact of Science on Society* 20(1970):29–44.
[11]David Barash, "Predictive Sociobiology: Mate Selection in Damselfishes and Brood Defense in White-Crowned Sparrows," in *Sociobiology: Beyond Nature/Nurture?,* ed. G. W. Barlow and J. Silverberg (Boulder, Colo.: Westview, 1980), 212.

[12]Thornhill, "Rape in Scorpionflies."
[13]Randy Thornhill and N. Thornhill, "Human Rape: An Evolutionary Analysis," *Ethology and Sociobiology* 4(1983):137.

spend part of the year paired off in monogamous couples, and Barash paid special attention to bachelor males that mounted coupled females without first going through the normal courtship ritual. He further recorded the response of the females' partners, which often insisted on mating immediately after the females had been "raped" by an intruding male. Barash argued that the behaviors he saw were "consistent with the sociobiologic theorem that animals should behave in ways consistent with maximizing their inclusive fitness."[14]

Sociobiologists do strange things with language. All three of my English language dictionaries define rape as "the crime of having sexual intercourse *with a woman* against her will" (emphasis added). The definition contains two parts: rape is something done to a woman (although in common use we also recognize male-male rape), and it involves her conscious state of mind. For it to be called *rape* it must be against her will. When scientists apply the word to fruit flies, bedbugs, ducks, or monkeys, the common definition expands to include all living beings (Barash even includes fertilization in higher plants!) and the idea of will drops out. Yet the "instinct" of a female bedbug to avoid forced intercourse certainly holds nothing in common with the set of emotions experienced by a woman who has been raped. Using the word *rape* to describe animal behavior robs it of the notion of will, and when the word, so robbed, once again is applied to humans, women find their rights of consent and refusal missing. Rape becomes just one more phenomenon in the natural world, a world in which natural and scientific, rather than human, laws prevail.

When attacked for applying loaded terms such as "slavery," which describe particular human relationships, to behavior in the animal world, Wilson replied by asking whether other overlapping phrases should be expunged from the scientist's vocabulary. "Do they," he wrote, "wish also to expunge communication, dominance,

monogamy and parental care from the vocabulary of zoology?"[15] After all, we are perfectly willing to say that animals are tired, hungry, or thirsty. Why not that they rape? As scientists, trained to recognize truth, we should be willing to call a spade a spade. David Barash writes:

> Some people may bridle at the notion of rape in animals but the term seems entirely appropriate when we examine what happens. Among ducks for example, pairs typically form early in the breeding season, and the two mates engage in elaborate and predictable exchanges of behavior. When this rite finally culminates in mounting both male and female are clearly in agreement. But sometimes strange males surprise a mated female and attempt to force an immediate copulation, without engaging in any of the normal courtship ritual and despite her obvious and vigorous protest. If that's not rape, it is certainly very much like it.[16]

The main difference, however, between observing that an animal is, for example, sleepy and that it rapes lies not in an accurate description of its behavior, as Barash suggests, but in the meaning of the words to human beings. The existence of sleep is for all humans a fact of life, controlling in some sense one's plans and daily activities. The existence of rape, on the other hand—or rather the fear of it—controls lives in quite another way. For example, it limits my evening activities, but it does not limit my husband's. It dictates the route I walk to work each day, but it does not dictate my male colleague's, who lives next door. It restricts what parts of the world I can travel to and with whom, but it does not restrict the male undergraduates whom I teach. It even prevents me from daydreaming too intensely when I walk about outside, lest I lose track for one fateful moment of a car slowing down as it passes or footsteps approaching from behind. Rape is not just another word. It signifies an important fear that affects my life, a fear that influences the lives of most women but few men in our culture.

---

[14]David Barash, "Sociobiology of Rape in Mallards: Responses of the Mated Male," *Science* 197(1977):788.

[15]E. O. Wilson, "Academic Vigilantism and the Political Significance of Sociobiology," *BioScience* 26(1976):187.

[16]Barash, *The Whisperings Within,* 54.

Students of animal behavior face a fundamental problem—how to name the observed activities of animals. The difficulty is not trivial; we are limited by one of the very things that separate us from other animals, the development and use of spoken language. When ethologists study a particular behavior, they think long and hard about the question and come up with various compromises, usually accompanied by long qualifications of what is *not* meant by the use of a particular word. In contrast many sociobiologists—especially those using examples from the animal world to draw analogies with human behavior—seem curiously oblivious to the problem. Indeed this is one of the major grounds on which such scientists have been attacked. In using the word *rape,* Barash, Symons, Thornhill, and others have transformed its meaning. First, to describe certain animal behaviors they use a word originally applied to a human interaction, one that includes within its definition the notion of conscious will. Then they employ the animal behavior (named after the human behavior) in theories about rape in human society. In the process they confuse the meanings of two different behaviors and offer a natural justification for a human behavior that Webster's calls criminal. *This linguistic hat trick characterizes virtually all of human sociobiology.*

Until recently the use of the word *rape* to describe animal behavior occurred only rarely, but the practice became increasingly more common after 1975. This timing takes on significance when one looks at what the feminist movement has had to say about it all. By the mid 1970s several scathing books on rape were either newly published or in the offing. Women's groups around the country started rape crisis centers and counseling programs, while protests against a legal system that protected the rapist but harassed the victim began in earnest. In short, rape became a hot topic. The sudden increase in the use of the word in the biological literature, as a response to the furor raised by feminists, was at the very least a non-conscious attempt to establish rape as a widespread natural phenomenon and thus deflect and depoliticize a subject of intense and specific importance to women. The attempt to defuse the political explosiveness of rape, thus trivializing its effect on women's lives, is what provokes such spontaneous anger from the critics of sociobiology. But angry though we may be, we must still contend with Barash's argument: if scientific observations reveal rape in nature, must we not face up to this reality?

DO ANIMALS REALLY RAPE?

Not surprisingly for a field that has flung its net so far and so wide, there are many kinds of sociobiologists, and they do not all agree with one another. Some use an approach called game theory to speculate about possible reproductive strategies. Others make arguments based on population genetics. Some are careful scientists making well-documented, detailed studies on specific animal behaviors, while remaining extremely cautious about applying their results to humans. Others are more than willing to leap from ants to chickens to baboons to humans and back again, with only the most casual glance at the intellectual chasms yawning beneath their feet. Before Wilson laid claim to sociobiology as a new field, warranting its own name and having its own unique literature and approach of study, scientists interested in evolution and animal behavior worked mainly in one of three traditions—population genetics, ecology, and animal behavior (known in the halls of academe as the field of ethology).

Randy Thornhill is an ecologist. During certain times of the year his research work takes him to the field daily, where he watches and records the behaviors of particular predatory insects from sunup to sundown.[17] When he's not actually observing the species of his choice he may be out sweeping the bushes with nets so that he can catch and classify the kinds of prey available to the flies that are the primary objects of his studies. Like

---

[17]Randy Thornhill, "Sexually Selected Predatory and Mating Behavior of the Hangingfly *Bittacua Stignaterus,*" *Annals of the Entomological Society of America* 71(1978):597–601.

any competent field biologist, he may develop theories in the field, but he uses his ingenuity to test them experimentally in the laboratory. Such is the case with his analysis of the behavior in scorpionflies which he labels rape.

As is the fashion with scientific publications, Thornhill first defines his topic and cites supporting examples from the literature. "Rape," he begins, "is forced insemination or fertilization." To substantiate his claim of rape in nature, he mentions in addition to observation of rape in ducks "behavior suggesting heterosexual rape" in fish.[18] Yet the fish to which he refers do not have internal fertilization; instead, they follow a mating ritual which serves to synchronize their behavior. Females and males release their gametes into the open sea, where the fusion of egg and sperm takes place. Sometimes an intruding male (one that has not done his courtship bit) rushes in, depositing his sperm near the eggs as they are shed into the water. It is this "stolen" fertilization—not involving copulation at all—which Thornhill finds suggestive of heterosexual rape. In this example, then, he equates fertilization with rape. He also invokes two instances of "homosexual rape." When I tried to follow up the first, a claim of homosexual rape in bedbugs, I found only a reference to an unsigned article in *Newsweek,* a most unusual source to cite in a scholarly publication. The second example came from a paper published in the journal *Science,* in which the authors assert the existence of homosexual rape in a parasitic worm and remark at length on its possible evolutionary origins, but never describe the behavior they so enthusiastically discuss.[19] As a result it is impossible to judge for oneself the propriety of the label.

In marked contrast, Thornhill clearly describes the events in his study. Most of the time male scorpionflies obtain food (usually dead insects) and secrete an attractant to entice females to feed and then copulate with the male. Some-

times, however, a male without a food offering rushes toward a passing female, attempting to grasp a wing or a leg with muscular claspers that form part of his genitalia. If he gets a grip he tries to place her in a position that would permit copulation, and he frequently succeeds. Females generally run from males without nuptial gifts, and ones grabbed in this manner fight strongly to escape. Thornhill argues that he can only label this foodless mating as "rape" if the female's escape behavior is genuine rather than "coy" resistance. To investigate he set up two situations in his laboratory. In one cage he put males and females together without any food, while in a second cage he introduced females, after giving the males a bunch of dead crickets which they each staked out, one-male–one-cricket.

Most (90 percent) of the males without food offerings tried to copulate with the females, but only 22 percent (eight out of thirty-six) succeeded, and of these only half actually transferred sperm into the female reproductive tract. The latter observation is the crucial one both for consideration of the possibility that such behavior is inherited and for a view of rape as a particular *reproductive* strategy. Thornhill then took the thirty-two females that had avoided mating in the cricketless cage and put them into the cage with the goodies, where most (twenty-seven out of thirty-two) mated almost immediately. Since he had thus shown that the same females that struggle to elude males without food offerings mate rapidly with males with food, he concluded that the females' previous avoidance behavior was not simple "coyness" and that rape had indeed occurred.

Thornhill writes, "Although successful rape [that is, including insemination] may be infrequent, it is an appropriate behavior for a male to adopt when he is aggressively excluded from possession of a dead insect."[20] In this context "appropriate behavior" means one that will increase the male's reproductive success, thus augmenting his "genetic fitness." By analogy, an

---

[18]Randy Thornhill, "Rape in Scorpionflies and a General Rape Hypothesis," *Animal Behavior* 28(1980):52.

[19]L. G. Abele and S. Gilchrist, "Homosexual Rape and Sexual Selection in Acanthocephalan Worms," *Science* 197(1977):81–83.

[20]Thornhill, "Rape in Scorpionflies," 55.

"unfit" male would be one that could not get his own food cache *or* manage to mate any other way.

Getting a food offering in the first place is a risky business. Males have even been known to attempt to rob dead insects from spider webs, often losing their lives in the process. Forced mating, then, might increase a male's relative fitness by helping him avoid such risks. If this were true, Thornhill asks, "Why do not all males use rape as their primary behavior?" The answer: a hypothesis that females that feed on food offerings lay many more eggs than ones that do not, the trade-off occurring between the risk taken in obtaining food and the enhancement in female fertility if she gets more to eat.* Thornhill further suggests that since no food is forthcoming, rape decreases female fitness—a point that is difficult to understand given that females mate up to five times per week and must obtain food on at least some of those occasions. This allegedly lowered female fitness, Thornhill believes, substantiates his assertion that the phenomenon under study is rape. As is characteristic of all sociobiological treatment of male-female interaction, Thornhill emphasizes conflict:

> Female fitness is probably reduced by rape because the female gets no food from the rapist and must therefore expend time and energy in finding a male with nuptial food or in finding food on her own in an environment with abundant predators. . . . Male fitness is enhanced by rape because predation-related risks . . . can be avoided.[21]

Since these males compete heavily with each other for food, many end up with none. An empty-handed male cannot convince a female he's worth the time of day. His unfitness is plain to see. Thornhill suggests that in species in which males normally make no nuptial offerings it is harder for a female to tell how fit he is, so that

males may get to mate just by doing a good job of courtship. In this case a less fit male can trick a female into mating with him because she can't be sure how fit he really is. "Thus,'" Thornhill argues, "selection for heterosexual rape should be stronger on males of species with male resource control than on males of other species."[22]

Thornhill does not shrink from the task of applying his work on rape in insects to the human condition. In an extensive discourse on human rape he and a co-author define rape as forced copulation which reduces the ability of the female to make her own reproductive choices. In explicating this definition they write:

> Copulation by a man with women who depend on him (e.g., a male employer copulating with his female secretary or a male slaveowner with his female slave) is not *necessarily* rape . . . by our definition because the female need not be denied the option of gaining benefits that exceed the costs to reproduction (job security or salary [secretary]; resources or higher status [slave]).

In the same paragraph they suggest that because high status men have so much to offer women who are dependent upon them, those women will rarely see copulation with their bosses or owners as maladaptive, but instead will use the interaction to further their own reproductive interests. Thus, according to Thornhill and Thornhill, "high status men probably rarely actually rape."[23]

In the Thornhills' world view human males "compete with each other for relative status, including wealth and prestige." Resulting from such competition is a gradation of successful males:

> At the top of this continuum are the big winners. . . . These males are represented by men with multiple wives in preindustrial human societies and by the highest executives in large corporations, powerful politicians, *leading scholars,* and outstanding athletes and entertainers in many industrial societies. [Emphasis added]

On the other hand, they see a large number of

---

*Evolutionary biologists consider fitness to be the ability of an individual to survive and reproduce. In estimating fitness one must consider an individual's life span, how many times it reproduces, how many offspring come from each mating, and how likely those offspring are to survive to reproductive age.
[21]Ibid., 55–56.

[22]Ibid., 56.
[23]Thornhill and Thornhill, "Human Rape," 141.

men who leave the competition with limited reproductive possibilities, a small amount of money, and a struggle to hold on to just one wife and a small family. At the bottom of the heap are "the big losers: those men who are excluded from a share in the wealth, prestige and resources, and thus access to desirable mates. . . . It is those human males who have the greatest difficulty climbing the social ladder who are most likely to rape."[24]*

As with many lines of reasoning in sociobiology, the Thornhills' offers the appearance of logic and simplicity although it is in fact a highly layered and encoded argument. In order to get a solid grip on it one must peel off the various underlying assumptions, place them in the context of the theory of evolution, and see which ones have evidence to back them up and which are nothing more than guesswork. We ought also to ask what kind of evidence Thornhill would need—at least for scorpionflies—to prove his hypothesis.

The Thornhills and others[25] make a startling claim. They argue that modern evolutionary theory holds within it the lesson that rape is but one of a number of co-equal reproductive strategies to have evolved through the millenia. They feel we must recognize this fact precisely because rape in our modern cultures is so reprehensible and hope to use "applied sociobiology" to help society deal with the problem. Their argument is that males try any means to "maximize inclusive fitness"; females try to acquire as many "parental resources" as possible; males look for "low-cost matings"; the female "reproductive strategy" is to seek the best possible male. Sociobiologists generally view reproduction in terms of male-female conflicts, of which rape is simply one example. Many modern Darwinists, however, believe that this sociobiological mode of

argumentation derives little support from Darwinian theory.

EVOLUTION: THE MODERN SYNTHESIS

Darwin documented the existence of variation in the natural world: for example, in one species of snail some individuals may have shells that coil to the left while others' coil to the right; in some regions of the eastern United States coal black "gray" squirrels are quite common; and most mammals have naturally occurring albino forms. Variation abounds in living organisms. Furthermore, as Darwin wrote in the *Origin of Species,* all living things "struggle" to stay alive. Many more offspring, eggs, seeds, or spores—the means of continuing the species—are produced each generation than can possibly survive.

> Can we doubt . . . that individuals having any advantage, however slight, over others would have the best chance of surviving and procreating other kinds? On the other hand, we may feel sure that any variation in the least degree injurious would be rigidly destroyed. This preservation of favorable individual differences and variations and the destruction of those which are injurious, I have called Natural Selection, or the Survival of the Fittest.[26]

While Darwin knew that animals varied and that at least some types of variations were heritable, he understood nothing about the mechanisms of inheritance. Furthermore, Darwin provided no experimental demonstration of natural selection in action. Thus his ideas met with strong resistance from two rather different quarters. On the one side were people who responded to the religious challenge brought by scientific theories of evolution; the attacks on Darwin from the clergy were strong indeed. But by the turn of the century the era of modern genetics picked up steam, and the theory of natural selection experienced attack as well from the scientific community on the grounds of in-

[24]Ibid.

*Note that this exposition implies also that social and economic class result from competition among men with different biological endowments. Social forces seem to play only a subordinate role in the formation of class and status hierarchies.

[25]W. M. Shields and L. M. Shields, "Forcible Rape: An Evolutionary Perspective," *Ethology and Sociobiology* 4(1983):115–36.

[26]Charles Darwin, *The Origin of Species by Means of Natural Selection* (1859); reprint, New York: Mentor, 1958), 87–88.

sufficient evidence. In fact it was not until seventy-five years after the first publication of the *Origin* that biologists reached some consensus about the general mechanisms of evolution through natural selection. The book responsible for bringing this unity, however temporary, was Julian Huxley's *Evolution: The Modern Synthesis;*[27] Wilson's title, *Sociobiology: The New Synthesis,* is a conscious variant on Huxley's, a title familiar to most biologists.

The period between the *Origin* and *The Modern Synthesis* was a busy one. To begin with the work of an obscure Czech monk named Gregor Mendel came to light. During the first decade of the twentieth century his research became not only widely known, but was a stimulus for an explosion of discoveries in the field of genetics. Scientists devised rules to describe the passage of genetic information from one generation to the next. They began to work out the pathways leading from a gene to some measurable trait, finding that the connections were not always direct. They began to devise mathematical accounts of how specific genes might maintain themselves in a population. And they discovered genetic mutation. Geneticists, so absorbed in their rapidly developing field, on the whole ignored Darwin's powerful use of data from natural history (about which this new breed of scientist knew relatively little). Instead they proposed that the mechanism of evolution involved something called *mutationism.* Natural selection might act as a negative pressure eliminating harmful mutations, but positive, creative change must, they held, occur through the continuous pressure of new, small, helpful mutations.[28]

At the same time that the Mendelians, working mostly with fruit flies, mice, and corn, established the particulate nature of inheritance of certain traits (Mendel's peas were either wrinkled or smooth, not intermediate), other geneticists realized that not everything behaved in such convenient fashion. Traits such as height result from the interactions of a number of different gene combinations with one another as well as with the environment. Humans are not either six feet tall or five feet tall. They form a continuum of variation from midgets to giants. Geneticists coming from an intellectual tradition somewhat different from that of the Mendelians termed such continually varying traits "quantitative" and developed mathematical methods of analyzing their inheritance.

Sociobiologists believe that most human behavior is genetically inherited. To the extent that this is correct, such behavior must be treated as a quantitative trait, since many genetic factors are certainly involved. Except when using metaphoric hyperbole no sociobiologist seriously argues that single genes determine complex human behaviors. The quantitative geneticists also used a statistical approach to the study of evolution. Instead of looking at the result of a mating between two individuals (for instance, a black and a gray squirrel), they asked questions about the distribution of genes in entire populations, developing concepts such as "gene pools" to describe the total genetic resources of a group of animals or plants which breed with one another. Looking at the collective genetic traits of a population is a key methodology of mainstream evolutionary theory. It grew out of the analysis of quantitative traits. Sociobiologists, however, write about behaviors as if they were particulate traits, even though they know this is an oversimplification. They end up, therefore, using evolutionary theory based on the inheritance of particulate traits to analyze behaviors that—if they *have* a genetic basis—must be multiply determined. In short, they inappropriately mix their analytical media.

During the first forty years of the twentieth century Mendelians and quantitative geneticists alternately quarreled with or ignored each other. Finally, out of the strife born of different traditions of knowledge came the Modern Synthesis so thoroughly considered in Huxley's book. It reformulated Darwin's proposals in up-to-date

---

[27]Julian Huxley, *Evolution: The Modern Synthesis* (New York: Harper Bros., 1943).
[28]G. Ledyard Stebbins, *Darwin to DNA, Molecules to Humanity* (San Francisco: Freeman, 1982).

terms: individuals within most sexually reproducing populations vary to some degree in their
genetic makeup. New genetic variants arise by
mutation; in addition variability increases because the chromosomes in which genes reside
constantly undergo rearrangements. Gene A
may have originally lain next to Gene b—and
may still in some members of a population—but
since homologous chromosomes interchange
parts in each generation through a process called
crossing over, in other individuals Gene A may
lie next to Gene b, and Genes A and b may
interact when they lie together in new, even unpredictable ways. Because during sexual reproduction chromosomes rearrange and change
their associations, the initial variation introduced by mutation increases greatly.

Sociobiologists frequently write about evolution as if it were a single, uniformly agreed-
upon theory. In fact, many currents, sometimes
conflicting, contribute to the stream of evolutionary thought. Although the Modern Synthesis brought Mendelians and quantitative geneticists into general agreement, even today
their intellectual descendants bring very different viewpoints to the study of evolution in
populations.[29] Arguments continue to rage over
the degree to which genetic variation is an ever-
present feature of populations, and whether
evolution proceeds through the effects of many
genes with minor effects working in concert
rather than through the appearance at auspicious moments in the life of a population of rare
genes with major effects. There is not yet *an*
accepted analysis of evolution but a number of
traditions of analysis, some predominating in
the United States, others in Europe.[30] If one
were to read only the sociobiological literature,
one would lose sight of the intellectual richness
of the study of evolution—missing would be
some of the difficult and fascinating intellectual

struggles in which students of evolution find
themselves.[31]

Sociobiologists focus on individuals' attempts
to *maximize* their genetic fitness. The Modern
Synthesis, however, contains no arguments
about perfection. Organisms do not strive to
maximize their ability to fit the environment in
which they find themselves; in fact, over the long
haul such maximization could spell extinction.
The more perfectly adapted an organism is to its
environment, the less flexibility it has should the
environment change. A versatile animal such as
a raccoon has managed rather well, even in the
heart of large cities, to live off of human refuse;
it remains annoyingly successful despite the constant diminishment of its original forest environment. In sharp contrast, the California con-
dor, shy and environmentally limited, is more
likely to end up like the passenger pigeon,
stuffed into a museum display cabinet.

The Indian and African rhinoceri provide another illustration of how the notion of maximization of fitness deviates from mainstream
evolutionary theory. Both use horns for defense,
but the Indian rhino has only one while the African sports two. Is there some reason that two
horns are more adaptive in Africa while one
horn promotes better survival in India? Probably not. It is more likely that one-horned, two-
horned, and hornless varieties of rhinoceros existed on both continents, but that in India by
chance the population experiencing selective
pressure had a higher frequency of the genes for
one horn, while the ancestral African population
happened to have had a higher starting frequency of genes for two horns. In each case there
may have been the same degree of selective pressure favoring horned over hornless varieties.
But in the Indian population, which already had
a higher frequency of single-horned genes, the
pressure selected for one horn; while in the African rhinos the quickest route to success was
through the increase in frequency of two-horned
individuals (see Figure 4-1). In other words,

[29]Ibid.
[30]Stephen Jay Gould and R. C. Lewontin, "The Spandrels of San
Marco and the Panglossian Paradigm: A Critique of the Adaptationist Programme, *Proceedings of the Royal Society of London B*
205(1979):581–98.

[31]Richard C. Lewontin, *The Genetic Basis of Evolutionary Change*
(New York: Columbia University Press, 1974).

there is more than one way to horn a rhino.[32] In fact in most populations of any size and complexity there are multiple ways to skin the selective cat and the one that is chosen is not always the best; it is the most quickly attainable.[33]

Sociobiologists emphasize natural selection to the exclusion of other mechanisms of evolution. Evolution can occur, however, without the intervention of either adaptation or natural selection. Among the best-studied examples are colonizations of previously uninhabited islands. Imagine an interbreeding population of birds living on the mainland. Within that population might exist genetic variations in feather color, for example a solid blue variety and a speckled pattern. Suppose that by chance a small number of the speckled birds got blown onto an island where no birds of that species previously lived. Should the birds survive, breed, and inhabit the island, the entire island population would be speckled rather than blue. A biologist who subsequently studied these two geographic locations would find two bird populations with different gene pools, one including two feather color variants, the other only one. Evolution—defined as a stable change in the frequency of genes in a population—has occurred. But the cause was a chance natural event, not natural selection. And the biologist studying the population—if he or she knew how it originated—would certainly not argue that speckled birds are better adapted to island life.

Island colonization illustrates but one of the ways in which evolution may proceed without either adaptation or natural selection, but there are many others. Consider albino animals of the arctic. Hungry predators may have unwittingly selected for the albino color variant by eating more of the easily visible dark-colored variants. But albinism, which affects coat color, also causes severe problems with eyesight; albino an-

imals generally cannot see as well as their colored counterparts. It is hard to imagine an adaptive "use" for poor eyesight. For arctic-dwelling mammals it just comes along as part of a package deal. Probably all genes are (like the gene for albinism) *pleiotropic,* that is, they have more than one effect. . . . Many traits common in populations of plants and animals have undoubtedly, as has nearsightedness in albinos, come along for the ride. Such traits have evolved, but they have not been selected for, nor are they adaptive.

In addition to evolution without natural selection, a population can also experience selection without adaptation, and adaptation without natural selection. A gene that doubles an individual organism's fertility would spread rapidly in a population. But if the population does not increase its food supply some of the extra animals produced will starve and the number of individuals who survive at any one time will remain more or less steady. While the population can in no way be said to have become better adapted, natural selection favoring individuals carrying the genes for higher fertility has certainly occurred.[34] Or, consider a species of shellfish which uses sand and mud grains to make its shell. By using local construction material, the animal ends up matching its background quite nicely, and the color coordination may well provide good camouflage. The well-suited shell color is an adaptation, but it has not occurred by natural selection. Instead it is a by-product of the fact that this particular shellfish uses the ground it sits on to build its shell.

The lesson from all of this is that one must proceed with caution when trying to decide whether the evolution of a particular trait has occurred by natural selection. It can even be difficult to know whether one has correctly identified a legitimate trait. Writings on the evolution of the human hand illustrate this particular dilemma. What was selected for? The whole hand, the opposable thumb, the flexibility of the fin-

[32]Richard Lewontin, "Adaptation," *Scientific American* 239(1978): 212–30.
[33]Sewall Wright, "The Roles of Mutation, Inbreeding, Crossbreeding and Selection in Evolution," in *Proceedings of the Sixth International Congress of Genetics* (ed. I. F. Jones), 1(1932):356–66.

[34]Gould and Lewontin, "The Spandrels of San Marco."

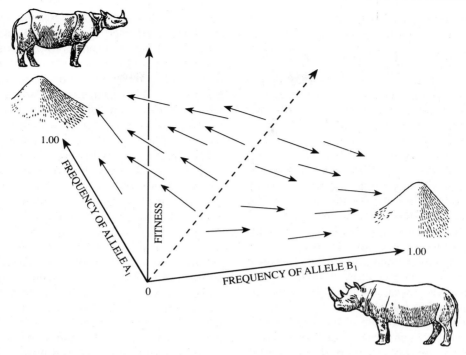

FIGURE 4-1   Alternate Evolutionary Paths of One- and Two-Horned Rhinoceri
Alternative evolutionary paths may be taken by two species under similar selection pressures. The Indian rhinoceros has one horn and the African rhinoceros has two horns. The horns are adaptations for protection in both cases, but the number of horns does not necessarily constitute a specifically adaptive difference. There are simply two adaptive peaks in a field of gene frequencies, or two solutions to the same problem; some variation in the initial conditions led two rhinoceros populations to respond to similar pressures in different ways. For each of two hypothetical genes there are two alleles: A_1 and A_2, B_1 and B_2. A population of genotype A_1B_2 has one horn and a population of genotype A_2B_1 has two horns.

SOURCE: Richard Lewontin, "Adaptation," *Scientific American* 239(1978):225. Copyright © 1978 by Scientific American, Inc. All rights reserved.

gers? We can never be sure. The problem arises because scientists are trained to break things down into component parts. The hand, however, functions as a whole unit, and losing sight of this can lead one into hopeless philosophical quagmires. The disagreements between evolutionary biologists who work by progressive atomization of traits and ones who believe most such traits to be artificial are profound and probably without resolution.[35]

The notion that evolution is best studied by

[35]Ibid.

identifying traits and then trying to figure out how they might help an organism better adapt to its environment predominates today in American scientific thought. But merely making up a plausible account will not do—good scientific inquiry requires careful consideration of nonadaptationist explanations, such as those just exemplified. Huxley understood this quite clearly, despite the fact that his book especially emphasized the processes of natural selection and adaptation. In its early pages Huxley explains the elements of proof in the study of evolution, emphasizing clearly that biology is first and foremost an experimental science:

> A particular shade of human complexion may be due to genetic constitution for fair complexion plus considerable exposure to the sun, or to a genetically dark complexion plus very little tanning; and similarly for stature, intelligence, and many other characters. *The important fact is that only experiment can decide between the two.*[36] [Emphasis added]

The phenomenon of industrial melanism comes about as close as one could hope to a fully proven case of evolution through natural selection. Living in the industrial regions of northern Europe is a moth called *Biston betularia,* commonly referred to as the peppered moth because of its light mottled appearance, a color pattern that blends in perfectly with the lichen-covered bark of trees in the area. As more and more industry developed in Europe, large areas became polluted with huge quantities of smoke particles, measurable in tons per square mile per month. As the particles darkened surfaces they (along with sulfur dioxide gas) killed the tree-growing lichen, exposing the dark underlying bark.[37] No record existed of a dark form of the peppered moth until the mid 1800s, when dark-colored variants appeared with some frequency and, in the most heavily polluted regions, became more common than the light form for which the moth had been named.

Geneticists interested in this moth established that the different colors were inherited. Following its initial appearance (presumably a spontaneous mutation), the first dark-colored moth spread much more rapidly in the population than would be expected if the dark moth and its descendants survived neither more nor less well than the lightly peppered variety. Scientists used ecological studies to decipher this puzzle. By watching the moths during the daytime when they are inactive and rest on tree trunks, it immediately became clear that the dark form was very difficult to spot in industrial areas where the bare, darkened bark served as the background, while in unpolluted regions the peppered variety blended in almost perfectly with the lichen-covered bark. Furthermore, they saw birds swoop in and eat resting moths. In an ecological experiment, one scientist marked and then released both darkly and lightly colored moths and retrapped them later, finding that in polluted areas he could recover fewer light than dark moths. The combination of observations led him to conclude that the birds ate more of the light moths in polluted regions, while the reverse was true in nonindustrial areas.[38]

Natural selection in the persona of hungry birds enabled the darkly colored variants to spread rapidly in the moth populations of industrialized England. Or, as a population geneticist would phrase it, a change in the environment led to a change in genotype frequency (more dark than light genes) within the population. The birds acted as selective agents: in unpolluted environments the light-colored moths had a selective advantage, making them fitter than the dark moths. The light moth living in unpolluted regions had a greater likelihood of producing more offspring than the dark moth; in polluted parts of the country the reverse was true.

A method of investigation emerges from this example. The population studied could be shown to have color variations (variation measured, rather than hypothesized). Breeding experiments established the genetic basis of the variation. The changes in gene frequency were measured, and the selective agents first hypothesized, then tested by field experiments. Even so it now turns out that selection has shown up at an unexpected stage of the moth's life cycle, a finding which even in this well-studied case leaves us partially ignorant of the workings of natural selection.

If the Modern Synthesis represents such a rich and complex body of thought and sociobiology

---

[36]Huxley, *Evolution: The Modern Synthesis,* 18.
[37]H. Kettlewell, "Darwin's Missing Evidence," *Scientific American* 200(1959):48–53.

[38]H. Kettlewell, "A Resume of Investigations on the Evolution of Melanism in the *Lepidoptera*," *Proceedings of the Royal Society of London B* 145(1956):297–303.

such an impoverishing oversimplification, why did Wilson's book and the others that followed receive such instant acclaim? It is of course true that the explanation and defense of the status quo contained within this body of writing offers a certain psychological and political sense of well-being, but that offers only a partial explanation of the phenomenon. The missing puzzle piece is that Huxley's Modern Synthesis did not solve all remaining questions about evolution. Sociobiology developed as one of a number of attempts to remedy the shortcomings of Huxley's account of evolution.

Evolution:
The Postmodern Dissolution

For about twenty years, the Modern Synthesis worked. In fact it worked so well that—in one of those contradictions that philosophers love—its very success brought new controversies. Using the Modern Synthesis as a framework, biologists analyzed a host of natural phenomena, putting meat on the bones of evolutionary thinking. It seemed reasonable to extend the insights gained about the process of evolution to the study of social behavior. And herein lay one of the troubles: behaviors were easy to describe, but accounting for their evolution was another matter altogether. For example, in her book on the mountain gorilla, Dian Fossey vividly describes the death of Digit, a male gorilla slaughtered by poachers as he defended a gorilla band consisting of his siblings, parents, and nonrelatives.[39] He did not just beat his chest and run, saving his life while permitting the others a chance at escape. Instead, he stood his ground and battled to the death. Digit's behavior appears to have been altruistic; he died to save the lives of the other troop members. His action, though, presents a puzzle to the evolutionist. If altruistic individuals are less likely to survive than "selfish" ones, *and* if the behavior in question is genetically determined, then how could it have become common in the population? More generally stated, the question becomes one about the evolution of cooperative behavior. That such behaviors evolved is certain. *How* is far from clear. This is one of the central problems sociobiologists have set out to solve.

The first stab at an answer came with the publication of the theory of group selection. It was proposed that natural selection could act on a group as a unit, selecting characteristics that might benefit the species as a whole even if it sacrificed some individuals. I remember grappling with this idea as a student, intrigued by the problem it addressed yet puzzled by the vague formulation of the solution. Biologists now agree that the idea of group selection, as originally put together, must be wrong. But from that idea has arisen a furious debate about the level of election. Does natural selection operate on whole species at once? On subspecies? Darwin thought it acted on individual organisms, but after Mendel's rediscovery many came to think of selection occurring for a particular constellation of genes (genotype). More recently, impassioned arguments have been offered for the idea that individual genes are the units of natural selection. Related to the disagreements over levels of selection are disputes about the definition of *fitness.* We must, then, continue to view sociobiological ideas as part of a heavily debated scientific controversy; to understand the elements of this debate we need to examine more closely the meanings of phrases such as *kin selection, inclusive fitness,* sexual selection,* and *parental investment.*

David Barash defines his view of the "Central Theorum of Sociobiology: Insofar as a behavior in question represents at least some component of the individual's genotype, then that behavior should act to maximize the inclusive fitness of the individual concerned."[40] Although sociobiologists write about the "maximization of inclusive fitness" as if it were accepted biological

---

[39]Dian Fossey, *Gorillas in the Mist* (Boston: Houghton Mifflin, 1983).

*Earlier in this [article, pp. 43–44] I introduced the more generally accepted concept of *individual fitness.*
[40]Barash, "Predictive Sociobiology," 211.

dogma, this new and controversial idea is one of the weakest links in the sociobiological chain of reasoning. We have already addressed some of the difficulties of the notion of maximization, and we must now consider what is meant by *inclusive fitness* and what it has to do with the "problem" of altruism.

An altruistic act lowers the actor's individual fitness (chance of survival), and that lowering ought to make it less likely that any possible genetic basis for the behavior survives in succeeding generations. Yet such behavior does exist. The solution to the problem, suggested by biologist W. D. Hamilton, lies in the related concepts of *inclusive fitness* and *kin selection.* For simplicity's sake let's imagine that the defense behavior of an adolescent male gorilla is encoded by a single gene, while remembering that animals within the troop are genetically interrelated. Because siblings, on average, have 50 percent of their genes in common, Digit's brothers and sisters stand a 50 percent chance of carrying the hypothetical "troop defense trait." Using greater precision than in the earlier proposal of group selection, Hamilton demonstrated mathematically that the troop defense trait could remain in a population generation after generation if the behavior increased the likelihood of sibling survival by more than two times, that is, by making it twice as likely that a family member with half the defender's genes would survive.

An analogous relationship would hold for altruistic acts affecting other family members. Nephews and nieces, for example, have on average one-fourth of their aunt's or uncle's genes. Thus, should the genes that hypothetically code for any act—for example, a warning call—even if the act led to the death of the caller, make it four times as likely for a niece or nephew to survive, the trait would remain in a population. Hamilton generalized these arguments into the concept of inclusive fitness, which holds that the effect of a genetically inherited trait can be measured by its effects on the fitness of an individual *and* on that individual's kin, depending on the degree of genetic relatedness of the kin.[41] With this approach fitness, rather than being an individual trait, becomes the property of several individuals related by family ties; selection for increased fitness occurs on an individual *and* its kin—hence the term *kin selection.* Hamilton's formulation was quite successful in explaining certain specialized problems in the behavior of social insects such as bees, ants, and termites.

Barash, however, raised Hamilton's limited concept of inclusive fitness to a central theorum. Indeed the invocation of inclusive fitness to explain the evolution of an enormous range of complex behaviors is one of the distinguishing features of sociobiology and, because it is not easily subject to experimental test, it is also one of its weakest. Barash himself recognizes the difficulty, "I know of few studies that have even measured individual fitness," he writes. "In most cases we must be content for now with measures that we *intuit* as being related to fitness . . . such as efficiency in foraging, avoiding predators, success in acquiring a mate, or often, simple copulation frequencies"[42] (emphasis added.* An argument relying on intuition rather than on something we can measure—however imperfectly—removes itself from the realm of conventional science, a realm in which one devises hypotheses and methods to test them, proving them "right" because they plausibly pull together most (but rarely all) available observations, or disproving them by finding they cannot handle a significant fact or observation. One standard method scientists use to shore up a position is to consider alternative hypotheses and show them wanting.

Barash, for example, uses the concept of inclusive fitness to talk about the evolution of menopause, a phenomenon that appears to be uniquely human. He wonders why women stop reproducing even though they may have as many as thirty years of life left. Since he figures

---

[41] Wilson, *Sociobiology: The New Synthesis.*
[42] Barash, "Predictive Sociobiology," 212.
*Measuring fitness is a difficulty for all of evolutionary theory. For a more detailed discussion of the problem see Appendix, pp. 223–24. [Not printed here.]

that everybody ought to be out there maximizing their fitness by constant reproduction, the puzzle seems great to him. Even allowing that older women face greater risks in childbirth is insufficient.

> Although the risks . . . are higher for older women . . . they should still be selected, as are men, to die trying. The genes carried by older women who average just one additional child because of some Herculean, possibly suicidal reproductive effort should still surpass statistically the genes carried by other women who elected instead to enjoy a peaceful, unencumbered but unproductive old age.*

Barash answers his own puzzlement by invoking inclusive fitness:

> As grandmothers, middle-aged women can provide for their fitness by caring for their children's children instead of bearing more themselves.[43]

He shores up this position by citing the universality of grandmothering, suggesting that his view of the origin of menopause is consistent with "the calculus of evolution."

And indeed it is. But so, too, are other explanations. Menopause might, for example, have both a biological and a cultural origin. Our protohuman ancestors never lived long enough to have more than a few postreproductive years. As humans developed the capacity for culture, however, they increased their average life span by improving their diet, building better shelters, and learning to cure the ill—all changes wrought by conscious human activity. Living long enough for the body to age and to enter that part of the life span in which menopause even shows up is recent (on the geological time scale) and is the result of human cultural activity. Menopause itself then is but a by-product of aging, which in turn became possible only through the advance of human culture.

I would argue with Barash that my explanation is more plausible than his. He, presumably, would disagree. I cannot think of any evidence

either of us could bring up that would resolve the issue. And that is my point: the argument has left the realm of conventional science since, except for restricted cases such as those dealt with by Hamilton, one must, as Barash admits, rely on intuition rather than experimentation. Thus a sociobiology that depends heavily on the maximization of inclusive fitness cannot convincingly lay claim to being scientific in the conventional sense.

Sociobiology and Sex

Darwinian theory has appeared again and again as ammunition in a social struggle over "the woman question." Should women go to college? Should they vote? Should they work outside the home? The storeroom of biological knowledge has undergone constant assault from raiding parties on both sides of the issue.[44] In addition to the "maximization of inclusive fitness," another weapon in the sociobiological arsenal is the concept of sexual selection. It all started with what Darwin viewed as the mystery of the universality of male excellence. Why should males be stronger and have larger antlers, horns, canine teeth, and on top of all that be the ones to sing beautiful courtship songs, to grow spectacular tail feathers, and to engage in strange behavior such as the mating displays of woodcocks and the intricate nest building of the bower and weaver birds? In some cases, such as that of the peacock, one might even expect natural selection to have eliminated the trait in question. Cannot a fox more easily spot and catch a peacock, brilliant as he is and weighed down by such an unmanageable tail, than he can a well-camouflaged peahen? How indeed did the peacock get to keep his feathers?

The answer to the problem, one emphasized

---

*Note how Barash equates human sexual activity with reproduction in this passage.

[43]Barash, "The Whisperings Within," 120–21.

[44]Janet Sayers, *Biological Politics* (London: Tavistock, 1982); Antoinette Brown Blackwell, *The Sexes Throughout Nature* (New York: Putnam, 1875; Westport, Conn.: Hyperion, 1976); Elizabeth Gamble, *Evolution and Woman: An Inquiry into the Dogma of Her Inferiority to Man* (London: Putnam, 1893; Westport, Conn.: Hyperion, 1976); and Frances Emily White, "Women's Place in Nature," *Popular Science Monthly* 6(1875):292–301.

strongly by modern sociobiologists, was something Darwin labeled *sexual selection.* Sexual selection has two components, intermale competition and female choice. Darwin recognized that large, specialized structures such as antlers in male deer were unlikely to have become common due to natural selection alone. Deer, for example, do not usually use antlers to protect themselves from attack, but depend more heavily on protective colors, alertness to surprise, and fleetness of foot—all characteristics likely to have become established through natural selection. What purpose then do antlers serve? Darwin saw but one—to enable males to spar with one another for mating rights with the females. In many species of deer there *are* ritual sparring matches each mating season. Darwin reasoned that the most successful combatants would get to mate earlier and more frequently, thus standing a better chance of passing on to the next generation those traits enabling them to win the contest in the first place. Too sophisticated a biologist to suppose that only antler size counted, he realized that sexual selection via male-male competition must have chosen a complex of traits which also included body size, vigor, and persistence.

Sexual selection was a complicated affair depending not only "on the ardor in love, courage and the rivalry of the males" but also on the "powers of perception, taste and will of the female."[45] For Darwin, female choice was key. Of what use would be a ritual "victory" if the female went off and mated with the loser? Postulating active female choice enabled one to understand that foxes have not eliminated long-tailed peacocks because the peahen's preference to mate with the most spectacular males has kept the genes for elaborate tail development present with high frequency in the population. Here is a case of balance between sexual selection and natural selection, predation working against males with spectacular tails, female choice working for them.

Darwin recorded many examples in which the male was more brightly colored or more highly specialized than the more juvenile-looking female. Extrapolating from these he suggested that in an evolutionary sense females represented the less variable, more juvenile or primitive state of the species. During evolution the male built more elaborate structures upon the simpler female baseline. (This idea is not unlike the embryological notion that the baseline of fetal development is female, discussed in chapter 3.) Not all nineteenth-century biologists bought Darwin's view. Alfred Russel Wallace, the most important nineteenth-century scientific interpreter of Darwinian theory, objected both to the idea that males were modified from a female base *and* to the notion that female choice played an important role in sexual selection.[46] Instead he felt that male structure and colors served as the starting point from which the different female coloration derived mediated by natural rather than sexual selection. Although he believed in sexual selection involving male-male competition, he held that dull-colored females evolved because their drabness provided good protective coloration. Over the millennia, no doubt, brightly colored females raised fewer offspring because predators spotted them more easily. Nature thus selected for drably attired females, leaving the brilliant males to offer beauty to the world. Wallace's dismissal of female choice found easy acceptance, and the idea of a female role in sexual selection did not regain popularity among biologists until the early 1970s.

Wallace's and Darwin's descriptions of the animal world of male and female reflected widespread views about women. The Darwinian female represented the stabler but also the more juvenile form of the species. Despite her own passivity, she played an active role in the establishment of many a spectacular male modification. Interestingly, Wallace's investment in the

---

[45]Charles Darwin, *The Descent of Man, and Selection in Relation to Sex* (1871; reprint, Princeton, N.J.: Princeton University Press, 1981).

[46]Alfred Russel Wallace, *Darwinism: An Exposition of the Theory of Natural Selection* (London: AMS, 1889); and Alfred Russel Wallace, *Tropical Nature and Other Essays* (London: AMS, 1878).

notion of female passivity made it impossible for him to buy the concept of active female choice in sexual selection. And unable to make that purchase, he had then to stock up on the idea that the male represented the basic species type from which the less brightly colored female deviated.

The reopening of the Darwinian debate, engendered by modern attempts to explain animal altruism, contributed to an intellectual climate in which reassessment of Darwin's proposals about sexual selection became inevitable. Huxley and Darwin both clearly separated natural from sexual selection. Huxley cited the example of elephant seals, in which the males are a great deal larger than the females. Both sexes reach far greater size than other seal species; these interspecific differences, Huxley felt, must be explicable in terms of natural selection. Given the lifestyle of the elephant seal, increased size must have provided some selective advantage over smaller forms. But the striking size difference between the sexes could not have evolved solely by the action of natural selection on the species—male and female—as a whole. Male elephant seals fight intensely with one another for control over large groups of females. The winners get to mate with large numbers of females, the losers with none at all. For elephant seals (but not, for example, for other harem-forming mammals*[47]) size is an important determinant of victory. The genes for increased size thus remain under heavy selective pressure and "the size . . . will tend to be pushed beyond the optimum, or what would be the optimum for other reasons."[48]

Sexual selectionists from Darwin to Edward O. Wilson have sought to explain the evolution of courtship displays. During such rituals males often strut about and show off any special courting colors (feathers, neck flaps, and so on) with great energy. Such behavior serves more than one function. To begin with it attracts the attention of members of the opposite sex. After the initial pairing, it helps to synchronize the couple's physiological readiness to mate: via the brain, visual stimuli can affect the pituitary gland to stimulate ovulation and thus increase the likelihood that fertilization will follow mating. It certainly wouldn't do, for example, for a male fish to shed his sperm into the open ocean *before* the female releases her eggs. Their courtship routine ensures that both eggs and sperm will end up in the right place at the right time. Natural selection was probably a major mechanism in the evolution of courtship displays, but some of the extreme displays such as the peacock's tail may well have become exaggerated through sexual selection—a selection that probably operated most strongly in species with strong intermale competition. Dr. Ernst Mayr, a highly respected modern Darwinist, sums it all up by explaining that the development of courtship displays and structures

> . . . was probably favored originally by natural selection to synchronize the physiological state of the two sexes, but . . . sexual selection is presumably super-imposed in all cases in which a male may gain reproductive advantage owing to an extreme development of an epigamic [courtship-related] character.[49]

Wilson describes the same events in different language. He uses the word *epigamic* to describe "any trait related to courtship and sex other than the essential organs and behavior of copulation":

> Pure epigamic display can be envisioned as a contest between salesmanship and sales resistance. The sex that courts, ordinarily the male, plans to invest less reproductive effort in the offspring. What it offers . . . is chiefly evidence that it is fully normal and physiologically fit. But this

*Jane Lancaster objects to the use of the word *harem*. She refers instead to one-male groups as those in which females are virtually self-sufficient, except for fertilization.
[47]Jane Lancaster, *Primate Behavior and the Emergence of Human Culture* (New York: Holt, Rinehart and Winston, 1975). Note that this completely alters the significance attached to the "fact" of a particular social organization.
[48]Huxley, *Evolution: The Modern Synthesis*, 525.

[49]Ernst Mayr, "Sexual Selection and Natural Selection," in *Sexual Selection and the Descent of Man*, ed. Bernard Campbell (Chicago: Aldine, 1972), 97–98, 320.

warranty consists of only a brief performance so that strong selective pressures exist for less fit individuals to present a false image. [The female] . . . will . . . find it strongly advantageous to distinguish the really fit from the pretended fit. Consequently there will be a strong tendency for the courted sex to develop coyness . . . its responses will be hesitant and cautious in a way that evokes still more displays and makes correct discrimination easier.[50]

Two things strike me about this passage. First, the role of natural selection in the evolution of courtship displays, clearly emphasized in Mayr's description, is lost from view in Wilson's. Sexual selection suddenly becomes the total picture, the *only* description of the evolution of courtship behavior. Second, the metaphor of consumption leaps off the printed page. "Salesmanship," "sales resistance," "invest," "warranty": the words jar compared to Darwin's lyric that females selected the most beautiful males. In a century's time the image of the female consumer shopping for the best mate has replaced that of the protectress of beauty and refinement. Missing, too, is the image of two sexes cooperating to bring forth the next generation. Instead Wilson presents courtship as a contest in which males and females are fundamentally at odds; *his* interest is to reproduce regardless of how fit he is, even if success entails trickery, and *hers* is to increase her fitness by exposing his deceit, choosing for herself the best possible mate.

Sociobiologists offer a simple physiological reason to explain why males and females have such different approaches to "maximizing their inclusive fitness." Females produce eggs, large cells stuffed full of nutrients which support the fragile life of the developing embryo. In an apparent trade-off between size and quantity, the females of most species produce relatively few such giant cells. A single female mammal, for instance, may make as few as four hundred in her lifetime. Males on the other hand produce millions of sperm, little bitty cells that stimulate egg development and transfer a set of the father's chromosomes to the new generation. Citing as evidence the difference in size and number of male and female sex cells, sociobiologists claim that females must invest more physiological energy in putting together an egg than males do in making a sperm. As an aside to the main explanation of their argument, I must point out that they provide no evidence to support this idea, apparently believing it to be obvious to even the most casual observer. How one weighs the energy costs of judicious manufacture of a small number of rather large, well-stocked cells against the profligate production of millions and millions of tiny ones, though, is far from clear. Be that as it may, the sociobiologists lean heavily on this nonaxiomatic axiom. A female, they say, starts out investing more in her sex cell and thus must protect her startup costs by making sure the egg gets the best sperm possible and by guarding the fertilized egg. If one adds on to the situation internal development and prolonged postnatal care, the differential becomes enormous. Here's how David Barash puts it:

> [The female] has much more invested in each of those eggs than [the male] has in his sperm and this asymmetry is particularly apparent in higher vertebrates. . . . Male birds and mammals produce sperm in incredible abundance with each ejaculation, and these sperm can be readily replaced. Males can usually walk . . . away from the consequences of a copulation. . . . The consequences of a bad decision . . . fall particularly heavily upon females and hence it is not surprising that they tend to be the more discriminating sex.[51]

At the time of fertilization females have already put more energy into gamete production and thus, so the theory goes, are less likely to abandon ship. In addition, females of many species carry the embryo inside them, or guard eggs while they develop. With passing time the energy invested in producing and then rearing to birth a fertilized egg increases the difference in female versus male investment. Thus, according

[50]Wilson, *Sociobiology: The New Synthesis*, 320.

[51]David Barash, *Sociobiology and Behavior* (New York: Elsevier, 1977), 147.

to sociobiological theory, a male can benefit by abandoning females early in the game, when he has invested little and she a great deal.

On the physiology of gamete production Barash and others have built entire edifices of behavior. This particular aspect of sociobiological theory bears intriguing similarities to one from the turn of the nineteenth century expounded by Patrick Geddes, a zoologist turned sociologist, and his student J. Arthur Thompson.[52] They argued that the sperm exhibits a catabolic or active quality while the egg is anabolic, passive, and well fed. From these differences in the metabolism of the male and female sex cells they deduced a host of behavioral differences found in adults: males are smarter, more independent, and more energetic than their patient, intuitive female counterparts. Although the sociobiological theory uses more up-to-date biological terminology and emphasizes courting and child-rearing behaviors rather than more general qualities such as intelligence, its biological content is no less naive than Geddes's and Thompson's eighty-five-year-old conceptualization.

Modern sociobiological theorists start with the gametes and end up explaining why females tend toward monogamy and males toward polygamy. Generally, they say, a female's reproductive physiology limits the number of offspring she can produce; she increases her fitness by ensuring that her young stand the best possible chance of survival and reproduction. Since in theory a single male can produce many more offspring than a single female, the quality of any individual offspring may not matter so long as he gets to make a whole lot of them. Thus males will mate without much discrimination and as often as possible, and any female will do, so long as she's young and healthy. Once a female has mated, though, she drops out of the running because her investment in the egg dictates that she take care of it rather than running off to mate again. So it pays for her to be highly selective, putting off the male until she can be sure he's a good choice. That polygyny is more common than polyandry, say sociobiologists, offers support for their assertions.

That polyandry exists at all, though, presents a puzzle. Certain shore birds, for instance, completely reverse sex roles. The female is larger and more brightly feathered and is the aggressive suitor. After mating with one male she leaves him behind to sit on the eggs and feed the hatchlings, while she moves on to a second and sometimes even a third round of mating and egg laying. The males in each case perform the child-care functions.[53]* Sociobiologists rationalize the existence of polyandry (which has evolved at least five different times in birds) by reference to another special invention, an account of sexual selection in terms of something they call "parental investment." "The relative parental investment of the sexes in their young," writes Professor Robert Trivers (who invented the idea), "is the key variable controlling the operation of sexual selection." Trivers hoped to offer a general theory to explain the wide variety of mating and child-care arrangements found in the natural world. He suggested that any time one sex (usually the female) invests more in reproduction and parenting, members of the other sex will compete among themselves (sexual selection) for mating privileges. The patterns seen in the world today, he suggests, were historically influenced by the differences in initial energy investments in differently sized sex cells. He defines parental investment as "any investment by the parent in an individual offspring that increases the offspring's chance of surviving (and hence reproductive success) at the cost of the parent's ability to invest in other offspring."[54] Investment starts with the production of the sex cell and ends when the parent is shed of its young.

Trivers plays out the consequences of this theory in a number of ways. Since sexual selection

---

[52]Patrick Geddes and J. Arthur Thompson, *The Evolution of Sex* (New York: Humboldt, 1890).

[53]R. Selander, "Sexual Selection and Dimorphism in Birds," in *Sexual Selection and the Descent of Man*, ed. Campbell.
*It is interesting to note that the females from these species produce more testosterone in their ovaries than do the males in their testes.
[54]Robert Trivers, "Parental Investment and Sexual Selection," in *Sexual Selection and the Descent of Man*, ed. Campbell, 139, 173.

occurs in cases for which the total parental invest-ment of each sex differs, these cases ought always to result in greater sexual dimorphism, that is, one sex being larger or more brightly colored than the other. Similarly, in species that are not partic-ularly dimorphic, the amount of parental care should be roughly the same for both sexes. He tests his hypothesis that the relative amount of parental investment controls sexual selection with the example of polyandrous birds, saying, in ef-fect, that they are the exceptions that prove the rule. For in this rare example in which the female invests less in parental care, she is the one to show the gaudy effects of sexual selection. Although this conveniently fits into part of his scheme, it does not explain how polyandry ever evolved to begin with. Female birds from polyandrous species, af-ter all, do produce eggs of enormous size and the males make tiny sperm. Using the gametic energy investment theory, polyandry ought not to hap-pen. And surprisingly, neither Trivers nor Wil-son—who offers an extended account of Trivers's ideas—seem worried about it.

The polyandry perplexity notwithstanding, Trivers has a lot to say about the relations be-tween the sexes. He develops his ideas about pa-rental investment to explain everything from philandering males who desert their mates and the sexual double standard to the deep humilia-tion felt by a cuckolded husband. True monog-amy, he writes, can't really exist because "male sex cells remain tiny compared to female sex cells. . . . The male's initial parental investment, that is his investment at the moment of fertiliza-tion, is much smaller than the female's, even if later, through parental care, he invests as much or more."[55] Thus a male, even a monogamous one, remains ambiguously committed because at any moment he can abandon an impregnated fe-male for a new mate and still come out ahead in the energy investment contest. The female is stuck with three choices. She can abandon her already considerable investment (ditch the kid) to search for a more faithful male. She can raise

the young alone; if she succeeds, the male who abandoned her lucks out—genetically speak-ing—and he may have managed to reproduce once or twice again in the meantime. Finally, the female can try to deceive another male into help-ing her out, a possibility with some likelihood of success if she doesn't already have eggs or off-spring to show for her troubles.

Trivers also offers us new insights into cuck-oldry, a word derived from the habit of the fe-male cuckoo of laying her eggs in the nests of other birds. The cuckoo hatchling invariably heaves its noncuckoo nestmates over the side of the nest and becomes the sole, enormous, ugly child of its still-doting foster parents. In modern usage a cuckold is the husband of an unfaithful wife—a far nastier and more humiliating state, apparently, than being the wife of a philanderer, for which in fact no word exists. In any organism in which fertilization is internal the male cannot be sure whose sperm did the fertilizing, so "to the degree that he invests in the care of the off-spring it is genetically advantageous for him to make sure that he has exclusive access to the female's unfertilized eggs."[56] Thus selection would favor the evolution of males that guard their females through territorial exclusiveness, dominance, or the development of long-term monogamous bonds. A cuckolded husband is far worse off, genetically speaking, than the wife of an unfaithful husband. She at least is certain that the children she bears are her own; he must take her word for it. In Trivers's view this bio-logical fact makes plausible the double standard and helps explain the severity of sanctions taken against sexually adventurous women.

PARENTAL INVESTMENT: WHAT IS THE EVIDENCE?

Trivers bases much of his work on animal stud-ies. Yet neither he nor other sociobiologists are timid about applying their ideas to humans. Wilson writes:

---

[55]Ibid., 145.

[56]Wilson, *Sociobiology: The New Synthesis*, 327.

The principal significance of Trivers' analysis lies in the demonstration that many details of courtship can also be interpreted with reference to the several possibilities of maltreatment at the hands of the mate. The assessment made by an individual is based on rules and strategies designed by natural selection. . . . Potentially the implications for the study of human behavior are very great.[57]

At one level it all seems quite plausible. Using the thread of internal consistency, sociobiological analyses bind together many seemingly disparate facts. A good explanation ought certainly to do just that—but, alas, *just* that is not enough. Viable theories require experimental testing in order to remove them from the realm of fantasy and place them in the world of science. Since evolution by natural selection requires favoring some genetic variants over others, the first and foremost criterion is the demonstration that the trait of interest is really under genetic control.

Attempts to demonstrate genetic control, however, encounter a number of serious difficulties. Consider two very different species of fish. One, the codfish, produces millions of eggs, spilling them without further attention directly into the open ocean, where the vast majority die. Another, the eelpout, produces only a few offspring which the female bears alive. Using the concept of parental selection one could explain the difference between these two fish, suggesting that the codfish adapted by producing large numbers of eggs while abdicating all parental responsibility. The eelpout, in contrast, invested more heavily in each egg but "saved" energy by producing fewer of them. The total energy cost for each species might be the same, the two lifestyles taking the appearance of coequal adaptive choices.

It might have happened that way, but it needn't have. In fact it would *only* have happened that way if the ancestral populations from which codfish and eelpouts evolved had equally variable gene pools for the traits of egg production and maternal care. If, however, the ances-

tral codfish population had a fair amount of genetic variation in egg production but relatively little variation with regard to maternal care, then it could not have chosen between two equally possible reproductive strategies. Instead natural selection could have acted only on egg production, since this was the only trait with genetic variants from which to choose. As the critic from whom I have taken this example put it, "Knowledge of the relative amounts of genetic variance for different traits is essential if evolutionary arguments are to be correct rather than simply plausible."[58] The example of the codfish and the eelpout, by the way, resembles that of the one- and two-horned rhinoceri, mentioned earlier in the chapter.

Another problem is that one cannot use knowledge about the genetic variance of a particular trait in a currently existing species to make accurate inferences about the trait's evolutionary origins. Consider further the evolution of the ancestral codfish. If there were a great deal of genetic variation for egg production and a strong likelihood that cod eggs would be snapped up by waiting predators, then those females genetically disposed to lay lots of eggs might have few surviving offspring, but they would in turn pass along the genes for greater egg production. At the same time, the genetic variants that produced few eggs would die out and that genetic variation would be lost from the population. Although it could be reintroduced by mutation or migration from a neighboring community, the net effect of selection would be to reduce the genetic variation in egg production. In fact a fundamental rule of natural selection is that the more highly selected a population, the lower the amount of genetic variation it contains. This accounts for the fact that animals that become too perfectly adapted face the probability of extinction, since as a population they lack the genetic resources to respond to changes in the environment.

Suppose that a sociobiologist wished to test

---

[57]Ibid.

[58]Richard C. Lewontin, "Sociobiology as an Adaptationist Program," *Behavioral Science* 24(1979):9.

his or her hypothesis that the codfish reproductive mode represents one end of a spectrum of possible adaptive choices open to fish. He or she could measure genetic variability in egg production in present-day populations. Finding little, the investigator could argue for the implication that in ancestral populations there must have been a great deal of variability, all eliminated in the interim by natural selection. On the other hand a finding that populations of codfish contain genetic variation for egg production would show that different levels of egg production are inherited and thus potentially susceptible to natural selection. Both results can be used to favor the idea of strategic choice in natural selection. In fact, "there is no conceivable observation about genetic variance at present that could prove the contention of past evolution of the trait."[59]

So how *can* one prove things about evolutionary history? In the case for the codfish one might, if exceedingly lucky, come upon some fossils in which soft parts were preserved. Such preservation happens rarely—most fossils consisting of mineral replacements of hard structures such as bones. But granting the possibility for the moment, it might be possible to find fossils of protocodfish which carried very different numbers of eggs and to gain from them some sense of how variable the ancestral population might have been. There is, unfortunately, no direct fossil record of behavior, no way to know whether the protocodfish exhibited variability in the amount of parental care lavished on its young. "Fossil behaviors" can only be inferred from physical evidence in the fossil record, and such interpretations must necessarily include considerable guesswork. Thus the sort of theorizing done by Trivers and others contains within it fundamental problems of proof. Stories about past evolutionary events will be the hardest to support, while assertions about behaviors seen in the wild today will at least be open to experimental examination. One such

behavior, to which we will now return, is the animal matings which some biologists have designated as rape.

RAPE: REPRISE

Thornhill hypothesizes that some male flies force themselves on females only when they have lost out in competition or nuptial food offerings. Since possession of a food source provides incontrovertible physical evidence—the male cannot easily deceive a female about his fitness. Failing in competition for food leaves male scorpionflies with two choices, rape or consignment to extinction. Such an analysis implies that behaviors which enhance reproductive fitness will be favored by natural selection. That rape in scorpionflies has evolved for just this reason becomes the unstated conclusion.

Although it is possible to test the *plausibility* of Thornhill's conclusions, he has not done so. His follow-up studies pursue quite a different tack. A first step would be to make sure forced copulation is a natural rather than an experimenter-induced event, for if it is but a laboratory artifact it loses all interest. On this point Thornhill's own writing is unclear. In one paper he reports observations of rape in nature in seven species of scorpionfly and in "most of the 18 species" he has studied in the laboratory.[60] But in another he mentions low frequencies of forced copulations in field enclosure experiments, while in open field experiments he observed no successfully completed forced copulation.[61] How robust (to use a favorite word of scientists), one wonders, is the claim that scorpionflies rape in the wild?

Leaving aside the actual biological importance of the observation, we can consider alternate explanations that are not based on fitness strategies. Thornhill mentions that males secrete a sub-

[59]Ibid., 10.

[60]Thornhill, "Rape in Scorpionflies," 53.
[61]Randy Thornhill, "*Panorpa* Scorpionflies: Systems for Understanding Resource-Defense Polygyny and Alternative Male Reproductive Efforts," *Annual Reviews of Ecology and System Matters* 12(1981): 355–86.

stance which attracts females to their food cache. Do females secrete a substance which stimulates male mating behavior? If this were the case it might be that most males would try to mate with any nearby female, although females resist matings with males that have no food to offer. Indiscriminate attempts to mate might occasionally succeed but would not represent a special adaptive strategy on the part of foodless males.

For rape to have evolved as an adaptive strategy it must be heritable. And if it were heritable it would be possible to raise up the offspring from females which have experienced forced copulation and to test their sons for such behavior. Do these sons also rape while those of "nonrapist" males do not? As the discussion of codfish and eelpout evolution points out, such a study would not prove that Thornhill was right about the *origin* of the field behaviors he first observed; but such experiments could at least make his theory minimally tenable.

If the scorpionfly studies leave something to be desired, Barash's work on mallards is far worse. He expands on the question of rape in ducks by worrying about the possible options of the victim's mate. Following observations of forced copulation in a population of ducks living in "a semi-natural urban environment," he recorded and interpreted the responses of the females' mates using "the sociobiologic theorem that animals should behave in ways consistent with maximizing their inclusive fitness." He suggests that a drake has two choices when "his" hen is attacked. Either defend her and drive off the attacker, or try to introduce his own sperm right after in the "hope" that the sperm would compete with those of the assailant. Barash's unstated assumption is that both the attacking behavior and the mate response represent evolved adaptation, and must therefore have a genetic basis. Since he observed both of his predicted behaviors, he felt justified in reaching the following conclusions:

An evolutionary perspective on behavior suggests that individuals will behave so as to maxi-

mize the difference between the benefits and costs associated with any potential act, with both benefits and costs evaluated in units of inclusive fitness. Rape of one's mate imposes a potential cost in that it increases the likelihood of another individual's fathering her offspring. The responses available to a rape victim's mate also carry benefits and costs and the observed pattern suggests that the mate behaves in accord with evolutionary prediction.[62]

Barash bases his discussion solely on what he finds to be consistent with the evolutionary possibilities he imagines. If the scheme fits, wear it; the evidence (or lack of it) be damned. Most unsettling, though, is his disregard of information pointing to a very different analysis of forced copulation in mallards. In fact, following the publication in the journal *Science* of his mallard article, two separate letters to the editor appeared, criticizing both the inadequacy of his data and, more fundamentally, the usefulness of the very phenomenon of "rape" for the sort of evolutionary analysis he attempts.[63]

As it turns out, rape in mallards is pathological. One careful study of ducks living under abnormal, high density conditions did indeed show some of the same behaviors observed by Barash. But they were far from adaptive. In fact the overall fertility in this particular crowded population was very low and the reproductive significance of violent mating attempts uncertain.[64] Barash, who provided no data on the density or the actual breeding success of the population he studied, dismisses the criticism that rape is a pathological response to overcrowding by saying that he certainly "would welcome studies in relatively undisturbed habitats." Barash cites one other paper as evidence that rape is common in ducks. This study too was done on urban ducks, but under relatively healthy conditions, and the cited researcher does indeed observe "rape" attempts.

[62]Barash, "Sociobiology of Rape in Mallards," 788, 789.
[63]J. P. Hailman, "Rape Among Mallards," *Science* 201(1978):280–81; and F. McKinney, J. Barrett, and S. R. Derrickson, "Rape Among Mallards," *Science* 201(1978):281–82.
[64]R. D. Titman and J. K. Lowther, "The Breeding Behavior of a Crowded Population of Mallards," *Canadian Journal of Zoology* 53(1975):1270–82.

But Barash fails to report a second key observation. The attempts were seasonal and only occurred at the very *end* of the breeding season. Thus they could not have had anything to do with increasing reproductive fitness, and seemed instead to be associated with the seasonal breakup of the breeding pair.[65]

In sum there are two quite extensive studies reporting forced copulation in mallards. One comes from a highly overcrowded population exhibiting a wide variety of pathological behaviors and low fertility (a fact which Barash fails to point out in his citation). It is well known that stress in animal populations can bring about aggressive and destructive behaviors, none of which result from natural selection for some alternative reproductive strategy. The second study suggests that forced intercourse may be an aggressive behavior associated with the yearly breakup of the breeding pair. Since it only shows up after reproduction is over for the year, it too fails to correlate with increased reproductive fitness. In other words, a quick check of Barash's "supporting" references makes clear that forced intercourse in mallards had nothing whatsoever to do with alternate reproductive strategies. The data render Barash's neat little scheme bankrupt.

Although Thornhill originally presented his ideas on human rape in underdeveloped form, he and Nancy Thornhill and William and Lea Shields recently published extensive accounts offering "an evolutionary perspective" in the same issue of a scientific journal. They uncritically cite the work on animal rape and go on to draw conclusions about humans. (The Thornhills' article was discussed earlier in this chapter.) The Shields suggest that human males employ one of three tactics to reproduce. The first of these, cooperative bonding, appears in our marriage system; the second, manipulative courtship, involves deceitful seduction, i.e., mating and running. Finally, if these tactics fail, forcible rape remains an option. Here is how they state their case:

Illustrating that rape is likely to be adaptive for males does not imply that *all* males will rape *exclusively* or *all* of the time. Intuitively, we feel that *individual humans* that possess *all three* of these mating tactics, each used in appropriate circumstances so as to minimize potential costs in a conditioned strategy, are likely to be more successful than males with a pure strategy (i.e., all males either rape or court honestly) and more stable than any polymorphic population (some males rape exclusively, others only court honestly).

Plainly put, all men have the potential to rape, and may be expected to do so if they can get away with it:

We suggest that *all* men are potential rapists. . . . We expect that the probability of a particular individual raping will be a function of the average genetic cost/benefit ratio associated with the particular conditions he faces.[66]

These authors do not argue that men consciously think through the possible genetic advantages of rape. Rather, they view this nonconscious calculation as an "ultimate cause," one that originated early in our evolutionary history. Rape, they acknowledge quite freely, may have "proximate causes" such as aggression, the desire to humiliate, or sexual gratification—just as many feminists have argued. But those proximate causes, say the Shields, represent evolution's way of carrying out its ultimate desire of maximizing genetic fitness.* Again, quoting from their article:

Ultimately men may rape because it increases their biological fitness and thus rape may serve, at least in part, a reproductive function, but in an immediate proximate sense it is as likely that they rape because they are angry or hostile, as the feminists suggest.[67]

The use of the ultimate-proximate distinction is

[65]T. Lebret, "The Pair Formation in the Annual Cycle of the Mallard, *Anas Platyrhynchos,*" *Ardea* 49(1961):97–158.

[66]Shields and Shields, "Forcible Rape: An Evolutionary Perspective," 119, 120.
*They also explicitly exclude nonadaptive rape, especially rape in which the victim dies, homosexual rape, and presumably—although they neglect it altogether—gang rape. They argue the legitimacy of the exclusion by saying that these forms of rape are rather rare compared to your run-of-the-mill daily rape.
[67]Ibid., 122.

clever, because it is totally unassailable. *Any* motivation for rape, regardless of how little it has to do with reproduction, can still be explained on an evolutionary basis by arguing that it is the proximate effector of the ultimate genetic cause!

All of this would be merely annoying were it not for the fact that it has immediate practical application. The Thornhills and the Shields deplore rape, but feel that society can figure out how to overcome its evolutionary heritage and put a stop to this morally heinous activity only if it acknowledges the accuracy of their theories:

> Our model . . . implies that reducing sexism, "raising the economic and social status of women and the consciousness of men," and rehabilitating the rapist . . . may have little more than minor effects on the incidence of rape. Only when efforts are directed at altering all of the genetic and environmental factors important in the natural control of rape would we predict success.[68]

Just what efforts do they suggest? If we set the cost of rape high enough, then the practice ought to diminish. One possibility is to increase drastically the severity of punishment for rape. This, the Thornhills acknowledge, might be difficult, especially given the trend away from life sentences for rape. As the Shields put it: "The application of the severest forms of retribution (e.g., execution or castration) . . . might carry many ethical, practical, and political problems."[69] The next best thing, then, would be to ensure *some* punishment; to stop rape, they suggest, we must achieve a high rate of criminal conviction complete with jail terms. This and this alone is what would work, according to the evolutionary hypothesis; yet how to achieve higher conviction rates *without* changing the social and economic status of women never seems to become an issue for these "theorists."

Neither the Thornhills nor the Shields discuss an alarming corollary to their evolutionary hypotheses, one that already plays itself out within the criminal courts. In fact they would probably refuse to acknowledge the relationship between their ideas and the releasing of rapists without jail terms on the condition that the convicts take the drug depo-provera to reduce their sexual drive. Yet this has happened. Item: A forty-one-year-old man convicted of raping his stepdaughter over a period of seven years received a one-year jail sentence under the condition that he take a drug to reduce his sex drive.[70] (That man, the wealthy heir to the Upjohn fortune, apparently represents a counterexample to the Thornhills's view that financially successful men don't rape.*[71]) Another rapist, convicted of raping the same woman on two different occasions and attempting it on a third, escaped jail altogether after his lawyer successfully argued that he suffered from uncontrollable biological urges. Instead the jury sentenced him to take depo-provera to control his need to rape. His lawyer argued that jail was not appropriate at all because the victim "came across consistent with what she underwent, which was not a particularly brutal rape; as rapes go, a relatively mild rape." A physician who touts the use of depo-provera to control rape says that some men have "unbearable physical urges. They have all been found to have unusually high levels of testosterone in their blood."[72]

If I were a clever (to say nothing of unscrupulous) lawyer, I would be heartened by reading the Shields's and Thornhills' work. Within it lies the ultimate evolutionary explanation for the supposed existence of men with strong biological urges to rape and the scientific basis for defending them when they do. If the builders of unfounded evolutionary theories about rape do

---

[68]Ibid., 132.
[69]Ibid.

[70]"Judge Orders 'Castration Drug' for Upjohn Heir," *The Providence Journal,* 31 Jan. 1984, pp. x–1.
*Public outcry in this case forced the judge to reconsider his initial ruling. It is perhaps ironic that Upjohn is the world's largest manufacturer of depo-provera, which—despite the fact that it is banned in the United States because it induces cancer in test animals—Upjohn sells to third-world countries as an injectable birth control drug.
[71]Phillida Bunkle, "Calling the Shots? The International Politics of Depo-Provera," in *Test Tube Women: What Future for Motherhood,* ed. Rita Arditti, Renate Duelli Klein, and Shelley Minden (London: Pandora, 1984), 165–87.
[72]CBS-TV, *60 Minutes,* vol. 16, no. 18, 15 Jan. 1984. Transcript.

not foresee how their work will be used and if they claim that it is not their fault, that they simply injected their hypotheses into the free marketplace of ideas where they could be tested and rejected if wrong, then they are at best fooling themselves. At worst, they engage in the most irresponsible sort of academic navel-watching. Rape, however, is not the only human activity about which sociobiologists write. Their ideas about human sexuality are far-reaching.

THE HUMAN BIOGRAM

Human sociobiology is a theory of essences. Wilson sets as his task the tracing of human qualities back through evolutionary time. "The exercise," he writes, "will help to identify the behaviors and rules by which individual human beings increase their Darwinian fitness through the manipulation of society. . . . We are searching for the human biogram."[†] In contrast to the uncertainty surrounding the chicken and her egg, it is clear that the human biogram precedes all other arrangements. "Our civilization is jerrybuilt around the biogram," asserts Wilson.[73] And by stripping away the cultural trappings characteristic of human societies, we can lay bare the human essence, that underlying genetic something which, after all is said and done, profoundly influences the social structures developed by members of the human race.

On the essence of male and female, sociobiologists have no dearth of opinions. To start with, men—more or less universally—are more sexually active than women, making it no surprise that among humans polygyny is far more frequent than polyandry. Then, too, men are less responsible, less nurturant, and less emotionally expressive,[74] while women are coy and sexually selective. All humans live in families with certain universal traits: in "an American industrial city, no less than a band of hunter-gatherers . . . during the day the women and children remain in the residential area while the men forage for game or its symbolic equivalent in the form of barter or money."[75] And, they tell us, while both males and females experience sexual jealousy when faced with an adulterous spouse, it "may be a more or less 'innate' response among husbands and a learned response among wives." Furthermore, the male desire for sexual variety is "natural and universal."[76] The male is more aroused by visual stimuli than is the female. Males are more naturally attracted to young and therefore highly fertile women. Since a male's fertility remains more or less constant over long periods of his life, youth is not a primary criterion for attracting the female. Instead she exhibits something Wilson labels *hypergamy*, the "female practice of marrying men of equal or greater wealth and status."[77] Such behavior follows from the existence of male–male competition. In nature, after all, most females get to mate, but whenever there is intermale competition the weaker, less fit males lose out. Wilson sees a human counterpart in societies that practice female infanticide among the upper classes. Sons survive and marry lower-class (hypergamic) females who—along with their dowries—move continually upward. The breeding system almost completely excludes poor males.[78]

When coming up with "universal" traits requiring explanation, many sociobiological accounts of human interactions so ignore the complexities of behavior and culture and make such selective readings of the literature, that it becomes a challenge to respond in any fashion other than unabashed astonishment. Although the problem of correctly describing human behavior is a serious one, the deeper issue lies with the very notion of human essence—not with the

[†]*Biogram* is a term used by Wilson; *biological programs* is its basic meaning.

[73]Wilson, *Sociobiology: The New Synthesis*, 548.

[74]B. A. Hamburg, "The Psychobiology of Sex Differences," in *Sex Differences in Behavior*, ed. R. C. Friedman, R. M. Rienhart, and J. R. L. Van de Wiele (New York: Wiley, 1974).

[75]Edward O. Wilson, *On Human Nature* (Cambridge, Mass.: Harvard University Press, 1978).

[76]Donald Symons, "Précis of *The Evolution of Human Sexuality*," *The Behavioral and Brain Sciences* 3(1980):176, 179.

[77]Robert Trivers, "Foreword," in R. Dawkins, *The Selfish Gene* (New York: Oxford University Press, 1976).

[78]Wilson, *On Human Nature*.

idea that there is a human nature, but with the thought that there is a *particular* human nature, visible when all culture and learning is stripped away.

Desmond Morris, in his book *The Naked Ape,* described human behavior as deriving directly from our ape-like biology. Most sociobiological writers would disagree—or so they say. Here's how Trivers puts it: "Sociobiology emphasizes facultative traits, based on genes, which permit individuals to adjust themselves . . . to a great array . . . of contingencies. . . . The fact that we are highly evolved social actors means that each of us has the genes with which to play almost all of the roles."[79] Wilson suggests that only 20 percent of what we are is attributable to genetic bias, 80 percent to cultural overlay. Trivers and Wilson certainly sound more reasonable than Desmond Morris, but what do they mean? If sociobiologists have discovered that humans can behave as both loving and rejecting parents and can be both violent and peaceful and can cheat and lie as well as cooperate, then they have said nothing that is not obvious to the most casual observer. The Quaker and the sniper coexist in every city in America. But sociobiologists say a good deal more than that: they say that what is universal is natural. And their universals include the double standard, sexually aggressive men, the sexual division of labor, conflict between male and female and between parent and child, and families in which men bring home the bacon while women care for the kids. We must consider the claim of essence from three interrelated viewpoints: (1) Is there any supporting evidence for the idea of universal human behaviors? (2) Do supposedly universal behaviors have the same meanings in different social contexts? (3) If there is some meaningful human universal, does that then imply its evolution through genetically based adaptation and natural selection?

In the radio and television series "Dragnet," Jack Webb kept asking for the facts ("the facts,

Ma'am, nothing but the facts"). And perhaps nowhere are the facts murkier than in the study of human universals. Even establishing that something as simple as the human smile is inborn rather than learned, and that it signifies happiness or pleasure in all human societies, is a complex undertaking. That it is probably unlearned can be ascertained from studying deaf, dumb, and blind children, who will smile quite unmistakably. That the smile is a sign of happiness can be ascertained by a variety of cross-cultural studies. But it is no easy task.[80] Among the behaviors considered by sociobiologists, something resembling agreement among groups as diverse as sociobiologists, feminist anthropologists, and Marxist sociologists exists about one: the division of labor by sex. With the exception of small groups such as the newly discovered Tasaday, all human societies seem to have some form of division of labor by sex. The problem is that no two societies have exactly the *same* form.[81] What's good for the gander in one culture is just fine for the goose in another. Nor is true as Wilson claims that men always earn the bread while women raise the children. In some cultures women are the merchants and financiers; in others men do the bulk of the child care. In fact how to interpret the sexual division of labor is a matter of considerable debate[82] and, although they never acknowledge their part in it, sociobiologists simply hold up one end of a diverse spectrum of thought on the topic.

The division of labor by sex embodies a seeming contradiction: it is a human universal but it has no universal meaning. Instead each culture has its own particular division of labor by sex (one that may be more or less rigid) and attaches

---

[79]Trivers, "Sociobiology and Politics," 37.

[80]R. Passingham, *The Human Primate* (San Francisco: Freeman, 1982).

[81]Michelle Rosaldo, "The Use and Abuse of Anthropology," *Signs* 5(1980):389–417.

[82]Karen Sacks, *Sisters and Wives: The Past and Future of Sexual Inequality* (Westport, Conn.: Greenwood, 1979); C. MacCormack and M. Strathern, eds., *Nature, Culture and Gender* (New York: Cambridge University Press, 1980); S. Ortner and H. Whitehead, eds., *Sexual Meanings: The Cultural Construction of Gender and Sexuality* (New York: Cambridge University Press, 1981); and Eleanor Leacock, *Myths of Male Dominance* (New York: Monthly Review, 1981).

to it its own set of interpretations. There may well be some human essence that leads to a division of labor by sex, yet there seems to be nothing in our nature which says what that division will be or how we will translate it into cultural meaning. It seems then that we can extract meaning only by examining the division in a particular social setting. But if this is true, what becomes of Wilson's biogram? I argue that it turns into one of two things—a tautology or (despite protests to the contrary) a prescription for human behavior.

Any harmony that might result from agreement that most cultures have a sexual division of labor dissipates completely when one looks at any of the other sociobiological "universals." Barash, for example, writes that sexual attractiveness to one's mate is a universal. One need only take note of cultures in which marriages are arranged at birth to question the accuracy of this generalization. But even if we were to grant the assertion we would still have to question its significance. There is certainly no generalizable standard of female beauty. In some cultures men find heavy women more sexually appealing than thin ones. In others the reverse is true. Within the Western European cultural tradition, the standard has differed in different historical periods. Barash would argue, though, that the specific standard is unimportant—that there *is* a standard is what counts. But one is then at a loss to know what he means. This fallback stance seems rather to return the argument to a tautological status. It is a little like holding up a pail before a thirsty person. "It is full," one might say. "With what?," would come the reply. For a person in need of a drink a pail filled with diesel fuel holds nothing of interest.

By insisting on understanding the meaning claimed for a human universal, it fast becomes clear that there is no single, undisputed claim about universal human behavior (sexual or otherwise). The notion of a naked human essence is meaningless because human behavior acquires significance only in a particular social context. This is the case even for clearly "biological" be-

haviors such as eating and drinking. All humans do both to keep alive. The ability to experience thirst is localized in a particular part of the brain. Yet the act of drinking has many meanings. We go out to a bar with friends not to quench our thirst but to be sociable. We raise our glasses in unison at a party to celebrate an important event, not to meet our physiological requirement for water. Even this act which *can* fill a biological need cannot be understood outside of its social context.

But suppose this argument is wrong, that one could identify a set of meaningful universal truths about human behavior. Then universality might indeed imply a human biogram, a muted genetic deep structure underlying the many-layered cultural overlay. And such a biogram might represent a set of genetically based adaptations to the selective forces that existed from one hundred thousand to four million years ago, when humans evolved from their primate cousins. But a human biogram might also have resulted from random genetic events which had nothing to do with adaptations and fitness maximization. Far too little is known about the origin of Homo sapiens to rule out such a possibility. Thus even if one were to grant a starting premise of human essence, it remains impossible to figure out which essences are adaptations arising under the pressure of natural selection, helping to increase fitness, and which just happened along for the ride. *Human sociobiology is a theory that inherently defies proof.*

Both of the above possibilities suggest a genetic basis for specific human behaviors. Yet a third option remains. Quite early in human prehistory protohumans could have learned certain behaviors and taught them to their offspring. If the present-day worldwide population of humans all evolved from a small progenitor stock (and on this point there is some, albeit far from unanimous, agreement), then certain kinds of behavior might be universal, yet learned rather than genetically programmed. Such an idea is not far-fetched. Today's primates learn social traits and teach them to the next generation. Rhesus monkeys raised in social isolation do not innately "know" how to interact with other rhesus. Nor do orangutan infants taken from their mothers innately know how to forage in the rain forest. They must be taught to do so by human surrogates before they can be returned to the wild.

Monkeys even have culture. They invent things and pass on their discoveries by nongenetic means. For example, a group of scientists spread grain on a sandy beach in order to attract wild Japanese macaques to a central location for observation. At first the members of the monkey troop tediously picked out the food, grain by grain. But one day a young female had a bright idea. She picked up a mixture of sand and wheat, rushed to the seaside, and threw it in the water. The sand sank and the wheat floated, and she simply scooped it from the surface. Her siblings learned the trick from her, followed by her mother and other juveniles. Males and older females without young were the slowest to pick up the new skill, but it is now handed down to succeeding generations. Yet an outside observer, seeing the universality of the event but not knowing its history, might hypothesize a genetic basis. (The inventor, by the way, was something of a monkey genius. Some years earlier she had learned and then taught the others to wash the sand from sweet potatoes left on the beach by the human investigators.)

Perhaps it doesn't really matter if a trait is genetic or learned. Maybe all that's important is that stable, widespread behaviors regardless of their cause have helped humans to survive and evolve. The whole debate may be much ado about nothing, but I think otherwise.

> Genes, being part of our bodies, live and die with us. They can be spread only through our offspring. Cultural templates are separate from our bodies. They can be multiplied, spread . . . during the lives of a single individual. Cultural evolution is therefore, far more flexible than biological evolution.[83]

Change, time, flexibility: in the controversy about genetic versus cultural evolution, these are the issues. Curiously the sociobiologists state with conviction that they are at one with their critics. Their cry is that in order to eradicate human social ills, we must first understand them. "Sociobiology," writes Barash, "helps to identify some of the possible roots of our injustice—male dominance, racism. . . . If any change is to occur . . . we would do well to understand the biological nature of our species."[84] Trivers, too, bridles at the thought that what he calls "Darwinian social theory" is politically reactionary. To the contrary, he suggests that "the concepts of parental investment and female choice provide an objective and unbiased basis for viewing sex differences, a considerable advance over popular efforts to root women's powers and rights in the functionless swamp of biological identity."[85] Self-knowledge must precede change—a most plausible theme.

Sociobiologists writing about humans do indeed take up the challenge of social change. "The major interest most of us have in rape," writes Donald Symons, "is in its total elimination." This he suggests could happen in one of two ways. Males and females could be kept separate, as they are in certain Moslem societies, building in effect a structural barrier to prevent rape; or, young boys could be bred with social inhibitions that would "produce men who want only the kinds of sexual interactions that women want." The problem is that the former course of action is unlikely in our culture, while the latter entails a loss of freedom—a price that may not be worth paying. Without explanation Symons asserts that the rearing conditions needed to eliminate rape "might well entail a cure worse than the disease."[86] Worse for whom, one might wonder.

In his discussions of social change Wilson uses a similar strategy. After stating his sincere interest in change he discusses the pros and cons of several options for achieving it. Finally, after

---

[83]Stebbins, *Darwin to DNA, Molecules to Humanity*, 399.

[84]Barash, *The Whisperings Within*, 235.
[85]Trivers, "Foreword," vi.
[86]Symons, *The Evolution of Human Sexuality*, 284, 285.

showing the pitfalls of each he reluctantly concludes that things really aren't all that bad as they stand. For example, he believes that slightly different inborn emotional dispositions account for the development of some of the "sexual universals" in which sociobiologists believe. Calling upon the hope offered by scientific truth, Wilson suggests that full recognition of these innate dispositional differences will help to light the path chosen by future societies: "In full recognition of the struggle for women's rights that is now spreading throughout the world, each society must make one or the other of the three following choices." Right now most societies "condition [their] members so as to exaggerate sexual differences in behavior." This, Wilson is well aware, usually leads to greater male domination and sexual inequality, although he holds out the hope that we could learn to safeguard human rights while savoring the richness of human difference. Alternatively, a society could bring up its children with an eye toward eliminating all sexual differences in behavior. Wilson fully believes this would be possible and that it might result in a more just, productive, and harmonious society. But—and this sounds the death knell for behavioral identity—"the amount of regulation required would certainly place some personal freedoms in jeopardy and at least a few individuals would not be allowed to reach their full potential." Finally, he proposes that we simply open all the doors but provide no special help for women to pass through them.[87] But here, too, there are pitfalls, for even with identical education and equal access Wilson thinks that their biological biases will leave men more likely to dominate in political life, business, and science and women more likely to do the child care.

One is thus left in a state of bewilderment. None of the options for change is perfect and some seem downright appalling. How *do* we recognize the spreading struggle for women's rights? In Wilson's view the best bet is to live with our differences: "I am suggesting that the contradictions are rooted in the surviving relics of our prior genetic history, and that one of the most inconvenient and senseless, *but nevertheless unavoidable,* of these residues is the modest predisposition toward sex role differences"[88] (emphasis added). From change to the status quo, from options to determinism, in one easy lesson.

There are variations on Wilson's theme. In the last chapter of his book *The Ape Within Us* John MacKinnon muses about the "Apes of the Future." He concedes that the ability to limit family size makes it "surely right" that women "should be granted" a chance to work outside the home—equal opportunity and all. Still, the future Ms. Average will be less aggressive, more emotional, and "her biological make-up has . . . designed her for fulfilling quieter, less spectacular roles. . . . For all her opportunity and capability Ms. Average is going to end up in a supportive domestic role." With one difference: in the past she received special recognition for that role but in her liberated future such special attentions will be lost, and she may be "haunted by the misery that she ought to be making more of herself." That, it seems, is what social change brings. Women's liberation won't wash. "Women's libbers"—as MacKinnon calls them—"will be constantly let down by their sex's biologically lower motivation for fighting for glory in the industrial head-hunt of the economic rat-race."[89]

The solution to the dilemma our future Ms. Average will face seems to lie in revaluing male and female roles. Just how we should do this MacKinnon doesn't say. But if only women were to receive more rewards for the wonderful things they do so specially, men and women could proceed with their various (complementary) activities. He proposes in essence a return to the two spheres of the Victorian era.

Sociobiological theory has already been put to

---

[87]Wilson, *On Human Nature,* 132, 133.

[88]Ibid., 135.

[89]John MacKinnon, *The Ape Within Us* (New York: Holt, Rinehart & Winston, 1978), 264–65.

social and political uses, for example in the movie *Doing What Comes Naturally*. With a background of voice-overs from interviews with Wilson, Trivers, and Dr. Irven de Vore (another outspoken sociobiologist), the movie shows male sheep locking horns, teenage girls and boys engaging respectively in coy and fickle behaviors, and scenes of massive bombings and battles in Vietnam. The message is so crudely put that the sociobiologists seen in the film publicly dissociated themselves from it.[90] But too late, alas. The film is still available, selling its message about female coyness, male aggression, and the inevitability of war. Others, too, have jumped onto the bandwagon. A psychiatrist has suggested that psychological disorders be reclassified using the concepts of adaptive strategies, survival, and inclusive fitness. "For example, a taxonomy might be developed which rated disorders in terms of their potential effects on inclusive fitness. A severely 'psychotic' man in his twenties would be seen as suffering from a major disorder because of probable poor reproductive success, while an equally 'psychotic' male over 50 years old who had no children would be seen as less severely ill."[91]

The major sociobiological theorists have expressed astonishment, outrage, and genuine anger at the force of expressly political attacks on their work. They had, they pointed out, not the least intention of working against social change. "While I was doing my own work," wrote Trivers, "it never occurred to me that the work was actually serving deeply regressive political aims."[92] And, indeed, I have every reason to take Trivers at his word. For apparently as these scientists developed their theories they never questioned their stance as politically neutral investigators interested only in empirical truth. Whatever science finds, after all, must be openly confronted. The truth is the truth, and if it's unpleasant so be it. Let's not kill the messenger because he bears sorrowful tidings.

But having been forced from the Eden of Scientific Purity into the political fray, the sociobiologists have taken up the challenge. Reserving the scientific mantle for themselves, they attack their critics as ideological, politically expedient, "intellectually feeble, and lazy."[93] Worse yet—they are Marxists (indeed some of them *are* Marxists, although they are also highly respected scientists). "Marxism and other secular religions offer little more than promises of material welfare and a legislated escape from the consequences of human nature,"[94] writes Wilson, who instead suggests we search for a new morality "based on a more truthful definition of man."[95] In thus claiming to have his finger on the scientific truth, Wilson hopes to discredit his detractors as "metaphysical" ideologues. But in launching the counterattack in this fashion he inevitably takes explicit political positions, contrasting his "analytic program of research on human society" with "the metaphysical truths of Marxism."[96] We have seen, however, that the programs for change proposed by people such as the Shields, Symons, Wilson, and MacKinnon always circle back to a suggestion that things aren't so bad as they stand. Furthermore, rather than confront their critics on scientific grounds, Wilson and others have launched their own political attacks. In taking their stand as scientific Custers opposing the Marxist Indian attack, they have declared themselves defenders of an ideology of scientific rationalism. Yet whether they like it or not, their claims about human nature fall so far

---

[90]In the October 1977 issue of *Anthropology Newsletter,* Wilson, DeVore, and Trivers wrote that they had nothing to do with making the film aside from providing interviews. They said, "We deplore the vulgar misrepresentation of the field by those who use this discredited film to imply that it represents an accurate statement of our ideas." This quote is not from the original source but is quoted in Ted Judd, "Naturizing What We Do. A Review of the Film *Sociobiology: Doing What Comes Naturally,*" *Science for the People.* Jan./Feb. 1978, 19.

[91]M. T. McGuire, "Sociobiology: Its Potential Contributions to Psychiatry," *Perspectives in Biology and Medicine* 25(1979):50–69.

[92]Trivers, "Sociobiology and Politics," 37.

[93]Ibid.

[94]Wilson, *On Human Nature,* 3.

[95]Ibid.

[96]C. J. Lumsden and E. O. Wilson, "Genes, Mind and Ideology," *The Sciences,* Nov. 1981, 8.

short of being scientifically defensible that one can only consider human sociobiology as a political science. It belongs in the arena of philosophical and political controversy far more than in that of scientific debate. The critics of sociobiology make no bones about their beliefs. It is high time that those who make pronouncements about human sociobiology own up to theirs.

5

ON THE EVOLUTION OF HUMAN SEXUALITY

DONALD SYMONS

Polygamy may well be held in dread,
Not only as a sin, but as a bore:
Most wise men with one moderate woman wed,
Will scarcely find philosophy for more . . .

. . .

. . . how the devil is it that fresh features
Have such a charm for us poor human creatures?

LORD BYRON, *Don Juan*

CONCLUSIONS

According to Rasmussen (1931), Eskimo men will "have intercourse with any woman whenever there is an opportunity" (p. 195); but neither Eskimo women nor women of other human communities will have intercourse at every opportunity. The ultimate causes of such sex differences are the differing reproductive opportunities and constraints males and females typically encountered during the course of evolutionary history. Shaw makes John Tanner say,

"if women could do without our work, and we ate their children's bread instead of making it, they would kill us as the spider kills her mate or as the bees kill the drone." But although evolutionary theory provides unparalleled ultimate explanations of many data on human sexuality, theory is in no sense more "real" than data. I argued, for example, that men tend to be sexually jealous of their wives because in ancestral populations the emotion of jealousy (in concert with other emotions) increased the probability that men would sire their wives' offspring; that is, I attempted to explain why this emotion

SOURCE: From *The Evolution of Human Sexuality* by D. Symons. Copyright © 1979 by Oxford University Press Inc. Reprinted by permission.

typically exists. But the evidence for its widespread existence comes from ethnography, not evolutionary biology, and it would be inaccurate to infer that a furious, cuckolded husband only imagines himself to be angry at his wife's sexual peccadilloes when, in some more profound sense, what he is "really" doing is promoting the survival of his genes. In fact, the opposite would be more accurate: sexual jealousy is real; this jealousy may or may not affect reproductive success; and how selection operated in times past is still more conjectural. Furthermore, an evolutionary explanation of why males tend to be sexually jealous has no implications for the question of how "free" they are to act or not to act jealously.

Throughout the Pleistocene boys and girls must have been reared differently, but it is most unlikely that these different rearing conditions were the sole developmental mechanism responsible for sex differences in sexuality. The data presented in previous chapters, and summarized in the last chapter, suggest some developmental fixity in sexuality (there are no myths of sleeping males who require a princess' kiss to awaken them: if males are still dozing at puberty they are awakened by nature). Very likely, many of these sex differences would prove to be innate—without apologetic quotation marks—if the environment were held constant. That is, males and females exposed to identical environmental conditions during ontogeny would develop different sexual behaviors, attitudes, and feelings. This does not necessarily mean that it would be impossible to rear boys and girls so that they developed identical sexualities, but simply that identical sexualities would not result from identical rearing conditions.

Because human sexual behavior is determined less by genes and gonadal hormones and more by learning than is the sexual behavior of any other animal species, human sexuality is often said to be released or emancipated from genes and hormones—culture and society, the great emancipators, having marched through the evolving cerebral cortex to sexual freedom. But culture and society are not entities: they are the cumulative material and symbolic products of individual human beings, no two of whom had identical reproductive "interests." Plasticity is a double-edged sword: the more flexible an organism is the greater the variety of maladaptive, as well as adaptive, behaviors it can develop; the more teachable it is the more fully it can profit from the experiences of its ancestors and associates and the more it risks being exploited by its ancestors and associates; the greater its capacity for learning morality, the more worthless superstitions, as well as traditions of social wisdom, it can acquire; the more cooperatively interdependent the members of a group become the greater is their collective power and the more fulsome are the opportunities for individuals to manipulate one another; the more sophisticated language becomes the more subtle are the lies, as well as the truths, that can be told. Hence I argued that the evolutionary elaboration of the cerebral cortical superstructure that makes human plasticity possible entailed a concomitant elaboration of a nonplastic motivational substructure. If selection has always been potent at the level of the individual, individuals must have "innate" mechanisms, probably best conceived as emotional/motivational mechanisms, to recognize and look after their own reproductive "interests." Thus humans cannot be merely passive vehicles by which society and culture perpetuate themselves, whether society and culture are understood as systems, as they often are, or as collections of discrete components, as Dawkins (1976) understands them. Dawkins argues that bits of culture are, like viruses, self-replicating parasites on human beings, but his analogy shows precisely why this view must be incomplete: in environments containing pathogenic viruses, selection favors the most resistant individuals.

Unlike most other mammals, humans mate year round. Unlike all other mammals, human females conceal, rather than advertise, ovulation. Unlike all other mammals, human reproductive competition occurred in social milieus of enormous complexity. It was, I believe, the complexity of sexual opportunity and constraint in natural human environments that made adaptive a human psyche uniquely informed by sexuality. That individual reproductive "interests" must in some degree conflict with one another may account for the intensity of human sexual emotions, the pervasive interest in other people's sex lives, the frequency with which sex is a subject of gossip, the universal seeking of privacy for sexual intercourse, the secrecy and deception that surround sexual activities and make the scientific study of sex so difficult, the universal existence of sexual laws or rules, and the fact that in our own society "morals" has come to refer almost exclusively to sexual matters. Neither adaptation to monogamous pair-bonds nor a history of noncompetitive promiscuity can easily account for the above facts about human sexuality, and these facts also constitute a challenge to group selection theories and to theories in which society is the source of human emotion.

The relations of society and culture to organic evolution are likely to be debated in the biological and social sciences for many years to come. Even at present, however, views of society that ignore organic evolution entirely can be seen to be inadequate, at least with respect to sexuality. It is generally believed, for example, that young women tend to be more sexually attractive than older women. But what is the source of this belief, and why is it maintained? Does a powerful, secret cabal of twenty-year-old women control propaganda? Do men promulgate this belief in order to reduce the competition for middle-aged women, whom they lust after in their hearts? In actuality, if one considers such concepts as the dirty old man, statutory rape, and psychosexual immaturity, it seems fairly clear that young women are perceived as attractive in spite of, not because of, normative and prescriptive rhetoric.

As discussed in Chapter Two, many social scientists, and probably most economists and psychologists, view society and culture as the cumulative products of individuals pursuing their own interests. But it has proved difficult to define "self-interest" in a way that is neither circular nor dependent on intuition and to specify the mechanisms by which individuals initiate, perpetuate, and change social forms. Although Bloch (1977) and Brown (n.d.) argue that inaccurate notions of time, society, and history are tools for perpetuating inequalities, these writers are appropriately vague about the actual mechanisms involved. Bloch writes that the perpetuation of institutionalized hierarchy is what the cognitive system that he calls social structure "is about." And Brown calls attention to the correlation between quality of historiography and openness of social stratification, but he does not argue that powerful individuals in hereditarily stratified societies necessarily either consciously perceive that accurate history would endanger their positions or make conscious efforts to suppress accurate history (though they may).

One reason the concept of self-interest is so difficult may be that, for the most part, self-interest is perceived and pursued unconsciously, making conspiracies without conspirators possible. Alexander (1974, 1975) has even argued that selection favored individuals who were ignorant of the "selfish" effects of their own behavior, since the sincere belief in one's own "altruism" makes one's deceptive performances more believable. Obviously selection could not have opposed awareness of abstract scientific notions like inclusive fitness any more than it could have opposed awareness of the atomic structure of matter, but even if "selfish" and "altruistic" are understood in their ordinary senses, Alexander's argument is not compelling. Our typically keen insight into other people's motives implies intense selection for social perceptiveness in times past (among preliterate peoples, reproductively successful headmen seem to be uncommonly politically astute and socially perceptive). But our failure to note that social perceptiveness is grounded in projection does not necessarily imply that selection actually disfavored self-insight. Karl Lashley pointed out that we are conscious primarily of the results, not the processes, of thought. Our ability to make almost any kind of judgment or calculation far exceeds our ability to understand how we make them. To know others is an adaptive necessity; to know thyself is an acquired taste.

The sex differences in human sexuality discussed in this book originated in the greater variability of male than of female reproductive success during the course of evolutionary history. One might, therefore, expect male sexuality to be more plastic and variable than female sexuality; for example, high- and low-ranking males might be expected to pursue different reproductive "strategies." Indeed, Crook (1971, 1972) suggests that among nonhuman primates high-ranking males freely use scarce resources, such as estrous females, while low-ranking males adopt "behavioral subterfuges" to gain access to these resources. Kaufmann (1965) characterizes some low-ranking male rhesus monkeys as "opportunistic" because they mate furtively and in concealment, and he notes that a low-ranking male may copulate when a female's regular partner is temporarily out of sight (also see Symons 1978a). Trivers (1972:146) writes: "If males within a relatively monogamous species are, in fact, adapted to pursue a mixed strategy, the optimal is likely to differ for different males. . . . Psychology might well benefit from attempting to view human sexual plasticity as an adaptation to permit the individual to choose the mixed strategy best suited to local conditions and his own attributes." And I suggested that the human male's desire for sexual variety might vary to some extent with opportunities to satisfy this desire (Chapter Seven). Nevertheless, contrary to expectation, the data on human sexuality indicate "that the range of variation in the female far exceeds the range of variation in the male" (Kinsey *et al.* 1953:537–38).

Some women in Kinsey's sample had never been aroused erotically, while others were aroused almost daily; of those who had been aroused, some responded only mildly to tactile or psychologic stimulation (visual and narrative stimuli and fantasy), while others responded instantaneously and intensely, and reached orgasm quickly; some who had been aroused by tactile stimuli had never been aroused by psychologic stimuli, while others could reach orgasm from psychologic stimuli alone. "There were females in the sample who had been more responsive to psychologic stimulation than any male we have known" (p. 540). Although the women in Kinsey's sample very rarely were interested in sexual variety *per se,* a few were as interested as any man. And, in cross-cultural perspective, among some peoples there is no concept of female orgasm, while among others all women are said to experience multiple orgasms.

Female sexuality seems to be generally less rigidly channeled than male sexuality. At swingers' parties in the United States, for example, over 90 percent of the (presumably heterosexual) women find that they enjoy sex with other women, while male swingers almost never have sex with other men (Bartell 1971). Recall, too, that AGS women were unequivocally happy about the changes cortisone therapy induced in their sexuality. They said that they liked being able to feel like normal women, but perhaps they also enjoyed the increased freedom from reflex-like responses to external stimuli and from internal sexual pressures. Neither their clitoral sensitivity nor, presumably, their capacity for sexual pleasure were impaired by cortisone: in essence, they lost sexual compulsion without losing sexual possibility.

Because the sexual variability of the human female far exceeds that of the male it is harder for women than for men to understand intuitively the sexual experiences and feelings of some members of their own sex:

> Because there is such wide variation in the sexual responsiveness and frequencies of overt activity among females, many females are incapable of understanding other females. There are fewer males who are incapable of understanding other males. Even the sexually least responsive of the males can comprehend something of the

meaning of the frequent and continuous arousal which some other males experience. But the female who goes through life or for any long period of years with little or no experience in orgasm, finds it very difficult to comprehend the female who is capable of several orgasms every time she has sexual contact, and who may, on occasion, have a score or more orgasms in an hour. To the third or more of the females who have rarely been aroused by psychologic stimuli, it may seem fantastic to believe that there are females who come to orgasm as the result of sexual fantasy, without any physical stimulation of their genitalia or of any other part of their body (Kinsey *et al.* 1953:538–39).

Perhaps female sexual variability accounts for the fact that one woman psychiatrist can argue, on the basis of the female's capacity for multiple orgasms, that human females are sexually insatiable (Sherfey 1972), while a second woman psychiatrist can question the very existence of multiple orgasms (Shainess 1976).

Some of the sexual variability of the human female probably represents adaptation. For example, although men and women are equally capable of experiencing intense sexual jealousy of a spouse, learning may play a greater role in determining the circumstances in which females experience jealousy; that is, sexual jealousy may be a facultative adaptation in the human female and an obligate adaptation in the human male (Chapter Seven). The probable ultimate explanation for this sex difference is that it has always been adaptive for men to be sexually jealous of their wives, while in some polygynous marriages it has not been adaptive for women to be sexually jealous of their husbands; furthermore, husbands' extramarital adventures have not *necessarily* constituted threats to their wives' reproductive success, hence females are adapted to learn to discriminate threatening from nonthreatening adultery. Similarly, criteria for evaluating sexual attractiveness probably develop in a more "innate" fashion in the human male than in the human female. For example, certain physical characteristics (especially skin quality) universally correlate with female age, and males very likely have "innate" psychological mechanisms for detecting

and responding to these characteristics, whereas the evaluation of male status and prowess presumably depends more on learning.

But facultative adaptations cannot, in my opinion, begin to account for the sexual variability of the human female. The fact of female sexual plasticity, which makes variability possible, is not in itself evidence for adaptation to exhibit variable sexual behavior (see Chapter Two); the enormous range of sexual variation observed among females may be primarily an artifact of artificial, postagricultural habitats. If one adopts Williams's dictum, "adaptation is a special and onerous concept that should be used only where it is really necessary," available evidence does not justify the conclusion that the female orgasm is an adaptation (Chapter Three). Parsimoniously interpreted, the data suggest that with sufficient clitoral stimulation any female mammal can experience orgasm, but that sufficient stimulation rarely or never occurs in a state of nature. With respect to humans, what happened in a state of nature is obviously conjectural, but since among most peoples sexual intercourse is completed primarily in terms of the man's passions and pleasures (Davenport 1977), it is a reasonable hypothesis that the human female's capacity for orgasm is no more an adaptation than is the ability to learn to read. If, throughout most of human evolutionary history, the potentials of females' sexuality were very rarely realized, these potentials would have been largely "invisible" to natural selection, and this may account for the astonishing sexual plasticity of the human female.

There are, I believe, several general implications in the line of reasoning pursued here. First, data, not theory and not analogies with nonhuman animals, reveal what human beings are like. Second, evolutionary analyses must consider the question of the environments for which organisms have been designed, however speculative such consideration may be. Structures, behaviors, and psyches that develop in unnatural environments may not have ultimate causes at all. Third, the tendencies to equate "natural" and "good" and to find dignity in biological adaptation can only impede understanding of ultimate causation and distort perceptions of nonhuman animals, preliterate peoples, and history. Finally, the *potentials* of a biological mechanism are not necessarily constrained by, and cannot necessarily be predicted from, the *purposes* for which the mechanism was designed by natural selection. Perhaps it is not excessively naïve to hope that a creature capable of perceiving the plowshare in the sword is also capable of freeing itself from the nightmare of the past.

REFERENCES

ALEXANDER, R. D.
  1971 The search for an evolutionary philosophy of man. *Proceedings of the Royal Society of Victoria* 84:99–120.
  1974 The evolution of social behavior. *Annual Review of Ecology and Systematics* 5:325–83.
  1975 The search for a general theory of behavior. *Behavioral Science* 20:77–100.
BARTELL, G. D.
  1971 *Group Sex: A Scientist's Eyewitness Report on the American Way of Swinging.* New York: Peter H. Wyden.
BLOCH, M.
  1977 The past and the present in the present. *Man* (N.S.) 12:278–92.
BROWN, D. E.
  n.d. Social stratification and historiography.
CROOK, J. H.
  1971 Sources of cooperation in animals and man. Pp. 237–60 in J. F. Eisenberg and W. S. Dillon, eds., *Man and Beast: Comparative Social Behavior.* Washington: Smithsonian Institution Press.
  1972 Sexual selection, dimorphism, and social organization in the primates. Pp. 231–81 in B. Campbell, ed., *Sexual Selection and the Descent of Man 1871–1971.* Chicago: Aldine.
DAVENPORT, W. H.
  1965 Sexual patterns and their regulation in a society of the southwest Pacific. Pp. 161–203 in F. A. Beach, ed., *Sex and Behavior.* New York: John Wiley and Sons.
  1977 Sex in cross-cultural perspective. Pp. 115–63 in F. A. Beach, ed., *Human Sexuality in Four Perspectives.* Baltimore: The Johns Hopkins University Press.

DAWKINS, R.
  1976 *The Selfish Gene.* Oxford: Oxford University Press.
KAUFMANN, J. H.
  1965 A three-year study of mating behavior in a free-ranging band of rhesus monkeys. *Ecology* 46:500–512.
KINSEY, A. C.; W. B. POMEROY; C. E. MARTIN; AND P. H. GEBHARD
  1953 *Sexual Behavior in the Human Female.* Philadelphia: W. B. Saunders.
RASMUSSEN, K.
  1931 *The Netsilik Eskimos: Social Life and Spiritual Culture.* Copenhagen: Gyldendalske Boghandel, Nordisk Forlag.
SHAINESS, N.
  1976 How "sex experts" debase sex. Pp. 122–25 in *Focus: Human Sexuality.* Guilford, Connecticut: The Dushkin Publishing Group.
SHAND, A. F.
  1914 *The Foundations of Character: Being a Study of the Tendencies of the Emotions and Sentiments.* London: Macmillan.
SHERFEY, M. J.
  1972 *The Nature and Evolution of Female Sexuality.* New York: Random House.
SYMONS, D.
  1978a *Play and Aggression: A Study of Rhesus Monkeys.* New York: Columbia University Press.
TRIVERS, R. L.
  1971 The evolution of reciprocal altruism. *Quarterly Review of Biology* 46:35–57.
  1972 Parental investment and sexual selection. Pp. 136–79 in B. Campbell, ed., *Sexual Selection and the Descent of Man 1871–1971.* Chicago: Aldine.

III

SEX AND THE
LIFE COURSE

INTRODUCTION

Anthropologists have long been interested in the ways that culture patterns the life course. Seemingly everywhere, people make a distinction between the statuses of preadults, adults, and the elderly. Yet, the criteria that are used to conceptualize the transition from one stage to the next vary widely, as do the number of life stages defined. Some of the criteria may be sociocultural (such as the ability to feed oneself), others psychological (such as the ability to "control" emotionality), and still others biological (such as the appearance of wrinkles).

Within any particular culture, divisions of the life course may change in response to broader cultural change. So, for example, Philippe Ariès (1962:25–32) argues that prior to the eighteenth century, childhood and adolescence were not clearly distinguished in the minds of most Europeans. He argues that until the eighteenth century, biological criteria (such as the onset of puberty) were less important than social criteria in the life-course progression. Childhood and adolescence both represented periods of dependency on adults, regardless of the state of puberty. One might suggest that this change to a more specific and biological definition of the transition to adolescence involved many factors: the industrial revolution and its attendant increase in specialization, the increasingly classificatory power of the biological sciences, or demographic changes coincident with an extended life span.

Age is used universally in the social division of labor. It reaches perhaps its most developed expression as a factor in social structure among the cultures of sub-Saharan Africa. For instance, the Nyakyusa of southwestern Tanzania formerly organized their chiefdoms into "age villages" (Wilson, 1963). At age 10 (or thereabout), each male child moved out of his parents' village and took up residence in a village of his peers. He would live with those members of his own age group for the remainder of his life, eventually marrying and raising children.

In a culture in which chronological time is clearly structurally important and is measured with great accuracy, we often think of age as an absolute measurement of time. Yet, age also is understood as a relative concept in the sense that it indicates membership in a social category. Regardless of absolute linear age, one's position in the life course is always established in reference to others in different positions—those who are older and those who are younger.

With each age status comes a different set of rights, duties, and responsibilities (roles). Thus, in America, it is generally considered unacceptable for children to consume alcohol. Alcohol consumption enters our lives as a right of those members with the status "adult." Similarly, sexual interaction among children is widely condemned in our society. That, too, is a behavioral aspect of adulthood in America.

This section of readings centers on questions relating sexuality to the definition and progression of the life course. How do societies around the world use sexuality in distinguishing life stages? What is the place of sexuality among children? Is the life course differentially divided for males and females?

Writing in the early part of this century, Bronislaw Malinowski considers the sexuality of children among the Trobriand Islanders of Melanesia. He notes that adults are comfortable in having children of all ages aware of adult sexuality. In fact, their experimentation with sexual contact prior to puberty is expected and accepted. As Malinowski says, "there is nothing . . . to determine how much or how little they will indulge in sexual pastimes" (p. 48). Malinowski also presents the Trobriand conception of the life cycle and discusses the role of sexuality among Trobriand youth.

Donald S. Marshall discusses a number of topics, from coital and orgasmic frequency to sexual attitudes, in his article about the Polynesian inhabitants of Mangaia. As do the other works in this section, Marshall's article emphasizes the role of childhood sexuality in contrast to the sexuality of adulthood. As Malinowski did, he often notes differences between Mangaian morality and that of a "European visitor."

David N. Suggs looks at the Tswana (or Kgatla[1]) of Botswana and reports how that society has changed with regard to its sexual morals and attitudes about premarital pregnancy. He also discusses the factors that define the life course for Tswana women, as well as their age gradation of knowledge. Whereas in 1933 Schapera found a mild disapproval of premarital pregnancy, Suggs' data suggest that now it has become not only acceptable, but expected as part and parcel of the transition to adulthood.

[1]Tswana is a name given to several formerly politically distinct groups of seTswana speakers in southern Africa. "Kgatla" is a designation of one such group.

REFERENCES

ARIÈS, PHILIPPE. (1962). *Centuries of Childhood: A Social History of Family Life.* New York: Vintage Books.

SCHAPERA, ISAAC. (1933). Premarital Pregnancy and Native Opinion: A Note on Social Change. *Africa,* 1:1:59–89.

WILSON, MONICA. (1963). *Good Company: A Study of Nyakyusa Age Villages.* Boston: Beacon Press.

SUGGESTED READINGS

Sexuality, Adolescents, and Young Adults

BARRY, HERBERT, III, AND ALICE SCHLEGEL. (1986). Cultural Customs That Influence Sexual Freedom in Adolescence. *Ethnology, 25*:2:Apr:151–162.

BROUDE, GWEN J. (1975). Norms of Premarital Sexual Behavior: A Cross-Cultural Study. *Ethos, 3*:3: Fall:381–402.

PARKER, RICHARD G. (1989). Youth, Identity, and Homosexuality: The Changing Shape of Sexual Life in Contemporary Brazil. *Journal of Homosexuality,17*:3–4:269–289.

THOMPSON, SHARON. (1990). Putting a Big Thing into a Little Hole: Teenage Girls' Accounts of Sexual Initiation. *Journal of Sex Research, 27*:3:341.

WORTHMAN, CAROL M., AND JOHN W. M. WHITING. (1987). Social Change in Adolescent Sexual Behavior, Mate Selection, and Premarital Pregnancy Rates in a Kikuyu Community. *Ethos, 15*:2:June: 145–165.

Sexuality through Adulthood

FRIEND, RICHARD A. (1990). Older Lesbian and Gay People: A Theory of Successful Aging. *Journal of Homosexuality, 20*:3–4:99–118.

TURNBULL, COLIN M. (1986). Sex and Gender: The Role of Subjectivity in Field Research. In Tony Larry Whitehead and Mary Ellen Conaway (Eds)., *Sex, Self and Gender in Fieldwork.* Urbana: University of Illinois Press.

6

PRENUPTIAL INTERCOURSE BETWEEN THE SEXES

BRONISLAW MALINOWSKI

The Trobrianders are very free and easy in their sexual relations. To a superficial observer it might indeed appear that they are entirely untrammeled in these. This, however, is not the case; for their liberty has certain very well-defined limits. The best way of showing this will be to give a consecutive account of the various stages through which a man and a woman pass from childhood to maturity—a sort of sexual life-history of a representative couple.

We shall have first to consider their earliest years, for these natives begin their acquain-tance with sex at a very tender age. The unregu-lated and, as it were, capricious intercourse of these early years becomes systematized in ado-lescence into more or less stable intrigues, which later on develop into permanent liai-sons. Connected with these latter stages of sex-ual life, there exists in the Trobriand Islands an extremely interesting institution, the bachelors' and unmarried girls' house, called by the na-tives *bukumatula;* it is of considerable impor-tance, as it is one of those arrangements sanctioned by custom which might appear on the surface to be a form of "group-marriage."

SOURCE: From *Savages in North-Western Melenesia* by B. Malinowski, pp. 44–64. Copyright © 1957 by Routledge & Kegan Paul, Ltd. Reprinted by permission.

THE SEXUAL LIFE OF CHILDREN

Children in the Trobriand Islands enjoy considerable freedom and independence. They soon become emancipated from a parental tutelage which has never been very strict. Some of them obey their parents willingly, but this is entirely a matter of the personal character of both parties: there is no idea of a regular discipline, no system of domestic coercion. Often as I sat among them, observing some family incident or listening to a quarrel between parent and child, I would hear a youngster told to do this or that, and generally the thing, whatever it was, would be asked as a favour, though sometimes the request might be backed up by a threat of violence. The parents would either coax or scold or ask as from one equal to another. A simple command, implying the expectation of natural obedience, is never heard from parent to child in the Trobriands.

People will sometimes grow angry with their children and beat them in an outburst of rage; but I have quite as often seen a child rush furiously at his parent and strike him. This attack might be received with a good-natured smile, or the blow might be angrily returned; but the idea of definite retribution, or of coercive punishment, is not only foreign, but distinctly repugnant to the native. Several times, when I suggested, after some flagrant infantile misdeed, that it would mend matters for the future if the child were beaten or otherwise punished in cold blood, the idea appeared unnatural and immoral to my friends, and was rejected with some resentment.

Such freedom gives scope for the formation of the children's own little community, an independent group, into which they drop naturally from the age of four or five and continue till puberty. As the mood prompts them, they remain with their parents during the day, or else join their playmates for a time in their small republic. And this community within a community acts very much as its own members determine, standing often in a sort of collective opposition to its elders. If the children make up their minds to do a certain thing, to go for a day's expedition, for instance, the grown-ups and even the chief himself, as I often observed, will not be able to stop them. In my ethnographic work I was able and was indeed forced to collect my information about children and their concerns directly from them. Their spiritual ownership in games and childish activities was acknowledged, and they were also quite capable of instructing me and explaining the intricacies of their play or enterprise.

Small children begin also to understand and to defer to tribal tradition and custom; to those restrictions which have the character of a taboo or of a definite command of tribal law, or usage or propriety.*

The child's freedom and independence extend also to sexual matters. To begin with, children hear of and witness much in the sexual life of their elders. Within the house, where the parents have no possibility of finding privacy, a child has opportunities of acquiring practical information concerning the sexual act. I was told that no special precautions are taken to prevent children from witnessing their parents' sexual enjoyment. The child would merely be scolded and told to cover its head with a mat. I sometimes heard a little boy or girl praised in these terms: "Good child, he never tells what happens between his parents." Young children are allowed to listen to baldly sexual talk, and they understand perfectly well what is being discussed. They are also themselves tolerably expert in swearing and the use of obscene language. Because of their early mental development some quite tiny children are able to make smutty jokes, and these their elders will greet with laughter.

Small girls follow their fathers on fishing expeditions, during which the men remove their

---

*The processes by which respect for tribal taboo and tradition is instilled in the child are described throughout this book, especially in ch. xiii. Custom must not be personified nor is its authority absolute or autonomous, but it is derived from specific social and psychological mechanisms. Cf. my *Crime and Custom,* 1926.

pubic leaf. Nakedness under these conditions is regarded as natural, since it is necessary. There is no lubricity or ribaldry associated with it. Once, when I was engaged in the discussion of an obscene subject, a little girl, the daughter of one of my informants, joined our group. I asked the father to tell her to go away. "Oh no," he answered, "she is a good girl, she never repeats to her mother anything that is said among men. When we take her fishing with us we need not be ashamed. Another girl would describe the details of our nakedness to her companions or her mothers.* Then these will chaff us and repeat what they have heard about us. This little girl never says a word." The other men present enthusiastically assented, and developed the theme of the girl's discretion. But a boy is much less in contact with his mother in such matters, for here, between maternal relations, that is, for the natives, between real kindred, the taboo of incest begins to act at an early age, and the boy is removed from any intimate contact of this sort with his mother and above all with his sisters.

There are plenty of opportunities for both boys and girls to receive instruction in erotic matters from their companions. The children initiate each other into the mysteries of sexual life in a directly practical manner at a very early age. A premature amorous existence begins among them long before they are able really to carry out the act of sex. They indulge in plays and pastimes in which they satisfy their curiosity concerning the appearance and function of the organs of generation, and incidentally receive, it would seem, a certain amount of positive pleasure. Genital manipulation and such minor perversions as oral stimulation of the organs are typical forms of this amusement. Small boys and girls are said to be frequently initiated by their somewhat older companions, who allow them to witness their own amorous dalliance. As they are untrammelled by the authority of their elders and unrestrained by any moral code, except that of specific tribal taboo, there is nothing but their

*That is, "classificatory mothers" mother, maternal aunts, etc. Cf. ch. xiii, secs. 5 and 6.

degree of curiosity, of ripeness, and of "temperament" or sensuality, to determine how much or how little they shall indulge in sexual pastimes.

The attitude of the grown-ups and even of the parents towards such infantile indulgence is either that of complete indifference or of complacency—they find it natural, and do not see why they should scold or interfere. Usually they show a kind of tolerant and amused interest, and discuss the love affairs of their children with easy jocularity. I often heard some such benevolent gossip as this: "So-and-so (a little girl) has already had intercourse with So-and-so (a little boy)." And if such were the case, it would be added that it was her first experience. An exchange of lovers, or some small love drama in the little world would be half-seriously, half-jokingly discussed. The infantile sexual act, or its substitute, is regarded as an innocent amusement. "It is their play to *kayta* (to have intercourse). They give each other a coconut, a small piece of betel-nut, a few beads or some fruits from the bush, and then they go and hide, and *kayta*." But it is not considered proper for the children to carry on their affairs in the house. It has always to be done in the bush.

The age at which a girl begins to amuse herself in this manner is said to coincide with her putting on the small fibre skirt, between, that is, the ages of four and five. But this obviously can refer only to incomplete practices and not to the real act. Some of my informants insisted that such small female children actually have intercourse with penetration. Remembering, however, the Trobriander's very strong tendency to exaggerate in the direction of the grotesque, a tendency not altogether devoid of a certain malicious Rabelaisian humour, I am inclined to discount these statements of my authorities. If we place the beginning of real sexual life at the age of six to eight in the case of girls, and ten to twelve in the case of boys, we shall probably not be erring very greatly in either direction. And from these times sexuality will gradually assume a greater and greater importance as life goes on, until it abates in the course of nature.

Sexual, or at least sensuous pleasure constitutes if not the basis of, at least an element in, many of the children's pastimes. Some of them do not, of course, provide any sexual excitement at all, as for instance those in imitation of the grown-up economic and ceremonial activities, or games of skill or childish athletics; but all sorts of round games, which are played by the children of both sexes on the central place of the village, have a more or less strongly marked flavour of sex, though the outlets they furnish are indirect and only accessible to the elder youths and maidens who also join in them. Indeed, we shall have to return later (chs, ix and xi) to a consideration of sex in certain games, songs, and stories, for as the sexual association becomes more subtle and indirect it appeals more and more to older people alone and has, therefore, to be examined in the contexts of later life.

There are, however, some specific games in which the older children never participate, and into which sex directly enters. The little ones sometimes play, for instance, at house-building, and at family life. A small hut of sticks and boughs is constructed in a secluded part of the jungle, and a couple or more repair thither and play at husband and wife, prepare food and carry out or imitate as best they can the act of sex. Or else a band of them, in imitation of the amorous expeditions of their elders, carry food to some favourite spot on the sea-shore or in the coral ridge, cook and eat vegetables there, and "when they are full of food, the boys sometimes fight with each other, or sometimes *kayta* (copulate) with the girls." When the fruit ripens on certain wild trees in the jungle they go in parties to pick it, to exchange presents, make *kula* (ceremonial exchange) of the fruit, and engage in erotic pastimes.*

Thus it will be seen that they have a tendency to palliate the crudity of their sexual interest and indulge by associating it with something more poetic. Indeed, the Trobriand children show a great sense of the singular and romantic in their

*For a description of the real *kula*, cf. *Argonauts of the Western Pacific*.

games. For instance, if a part of the jungle or village has been flooded by rain, they go and sail their small canoes on this new water; or if a very strong sea has thrown up some interesting flotsam, they proceed to the beach and inaugurate some imaginative game around it. The little boys, too, search for unusual animals, insects, or flowers, and give them to the little girls, thus lending a redeeming aesthetic touch to their premature eroticisms.

In spite of the importance of the sexual motive in the life of the youngest generation, it must be kept in mind that the separation of the sexes, in many matters, obtains also among children. Small girls can very often be seen playing or wandering in independent parties by themselves. Little boys in certain moods—and these seem their more usual ones—scorn the society of the female and amuse themselves alone. Thus the small republic falls into two distinct groups which are perhaps to be seen more often apart than together; and, though they frequently unite in play, this need by no means be necessarily sensuous.

It is important to note that there is no interference by older persons in the sexual life of children. On rare occasions some old man or woman is suspected of taking a strong sexual interest in the children, and even of having intercourse with some of them. But I never found such suspicions supported even by a general consensus of opinion, and it was always considered both improper and silly for an older man or woman to have sexual dealings with a child. There is certainly no trace of any custom of ceremonial defloration by old men, or even by men belonging to an older age class.

AGE DIVISIONS

I have just used the expression "age class," but I did so in a broad sense only: for there are no sharply distinguished age grades or classes among the Trobriand natives. The following table of age designations only roughly indicates the stages of their life; for these stages in practice merge into one another.

The terms used in this table will be found to overlap in some instances. Thus a very small infant may be referred to as *waywaya* or *pwapwawa* indiscrimately, but only the former term as a rule would be used in speaking of a fœtus or referring to the pre-incarnated children from Tuma.* Again, you might call a few months' old child either *gwadi* or *pwapwawa*, but the latter term would be but seldom used except for a very small baby. The term *gwadi* moreover can be used generically, as "child" in English, to denote anything from a fœtus to a young boy or girl. Thus, it will be seen that two terms may encroach on each other's field of meaning, but only if they be consecutive. The terms with sex prefixes (4) are normally used only of elder children who may be distinguished by their dress.

There are, besides these more specific subdivisions, the three main distinctions of age, between the ripe man and woman in the full vigour of life and the two stages—those of childhood and of old age—which limit manhood and womanhood on either side. The second main stage is divided into two parts, mainly by the fact of marriage. Thus, the words under (5) primarily

*Cf. ch. vii, sec. 2.

designate unmarried people and to that extent are opposed to (6a), but they also imply youthfulness or unripeness, and in that respect are opposed to (6).

The male term for old age, *tomwaya* (7) can also denote rank of importance. I myself was often so addressed, but I was not flattered, and much preferred to be called *toboma* (literally "the tabooed man"), a name given to old men of rank, but stressing the latter attribute rather than the former. Curiously enough, the compliment or distinction implied in the word *tomwaya* becomes much weaker, and almost disappears in its feminine equivalent. *Numwaya* conveys that tinge of scorn or ridicule inseparable from "old woman" in so many languages.

THE AMOROUS LIFE OF ADOLESCENCE

When a boy reaches the age of from twelve to fourteen years, and attains that physical vigour which comes with sexual maturity, and when, above all, his increased strength and mental ripeness allow him to take part, though still in a somewhat limited and fitful manner, in some of the economic activities of his elders, he ceases to be regarded as a child *(gwadi),* and assumes the

TABLE 6-1 Designations of Age

1. *Waywaya* (fœtus; infant till the age of crawling, both male and female).		· I. Stage: *Gwadi*—Word used as a generic designation for all these stages 1–4, meaning *child,* male or female, at any time between birth and maturity
2. *Pwapwawa* (infant, till the stage of walking, male or female).		
3. *Gwadi* (child, till puberty, male or female).		
4. *Monagwadi* (male child)	4. *Inagwadi* (female child)	
5. *To'ulatile* (youth from puberty till marriage)	5. *Nakapugula* or *Nakubukwabuya* (girl from puberty till marriage)	II. Stage: Generic designations— *Ta'u* (man), *Vivila* (woman).
6. *Tobubowa'u* (mature man)	6. *Nabubowa'u* (ripe woman)	
6a. *Tovavaygile* (married man)	6a. *Navavaygile* (married woman)	
7. *Tomwaya* (old man)	7. *Numwaya* (old woman)	III. Stage: Old age.
7a. *Toboma* (old honoured man)		

position of adolescent *(ulatile* or *to'ulatile).* At the same time he receives a different status, involving some duties and many privileges, a stricter observance of taboos, and a greater participation in tribal affairs. He has already donned the pubic leaf for some time; now he becomes more careful in his wearing of it, and more interested in its appearance. The girl emerges from childhood into adolescence through the obvious bodily changes: "her breasts are round and full; her bodily hair begins to grow; her menses flow and ebb with every moon," as the natives put it. She also has no new change in her attire to make, for she has much earlier assumed her fibre skirt, but now her interest in it from the two points of view of elegance and decorum is greatly increased.

At this stage a partial break-up of the family takes place. Brothers and sisters must be segregated in obedience to that stringent taboo which plays such an important part in tribal life.* The elder children, especially the males, have to leave the house, so as not to hamper by their embarrassing presence the sexual life of their parents. This partial disintegration of the family group is effected by the boy moving to a house tenanted by bachelors or by elderly widowed male relatives or friends. Such a house is called *bukumatula,* and in the next section we shall become acquainted with the details of its arrangement. The girl sometimes goes to the house of an elderly widowed maternal aunt or other relative.

As the boy or girl enters upon adolescence the nature of his or her sexual activity becomes more serious. It ceases to be mere child's play and assumes a prominent place among life's interests. What was before an unstable relation culminating in an exchange of erotic manipulation or an immature sexual act becomes now an absorbing passion, and a matter for serious endeavour. An adolescent gets definitely attached to a given person, wishes to possess her, works purposefully towards this goal, plans to reach

the fulfilment of his desires by magical and other means, and finally rejoices in achievement. I have seen young people of this age grow positively miserable through ill-success in love. This stage, in fact, differs from the one before in that personal preference has now come into play and with it a tendency towards a greater permanence in intrigue. The boy develops a desire to retain the fidelity and exclusive affection of the loved one, at least for a time. But this tendency is not associated so far with any idea of settling down to one exclusive relationship, nor do adolescents yet begin to think of marriage. A boy or girl wishes to pass through many more experiences; he or she still enjoys the prospect of complete freedom and has no desire to accept obligations. Though pleased to imagine that his partner is faithful, the youthful lover does not feel obliged to reciprocate this fidelity.

We have seen in the previous section that a group of children forming a sort of small republic within the community is conspicuous in every village. Adolescence furnishes the community with another small group, of youths and girls. At this stage, however, though the boys and girls are much more bound up in each other as regards amorous interests, they but rarely mix in public or in the daytime. The group is really broken up into two, according to sex. To this division there correspond two words, *to'ulatile* and *makubukwabuya,* there being no one expression—such as there is to describe the younger age group, *gugwadi,* children—to define the adolescent youth of both sexes.

The natives take an evident pride in this, "the flower of the village," as it might be called. They frequently mention that "all the *to'ulatile* and *nakubukwabuya* (youths and girls) of the village were there." In speaking of some competitive game, or dance or sport, they compare the looks or performance of their own youths with those of some other village, and always to the advantage of their own. This group lead a happy, free, arcadian existence, devoted to amusement and the pursuit of pleasure.

Its members are so far not claimed by any

*Cf. ch. xiii, 6, and ch. xiv.

serious duties, yet their greater physical strength and ripeness give them more independence and a wider scope of action than they had as children. The adolescent boys participate, but mainly as freelancers, in garden work, in the fishing and hunting and in oversea expeditions; they get all the excitement and pleasure, as well as some of the prestige, yet remain free from a great deal of the drudgery and many of the restrictions which trammel and weigh on their elders. Many of the taboos are not yet quite binding on them, the burden of magic has not yet fallen on their shoulders. If they grow tired of work, they simply stop and rest. The self-discipline of ambition and subservience to traditional ideals, which moves all the elder individuals and leaves them relatively little personal freedom, has not yet quite drawn these boys into the wheels of the social machine. Girls, too, obtain a certain amount of the enjoyment and excitement denied to children by joining in some of the activities of their elders, while still escaping the worst of the drudgery.

Young people of this age, besides conducting their love affairs more seriously and intensely, widen and give a greater variety to the setting of their amours. Both sexes arrange picnics and excursions and thus their indulgence in intercourse becomes associated with an enjoyment of novel experiences and fine scenery. They also form sexual connections outside the village community to which they belong. Whenever there occurs in some other locality one of the ceremonial occasions on which custom permits of licence, thither they repair, usually in bands either of boys or of girls, since on such occasions opportunity of indulgence offers for one sex alone (see ch. ix, esp. secs. 6 and 7).

It is necessary to add that the places used for lovemaking differ at this stage from those of the previous one. The small children carry on their sexual practices surreptitiously in bush or grove as a part of their games, using all sorts of makeshift arrangements to attain privacy, but the *ulatile* (adolescent) has either a couch of his own in a bachelors' house, or the use of a hut belonging to one of his unmarried relatives. In a certain type of yam-house, too, there is an empty closed-in space in which boys sometimes arrange little "cozy-corners," affording room for two. In these, they make a bed of dry leaves and mats, and thus obtain a comfortable *garçonnière,* where they can meet and spend a happy hour or two with their loves. Such arrangements are, of course, necessary now that amorous intercourse has become a passion instead of a game.

But a couple will not yet regularly cohabit in a bachelors' house *(bukumatula),* living together and sharing the same bed night after night. Both girl and boy prefer to adopt more furtive and less conventionally binding methods, to avoid lapsing into a permanent relationship which might put unnecessary restraint upon their liberty by becoming generally known. That is why they usually prefer a small nest in the *sokwaypa* (covered yam-house), or the temporary hospitality of a bachelors' house.

We have seen that the youthful attachments between boys and girls at this stage have ripened out of childish games and intimacies. All these young people have grown up in close propinquity and with full knowledge of each other. Such early acquaintances take fire, as it were, under the influence of certain entertainments, where the intoxicating influence of music and moonlight, and the changed mood and attire of all the participants, transfigure the boy and girl in each other's eyes. Intimate observation of the natives and their personal confidences have convinced me that extraneous stimuli of this kind play a great part in the love affairs of the Trobrianders. Such opportunities of mutual transformation and escape from the monotony of everyday life are afforded not only by the many fixed seasons of festivity and permitted licence, but also by that monthly increase in the people's pleasure-seeking mood which leads to many special pastimes at the full of the moon.*

Thus adolescence marks the transition between infantile and playful sexualities and those

*Cf. ch. ix.

serious permanent relations which precede marriage. During this intermediate period love becomes passionate and yet remains free.

As time goes on, and the boys and girls grow older, their intrigues last longer, and their mutual ties tend to become stronger and more permanent. A personal preference as a rule develops and begins definitely to overshadow all other love affairs. It may be based on true sexual passion or else on an affinity of characters. Practical considerations become involved in it, and, sooner or later, the man thinks of stabilizing one of his liaisons by marriage. In the ordinary course of events, every marriage is preceded by a more or less protracted period of sexual life in common. This is generally known and spoken of, and is regarded as a public intimation of the matrimonial projects of the pair. It serves also as a test of the strength of their attachment and extent of their mutual compatibility. This trial period also gives time for the prospective bridegroom and for the woman's family to prepare economically for the event.

Two people living together as permanent lovers are described respectively as "his woman" *(la vivila)* and "her man" *(la ta'u).* Or else a term, also used to describe the friendship between two men, is applied to this relationship *(lubay-,* with pronominal suffixes). In order to distinguish between a passing liaison and one which is considered preliminary to marriage, they would say of the female concerned in the latter: *"la vivila mokita; imisiya yambwata yambwata"*—"his woman truly; he sleeps with her always always." In this locution the sexual relationship between the two is denoted by the verb "to sleep with" *(imisiya),* the durative and iterative form of *masisi,* to sleep. The use of this verb also emphasizes the lawfulness of the relation, for it is used in talking of sexual intercourse between husband and wife, or of such relations as the speaker wishes to discuss seriously and respectfully. An approximate equivalent in English would be the verb "cohabit." The natives have two other words in distinction to this. The verb *kaylasi,* which implies an illicit element in the act, is used when speaking of adultery or other forms of non-lawful intercourse. Here the English word "fornicate" would come nearest to rendering the native meaning. When the natives wish to indicate the crude, physiological fact, they use the word *kayta,* translatable, though pedantically, by the verb "copulate with."

The pre-matrimonial, lasting intrigue is based upon and maintained by personal elements only. There is no legal obligation on either party. They may enter into and dissolve it as they like. In fact, this relationship differs from other liaisons only in its duration and stability. Towards the end, when marriage actually approaches, the element of personal responsibility and obligation becomes stronger. The two now regularly cohabit in the same house, and a considerable degree of exclusiveness in sexual matters is observed by them. But they have not yet given up their personal freedom; on the several occasions of wider licence affianced couples are invariably separated and each partner is "unfaithful" with his or her temporary choice. Even within the village, in the normal course, the girl who is definitely going to marry a particular boy will bestow favours on other men, though a certain measure of decorum must be observed in this; if she sleeps out too often, there will be possibly a dissolution of the tie and certainly friction and disagreement. Neither boy nor girl may go openly and flagrantly with other partners on an amorous expedition. Quite apart from nocturnal cohabitation, the two are supposed to be seen in each other's company and to make a display of their relationship in public. Any deviation from the exclusive liaison must be decent, that is to say, clandestine. The relation of free engagement is the natural outcome of a series of trial liaisons, and the appropriate preliminary test of marriage.

THE BACHELORS' HOUSE

The most important feature of this mode of steering towards marriage, through gradually lengthening and strengthening intimacies, is an institution which might be called "the limited bachelors' house," and which, indeed, suggests at first sight the presence of a "group concubinage." It is clear that in order to enable pairs of lovers permanently to cohabit, some building is needed which will afford them seclusion. We have seen the makeshift arrangements of children and the more comfortable, but not yet permanent love-nests of adolescent boys and girls, and it is obvious that the lasting liaisons of youth and adult girls require some special institution, more definitely established, more physically comfortable, and at the same time having the approval of custom.

To meet this need, tribal custom and etiquette offer accommodation and privacy in the form of the *bukumatula,* the bachelors' and unmarried girls' house of which mention has already been made. In this a limited number of couples, some two, three, or four, live for longer or shorter periods together in a temporary community. It also and incidentally offers shelter for younger couples if they want amorous privacy for an hour or two.

We must now give some more detailed attention to this institution, for it is extremely important and highly significant from many points of view. We must consider the position of the houses in the village, their internal arrangements and the manner in which life within the *bukumatula* shapes itself.

In the description of the typical village in the Trobriands (ch. i, sec. 2), attention was drawn to its schematic division into several parts. This division expresses certain sociological rules and regularities. As we have seen, there is a vague association between the central place and the male life of the community; between the street and feminine activities. Again, all the houses of the inner row, which consists principally of storehouses, are subject to certain taboos, especially to the taboo of cooking, which is believed to be inimical to the stored yam. The outer ring, on the other hand, consists of household dwellings, and there cooking is allowed. With this dis-

tinction is associated the fact that all the establishments of married people have to stand in the outer ring, whereas a bachelor's house may be allowed among the storehouses in the middle. The inner row thus consists of yam-houses *(bwayma),* personal huts of a chief and his kinsmen *(lisiga),* and bachelors' houses *(bukumatula).* The outer ring is made up of matrimonial homes *(bulaviyaka),* closed yam-houses *(sokwaypa),* and widows' or widowers' houses *(bwala nakaka'u).* The main distinction between the two rings is the taboo on cooking. A young chief's *lisiga* (personal hut) is as a rule used also to accommodate other youths and thus becomes a *bukumatula* with all that this implies.

At present there are five bachelors' establishments in Omarakana, and four in the adjoining village of Kasana'i. Their number has greatly diminished owing to missionary influence. Indeed, for fear of being singled out, admonished and preached at, the owners of some *bukumatula* now erect them in the outer ring, where they are less conspicuous. Some ten years ago my informants could count as many as fifteen bachelors' homes in both villages, and my oldest acquaintances remember the time when there were some thirty. This dwindling in number is due, of course, partly to the enormous decrease of population, and only partly to the fact that nowadays some bachelors live with their parents, some in widowers' houses, and some in the missionary compounds. But whatever the reason, it is needless to say that this state of affairs does not enhance true sex morality.

The internal arrangements of a *bukumatula* are simple. The furniture consists almost exclusively of bunks with mat coverings. Since the inmates lead their life in association with other households in the day-time, and keep all their working implements in other houses, the inside of a typical *bukumatula* is strikingly bare. It lacks the feminine touch, the impression of being really inhabited.

In such an interior the older boys and their temporary mistresses live together. Each male owns his own bunk and regularly uses it. When a couple dissolve their liaison, it is the girl who moves, as a rule, to find another sleeping-place with another sweetheart. The *bukumatula* is, usually, owned by the group of boys who inhabit it, one of them, the eldest, being its titular owner. I was told that sometimes a man would build a house as a *bukumatula* for his daughter, and that in olden days there used to be unmarried people's houses owned and tenanted by girls. I never met, however, any actual instance of such an arrangement.

At first sight, as I have said, the institution of the *bukumatula* might appear as a sort of "Group Marriage" or at least "Group Concubinage," but analysis shows it to be nothing of the kind. Such wholesale terms are always misleading, if we allow them to carry an extraneous implication. To call this institution "Group Concubinage" would lead to misunderstanding; for it must be remembered that we have to deal with a number of couples who sleep in a common house, each in an exclusive liaison, and not with a group of people all living promiscuously together; there is never an exchange of partners, nor any poaching nor "complaisance." In fact, a special code of honour is observed within the *bukumatula,* which makes an inmate much more careful to respect sexual rights within the house than outside it. The word *kaylasi,* indicating sexual trespass, would be used of one who offended against this code; and I was told that "a man should not do it, because it is very bad, like adultery with a friend's wife."

Within the *bukumatula* a strict decorum obtains. The inmates never indulge in orgiastic pastimes, and it is considered bad form to watch another couple during their love-making. I was told by my young friends that the rule is either to wait till all the others are asleep, or else for all the pairs of a house to undertake to pay no attention to the rest. I could find no trace of any "voyeur" interest taken by the average boy, nor any tendency to exhibitionism. Indeed, when I was discussing the positions and technique of the sexual act, the statement was volunteered that there are specially unobtrusive ways of doing it

"so as not to wake up the other people in the *bukumatula.*"

Of course, two lovers living together in a *bukumatula* are not bound to each other by any ties valid in tribal law or imposed by custom. They foregather under the spell of personal attraction, are kept together by sexual passion or personal attachment, and part at will. The fact that in due course a permanent liaison often develops out of a temporary one and ends in marriage is due to a complexity of causes, which we shall consider later; but even such a gradually strengthening liaison is not binding until marriage is contracted. *Bukumatula* relationships, as such, impose no legal tie.

Another important point is that the pair's community of interest is limited to the sexual relation only. The couple share a bed and nothing else. In the case of a permanent liaison about to lead to marriage, they share it regularly; but they never have meals together; there are no services to be mutually rendered, they have no obligation to help each other in any way, there is, in short, nothing which would constitute a common ménage. Only seldom can a girl be seen in front of a bachelors' house, and this as a rule means that she is very much at home there, that there has been a liaison of long standing and that the two are going to be married soon. This must be clearly realized, since such words as "liaison" and "concubinage," in the European use, usually imply a community of household goods and interests. In the French language, the expression *vivre en ménage,* describing typical concubinage, implies a shared domestic economy, and other phases of life in common, besides sex. In Kiriwina this phrase could not be correctly applied to a couple living together in the *bukumatula.*

In the Trobriands two people about to be married must never have a meal in common. Such an act would greatly shock the moral susceptibility of a native, as well as his sense of propriety. To take a girl out to dinner without having previously married her—a thing permitted in Europe—would be to disgrace her in the eyes of a Trobriander. We object to an unmarried girl sharing a man's bed—the Trobriander would object just as strongly to her sharing his meal. The boys never eat within, or in front of, the *bukumatula,* but always join their parents or other relatives at every meal.

The institution of the *bukumatula* is, therefore, characterized by: (1) individual appropriation, the partners of each couple belonging exclusively to one another; (2) strict decorum and absence of any orgiastic or lascivious display; (3) the lack of any legally binding element; (4) the exclusion of any other community of interest between a pair, save that of sexual cohabitation.

Having described the liaisons which lead directly to marriage, we end our survey of the various stages of sexual life previous to wedlock. But we have not exhausted the subject—we have simply traced the normal course of sexuality and that in its main outlines only. We have yet to consider those licensed orgies to which reference has already been made, to go more deeply into the technique and psychology of love-making, to examine certain sexual taboos, and to glance at erotic myth and folk-lore. But before we deal with these subjects, it will be best to carry our descriptive narrative to its logical conclusion—marriage.

REFERENCES

MALINOWSKI, BRONISLAW. (1922). *Argonauts of the Western Pacific.* London: George Routledge and Sons.

MALINOWSKI, BRONISLAW. (1926). *Crime and Custom in Savage Society.* New York: Harcourt, Brace & Co.

7

SEXUAL ASPECTS OF THE LIFE CYCLE

DONALD S. MARSHALL

The Mangaian is born, as he lives and loves and dies, in the midst of his clustered kinsmen. The woman in labor is surrounded by family members; assistance is given to her by the grandmother and the husband or father—and by the midwife. More powerful than the physical presence of these kinfolk is the social warmth and approval that envelop a newborn child. For the new member is additional insurance of the continued existence of the family. He is an added source of strength and power, an increment to their means of subsistence. In fact, he is the foundation of the marriage bond itself—which his conception may have caused to be formalized. Far from serving as a potential wedge between parents, as can occur in other societies—including our own—the birth of the child serves both to strengthen ties of sexual affection between mother and father and to extend the web of kinship; the child's conception has made more attractive, rather than less so, the sexual relations between the couple.

The Mangaian couple copulates regularly, up until the onset of labor pains. Some Mangaian men prefer intercourse with their wives during this period of pregnancy to that during any other

SOURCE: "Sexual Aspects of the Life-Cycle" from *Human Sexual Behavior* by Donald S. Marshall and Robert C. Suggs. Copyright © 1971 by the Institute for Sex Research, Inc. Reprinted by permission of Basic Books, a division of HarperCollins Publishers Inc.

time, for the woman's privates are believed to become "wetter, softer, fatter, and larger"; natural secretions provide the lubrication that Mangaian lovers prefer. Some slight adjustments in coital position are made, with the rear approach (pāto'e) being used more frequently than otherwise. There is a belief shared by some Mangaians that frequent copulation up until the time of delivery eases the path of the child (though some differ, and abstain from coitus with their wives—out of the jokingly expressed fear that "the baby will bite"). Copulation between the couple may be resumed within a few days after delivery, although the cultural ideal is to wait for three months or so.

Boys and girls may play together until they are three or four years of age. But between ages four and five, they separate into those sex-age groups that will distinguish them socially for the rest of their lives. Brothers and sisters, sweethearts and lovers, husband and wife, mother and father, old man and old woman—such pairs rarely mix together socially in public, despite their intense private relationships. A six-year-old Mangaian brother and his three-year-old sister would no more walk together hand in hand along the main street of the town than would the dignified Mangaian deacon think of walking down the same street with his wife on his way to church. Seeing such behavior by my children, my principal informant expressed this "don't" of the cultural system thus: "No Māori brother and sister allowed to go together like that!"

The bare bottom and penis of the preschool Mangaian boy are only covered when going to church or on other formal occasions. Mothers attempt to justify this undress to the European visitor by saying that it's "hard to teach them to wear trousers." But there is no real shame associated with seeing a child's penis before he has been superincised, at about age twelve (or in seeing a little girl's genitals—up until she has reached age four or five). However, if the boy child has been circumcised in the European fashion at birth, he must then keep his organ covered. For it is the glans of the penis that must not be seen. Normally, this is covered up by the foreskin of the nonsuperincised male youth; but when this skin is cut, the penis then has "no hat," as the Mangaian expression goes, and must no longer be viewed by anyone.

Young children imitate the work and activities of their elders as a basis of play. In the course of this, according to some informants, they are thought to play at copulation. But this activity is never seen in public. In a somewhat different sense, the adult act itself is never socially acknowledged in public. For the Mangaian enjoys an extraordinary sense of "public privacy." He may copulate, at any age, in the single room of a hut that contains from five to fifteen family members of all ages—as have his ancestors before him. His daughter may receive and make love with each of her varied nightly suitors in that same room. Clothes are changed and accidents, such as public loss of a menstrual pad, may happen. But under most conditions, all of this takes place without social notice; everyone seems to be looking in another direction.

Despite varied sexual activities that occur continuously within the one-room houses, it is outside of the home that the child learns more intimate details of sex and their results—such as "where the babies come from." This knowledge is achieved at about age eight or nine. For just as brother and sister are not seen together in public, so they do not discuss sexual matters together, nor do they joke together. Brothers do not advise brothers, nor do closely related agemates joke with one another. Mothers and daughters or fathers and sons do not discuss sexual matters with one another—or even with the older persons among whom they work.

These "do's" and "don'ts" of what is permissible at home and what must be discussed elsewhere produce odd contrasts. Offsetting the lack of discussion of sexual matters within the family are actual sexual acts that regularly take place in the home and the lingual manipulation of the penis of small children by women of the family. Just as anomalous is the cultural atmosphere of the Mangaian community itself. Despite lack of public social contact between sexes of all ages, there is a continual public evocation of sex. The slightest attention of an unrelated boy to a girl will raise the buzz of gossip, whether based upon a public compliment or a casual touch or smile. And a very common technique of active leadership is to introduce a sexual joking element into the public situation. The district chief, the territorial governor, the church elder, the proud storekeeper—each knows that a risqué remark, a suggestive comment, or a timeworn sexual proverb provides the element of public amusement that is required to keep things moving. As my pastor-friend and host noted, proverbs are *not* religious in this community, although local activities are geared to a religious calendar cycle. Such proverbs would, he explained, "only make the deacons and a pastor happy"—one needs a sexual story to "make all the people happy and work fast." The Mangaian proverb or story must have a biological, a scatological, or a sexual basis if it is to be used to get people in the mood for group work. The work leader must have a strong voice and a "good sense of humor"—that is, a good store of sexual proverbs and stories—or the work "never gets done." Hence, one may find oneself sitting in the village pastorate, listening to the local minister tell the anthropologist and visiting pastors a ribald story of how the island of Manihiki became renowned as a "finger work" island; while, from the next room, comes the sound of his daughter reading her Bible aloud. Or one may watch, over and over again, as the *Ekalesia* of the church increase their work efforts threefold in response to the ribald implication of a deacon's publicly told story.

Further compounding this apparent ambivalence in social attitudes is a typical Polynesian concern with the sexual genitalia and lack of concern with the rest of human anatomy. The Mangaian is completely flabbergasted at the American and European male's interest in the female breast, for the Polynesian considers this organ to be of interest only to a hungry baby. Yet, the Mangaian male is as fully concerned with the size, shape, and consistency of the mons Veneris as is the American male with the size, shape, and consistency of the female bust. Moreover, the Mangaian concern with sex is supplemented by considerable knowledge of the genital organs; the average Mangaian youth has fully as detailed a knowledge—perhaps more—of the gross anatomy of the penis and the vagina as does a European physician. In fact, the Mangaian vocabulary contains terms for features of the genitalia that users of English have not found necessary to specifically name or classify; for example, *tipipā*, the ridge of the glans of the penis, *ngutupakō*, the exposed area of the glans of the nonsuperincised penis; *keo* and *keokeo*, modifying terms for the shape of the clitoris. For the clitoris itself there are several synonyms (*kaka'i, nini'i, tore, teo*, etc.), as there are for the cunnus (*kāwawa, mete kōpapa, 'ika*). One indication of the significance attached to sexual organs is found in the fact that the clitoris, which is said to be some three-quarters of an inch long, is classified as either one or another degree of "sharpness" or is considered to be "blunt"; alternate terms describe it as "projecting," "erecting," or "protruding." (This fact may be functionally and physiologically related both to the deliberate manipulation of children's sexual organs by older people in an attempt to change their size and to the activity rate to which they are subjected.)

The principal sexual factor in the development of the Mangaian personality is, thus, the early and constant exposure to patterned ambivalence. There is an emphatic social division of the sexes, in an atmosphere redolent with cultural emphasis on sexual organs and sexual intercourse; unique modesty as to exposure of adult organs (Polynesian men are horrified at European casualness in exposing the penis in urination) is contrasted with extreme sensuousness in local dance and explicitly detailed accounts of sexual acts and organs in folktales; the utmost lack of interest in modern European-style clothing is offset by lavish use of perfumed scents and flowers; perhaps most importantly, intricate incest prohibitions are contrasted with the restriction of most social contacts to those that take place only between kinsmen.

A Mangaian boy supposedly first hears about masturbation (tītoi, kurukuru, or pa'ore; sometimes referred to in the village of Oneroa as "Ivirua poetry"—Ivirua being a neighboring village) sometime between the ages of seven and ten. He discusses it with his friends and, eventually, he experiments with himself while off feeding the pigs or fishing. Boys are often stimulated to do this by hearing the young men (māpū) talk about sex. Boys may masturbate themselves an average of two or three times a week; excessive masturbation is thought to expose the glans of the penis (ngutupakō) prior to superincision. Mangaians believe that boys with few friends tend to masturbate more than those who spend more time with other children. After erection, even without masturbation, the boy is said to notice the "pressure of fluid" on the penis. (This is different from the "morning erection," which goes down without trace after urination.) Boys also begin to experience nocturnal emissions ("wet dreams") at this age, although they tend to blame these upon the visits of variously described, but always sexually avaricious, "ghost women." The emission in wet dreams and the subsequent waking up always occur, however, before the penetration is made. Nocturnal emissions are much more frequent when the men are denied free access to women, as on the labor island of Makatea. Later, the Mangaian boy will frequently be brought to erection by sexual talk or even by sight of a girl.

Girls also masturbate (tīrau) by thigh pressure or by rocking on their heel. This female masturbation is known to have been practiced from life history data, and it has been witnessed in public by Europeans, in contrast to the privacy of the boy's behavior. But I have too few data available to discuss it more fully. And I have never seen, or known anyone who actually claims ever to have seen, boys masturbating publicly. Although parents may try to stop children from masturbating, once they know of it, their efforts are not very

heavy nor their punishment severe. And, if without a girl, the older boy or traveling husband may masturbate. Only the hand is used, without elaborate devices. There is accompanying imagery of girls or thinking about the orgasm.

It is important to note that, up until recent years, very small children were taught who their kinsmen (taeake) were and learned their genealogy ('akapapa'anga) in great detail. This practice has now fallen away, leading to unfortunate results that will be discussed later in this chapter.

SUPERINCISION

Some Mangaian boys experiment with sexual intercourse prior to superincision. But such "new boys" must content themselves with sexually knowledgeable and promiscuous older women and widows of the village, rather than copulate with either the younger girls or with what are referred to as the "good girls." Most boys wait until age thirteen or fourteen to commence their sexual adventures (kitenākenga), following the act of superincision. The Mangaian girls' personal knowledge of, and appetite for, sex also begins at this age, about the time that they have begun to menstruate. (Some girls experience very severe menstrual cramps, sufficient to require bed care.)

Mangaians recognize the arrival of male puberty by two signs: the growth of pubic hair and (they say) an ability to "retract the foreskin of the penis." These signs presage the approach of the most traumatic, most clear-cut, and most meaningful of the Mangaian males' varied "rites of passage": the superincision, which marks the transition from boy to man. There are, of course, several subphases of boyhood and adulthood, but the critical transition is that of the youth with an uncut smegma-sullied penis to the adult with a clean and virile male organ.

At the same age that girls are experiencing the onset of menstruation and are beginning to have their initial sexual experience, the Mangaian boy is subject to aggressive social pressure from his male age mates and the jeers of village females. He may be accused of a lack of courage and of having a stinking penis *(ure piapia)*. It is not long before he himself, or his father or uncle, decides that he must undergo the superincision operation *(te'e)*. If he waits too long, he may be forcibly knocked out and operated on by his age mates. But most boys succumb at an early age to the pressures of society and custom. Typically, the sequence today is as follows. When a father notes his son coming of age, perhaps because of the social stigma of his son's nonsuperincision, he starts "feeding a pig" for the boy and has a word with a cousin or an older brother of the son, who will "give the idea" to the boy. The father then brings in an expert from outside the immediate family to take care of the actual details and to carry out the operation; two experts may, in fact, be required: one to make the cut, another to tie the bandages. There are several of these superincision experts *(ta'unga te'e)* in the villages today. (Once these were special "priests" called *waikea*.)

The expert approaches the boy and lets him know that the father has actually initiated arrangements for the operation. It is he who makes the cut who is the most important source of the boy's information about sexual behavior, of "what to do with women," and who may actually arrange for the woman who will remove the superincision scab and provide more practical instruction in sexual matters. This was, say my informants, "like a law before" (that is, it was once a publicly acknowledged, explicit cultural pattern). Variant forms of the custom are found elsewhere in central Polynesia, such as the Society and Austral Islands (Marshall 1961, n.d.).

The superincision operation itself, which may be performed upon one boy or upon a group of age mates, takes place in a secluded spot. Preferably, this is by the sea; alternatively, it may be by a mountain stream. The cut was formerly made with a flake of a semi-flintlike local stone *(ruarangi)*; in a few cases this stone is still used. But most modern "experts" prefer an imported straight razor; although they recognize that there

is more danger of infection, the cut is more easily made. In addition, a superincision anvil is required. Formerly, this anvil is said to have been made of stone; now, it is whittled from coconut shell to about the size and shape of the bowl of a tablespoon. The shell anvil serves to protect the glans of the penis and to provide a firm surface upon which to make the cut. Many experts carefully study the organ and lay out a line on the surface of the skin in order to avoid cutting veins; others are less careful. In any event, severe hemorrhaging may take place, during and after the operation. The foreskin is retracted, and the anvil inserted; then the skin of the penis is pulled tightly over it and slit down the medial dorsal line through the white cartilaginous underlayer—stately, right up to the stomach, in most cases. The more carefully done and the more lengthy the incision, the neater is said to be the final result. Mangaian men are quite concerned over the appearance of the superincised organ. An insult of major social magnitude, only slightly less severe than reference to a man's smegma, is to imply that a man has a "dog-eared" penis, with pendulous skin below the shaft.

Severe pain characterizes the superincision operation, and the youth runs directly into the sea or the stream for relief—at the same time exultantly proclaiming, "Now I am really a man."

After the cut has been cleansed with water, the superincised organ is soothed with a poultice of coconut oil, sandalwood powder, and succulent leaves that have been chewed to release their juice. Then a leaf that has had a hole cut in it is wrapped around the organ, the expert being careful to lay open the cut at the same time so that the contractions of healing will expose the glans. The organ is wrapped with cloth, now purchased specifically for the operation, and then tucked up under the belt of a loincloth that also has been made up from specially purchased cloth. Then the boy returns home, meeting with apparent indifference his family's studied lack of notice of his condition.

During the first day following the operation,

any foods may be eaten. But for two weeks following this first day, the boy must carefully avoid those foods characterized by Mangaians as "hot" (meat, coconut sauce, salt, tea) and eat only "cold" foods (taro and taro leaf greens). His mother, who supposedly does not know what has happened, cooks special "nonhot" foods, which she puts in a "special place" for him; usually, however, the boy is not particularly interested in eating, owing to the pain of the cut area. Twice a day the superincised youth must bathe his cut in the sea, no matter what the weather or what his other problems, and then have the wound redressed by the expert. A yellow powder found on the base of the coconut frond or on the leaves of the mountain fern is sprinkled on the wound at this time, in order to produce the proper scab *(tōpā)*. Blisters, which may have been caused by urine coming in contact with the cut, are reduced and treated with the use of heated stones *(māinaina);* infections may be treated with wads of spider web.

But more important than physiological treatment (from the sociocultural standpoint) is the knowledge of sexual matters and the training in sexual behavior given to the youth by the circumcision expert. Not only does this detailed information concern techniques of coitus but it is also said to include the means of locating a "good girl." The expert teaches the youth (as the elderly woman instructs the young female) about such techniques as cunnilingus, the kissing and sucking of breasts, and a means of achieving simultaneous mutual climax, as well as how to bring the woman to climax several times before the male partner permits himself to achieve the goal. Some of this instruction is by straightforward precept, some by the use of figurative stories. Among lore taught is that related to the use of raw eggs, believed by Mangaians to make men more virile and to aid women in speeding up their orgasms.

This period of formal instruction is followed some two weeks after the operation, by a "practical exercise" in copulation, the purpose of which is to have the superincision scab removed by actual sexual intercourse. The intercourse, often arranged by the expert, must be with an experienced woman; formerly she was an appropriately related kinswoman, but now she may be any mature and experienced female, including the village trollop. There is said to be a special thrill involved for the woman, although there are also some indications that many women object to the role. Of significance to the youth is the coaching he receives in the techniques that he has learned about from the expert. The woman teaches him to hold back until he can achieve orgasm in unison with his partner; she teaches him the techniques involved in carrying out various acts and positions about which the expert has advised him—especially the matter of timing *(kite i te tā'ei).* A touch of the old ceremony is often preserved in that the woman may insist upon carrying out this practical instruction on the beach, at a place where water seeps through the sands. Here the mistress and the pupil, these Polynesian "children of the sea," are in contact with the mother waters.

The newly cut male organ itself provides other rewards. Socially, perhaps more than biologically, it provides the youth with the mandatory cleanliness for acceptability as a sexual partner. Psychologically, the youth believes that it enables him to better thrill his partner, to permit him to make the sexual act more vigorous, and to enable him to bring his partner to orgasm three times as compared to his once. And, if the cut has been properly made and the scab properly removed by an experienced partner, the organ in itself is thought to be beautiful.

In modern times, the last day that the expert takes care of the boy is marked by a feast given for both the boy and his mentor. The father acknowledges the help given to his son and sends part of the pig to the expert's home. (When the pig is killed and cooked, the superincision expert receives the head—the part of honor—and one of the thighs; the bandager receives another of the thighs). This feast is the signal for the boy to be called a man by the people.

Not all individuals experience the ideal pattern

as generalized above. Although at least 95 percent of Mangaian men are said to be cut, a very few are able to resist for their entire life the social shame and scorn and mockery heaped upon unsuperincised males; some few others may resist it until they have become fathers. (The most successful and sought after young girl-chaser during my last visit to Mangaia had not yet been circumcised.) Now that there are European-trained medical practitioners on the island with modern drugs and techniques, some infants are being circumcised at birth rather than superincised at puberty. And there is a tendency to cut the penis at an ever more youthful age; some Mangaian youths of ten years are now undergoing the ordeal, to the despair of the old men. (One of the governors attributes a supposed decline in local physique and athletic prowess to the earlier age of superincision.) In "the old days," they say, the act awaited a boy's training as a warrior and was carried out "in secrecy," at anywhere from fifteen on up to thirty-six years. And warriors abstained from sex for from three to seven days before battle, lest they lose their physical power. Now the superincision is "announced" to the village by the killing of a pig; a practitioner may use a local anesthetic rather than go off to a lonely place by the sea; and he may make the Jewish cut. With these "new medicines" the youth can "eat any food." Methylate may be used instead of the chewed medicines of leaves and powder; and some boys no longer lose their scab in actual sexual intercourse. Some boys now make the cut upon one another, rather than have an expert assist them.

Once he is made acceptable by superincision, a boy leaves off masturbation in favor of girls; he aggressively seeks them out or is sought out by them. Soon copulation becomes an every-night affair.

SEXUAL ATTITUDES

Copulation is a principal concern of the Mangaian of either sex. This concern is evident in the number of words for coitus, for the sexual parts of the body, and for sexual activities and other intimate matters in the Mangaian insults. To tell a man *maumau 'ua te ure i āau'* is to tell him, insultingly, that he's lazy and that he's letting his penis go to waste, letting it "get rusty." For the act of coitus or copulation itself there is a formal specific word, *ai,* that is related only to the human act. *Oni* is the formal word for animal copulation, although this word may be used for human intercourse in a joking sense. There are innumerable synonyms including some that are similar to English usage. "To sleep" *(moe)* and "to lie down" *(takoto)* also mean "to copulate" and are often used as socially acceptable or "polite" terms. And the terms for "male" *(tāne)* and "female" *(wahine),* when used by a member of the opposite sex, may also infer copulation. The twenty-seventh night of the lunar month (also called *tāne*) is considered "an especially good night for searching out women," as well as for net fishing.

The Mangaians' approach to sex must be as indirect as the final proposition is direct. There is no dating whatsoever (in the American sense) between youths of the two sexes. In this day of public elementary school and general knowledge of writing, a note carried by an intermediary or left in a hidden location may ask the direct question; rarely would it be handed directly from writer to receiver. The slight pressure of a finger or arm in dancing, the raising of an eyebrow, the showing of a seed pod or flower cupped in the hand so as to provide a sexually suggestive sign are all that is required to raise the question in this society where boy is not seen with girl in public. Or (as will be seen later in the discussion of *motoro*) the boy (or girl) may simply go at night to the house and bed of the sought-after partner. Today the phrases "I love you" or "I want you" play a role in the note or the go-between's message, for "sweet talk" is recognized as a necessary social lubricant. But such phrases mean only "I want to copulate with you."

Whatever the indirect approach or whoever the social go-between, the proposition raised is direct and unmistakable. There is no contact between the sexes, no rendezvous, no equivalent of our "necking" that does not culminate directly and immediately in copulation. Coitus is the only imaginable end for any kind of sexual contact among Mangaians. Less than one out of a hundred girls, and even fewer boys—if, indeed, there are any exceptions in either sex—have *not* had substantial sexual experience prior to marriage. Although the sexual act is understood to be related to childbirth, Mangaians believe that if one spreads the relationship between varied partners and avoids continuous or regular intercourse with the same partner, pregnancy will not result. They also maintain that although sexual intercourse is one of the prerequisites between partners in formal marriage or in mating, it in itself bears no implication of love or connotation of marriage.

COITUS

Little stimulation is required to prepare the Mangaian male for sexual intercourse; custom and habit seem sufficient. However, the Mangaian does admit to increased sexual excitement and desire upon hearing music. Somewhat more exciting is the sight of the nude female body—a knowledge used by Mangaian females to arouse flagging interest in their partners. Perfume, the sight of a woman's well-rounded hips, and the actions of the Polynesian dance also incite the male Mangaian to thoughts of copulation, as does the sight of female genitalia—particularly a prominent mons Veneris. The rotating motion of his partner's hips in the actual sex act is what then spurs the Mangaian male on to greater sexual achievements; female passiveness dampens the male's abilities. Most particularly, the Mangaian is sexually excited by the sounds of others copulating, especially by the sound of moist genitalia coming together (*'ikawaiwai*).

With the exception of copulation between married partners or *motoro* partners, which takes place in the home, sexual connection between young Mangaians takes place in out-of-the-way places: on the beach, in the woods, out of the village in "the bush," and in empty houses. Most of it occurs at night, but some takes place during the day—if other circumstances are right. The act may take only minutes to complete, or the session can be prolonged over several hours and (successively) be carried on all through the night. As the male youth has been instructed by the older male, the young female by the older women, and the male youths have been schooled in practice as well as theory at the period of their *te'e,* little time need be devoted to self-discovery.

There is seldom any kissing or affectionate foreplay and demonstration prior to coitus. (Polynesians did have the *'ongi* [*PPN *hongi*]*— improperly called "nose rubbing," actually a kind of sniffing of the scent of one another—but it was more a demonstration of kinship affinity and formal emotion than of sexual intent.) Although the concept of lip kissing has recently begun to be used with approval on Mangaia, stimulated by the moving pictures and/or by experience overseas or with European partners on the other Cook Islands, the older Mangaian female still cannot understand why her youthful partner attempts to kiss her just prior to climax; kissing appears to be restricted to the present younger generation. Sexual intimacy is *not* achieved by first demonstrating personal affection; the reverse is true. The Mangaian, or Polynesian girl takes an immediate demonstration of sexual virility and masculinity as the first test of her partner's desire for her and as the reflection of her own desirability. (In fact, the Cook Island female may test the male's desire rather severely, as did the Aitutaki girl who went for several days without washing her privates and then insisted that her would-be lover perform cunnilingus upon her before admitting him to more intimate acts of coitus.) One virility test used by Mangaian women is to require a lover to have successful sexual intercourse without making contact with any part of the part-

*PPN = proto-Polynesian; * = reconstructed word.

ner's body other than the genitalia. Personal affection may or may not result from acts of sexual intimacy, but the latter are requisite to the former—exactly the reverse of the ideals of western society.

The foregoing is not to be construed as meaning there is no Mangaian sexual foreplay; it indicates that the component of affection is separate from the coital act, at least as far as the young Mangaian is concerned. In fact, there is a considerable technique involved in Mangaian coital foreplay, even though the preliminary period may be brief. Such foreplay, directed toward achieving a heightened erotic interest and bringing about the full arousal of passion before actual copulation, includes the manual and lingual caressing of each other's nipples by the partners of either sex and manipulation of the genitalia of one another by both partners. Not only is erection of the nipples desired, but some of the sexual foreplay is aimed at moistening the sexual parts to make it easier to come together. For this same reason there is penilingual and cunnilingual foreplay, although some informants said these later may be used to achieve climax—"if the two partners like each other very much." In addition, the young Mangaian male may use erotic words and "dirty talk" to excite his partner and to make her "hotter." But, in the main, the Mangaian (and the Polynesian) rejects the use of very much sexual foreplay, as this would take away from the pleasures of actual copulation; it takes place largely after the first act and is a prelude to the next. One informant noted, "Fooling around would cut down the time that we could actually go in and out." The man who incites a girl to sex and then "wastes her time" with too much preliminary fooling is likely to be pushed away and called *ure paruparu,* "limp penis," by the disappointed girl, as she runs away. This insult is his penalty for not having immediately "got on with the work." The "good man," as the term is used by informants, can go and stop, play and go, continuing each act for fifteen minutes or a half hour. But even between married partners the first foreplay is likely to be only

for a five-minute period—"enough to warm her up."

Setting aside experimental sessions of the very young and the just-mated, Mangaians are not very concerned with the use of a variety of positions for the coital act. The use of the more elaborate positional variations and a desire to watch the partner's nude body are related to the newly mated, as is copulation in the daytime. After the first five years or so of partnership, these aesthetic devices are dispensed with. Conversely, coitus between two youthful partners who are not well acquainted will not be in the nude; any of their small talk or caressing will follow the first penetration and orgasm.

The Mangaian prefers sexual intercourse without the inconvenience of clothing, but he is also concerned lest he be seen. "Be careful—much talk around the island if you are seen." Hence, this social pressure serves to restrict most mature marital coitus to the night-time hours and often to "under-the-cover" of bedclothes. Again, there is little real desire to actually watch one's partner during the act; the principal interest is in "making every part of the body move." The principal requirement of the female (and the reason that the Mangaian male dislikes coitus with a European female) is that the woman "must move"—there must be plenty of pelvic action to satisfy her lover. Without question, the essential and principal component of Mangaian sexual ability and interest is not the foreplay or between-play, not the nakedness, not the scene or the props, and certainly not the position. Rather, it is the ability to continue the in-and-out position of coitus over long periods of time.

All of the principal varieties of coital position are practiced by Mangaians: the partners facing each other or in the same direction while lying on their side *(aikaukau);* the male lying prone on top of the woman while facing one another (the most common position) or vice versa *(aitīra'a);* both partners standing, facing one another *(aitū);* the woman bending over and the male mounting from behind *(ai'aka'oro);* penilingus *(kaiure);* cunnilingus *(kai'ika);* soixante-neuf.

There is no recorded term for the latter, despite informant statements that the act is performed; however, the Mangaian fighting words (used as an insult on other islands), *"Mangaia Kai Kiore,"* though ostensibly translated as "Mangaians eat rats," are a not-too-well-veiled allusion to genital-lingual practices. Anal intercourse, axillary intercourse with penis held between breasts, thighs, feet, or in armpits, and other noncunnal means of sexual relief, including mutual genital manipulation to climax and masturbation, are used during the menstrual period—despite the older generations' horror at the concept of sexual contact during menstruation. (Mangaian grandfathers indicate that they were advised by their sexual mentors that copulation during menstruation was the cause of venereal disease.) The manual techniques are said to be used less frequently than in the northern Cook Islands. Europeanized Mangaians dislike discussing these variant positions.

The Mangaian desires a well-lubricated sexual path and may use his own saliva or a concoction of the viscous chewed bark or stalk of the hibiscus tree to assist him. Mangaians also say that a youthful or small female may require lubrication of her privates with soap, prior to intercourse.

Once penetration has been made, the male realizes that his action must be continuously kept up in order to bring his partner to climax (as has been pointed out by Kinsey). He may deliberately "think of other things" to avoid premature ejaculation; he may also fantasy to more rapidly bring on the climax. During copulation there is talk, the passing of compliments, and a good deal of moaning and sighing. Biting, or more particularly a strong sucking on the flesh of the body, may also accompany the sexual act. (The latter produces a red welt "bee sting," which provides evidence of one's sexual activities—to the annoyance of the church members when these occur on the elder members of the community.) Biting of the partner's body is a common expression of passionate involvement in the sexual act, as is oral-genital intercourse. My princi-

pal Mangaian informant (with whom I had previously been working on setting up an electric generator and voltmeter for my field equipment) expressed himself metaphorically as follows. When you "play" between the sexual acts, as in the oral-genital contact, your "voltage goes high," and "high voltage stops the smell" and the partners "do anything." But once the climax arrives, "the voltage drops down." However, when the "voltage is high," a "good man" will be able to continue his actions for fifteen to thirty minutes or more, and in the middle of this "a woman thinks she's urinating—but that's not urine." (But it is *not* the orgasm, according to Mangaians—it is "another type" of sensation.) Above all, the man's goal is to continue the coital action—"the longer you go, the more the pleasure"; "the man who goes only a short time does not 'love' (that is, want to please) his woman." Young couples may carry this act to climax three to five times in an evening. But marriage and the concomitant presence of children, and the increasing need for continuous physical exertion of work, reduce the number of climactic acts. There is also a decrease in the talk, stroking, and (for today's younger couples) the kissing between partners.

There is no indication of group intercourse on Mangaia other than the gang rapes, which will be discussed later in the chapter.

Currently, the most favored coital position on Mangaia is that of the couple prone, facing one another; most frequently the male assumes the superior role, although the female commonly assumes it also. The second most frequently practiced position is that of the woman bending over from the standing position, the man approaching her from the rear. Third most frequent (practiced, for the most part, when the woman is pregnant) is the position of the couple lying on their side with both partners facing in the same direction, the male approaching his partner from the rear (*pāto'e;* this is *not* anal penetration). Very much less frequently practiced is the variant of the side position, in which partners face one another. Fourth most common of the positions (but very infrequently practiced) is that of the female facing down, prone, with the male approaching from the rear. Today, although the sitting or the "oceanic" position is "tried" among the newly mated, it is rarely practiced. But it is important to note that it is specifically acknowledged by informants that, "the older people, they 'know' (i.e., 'believe') that this is the best."

THE ORGASM

Despite the fact that the Mangaian male and female realize that orgasm is a culminating peak of the sexual act, it is not the sole goal to be achieved. As indicated above, the interplay of copulation and the prolongation of this interplay are the focus of the act. The Mangaian says that the orgasm "feels good" and "we enjoy it"; but he has not built up the elaborate concern with it that characterizes the American folklore of sex. This is, perhaps, due to the fact that it is so universally achieved among Polynesians of both sexes. It is stated that the orgasm must be "learned" by a woman and that this learning process is achieved through the efforts of "the good man." Formerly, it was the older woman who taught the young girls to achieve orgasm. Now, if one man is not successful in teaching this to her when she is young, then another man will soon take his place and provide more adequate tutelage.

The Mangaian male is not known to achieve the so-called extended orgasm, the effects of which in of itself—separately from the coital buildup—supposedly last from half an hour to one hour. (It has been reported for the premodern period by one worker on another Polynesian island on the basis of informant statements.) However, Mangaian men indicate that this extended orgasm—which they translate by the English term "knockout"—has been observed among their womenfolk. In any event, the Mangaian male lover aims to have his partner achieve orgasm *(nene)* two or three times to his once. But

the ultimate and invariable goal of two lovers is to so match their reactions that when the male finally does permit himself to reach climax it is achieved simultaneously with the peak of his partner's pleasure. The older males indicate that even though the young *māpū* has not yet learned to care much for his partner's pleasure, he will still concern himself with bringing her to climax, in order to "hold" her and to preserve his own reputation. Men say that they are always careful of "women's talk," in order that the female will "pass on the good name" of the male. For the Mangaian believes that once he gives his girl the climactic pleasure, she "cannot keep away from him"—unless someone else deliberately "holds her back" by bettering the other male's performance. But it was generally agreed among my several informants that the really important aspect of sexual intercourse for either the married man or the more experienced unwed male is to give pleasure to his wife or woman or girl—the pleasure of the orgasm; supposedly this is what gives the male partner his own pleasure and a special thrill that itself is set apart from his own orgasm. In this connection, it appears to be an accepted cultural fact that following an argument between the couple, Mangaian (and central Polynesian) women in general must have intercourse with their partners before they can "make up." For, the women say, this copulation is proof that the male is still "in love" (desires her).

A consensus of the formal Mangaian sexual discussion group, in analyzing the phenomenon of orgasm, was that the "average" number per night or week was as set forth in the following tabulation.

TABLE 7-1

Approximate Male Age	Average Number of Orgasms per Night	Average Number of Nights per Week
18	3	7
28	2	5–6
38	1	3–4
48	1	2–3

Individual informant data and other sources of information, not only from Mangaia but from elsewhere in central Polynesia, indicate that these estimates are probably reasonably valid. However, I would, myself, tend to reduce slightly the younger male figures on frequency per week, because of situational factors that preclude continual night after night copulation. But I would tend also to raise slightly the frequency figures for the older males, because of the apparent strong demands of older Polynesian females. Further, one must keep in mind the variability between individuals. Some men may come to orgasm four times a night, every night; others, only once a night, two or three times a week. These data should be borne in mind during the discussion of impotency and sterility.

It is significant to note that the Mangaian males very definitely believe that men tend to want sexual activity more frequently than do their women but that women tend to "hold them back" from full sexual indulgence. Some husbands, however, may "beat the wife into submission." And, in contrast to western sexual folklore, Mangaians believe that it is the female who becomes thin from sexual exertion; males boast, *Me ū ana i a tāua, 'ua topa te to'e*—"If we two thump together (I will go so many times that) her rectum will fall out." And, again in contrast to western sexual folklore, the Mangaian emphasis is not upon the number of times a night that a male can achieve climax; rather, he sets his sights on the number of nights in the week that he is capable of coitus. In his teens and twenties, he aims at an every night capability; it is in the thirties and forties that he starts to "miss" nights. He also judges potency by his ability (or that of others) to get the same woman pregnant twice in one year, as well as to "make a girl grow thin."

REFERENCES

MARSHALL, D. S. 1961. *Ra'ivavae: An Expedition to the Most Fascinating and Mysterious Island in Polynesia.* New York: Doubleday.

n.d. "Polynesian Sexual Behavior." Manuscript.
n.d. "The Village of God: An Ethnography of Mangaia." Manuscript.

8

FEMALE STATUS AND ROLE TRANSITION IN THE TSWANA LIFE CYCLE

DAVID N. SUGGS

In a review of anthropological data on the climacteric, Griffen (1978) notes that there is a dearth of material pertaining to post-menopausal women in the ethnographic record. She correctly attributes this partially to "the anti-woman, anti-aging biases within U.S. culture, the culture in which so many ethnographers have been trained" (Griffin 1978:51). In line with current efforts to amend this situation (see e.g., Beyen 1986, Davis 1986, Lock 1986), this paper examines adult female status and role transition in terms of life-cycle progression among the Kgatla of Botswana.[1]

The data derive from a year's research in Mochudi, Botswana. Structured interviews were conducted with a total of 60 women, 30 pre-menopausal and 30 postmenopausal. Due to budgetary constraints, the sample is not necessarily representative of all Kgatla women. Those in my sample are teachers, nurses, shop owners,

[1] I thank Brian du Toit for his helpful criticism of an earlier draft of this paper and Sharon Anderson for her help in the planning of the research. I also wish to acknowledge the help of Yvonne Suggs, Sona du Toit, and Thea De Wet in the field. Finally, I thank Dr. M. Jack Suggs and Dr. J. O. Williams, whose financial assistance made this work possible.

SOURCE: From "Female Status and Role Transition in the Tswana Life Cycle" by D. N. Suggs, *Ethnology Vol. XXVI, No. 2,* April 1987. Copyright © 1987 by the University of Pittsburgh. Reprinted by permission of the author.

and entrepreneurs, and are therefore most representative of the educated elite of Mochudi.

Throughout the discussion, results of the investigation are compared with previous literature on the Tswana. Isaac Schapera devoted considerable attention to women's roles, and information from his ethnographic materials (Schapera 1933, 1959, 1966) serves as a baseline for the documentation of culture change. Izzard's (1982) study of women's roles in Botswana emphasizes the primacy of labor migration and education as etiological factors impacting the status of women. Comaroff and Roberts (1977) note the importance of these factors as well, but stress the salience of changes in the Tswana marriage patterns as they relate to resource management. The data presented below support both of their arguments, enlarging specifically on the importance of change in the pattern of age-based resource control as it affects the status of women throughout the life course. It is argued that the primary areas of change in women's status and roles have been (1) the resulting devaluation of marriage as a prerequisite for motherhood and definitional characteristic of adulthood, and (2) a concurrent increased emphasis on women's productive and managerial roles in the definition of female adulthood.

FEMALE LIFE STAGES

The Kgatla divide the human life span into four major stages. For women, these stages are termed *mosetsana*,[2] *lekgaribe, mosadi,* and *mosadi mogolo.* These correspond roughly in relative age to the western categories of girl, adolescent, woman, and old woman. But while the correspondence is noted, age is shown to be of secondary importance in a woman's movement through these stages. Competence in decision-making and judgment, motherhood, household provisioning, and the establishment of managerial household

[2]For a discussion of sample selection and characteristics, as well as the status of mosetsana, see Suggs 1986.

independence are primary agents in life-cycle transition.

Lekgaribe (pl. *Makgaribe*)

Menarche occurs among the Kgatla without any real sense of celebration, although it is this event which marks the end of *mosetsana* status. Once menstruation begins, a girl will be told that she is "now a woman." All but three of the women spoken with responded to the question of "when does a girl become a woman?" by saying "at first menstruation." Yet, they also qualified the remark with such statements as "but not a real *mosadi* until she can think straight" and "but not a responsible adult yet."

Some women said that while menarche marked the beginning of womanhood, a girl at that time becomes *lekgaribe.* The term was loosely translated to me as meaning "young woman," "unmarried woman," and "carefree older girl." Thus, the age range for the lekgaribe stage is roughly the teen years, extending into the early twenties when childbirth or marriage bring it to a close. While not all, or even a majority of those spoken to, gave this term as a separate stage in the life cycle, it is certain that they would not look at a teen who was known to have just begun menstruating and say that she is truly a woman. On the contrary, one is told repeatedly that merely menstruating does not make one mosadi. This will be made explicit below. For now, it is sufficient to note that the data support the generalization for a term *(lekgaribe)* given by only a few as being categorically substantial.

When a girl attains menarche, she may already have learned of its significance from friends. In such a case, she may simply keep the knowledge to herself and go on about life as usual. But it is much more common for her not to know anything about menstruation. The Kgatla value age-specific knowledge greatly and, while matters dealing with sexuality may be spoken about among peers, such topics are rarely and only situationally discussed between generations. As one reaches the stage where the knowledge in question is of personal use, the older people impart it to them. Until they have attained that stage, it is "not yet their time."

For this reason, women commonly reported being frightened at menarche. Out of the total sample, only nine reported that they had known with certainty what it was. Most feared that they were suffering from an illness. "No, I didn't know this thing. I only remember running home to my mother and crying to her that I had done nothing but was bleeding to death." "Oh, yes, I went to my grandmother and she said that I was not ill, but was growing up." "I was very frightened. I didn't want to tell anyone because I thought I would have to go to hospital." "I had been playing very roughly that morning. I cried so hard because I thought I had ruptured something."

Some few women (three from my sample) say nothing to anyone about it at first. After a while they learn from their friends that they are not unique. Most go to their mother, grandmother, or elder sister and report what happened.

Girls are inevitably told several things at this time. They are first told that they must not "play" with boys any longer. "We are all told this one thing; if you now play with boys you will get a baby." They are then typically told that now they are like mosadi and must learn to behave like mosadi (in other words, play less and be more responsible). They are told how to keep themselves clean during menstruation and how to carefully dispose of their "cloths" so that no sorcerer may obtain them and thereby do them damage.

If she is from a more traditional family, a girl will be taken to her mother's sister or to her maternal grandmother. There the older woman will spread cow dung on her chest in the shape of an X. This is said to delay the continuation of menstruation after the first menses and to lessen the likelihood of physical discomfort accompanying menstruation when it comes again. While Schapera (1966:222) reports this to be common (with regard to child-spacing), it is now rare. Only twelve of the older women and three of the

younger ones report having this ritual performed.

Makgaribe past the ages of sixteen to seventeen are considered marriageable, although few will be married before age eighteen and most will be in their twenties. Working in the 1930s, Schapera (1966:248) reports that the lekgaribe spent her days involved in the domestic chores of the household; sweeping, cleaning, washing, chopping wood, cooking, and caring for the males. If she is not a student or domestic servant in another household, today's lekgaribe does the same. Like the mosetsana, the lekgaribe is under the immediate authority of her parents. "The lekgaribe is needing control; mosadi is her control."

Unlike the period of childhood, the lekgaribe years are a time of increasing independence and responsibility. The adolescent often will do some of the buying at the store, finding time to chat with friends as she does so. Commanding the respect and obedience of younger siblings, she will play less and less. Concomitantly, she will spend more of her time working. Now she can engage in the heavier activities such as chopping firewood and stamping grain. She may also learn some of the more artistic responsibilities of women, such as smearing a new lapa floor or sewing. She will spend much more time cooking than her younger sisters and, like them, continues to fetch water, sweep, and engage in the lighter tasks of home management. She also is given more responsibility in terms of crop production, helping in all of the work from planting to harvesting. By the end of the lekgaribe years she is usually capable of performing all of the tasks of home management and production but does so under the direction of her mother.

Also, at this time a young woman is likely to begin to have serious boyfriends. They will come to visit her in the evenings if her parents allow it. If not, then the young man will wait until she leaves the lapa—most usually to fetch water—and will then seek her out and ask her to meet him some evening. (So common is this strategy, that when a teacher at one of the secondary schools asked his students if they knew how to avoid pregnancy, one of the young women replied, "Don't go to fetch water.") In any case, the lekgaribe years are a time of sexual experimentation. Ninety percent of the women in the sample first engaged in sexual intercourse during this life stage.

Part of a young woman's increasing independence is her ability to come and go more freely, particularly on weekend nights. Schapera reports young people attending "concerts"—gatherings where the young women joined young men in singing and dancing. Today, the concerts are for the most part gone. In their place are the community center dance halls and the "disco." Parents rarely approve of their older children, male or female, attending the disco but it is a popular spot among the older teens. If the lekgaribe does not go to the community centers or disco, the village offers many secluded areas where she can meet with friends or boyfriends. Thus, while parents continue to control her movements, they do so with greater leniency than before.

Some 20 percent of the women spoken with remember the lekgaribe years as their best. One woman's response in particular covered the range of their responses well: "It is too nice, lekgaribe. You are still young and with your parents, so you are loved and cared for. But you are big now. You are knowing how to be a person. Later, you will worry always about your children and your crops and where your husband is. The lekgaribe, she is free of such concern. She worries about nothing. Hers is just to dream."

The lekgaribe who is also a secondary school student will not escape domestic duties entirely. Those whose families live in Mochudi will continue to aid in household work both before and after school hours. Those who come from a different village and board at the school will be spared the stamping of grain and chopping of firewood. But theirs is the responsibility for keeping their hostel clean and their clothes washed.

Thus, the lekgaribe phase is a time of incipient adulthood when one assumes more and more competence in women's roles. It is a time of experimentation with selfhood and sexuality. The phase can theoretically come to an end in one of three ways; pregnancy, marriage, or the establishment of an independent household. Practically, for the majority of the Kgatla it will end at first pregnancy.

Mosadi (pl. Basadi)

The seTswana term for "woman" is *mosadi* (the one who stays or remains). The implication, I was told, is that it is the woman's responsibility to care for home and for family. Women universally are given some degree of domestic status, although the roles associated with the status vary. Ask the women of Mochudi what makes an ideal *mosadi* and they will first tell you that she keeps a clean, well-organized, and hospitable home while seeing that her family is fed and is comfortable. In Mochudi, a woman's greatest pride is her home; it is her arena of control and commonly her domain of greatest independence. Its organization visually represents her ability to think, decide, and act responsibly. The ability to act responsibly is what most women see as the mark of adulthood. As one woman put it, "You become *mosadi* when you know the difference between right and wrong. But if you don't have your own house, you have no respect, no authority, and no peace." As noted above, the women in my sample represent the educated women of Mochudi most fully; they are teachers, nurses, and entrepreneurs but simultaneously perform the traditional roles assigned to women. Still, their self-expressed central role is that of caretaker or manager of home and family.

This, then, suggests that two much desired statuses are wife and mother. While the latter is of tremendous importance, the women of Mochudi view marriage with some ambivalence. This is a significant change from the situation described by Schapera (1959:38) where "few people, if any, fail to get married before reaching middle-age."

The high rates of labor migration have contributed strongly to an increase in unmarried women in Mochudi. Izzard (1982:664–665) has examined the issue in depth:

> The absence of men had a considerable impact on the role of women as wives and as mothers. [Out-migration] resulted in a reduction of the marriage rate . . . and an increase in the number of deserted wives. The likelihood of a woman assuming the role of wife changed, as did the circumstances in which she held this position, whilst there were concomitant adjustments in attitude toward marriage . . . [Women] no longer saw marriage as the chief means with which to enhance their status in society. The role of mother assumed greater significance in the face of the declining importance of 'the wife,' and the two roles became isolated from each other.

In an outstanding analysis of the change in marriage patterns among the Tswana, Comaroff and Roberts (1977:101) point specifically to the effects of labor migration on the males' control of sexual access to females:

> The incidence of labor migration has grown steadily and . . . sexual access has become more difficult to regulate. . . . Apart from the fact that a high proportion of women spend long periods away from parental control, the absence of many of their close relatives when they are themselves at home means that the careful watch which was formerly maintained over their socialization is now considerably relaxed. Moreover . . . because of the enforced emigration of many males, the number of female-headed households in which unmarried women live independently of any male guardian has risen. In short, there has been a widespread loosening of the control of senior kinsmen over the younger generation, a tendency which has been expressed both in structural terms and in patterns of socialization.

Comaroff and Roberts (1977) suggest that a further result has been a change not only in the rate of marriage, but also in the form of marriage. Traditionally, Kgatla males could utilize polygyny as one means of "accumulating a wide-ranging network of supportive [affinal] bonds" (Comaroff and Roberts 1977:116). While the need for these bonds remains polygyny is no longer a viable option. They suggest that as polygyny declined individuals who sought to manipulate conjugal bonds as a strategy for re-

source management found a practical solution in serial monogamy. Where before they had manipulated conjugality through negotiation of the rank of wives, serial monogamy allows for the manipulation of the status of wives. Historically, as this practice became more common, "the emergent statistical regularity . . . became a recognized and culturally meaningful expectation" (Comaroff and Roberts 1977:118). Thus, if a man enters a prospective union and subsequently finds it to be less than advantageous, he will seek to terminate the union or to construe it as a nonmarital relationship. This has resulted in an increase in the number of marriage disputes brought before the traditional courts (Comaroff and Roberts, 1977:119).

In addition, it has resulted in marriage being a much more tenuous means to security for Kgatla women, a fact that did not go unnoticed by the post-war chiefs. In response, they instituted the jural maturity of women and legal means for women to receive compensation for any births out of wedlock where the man had no intention of completing the marriage process. This ambiguity in the status of a union is undoubtedly one source of the women's ambivalence toward marriage.

Another factor of obvious importance is the educational advances of women. Specifically, education has provided women with the opportunity to support themselves and their children through their own labor. This is a degree of independence unmatched in the traditional system. Predicting such change in the 1930s, Schapera (1959:29) wrote, "[t]he cumulative effect of education . . . must almost inevitably make itself felt in a reorganization of women's place in society."

In 1985, this is exactly what has occurred, most particularly with regard to the decreasing significance of marriage as a definitional criterion for female adulthood. "Traditionally, the status of women was prescribed solely by their relationship to men, as their wives and as the mothers to their children" (Tsimako 1980:5, cited in Izzard 1982:664). The educational gains and the redefinition of the jural status of women have led to women's ability to form an independent household without marriage. "This situation [female-headed households] was unheard of in earlier times. It not only gave women greater authority within the confines of the family, but also enhanced their overall status in society" (Izzard 1982:666). The magnitude of this change is apparent when one realizes that according to Schapera marriage was the essential route to the status of independent household manager. Schapera reports the following, "As long as the wife [sic] lives in her parents' home, she remains under the immediate authority of her father" (1966:102). "Marriage effects a change in the legal and social status of both husband and wife. They . . . play the part of full adult members of the community" (1959:150). "[A woman's] lot is on the whole much easier when her husband sets up his own home and she becomes its mistress" (1959:149). "[H]er status . . . is improved by the establishment of [this] household, for she now . . . acquires a new authority in domestic affairs" (1966:104).

Today a woman need not marry to establish her own household provided she has the funds to build it, the experience to run it, and the will to do so. Indeed, of the 10 percent of the sample who were never married, only two were in their natal households, and one of these was currently building her own home. As is noted below, marriage does speed up a woman's attainment of the status of independent household manager but lack of a husband does not preclude its achievement. The point is that there is today a decreased emphasis on marriage as a definitional characteristic of women. This does not mean that the women of Mochudi are now prepared to simply eschew marriage. Rather, it means that the decreased likelihood has resulted in the de-emphasis of marriage as the primary route to fulfillment and adulthood. Ideally, every mosadi prefers to be married; practically, it is neither achievable nor desirable for every mosadi. An unmarried mosadi is no less a "woman" for being so.

This is evidenced strongly in the responses to an eight-item role index constructed for this research. When given the statement, "Unmarried women are more likely to feel empty or incomplete than married women," a quarter of the postmenopausal women disagreed and a third of the premenopausal women disagreed. It is not surprising that the majority agree with this statement. After all, marriage is a universal institution and remains the ideal state for child-bearing in Mochudi. Yet, a substantial minority of both the young and old women do not see it as necessary for female fulfillment. Among the comments of the postmenopausal group are the following. "They are just the same; married or not, they are first mothers." "Life wants two people. It is only natural. But today, I don't know. . . . Some enjoy being single." "A single woman is proud and happy. Why shouldn't she be? She has her children and does exactly what she wishes to do." "Many men here just treat you poorly. Then, it is better to be single." The premenopausal women are even more explicit in their ambivalence. "Today, women are very clever and can handle themselves." "An unmarried woman is a free woman. That is a happy woman for certain." "Look at the educated woman who is unmarried. She is very rich."

But the status of mother is of paramount importance in the definition of womanhood. The general opinion among both young and old women is that a woman is never complete and never happy without having children. Children are valued on several levels; as objects of love, as continuation of family, as extra hands while one is working, and as security in old age. As one person stated the importance of motherhood, "Only women can do this thing. Those who can not are not wholly women. They work for nothing and die for nothing." In the words of another, "To be a woman one must bear children. That is the first work of a woman."

Thus, in response to the question, "Is a woman who has not had children a complete woman?" 90 percent of all the women in my sample said, "No." "She will just be lonely and jealous of those who have babies." "Who will she send on errands? Who will help her? Who will love her? No one." "Without children a woman has no one in old age." "I am called MmaKaliso.[3] It is a disgrace to be an adult and be called by your birth name alone." "You know a cow is a good cow if it has a calf (Tswana proverb)."

Yet, there are some important changes in regard to motherhood, not the least of which is an emergent value on limiting the number of children born. Of the premenopausal women, only one said there was no value in birth control and family planning, quoting a Tswana proverb: "One eye gets all of the injuries." The reasoning of the other young women was pragmatic. One woman's response in particular sums up their attitudes. "Things will get bad nowadays if you have more than four children. You can not feed them all or clothe them or educate them. Some of the children will suffer because of this. Besides, you never know when you will get rascals for children. By having less children you get fewer rascals because you raise the ones you have better."

While the older women were not as homogeneous in their opinions, 76 percent still stated that it was better to have fewer children. "Limiting the number of children makes them listen better and easier to maintain." Of the 24 percent who saw no value in birth control, the reasoning varied. "It is why women live—to have children." "If God wants you to have seven and you decide to have only two, then He will take those two away from you as punishment." "The more children you have, the more love you have."

The interplay between traditional values and the changing attitude with regard to family planning is clear in the responses to two other questions which were asked. The question, "What would your neighbors say if you did not have (any) children?" yielded various responses, almost all pejorative. "I don't know exactly what they would say but I know they won't like it." "They will just pity you." "They will say that

you are a mule" (i.e., that you are sterile and have slept with too many lovers). "They laugh at such a one behind her back and say that she is cursed." "They will just treat this woman like a child." "They call you *ntswa* (dog) and they treat you like one." "They call you *mmopa*" (clay pot, see Schapera 1959:155). Clearly a woman is expected to have some children.

But with the change in attitude, now one must not have too many, either. While a few women said that a woman would be praised if she had more than ten children, most said that such a woman would be considered foolish and irresponsible. "They would say *Ijojojojo*, this one can not count." "They would say that she doesn't know how to close her thighs." "They would say that she will not be able to maintain them." "They say, 'Ao! This one must love rascals'" (implying that she will not be able to raise so many properly). "They will call her *mmalesaisai* (mother of a colony of ants). No, those children will steal."

The limitation of family size will undoubtedly have some important repercussions for the future. While the women of Mochudi recognize its educational and economic advantages, some worry that it will further emphasize the individuation of households and the declining importance of the extended family in Botswana. Already, traditional family structures are undergoing alteration as more people move to the new areas on the outskirts of Mochudi proper. More important is the fact that the better educated tend to move to the urban areas where employment suiting their education is centered. If all of the children are educated due to better maintenance of smaller families, then the towns stand to lose a significant portion of their population in the future. And, as the extended family is the basis for the care of the aged in traditional Tswana society, more children may move away and leave their responsibility for their elders behind. Some of the older women of Mochudi believe this to be the case now.

The primary social difference between men and women, from the Tswana point of view, is

---

[3]MmaKaliso translates as Mother of Kaliso. It is honorific to call a woman by the formula Mma plus the name of her first-born.

the following. "Men have the power, women just have the work." It does not take much observation to confirm this. Men tend cattle, plough, and may work in employment. Some few also chop firewood. Ideally, their labor is limited to heavy work and family provision via livestock management and/or wage labor. Women sweep, wash clothes and utensils, plant fields, tend and harvest them, cook, market, collect, carry, and chop firewood, build rondavels, and smear floors. In short, they handle virtually all of the day-to-day necessities. Even if employed, women will make every effort to continue to farm their own fields; if they can not, then they will have others do it and share in the harvest. The ability to grow enough food to feed themselves and their families is highly regarded. With or without education and/or employment, Tswana women are providers and they view their role in provision as complimentary to that of men.

With 38 percent of the men who are between the ages of fourteen and 54 absent from the country, Kgatleng district has the highest rate of labor migration in Botswana (Brown 1980:3). Brown notes in her study of women in agriculture that women and children are often dependent upon the remittance of funds from their migrant sons and husbands. She (Brown 1980:5) further notes that "[i]t seems that it is the exceptional migrant son who sends or brings money, food, or clothing home regularly." While I have no figures to document the validity of this statement, there is little doubt that it represents the collective opinion of the women in the sample. As one informant puts it, "You raise them. You see that they are prepared for life. Some will remember and will be helpful but most just go away and forget you. Young men can not be bothered with serious things."

While 90 percent of the postmenopausal women in the sample agreed with the statement, "It is the husband's duty to support his wife and family," only 71 percent of the premenopausal women agree. Those in both groups who disagreed stated consistently that they saw the sup-

port of the family as the duty of both husband and wife. This reflects the growing number of wives who are educated and gainfully employed, as well as the increase in female-headed households (Brown 1980). None of the unmarried women sampled felt it the sole duty of the husband to provide support.

Because of the assumption of employment by women, only 35 percent of the older women agreed with the statement, "A woman's place is in the home." A mere 18 percent of the younger women agreed with this statement. Both groups stated that the woman's role in extradomestic employment was necessary and accepted. So, while motherhood is certainly one of the most important roles a woman has, many are quick to point out that it is not the only role of importance. One woman's statement is representative of this opinion. "In the past it [motherhood as woman's most important task] used to be like that. Today, women must work. Many do not have husbands. How else would they feed their children? Even those who have husbands will work. It is a good thing; it helps the children. So, yes, raising children is a most important task of women, but not the only one."

Practically none (4 percent) of the women I spoke with said that a mother with young children should not work. They almost all agreed that not working would be better because, then, "her word becomes their word very early." But the Kgatla are also realists. When a mother works, the children have more and better food, clothing, and life chances. In short, *mosadi* no longer means "the one who remains [at home]" in an exclusive behavioral sense.

These three roles—independent household manager, mother, and provider—do not, of course, exhaust the list of statuses available to Tswana women but they are central. A true *mosadi* is, from the Tswana point of view, all of them. Without the attainment of any single one, a woman feels diminished and the women in her community concur. All other roles are secondary relative to these three and for some are perhaps even expendable.

The three roles are achieved in a sequential manner. It was earlier noted that one begins helping in provision at an early age; preteens can help to weed crops and keep pests out of the fields. Teens participate in all farming activities and by the late teens a woman is fully capable of responsibly performing all of the roles traditionally assigned to women as providers. Also, an adolescent girl begins to help looking after younger siblings at an early age. Thus, she learns some of the caretaking roles of motherhood concurrently. But while she learns this part of her mothering role as a young girl, a woman usually does not attain the status of mother until her early twenties, the mean age for first birth in the sample being 23. At this age she is more likely to be single than married. Again, the percentage of unwed mothers in Mochudi is unusually high. This too marks an important change in women's roles in Mochudi.

Schapera devoted considerable space to marriage and childbirth, linking them as conceptually inseparable:

> Marriage according to the Tswana is designed primarily for bearing children; and if a woman fails in [bearing children] her lot is hard (1959:155).
> [Marriage] permits a woman to bear children without involving her in the disgrace that would ensue if she were unmarried (1966:38).

Indeed, at the time of Schapera's research, premarital births were negatively sanctioned among the Kgatla. He notes that prior to European contact there were strong sanctions against both mother and child (Schapera 1933:64–68). But, he noted, this was rapidly fading:

> [P]remarital sexual relations, formerly severely condemned, have become almost a matter of course, and many girls [sic] bear children out of wedlock (1966:19).
> [S]o many unmarried girls have born children . . . that the traditional penalties against them are no longer enforced. [Still, unwed mothers] are not often regarded as desirable brides [and] the offspring of casual and unrecognized liaisons . . . are despised (1966:45).

Today, birth outside of wedlock is quite simply a statistical norm, an accepted if not completely welcome commonality. Children born to unwed mothers are not despised in any way; rather, it is expected that women will have children prior to their marriage. One informant puts it this way. "A woman desires to have children even more than she desires a husband. A husband may desert you, a husband may beat you, a husband will betray you. A child only loves you and will know you as mother whether you are young and beautiful or old and ugly."

Nor is a woman who gives birth out of wedlock a less desirable bride. Of the married women in my sample, 47 percent had a child at the time of their marriage. Not once was pregnancy given as a cause for marriage. In fact, of those who were pregnant at the time of their betrothal, all but one had previously given birth. While Schapera (1966:45) noted premarital pregnancy to be disadvantageous for future marriage, some of the women I spoke with claimed it was an advantage. "A man wants a wife who will bear out (sic) children. If you have children, he will see that you are healthy and will want you as a wife." Thus, while the mean age of first birth is 23, the mean age of marriage for the sample is 25.

A woman rarely used to have her own compound immediately following marriage. Traditionally, sons brought their wives into their parents' household. "After [*go ralala,* a form of cohabitation] the young couple would go to live at the home of his parents" (Schapera 1959: 135). There, a new wife's lot was not to be envied, for she became "in effect . . . the general servant of the household" (Schapera 1959:149).

Thus, again, traditionally a woman married and looked forward to a time in the future when she would have her own household. Today, this is less common. Married couples typically start their own household before or immediately after marriage. If a woman does not marry, it is unlikely that she will have her own compound before age 30 but she will most likely have it eventually. While Brown (1980:6) reports that for most Kgatla women the establishment of an independent household is difficult and unlikely before age 40, the more educated women find it to be relatively easy. This is particularly true following cohabitation with a man who has, in the past, expressed an intention of marriage which was subsequently withdrawn. As Comaroff and Roberts (1977) note, this is an increasingly common occurrence. The only expressed obstacle to independent living faced by women is the investment of funds and time in house construction.

So, the woman first becomes proficient at providing, then becomes a mother, and lastly an independent household manager. The sequence of status advance is the same as in Schapera's day, although the specific mechanisms for their achievement have undergone great changes, the most important being that marriage is no longer necessary for the attainment of any, while formerly it was the key to progression into adulthood.

On the basis of the foregoing, some readers might be drawn toward the conclusion that the Kgatla are responding to these changes with matrifocal tendencies. But, if one takes Gonzalez (1970) as a point of departure, any portrayal of the Kgatla as being matrifocal is misleading. That is, while they obviously share some characteristics with matrifocal systems (e.g., closest bonds between uterine siblings and the mother as a more stable presence), on most grounds the Kgatla system is decidedly not matrifocal.

Gonzalez (1970:233–234) argues that by definition in matrifocality (1) the "protective male" is important primarily as "mother's husband," (2) kin relationships beyond the household are defined largely in terms of the mother, (3) extended family members, when present, are most typically "relatives of the mother," and (4) mothers are seen as "most dominant" and the disciplinarians. Yet, in the Kgatla system, on the assumption that bridewealth will be transferred, (1) the children identify primarily with the father's kin; if bridewealth is not transferred, then the children identify with the mother's patriline, (2) extrahousehold kin relations are defined first

with reference to patriline, (3) extended family members, when present may be relatives of either parent but are more commonly those of the father, and (4) fathers, when present, are viewed as the "most dominant" and the disciplinarians.

It is interesting to compare the similarities shared by matrifocal families and female-headed households in Botswana but even here the analogy is at best a slender one. For example, that the bonds between uterine siblings are stronger than those between siblings who share only a father has little to do with the relative absence of males or the stability of females in the household. On the contrary, such bonds were strong prior to the structural changes under discussion and resulted from competitive interests in the devolution of polygynous fathers' resources (Comaroff and Roberts, 1981). In short, to discuss Kgatla female-headed households, ambivalent attitudes to marriage, or the relative absence of fathers from the household as being matrifocal tendencies implies much more than the data warrant.

The place of menstruation and menopause in the definition of womanhood in Mochudi is discussed fully in Suggs (1986). But since the Bakgatla conceptualize the loss of reproductive ability as the onset of old age, it is appropriate to note that while there is no real specific role gain coincident with menopause in Mochudi, there is certainly no role loss. The only remnants of the advantages of aging noted by Schapera (1959, 1966) which could be elicited from the old women themselves were the right to eat certain foods (although only one woman knew what they were), wash a corpse for burial, and bury an aborted fetus.

There is a coincidental increase in generalized social respect at this time. Around the time of menopause, a woman feels at the peak of her competence and members of her community expect her to be. She has continuity in her role as mother in the sense that grandchildren often live with her, and in the sense that her advice is respected by her daughters. It is not until much later that she will lose her role in provision and she does so only with the onset of infirmity due to advanced age. Likewise, she will continue to manage her own home until she feels unable to do so. Many never give up their homes. These are the criteria by which women define themselves as women and thus they remain following menopause.

Mosadi Mogolo (pl. *Basadi Bagolo*)

As the various factors noted above have changed the criteria of womanhood, so have they also changed the position of old women in Tswana society. A woman assumes the role of mosadi mogolo as she loses her capacity to perform the roles of mosadi. Just as women attain the roles of an adult woman sequentially, so they usually relinquish them sequentially, although not in the reverse of the order in which they were attained. Thus, being adult is a systematic process rather than a state and being old is basically a reversal of these processes. As the movement to adulthood is marked by increasing independence and responsibility, so the movement to old age is marked by increasing dependence and decreasing competence.

It is not surprising, then, that a woman does not voluntarily assume the status of mosadi mogolo. As is made explicit below, older women no longer hold the positions of authority described by Schapera (1959, 1966) nor do they look forward to rest. "Mosadi mogolo is just like a baby." "Mosadi mogolo can no longer think for herself." "A woman used to enjoy being old. Our grandparents were old very quickly. But, today it is not good to be an old person." "Mosadi mogolo can not even bend down to cut her toenails." "Mosadi mogolo? There is a useless thing."

Both premenopausal and postmenopausal women were asked at what age a woman is considered to be mosadi mogolo. The mean response for each group was age 60, although the range runs from 40 to 80. The general consensus among all the women, however, is that chronological age ultimately has very little to do with

the status. Rather, it depends upon a combination of what one can do and how one behaves.

Menopause is seen by many as the first sign of old age. As menarche indicates incipient adulthood, so menopause marks incipient old age. The Kgatla recognize that the age at menarche has decreased since contact with European culture and a few women suggested that the same thing had occurred with regard to age at menopause. To one woman in particular this was a cause of some concern. "We used to stop menstruating at age 60 or even 65 but since mixing with you people [whites] we get it too early! Look at how old I am. My grandmother looked much younger at my age and that is because she didn't menopause so soon." But, in general, women do not think of the signs of old age (wrinkles, grey hair, tiredness, etc.) as resulting directly from menopause.

Just as women would not really consider a girl to be mosadi at menarche, so they do not really consider a woman to be mosadi mogolo at menopause. This is due to the realization that while menopause results in a woman's inability to bear more children, it does not result in the loss of her role as mother. First, as was noted above, a middle-aged woman is considered to be at the peak of her competence. A daughter who is relatively inexperienced in motherhood will look to her for guidance and counseling with regard to child care. Menopausal and postmenopausal women have, on the whole, a great deal of influence in the raising of their grandchildren. In fact, they retain much of the caring/socializing roles of motherhood (such as tending infants) even in advanced age.

Second, and most important, daughters who are away from the village (at the lands or in urban areas) typically leave some or all of their children with their mother. This is doubly advantageous; the mother has the freedom to work without having to invest in child care and the grandmother has extra hands around who can be sent on errands and help in household tasks. It is not uncommon for a child to be raised primarily by a grandmother. This is a source of great pride among older women. "Kaliso was raised by me. Though he is the child of my daughter, he listens only to me. If my daughter comes to visit and tries to hold him, he gets very angry. I am his mother." "Oh, yes, my granddaughter considers me her mother. She says that when she finishes school, she will then take care of me. Really, I am just the child's mother." Of the postmenopausal women in my sample, fully 79 percent had grandchildren (or children of other relatives) living with them.

While the Kgatla do not think mosadi mogolo is physically capable of doing much, they all agree that she is helpful in raising children. Her role in this regard becomes limited as her strength declines but it is nonetheless esteemed, for she is the "doorway to tradition." "One thing only she is very good at doing. She can tell proverbs and Tswana stories to the little children. Her age and experience give her this right." "She is very important in teaching our children their history." Thus, while she will eventually abandon the strenuous activities associated with motherhood, she retains one of the central aspects of it—that of teaching children right from wrong—until death.

A woman will retain her role in provision for as long as she is physically capable of doing the work. In Schapera's (1966:285) data one finds the opposite impression. "As she grows older and her children begin to relieve her at work, she gradually attains a more comfortable position." There are several explanations as to why this is no longer the case.

The traditional role of young wife was general household servant, the person in control of her work was the mother-in-law. Combined with her control of any unmarried daughters, a woman's progression to middle- and old-age meant increased power, increased security, increased independence, and increased freedom. As her own children grew and as her family expanded, she was able to delegate more tasks of a tedious or strenuous nature to those in her charge. She attained increasing competence and moved from the role of advice-receiver to advisor. And, as her daughters married and moved out, her sons

provided her with a replacement workforce by bringing daughters-in-law into her household. In short, old age status was valued as an enhancement of increasing autonomy and as a movement towards the enhancement of her managerial role.

Today, the Tswana do not so commonly practice patrilocal post-marital residence. Of the premenopausal women in my sample, only 21 percent did not establish their own household immediately upon marriage. This reflects, again, the decreasing importance of the extended family and the individuation of households, a trend that Schapera (1966:329) saw the beginning of: "[T]he family is no longer so greatly submerged in the kinship group, but is tending to acquire more individuality, and [this may lead to] important changes in the status of women." Indeed, as it has resulted in an earlier household independence for young women, it has removed a major portion of the power base of older women; that of the control of daughters-in-law in work. This in turn has led to the increased emphasis on the importance of providing as a role associated with womanhood.

As a woman reaches age 60 and beyond, her ability to work in the fields diminishes, as does her capacity for the more strenuous household tasks (e.g., stamping or chopping wood). The Kgatla see this loss in work capacity as definitionally characteristic of mosadi mogolo. "Mosadi is strong, mosadi mogolo is not strong. She can not do the work of mosadi." "Mosadi's muscles become mosadi mogolo's wrinkles." "Mosadi mogolo can no longer give. She only takes." "They don't do anything. If you expect them to do anything they will just say 'No, I am not your Sarwa'."[4] "In her heart, she wants to work but can not. She may sweep a little or wash a few dishes but she cannot work hard like before." "Hers is just to rest."

For some women, their removal from farming, stamping, and the like is the end of their role loss. Some are able to continue to manage their

---

[4]Sarwa is the seTswana term for the San peoples, traditionally servants to the Tswana. The statement is, in essence, a racial slur and an insult to a Tswana.

home with the help of children or by paying for help. While such women are basadi bagolo, they are ambiguously so. "Now, my mother is 65 and can no longer tend crops. Her health is sometimes poor and she is getting weak. She is mosadi mogolo but if you saw her home, you would say 'Ao! This home is spotless! She is not so old after all'." One of my informants commented insightfully on the basadi bagolo who maintain their household independence. "These older women become obsessed with cleanliness. But, really, it is only because they are not capable of doing other work and it keeps them happy to be busy."

For other women, weakness and infirmity lead to the loss of their abilities to cope with home management, as well. Even though descent is traced through males, an older woman who must give up her home usually prefers to live with a daughter. This was explained in two ways. The most common response is that while a son and his wife could care for her, they will not anticipate her needs as well as a daughter. A few women added that this is the result of the traditional patrilocal postmarital residence yielding resentment from daughters-in-law, a condition that is not conducive to quality care.

In Schapera's Mochudi, there would have been less need for the woman to give up her home. Then, the extended family would have ample members to help care for her. Therefore, the increasing number of widows living in their daughters' households is probably a result of the decline in kinship functions.

The abandonment of household independence is more than a loss of home. It is also a loss of control and authority in resource usage. When asked, "Who has more authority in the household, mosadi or mosadi mogolo?", almost all of the respondents (86 percent) answered "mosadi." "An old woman can not work or provide or do anything. She can't even think straight anymore." "Mosadi mogolo has no authority. That would be like giving authority to the children." Further investigation of this surprising pattern revealed that the key to household authority is household management. "Well,

actually it depends. If mosadi lives with mosadi mogolo, the old woman controls it all. If mosadi mogolo lives with mosadi, it is the other way."

Traditionally, almost complete control of resources—lands and cattle—rested in the hands of the older people. Thus, as long as they lived in their home they maintained authority through the distribution of these resources. Today, with the steadily rising importance of wage income and the increasing opportunities for wealth created by education, the young people may control as much or more in the way of resources than the older people. Thus, the position of the aged is less valued and their authority is undercut.

Today, "rest" among the Kgatla is associated with the concept of dependence. The more one rests, the more one is seen as dependent. The more one is considered dependent, the lower one's status becomes. With the abandonment of the household managerial role, a woman's dependence is considered to be roughly equivalent to that of a child. "She is just like a baby again." "She wants you to care for her just as you would a newborn." "She becomes very cross, just like a child." "She is very jealous. If you bring a child a piece of fruit, [mosadi mogolo] will just pout and say, 'Where is my piece of fruit?'."

CONCLUSIONS

Comparison of these results with the work of Isaac Shapera indicates a significant degree of change in Tswana women's status and roles over the past 50 years. Clearly, wage-labor migration and education have led to the redefinition of womanhood throughout the adult phases of the life cycle. The same forces have led to decreased opportunities for marriage and, as Comaroff and Roberts (1977) suggest, the emergence of serial monogamy as a viable male option in resource management. This, in turn, has contributed to the establishment of jural maturity for women and an increasing ability for women to form their own households. It is clear from the responses of the women themselves that another significant result has been the removal of marriage as a requirement for the attainment of complete adult status. A further result has been the relative loss of the power of resource control by the elderly and a subsequent emphasis on managerial independence in women's roles. This, in turn, has resulted in a decrease in the authority of the older women in controlling the labor of their daughters-in-law. Thus, what the younger women of Mochudi have gained represents not only increasing independence vis-à-vis the control of men, as Comaroff and Roberts (1977) suggest, but also greater autonomy with regard to the control of older women. Finally, an end result is the devaluation of the roles of elderly women as compared to those reported by Schapera.

From the discussion presented above it should be clear that the female life cycle among the Tswana is more accurately described in terms of relational transitions than in progress of years. Unlike the Western conception of a linear life span, the Tswana conceptualize what might best be described as a dependence loop. That is, it consists of the transitions from dependence to independence, circling back to dependence in the end.

In this light, mosetsana as a stage is one of total dependence. One can not then care for one's self or others, does not know right from wrong, is thus irresponsible, must be cared and provided for, and must accept the direction of elders. Lekgaribe as a stage is one of independent dependence. That is, while one is still not considered to be totally responsible and relies largely on the decisions of elders, one is learning more about caring and providing for self and family. One has charge of younger siblings and a greater freedom of movement. Mosadi as a stage is one of dependent independence if marriage occurs. While one basically defers to the final decisions of one's husband, one also now has control over house, fields, and children. Mosadi is responsible and, understanding right from wrong, imparts her knowledge and skills to those in a dependent stage. With the decreasing occurrence of marriage and emergent jural maturity, many actually attain a virtually complete independence with the establishment of their own households. Mosadi mogolo as a stage represents the closing of the circle in a sequential and gradual return to dependence.

REFERENCES

BEYEN, Y. 1986. Cultural Significance and Physiological Manifestations of Menopause. Culture, Medicine, and Psychiatry 10:47–72.

BROWN, B. 1980. Women, Migrant Labor, and Social Change in Botswana. Boston University African Studies Center Working Papers No. 41. Boston.

COMAROFF, J. L., AND S. ROBERTS. 1977. Marriage and Extra-marital Sexuality: The Dialectics of Legal Change among the Kgatla. Journal of African Law 21:97–123.

———— 1981. Rules and Processes: The Cultural Logic of Dispute in an African Context. London.

DAVIS, D. 1986. The Meaning of Menopause in a Newfoundland Fishing Village. Culture, Medicine, and Psychiatry 10:73–94.

GONZALEZ, N. 1970. Toward a Definition of Matrifocality. Afro-American Anthropology, eds. N. Whitten, Jr. and J. Szwed, pp. 231–243. New York.

GRIFFEN, J. 1978. A Cross-cultural Investigation of Behavioral Changes at Menopause. Women's Stud-

ies, eds. K. Blumhagen and W. Johnson, pp. 47–54. London.

IZZARD, W. 1982. The Impact of Migration on the Roles of Women. Migration in Botswana: Patterns, Causes, and Consequences. Central Statistics Office, Ministry of Finance and Development Planning, pp. 654–718. Gaborone.

LOCK, M. 1986. Ambiguities of Aging: Japanese Experience and Perceptions of Menopause. Culture, Medicine, and Psychiatry 10:23–46.

SCHAPERA, I. 1933. Premarital Pregnancy and Native Opinion. Africa 6:59–89.

———— 1959. A Handbook of Tswana Law and Custom. London.

———— 1966. Married Life in an African Tribe. Evanston.

SUGGS, D. N. 1986. Climacteric among the "New" Women of Mochudi, Botswana. Doctoral Dissertation. University of Florida. Gainesville.

IV

SEX AND THE NATURE OF GENDER

INTRODUCTION

It is widely believed by Americans that men are "naturally" more interested in sex than women are and that men are "naturally" dominant in sexual interactions. Yet, it does not take a great deal of searching in the ethnographic record to find grounds for questioning these beliefs. For example, among many groups in Melanesia, there is a belief that semen is not naturally produced by men's bodies, but can only be acquired from others (that is, adult men) in finite quantities (see, for example, Herdt, 1984). Because semen is seen as the generator of masculine "life force," these Melanesian men are careful about expending it too freely. Given that an individual man possesses a limited amount of semen, women come to be seen as creatures who demand that men subject themselves to the dangers of sexual intercourse and the loss of semen. Such a view hardly fits the "natural" interest and dominance perspective so often taken for granted in North America.

In the introduction to Part II, we mentioned that the nature versus nurture debate has found fertile ground in anthropological studies of sexuality. This is nowhere more evident than in the area of gender studies. There is a large body of literature in the social and behavioral sciences that focuses on gender roles, and the interested student will find several volumes of readings, as well as literature reviews, on this important topic. This part, however, is designed specifically to address some of the gender issues related to sexual behavior.

These articles examine the extent to which particular and differential sexual behaviors are normatively defined in gender roles. Issues discussed in this section include: the myth of inevitable male sexual dominance, differential socialization of men and women in matters sexual, differential control over sexual access, and the effects of social and technological change on gender roles.

Marjorie Shostak provides a captivating description of sexual socialization in an egalitarian society, the !Kung of the Kalahari. She uses first-person narratives, or "memories," of a !Kung woman entering menopause, who reflects on her childhood, her early sexual encounters, and her first marriage. Insight regarding questions of sexuality and marriage relationships gained from this hunting and gathering culture make for interesting comparisons with practices in industrial societies.

Margaret Mead describes gender roles among the Tchambuli of New Guinea. The ideal Tchambuli man is charming, graceful, and coquettish. Attending to personal appearance, dancing, gossiping, exhibiting jealousy, and engaging in petty bickering—especially between younger and older men—consume most of the men's time and energies. On the other hand, women, working in cooperative groups, primarily are concerned with providing a living for their families. In considering this description of dominant Tchambuli women, who are not "passive sexless creatures," one cannot help but think of Mead's own self-image as presented in her autobiography, *Blackberry Winter* (1972).

Maxine L. Margolis and Marigene Arnold describe and analyze the all-male stripper show designed for a female clientele. Do male stripper shows really turn the sexual tables, or do such shows reinforce conventional role elements and sexual scripts? Whereas the entertainment provided by the male "Feelgood Dancers" may appear to be a role reversal, Margolis and Arnold conclude that it actually reinforces the American male dominance and female subordination of the traditional gender hierarchy.

REFERENCES

HERDT, GILBERT H. (Ed.). (1984). *Ritualized Homosexuality in Melanesia.* Berkeley: University of California Press.

MEAD, MARGARET. (1972). *Blackberry Winter.* New York: Morrow.

SUGGESTED READINGS

BROUDE, GWEN J. (1990). Protest Masculinity: A Further Look at the Causes and the Concept. *Ethos, 18*:1:103–122.

BUCKLEY, THOMAS, AND ALMA GOTTLIEB. (Eds.). (1988). *Blood Magic: The Anthropology of Menstruation.* Berkeley: University of California Press.

FRIEDL, ERNESTINE. *Women and Men: An Anthropological View.* New York: Holt, Rinehart & Winston.

HERDT, GILBERT H. (1986). *The Sambia: Ritual and Gender in New Guinea.* New York: Holt, Rinehart & Winston.

ORTNER, SHERRY B., AND HARRIET WHITEHEAD (Eds.). (1981). *Sexual Meanings: The Cultural Construc-*

tion of Gender and Sexuality. New York: Cambridge University Press.

ROSCOE, WILL. (1991). *The Zuni Man-Woman.* Albuquerque: University of New Mexico Press.

VANCE, CAROLE S. (1984). Pleasure and Danger. In Carole S. Vance (Ed.), *Pleasure and Danger* (pp. 1–17). Boston: Routledge & Kegan Paul.

WHITING, BEATRICE. (1979). Contributions of Anthropology to the Study of Gender, Identity, Gender Role and Sexual Behavior. In Herant A. Katchadourian (Ed.), *Human Sexuality* (pp. 320–351). Berkeley: University of California Press.

9

A !Kung Woman's Memories of Childhood

Marjorie Shostak

The !Kung have engendered a great deal of interest during the past twenty-five years. Research, such as that set forth in this volume, has been done on their social structure, cultural institutions, subsistence ecology, physique, health, and growth, providing a broad base from which to understand the !Kung way of life. The most striking features of the adult society include hunting and gathering, frequent mobility and fluid band structure, lack of privacy, sharing of food and possessions, ample leisure time, the birth of children every three or four years, and a 50 percent mortality before adulthood; childhood is marked by late weaning, multiple caretaking, multiaged play groups, sex play, lack of responsibility throughout adolescence, and occasional early marriage for girls.

All these aspects have been noted and discussed by Western scholars, but how is this way of life experienced by !Kung women and men? How do they perceive their childhoods, their families and friends, death, birth, hunting and gathering as a way of life? How do they feel about themselves? As essential as these questions are, almost no attention had been given them. I wanted to try and find some answers

SOURCE: Reprinted by permission of the publishers from *Kalahari Hunter-Gatherers* by Marjorie Shostak, Cambridge, Mass.: Harvard University Press. Copyright © 1981 by Marjorie Shostak.

Girls dancing the springhare dance

before the acculturation process that has been gradually changing the traditional !Kung way of life, and that of all other known hunting and gathering societies, had progressed so far as to make a search of this kind impossible. Therefore, while in the field from 1969 to 1971, I undertook an exploration of the inner experience of being a !Kung. What follows is a description of how I used the interview technique to approach this problem and a presentation of edited sections from interviews with one woman. Her memories of early childhood and adolescence have been selected for this chapter.

When I first started to live among the !Kung, I hoped to be able to establish informal relationships with several people in which we would exchange feelings about experiences we shared in common and those that were different. As I became fluent in the language, however, I realized this was not possible. Apart from being a foreigner, I was seen as someone with unlimited wealth, who did not freely share her possessions as they did (for the most part) among themselves. If I wanted something from them, they in turn wanted something back from me. After considering carefully how payment might affect both the type of information I wanted and the delicate economic balance of a seminomadic people, I finally decided that some form of payment would be appropriate. People felt this was fair and became more responsive to my probing. After a period of experimenting with different interview techniques, I settled on one which I used for all subsequent, long-term interviews: I would ask someone to "enter talks" with me, and for an hour or more at a time over a period of about two weeks, we would sit talking while I taped the conversation. By the end of a full set of interviews, I would have spent, on the average, twenty hours with each person.

Because of the intimacy required by this technique, I could not select my subjects completely objectively. After interviewing one man, I quickly learned that I could not achieve the same degree of intimacy with men. This was probably due to !Kung men's reticence in talking about masculine concerns with women, and to our mutual embarrassment in dealing with intimate matters. The women I chose were ones with whom I felt I could establish a good rapport, and ones who would reflect the widest range in !Kung conditions of life. Therefore, my sample included both fertile and barren women; married and, as yet, unmarried; happy and, as it seemed to me, unhappy; and women of a wide range of ages.

All the women I approached were eager to participate, partly for the payment and partly for the chance to talk about themselves. At the onset, I told each woman that I wanted to spend many days with her about her experiences. I mentioned some of the topics I hoped to discuss: memories of early childhood; feelings about parents, siblings, relatives, and friends; adolescence and experiences with other children; dreams; marriage; the birth of children; sex; relationships with husband and/or lovers; feelings about the death of close family members; and thoughts about the future. I made it clear that anything she told me would not be repeated while I was living there and that the purpose of our talks was so women in my country could learn about !Kung women's lives.

Although the interviews began with my mentioning the kinds of things I wanted to discuss, I encouraged the women to initiate the conversations themselves. I felt that the way one memory led to another was of potential importance, and I tried to interrupt as little as possible. Aside from asking questions of clarification, I asked women to expand on topics which seemed interesting or important, but which might have been spoken about only briefly. When a woman found it difficult to sustain a topic or start a new one, I suggested other directions. With some women, I had to direct each interview, while others, once they understood the procedure, were able to go ahead with little assistance.

I interviewed eight women, and a unique relationship developed with each. This was not only because we spent close to twenty hours talking together, but also because of the marked personality differences among the women. Generally, as I learned to see the subtleties in the way each woman expressed herself, I was able to understand her better and, presumably, ask better questions. In turn, as each woman came to realize that I kept her confidences, she learned to trust me more. The women often openly expressed their pleasure in talking with me. They were proud they had been chosen to teach me about their customs and experiences. They told me that the things we discussed would never be spoken about with a man, because men had "their talk" and women, theirs. They became silent whenever a man walked by the hut we were in. It would be in a low and excited voice that a woman told me her lover's name, or discussed an early sexual experience, or talked of the time she went from the village, by herself, to give birth to her child.

Talking about experiences and telling stories is one of the main sources of entertainment for the !Kung. They have no written forms in which to express themselves; people sit around for hours talking to one another. It is common when a man describes a hunt or a woman describes something that happened while she was out gathering food, to see the speaker gesture broadly, suddenly raise or lower his voice and imitate sounds of animals, birds, and physical movements. Elements of the stories are repeated over and over again, and there is much use of exaggeration and hyperbole. Stories are usually accompanied by drama and excitement.

As with any skill, some people are more proficient at it than others. Among the eight women I interviewed, one woman was exceptional in her ability to tell a story vibrantly, expressively, and dramatically. I will refer to her as N≠isa. Her life has been difficult: in her fifty years she has experienced the death of all three of her children, her much loved husband, and both her parents. Her only living relatives are two brothers, one older and one younger. Although she derives pleasure from being a "substitute mother" for her brother's two small daughters, she feels her life is somewhat empty, that few people care if she lives or dies. She envies a woman of her age in another village who not only has seven children living nearby and many grandchildren, but whose father, husband, and older brother are alive as well. N≠isa feels that God has abandoned her; she does not understand why he has refused to help.

Like most !Kung women, N≠isa loves and has always wanted to have children. Although she was married five times, her only children came from her third marriage. She had been married twice before she reached menarche. These marriages were unstable and brief (see note 17). After her third husband (the father of her children) died, she married for the fourth time. During this fourth marriage she did not conceive again, and, because of other difficulties, they separated. By the time she married her present (fifth) husband, all three of her children had died. She became pregnant for the last time in this marriage but miscarried. Though she wanted to have another baby, she was not able to conceive again. At the time of our interviews she was going through menopause, causing her much emotional, and some physical, pain. Now she knew she would never have another child.

In addition, N≠isa seemed to be questioning her sexual role. Along with the difficulties brought on by the onset of menopause, her husband, within the previous months, had not shown much interest in having sexual relations with her, or, she believed, with other women. He complained about being tired and old, while she often felt full of sexual energy. She wavered between thinking of herself as an old woman, and as one attractive (and attracted) to men. She still had a few lovers, as she had had for years, but none seemed steadily interested in her, as others had been when she was younger. On occasion, she said she did not feel healthy and that she was too thin to continue the relationships she already had. At other times, she talked positively about the prospects of new men in her life and said she would start "looking again" when our interviews were finished.

N≠isa's life has been a full though difficult one, marked throughout by death and sorrow. Yet, despite the pain and despite her present loneliness, she has been able to find humor and value in her experiences. Even had she not been so gifted in her ability to express herself, her interviews would be a valuable document. But the combination of this attitude, her expressive gift, and her confidence, intelligence, and sensitivity make her narrative an exceptionally moving account of the life of a courageous woman.

This is what I wanted. I hoped getting behind objective facts, getting "into" who the people are would provide a deeper insight into !Kung life. But, more important, I hoped it would touch us *humanly,* in terms of the felt experience, in a way a body of strange facts cannot. Such facts often emphasize differences rather than similarities.

N≠isa's twenty hours of tape produced 350 single-spaced pages of typewritten transcript, written mostly in English, with some !Kung expressions retained so that the final version would reflect nuances unique to the !Kung language. Achieving a fluid English reading in the final version involved modifying or deleting awkward elements in the first transcription, particularly my interruptions for clarifications and the excessive repetition of words and phrases. Although repetition is a natural way to emphasize ideas in the !Kung language, it is unnatural in ours. Wherever possible, I have incorporated literal translations of !Kung idioms.

The texts presented here are edited excerpts of close to half of all N≠isa's memories of her childhood. (The entire collection of these early memories comprises about one-third of the total narrative.) They do not reflect the order in which they appeared in the interviews; here, they are organized chronologically. In a few cases, a memory presented as a continuous narrative is, in fact, taken from two different accounts of the same incident. Apart from these changes, the excerpts are faithful to N≠isa's narrative.

The memories are organized into four sections as follows: (I) weaning and her relationship with her younger brother; (II) relations with other family members; (III) experiences with other children; (IV) marriage. Both N≠isa's style of narration and the content of her stories raise a number of important questions about the factual validity of her narrative. It is not necessary to take literally everything she says for reasons which will become clear in the discussion found at the end of each group of memories.

PART I: WEANING AND HER RELATIONSHIP WITH HER YOUNGER BROTHER[1]

(1) Long ago my mother gave birth to my younger brother Kumsa. I wanted the milk she had in her breasts and when she nursed him, my eyes watched as the milk spilled out. I cried all night, cried and cried, and then dawn broke.

Some mornings I just stayed around and my tears fell and I cried and refused food. That was because I saw him nursing, I saw with my eyes the milk spilling out. I thought it was mine.

Once, when my mother was with him and they were lying down asleep, I took him away from her and put him down on the other side of the hut. Then I lay down beside her. While she slept, I squeezed some milk and started to nurse and nursed and nursed and nursed. Maybe she thought it was him. When she woke and saw me, she said, "Where . . . tell me . . . tell me where did you put Kumsa? Where is he?"

I told her he was lying down inside the hut. She grabbed me and shoved me. I landed far away from her; I lay there and cried. She took Kumsa, put him down beside her, and insulted me by cursing my genitals.

"Are you crazy? By your large genitals,[2] what's the matter with you? Are you crazy that you took a baby and dropped him somewhere else and then lay down beside me and nursed? I thought it was Kumsa."

I stayed there crying and crying, and then I was quiet. I got up and just sat, and when my father came home, she told him:

"Do you see what kind of mind your daughter has? Hit her! Hit her, don't just look at her. She almost killed Kumsa. This little baby, this little thing here, she took from my side and dropped him somewhere else. I was lying here holding him and was sleeping. She came and took him away, then left him, and lay down where he had been and nursed me. Now, hit her!"

I said, "You're lying! Me . . . daddy, I didn't nurse. I refuse her milk and didn't take him away from her."

He said, "If I hear of this again, I'll hit you. Now, don't ever do that again!"

I said: "Yes, he's my little brother, is he not? My brother, my little brother, and I love him. I won't do that again. He can nurse all by himself. Daddy, even if you're not here, I won't try to steal mother's breasts. That's my brother's milk. But when you go to the bush, I'm going to follow along with you. The two of us will go and kill springhare, and you will trap a guinea fowl and then give it to me."

We slept. When dawn broke my father and my

---

[1]Memories 1 and 2 probably took place when N≠isa was three or four years old; memories 3, 4, 5, and 6 when she was about six or seven.

[2]Insults making reference to the genitals are common and are given either in jest or in anger. Even when expressed angrily, they are not very serious.

older brother went and I ran behind. I knew that if I stayed in the village, mother would stinge [3] her milk and wouldn't let me nurse. But when my older brother saw me, he pushed me away and told me to go back to the village, because the sun was too hot, and he said it would kill me.

(2) It was like that even before he was born, when mother tried to wean me. One night, my father took me and left me in the bush.[4] Mother was pregnant, and I cried because I wanted to nurse. When night sat, my father shook me and said,

"I'm taking you and leaving you in the bush so a hyena will kill you. Hyena! There's meat over here! Come and take it!

"Are you a little baby? If you nurse the milk that belongs to your little sibling, you will die."

He set me down in the bush and began to leave. I started to run and ran past him. Crying, I ran back to mother and lay down beside her. I was afraid of the night. I ran back and lay beside her. When my father came back, he said, "I'm going to hit you! You can see that your mother's stomach is big, yet you still want to nurse. Your sibling's milk will kill you."

I cried and cried and finally was quiet. Then father said, "Now, stay quiet and lie down. Tomorrow I will kill a guinea fowl and give it to you to eat. Today your mother's breasts are bad for you."

I heard what he said and was quiet. The next morning he killed a guinea fowl, and when he had cooked it, he gave it to me to eat. But when I finished, I still wanted to take mother's nipple. He took a piece of leather and hit me.

"N≠isa, are you without brains? Why don't you understand? Why do you want your mother's breasts again and again. Leave her breasts be."

I cried and cried. She was pregnant with Kumsa, wasn't she? I cried, and soon I was quiet. I ate many other things because it was the rainy season, but I still asked to nurse. Mother said, "Daughter! these things are things of shit! Shit, and you don't eat it. It kills you. Yes, it is shit, and it smells terrible. If you nurse, you'll go, 'whgaaah, whgaaah' and will throw up."

I said, "No, no. I won't throw up. I'll just nurse and drink the milk."

She refused, "You don't know what you're talking about. I'll explain to you. If you nurse the milk you'll die! Tomorrow your father will kill another springhare, and he will give it to you."

When I heard that, my heart was happy.

(3) One day my older brother ≠Dau went out, and while he was digging some //xaru bulbs, he saw a duiker and struck and killed it with an arrow. I was playing when he came back. He skinned it and gave me the feet, and I went and roasted them. He took some meat off the leg and gave that to me, too. I roasted it with the other, and then I ate and ate and ate. Mother asked me for some, but I refused.

"Didn't you stinge your breasts? Didn't I say I wanted to nurse and you stinged the milk? Are your breasts a good thing? No, your breasts are a bad thing, and I alone will eat this meat. I won't give you any. Just ≠Dau and I will eat it, and you won't."

(4) My youngest brother Kumsa grew up and when he was just walking, my mother was pregnant with my younger sister, the one who died when she was still a little girl. When mother was pregnant this time, I was older and hated Kumsa. I always did bad things to him. We hated one another. When Kumsa said he wanted to go to mother and nurse, I picked him up and dropped him down somewhere in the bush. I hit him and pushed him down and told him that mother was pregnant and that he shouldn't nurse.

(5) Some people just live, and others live and set animal and bird traps. If it is your father who is carrying the animals back home, you say to yourself, "My father is bringing home meat, and when he comes back I can eat it, and I can also stinge it."

Because when you are a child, you play, and you also do bad things to one another. You do bad things to someone, and he does bad things back to you. You tell him, "My father brought back meat and I won't let you have any of it."

You are mean to one another and hit and fight all the time. My younger brother Kumsa and I were like that. We hit one another. Sometimes I bit him and said, "Ooooh . . . what is this thing that has a horrible face and no brains and is mean? Why is he so mean to me when I'm trying to rest?"

He'd say he would hit me. I'd say I would hit him. We stayed together and played like that.

---

[3] "Stinge": the word "kxung," to be stingy, or to withhold, is repeatedly used as a verb throughout the narrative. "Stinge" seemed to me the closest possible English rendering.

[4] The bush is a general term referring to all land beyond the village camp boundary.

(6) Once when our father brought back meat, we both said, "Daddy . . . daddy . . . !" When I heard my brother say "Daddy . . . daddy . . . !", I said, "Why are you greeting my father? He is *my* father, isn't he? You can only say, 'Oh, hello father'."

He said, "Daddy . . . daddy! Hello, daddy!"

I said, "Be quiet! I alone will say hello to him. Why are you greeting him? When I say 'Daddy . . . daddy . . . !', you be quiet. Only *I* will talk to him. Is he your father? I'm going to hit you!"

We argued and argued and argued. Later mother began cooking the meat father had brought back. She put a few pieces in the coals, and the rest she put in a pot. When the meat in the coals was done, she brushed the ashes off and gave me some. I sat and ate it, but while I was eating, Kumsa grabbed it and ran away. I ran after him, got it back, and bit him. He started to cry and I left him. I came back and cooked the piece again, then finished it.

When the meat in the pot was done, they took the pot out of the fire and gave me a plate of meat that I was supposed to share with Kumsa. I refused:

"I refuse Kumsa, his fingers are dirty. Kumsa has dirty fingers and I won't eat out of this plate with him. I'm going to eat out of this plate myself. Take some of it and give it to your son. Why should Kumsa and I eat together?"

Then we both ate. Kumsa and I were without brains, we were always fighting with one another. I hated him, and Kumsa, he hated me.

DISCUSSION

The memories in Part I raise a number of questions that are difficult to answer. First, can we assume that N≠isa remembers in such detail, not only the event of being weaned, but verbatim accounts of conversations between her parents, her brother, and herself? It seems unlikely. Late weaning (age three or four) makes it possible that at least some of the feelings could have been remembered. But the exact detail in which N≠isa describes these events is best regarded as her own stylistic invention. N≠isa enjoyed the interview situation with the machine that "grabs your voice," and this, as well as her desire to tell her stories dramatically, may account for her seemingly unusual memory. However,

other women I spoke with said, quite directly, that people do not remember anything from when they are such little children. It seems fair to assume then, that her earliest memories are a combination of facts, generalized experiences, and fantasy. (Verbatim accounts of conversations characterize her entire narrative. Even from later sections, much of this is probably reconstruction rather than actual memory.)

The second memory in which she said her father took her out to the hyenas because she was bad, raises the question of exaggeration. This is almost certainly the remembered fantasy of a little girl who was deeply frightened of her father's verbal threats. He might have gone as far as to pick her up, perhaps he even took her out of the hut, but it is very doubtful that the event took place as she described it. As indicated in Draper's and Konner's accounts (Chapters 9 and 10) of child-training practices, the !Kung are very lenient and indulgent with their children and rarely are observed using any form of physical punishment. This second memory can best be seen as the product of the fanciful imagination of N≠isa the little girl who eventually believed her own fantasy, or N≠isa the woman exaggerating a feeling that she still remembers from her childhood. This kind of exaggeration, especially when it involves parental physical punishment, will be encountered repeatedly throughout the sections that follow.

N≠isa's parents seem severe in the first weaning memory but they were very concerned that she stop nursing. The !Kung believe that a child should be weaned as soon as the mother realizes she is pregnant again. The milk that remains in her breast is thought to belong to the fetus and not to the child. If the child continues to nurse, they believe that the life or health of either the child or the fetus may be endangered or that the infant will be born wanting to injure his older sibling. Observations of the weaning period confirm the feelings of misery N≠isa expressed. Konner (1972) describes this stage as one in which children usually are depressed and resentful of the birth of the new sibling. N≠isa still carries some of these feelings with her. She believes that her relatively slight build and short stature came from having been weaned too early and from not having been given enough to eat.

!Kung children are encouraged to share things from infancy, because exchanging food and possessions is so basic to adult social interactions. Among the first words a child learns is *"na"* ("give it to me") and *"i"* ("here, take this"). This type of socialization is hard for children, especially when they are expected to share with someone they resent or dislike. Then, giving or holding back becomes a way of exercising power and expressing anger. Evidently, this is what is occurring with her brother, in memories 3, 5, and 6.

PART II: RELATIONS WITH OTHER FAMILY MEMBERS[5]

(7) During the time I cried because I wanted to nurse and couldn't, I sometimes took food from our hut when mother was away gathering. My parents hit me when I took things; they left me alone when I didn't. Some days I remained in the village and I didn't take and ruin[6] their things. Other days, when they were not there, I did. That's when they hit me and said I was without brains.

Once my mother took a digging stick and hit me. She hit me so hard my back hurt. I cried and cried and cried. Then I was sick.[7] My father said to her: "What did you do? You took your digging stick rather than a soft branch and hit the child? You hit that small child with a stick? You might have broken her back!"

I said, "I won't eat any of your //xaru bulbs. I'm going to go and eat grandma's //xaru."

I went to the village where mother's mother lived and told myself I would eat with her. When I arrived at her hut, grandma roasted //xaru, and I ate and ate and ate. I slept beside her and lived there for a while.

Once, when it was getting dark, I got up and

walked back to mother's hut and lay with her and father. Another day, when they were away, I climbed the tree where the little pouch hung and took the //xaru again. I took the big bulbs and put them in a little pouch my father had sewn for me. I sat there and ate them, and when my parents returned they accused me of eating the //xaru again. I said I didn't. They said I did. Then I started to cry; my father hit me and my mother yelled at me: "Don't take things! You don't understand? I tell you and you don't understand. Your ears don't hear me when I talk to you."

I thought: "Uh-uhn, mother's making me feel terrible. I'm going to go stay with grandma again. Mother says I take things and hits me until my skin hurts. I'm going to go to grandma's and sleep beside her. She will prepare //xaru for me to eat."

I went to my grandmother's, but she said: "No, I can't take care of you. If I try, you will be hungry because I am old and just go gathering one day at a time. In the morning I just rest. While we sit together, hunger will kill you. Now, go and be good. Sit nicely beside your mother and father."

I said, "No, they will hit me. Today my skin hurts and I want to stay with you."

I stayed with my grandmother for a while that time. Then, one day, she said she was taking me back to my parents' village. She carried me there and gave me to my mother. Then she said: "Daughter, today I refuse N≠isa because I can't take care of her well. She's just a child, and you shouldn't hit her and hit her. If she is someone who likes food—then she *likes* it—and has a good appetite. Some of you are lazy and left her without enough to eat and she didn't grow well. Maybe that's what happened. When I used to take care of her, there was a lot of food, and I fed her well. She grew up with me for a while and when she went back with you, you killed her with hunger. With your own hands you hit her as though she weren't a !Kung. She cried and cried and was just a little thing. Yet, you yelled at her."

When my grandmother said that, I was happy. I held happiness in my heart because grandmother scolded mother. That made me so happy and I laughed and laughed. Then grandmother went back to her village. When she left, I cried. My father scolded me. "When you left us, we missed you. We wanted you to come back. Yes, your mother even came and looked for you. But today you refuse to be with her. Your mother was the one who gave birth to you. Now you'll start to do things with her and go gathering with her."

---

[5]N≠isa was probably between the ages of five and seven in memories 7, 8, 9, and 10.
[6]"Ruin": the !Kung word *k"xwia* meaning general disruptiveness.
[7]The !Kung believe that the expression of intense anger is sometimes followed by sickness in the person to whom the anger was directed.

But I cried and cried and refused to be with her. I said, "Mother, let me just stay with grandmother. I want to follow her to her village."

My father said, "Be quiet, quiet. There is nothing here that will hit you. Now, be quiet."

Then I was quiet, and my father dug //xaru and *chō* bulbs and I ate them. I ate the roots and bulbs and nuts they gathered, and they didn't scold me.

When I was growing up, I sometimes stayed with my mother's sister for days at a time and then went back to my mother. I stayed with her for a while and then passed on to my grandmother. I would go there for many days. Everybody helped bring me up—my mother's sister, my father, my mother, my grandmother. Look at how I am today. I'm very small. That's because people brought me up badly. I was too difficult for them.

(8) Let me tell you about my mother, my father, and myself. My father sometimes hit me. I remember the day I broke the ostrich eggshell water container. The shell was on the ground, and I picked it up and carried it in my kaross to get water. But it fell and broke! When I came back, my father took a thin branch and told me he was going to beat me. So, pffht! I ran away.

Another day, when I went again to get water, I took another eggshell and BAMM! But I said, "Today I won't run. Even though father may beat me, I won't run."

He did hit me, and I said I didn't care. But I cried and cried, and he hit me, and I cried. Then it was over. Whenever they asked me to take an ostrich eggshell and bring back water, I refused. When I did go to the well, I just took my thumb piano[8] with me, drank some water, then left and went home. I wouldn't collect water for them. I thought, "If they want me to get water in the ostrich eggshell, I refuse."

I stayed behind with the other people, and only mother went to fill the containers. Because if I went, I might break another eggshell, and they'd hit me.

I told them I wouldn't help them, that I wouldn't touch their ostrich eggshells because I was afraid they'd beat me. Instead, I took a small can, if I had one, and drank water from that. I was afraid.

We continued to live there, but I didn't touch any more ostrich eggshell containers.

(9) One day we were walking, gathering food, and the sun was burning. It was the hot, dry season, and there was no water anywhere. The sun hurt! As we walked along, my older brother saw some honey. He and my father took it from the tree, and we ate it. I was so thirsty I practically drank it! I carried some with me, and we continued to walk. Thirst was killing mother, and I was crying for water. I cried and cried. We rested somewhere in the shade and there was still no water. My father said to my older brother, "≠Dau, your mother and I will remain in the shade of this baobab tree. Take the water containers, go and fill them with water. There is a big well way over at the Homa[9] village."

≠Dau got up, took the ostrich eggshell containers, took a clay pot, and went. I was lying down, thirst killing me. As I lay there, I thought, "If I just stay here with mother and father, I will die of thirst. Why don't I go with ≠Dau, go and drink some water?"

As soon as I thought that, I got up and ran. I cried after him and ran and cried and ran and followed his tracks. He still didn't hear me. I kept on running and cried after him. When he finally heard me, he turned around and saw me behind him and said, "N≠isa's here? What am I going to do with her now?"

When I finally caught up with him, he picked me up and carried me on his shoulder. My older brother liked me. The two of us together and walked and walked and walked until we finally reached the water well. When we got there, we drank. I drank the water and my heart was happy. Then we filled the containers. ≠Dau got them together, picked them up, picked me up, and carried me on his shoulders.

We started walking back and walked and walked, and then he put me down. I ran along with him and soon I started to cry. He told me: "N≠isa, I'm going to hit you. I am carrying these containers and they're very heavy. Now, keep running along, and let's get back to mother and father and give them some water. Thirst will kill them. What are you crying about? Are you without any sense?"

I said, "No! Pick me up. ≠Dau, pick me up and carry me on your shoulders."

He refused, and I cried. I ran along with him and cried and ran and cried. After a while he said

---

[8]Thumb piano: a musical instrument now very popular among !Kung children. It is questionable whether this is actually the instrument she played because the thumb piano is believed to have been introduced more recently.

[9]"Homa": fictitious village name.

he would carry me again. He picked me up and put me on his shoulders and carried me a long way. It was far! Then he set me down again, and I ran until I was tired, and he picked me up and carried me. We finally brought the water back to our parents. Then we drank it and they said, "Yes our children brought water back and did well—we are alive once again." . . .

(10) The rainy season came. The sun rose and set, and then the rain spilled itself, and it fell and kept falling. It fell tiresomely, without ceasing, and it seemed to tease people like a naughty child. The water pans were full and my heart was happy, and we lived and ate mongongo nuts. We ate more and more mongongos, and they were delicious. I was like a dog wagging my tail, and I ran around and wagged my tail. Really!! I went like that with my tail, just like a dog.

My heart was so happy because water had come that day. Yes! I was also thankful. We ate caterpillars,[10] ate many of them, and people collected food; people just kept collecting food. And there was meat, because people had killed meat, and it was hung up. My heart was so happy. I ate meat and wagged my tail. I laughed with my little tail and laughed a little donkey's laugh, a little thing that is. I wagged my tail and said, "Today I'm going to eat caterpillars. CA-TER-PIL-LL-LEEERRRS!"

I ate them, and people kept roasting them in the coals and cooking them, and I kept eating them and ate and ate and ate them and then went to sleep.

DISCUSSION

Again, in this section, N≠isa makes some puzzling statements. The first is about being beaten for having broken the ostrich eggshell water container. It is likely that she was severely scolded for breaking it since emptied eggshells are relatively scarce and are used for carrying and storing water. That she was actually physically beaten, however, is conceivable but doubtful. As in the hyena memory in Part I, memory 2, this is probably an exaggerated account of threats that were internalized and carried out only in the imagination of a little girl.

[10]The caterpillars eaten by the !Kung are about two inches long and have smooth skins. They are considered a great delicacy.

N≠isa makes still another statement that is surprising—that she was punished for taking food. It is difficult to believe that she was either beaten or scolded because parents are concerned that their children have enough to eat and food is given freely. When parents go away for the day, they either leave food for their children or arrange for someone else to feed them. If there is a scarcity of food, it is the children who get preferential treatment. Draper (1972) did observe withholding of food as punishment for wasting or destroying food, but this was short-lived, and there are no observations of beating for taking food. This is why N≠isa's account of her parents' reaction to her taking the //xaru when they were away is difficult to understand. One explanation could be that //xaru has some significance we do not yet know about and that parents do not want their children eating large quantities of it. This seems plausible because it is the only food N≠isa described being scolded for taking.

Another possible explanation involves N≠isa's relationship to her mother. Her memories suggest that this was a time of great tension between them. She portrayed her mother as someone who was always hitting, scolding, and criticizing her. She portrayed herself as someone who kept doing things her mother did not like, especially involving food: she took food which, for some reason, her mother did not want her to have; and, as indicated in other memories, she took food from other people's huts as well. These tensions may have distorted her view of this period and resulted in her remembering only the hostile feelings that existed between them. Whether it was her feelings of being unloved, or some resentment held over from the time of weaning, or simply the general !Kung anxiety about food availability that may have caused her to exaggerate, it is impossible to determine. It is also conceivable that her accounts are accurate; it is possible that her family was unusual in this regard. Also, physical punishment could be so rare that it is almost never observed, and yet be very important in the memories of a child. It is difficult to separate fact from fantasy.

In Part I, memory 3, N≠isa refused to give her mother meat. In this last section, she refused to get water after having been scolded. She also left her mother's home for her grandmother's because she did not like the way she was being treated. Leaving was made somewhat easier by the !Kung tradition of multiple caretaking. Children often spend extended period with close relatives, and at least some do this when there are tensions resulting from the birth of a sibling. These actions, though, are indications of N≠isa's emerging independence as she learns to assert herself against the authority of her parents. !Kung children are encouraged to respect their own needs and may refuse to do things they feel strongly enough against, even when the requests come from their parents. Unlike western children, !Kung children are not strongly pressured to obey authority (see Draper, Chapter 9). This is reflected in the adult band structure in which there is no real chief.

At the time a child is weaned from the breast (usually when the mother realizes she is pregnant), he is still carried in her kaross while she engages in daily activities. This continues throughout her pregnancy and often even after the next child is born. Children love to be carried; they love the contact with their mothers, and they love not having to walk under the pressure of keeping up. But as a child grows older and gets heavier, and the demands of the younger child become greater, mothers begin to expect the older child to walk beside them.

This being "weaned from the back" (Draper 1972) elicits, in a slightly lessened form, similar kinds of behavior that weaning from the breast did: the child throws temper tantrums, refuses to walk by himself, demands to be carried, and refuses to be left in the village while his mother goes gathering. The adjustment, a difficult one for the child, is made easier by other people carrying him. This is why memory 9, in which N≠isa's brother carries her to the water well, is recalled with such tenderness.

PART III: EXPERIENCES WITH OTHER CHILDREN[11]

(11) When a child sleeps beside his mother, in front, and his father sleeps behind and makes love to her, the child watches. Perhaps this is the way the child learns. Because as his father lies with his mother, the child watches. The child is still senseless, is without intelligence, and he just watches.

Then, when he and the other children are playing, if he is a little boy, he takes his younger sister and has sex[12] with her. Because he saw his mother and father do that. So he takes her. And as he grows, he lives in the bush and continues to play, now with other children, and they have sex with each other and play and play and play. They take food from the village and go back to the bush and continue their games. That's the way they grow up. When the sun is low in the sky they return to the village and sit down. They return when evening is just beginning to set and play in the middle of the village. That's what they do.

(12) I remember my parents when they lay together. Night . . . at night my father lay with my mother. I still wouldn't have fallen asleep; I'd just be lying still. My father slept with her, and I watched. Why wasn't my father concerned about me, that I might be up? I was fairly old by then. Why wasn't he respectful of me? Why wasn't he respectful? Adults should be concerned that a child may be awake. I couldn't sleep, and why were they making love? That's what I thought. I thought that my mother and father didn't care if I were dead asleep or not. If they had, then they could lie together, and no one would hear; then I'd be asleep and wouldn't wake up. That's what I thought.

Then, long ago, I refused to sleep in their hut. I said, "No. Today I won't lie down with mother and father. Today I will sleep alone in another hut."

I refused to stay with them because they weren't respectful of me.

(13) A child that is nursing doesn't know anything because he still has no intelligence. When

---

[11]N≠isa was from six to twelve years old during the episodes in this section.

[12]The expression "tchi" literally means sexual intercourse, but in reference to children it only means experimental sexual play without actual intromission.

Playing the Antbear game. "It" burrows under the legs

he is nursing, he has no thoughts. The milk is the only thing he knows. Then he learns to sit. Even when he sits, he still doesn't think about things because his intelligence hasn't yet come to him. Where could he take his thoughts from? The only thought is nursing. But when he grows and is bigger, and he is walking, he has many thoughts. His thoughts now exist, and as he sits, he thinks about the work[13] of sexual intercourse. He sits and thinks about it, and if he is a little boy, he plays with the other children and teaches it to himself. The little girls also learn it by themselves.

They play and play and have sex with one another, and when they see a little girl by herself, they take her. She cries and cries. That's how

[13]The !Kung word *"///"xwasi-"* literally means "to work" and is used humorously in this context.

boys teach themselves, and that's how girls teach themselves. They play and play and teach themselves. Little boys are the first ones to know its sweetness. That's why they do that when they play. Yes. A young girl, while she is still a child, her thoughts don't know it. A little boy has a penis, and perhaps, while he is still inside his mother's belly, he already knows about having sex. Because boys know how to do things with their genitals. They take little girls and push them down and have sex with them. Even if you are just playing, they do that.

Sometimes the boys ask if you want to play a game with your genitals, and the girls say no. They say they don't want to play that game, but they'd like to play other games. The boys tell you that having sex is what playing is all about.

I didn't know about it, and they taught it to me. After they taught me and taught me, I didn't cry. Some of the others knew about it long before I did, they had taught themselves and knew it. The little boys used to ask me why I always cried when they played. I said, "You all . . . you all are playing and say we should have sex together. That's why I'm crying. I'm going to tell mother you said we should do that."

Some days I refused and remained in the village and just stayed with mother. Some days I went with them. Sometimes I refused to play, other times I agreed. The little boys entered the play huts where we were playing, and then they lay down with us. My boyfriend came to see me and we lived like that and played. We would lie down and they would have sex with us.

(14) /Ti!kay taught it to me and because of that I liked him. I really liked him! When we played, the other children said I should play with someone else, but I refused. I wanted /Ti!kay only. I said, "Me, I won't take a horrible man."

They teased /Ti!kay, "Hey . . . /Ti!kay . . . you are the only one N≠isa likes. She refuses everyone else."

He taught me about men. We played and played, and he grabbed me, and we played and played. Some days we built little huts, and he took me. We played every day. I used to think, "What is this thing that is so good? How come it is so good and I used to refuse it? The other children knew about it and I had no sense. Now I know when you are a child, this is something you do. You teach it to yourself."

(15) We left the area where I played with /Ti!kay and the other children and went to live somewhere else, far away. When we got there, I thought about my friends and said, "I miss the children I used to play with. Mother, say we can go. Mother, father, let's go back east."

When they asked me why, I said, "So I can find the children I used to play with. I've come here and don't see any children."

They told me, "Yes, we'll go. We'll go where you want—we'll go to your cousins Dem and /Tasa. You can play with them."

I said, "No, I refuse! Let's go to the east so I can find the children I used to play with. I don't want to play with my cousins in their village."

I cried and cried, but they wouldn't go as far away as I wanted. They said I was being silly and that we would go to where my cousins lived.

When we got there, I just watched my cousins and their friends. I watched and watched and said to myself that I wouldn't play with them.

Then /Tasa came and took me from my hut and asked me to play with her. I refused. Then she asked me to go and play with her in the water, but I refused that too.

At first I refused everything, then later I went with her to where her friends were playing and I joined them. They didn't have sex with one another. Maybe they didn't know it. We went to the water pan and played and then returned. We stayed in the village and rested. Then we went again to the water pan. We just stayed around and played and played and played.

(16) When you are a child you play at nothing things. You build little huts and play. Then you come back to the village and continue to play. If people bother you, you get up and play somewhere else.

Once we left a pool of rain water where we had been playing and went to the little huts we had made. We stayed there and played at being hunters. We went out tracking animals and when we saw one, we struck it with our make-believe arrows. We took some leaves and hung them over a stick and pretended it was meat. Then we carried it back to our village. When we got back, we stayed there and ate the meat and then the meat was gone. We went out again, found another animal and killed it. We threw more leaves over a stick, put other leaves in our karosses,[14] and brought it back. We played at living in the bush like that. We pretended to get water and we ate the meat. That's how we played.

We made believe about everything. We made believe about cooked food, and then we took it out of the fire. We had a trance dance,[15] and we sang and danced and danced and sang, and the boys made believe they were curing us. They went— "Xai———i! Kow-a-di!"[16]

They cured us, and we sang and danced and danced, danced all day. Sometimes the sun set while we were visiting in our friends' village, but even though night sat, we stayed in the center of the village and played. We stayed into the night, dancing and singing and finally left one another and went to sleep. We were up again in the morning and started playing again. Sometimes we played with the children from another village, sometimes we just played by ourselves in the

---

[14]The kaross *chikn!a* is a skin worn by women. When it is tied around the waist and neck, a pouch is formed in which children and food are carried.

[15]Trance dance: see Katz (Chapter 11).

[16]*"Xai, kow-a-di":* cried out during the trance dance by a man in trance and in the act of curing.

bush. That's what we did, and that's how we lived.

We took food from the village, went to our little village, and shared it with one another, ate it and gave it and took it. We stayed together and danced and sang and played. Most of the time we played the play of children, that of having sex with one another. We all did that. That was our work. Did we have any sense? No, we didn't have any sense and just did our work.

(17) One day, when I was fairly big, I went with some of my friends and with my younger brother and my younger sister away from the village and into the bush. We walked a long way. As we were walking, I saw the tracks of a baby kudu in the sand. I called to everyone and showed them. "Everybody come here! Here are tracks of a baby kudu. Let's see if we can find it."

We walked along, following the tracks, and walked and walked and walked. As we followed the tracks around, we saw, in the shade of a tree, the little kudu dead asleep. I jumped and tried to grab it. It cried, "Ehnnn . . . Ehnnn. . . . "

I cried out as it freed itself and ran away. I hadn't really caught it well. We started following the new tracks. I ran on ahead of everyone, ran so hard and so fast that I was alone. I came on it, jumped on it and then killed it. I grabbed its legs and carried it back. I was breathing very hard. "Whew . . . whew . . . whew . . . whew . . . whew . . . !"

When I came to where the rest of them were, my older cousin said to me: "My cousin, my little cousin killed a kudu! The rest of you here, what are you doing? How come we men didn't kill the kudu? This young girl has so much 'run' in her that she killed the kudu!"

I gave the animal to my cousin, and he carried it. On the way back to the village, we saw another small animal, a steenbok. One of my girlfriends and her older brother ran after it, and then he killed it. That day we brought a lot of meat back with us to the village. We cooked it and had plenty to eat.

DISCUSSION

The !Kung have little privacy, either in the village or within the family. Parents and children sleep together in huts that have no dividers or private sections. This arrangement is inconvenient for parents when they want to engage in sexual activities. Occasionally they go to the bush to make love; most of the time they wait until they think their children are asleep and try to be discreet. But !Kung children are curious and have many opportunities to observe their parents' lovemaking. Several of the other women interviewed expressed feelings similar to the ones N≠isa described. One woman remembered telling her mother, the morning after observing her parents' lovemaking, that she refused to help any more because her mother had engaged in sexual activity the night before. Her mother scolded her and told her not to mention that kind of thing again. N≠isa's behavior in memory 12 is typical of older children, who often move out of their parents huts and build small huts of their own, or share them with other adolescents.

!Kung children are sexually aware at a very early age because of the relative openness and acceptance of adult sexuality. They also have many opportunities to experiment with what they have observed. All the women I interviewed said that their childhood sex play included sexual intercourse. Parents say they do not approve of this among young and adolescent children; they say it is a good thing to do only when you are older. But the parents played this way when they were children and, although they usually deny it, they know their children are playing the same way. As long as it is done away from adults, children are not prevented from participating in experimental sexual play. If they are seen by an adult, they are scolded and told to play "nicely" (that is, nonsexually).

!Kung children have few responsibilities. They spend their time watching and participating in some adult activities and playing in small groups of children of different ages. For the most part, their games do not reflect a separate children's culture. They are usually imitations of adult activities: hunting, gathering, singing adult songs, trancing, playing house, and playing marriage. Many times, as in the case of gathering food or as described in memory 17 (when N≠isa killed the kudu), the children actually perform subsistence activity, rather than merely playing at it.

The memory in which N≠isa kills the kudu (17) also sheds light on the process through which !Kung boys and girls come to think of themselves as men and women. While it was made clear to the boys that they should have been the ones to kill it, N≠isa herself was highly praised for her success and not made to feel ashamed of doing something "unfeminine." Unlike our own society where names like "tomboy" and "sissy" serve to make boys and girls play separately and avoid each other's activities, !Kung boys and girls play together and share most games.

In these memories, and in others not presented here, N≠isa portrays many of her childhood experiences as occurring away from the village. Memory 17 describes them following animal tracks far into the bush; memories 13–15 describe the children participating in sexual activities that would be disapproved of were adults present. These memories suggest that children either spend more time away from their parents' supervision than Draper observes (Chapter 9), or that the experiences they have at these times are among their most vividly remembered.

PART IV: MARRIAGE[17]

(18) When adults talk to me, I listen. Once they told me that when a young woman grows up, she takes a husband. When they first talked to me about it, I said, "What? What kind of thing am I that I should take a husband? Me, when I grow up, I won't marry. I will just lie by myself. A man, if I married him, what would I think I would be doing it for?"

My father said: "N≠isa if you agree, you will marry a man and get food and give some to him, and he will eat it. I, I am old. I am your father and am old; your mother's old, too. You will get married, gather food and give it to your husband to eat. He also will do things for you—give you things you can wear. But if you refuse to take a

[17]N≠isa was probably about thirteen years old in memory 18 and fifteen years old in memories 19, 20, 21, 22, and 23.

husband, who will get food and give it to you to eat? Who will give you things that you shall have? Who will give you things that you will be able to wear?"

I said to my father and mother: "No. There's no question in my mind—I refuse a husband. I won't take one. What is it? Why should I take a husband? As I am now, I am still a child and won't marry. Why don't you marry the man you want for me and sit him down beside father? Then you'll have two husbands."

Mother said: "You're talking nonsense. I'm not going to marry him, you'll marry him. A husband, I want to give you. You say I should marry this other man? Why are you playing with me with this talk?"

I said: "Yes, that's what I am saying. Because you can see I am only a child, and yet you say I should get married. When I grow up and you tell me I should marry, then I will agree. But today I won't! I haven't passed through my childhood and I won't take a husband."

We continued to live and lived on and on and returned to just living. Then she talked about it again. "N≠isa, I should give you a husband. Which man shall I give you?"

I knew which man she wanted me to marry. I said, "I refuse that man."

She said, "Marry him. Won't you marry him?"

I said, "You marry him. Marry him and set him beside father."

I stopped talking. I felt ashamed, and was silent. I said to myself, "What am I doing? Later I will still go back to mother. When I speak like that, am I not shitting on her?"

I thought that. Then we all went to sleep. We continued to live and just kept on living and more time passed.

(19)[18] Long ago my parents and I went to the

[18]N≠isa was married five times in all. At the time of the interviews, she was living with her fifth husband. /"Tashay, whom she meets and married in memories 22–26, was her third husband. She was about thirteen years old the first time she married. This marriage lasted only a few days because her husband, who was much older, had an affair with an older woman. Traditionally, when a grown man marries a young girl, an older woman is asked to spend the first few nights with the couple. This gives the girl a sense of protection and helps her adjust to her new situation. In N≠isa's case, however, the older woman contributed to the break-up of the marriage. The woman, one of N≠isa's relatives, had been N≠isa's husband's lover prior to the marriage. During the first few nights, they engaged in sexual relations in the hut. N≠isa told her parents about it, and they dissolved the marriage.

village where old Kan//a and his son /"Tashay were living. My friend N!huka and I had gone to the water well to get water and he and his family were there, having just come back from the bush. When /"Tashay saw me, he decided he wanted to marry me. He called N!huka over and said, "N!huka, that young woman, that beautiful young woman . . . what is her name?"

N!huka told him my name was N≠isa, and he said, "That young woman . . . I'm going to tell mother and father about her. I'm going to ask them if I can marry her."

N!huka came back. We continued filling the water containers, then left and walked the long way back. When N!huka saw my mother she said, "N≠isa and I were getting water and while we were there, some people came to the well and filled their water containers, and a young man saw N≠isa and talked about marriage. He said his parents would ask you for N≠isa in marriage."

I was silent, just quiet. Because when you are a child and someone wants to marry you, you don't talk. At first my heart didn't agree to it. When they first talked about marriage, I didn't agree.

The next night there was a dance and we were singing and dancing, and he and his parents came from their camp and stayed with us at the dance. We danced and sang and danced and sang, and we didn't stop. N!huka and I sat together. /"Tashay came over to me and took my hand. I said: "What . . . what is it? What kind of person is this? What is he doing? This person . . .

N≠isa's next marriage, begun about a year later, lasted a few months and ended in a dispute about food. Because there is an imposed scarcity of women of marriageable age (due to polygamy), a son-in-law has to prove himself worthy of his wife (L. Marshall, 1959; Lee, 1974). In N≠isa's father's eyes, her second husband did not fulfill his responsibilities. They quarreled over some meat that the son-in-law had brought with him from his parents' village. Her father asked for a portion, and her husband said he would give it to him in the morning. When her father then pressed him for a share, her husband refused. Her father took this refusal as an insult and said it showed he would not take care of his daughter and her family in the future. Much to N≠isa's delight (she still did not feel ready to be married), her father told him the marriage was finished and that he should leave.

N≠isa married her third husband, /"Tashay, when she was about fifteen. Her breasts had begun to develop, but she had not yet reached menarche. In the marriage negotiations described in memory 19, N≠isa's father blames her for having left her previous husbands and accuses her of being fickle, although he and his wife had actually terminated both previous marriages. When parents discuss marriage plans with their daughter's prospective parents-in-law, it is usual for them to deprecate her. This is in keeping with the general !Kung concern to avoid being thought of as acting "proud."

this person . . . how come I'm sitting here and he came and took hold of me?"

N!huka said, "That's your husband . . . your husband has taken hold of you, is that not so?"

I said, "Won't he take you? You're older, and he'll marry you."

She said, "What! Isn't he my uncle? I won't marry my uncle. Anyway, he is asking you to marry him."

His parents went to my mother and father. His father said: "We have come here, and now that the dancing is finished, I want to speak to you, to /Gau and Chu!ko, N≠isa's father and mother. I will speak with you. Give me your child, the child you gave birth to. Give her to me, and I will give her to my son. Yesterday, while we were at the well, he saw your child. When he returned he told me that in the name of what he felt, that I should today come and ask for her. Then I can give her to him. He said I should come for her."

My mother said, "Yes . . . but I didn't give birth to a woman, I bore a child. She doesn't think about marriage, she just doesn't think about the inside of her marriage hut."

Then my father said: "Yes, I conceived that child as well, and she is a person who doesn't think about marriage. When she marries a man, she leaves him and marries another man and leaves him and gets up and marries another man and leaves him. She refuses men completely. There were two men whom she already refused. So, when I look at N≠isa today, I say she is not a woman. There is even another man, Dem, his hut is over there, who is asking to marry her. Dem's first wife is giving her things. When Dem goes gathering and comes back, he gives things to his wife so she can give them to N≠isa. He asks N≠isa to sit with them. He wants her to stay and be a second wife. He wants her to take the food from his wife, so they can all eat together. But when his wife undoes the kaross and gives N≠isa food, she throws it down, ruins it in the sand, and kicks the kaross. It is because of that I say she is not a woman."

My father told that to /"Tashay's father. Then his father said: "Yes, I have listened to what you have said. That, of course, is the way of a child; it is a child's custom to do that. She gets married many times until one day she likes one man. Then they stay together. That is a child's way."

They talked about the marriage and agreed to it. All this time I was in my aunt's hut and couldn't see them, I could just hear their voices. Soon, I got up and went to my father's hut where they were talking. When I got there, /"Tashay was looking at me. I sat down. Then /"Tashay's mother said, "Ohhhh! How beautiful this person is! You are a young woman already. Why do they say that you don't want to get married?"

/"Tashay said, "Yes, she has just come in. I want you to take her and give her to me."

(20)[19] There were a lot of people there, everyone came. All of /"Tashay's friends were there, and when they saw me, they told him he was too old for me. Each one said he wanted to marry me himself. His younger brother and his nephew were sitting around talking that way.

I went into my mother's hut and sat there. I was wearing many beads and my hair was covered with ornaments. I went and sat beside mother. Another one of /"Tashay's friends came over and started talking as the others had, and I felt confused and couldn't understand why this was happening to me.

That night there was another dance and we danced and other people fell asleep and others kept dancing. In the morning they went back to their camp and we, to ours, and then we went to sleep. When the morning was late in the sky, his relatives came back. They stayed around and his parents told my aunt and my mother that they should all start building the marriage hut because they wanted to leave for another village. They began building the hut together, and everyone was talking and talking. There were a lot of people there. Then all the young men went and brought /"Tashay to the marriage hut. They stayed around the hut together near the fire. I was at mother's hut. They told two of my friends to go get me and bring me to the hut. I

[19]The !Kung have a simple marriage ceremony which takes place over a two-day period. When both sets of parents have agreed to the marriage, the two mothers work together and build a marriage hut for the couple. The !Kung believe that the sun is death-giving because it dries up all the water, and consequently, during this day, the girl keeps a covering over her head so that the sun will not shine on her. Once the sun has set, a firebrand from the fire of each set of parents is brought over to light the fire in front of the marriage hut. Women friends and girlfriends go to where the girl has been waiting, pick her up so that her feet do not touch the ground, and carry her to the marriage hut. They leave her inside, and she lays down with the cover still over her. Male friends escort the boy, and he sits down outside the hut with his friends. Boys and girls sit by the couple's fire and have a good time: they sing, play music, and eat whatever they have. Neither the couple nor their parents joins them in these activities. Late in the night the boy goes into the hut to sleep, but not to make love. The next morning oil and red powder are rubbed over the bodies of the couple by female relatives of both. This marks the end of the formal ceremony (L. Marshall, 1959).

said to myself, "Oooooh . . . I'll run away to the bush."

When they came for me they couldn't find me. I wasn't by the fire.

"Where did N≠isa go? It's dark now, isn't it? Doesn't she know that things may bite and kill her when it is dark like this? Has she left?"

My father said, "Go tell N≠isa that if she behaves like that, I will hit her, and she won't run away again. What's the matter with her that she ran away into the bush?"

I had already gone. I stayed away a long time. I heard them calling. "N≠isa—a! N≠isa—a!"

They were looking for me. I just sat, sat by the base of a tree. I heard my friend, N!huka, call out. "N≠isa—e . . . N≠isa—e . . . my friend . . . there are things there which will bite and kill you. Now leave there and come back here."

They looked for me and looked and looked, and then N!huka came and saw me. I ran away from her, and she ran after me and chased me and then caught me. She called out to the others. "People! N≠isa's here! Everyone come over here, come, take her. N≠isa's here!"

They came and brought me back. Then they lay me down inside the hut. I cried and cried, and people told me: "A man is not something that kills you; he is someone who marries you, and he becomes like your father or your older brother. He kills animals and gives you things to eat. Even tomorrow; but because you are crying, when he kills an animal, he will eat it himself, and won't give you any. Beads, too. He will get some beads, but he won't give them to you. Why are you afraid of your husband and why are you crying?"

I listened and was quiet. Then he and I went and slept inside the hut. He slept by the mouth of the hut, near the fire. He came inside after he thought I was asleep. Then he lay down and slept.

I woke while it was still dark and said to myself "How am I going to jump over him? How can I get out and go to mother's hut?"

That's what I was thinking in the middle of the night. Then I thought, "This person has married me . . . yes . . . " I lay there. I lay there and thought some more. "Why did people give me this man in marriage? The older people say he is a good person and. . . . "

I lay there and didn't move. The rain came and beat down. It fell and kept on falling and falling and then dawn broke. In the morning, he got up first and went and sat by the fire. I was frightened! I was afraid of him and lay there and didn't get up. I waited for him to go away from the hut and when he went to urinate, I left and went to mother's hut. I went there and sat down inside her hut.

That day all his relatives came to our new hut—his mother, his father, his brothers . . . everyone! They all came. They said, "Go tell N≠isa that she should come and her in-laws will put the marriage oil on her. Can you see her over there? Why isn't she coming out so we can put the oil in her new hut?"

I refused to go there. Then my older brother said, "No, no. N≠isa, if you continue like this, I'll hit you. Now get out there and go sit down. Go over there and they will put the oil on you."

I still refused and just sat there. My older brother took a switch and came over to me. I got up because I was afraid of the switch. I followed him and walked to where the people were. My aunt put oil on /"Tashay, and his relatives put oil on me. Then they left, and it was just /"Tashay and me.

(21) We lived together and after a while /"Tashay lay with me. Afterward, my insides hurt. I took some leaves and tied them with a string around my stomach,[20] but it continued to hurt. The next morning I went gathering and collected some mongongo nuts and put them in my kaross. Meanwhile, I was thinking to myself, "Oooohhh . . . that man made my insides hurt. He made me feel pain today."

The next evening we lay down again. This time I took a leather strap, tied it around a piece of wood and then secured it to my genitals; I wanted to withhold my genitals. The two of us lay down and after a while he was looking for my genitals, and he felt the leather strap there. He said, "What . . . did another woman tell you to do this? Yesterday you lay with me so nicely when I came to you. Why are you today tying a piece of wood to your genitals? What are you holding back?"

I didn't answer. Then he said, "N≠isa . . . N≠isa. . . . "

I said, "What is it?"

He said, "What are you doing?"

I didn't answer him. I was quiet.

"What are you so afraid of that you tied your genitals with a piece of leather and with a branch?"

I said, "I'm not afraid of anything."

He said: "No, no. Tell me what you are afraid of. Why did you tie a branch to your genitals. In the name of what you did, I am asking you.

"What are you doing when you do something like that? You are lying with me as though you were lying with a Bantu, a stranger. Why did you tie a branch to your genitals?"

I said: "I refuse to lie down because if I do, you will take me. I refuse! I refuse your touching my genitals because when you lay with me yesterday, my insides hurt me. That's why I am refusing you today, and you won't have me."

He said: "You're not telling the truth, now untie the leather strap. Untie the strap from around your genitals. Do you see me as someone who kills other people? Am I going to eat you? Am I going to kill you? I'm not going to kill you. Instead, as I am now, I have married you and want to make love to you. Don't think I would marry you and not sleep with you. Would I have married you just to *live* with you? Have you seen any man who has married a woman and who just lives with her and doesn't have sex with her?"

I said, "No, I still refuse it! I refuse sex. Yesterday my insides hurt, that's why."

He said, "Mm. Today you will just lie there by yourself. But tomorrow I will take you."

I continued to refuse him and we just lay down. Before we went to sleep, he untied the strap and said, "I'm going to destroy it. If this is what use you put it to, I am going to untie it and destroy it in the fire."

Then we went to sleep and slept. He didn't take me, but he untied the strap because he was big and I was afraid of him. We went to sleep and got up the next morning. The men went out that day and then returned. That night /"Tashay and I entered the hut again and lay down together. I just lay there and after a while he touched my leg. I didn't move. I thought to myself, "Oh, what I did last night won't help me at all, because this man will hurt me. Then I'm going to give it to him, and he will have it. Some day it will no longer hurt me."

I said to him: "Today I'm going to lie here, and if you take me by force, you will have me. You will have me because today I'm just going to lie here. You are obviously looking for some 'food,' but I don't know if the 'food' I have is 'food' at all, because even if you have some, you won't be full."

Then I just lay down and he did his 'work.' Afterward he lay down.

---

[20]The !Kung, when they are sick, sometimes tie a piece of rope or leather around the body part that ails them.

(22) We lived together after that, but I ran away again and again. Once I ran away and slept in the bush and they found me in the morning. When my older brother said he was taking me back, I threatened to stick myself with a poison arrow. He got very angry and said: "If you try to stick yourself with an arrow, then I'll beat you, and you'll understand what you were doing. As you stand here, you are talking very badly about what you are going to do to yourself. You are a person, a woman, and when you are alive, you don't say those things. When you are alive, you should be playing.

"All your friends have gotten married and N!huka, too, she is going to marry your uncle and sit beside him. Don't say you won't come back to the village, because you and N!huka will have your own huts. Will your friend have a hut, and you won't? That's all. As I am ≠Dau, your older brother, that's what I have to say."

I said: "Yes. This friend of mine has taken a husband, but surely she is older than I am. She is a grown woman. Me, I'm a child and don't think I should be married. Why have you come to ask me these things again?"

He said: "Put the *sha* roots you collected in your kaross and let's go. The person who sits here is your *husband!* He isn't anyone else's husband. He is the man we gave you. You will grow up with him, lay down with him, and give birth to children with him."

(23) When we returned to the village, I didn't go to my hut, but went and stayed at mother's hut. I went inside and rested. /"Tashay went to our hut and stayed there. He called to me. "N≠isa . . . N≠isa. . . ."

I asked him what he wanted and left my mother's hut and went over to him. He gave me some *sha* roots he had dug. I took them, gave some to mother and went back to her hut and stayed there. Late afternoon, when dusk was standing, I went back to our hut and roasted some food. I took the food out of the coals and gave him some and set mine aside to cool. When it was ready, I ate it.

I ran away a few more times. I used to cry when he lay with me and kept saying no. People talked to me about it. Let me tell you what they said.

My mother said, "A man . . . when you marry a man, he doesn't marry your body, he marries your genitals so he can have sex with you."

And my aunt told me, "A man marries you

and has sex with you. Why are you holding back? Your genitals are right over there!"

I answered, "I am only a child. This person is an adult. When he enters and takes me, he tears my genitals apart."

We lived and lived, and soon I started to like him. After that I was a grown person and said to myself, "Yes, without doubt, a man sleeps with you. I thought maybe he didn't."

We lived on, and then I loved him and he loved me, and I kept on loving him. When he wanted me, I didn't refuse and he slept with me. I thought, "Why have I been so concerned about my genitals? They are, after all, not so important. So why was I refusing them?"

I thought that and gave myself to him and gave and gave. I no longer refused. We lay with one another, and my breasts had grown very large. I had become a woman.

DISCUSSION

Although the recent trend has been for !Kung women to marry when they are older, women of N≠isa's generation were occasionally married between the ages of thirteen and fifteen (Howell, Chapter 6). Parents are usually responsible for arranging the first marriage and later marriages if the couple is still young (see also L. Marshall 1959), but, as indicated in memory 18, their decision is not final. If the girl is strongly opposed to it, the marriage will not take place. When young girls do get married, it is usually to a man seven to fifteen years older. These first marriages are very unstable, and many break up within a short period of time (Lee 1974).

One of the questions raised by N≠isa's account of her marriage is why, if she experienced so much premarital sex play, was she anxious about marrying and having intercourse with her husband? The circumstances of the marriage suggest some possible explanation! Although she agreed to marry /"Tashay, she had hardly spoken to him before they were left together in the hut. The next morning, when the final ceremony was to be performed, she ran away, demonstrating her reluctance to leave her parents and her modesty in not accepting her new husband too easily (see also Marshall 1959). Her husband was probably some years older than she was and expected to sleep with her immediately. From the description of her discomfort after he had slept with her the first time, he must have been larger, genitally, than the boys she had had experience with. He threatened her with force. He also insisted that she sleep with him quite frequently. All these things, combined with the fear of having to eventually leave her parents for him, made her frightened of staying with him and appears to account for her repeated running away. The fact that she kept going back to him suggests her ambivalence rather than her dislike of him.

It could also be that she was generally frightened by any kind of new sexual experience. There is evidence for this in her first descriptions of learning to play sexual games with other children (Part III, 13). She described herself as always saying no, crying and running back to tell her mother, being frightened while most of the other children were participating, and needing a lot of encouragement before she could accept and finally enjoy this sexual play. Perhaps her fear of the unfamiliar is at work in both sets of memories.

By the last memory, N≠isa is still not a fully matured woman; she is only on the verge of menarche. But this memory presents her first successful efforts at staying with a man and her gradual moving away from her mother. She begins to accept a new person to take the place of her family.

SUMMARY

N≠isa is an exceptionally articulate person, and much of her narrative is highly idiosyncratic; nevertheless, the events of her childhood, as she described them, resemble those of other !Kung women and touch upon a number of fundamental features of their life.

(1) Weaning from the breast, the birth of a sibling, and weaning from the back enforce on the !Kung child adjustments that are very diffi-

cult to make, and they spark off periods of intense unhappiness. N≠isa's descriptions confirm observations by Draper and Konner of the frustration children experience during these times. Looking back, adults see these events as having had a formative influence on their lives.

(2) Children are expected to share things with others even when they are very young. They discover, as N≠isa did, that giving and withholding things is a powerful vehicle through which anger, jealousy, and resentment, as well as love, can be expressed. This behavior is of great importance because it becomes the only means of distribution of goods in the adult economy.

(3) The general !Kung concern about, and pleasure in, food is already present in childhood. N≠isa's memories confirm Lee's observations that they express anxiety about their food supply in spite of the fact that they have enough to eat (Lee 1968a).

(4) As reflected in N≠isa's confrontations with her parents, individualism is encouraged and strict obedience of parental authority is considered neither necessary nor desirable. This has the effect of ensuring a very wide range of personalities among the !Kung living in small, isolated groups. N≠isa's tales of physical punishment are puzzling, since it has not been observed by Draper or Konner. This contradiction should be resolved by further research.

(5) Children play in groups with other children much of the day. Because no formal teaching is done, it is in these groups that children acquire a good deal of the information, habits, and skills they need to survive in their environment and to become proper members of their culture. Unlike our own (middle-class) society, such groups perform actual subsistence activities and actual sex play, including sexual intercourse. In N≠isa's accounts children spend much of the time away from adult supervision, although, as Draper points out (Chapter 9), they are seldom far from adult help, if needed.

(6) N≠isa's memories of her early marriages show some of the stresses involved when young girls marry men much older than themselves.

Because young girls are in demand, due to the existence of a small percentage of polygamous marriages, the girl's parents exercise a good deal of control over their son-in-law and can afford to be exacting. Early marriages are unstable (Lee 1972a, 1974; Howell, Chapter 6).

(7) N≠isa's descriptions of the way girls learn about sex and of her relationship with her husband /"Tashay suggest that relations between the sexes are not egalitarian, and that men, because of their greater strength, have power and can exercise their will in relation to women. This confirms Marshall's (1959) finding that men's status is higher than women's. Still, it must be said that women have considerable voice in group affairs and considerable control over their own lives (that is, in terminating an unsatisfactory marriage). In these respects they may be more egalitarian than most other societies, including our own.

While the factual confirmations and controversies raised by interviews such as these are important, the immediacy of feeling and poetry that is contained in a person's account of his life is at least equally important. Reading, "Look how I am today, I'm very small. That's because people brought me up badly. I was too difficult for them," is more informative than an ethnographer's guess as to the effects of weaning in relation to a person's self-concept; reading, "The rainy season came . . . My heart was so happy and I ate meat, wagged my tail and imitated a dog. I laughed with my little tail and laughed a little donkey's laugh . . . ," reveals more profoundly how the !Kung feel about the beginning of the rainy season than a description of their concern about water availability. In an individual's narrative expression of feeling, we can begin to grasp emotionally what it may be like to be a !Kung.

This is important because all too often "primitive" people are dismissed as being so different that it would be difficult to determine or identify with what they feel. This study has carried us beyond this prejudice by presenting the !Kung as *people:* reluctant to leave friends, sometimes loving and sometimes angry with those they love, sad and happy at the changes of the seasons, wanting to live good lives. Underneath all the obvious differences, they are, after all, not so very different from ourselves.

REFERENCES

DRAPER, P. 1972a. !Kung Bushman Childhood. Ph.D. dissertation, Harvard University, Cambridge, Mass.

HOWELL, NANCY. 1976. The population of the Dobe area !Kung. In R. B. Lee and I. DeVore, eds., *Kalahari Hunter–Gatherers,* pp. 137–151. Cambridge: Harvard University Press.

KATZ, RICHARD. 1976. Education for transcendence: !Kia-healing with the Kalahari !Kung. In R. B. Lee and I. DeVore, eds., *Kalahari Hunter–Gatherers,* pp. 281–301. Cambridge: Harvard University Press.

KONNER, M. J. 1971. Infants of a foraging people. *Mulch* 1:44–73.

——— 1972a. Review of Baby and Child Care, Benjamin Spock, M. D. *Mulch* 2:70–78.

——— 1972b. Aspects of the developmental ethology of a foraging people. In N. G. Blurton Jones, ed., *Ethological Studies of Child Behaviour,* Cambridge: Cambridge University Press.

LEE, R. B. 1968a. What hunters do for a living, or how to make-out on scarce resources. In R. B. Lee and I. DeVore, eds., *Man the Hunter,* pp. 30–48. Chicago: Aldine.

——— 1972a. The !Kung Bushman of Botswana. In M. Bicchieri, ed., *Hunters and Gatherers Today,* pp. 327–368. New York: Holt, Rinehart & Winston.

——— 1974. Male-female residence arrangements and political power in human hunter-gatherers. *Archives of Sexual Behavior* 3:167–173. Original from a paper presented at the workshop "Male-Female Behavior Patterns in Primate Societies" at the IV International Congress of Primatology (honoring Sherwood L. Washburn), Portland, Oregon, August 1972.

MARSHALL, L. 1957a. The kin terminology system of the !Kung Bushmen. *Africa* 27(1):1–25.

——— 1957b. N!ow. *Africa* 27(3):232–240.

——— 1959. Marriage among the !Kung Bushmen. *Africa* 29:335–365.

10

THE CONTRASTING ROLES OF TCHAMBULI MEN AND WOMEN

MARGARET MEAD

As the Arapesh made growing food and children the greatest adventure of their lives, and the Mundugumor found greatest satisfaction in fighting and competitive acquisition of women, the Tchambuli may be said to live principally for art. Every man is an artist and most men are skilled not in some one art alone, but in many: in dancing, carving, plaiting, painting, and so on. Each man is chiefly concerned with his role upon the stage of his society, with the elaboration of his costume, the beauty of the masks that he owns, the skill of his own flute-playing, the finish and *élan* of his ceremonies, and upon other people's recognition and valuation of his performance. The Tchambuli ceremonies are not a by-product of some event in the life of an individual; that is, it cannot be said that in order to initiate young boys the Tchambuli hold a ceremony, but rather that in order to hold a ceremony the Tchambuli initiate young boys. Grief over a death is muffled and practically dissipated by interest in the ceremonial that surrounds it—which flutes are to be played, which masks and clay heads are to decorate the grave; in the etiquette of the groups of formally mourning women, who are given charming little souvenirs of reeds to remember

SOURCE: From *Sex and Temperment in Three Primitive Societies* by M. Mead, pp. 245–264. Copyright 1963 by William Morrow and Company, Inc., New York. Reprinted by permission.

the occasion by. The women's interest in art is confined to sharing in the graceful pattern of social relations, a small amount of painting on their baskets and plaited cowls, and chorus dancing; but to the men, it is the only important matter in life.

The structure of the society is patrilineal. Groups of men all related through male ancestors, and bearing a common name, own strips of territory that stretch from the hill-tops, where occasional gardens are made, down through the wooded mountain-side where the women's houses are built, to the lake-shore, where each clan or sometimes two adjacent clans, building together, have their men's club-house. Within this group of related males there are certain taboos. An eldest son is embarrassed and shy in the presence of his father, and his next younger brother observes the same sort of behaviour towards him. The possibility of inheritance is the subject of their embarrassment. The younger sons, far removed from considerations of the succession, are easy with one another. Relationships between a man and his brother's son are also friendly, and these men—whose position is vividly described by the pidgin-English term "small papa"—intervene between small boys and their self-appointed and light-hearted disciplinarians, the bigger boys. The membership in these men's houses varies, and quarrels are frequent. Upon the merest slight—a claim of precedence that is not justified, a failure of the wife of one man to feed the pigs of another, a failure to return a borrowed article—the person who cherishes a sense of hurt will move away, and go to live with some other clan group to which he can claim relationship. Meanwhile there is a strong social feeling that such behaviour is bad, that the men of a clan should sit down together, that in a large number of older men lies the wisdom of the ceremonial house. When illness or misfortune occurs, the shamans explain that the shamanic spirits and the ghosts of the dead that hang about the house-posts are angry because one or more members of the clan have moved away. The solidarity of any of these groups of men is more apparent than real; it is as if all of them sat very lightly, very impermanently, on the edges of their appointed sitting-shelves, ready to be off at a look, a touch, a word of hostility.

Each clan possesses certain privileges: long lists of names that it is privileged to give to the children of all women of the clan; clan songs, and a mass of ceremonial possessions, masks, dances, songs, flutes, slit drums, special calls; and a set of supernaturals of its own, *marsalais* of the lake, sometimes one of the shamanic spirits, and other minor supernaturals whose voices are heard through flute and the drum and the bull-roarer. The men's house of one clan insists that masked dancers who pass that way must stand for a moment beside the standing stones that are set up outside; other ceremonial houses have the privilege of swinging the bull-roarers for high water.

In addition to the clan organization there are various other formal ways in which the society is organized. There is a dual organization; all the members of one clan usually belong either to the Sun or to the Mother people, but occasionally a clan is split in half and one half belongs to each. Marriage should be across the dividing-line of the dual organization, but is not always so. These two divisions also have many ceremonial rights and possessions, the latter usually being kept in one of the men's houses. Each man also belongs to several other groups, in which he plays a special part in initiatory ceremonies and in feasts of other kinds. Although his clan membership is perhaps the most fixed of his allegiances, he can also think of himself as proud of and ennobled by the ceremonial display of any one of these other cross-cutting associations. He may also have his feelings hurt as a member of any of these groups, and by proclaiming his partisanship in one kind of ceremonial dispute become involved in coldness and disgruntlement with his associates in some other activity. Each man has a high feeling of the importance and the value of each one of these allegiances. He is like an actor who plays many parts, and can, for the duration of any play, identify himself with the rest of the company. One day as a member of the Sun moiety he objects because the members of the Mother moiety have got out their flutes for a funeral when it was not their turn; a week later all of this is forgotten in a furore over the way the other initiatory group behaved at a small initiation-feast. Each of these passing and incompatible loyalties serves to confuse the others; the same man is his ally one day, his opponent the next, an indifferent, carefully nonchalant bystander on the third. All that remains to the individual Tchambuli man, with his delicately arranged curls, his handsome pubic covering of a flying-fox skin highly ornamented with shells, his mincing step and self-conscious mien, is the sense of himself as an actor, playing a series of charming parts—this and his relationship to the women.

His relations to all other males are delicate and difficult, as he sits down a little lightly even in his own clansmen's house, and is so nervous and sensitive that he will barely eat in the houses of other clans, but his relations to women are the one solid and reliable aspect of his life. As a small child, he was held lightly in the arms of a laughing casual mother, a mother who nursed him generously but nonchalantly, while her fingers were busy plaiting reeds into sleeping-baskets or rain-capes. When he tumbled down, his mother picked him up and tucked him under her arm as she went on with her conversation. He was never left alone; there were always some eight or ten women about, working, laughing, attending to his needs, willingly enough, but unobsessively. If his father's other wife failed to feed him as generously as his mother, his mother needed only to make the light reproach: "Are children plentiful that you should neglect them?" His childhood days were spent tumbling about the floor of the great dwelling-house, where his antics were privileged, where he could tickle and wrestle with the other children. His mouth was never empty. Women weaned their children as carelessly and casually as they nursed them, stuffing their mouths with delica-

cies to stop their crying. Afterwards the women fed them bountifully with food, lotus-stems, lily-stems, lotus-seed, Malay apples, pieces of sugar-cane, and a little boy could sit and munch in the great roomy house filled with other children of his kin and with groups of working, kindly women. Sometimes there was a ceremony, and his mother took him with her when she went to spend the day cooking in another house. There, in a larger crowd of women, with more children rolling about on the floor, he also munched. His mother took plenty of dainties along in her basket, to give him whenever he cried for them.

By the time a boy is seven or eight, he is beginning to hang about the edges of the men's ceremonial life. If he goes too close to the men's house during a ceremony, he will be chased away, although on ordinary occasions he can slip in and hide behind a small papa's protection. The older boys will haze him lightly, send him on errands, throw sticks at him, or beat him if he disobeys. Back he runs, scurrying up the hill-side to his mother's house, whither the big boys will not pursue him. The next time that he and those big boys are in a woman's house together, he will take advantage of the older boy's embarrassment; he will tease and plague him, caricature his walk and manner—with impunity; the older boy will not attack him.

At some point when he is between eight and twelve, a period that is not determined by his age so much as by his father's ceremonial ambitions, he will be scarified. He will be held squirming on a rock while a distantly related maternal "uncle" and an expert scarifier cut patterns on his back. He can howl as much as he likes. No one will comfort him, no one will attempt to stop his howls. Nor will anyone take any delight in them. Casually, efficiently, performing as relatives their ritual duty, for which they will receive graceful recognition, or performing their duty as artists, they cut patterns on the little boy's back. They paint him with oil and turmeric. All about him is an elaborate ceremonial pattern that he does not share. His father gives presents to his mother's brother. His mother's brother's wives are given beautiful new grass skirts, new rain-capes, new carrying-baskets. His scarification is the occasion for all this display, but no one pays any attention to him.

There follows a long period of seclusion. At night he is allowed to go home to sleep, but in the chill morning, before dawn, he must creep away from the women's house, wrapped from head to foot in a great coarse rain-cape. His body is smeared with white clay. All day he must stay inside the men's house. Every fourth day he washes and assumes a new coat of paint. It is all very uncomfortable. Sometimes two men of the same clan combine to scarify their sons, but as often a boy is initiated alone. There is no suggestion that this is done for his welfare. Nor is there any suggestion that the adults are interested in the discomfort of his position or the pain of his scarifications. All about him goes on the discussion of ceremonial policy, and if his father can make a more effective ceremony by waiting for three months to wash him, he waits. The child is not considered. Or in a great pet over some slight or indignity put upon him by those who should assist him in the ceremony, the father incontinently washes the child within a week or so after his scarification. The washing is ritual, and ends the period of seclusion. The boy's mother's brother presents him with an elaborately woven belt, shell ornaments, a beautifully incised bamboo lime-gourd with a lovely filigree spatula. He may now walk about with these under his arm, accompanying parties of people who take food or *talibun* and *kinas* to other people in his name. After this he is supposed to spend more time in the men's house, but he still takes refuge among the women whenever possible. He grows gradually into young manhood; his father and elder brothers watching jealously his attitude towards their younger wives and suspecting him if he walks about upon the women's roads.

The women remain, however, a solid group upon whom he depends for support, for food, for affection. There is no split between the women of his blood-group and the wife whom he marries, for he marries a daughter of one of his mother's half-brothers or cousins. He calls her by the name by which he calls his own mother, *aiyai*. All of the little girls of his mother's clan, to all of whom he looks hopefully, he addresses as *aiyai*. One of his "mothers" will some day be his wife. The gifts that his father gave in his name when he was very small, the gifts which he is now being taught to take himself to his mother's brothers, these are the earnest of his claim upon a woman of his mother's clan. In this way, one clan is linked with another from generation to generation, the men of one clan having a lien upon the women of the other.[1] Women are therefore divided for him into the group upon which he depends; these are all considered as of the order of mothers and include his mother, his mother's sisters, his father's brothers' wives, his mother's brothers' wives, and the daughters of his mother's brothers. Towards his father's sister and his father's sister's daughter his behaviour is more formal, for these can never be either mother, wife, or mother-in-law, the three relationships that Tchambuli feeling groups together. For the actual marriage, in addition to the presents that have been sent on ceremonial occasions the bride must be paid for in many *kinas* and *talibun,* and for this payment the young man is dependent upon his immediate male kin. An orphan, if he is allowed to live, has small hope of obtaining a bride while he is a young man. He is no one's child; how, indeed, can he hope to have a wife?

As the young man's attitude towards the women is single-hearted, rather than complicated with different conflicting attitudes appropriate to mother, sister, wife, and mother-in-law, so also the women in the house in which he has been brought up are a solid unit. When a girl marries, she goes not into the house of strangers but into the house of her father's sister, who now becomes her mother-in-law. If a man has two wives they usually, although not always, come from the same clan, and are sisters as well as

[1]For a discussion of this lien system see Dr. Fortune, "A Note on Cross-Cousin Marriage," *Oceania,* 1933.

cowives. To have been cowives, even although separated by death of the husband and subsequent remarriage, is regarded as a great tie between women. The prototype of Tchambuli polygyny is a pair of sisters entering as brides a house into which one or more of their father's sisters have married before them; in which the old woman who sits by the fire, and occasionally utters a few carping comments, is a woman of their clan also, and so will not deal harshly with them. And this unusual picture of great amity and solidarity within the two feminine relationships that are often most trying, that of cowives and that of mother-in-law and daughter-in-law, pervades the interrelations of all women. Tchambuli women work in blocks, a dozen of them together, plaiting the great mosquito-bags from the sale of which most of the *talibun* and *kina* are obtained. They cook together for a feast, their clay fire-places (circular pots with terraced tops, which can be moved from place to place) set side by side. Each dwelling-house contains some dozen to two dozen fire-places, so that no woman need cook in a corner alone. The whole emphasis is upon comradeship, efficient, happy work enlivened by continuous brisk banter and chatter. But in a group of men, there is always strain, watchfulness, a catty remark here, a *double entendre* there: "What did he mean by sitting down on the opposite side of the men's house when he saw you upon this side?" "Did you see Koshalan go by with a flower in his hair? What do you suppose he is up to?"

As a boy grows up he sees the world into which he will enter as a network of conflicting courses, each one adorned with airy graces. He will learn to play the flute beautifully, to play the flute that sounds like a cassowary, the flute that barks like a dog, the flutes that cry like birds, the set of flutes that are blown together to produce an organ-like effect. If he is politic, if he is well liked, he may have two wives, or even three, like Walinakwon. Walinakwon was beautiful, a graceful dancer, a fluent speaker, proud, imperious, but withal soft-spoken, and resourceful. In addition to his first wife, who had been given

him as a child by his mother's clan, two other women had chosen him as a husband. He was a fortunate man. All three of his wives could plait mosquito-bags, and Walinakwon was therefore in a fair way to become a rich man.

For although Tchambuli is patrilineal in organization, although there is polygyny and a man pays for his wife—two institutions that have been popularly supposed to degrade women—it is the women in Tchambuli who have the real position of power in the society. The patrilineal system includes houses and land, residence land and gardening-land, but only an occasional particularly energetic man gardens. For food, the people depend upon the fishing of the women. Men never fish unless a sudden school of fish appears in the lake, when they may leap into canoes in a frolicsome spirit, and spear a few fish. Or in high water when the shore-road is become a water-way, they may do a little torch-light fishing for sport. But the real business of fishing is controlled entirely by the women. For traded fish they obtain sago, taro, and areca-nut. And the most important manufacture, the mosquito-bags, two of which will purchase an ordinary canoe, are made entirely by women. The people in the middle Sepik purchase these mosquito-bags, in fact they are so much in demand that purchasers take options on them long before they are finished. And the women control the proceeds in *kinas* and *talibun*. It is true that they permit the men to do the shopping, both for food at the market and in trading the mosquito-bags. The men make a gala occasion of these latter shopping-trips; when a man has the final negotiations for one of his wives' mosquito-bags in hand, he goes off resplendent in feathers and shell ornaments to spend a delightful few days over the transaction. He will hesitate and equivocate, advance here, draw back there, accept this *talibun,* reject that one, demand to see a more slender *kina* or one that is better cut, insist on changing half of the purchasing items after they have been spread out, have a very orgy of choice such as a modern woman with a well-filled purse looks forward to in a shopping-trip to a big city.

But only with his wife's approval can he spend the *talibun* and *kina* and the strings of *conus* rings that he brings back from his holiday. He has wheedled a good price from the purchaser; he has still to wheedle the items of the price from his wife. From boyhood up, this is the men's attitude towards property. Real property, which one actually owns, one receives from women, in return for languishing looks and soft words. Once one has obtained it, it becomes a counter in the games that men play; it is no longer concerned with the underlying economics of life, but rather with showing one's appreciation of one's brother-in-law, soothing someone's wounded feelings, behaving very handsomely when a sister's son falls down in one's presence. The minor war-and-peace that goes on all the time among the men, the feelings that are hurt and must be assuaged, are supported by the labour and contributions of the women. When a woman lies dying, her thought is for the young boys whom she has been helping, her son, her sister's son, her husband's sister's son; how will this one, who, it is true, is an orphan also and has no one to help him, fare when she is dead? And if there is time, she will send for this handsome stripling or accomplished youth, and give him a *kina* or so, or some *talibun*. Such a handsome one is sure to arouse jealousy, to get into scrapes; he must be provided with the means by which to bribe his way back into favour.

The women's attitude towards the men is one of kindly tolerance and appreciation. They enjoy the games that the men play, they particularly enjoy the theatricals that the men put on for their benefit. A big masked show is the occasion for much pleasure. When a *mwai* dance is made, for instance, it means that a group of women dance about each of the sets of masked dancers. These masked figures wear wooden masks balanced in the midst of a head-dress of leaves and flowers in which dozens of slender little carvings are thrust on sticks. They have great paunches made up of a long row of crescent-shaped *kina* shells, which extend below their waists rather like elephants' tusks. They

wear bustles in which grimacing carved faces are stuck. Their legs are concealed with straw leggings, and they descend from a platform, which has been specially built with a back-drop resembling the distant mountains. The two male masks carry spears, the two female masks carry brooms; trumpeting and singing esoteric songs through little bamboo megaphones, they parade up and down a long cleared way that is lined with watching women and children. The masks are clan-owned, and when their own masks appear, the women of that clan and other women also go out and dance about them, making a gay chorus, and picking up any feathers or ornaments that fall from them. There are no men upon the dancing-ground except the four men hidden within the mask—older men in the male masks, young and frivolous ones within the female masks. These young men take a strange inverted pleasure in thus entering, in semi-disguise—not wholly in disguise, for most of them have whispered the details of their leggings to at least one woman—into the women's group. Here masked they can take part in the rough homosexual play that characterizes a group of women on any festive occasion. When there are no masks on the dancing-ground, the women play among themselves, jocosely going through pantomimes of intercourse. When the masked figures appear, the women include the female masks in their play, but not the male masks. The women treat these latter with gentle, careful gravity, lest their feelings be hurt. To the female masks the women give very definite attention, poking them with bundles of leaves that they carry in their hands, bumping against them in definitely provocative positions, tickling and teasing them. The *double entendre* of the situation, the spectacle of women courting males disguised as females, expresses better than any other ritual act that I witnessed the complexities of the sex-situation in Tchambuli, where men are nominally the owners of their homes, the heads of their families, even the owners of their wives, but in which the actual initiative and power is in the hands of the women. To the male mask the women give lip-service, and some of them, usually the older and graver women, dance with it; they pick up its ornaments when they fall. With the female masks they display aggressive sexual desire, and flaunt their right to initiative. After all, the young men can only whisper to the women in which masks they plan to dance and how their legs may be distinguished. Then, imprisoned in the clumsy, unstable, top-heavy masks and partially chaperoned by the older men who are dancing in the male masks, they can only parade blindly up and down the dancing-ground, waiting for a whisper and a blow to advise them that particular women have pressed against them. These ceremonies usually break up in a far shorter number of days than the original plan provides for, as rumours of liaisons flutter about to frighten the older men, who decide that they have lured their wives out on the dancing-ground for no good purpose. For even if no new alliance has sprung up under cover of the dancing, the dance of the women is itself designed to produce a high degree of sexual excitation, which may become an explosive in the days to come. It is the young wives of old men who enjoy these ceremonies most.

These festivals are a break in the vigorous workaday life of the women. Swift-footed, skillful-fingered, efficient, they pass back and forth from their fish-traps to their basket-plaiting, from their cooking to their fish-traps, brisk, good-natured, impersonal. Jolly comradeship, rough, very broad jesting and comment, are the order of the day. To each household is added once in so often a child-bride, a girl who at ten or eleven is sent to marry her cousin, one of the sons of the household. The bride is not difficult for the women to assimilate. She is their brother's child, they have known her always; they welcome her, teach her more skills, give her a fire-place at which to cook. And whereas the lives of the men are one mass of petty bickering, misunderstanding, reconciliation, avowals, disclaimers, and protestations accompanied by gifts, the lives of the women are singularly un-clouded with personalities or with quarrelling. For fifty quarrels among the men, there is hardly one among the women. Solid, preoccupied, powerful, with shaven unadorned heads, they sit in groups and laugh together, or occasionally stage a night dance at which, without a man present, each woman dances vigorously all by herself the dance-step that she has found to be most exciting. Here again the solidarity of women, the inessentialness of men, is demonstrated. Of this relationship the Tchambuli dwelling-house is the symbol. It presents the curious picture of the entire centre firmly occupied by well-entrenched women, while the men sit about the edges, near the door, one foot on the house-ladder almost, unwanted, on sufferance, ready to flee away to their men's houses, where they do their own cooking, gather their own firewood, and generally live a near-bachelor life in a state of mutual discomfort and suspicion.

Tchambuli young men develop their attitudes towards one another in the highly charged atmosphere of courtship, in which no one knows upon whom a woman's choice will fall, each youth holds his breath and hopes, and no young man is willing to trust another. Such courtship arises from the presence of widows or dissatisfied wives. The dissatisfied wives are created by the same fidelity to a pattern without regard for practical considerations that occurs in the exchanges in Mundugumor. If among the "mothers" of his generation, one of whom he has a right to marry, there is no girl a little younger than a boy, his mother's clan will give him a girl who is a little older. While he is still adolescent, insecure, frightened of sex, she matures, and becomes involved in a liaison either with one of his brothers or possibly with an older relative. His mother's brothers will try to prevent this; they will publicly deride the boy who does not enter his betrothed wife's sleeping-bag, and threaten him that trouble will result and she may be lost to another clan. The boy, shamed and prickly with misery, becomes more tongue-tied, more recalcitrant than ever to his wife's advances. Then some rearrangement, her marriage to another man of the same clan, is likely to follow. With a young widow also, it is the girl's choice that is decisive, for men will not be foolish enough to pay for a girl who has not indicated her choice of a husband by sleeping with him. It will be, as they say, money thrown away. A young widow is a tremendous liability to a community. No one expects her to remain quiet until her remarriage has been arranged. Has she not a vulva? they ask. This is the comment that is continually made in Tchambuli: Are women passive sexless creatures who can be expected to wait upon the dilly-dallying of formal considerations of bride-price? Men, not so urgently sexed, may be expected to submit themselves to the discipline of a due order and precedence.

Yet the course of true love runs no smoother here where women dominate than it does in societies dominated by men. There is sometimes a tendency in describing marriage arrangements to consider that one of the inevitable effects of the dominance of women is the woman's freedom to marry whom she will, but this is no more a necessary aspect of women's power than the right of a young man to choose his wife is an inevitable result of patriliny. The social ambitions of a mother may ruin her son's marriage under the most patriarchal form of society, and in Tchambuli neither men nor women are minded to give young people any more rein than they can help. The ideal is to marry pairs of cousins as children and thus settle at least part of the difficulty. The opportunities that polygyny offers wait, then, upon the ripening of the boy's charms. The older men see with jaundiced eyes the beauty and grace of their younger brothers and later of their sons, a beauty and grace that will soon displace them in the eyes of women, especially of their young wives, whose favour they had perhaps caught in the last flutter of powerful middle age. The young men say bitterly that the old men use every bit of power and strategy which they possess to cut out their young rivals, to shame and disgrace them before the women.

The method of discrediting a young rival that the men find readiest to their jealous hands is

the accusation of being an orphan. If a boy's father is alive, he will contribute perhaps 10, perhaps 20, percent of the bride-price, seldom more, and the other men of the clan contribute the rest. The principal contribution is made by the man or men whose marriages were mainly financed by the bridegroom's father. The state of being an orphan, then, does not mean that the boy is actually unable to pay a bride-price, but merely that he is in an exposed state of which the other men can take advantage. And cruelly the old lascivious man, nearing his grave, will use this power to interfere between an orphan boy of his clan and the young widow who has expressed a preference for that boy. One of these dramas was played out in detail while we were in Tchambuli. Tchuikumban was an orphan; his father and mother having both been killed in head-hunting raids, he belonged to a vanishing clan. But he was tall and straight and charming, although more arrogant and masterful than Tchambuli men usually are. Yepiwali was his "mother," a girl of his mother's clan, but she had been married as a child in a distant part of the settlement, and Tchuikumban has seen little of her. Then, just about the time we arrived in Tchambuli, the two potential mates, Yepiwali now a widow for many moons, Tchuikumban an orphan of a poor clan and with no betrothed wife, found themselves seeing each other daily, Yepiwali, suffering from a bad framboesia sore, was visiting her own parents, and Tchuikumban was helping work on the new men's house of Monbukimbit, a service that all uterine nephews owe to their mother's brothers. Yepiwali saw him and he found favour in her eyes. She told an older woman that Tchuikumban had given her two bead armlets. This was not true, but was a boast that she intended to capture his favour. Then she sent the head of a fish to Tchuikumban through his brother-in-law. Tchuikumban ate the head of the fish, but did nothing in reply to her overtures. A few days later, Tchuikumban was given a pair of snake-birds. Yepiwali heard of it and she sent word to him: "If you have any bones, send me some of that snake-bird in return for my fish." So Tchuikumban sent her half the breast of a snake-bird. The next day he made a journey to Kilimbit hamlet, and passed Yepiwali on the road. He did not speak to her, nor she to him, but she noted the new white belt that he was wearing. That night she sent word to him that if he had any bones, he would send her that belt, and some soap and matches.[2] This he did.

About this time, the father of Yepiwali decided that the need to remarry her was urgent. Rumours of her liaisons were rife, and it was not safe to leave her so long unmarried. He could not discuss her marriage with her himself, but he sent for a male cousin, Tchengenbonga, whom she called "brother," to do so. Tchengenbonga asked her which of her "sons" she wished to marry, and she said that Tavalavban had tried to win her affection, he had passed her on a path and held her breasts, but she didn't like him. She showed Tchengenbonga the gifts that she had elicited from Tchuikumban and said that she would like to marry him. Tchengenbonga asked her for the belt, and she gave it to him. Tchuikumban saw the belt on Tchengenbonga but said nothing. Soon after this there were offers for Yepiwali's hand from a man from another tribe, but after prolonged negotiations these were refused—not, however, before her choice of Tchuikumban had been published. The question of paying for her came up among Tchuikumban's relatives, and they refused to pay for her, because she did not know how to make mosquito-baskets. They were not going to have one of their boys marrying a woman who would not be a good provider. His foster-father was merciless: "You are an orphan. How can you expect to marry a wife of your own choice? This girl is no good. She is worn out with loose living. She cannot weave. How will it profit for you to marry her?" He reduced Tchuikumban to sulking misery. Soon after this Tchuikumban encountered Yepiwali on a deserted path; she paused and smiled at him, but he fled, too

ashamed of his miserable status as an orphan to stay and make love to her. Yepiwali lost her patience. She had chosen this man, and why did he hesitate? She sent a message to the men of the next hamlet, together with two baskets of food, saying that since the men of her own hamlet had no bones, one of them might come and carry her off. Her relatives became alarmed. She was watched more closely. Then in the midst of the ceremony and confusion of a house of mourning, word got about that Yepiwali had been meeting someone clandestinely, and this someone turned out to be Akerman, an older man of the clan who had the right to marry her. Still longing for Tchuikumban, although in a fine rage with him and with all of the young men, she was led away to marry Akerman, followed by the consoling word of an older woman: "The other wife of Akerman is your father's sister. She will be kind to you and not scold you because you do not know how to make baskets." The other wife of Akerman made good baskets, Akerman was old and rich, and it was no one's concern if he took a young wife. So the love-affair was defeated because his relatives shamed Tchuikumban in terms of his orphanhood and because Yepiwali was not able to provide for a young husband.

So the conflict over women, outlawed in Arapesh because of the emphasis upon finding wives for sons and so important a part of the struggle and clash of life in Mundugumor, exists too in Tchambuli, where young men and old struggle stealthily for the possession of women's favours—but the struggle is for the most part an underground one. It is not a fight but a secret competition, in which young men and young women are both likely to lose to the will of their elders.

Relevant also to the position of the sexes are the secrets of the men's cults and the sanctity of the men's houses. These men's houses, which combine the functions of club and green-room, places where men can keep themselves out of the women's way and prepare their own food, workshops and dressing-rooms for ceremonies, are not kept inviolate from a woman's entrance on

---

[2]Traded from our house-boys.

certain ceremonial occasions. For the scarification of a child, the woman who carries the child enters the men's house in state, and sits there proudly upon a stool. If there is a quarrel, the women gather on the hill-side and shout advice and directions into the very centre of the house where the debate is going on. They come armed with thick staves, to take part in the battle if need be. The elaborate ceremonies, the beating of water-drums, the blowing of flutes, are no secrets from the women. As they stood, an appreciative audience, listening solemnly to the voice of the crocodile, I asked them: "Do you know what makes that noise?" "Of course, it is a water-drum, but we don't say we know for fear the men would be ashamed." And the young men answer, when asked if the women know their secrets: "Yes, they know them, but they are good and pretend not to, for fear we become ashamed. Also—we might become so ashamed that we would beat them."

"We might become so ashamed that we would beat them." In that sentence lies the contradiction at the root of Tchambuli society, in which men are theoretically, legally dominant, but in which they play an emotionally subservient role, dependent upon the security given them by women, and even in sex-activity looking to women to give the leads. Their love magic consists in charms made of stolen stones that the women use for auto-erotic practices: this the men deeply resent, feeling that they should benefit by the greater sexual specificity and drive of the women. What the women will think, what the women will say, what the women will do, lies at the back of each man's mind as he weaves his tenuous and uncertain web of insubstantial relations with other men. Each man stands alone, playing his multiplicity of parts, sometimes allied with one man, sometimes with another; but the women are a solid group, confused by no rivalries, brisk, patronizing, and jovial. They feed their male children, their young male relatives, on lotus-seeds and lily-roots, their husbands and lovers upon doled-out pellets of love. And yet the men are after all stronger, and a man can beat his wife, and this possibility serves to confuse the whole issue of female dominance and masculine charming, graceful, coquettish dancing attention.

11

TURNING THE TABLES? MALE STRIPPERS AND THE GENDER HIERARCHY

MAXINE L. MARGOLIS / MARIGENE ARNOLD

Anthropologists have long asserted that all societies differentiate their members by gender. Some activities and occupations are defined as "masculine," others as "feminine." That these definitions are largely arbitrary is suggested by the fact that what is obviously a masculine activity to one group, is just as obviously a feminine one to another group. Thus, among the Pueblo Indians of the American southwest only men weave, while their Navaho neighbors insist that women are clearly the superior weavers. Societal ideologies justify such divisions of labor by appealing to sexual stereotypes. Women are said to

be "naturally" better than men at whatever tasks a given society assigns to the feminine realm, while men's "innate" talent is said to be just as unambiguously displayed in tasks that that society defines as masculine.

The United States has not been exempt from ideologies that rationalize the sexual status quo. In American society of the 1950s, for example, the "ideal" family was synonymous with the "ideal" gender hierarchy. Thus, men were to be breadwinners, women housewives and domestic consumers, with a clear cultural preference for the male role. Moreover, the woman who dared

SOURCE: From "Turning the Tables? Male Strippers and the Gender Hierarchy" by M. L. Margolis and M. Arnold in *Gender Hierarchies* by B. D. Miller (Ed.). Copyright © 1992 by Cambridge University Press. Reprinted with the permission of Cambridge University Press.

151

to cross over the sexual boundary line and seek a career, was decried and labeled a "feminist neurotic" (Margolis 1984:218–225).

In a classic article the anthropologist Jules Henry neatly summarized the gender hierarchy in the United States: A "man validates himself by working and supporting," Henry wrote, "a woman validates herself by getting a man. A man does, a woman is. Man performs, woman attracts" (1973:135).

While there have been significant social and economic changes in American society since the rebirth of the feminist movement in the late 1960s, elements of the traditional gender hierarchy are still very much with us. Sey Chassler, former editor of *Redbook* writes:

> The women's movement has made some remarkable changes in our lives, but it hasn't changed the position of the male much at all. Men still make the moves. They are the ones who, in their own good time, move in. And in their own good time, move out. Someone makes the rules, someone else does as she is told. . . . As men we are surely in charge. It comes with the territory (1988:173).

The gender hierarchy is expressed in diverse realms. In many societies, for example, and ours is no exception, sexual activity is symbolic of men's control over women. One anthropologist writes that "the essential formal characteristic of the sex act . . . is the exploitation of women by men" (Kemnitzer 1977:294). Men are expected to initiate sex and women are expected to submit. Men are the consumers, women the providers.

In this country even the right to ogle the opposite sex has been, until recently, the exclusive province of men. As Laura Mulvey, a film editor and director puts it:

> In a world ordained by sexual imbalance, pleasure in looking has been split between active/male and passive/female. The determining male gaze projects its fantasy onto the female figure, which is styled accordingly. . . . Women displayed as sexual object is the leitmotif of erotic spectacle; from pinups to striptease, from Ziegfield to Busby Berkeley, she holds the look, plays to, and signifies male desire (1977:418).

This chapter examines what appears to be a reversal of this aspect of the traditional gender hierarchy in America by describing the role of male striptease dancers who play to female audiences. Here men would appear to be the sexual objects, the passive caterers to women's needs. In such performances, it is male, rather than female bodies that are put on display and judged.[1]

Our aim is to analyze the male strip show within the broader context of gender hierarchies in the United States. In order to do this we compare male strip shows with the more traditional ones that feature female dancers. Female strippers are said to be symbols of the sexual objectification of women (Lewin 1984). Moreover, their jobs have a tendency, in the words of one feminist-historian, " . . . to reproduce in the cruelest possible way the structure of patriarchal power and female dependence" (Kessler-Harris 1985:12).

If this is true, and we believe that the few studies of female strip shows support this interpretation, our question then is, are male strip shows in any way analogous to their female counterparts? We focus primarily on the issue of control during the men's performance because we see control as an important clue to power relations and, therefore, to gender hierarchy. We ask what, if any, are the differences between audience-performer interaction in shows featuring male and female strippers? Our assumption is that if the male strip show does indeed represent a true inversion of the traditional gender hierarchy, it should be a mirror image of the female strip show with only the sex of the performers and the audience reversed.

THE MALE STRIP SHOW

Before presenting our findings which are based partly on participant observation in a discotheque featuring male strip shows, we provide

[1]We appreciate the helpful suggestions of many of the participants in the Wenner-Gren symposium as well as the insightful comments of Professor David Suggs of Kenyon College.

some background on the phenomenon itself. Bars and nightclubs featuring male strippers were first established sometime during the mid to late 1970s. While their total number in the United States is impossible to estimate, they appear to be widespread. They are not limited to the sophisticated metropolitan centers of the two coasts or to big cities in general (*Time Magazine,* 1979:69). Male strip shows have mushroomed in suburban areas and small cities in the Midwest and South including University City, a town of about 100,000, where we conducted our research.[2] Patrons of these establishments are of all ages, although our own study is heavily weighted towards college age women because of the makeup of University City's population.

As a general rule, the owners of bars and nightclubs that feature male strippers restrict their clientele to women. A number of explanations are given for this policy. Some club owners say they want to avoid attracting male customers who are gay, while others claim that the all-woman policy serves to keep out straight men who make their female clientele uncomfortable and who occasionally become violent (Brackley 1980:70). Then, too, some women customers aver that because of the absence of men in the audience they feel safer and more relaxed in these establishments than they do in regular bars (*Chicago Tribune* 1980:1).

Through zoning ordinances and license challenges a few communities have attempted to shut down businesses featuring male strippers, although it is not clear if these efforts are greater than those to control the more traditional female strip joints and topless bars (Brackley 1980:69). It is true, however, that in one small city in the Northeast male strippers were arrested for "disseminating obscene materials" while the city fathers have made no similar attempt to limit the right of female performers to remove their clothes in public or the right of male customers to watch them (*New York Times*

1980:A29). In a Chicago suburb a male strip joint was closed less than two weeks after opening purportedly because it lacked a "special use permit." Yet, according to the city manager the true reason was that the nightclub did not "offer the type of show generally identified with our hometown atmosphere." "I don't know," he said, "maybe there's some male chauvinism behind this. We say belly dancers are okay but when men do the same thing, we say it's obscene" (*Chicago Tribune* 1980:2).

THE SHOW AT GINNIE'S

Our research was conducted at Ginnie's, a discotheque that features a male strip show one night a week. It strictly enforces an all-female policy during the two-hour show, but permits men in immediately following the performance. Its advertisements, in fact, invite men "to come dance and romance with the ladies who have experienced the ultimate 'Male Review.' "

Ginnie's charges $5.00 admission for the show itself which includes the cost of unlimited quantities chosen from a list of alcoholic beverages and soft drinks. In addition, customers are expected to tip the male dancers as well as the waiters, an expectation of which they are reminded constantly by the disc jockey.

Most women come to the show in groups of threes and fours. We observed no lone women customers at Ginnie's, a point to which we will return later. Attendance is often in celebration of the birthday of one of the women. There have been reports that friends of a recently divorced woman will invite her to a male strip show to mark her new status (*Time Magazine* 1979:69).

The performance at Ginnie's takes place on a small dance floor lined on two sides by banquettes on which patrons may sit. These are the seats of choice for some customers who arrive up to an hour before the doors open so that they may dash in and reserve them for themselves and their friends. There are also small tables on one

---

[2]University City is a pseudonym as is Ginnie's, the club featuring male strip shows in which we did our research. The research was conducted during the spring and winter of 1985.

side of the dance floor as well as on two balconies overlooking it.

As the sixty or seventy patrons are seated and place their drink orders against the din of loud rock music, a disc jockey begins to work the audience. "This is ladies' night out," he proclaims. "You deserve a night out." The refrain, "ladies, this is *your* night," is repeated throughout the performance. We agree with other researchers that the "equal time for women" theme is a salient feature of the male strip show (Petersen and Dressel 1982:189). Following the popular media's portrayal of the male strip show as part of the feminist movement's demand for women's equality, Ginnie's female audience is obliquely told that attendance at such a show is a liberating experience (*Time,* August 6, 1979; Snider, 1980).

The show is presented by five male performers collectively known as the "Feelgood Dancers." Each show begins with the same scenario: four of the five dancers, wearing white tuxedos and top hats and carrying long-stemmed carnations, enter the bar area and begin distributing flowers and kisses to patrons. The four work their way to the dance floor where they proceed to dance and strip. This opening number sets the stage for the rest of the performance. An aura of romance and chivalry is created which will be mixed throughout the evening with more overt sexuality and male aggressiveness.

After the opening number each dancer returns twice, dressed in a variety of elaborate costumes—a sailor, a construction worker, an explorer, a fireman, an American Indian, Charlie Chaplin, Conan the Barbarian, and a Kung Fu in leather. Each dancer is introduced by the disc jockey, makes his way to center stage, and does a bump and grind performance while stripping off layers of clothes until he is wearing only a g-string. Total nudity is not a feature of the show.[3]

These performances take place against a backdrop of loud frenzied music and the non-stop encouragement of the disc jockey. "The more you scream, the more you see," he urges his audience over and over again. Customers are told they must continually yell and clap to show their appreciation of the performers. The message is that the audience must behave in a certain way in order to get the desired results—presumably having the dancers strip down to their g-strings.

There is constant sexual banter and double entendres. The audience is told that the explorer "has a large animal which he is going to show us tonight." When two dancers appear in striped uniforms, the deejay warns: "Watch out, ladies, these guys have been in prison for twenty years."

A central feature of the performance is the dancers' singling out women in the audience for attention. Once a dancer has completed his strip and is wearing only a g-string he will start to "work" the crowd, moving from table to table where he accepts dollar bills which the patrons stuff into his g-string. Each tip is followed by a kiss. Some women in the audience hold up dollar bills and the dancer will usually move to their tables. However, each dancer also singles out patrons by leaping on a table or the railing around the balcony and focusing his gyrations at a particular woman who is sometimes embarrassed into making a physical and monetary response as the only way to be left alone. The finale features all of the performers simultaneously going from table to table to pick up additional tips and by the end of the show their g-strings are overflowing with dollar bills.

GENDER AND CONTROL IN THE FEMALE STRIP SHOW

Earlier we suggested that the male strip show, in which women as consumers take the active role and men as providers take the passive one, appears to be a reversal of the traditional American gender hierarchy. Before analyzing this point, however, the male strip show can be put into sharper focus by comparing it to the traditional

---

[3]Total nudity also was not a feature of the strip shows observed by Petersen and Dressel (1982). However, there are shows in which the male dancers completely strip. It is our impression that the latter are confined to large cities.

female strip show with particular attention being paid to the interactions between the performers and the audience.

Despite its ubiquitous and long term presence on the American scene, relatively little social science research has been done on the female strip show. Moreover, with few exceptions, most work has focused on stripping as a "deviant" profession (Boles and Garbin 1974b, 1974c; Carey, Peterson and Sharpe 1974; McCaghy and Skipper 1972; Skipper and McCaghy 1970). Aside from an article by Boles and Garbin (1974a) and a personalized account of Boston strip joints by Lewin (1984), no researchers have investigated the actual performances in bars with female strippers or the patterns of dancer-customer interactions in these establishments.

It is clear from the few studies of behavior in nightclubs featuring female strippers that one of the principal functions of the performers is to encourage customers, most of whom are men, to buy drinks. In some clubs there is a distinction between "featured strippers" who draw customers because of their abilities as performers and "house girls" who also dance, but whose main responsibility is to mingle with customers and get them to buy drinks. House girls may help tend bar, wait on tables, and seat customers. They are also expected to interact with the audience on a personal level, particularly if requested to do so by a customer (Boles and Garbin, 1974a).

Female strippers often adopt distinctive personae in their acts—the vamp, the baby doll, the ice queen—donning elaborate costumes and exaggerated face makeup. They also almost invariably use stage names appropriate to their chosen persona—Cleopatra, Lolita, Crystal, and so on. Nevertheless, according to Boles and Garbin, "the very image strippers are attempting to create may be destroyed in the process of sitting with members of the audience" (1974a:139). A number of the dancers indicated that they found this requirement distracting because it breaks down the social and physical distance that usually exists between performer and audience and interferes with their self-image as entertainers.

This lack of distinction between performer and audience seems to be a problem endemic to female strip shows. In *Naked Is the Best Disguise* (1984), a study of bars featuring such shows in Boston, Lewin describes how female strippers try to keep their sense of dignity and self-esteem by setting limits on their interactions with male patrons. Here too, the stripper is expected to entertain male clients when she is not performing and her success is, in part, judged by the number of drinks clients buy for her. In fact, this feature is so central to the job that strippers were warned that if they "couldn't please customers"—as measured by how many drinks were bought, they would be let go (1984:37).

While strippers are expected to joke and banter with their customers, the degree to which touching and other sexual activities take place between stripper and customer seems to vary with the type of establishment. In the clubs studied by Boles and Garbin the strippers rarely permitted men to touch them (1974a), while in one of the "combat zone" bars Lewin investigated, a private back room was available for sexual trysts.[4] But even here Lewin describes the strippers attempts to set limits, or what one of them called the need to have "a gimmick." One stripper, for example, permitted male customers to touch her, but refused to touch them, while another touched the men but would not allow them to fondle her. Still another would engage in a variety of sexual activities but drew the line at sexual intercourse claiming (falsely) that she had a venereal disease (1984:43).

The men who attend female strip shows appear reluctant to show any appreciation for the performance. They must be shamed into applause either by the establishment's manager or by other dancers. An overt display of appreciation might demonstrate the female dancers' power over the male audience.

Perhaps because of the problematic nature of

---

[4]The "combat zone" in Boston is an area of the city so designated because it has been zoned for bars featuring strip shows, pornographic book shops and other forms of "adult" entertainment. It is also a center of prostitution and drug traffic.

the relationship between audience and performer in bars featuring female strip shows, any action by a member of the audience, no matter how inadvertent, that appears hostile may provoke the stripper's wrath. This is particularly true of female customers. At the slightest sign of hostility or rejection, the stripper will immediately react with a verbal assault, often making a disparaging remark about some inadequacy in the customer's anatomy.

At times strippers have to contend with customers who leap on the stage either because they want physical contact with the dancer or are inebriated and want to be part of the show (Boles and Garbin 1974a:140). In either case, the performer-audience distinction is breached and the dancer loses at least temporary control over the show.

The question of control—who has it and how it is maintained—seems to be a recurrent issue in the context of female performers playing to (largely) male audiences. Lewin sees the stripper retaining control over her performance, at least in her own mind, by deciding how explicit her "floor show" will be. After stripping, the dancer sits on the floor and exposes her genitals. By varying the degree and length of exposure, she sees herself as being "in control" (1984:73–74). Whatever one thinks of this feeble attempt at control, in other circumstances the audience clearly has the upper hand. A waitress in a University City establishment featuring a "miniskirt contest"—which is actually an amateur strip show—noted that "the strippers do what the crowds want. Every time one girl shows a little, the next one has to show more." And since this is a contest, those who show the most receive the most applause and are the most likely to win. According to the same informant, men watching the miniskirt contest "are not easily satisfied and usually try to get the contestants to show more" (Schultz 1985:1, 8).

In some respects the audience controls the female stripper, but control over the audience in these establishments is exerted by male bouncers (Lewin 1984:173). The owner of the mini-

skirt contest bar claims that bouncers are essential for restraining unruly men in the audience who try to touch the dancers, behavior that is forbidden by house rules (Schultz 1985:8). Thus, in the female strip show some members of the male audience try to have their way with the performers and audience behavior is kept in check only by muscular male bouncers.

The permeable boundary between audience and performer and the issue of control are not the only problematic aspects of the female strip show. According to Boles and Garbin, the main complaint of the female strippers they studied was that they were "objectified" by their audiences; that they were " . . . treated as instruments rather than as persons valuable in themselves" (1974a:141). Dancers are propositioned indiscriminately by men in the audience under the assumption that strippers are, by definition, prostitutes. The same negative stereotypes hold for contestants in the miniskirt contest, many of whom are college students. According to the owner of the club which holds the contests, these attitudes have presented problems: "We've had the girls out getting something to eat and because they dance in the miniskirt contest the guys treat them like some sleazy whore" (Schultz 1985:8).

Performers bridle at these attitudes and even those who do accept money for sex resent the lack of "courting behavior" on the part of male customers (Boles and Garbin 1974a:141). "I'm not a sleaze bag or a slut," protested one miniskirt contestant who said that although she entered the contests only in hopes of winning money, she always felt reservations when she performed (Schultz 1985:8).

The belief that female strippers are available sexually is related to the general denigration of stripping as an occupation (Bryant 1982:151–52). The dancers deeply resented the question: "What's a nice girl like you . . . ?" and miniskirt contestants previously acquainted with men in the audience often heard the refrain: "I thought you had more class than that . . . " (Boles and Garbin 1974a:141; Schultz 1985:8).

Given these tensions it is not surprising that researchers have described the atmosphere in bars with strip shows as suffused with hostility and even violence. Dancers will routinely insult members of the audience who act uninterested in their performance or who offend them in some other way. Lewin (1984) describes many violent incidents between strippers and customers as well as between customers and bouncers. Boles and Garbin (1974a) note that the level of violence varies from club to club and that the greatest displays of anger are between customers and performers. In fact, most clubs serve drinks in plastic glasses so as to lessen the chance of serious injury during fights.

Finally, it is evident that the context and structure of the stripper's job replicates the external gender hierarchy of male dominance and female submission in a number of ways. Male club owners and managers maintain tight control over the female performers. "Club rules" which dictate the strippers behavior are strictly enforced. For example, pay is withheld if strippers are unable to convince customers to buy a specified number of drinks. Strippers are expected to do nothing that will displease customers and to use their "womanly wiles" to get them to spend as much money as possible. It is a stripper's duty to cajole her customers into buying drinks; a common strategy is to evoke the male client's sympathy and plead for support. Lewin notes that no matter how old, sickly or unattractive, male customers can still "buy illusions of power," while female performers generally feel powerless and exploited (Lewin 1984:36, 122, 124, 145).

GENDER AND CONTROL IN THE MALE STRIP SHOW

We now return to our analysis of the male strip show. Briefly put, we found that the purported role reversal in the male strip show is illusory. The male strip show is not a mirror image of the female strip show with a mere inversion of the sex of the audience and the performers.[5] Moreover, because the male strip show contains elements reminiscent of traditional gender hierarchies in the United States, the popular media's widely touted interpretation of it as a symbol of women's liberation rings false.

A number of factors contribute to our conclusion that the structure and content of the contemporary male strip show is characterized by antiquated sex role expectations. For one, through a variety of mechanisms, both the male dancers and the other employees of Ginnie's, the establishment in which we did our research, direct and manage the female audience in such a way as to recreate the traditional gender hierarchy of male dominance and female subservience.

The first indication to Ginnie's female customers that their behavior is subject to external control is the requirement that they line up in a public corridor to await the door's opening at 9 P.M. After they enter and are seated the disc jockey takes command. First, he repeatedly reminds the audience to tip the waiters. While this may be a response to the stereotype that women do not tip, it is a patronizing gesture. The deejay also enjoins the audience to behave in a certain way in order to get the dancers to strip. Again and again he says, "they won't take it off if you don't scream." Then, too, by emphasizing the male dancers' sexual starvation—in the case of escaped convicts and sailors returning after years at sea—or their sexual endowments, and, by extension, prowess—a sheriff with a six-shooter and a lion tamer with a large animal—the disc jockey verbally creates scenarios in which the male dancers would be expected to be the sexual assailants. Thus, the image of the dancers, rather than being sexual providers as implied in gender role reversal, are instead depicted as sexual aggressors.

The dancers themselves add to this sense of

[5]The role of gigolo would also seem to be a role reversal but for the combat zone in Washington, D.C., Weatherford reports that "[in] the terminology of the street . . . these men were pimps rather than gigolos because the word *pimp* implied control over the woman rather than just serving her. According to this distinction, the man who took a woman's money was 'pimping' her. . . . " (1986:179).

control. One performer indicated this when he said, "Compared to most topless nightclubs we put more emphasis on costumes and choreography. You can control your audience by the way you present yourself" (Schultz 1985:1). As we have seen the male dancers choose the women they play to and some women are embarrassed into making a monetary response to the dancer's attentions. Quite unlike the cajoling stance of the female stripper, the male stripper seems to be demanding payment for his performance.

There are still other aspects of their performance that enhance the feeling that the male dancers are in charge of the action. First, they are all well-muscled. This fact contributes to the sense that they are stronger than the clients and could presumably overpower them at will. In addition, they enhance their size by dancing on tables and balconies, thus, positioning themselves above the female audience for much of the performance. A dancer often gets a woman from the audience to remove a piece of his clothing; when this is done he invariably stands on a chair and towers above her. In one instance a woman who got up from her chair to kiss a dancer was taller than the dancer; he immediately hopped on a chair before he kissed her. While this incident may have been merely a whimsical moment in the show, it, along with the other behaviors we have described, may be taken as symbolic of differential male and female power.

Nowhere is this more apparent than in the "dive bomb" method of tipping the dancers. From the start of the show the deejay extols patrons to be creative in their tipping and cajoles them to be the first to "dive bomb." Early in the show women stuff tips into the sides and back of the dancers' g-strings; later in the evening and, presumably with the assistance of alcohol, dive bombing begins. To dive bomb, a woman puts a dollar bill in her mouth, gets down on the floor on her knees and sticks the bill into the front of the dancer's g-string. This action, which mimics fellatio, is symbolic not only of women's subservience, but of their sexual availability and vulnerability.

Audience control, then, does not seem to be a major problem for the male strippers at Ginnie's.[6] Perhaps because their command of the situation is not in doubt, the deejay encourages women in the audience to touch the male dancers, behavior that is strictly forbidden in establishments featuring female strippers. In other words, physical contact with the dancers is not seen as threatening because it is not likely to be disruptive as it might be were the sexes of the customers and performers reversed. This interpretation is supported by the comments of the owner of another University City nightclub that features male strippers who work the audience in the manner described above. When asked why he does not have an equivalent show with female dancers, he replied that "a woman going out into the crowd is going to get abused. We can intercede but if some guy in the audience grabs [her], it may take four bouncers to get him off, and by that point the damage has been done" (Schultz 1985:8).

Then, too, the audience/performer dichotomy is far better defined in the male strip show than in the female strip show because the male dancers interact with the female clientele only as performers. They do not wait on tables, nor do they sit with female customers after the show and encourage them to buy drinks. Unlike many female strippers, male strippers are not obliged to wait in attendance on an audience of the opposite sex. It is presumed that they can please the female clientele with the artistry of their performances; they are not called on to interact with members of the audience on a more personal level.

Distinctive patterns of attendance at the male and female strip shows also are related to the issue of control. As mentioned earlier, we observed no lone women at Ginnie's. Similarly, Petersen and Dressel (1982) note that during

---

[6]Audience control did present more of a problem in the club featuring a male strip show that was studied by Petersen and Dressel. They note that some female customers were verbally and physically aggressive towards the dancers, pinching or scratching them, pulling at their g-strings, and insulting the dancers' physical attributes (1982:201). We never witnessed any comparable behavior at Ginnie's.

eight months of visiting the male strip club in which they conducted their research they never once observed a woman attending the show alone. This is in marked contrast to the bars featuring topless waitresses or female strip shows. In these establishments the lone male customer seems to be the norm. Although Lewin (1984) provides no specific figures in her description of the audience in bars featuring female strippers, she gives the strong impression that most of the men come to the bars alone.

There are several possible interpretations of the phenomenon of "group female" versus "solitary male" attendance at these performances. Perhaps it is simply the relative novelty of male strip shows that induces women to go to them with their friends; attendance in a group lessens an individual's feeling of discomfort in a new situation. Conversely, because female strip shows have been around for years, the lone male attending a performance is likely to find himself in familiar surroundings.

We believe, however, that there are more profound social and psychological explanations for this pattern of attendance. Given the norm of male control, women who go to male strip shows seeking a reversal in erotic roles may feel more at ease in a setting of group solidarity than of individual liberation. The "safety in numbers" dictum may well apply here as a logical outgrowth of traditional patterns of female socialization in the United States. Then, too, perhaps women go to these performances accompanied by their friends because of the hoary notion that a sexually assertive woman is "out of control." By attending a performance alone, a woman may fear that she would be making a social statement that she "needs" more satisfaction than the vicarious sexual expression obtained from the male strip show itself.

We are on more tentative ground in trying to explain the lone male pattern of attendance at female strip shows. Men may worry that attending a strip show sullies the ideal of the macho American male as a sexual dynamo capable of seducing women at all times. In line with this idealized image of masculinity, why should the vicarious eroticism of viewing nude or semi-nude female performers be necessary for a 'man's man'? Is going to a strip show, then, an activity best concealed from (male) friends? The question also arises of how a man would react to a friend getting comparatively more attention from a female dancer. Is the solitary male unwilling to share the attention of the dancers qua sexual beings? While we are uncertain as to which of these interpretations is the most accurate one, we are convinced that the marked gender differences in patterns of attendance at these performances are not random.

The self-images of the male strippers and their profession also diverge significantly from those of their female counterparts. Unlike the negative feelings expressed by the female strippers, the male dancers seemed to enjoy their work. "I love what I'm doing," said a male stripper in a Chicago club. "You see, I really love the ladies" (*Chicago Tribune* 1980:2). Said another, "It's basically a man's dream. . . . The opportunities come fast and furious" (quoted in Petersen and Dressel 1982:194). Nor do they appear ashamed of their jobs: "Everybody I know knows what I do and most of them have seen the show, including my mother," boasted yet another (quoted in Schultz 1985:8). Moreover, the job seems to evoke interest because of its novelty. "When I tell people I'm a dancer, they say 'How interesting, tell me about it,' " according to one of the Feelgood Dancers.

These attitudes are reflections of the American gender hierarchy. Why are similar activities judged so differently when they are performed by males and females? Why is comparable behavior admired in men and denigrated in women? Why are women strippers characterized as "sluts" and "sleaze bags," while men strippers are seen as artistic and sexy? Why are the male dancers not "fair game" to the audience like the female dancers are? Surely, if the male strip show were really an analogue of the female strip show we would not see such a marked contrast in attitudes towards the performers and the job itself.

There is also the issue of economic compensation. While it is difficult to come up with accurate figures for the earnings of male and female strippers, there is some evidence that the men, on average, earn much more than the women do. One of the Feelgood Dancers said that he never earned less than $120 a night and could earn up to $200 when he performed on a "hot night" in a club in a larger city (Campbell 1985). These figures are comparable to those cited by other male strippers (Bryant 1982:197).

The pattern of compensation in one nightclub that features both male strippers and a miniskirt contest is telling. The male dancers earn $600 from salary and tips for four shows, while the female contestants, in what amounts to an amateur strip show, get $10 for entering the contest and compete for first, second, and third prizes of $200, $50, and $25 respectively (Schultz 1985:8). As a result of this arrangement, although both men and women provide the night's entertainment, aside from a token payment, the women are not compensated for their performance unless they win one of the prizes.

In *Naked Is the Best Disguise*, Lewin explains what female strippers must do for their earnings. In addition to a salary of $40 a day, they receive a commission on the drinks they induce customers to buy for them. They earn $1 on every $6 drink, but only if they fill their quota of twelve drinks for the evening; no commission is paid if less than twelve drinks are sold. Moreover, she makes it clear that in some establishments the size of a stripper's "tips" is proportional to her willingness to be fondled by male customers (1984:36–37).

Finally, there is a very telling theme in some of the print and broadcast advertising for male strip shows, a theme that would be nearly unimaginable in ads for their female counterparts. The advertisement that Ginnie's directs at potential male customers is illustrative. It urges men "to come dance and romance with the ladies who have just experienced the ultimate Male Review." A radio spot for Dazzles, another club that features a male strip show and allows men in afterward has a similar, albeit, more explicit, come on: "Men, you have two things to look forward to: a most sophisticated nightclub and some *very* excited women."

The common leitmotif here is that witnessing a performance by male strippers "readies" women sexually for other men. One interpretation of this message is that male strip shows *ultimately* benefit men by making women who view the shows more sexually available to them. The salience of this point in terms of the perpetuation of the gender hierarchy becomes explicit if we imagine the likelihood of a similar advertisement being directed at women. What are the chances that the print or broadcast media would run ads that try to induce women "to dance and romance the [gentlemen] who have just witnessed the ultimate [Female] Review"?

Thus, although the media paints the male strip show with an "equal time for women" motif, we find this to be a deceptive commentary on a phenomenon that, in fact, symbolically recreates traditional gender roles. It is true that the shows contain a reversal in the sense that women are encouraged to look at and enjoy male bodies—a recent innovation. Nevertheless, the male dancers adopt an active, aggressive stance throughout the performance. It is they who select female members of the audience for attention, an audience that is kept in check by constantly being told how to behave through the patronizing and infantilizing prattle of the disc jockey.

Then, too, male dancers are seen in an entirely different light than their female analogues. Their status is not degraded through participation in the strip show and their jobs are even viewed as novelties. They earn more money than female strippers and they are never required to wait on and socialize with members of the audience. Finally, they are responsible, at least in a symbolic way, for "turning on" the client for the ultimate benefit of her boyfriend or of some other male. And so despite a surface appearance of the male strip show as a "liberating" experience for women, role reversal is illusory and the deeply embedded gender hierarchy is reenacted and upheld.

TURNING THE TABLES?

As social scientists and feminists, our description and analysis forces us to conclude that the male strip show is yet one more example of the traditional gender hierarchy in action. Nevertheless, Ginnie's is always packed, many of the women attend time and time again, and the crowd appears to enjoy itself tremendously. What explains the disparity between our interpretation of the show and the audience's evident enjoyment of it?

Several elements of the male strip show help explain the enthusiasm of Ginnie's patrons. One analyst claims that while "men watching [female] strip shows tend to be aroused . . . women tend to treat the whole thing [i.e. male strip shows] as a joke" (Faust 1980:37). While our informal interviews with patrons do not indicate that the show at Ginnie's is seen as a joke, it certainly is perceived as fun. Moreover, there is the novelty of women being encouraged to enjoy viewing scantily clad male bodies.

Then, too, the environment during the show, though meant to be erotic, is perfectly safe. The sense of security, in fact, has been cited as an explanation for why the "new erotica" is so popular with women; they can rent x-rated, romance-oriented movies and watch them on their VCRs in the privacy of their own homes (Leo 1987:63).

There is also the question of whether Ginnie's show would have succeeded had it actually featured a true gender role reversal. Beginning with Kinsey, all research on the matter indicates that men and women, at least in the United States, respond to very different sexual stimuli (Faust 1980; Whitehurst and Booth 1980; Frayser 1985; Weatherford 1986; Leo 1987). Keith McWalter expresses the difference best:

> Men's sexual response is triggered predominantly by visual stimulation [but] . . . women are creatures of gestalt, aroused by the full range of the senses and the heart and brain besides (1987:138).

Another analyst claims that "most erotica fits into our cultural stereotypes of men and women and reinforces the conventional elements of such scripts" (Gagnon cited in Whitehurst and Booth 1980:144). This aptly describes the show put on by the "Feelgood Dancers." The performance plays up gender stereotypes, reinforces "conventional elements" and, in fact, is more reminiscent of a Harlequin Romance novel than of a female strip show.

Like the male strip show, the issue of control also arises in women's magazines, romance novels, and the like. They portray

> sex and violence in such a way that heroines are often raped, but 'never ruined'; their experiences explore a wide range of sexual activities for women, but only in contexts over which the women have no control. . . . They absolve women from the responsibility of choice in sexual relationships and provide vicarious satisfaction for women who have no intention of being permissive in "real" life (Frayser 1985:421).

Thus, the successful formula for the romance novel and other entertainment directed at women also works well for the male strip show.

A similar point is driven home if we try to conceive of a true gender role reversal in a sexual context:

> Imagine two doors: in front of each door is a line of people; behind each door is a room; in each room is a bed; on each bed is a person. The line in front of one room consists of beautiful women, and on the bed in that room is a man having intercourse with each of these women in turn. One may think of any number of things about this scene. One may say that the man is in heaven, or enjoying himself in a bordello; or perhaps one might wonder at the oddness of it all. One does not think that the man is being hurt or violated or degraded—or at least the possibility does not immediately suggest itself. . . .

> Now consider the other line. Imagine that the figure on the bed is a woman and that the line consists of handsome, smiling men. The woman is having intercourse with each of these men in turn. It immediately strikes one that the woman is being degraded, violated, and so forth—"that poor woman" (Baker 1988:293).

We are forced to conclude, then, that although sexual behavior has changed since the sexual revolution[7] attitudes towards active female sexuality have not kept pace. The male strip show, like the fun-house mirror, distorts the fact that, sexually, we still live in a "man's world."

[7]The AIDS scare may be reversing these changes.

REFERENCES

BAKER, ROBERT. (1988). Pricks and Chicks: A Plea for Persons. In *Racism and Sexism: An Integrated Study.* P. S. Rothenberg, Ed. Pp. 280–295. New York: St. Martin's Press.

BOLES, JACQUELINE AND ALBENO P. GARBIN. (1974a). The Strip Club and Stripper-Customer Patterns of Interaction. *Sociology and Social Research* 58:136–144.

———. (1974b). The Choice of Stripping for a Living. *Sociology of Work and Occupations* 1:110–123.

———. (1974c). Stripping for a Living: An Occupational Study of the Night Club Stripper. In *Deviant Behavior: Occupational and Organizational Bases.* C. D. Bryant, Ed. Pp. 312–335. Skokie, IL: Rand McNally.

BRACKLEY, JUDITH. (1980). Male Strip Shows: What Women See in Them. *Ms. Magazine* IX (November):68–70, 84.

BRYANT, CLIFTON. (1982). *Sexual Deviancy and Social Proscription: The Social Context of Carnal Behavior.* New York: Human Sciences Press.

CAMPBELL, LORI. (1985). You've Come a Long Way Baby: Three Men Who've Turned the Table on Female Roles. *The Independent Florida Alligator* (February):5.

CAREY, SANDRA H., ROBERT A. PETERSON AND LOUIS K. SHARPE. (1974). A Study of Recruitment and Socialization in Two Deviant Female Occupations. *Sociology Symposium* 11(Spring):11–24.

CHASSLER, SEY. (1988). Listening. In *Racism and Sexism: An Integrated Study.* P. S. Rothenberg, Ed. Pp. 167–175. New York: St. Martin's Press.

Chicago Tribune. (1980). Girls' Night Out: A Bump and Grind. April 20:1–2.

FAUST, BEATRICE. (1980). *Women, Sex and Pornography: A Controversial and Unique Study.* New York: Macmillan.

FRAYSER, SUZANNE G. (1985). *Varieties of Sexual Experience: An Anthropological Perspective on Human Sexuality.* New Haven: HRAF Press.

HENRY, JULES. (1973). *On Sham, Vulnerability and Other Forms of Self-Destruction.* New York: Vintage.

KEMNITZER, DAVID S. (1977). Sexuality as a Social Form: Performance and Anxiety in America. In *Symbolic Anthropology: A Reader in the Study of Symbols and Meanings.* J. L. Dolgin et al., Eds. Pp. 292–309. New York: Columbia University Press.

KESSLER-HARRIS, ALICE. (1985). Selling Sex, Buying Power? *The Women's Review of Books II* (February): 12.

LEO, JOHN. (1987). Romantic Porn in the Boudoir. *Time* (March 30):63–65.

LEWIN, LAURI. (1984). *Naked Is the Best Disguise.* New York: Morrow.

MARGOLIS, MAXINE L. (1984). *Mothers and Such: Views of American Women and Why They Changed.* Berkeley: University of California Press.

McCAGHY, CHARLES H. AND JAMES K. SKIPPER, JR. (1972). Stripping: Anatomy of a Deviant Life Style. In *Life Styles: Diversity in American Society.* S. D. Feldman and G. W. Thielbar, Eds. Pp. 362–373. Boston: Little, Brown.

McWALTER, KEITH. (1987). Couch Dancing. *New York Times Magazine* (December 6):138.

MULVEY, LAURA. (1977). Visual Pleasure and Narrative Cinema. In *Women and the Cinema: A Critical Anthology.* Karyn Kay and Gerald Peary, Eds. Pp. 412–428. New York: Dutton.

New York Times. (1980). Banned in Lawrence. (March 27):A29.

PETERSEN, DAVID M. AND PAULA L. DRESSEL. (1982). Equal Time for Women: Social Notes on the Male Strip Show. *Urban Life* 11(2): 185–208.

SCHULTZ, ANNETTE. (1985). Skin Shows: The Double Standard. *The Independent Florida Alligator,* (September 6):1, 8.

SKIPPER, JAMES K., JR. AND CHARLES H. McCAGHY. (1970). Stripteasers: The Anatomy and Career Contingencies of a Deviant Occupation. *Social Problems* 17:391–404.

SNIDER, BETTY. (1980). Girls Night Out. *Oui* 9:107–110, 112, 128.

Time Magazine. (1979). And Now, Bring on the Boys. (March 6):69.

WEATHERFORD, JACK McIVER. (1986). *Porn Row.* New York: Arbor House.

WHITEHURST, R. V. AND G. V. BOOTH. (1980). *The Sexes: Changing Relationships in a Pluralistic Society.* Agincourt, Ont.: Gage.

V

SEX AND THE NATURE OF FAMILY

INTRODUCTION

Procreation is a primary function of the family in all societies, for without a new generation, a society will cease to exist. Moreover, cultural traditions and environmental exigencies may combine to affect sex and procreation, as well as to affect the very nature of the family.

Kathleen Gough (1971) has defined a family as "a married couple or other group of adult kinsfolk who cooperate economically and in the upbringing of children and all or most of whom share a common dwelling." Clearly a universally applicable definition of marriage cannot depend on a specific social function (such as the legitimization

of children), since for any given function there is always an exception (for example, the Nayars). However, traits such as economic cooperation, the primary responsibility for childrearing, and common residence certainly are widespread.

How the family is structured may vary greatly from one society to another. For example, an individual may live with a single spouse, multiple spouses, or even no spouse. Thus the opportunities for sex and the understanding of what is appropriate with regard to sex may be expected to vary.

Belief systems may also affect sexual practices within the family. Parallel beliefs about procreation frequently coexist within a culture. It is likely that, in all societies, the relationship between sexual intercourse and procreation is recognized. However, folk explanations to account for conception and birth may provide meaning to life and reproduction. This complexity of beliefs can lead to confusion on the part of ethnographers, whose questions about sex and procreation may be answered differently by individual members of a society. Furthermore, there is often a discrepancy between the expression of beliefs and the description of behaviors and actual sexual practices.

This section discusses issues of sexual behaviors and beliefs as they relate to marriage and family. While examining topics such as procreative beliefs, demographic issues, and multiple marriage, these readings also illustrate important relationships between biology and culture, between culture and material exigencies, and between belief and behavior.

Stanley A. and Ruth S. Freed's article explains the seemingly paradoxical fact that poor rural families in India have many children in spite of the high costs and high risks of food shortages. The Freeds show that sons provide parents with social security in their old age, indicating that a high birthrate and a high male to female ratio is adaptive. This material analysis helps to explain the rejection of attempts at population control in India; what's good for the society may not be good for the individual family. The reverse also may be true.

Isaac Schapera describes some notions about procreation and contraception prevalent among the Kgatla peoples of Botswana in the 1930s. For example, the Tswana (Kgatla) believe that a single copulatory act cannot result in pregnancy. Schapera also demonstrates that as knowledge changes and new technologies are introduced (such as condoms), cultural practices may change in the face of resistance—especially by those benefiting from the status quo (for example, the ruling males).

E. Kathleen Gough uses ethnographic data on the Nayars to develop a definition of marriage. Childbirth is central in her definition of marriage. Although her logic seems appropriate given the ethnographic data available in the 1950s, one wonders how she might respond to the increasingly common practice of "marriage" between two men or between two women in Western societies.

Douglas R. White and Michael L. Burton provide an analysis of the causes of polygyny. Polygynous marriage is a wealth-producing strategy among sub-Saharan African peoples. Peoples of the New World exemplify a different type of polygyny. The article demonstrates that what constitutes a family—in terms of the number of wives a man may have simultaneously—is related to structural and environmental variables. Thus, what is thought natural and appropriate in a society may be a result of causal forces affecting societal survival.

REFERENCES

GOUGH, E. KATHLEEN. (1971). The Origin of the Family. *Journal of Marriage and the Family,* pp. 760–770.

SUGGESTED READINGS

BROUDE, GWEN J. (1987). The Relationship of Marital Intimacy and Aloofness to Social Environment: A Hologeistic Study. *Behavior Science Research, 21:*(1-4):50–69.

BROUDE, GWEN J. (1988). Rethinking the Couvade: Cross-Cultural Evidence. *American Anthropologist, 90:*4:902–911.

EMBER, CAROL R. (1978). Men's Fear of Sex with

Women: A Cross-Cultural Study. *Sex Roles, 4*:5: 657–678.

GREGOR, THOMAS. (1973). Privacy and Extramarital Affairs in a Tropical Forest Community. In Daniel R. Gross (Ed.), *Peoples and Cultures of Native South America* (pp. 242–260). Garden City: Doubleday.

HARRELL, BARBARA B. (1981). Lactation and Menstruation in Cross-Cultural Perspective. *American Anthropologist, 83*:796–823.

LEAVITT, STEPHEN C. (1991). Sexual Ideology and Experience in a Papua New Guinea Society: Anthropology Rediscovers Sex. *Social Science and Medicine, 33*:897–907.

SCHAPERA, ISAAC. (1941). *Married Life in an African Tribe.* New York: Sheridan House.

12

"One Son Is No Sons"

*Despite increased acceptance of sterilization and a lowered birthrate,
India's massive population growth remains unchecked*

Stanley A. Freed / Ruth S. Freed

Devi and her five children were sitting in their village home in north India watching "Star Trek" on television. Caught up in the adventure, the children struggled to understand the English words. Their mother, meanwhile, was explaining why she was not interested in the government's program of birth control. Noting that her first four children had been girls, Devi said, "I would have gotten sterilized if I had had sons instead of daughters in the beginning. My six-year-old son is very weak physically, which is why I want to have one more son. Girls get married and leave the village to live with their husbands; they are no longer your own. A son in the family is necessary."

Already endowed with five children and intending to have at least one more, Devi and her husband contribute to making India a demo-

Stanley A. Freed is a curator and Ruth S. Freed is a research assistant in the American Museum's Department of Anthropology. This article is based on the authors' study, "Fertility, Sterilization, and Population Growth in Shanti Nagar, India: A Longitudinal Ethnographic Approach," published in The Anthropological Papers of the American Museum of Natural History, vol. 60, part 3, pp. 229–286, 1985.

Source: From "Population Control: One Son Is No Sons" by S. Freed and R. Freed in *Natural History 94*, 1984, pp. 10–13. With permission from *Natural History*, Vol. 94, No. 1. Copyright the American Museum of Natural History, 1985.

graphic giant second only to China. In 1981, India had 684 million inhabitants, about 15 percent of the globe's population. This figure includes 136 million persons added since the census of 1971, an increment larger than the total population of Brazil, which ranks sixth in the world. The current annual increase of about 15 million is more than double the population of New York City. India's population, now estimated at 735 million, will approach one billion by 2001 and may surpass China's soon after 2025.

Devi and her husband are not illiterate, poverty-stricken villagers, often thought to be at the heart of India's problem of massive population growth. Devi finished five years of school, and her husband is a high school graduate with a well-paying clerical job in Delhi and a sizable farm in a nearby village. The family is quite prosperous. What impels people like Devi and her husband to continue to have large families in an era of largely free, easily available contraception is that sons are the only dependable insurance against misfortune, poverty, and the disabilities of old age. The vast majority of Indians have no social security, private pension plans, or annuities; they rely instead on their sons. Few couples are satisfied with just one son, for the rate of infant mortality, while steadily declining, is still high enough to make parents with only one son very anxious. "One eye is no eyes, and one son is no sons," runs a popular saying. People try to have two or three sons, hoping that one of them will survive to care for them in their old age.

While a great deal of modernization has taken place in India since independence in 1947, the basic economic arrangements, values, and family roles, which tend to support the desire for a large family, have been generally stable. Even though India's birthrate has dropped and the use of contraception has mounted, India's average annual rate of population growth increased slightly from the 1960s to the 1970s—from 2.20 percent to 2.23 percent—because of lowered mortality. It is this stubbornly high rate of population growth—three times the estimated rate for the United States in 1981—that the government of India is

fighting to control. As the late Prime Minister Indira Gandhi was fond of saying, India adds an Australia a year to her population.

In 1951, the year of the first Indian census after independence, the size of the population was of sufficient concern to lead to a national program of family planning, but it was presented in terms of maternal and child health care rather than fertility control. Serious efforts to reduce fertility did not begin until the mid-1960s. The endeavor to check population growth was most intense during the political Emergency legally proclaimed by Prime Minister Gandhi on June 25, 1975, after a period of political unrest and demands that she resign. During the 21-month period of the Emergency, which lasted until March 21, 1977, couples were strongly urged—by publicity, plus a combination of cash payments and various disincentive measures—to undergo sterilization. The governmental slogan "Two or three children, enough!" was widely disseminated. Because the program was often perceived as coercive, the ruling Congress Party suffered a temporary electoral defeat. Despite the popular reaction against the excesses of the Emergency, however, the government of India did succeed, much faster than might otherwise have happened, in establishing sterilization as a routine and acceptable option for couples wishing to terminate childbearing.

Today sterilization is the principal contraceptive technique used in India. Because it permanently ends childbearing, parents do not use it until they have all the children they want or think they will need. The present government, concerned with fertility control, extols and publicizes the small family of two or three children. Indian parents think in terms of two sons and one daughter as the ideal "small" family, but in trying for at least two sons they end up with an average of about 4.2 children. In general, the minority of Indian parents who choose to be sterilized do so about two children too late from the government's point of view, and the large majority shun sterilization altogether, wanting to be very sure that they will never be left without at least one son. "To be sterilized is to tempt fate" summarizes a common attitude.

The government would like to achieve a family norm of two children by the turn of the century, at which point India's population would begin to stabilize, reaching a plateau of 1.2 billion by the middle of the twenty-first century. Is this goal realistic? The answer must be sought chiefly in India's villages, where 76 percent of the population lives. At various times during the 25-year period from 1958 to 1983, we have had the opportunity to investigate population growth in a north Indian village we call Shanti Nagar (the name is fictitious). The study is of particular interest because it encompasses the demographic watershed between the time that family planning barely existed and the period when fertility control became a serious governmental concern and sterilization was established as the major contraceptive technique. Although one should be cautious about drawing conclusions from a single village, the study of a small community such as Shanti Nagar provides an appreciation of the motives and attitudes that underlie people's everyday decisions about childbearing, family size, and sterilization.

Shanti Nagar is typical of the region that includes the northern states of Punjab, Haryana, western Uttar Pradesh, and the Union Territory of Delhi. From the 1950s to the 1980s, Shanti Nagar has undergone an economic revolution. The village has acquired electricity, brick houses have replaced mud houses, and streets have been paved. In agriculture, bullock power and hand labor have largely given way to machinery. Paved roads and increased bus service make it easier to commute to urban areas, where many men have jobs. Radios are now commonplace, there are some TV sets, and newspapers are delivered daily. The educational level has risen dramatically for both men and women. The village has become more prosperous and better informed about government programs.

Although one would expect that the modernization of education, communications, and the economy would significantly alter family life, the village family has generally maintained its traditional form and functions. A single Indian family may include more people than just a couple and their children: often a family is composed of a couple, their married son (or sons), and his wife and children. Sometimes two or more married brothers live as members of the same family, the eldest brother acting as family head. Families are relatively large by American standards, consisting on average of more than seven members. Men are young when they marry, and women are very young, often beginning their married lives shortly after first menstruation. Men continue to live at their parental home after marriage and bring their brides to live with them. Women are expected to begin childbearing as soon as possible, for both the economic and political strength of a family and a woman's own status depend on the number of sons. "Marriage is not for pleasure," say the villagers. "It is the duty of a wife to have children."

Because attitudes in the 1950s were so strongly in favor of having a goodly number of children, we would have given family planning and, particularly, sterilization little chance of making significant headway. Therefore, when we returned to Shanti Nagar in 1978 after an absence of twenty years, we were startled to hear so many people discussing their own sterilizations or those of their neighbors. We eventually found that there were 68 sterilizations involving both males and females, tantamount to 26 percent of the women of childbearing age (15 to 45 years) at the time. By late 1983, there were 93 sterilized individuals.

Sterilization has run an uneven course in Shanti Nagar. It was accepted slowly at first. From 1968 to 1974, 3.4 individuals on the average were sterilized annually. Then came the twenty-one months of the Emergency, which began in 1975, and the average number of persons who underwent sterilization jumped to about 20 per year. After the Emergency, the figure returned almost to the pre-Emergency norm: from 1977 to late 1983, 4.7 persons were sterilized per year. The big jump in sterilizations during the Emergency was due to the strong campaign mounted by the government. Governmental pressure was especially effective with men holding government jobs. Most of the men sterilized during the Emergency were in government service.

When the Emergency ended, there was a noteworthy change in the proportion of men to women undergoing sterilization. Prior to 1977, 53 percent of the operations were performed on men; for the period from 1977 to late 1983, this figure had fallen to 15 percent. The shift is probably related to the introduction of the surgical technique of laparoscopy, which has made female sterilization easier. The government also suggested a somewhat higher payment to women undergoing sterilization, compared with the incentive to men. Moreover, villagers may not have been entirely convinced that a vasectomy was foolproof. If a vasectomy is done improperly, a pregnancy can follow, exposing the unfortunate woman to suspicion of adultery and to village gossip and scorn. Why take that chance when a tubectomy will avoid the problem?

Most of those in Shanti Nagar who discussed reasons for not being sterilized or for postponing the operation cited an insufficient number of sons. On the other hand, the expense of raising children was overwhelmingly the main reason that villagers gave for undergoing sterilization. Couples also frequently cited the governmental sterilization campaign, principally its coercive aspects, as a motive for being sterilized, and a few people mentioned that sterilization was seen as the solution to specific health problems of women.

The emphasis on economic reasons focuses attention on the changing value of child labor. In rural India, where children participate on the family farm from an early age, the value of their labor remains considerable. However, the modernization of agriculture has reduced the need for child labor. At the same time, there has been an increase in employment opportunities that require an educational qualification. Many parents

aspire to better jobs for their children and prefer fewer, more educated children to more numerous, uneducated offspring. Few can afford to educate all the children that they can possibly have.

The findings from Shanti Nagar suggest that a significant drop in the growth rate of the population cannot be expected in the near term. The parents in Shanti Nagar who chose sterilization did so generally after having four or five living children, and it must be borne in mind that most couples have not been sterilized. Overall, completed families in the 1970s were larger than those of the 1950s (averaging 5.2 versus 5.0 living children). Even the women who were sterilized (or whose husbands were sterilized) in 1978 had almost as many living children (an average of 4.9) as had the women with completed families in 1958, almost all of whom used no contraception.

On the other hand, persons who anticipate at least a slight downturn in the rate of population growth can find some grounds for optimism in the statistics from Shanti Nagar. In 1978, sterilized mothers had fewer living children than nonsterilized mothers who had completed their childbearing (4.9 versus 5.5 on the average). Moreover, the effect of sterilization is becoming more pronounced: from the end of the Emergency in 1977 until late in 1983, couples underwent sterilization at a younger age and had fewer children than before 1977. But they still averaged 4.3 living children, enough to produce a rather high rate of population growth.

Sterilized couples had, on the average, about three sons and two daughters, an imbalance that appears to be increasing. From 1977 to 1983, sterilized couples averaged twice as many sons as daughters. This sexual disparity is no accident: couples aim for between two and three sons before undergoing sterilization, but almost no one desperately wants more than one daughter. It is important to note that sterilization by itself cannot influence the sex of children. However, if either by random chance or active intervention a couple has more sons than daughters, a sterilization operation makes the situation permanent, provided that there are no untimely deaths of sons. As is common in northern India, Shanti Nagar has slightly more males than females, a difference usually explained by the preference for sons and the suspected mistreatment of female children. It is also possible that female infants are undernumerated in censuses. One explanation does not preclude the other and both may be involved.

From an American and Western European perspective, one might assume that population control could be achieved in India by instituting a system of social security, such as is found in the United States, to reduce the need for so many sons and make the two-child family possible for many couples. In developed countries, much of the economic support and care of the aged comes from outside the family; children may assume minor financial and custodial roles or none at all. This feature of Western society is not of recent origin: it appeared in England, for example, several centuries before the Industrial Revolution, the source of sustenance shifting through the centuries from the manor and the guild to the parish and to the state. But India is a different world, where the care and support of the aged have always been a family affair. Indians do not believe that the government or anyone but their sons will take care of them when they are old. Their experience is that governments and policies change too frequently to be trustworthy in the long term. A family with fewer than two sons makes no sense to most Indians. This attitude would persist even if the resources to institute a system of social security could be found.

Many Western analysts also assume that economic development to improve the standard of living will solve the problem of population growth in India. However, there is no evidence from Shanti Nagar or elsewhere in India that motivation to limit family size to two or three children develops after a certain economic status has been attained. Even the effect of the education of women—perhaps the most promising of the socioeconomic factors thought to lower fertility—is somewhat ambiguous in India and, in any case, has little impact until women achieve the college level and begin to work outside the home. In all probability, it will be a long time before a significant proportion of rural Indian females are sent to college.

Although sterilization is increasing in India and the birthrate has been declining for some time, these developments do not presage an imminent solution to the problem of India's population growth. For our part, we would be inclined to keep a sharp eye on the average size of completed families, for this statistic will provide greater insight into India's demographic future than the drop of a few points in the birthrate. If parity at completed childbearing shows signs of stabilizing at between four and five children, India will continue to live up to its reputation as a demographic juggernaut. In that case, India's currently voluntary program of family planning might have to be replaced by more Draconian measures, like those instituted in China. The Indian government fell from power when it previously tried to introduce a stringent program of fertility control. The challenge is to try to control population growth in a democracy where families of four or more children are, for very good reasons, considered necessary.

13

SOME KGATLA THEORIES OF PROCREATION

I. SCHAPERA

The material presented below was obtained in the course of fieldwork carried on intermittently during the years 1929–35 among the Kgatla (Bakgatla-bagaKgafela) of Botswana. As I do not know if all or even some of the beliefs recorded then are still current among the people, I have used the past tense throughout, to indicate that what is said here relates to a period of more than forty years ago.

Much of this material has already been summarized in previous publications (notably Schapera 1933 and 1940), but the present paper gives considerably more detail and also includes

some new information. By its very nature such material could only be obtained by talking to people, and not by 'participant observation' or similar techniques. The reader is therefore entitled to ask how many informants were used, who they were, and what each of them said. In the following list, which answers the first two questions, principal informants are identified by means of asterisks after their names. The others contributed isolated or scrappy details only, generally mentioned casually while we were discussing some other topic. The names of males are printed in small capitals, those of females in

SOURCE: From "Some Kgatla Theories of Procreation" by I. Schapera in *Social Systems and Traditions in South Africa* by J. Argyle and E. Preston-Whyte (Eds.). Copyright © 1978 by Oxford University Press, Capetown. Reprinted by permission.

lower case. All quotations are free translations of the original Kgatla version. Where relevant I have also added the date of the interview.

Dingaka ('doctors'): MAGOLENG LEFI, NATALE MOREMA*, RAKGOMO SEGALE, RAPEDI LETSEBE*, SEBAITSENG MODISE, SEPHARE SEPHARE. (RAKGOMO was elderly, the others all middle-aged.)

Elderly persons: Mmampotele Modikwe*, Mmasenwelo Tladi, MORUE MODIBEDI*.

Middle-aged: (Ex-chief) ISANG PILANE, Mathee Ramatlai*, Mmapoonyane Ramodisa, Mmatsholofelo Ratsatsi, Mosalakwe Tshwene.

Young: (married) Manyama Mosaate*, Ntebeng Molefe*; (unmarried) LESAANE MAKGOTSO*, MAGANELO PILANE, Marutshwi Mpane, MOLEFE SEGOGWANE*, Motlhodi Kedisang, Seanokeng Motoma, SEIKANELO LEBOTSE, SOFONIA POONYANE*, Tsholofelo Ratsatsi*.

The list, it may be claimed, is reasonably representative of both sexes and various age-groups. But I cannot maintain that what my informants said is necessarily valid for the Kgatla as a whole (except perhaps when their statements were confirmed independently by others). For this reason I have entitled the paper 'Some Kgatla Theories . . . ' and not simply 'Kgatla Theories . . . '.

CAUSES OF CONCEPTION

Kgatla theories of conception were summarized as follows (11.2.1930) by MOLEFE SEGOGWANE, an unmarried youth (age-set Chama created in 1928), who had been to school abroad:

> Children are told by the women that an old woman goes to a pool and from its side gets some fine stones (so that the child may be fine), which she throws into the water. She has a wooden spoon, with which she stirs the water near her. While doing so she sings: *Noga leledu, noga leledu, tswa metseng, tswa metseng, regobone,* 'Bearded snake, bearded snake, come from the water, come from the water, that we may see you.' Then, they say, a snake will bring out a child to her. She takes the child up to a cave in the hills and leaves it lying there, wrapped in

blankets. Then she comes at night to fetch it, and brings it to its mother.

Adults believe that children are produced by copulation, from a mixture of the man's semen (*marere*) with the blood inside the woman's womb (menstrual blood, *mosese*). The semen goes into the womb (*tsala*) and rests there until, after the fourth time or so of intercourse, it is sufficient in quantity. Then a mixture takes place. This mixture is not formed at the first co-ition, but after several; and when it has occurred, the woman ceases to menstruate. . . . She dates her pregnancy from the cessation of her menses, and starts counting the new moons; and when eight months have passed, she knows that she will bear her child in the ninth.

The first part of this statement was confirmed independently by two other unmarried members of the Chama age-set:

> (SOFONIA, 25.6.1931): When small children ask where a baby comes from, they are told that it comes from a well. They often ask each other, 'When is mother going to take a baby from the well,' and also, 'From which well did your mother take it?' Then the bigger children tell them, 'No, a baby comes from its mother's stomach.'
>
> (LESAANE, 25.12.1933): When children ask where a baby comes from, they are told that it comes from deep waters. You will hear one child say to another, 'My mother says that my little brother came from the well.'

All adult informants agreed that conception resulted from the passage of semen into the womb; this belief was in fact reflected in various contraceptive practices (see p. 179). As shown by the following simple statements (others are quoted later), they generally also agreed that children are formed by a mixture of semen and menstrual blood, i.e. of the man's 'blood' (see p. 173) and the woman's:

> 'A man sleeps with his wife in order to make a child, and if their bloods agree the woman will become pregnant and stop menstruating' (LESAANE);
>
> 'When a boy and a girl copulate their bloods coalesce into a big lump (*letlhole*), and this will grow until it becomes a child' (Tsholofelo).

According to some informants a single act of coitus was enough to cause pregnancy, 'if there is nothing wrong with husband and wife' (NA-TALE) or 'if their bloods agree' (LESAANE, Tsholofelo). But most of them said, like SEGOGWANE, that repeated coition was necessary, say 'for at least three successive nights' (SOFONIA) or 'for three or four nights running' (RAPEDI), in order that enough semen could accumulate in the womb. This particular belief was expressed as follows by two unmarried young women:

(Motlhodi, 5.3.1934): When I slept with a boy for the first time, . . . before he put in his 'thing' (*selo sagagwe*) I was afraid and said, 'Won't you make me pregnant?' He replied, 'No; a person impregnates someone (*motho akgorisa motho*) only after sleeping with her three or five times (*gararo kampo gatlhano*).'

(Marutshwi, 15.9.1934): I believe that the first discharge [ejaculation] can never make one pregnant, even if the boy's blood is very 'sharp.' But if he sleeps with you three nights in succession, then he has filled your womb and you will become pregnant.

Kgatla apparently did not have one specific name for semen. Because it comes out through the urethra it was sometimes called by the same terms as urine (*moroto, motlhapo*), and because of its texture it was sometimes called 'mucus, slime' (*marere, marerenyana, maregerege)*. Other names, each mentioned by single though different informants, were *mothunyo* (discharge, lit. shot); *bothata* (strength); *bonna* (manhood); and *letshekgetshekge* ('slimy stuff'). Many people also referred to it as *madi*, 'blood.' This does not mean that they identified it with ordinary blood. Manyama said the name was used 'just to distinguish it from urine'; Motlhodi referred to it more precisely as *madi amasweu* 'white blood'; MORUE similarly distinguished it as *madi amagola,* 'the blood of growth', i.e. the blood that forms a person; RAPEDI spoke of it in one context as 'porridge' (*bogobe*) stored in the womb after coition; and Mmampotele said that a child's flesh was made by its father 'because of the heavy lumps he puts into his wife.'

The only information given to me about its source is contained in the following statements: 'Semen (*moroto*) is blood (*madi*) that comes from the veins all over the body and takes a line going straight to the penis' (SOFONIA); 'It is prepared by the testicles and stored in the scrotal sac, but I don't know how' (LESAANE); 'It comes from the waist and hips' (Manyama). SOFONIA said also that during coition 'the girl's blood goes into your body to call your blood; then if you don't drop it out [by coitus interruptus] it all goes into the girl's body to make a child.' The belief that the woman's blood enters the man's body and 'calls' his blood was confirmed by several other informants (e.g. RAPEDI, Mmapoonyane, and LESAANE).

People were usually definite about the role of menstrual blood in conception. They said, firstly, that a woman stops menstruating on becoming pregnant, and in fact realizes or suspects her condition because of that. Thus, according to Manyama (25.8.1934):

A woman knows she is pregnant when she misses her period. If she ordinarily misses a period, it may be just because she is sick and her blood is no good; but then she will get well again. But if she has recently met a man, then she knows she is pregnant, because she used to get her periods regularly.

Similar statements were made by others, including for instance SEGOGWANE, SOFONIA, RAPEDI, SEPHARE, and the two quoted in the following paragraph (LESAANE and Tsholofelo).

Secondly, as SEGOGWANE said (see p. 172), it was believed also that menstruation stops after conception because the woman's blood helps to make the child. The following are other statements to the same effect:

(LESAANE, 13.1.1934): When a child is born we know that its father and mother both contribute to its physique. Its flesh comes from the father, and its blood from the mother. We say that the woman forms the blood because before she conceives she menstruates regularly, and that is nothing but blood; but after she is pregnant her menses stop and the child starts to be formed. It is therefore obvious that she sacrifices her blood for the child.

(Tsholofelo, 22.1.1934): When a girl sleeps with a boy, nothing comes out of her [similar to ejaculated semen]. This is because the blood she normally sheds while menstruating is that which forms the child when it meets the blood of the boy.

Menstrual blood was usually spoken of by the same term as ordinary blood, viz. *madi.* 'There is no difference between the two, they are just the same, for they come from one body' (Manyama). It was occasionally also termed *motlhapo* (flux, urine) or *moroto* (urine). All three terms, as we have seen, were likewise used for semen. (The last two are derived respectively from *-tlhapa,* wash, and *-rota,* urinate.) Menstruation itself was sometimes referred to as *gotlhapa metse,* lit. 'to wash water'; *gobona mosese,* 'to see the skirt'; or simply *mosese,* 'skirt.' But the most common terms were *bolwetse bakgwedi,* 'sickness of the moon' (or 'monthly sickness'), and *gobona kgwedi,* 'to see the moon'; and when a woman had her periods people often said of her, *oile kgweding,* 'she has gone to the moon.'

As this indicates, menstruation was known to have a lunar cycle. The following is the only explanation given to me: The blood passes into the womb *momaleng,* 'from the intestines' (Manyama) or *moditshekeng,* 'from the veins' (Seanokeng), and accumulates there every month to form a clot (*lehuto,* knot), which then breaks up and flows away (except after conception and recent childbirth). 'People say that a woman is full of blood and if she does not menstruate regularly she will probably die; her blood must therefore be diminished so that she can live' (SEGOGWANE). This particular statement lacks confirmation. The term *lehuto,* incidentally, was sometimes also used for menstrual blood 'while it is still in the womb.'

The relationship between childbirth and menstruation was reflected in several additional beliefs. Informants said that a woman cannot bear children unless she menstruates, and barrenness in young or middle-aged women was sometimes held to be due to menstrual irregularities (see p. 176). They said also that women past the menopause can no longer have children. For instance:

(SOFONIA, 16.4.1931): If a woman does not menstruate she won't bear children. They say it

prepares the womb. But if she is an old woman who no longer menstruates, they say of her *ofeletswe keletsalo,* 'she has finished with child-bearing.'

(Manyama, 11.6.1931): Menstruation is due to God, so that you can get a child. If you don't menstruate you can't have a child. If you have been bearing children and then afterwards you don't menstruate any more, you know that you have finished with children, you won't bear any more.

(LESAANE, 15.1.1934): When women get old they stop menstruating. This shows they will no longer bear children. We don't know why it happens. It is just according to the will of God.

(Mmampotele, 30.1.1934): There are some women who have never menstruated since they were born. We call such a woman *mosadi sekamonna,* 'a man-like woman.' She will never bear a child; she is no good.

It was likewise held that a girl cannot conceive until she has started to menstruate. This explains the tolerance shown by some adults for the sexual play of children, which often included attempts at copulation.

(LESAANE, 20.12.1933): Love among children is treated very lightly, and so is *thobalo* (sexual intercourse, lit. 'sleeping, sleep') . . . Because they are still young, adults say nothing, even though aware of what is going on. There will be no consequence, because the children are still immature. Their genitals are still *kwasefalaneng* ('in the granary'); the girl has not yet menstruated, nor does the boy have any semen.

(Tsholofelo, 22.8.1934): Even if children copulate like adults nothing can go wrong, for at this time the girls are still called *basimane* (boys), because they do not yet menstruate. So it doesn't matter how they sleep, there can be no trouble.

(Manyama, 25.8.1934): A girl can't have children before she menstruates. That is the work of God. Until then she can sleep with boys as often as she likes, but it makes no difference.

But when a girl's breasts began to swell, and especially when she menstruated for the first time, she was generally warned about the dangers of sexual intercourse:

(SOFONIA, 18.1.1934): As girls grow, their mothers say to them, 'The day you menstruate you must know that you can now conceive; before this you can't.'

(Tsholofelo, 19.1.1934): We know that when a girl's breasts grow big she will soon menstruate.

Now she must be careful of boys; she is a complete woman, for if she sleeps with a boy she can conceive.

(Mosalakwe, 24.8.1934): As soon as girls get their periods they must no longer sleep with boys. This is a proper *moila* (taboo). Older girls warn them that as soon as they get that flow they must not again meet boys: 'If you dare to sleep with them you will become pregnant, and then get into trouble.'

There were apparently no similarly distinctive criteria by which people knew when a boy was old enough to beget. The following are the only statements I have about this:

(Manyama, 25.8.1934): Small boys can't make children. They can ejaculate, but very little. Small boys don't have semen, they get it as they grow older.

(SOFONIA, 6.9.1934): Boys at cattleposts sometimes play about in each other's presence with their penises. They roll back their foreskins, and in some cases they find white stuff round the glans. They say that shows *bonna* (manhood), and each comments about the other's. They know that when they have this they can *kgorisa* (impregnate), but not before. If one hasn't got it his mates laugh at him and call him *mosimanyana* (little boy).

(MORUE, 11.9.1934): We don't see by any signs that a boy is capable of begetting, except when he has grown big. We just guess that he is big enough to make a child. It is not as with girls, whom we see menstruate. When a boy is still small he can't make a child, perhaps because he has not got enough *madi* (blood, viz. semen).

It was recognized also that old men could sometimes no longer 'make' children. It was even usual for such a man to let a younger relative or friend have access to his wife in order to 'raise seed' for him. But I received no special explanation for this loss of potency, apart from what informants said about impotence in general (see p. 178).

BARRENNESS

Kgatla theories of procreation were further reflected in various beliefs and practices relating to barrenness (*boopa*). All married people were said to want children, and a wife was expected to bear as many as she could, provided only that she did not become pregnant while still suckling an infant. A young bride when taken to her husband's home on the first afternoon of the wedding ceremonies was given a young baby to hold as she entered his hut. This rite, performed 'so that she too must get a child' (SOFONIA), symbolized the hopes now centred on her. It was her husband's duty to sleep with her regularly, and if he stayed away too long from her, for instance at work abroad, public opinion did not usually condemn her for taking a lover by whom she could continue to bear.

A woman with many children was highly honoured. If she had none at all she was an object of pity, often tempered with scorn; her husband's relatives, in particular, would sometimes reproach her openly and treat her unkindly. In the old days there was apparently even a special mode of burying such a woman when she died: 'they used to bind her right arm on her back, as if it was her child' (SOFONIA); 'she was buried with her hands at her back' (Mmatsholofelo).

The term for a barren person, *moopa*, was not applied to anybody either too young to have children or too old to have any more. It was normally restricted to those, whether men or women, who after several years of marriage had not yet produced any at all. Such people were not very numerous. Genealogical data I collected in 1931–2 showed that, of 462 married women then alive, 47 (10 per cent) were barren at the time of investigation. But these included many who, judged solely by their ages, could possibly still conceive. Of the 184 women past the menopause, only seven (4 per cent) had never been mothers.

If after a year or two of marriage a woman had not yet become pregnant, her husband usually called in a 'doctor' (*ngaka,* professional magician) who knew how to deal with such cases. The doctor ascertained the cause of the trouble by divination. Occasionally he found nothing wrong with either husband or wife except that 'their bloods do not agree.' He would then perform the rite of *gokopanya madi,* 'uniting the bloods': he cut each on the mons pubis and then, with his finger, transferred blood from the woman's wounds on to the man's, and vice versa. 'When the cuts heal, the couple sleep together, and they will have a child later on' (Mathee). But apparently not always: 'sometimes he cannot manage to make their bloods like each other, and so they will remain without children' (Tsholofelo).

Most commonly, however, the divination indicated that the fault lay with the wife. The causes usually mentioned were summarized as follows by Ntebeng (29.12.1933):

> If a woman does not bear children, it may be that while still unmarried she had many lovers; the bloods of all these men coming into her disagree (*gaadumellane*), and so her womb becomes spoiled (*tsala yagagwe easenyega*). Or she may have spoiled it herself, if she became pregnant, by drinking medicines *gontsha mpa* (to take out her belly, i.e. to induce an abortion).
>
> Her barrenness is sometimes due to the fact that her womb is withered (*eswabile*): it is narrow and its mouth is small, so that it does not open wide [to receive the semen]. Or on the other hand it does not close after she has slept with a man, but remains wide open; it is then said to have been worn smooth (*gatwe gogotlhilwe*), so that the semen all flows out of it, and this prevents her from conceiving.
>
> Sometimes she may have been bewitched by an enemy who got hold of the rags she wears [as pads] when menstruating.
>
> Her husband calls a doctor, who will say what is wrong. He gives them medicines and then, if God wills, she will get a child.

As this summary indicates, a woman's barrenness could be attributed to purely biological factors. She might never have menstruated at all (SOFONIA, Manyama, Mmapoonyane) or 'her blood may have gone bad' so that she menstruated excessively (MAGOLENG). Or, as mentioned by Ntebeng, something might be wrong with her womb. This was confirmed by other informants. For instance, Chief ISANG said (31.12.1933):

> It is believed that there is in the womb a sort of snake (*noga*), which either bites or spits out the blood of the man and prevents it from com-

ing inside. They speak of it as being there only when the woman is barren. The doctor then says he will have to kill it by medicine.

Sometimes the semen is rejected when the womb is 'sick' inside: it may be twisted, so that the semen is blocked from passing into the interior and is thrown back again; or it may have pimples or sores, which make the woman unable to hold the man's semen.

Mathee, whom I questioned on the point (12. 1.1934), did not know of the belief about the 'snake'; and NATALE, himself a doctor, said in this connexion (22.1.1934), 'There is nothing like a snake in the womb; "snake" is only a nickname given to it because it spits out the man's blood.'

There was widespread agreement that this rejection of semen by the womb was perhaps the most common cause of barrenness in women. The phenomenon was termed *pusa*, repulsion (from *-busa,* send back, cause to return). It was variously described as follows:

> (MAGANELO, 22.8.1932): *Pusa* is when a girl can't hold a boy's semen, it flows out of her. That is why some women cannot bear children.
>
> (LESAANE, 28.12.1933): Semen changes into 'blood' when it gets into a girl's womb. If it does not mix properly with hers she won't get a child; she will excrete the semen, her womb cannot hold it.
>
> (Mathee, 12.1.1934): *Pusa* means that when a man sleeps with his wife his semen flows out again after it has entered.
>
> (Ntebeng, 13.1.1934): *Pusa* is a sickness inside a woman. They say this when a man meets a woman and leaves his blood in her, and she sends it back again; her womb stops the blood and throws it out.

Pusa was said to be due sometimes to anatomical abnormality, either innate (as suggested above) or produced by means of sorcery. The most usual explanation, however, was that it resulted from premarital promiscuity. Some people stated merely that if the girl had many lovers her womb became spoiled, because the different 'bloods' ejaculated into it 'disagreed' with one another. Others added that, in consequence, she was unable to retain the 'bloods' and kept on expelling them.

Another alleged cause of barrenness was induced abortion. Most of the medicines used for this purpose (cf. Schapera 1940:223–4) did nothing more than 'spoil the woman's blood' for the time being, i.e. they did not prevent her from conceiving again. But some were said to cause permanent sterility: 'they polish (-*dila*) the womb, so that everything is smooth on top and the semen flows off' (Mmampotele). The woman could also become and remain barren if she secretly buried the foetus in open ground:

(Mathee, 12.1.1934): There are many girls here who do not bear children after marriage. They are barren because when they were still young they led a loose life. Then they became pregnant, and through fear of the consequences (wrath of their parents, expulsion from church membership, and mockery of other girls), they worked on their stomach for several days until the foetus (*madi,* blood) came out. The girl then wrapped up the 'blood' in an old underskirt, dug a hole, and buried it there, without telling her parents. This is called *goiphitlhela* (to hide oneself). After this she can no longer bear a child, no matter for with whom she sleeps. It is just like anthrax (*lebete*) in cattle: when a cow dies of anthrax, its spleen (*lebete*) is buried in a hole made in the ground, and then the disease will not attack the cattle again.

It should be added here that abortions, miscarriages and stillbirths all had to be buried in a particular way inside a hut, otherwise the mother 'will bear no more children'; they also had to be buried by women past the menopause, and not by one of child-bearing age, or 'she will stop having children' (Mathee, Mmasenwelo).

Kgatla believed also that a woman could be made barren by the actions of other people. This, informants said, usually took the form of sorcery (*boloi*). To achieve this aim the sorcerer (*moloi*) had to get hold of and 'doctor' something associated with the woman, such as her menstrual pads, the afterbirth of a child she had just borne, or the 'blood' that came from her if she miscarried. He could thus stop her from having any more children, or, if she was newly married, from having any at all. In an inheritance dispute heard in the chief's court in October 1935 (*Andrea Tlhowe* v. *Gaenaope*), a young widow asserted that she was barren because, soon after she was married, her father-in-law had stolen and doctored her husband's belt.

Sorcery sometimes caused the woman to menstruate excessively, 'so that her blood does not coalesce with the man's, but keeps on breaking up and coming out' (NATALE). It could also 'turn her womb upside down' (-*ribega tsala*), and so prevent the semen from getting in (SOFONIA, Manyama). Another possible effect was described as follows by Mmampotele (30.1.1934):

When a girl menstruates one month but not the next, and then again, we call this *gokgora seome* (to eat a little food and satisfy one's appetite, but to become hungry again soon afterwards). Such a girl has been bewitched by means of the little animal *senanatswii* [a small variety of frog]. If she gets married, she will give birth to only one child, and then stop altogether. They will try to *remela* her [doctor her for barrenness], but she will not get healed.

As mentioned above, some forms of barrenness were considered incurable. This applied chiefly, but not only, to those caused by sorcery. Most other forms, it was said, could be cured. The treatment was known technically as -*remela* (from -*rema,* to cut or chop, e.g. branches of a tree). The name, MAGANELO explained, 'does not mean that branches are cut for an enclosure in which husband and wife must live alone; it means that they must isolate themselves from bad ways and take care of each other, i.e. they must abstain from adultery until they bear a child.' The sexual taboo was confirmed by MAGOLENG, who said that if the husband violated it 'the wife's blood will break and she will be unable to conceive.' A child born as a result of the treatment was termed *ngwana wameremelo* (from -*remela*). 'People say it is more delicate than others' (MORUE).

Of six doctors questioned at various times (RAKGOMO, MAGOLENG, RAPEDI, SEPHARE, SEBAITSENG, and NATALE), only the first-named denied knowing how to deal with cases of barrenness.

The others all said that their treatment consisted mainly in giving the woman medicines—'to clean out her womb, which has been dirtied by a man with bad blood' (RAPEDI); 'to clean out her stomach' (SEPHARE); 'to dry her womb, so that the blood should not keep running out,' i.e. to inhibit her menses (NATALE). Three (MAGOLENG, SEPHARE and NATALE) stated that the same medicines, or some of them, also had to be taken by the husband.

The medicines used invariably included portions, mostly roots, of one or more plants. Judging from the names given, some of which were esoteric, no two doctors relied on the same plants, SEBAITSENG, for instance, made his medicine from roots of *pelobotlhoko* (*Geigeria passerinoides*), whereas SEPHARE used roots of *mothata* (*Pappea capensis*) and *monokana* (*Heeria* sp) and leaves of *mosimama* (*Senecio laxiflorus*). Usually the medicine (sometimes whole, sometimes in powdered form) was either boiled or steeped in water. This the patient had to drink, once or twice daily, for periods ranging from 'three or four days' (MAGOLENG, NATALE) to 'a month' (SEPHARE) or 'until no longer needed' (RAPEDI). Some doctors (MAGOLENG, SEBAITSENG and NATALE) supplemented it with another medicine that was added to sorghum porridge, the staple food.

An additional ingredient of the medicines used by both SEBAITSENG and NATALE was the womb of a female goat that had borne one or more kids. It may be noted in this context that according to Chief ISANG (31.12.1933) some doctors also used a goat for diagnosing the cause of a woman's barrenness. They gave the goat medicines to drink, and made it lie next to her 'for half an hour or so.' Then they killed it, skinned it carefully, cut it open, and inspected the womb. From this they could tell what was wrong with the woman's womb, for instance if it was 'twisted' or had 'pimples or sores.' They knew accordingly what treatment to use. ISANG said he had seen this method successfully employed by a doctor named SEGAI.

The treatment sometimes included other features. Medicines burned in a potsherd, next to

which the woman had to sit, wrapped in blankets, 'so that she can -*aramela* (inhale) the smoke and have it round her body' (MAGOLENG, SEBAITSENG). Or the doctor might rub powdered medicine into small cuts he made 'on her belly, near the navel' (SEBAITSENG) or 'on the back, between the shoulder blades' (SEPHARE). NATALE used a homeopathic rite: he told the woman that after boiling the roots and removing them from the water she must bury the sodden mass in a hole dug in an antheap; then, while she continued drinking the water daily, 'the roots will start to swell, and so also will the womb.'

NATALE's treatment for *pusa* (see p. 176) seems worth recording more fully because of its ingenuity. Here is a paraphrase of his description (22.1.1934):

> He gave the woman a powder made from the roots of the bush *ntswelebogale*. She mixed some of it daily with a little porridge, which she and her husband had to eat early in the morning 'for about two weeks.' He also gave her a thick 'cork' (*sethiba*), whose main ingredient was 'the womb of a she-goat that has had kids once or twice.' Bits of the womb were roasted and powdered and, together with some *ntswelebogale* powder, were mixed with the goat's fat and moulded into shape. The woman had to insert this 'cork' into her vagina immediately after coition, as soon as her husband withdrew his penis. Its function was 'to prevent his blood from flowing out; the blood touches the cork, which makes it run back into her womb.' She kept it in position all night through, though if her husband wanted to 'use' her again that night she took it out immediately before coition and replaced it immediately afterwards. In the morning she took it out, wrapped it in a cloth, and 'hides it somewhere in the hut,' ready to use again when needed. She continued using it like this 'until she knows that she is pregnant.'

It was less common, though by no means unknown, for a childless marriage to be attributed to a husband's impotence. The cause usually mentioned was the 'spoiling' of his blood through coition with a ritually-impure woman, especially a widow. He could then perhaps be cured by one of the treatments used in cases of infection by 'hot blood' (cf. Schapera 1940:194–6). An unfaithful husband could also be made impotent by the sorcery of his jealous wife. A third possible cause, mentioned only by LESAANE, was organic disease. He instanced a man named Bopapi, of Odi village, who suffered from *nkwana,* 'a sickness which ate out the innerparts of his nose, so that it became flat and he could not speak or breathe properly. This affected his main system: he would copulate, but he could not have an orgasm.'

Kgatla further believed that impotence is sometimes innate. It was then held to be incurable.

(Mathee, 12.1.1934): A man is sometimes born impotent (*moopa*). This can be noticed when he is still a small boy. Whenever he urinates his little penis does not rise (*ntsutswanyane yagagwe eseke etsoge*). So they say he has been fashioned like that by God, who did not give him strength (*obopilwe keModimo, mme osamha thata*), and when he sleeps with a woman he does not get an erection. When a man is like this, doctoring is of no use. He cannot be cured.

(LESAANE, 13.1.1934): When a boy is still young it is easily seen that he won't be able to beget children. By the law of nature his penis should be stiff when he urinates, and relax again afterwards. But if it dangles loosely when he urinates, then we know he won't be potent. Or if he does not get an erection when he sees girls, then we also know that he hasn't got any strength.

METHODS OF CONTRACEPTION

The interval between one birth and another was usually longer than is physically possible. An important reason was the rule that a woman should not become pregnant again before having weaned a sucking child. This she seldom did until it was able to walk steadily at the age of about two or three years. Should she conceive sooner, it was said, the child at her breast would suffer.

Since at the time of my fieldwork few Kgatla yet reckoned their ages in terms of calendar years, I could not get much quantitative information about the spacing of births. The only fairly reliable data I have are for 26 families,

each of three or more children whose dates of birth were recorded in the church baptism registers (1880–1935). According to this source, the intervals (in years) between successive births were numerically distributed as follows:

TABLE 13-1

Years	Births	Percentages
1	5	4,3
2	50	43,5
3	38	33,0
4	15	13,0
5	6	5,2
6	1	0,9
	115	99,9

The figures, because of their source, do not include records of miscarriages and stillbirths. They are therefore not a complete guide to the spacing of pregnancies. Nevertheless it seems reasonable to conclude from them that, in general, most children were born two or three years after their immediate predecessors.

A husband's often lengthy absence at work abroad must have helped to bring this about, assuming of course that his wife remained chaste while he was away. But a much more widespread, and older, cause was that the Kgatla knew and practised various methods of contraception.

The most common was coitus interruptus. This was variously termed *gontshetsa madi kwantle,* 'to take the "blood" outside'; *gotsholla mophateng,* 'to spill (the semen) on the sleeping-mat'; or *gotsholla kwantle,* 'to spill (the semen) outside.' It was widely practised not only by married people, especially while the wife was suckling a child, but also by unmarried lovers. The necessary action had to be taken by the man; an unmarried girl, for instance, would sometimes yield to his advances only if he promised to do so.

(SOFONIA, 24.4.1931): When a boy wants to sleep with a girl she may at first refuse, saying,

'What will you do if I become pregnant?' He replies, 'Only fools make girls pregnant (*gokgorisa dithomo*), I would not do so; I shall discharge outside you (*ketlantshetsa kwantle gagago*) the stuff that causes pregnancy (*selo sesekgoriset-sang*).' Then the girl agrees. The boy sleeps with her, and spills his semen outside (*otshollele moroto kwantle*). Then the girl thinks he is all right, he will never make her pregnant.

(Ntebeng, 13.1.1934): When a wife is still suckling a child her husband will try to ensure that he does not 'come' properly into her. Some men send their semen on to the ground; others put it in, but not properly, i.e. they withdraw the penis as they ejaculate. Or, if the woman herself does not want to become pregnant again, as soon as she feels that he is going to ejaculate she moves her hips slightly, so that his penis slips out of her vagina and the semen is spilled on to her loins. That is what I myself do.

(Tsholofelo, 25.1.1934): If a girl does not want to become pregnant when sleeping with a boy, she tells him not to stay on her too long, so that his *bonna* ('manhood,' semen) should not come into her.

Ntebeng's statement about the woman herself taking evasive action was confirmed by other informants:

(LESAANE, 19.1.1934): Married women, when they want to avoid conception, feel from the stiffening of the man's body that he is about to ejaculate. Then they move their hips slightly, so as to throw out the penis and let the semen spill outside just at the mouth of the vagina.

(Manyama, 15.8.1934): When people have sexual intercourse it is the man who should stop himself from ejaculating into the vagina. But the woman can (also) stop it. When she feels him pushing more hurriedly, and so knows that he is about to ejaculate, she quickly turns on her side and pushes him off. But if you do this he usually quarrels with you and says, 'When I am enjoying myself you stop me by doing so.'

Should the man nevertheless ejaculate into her, the woman could try other expedients. According to male informants, 'immediately after copulation she goes outside and pisses to get rid of the semen' (SEIKANELO), or 'she turns on her belly after sleeping with the man, then his blood flows out and she cannot become pregnant' (NATALE). Female informants gave a little more detail:

(Ntebeng, 23.1.1934): If a girl does not want to conceive, she goes outside to urinate after the boy has slept with her, and so gets rid of his semen too. Or she lies on her belly so that all the semen he has put into her must flow out.

(Marutshwi, 15.9.1934): As soon as the boy stops shaking on you [i.e. immediately after he ejaculates], you must not let him keep his penis inside. You quickly pull your thighs together and push him out; then you turn over quickly on to your belly, to let his 'blood' flow out. If you let him stop there it's your own look-out (*kesagago*), you are going to get pregnant, because that thing of his [the penis] pushes the blood inside.

Another practice, described by two unmarried youths only, was the use of medicines:

(SEGOGWANE, 5.2.1930): The woman eats the roots of the *bogoma* shrub [*Setaria verticillata*], or she may grind the roots of *phukutsa* [a purgative, unidentified] and put the powder into water, which she drinks just after copulating.

(SOFONIA, 10.7.1930): *Magwane* (adolescent youths) sometimes give girls roots to chew, either before sleeping with them or immediately afterwards, so that they won't conceive. Sometimes a boy takes the twigs of the *phukutsa* plant and boils them in a pot. He then mixes the foam with hot water, which he gives to the girl to drink straight after copulation. It prevents her from having a baby.

The methods so far described were all traditional, and some were said to be taught to children by their parents or other elderly relatives. In about 1930 youths who had either worked abroad or been to school there also began to use condoms (which they called by the English name 'French letters'). These they obtained in the towns, or from local traders (one of whom first stocked them in 1932). They regarded this method as more reliable than coitus interruptus, but (as indicated below) girls apparently disliked it. I did not hear of its being used by married people.

(MAGANELO, 21.8.1932): A few educated young men use French letters when sleeping with girls. They say that some girls like them, but that others object violently, through fear of one breaking and bits coming into the womb.

(LESAANE, 18.1.1934): French letters are a recent innovation. But girls regard them as very dangerous, having heard that sometimes they get broken inside the girl and then she dies. If you tell a girl that you are going to use one, she will utterly refuse to let you sleep with her. That once happened to me. So you never tell the girl, you just slip it on.

What some other people thought of condoms was shown in the following incident, recorded by SOFONIA (12.9.1934). During a seduction case tried in Makgophana ward court, the girl alleged that the youth, when asking her to sleep with him, produced *sengwe sesetlhanyana,* 'something yellowish,' which he said would prevent her from conceiving. 'But I refused it, telling him I don't like it.' Then one of the men in court asked that this particular bit of evidence should be ignored and not pursued further, 'because the chief would not like it, it had not been heard of in the village before.'

REFERENCES

SCHAPERA, I. 1933 — Premarital pregnancy and native opinion: a note on social change. *Africa,* **6,** 59–89.

—— 1940 — *Married Life in an African Tribe.* London: Faber & Faber.

14

THE NAYARS AND THE DEFINITION OF MARRIAGE

E. KATHLEEN GOUGH

The problem of a satisfactory definition of marriage has vexed anthropologists for decades and has been raised, but not solved, several times in recent years.[1] Over time it became clear that cohabitation, ritual recognition, definition of sexual rights or stipulation of domestic services each had too limited a distribution to serve as a criterion for all the unions anthropologists intuitively

felt compelled to call 'marriage.' For good reason therefore the *Notes and Queries* definition of 1951 makes no reference to any of these: 'Marriage is a union between a man and a woman such that children born to the woman are recognized legitimate offspring of both parents.'

Admirably concise though it is, this definition too raises problems in a number of societies. The Nuer institution of woman-marriage-to-a-woman would be a case in point. Here, both parties to the union are women yet, as Evans-Pritchard (1951, pp. 108–9) has shown, the legal provisions of the union are strictly comparable to those of simple

[1]The fieldwork on which this paper is based was carried out in three villages of Kerala between September 1947 and July 1949 with the aid of a William Wyse Studentship from Trinity College, Cambridge. Writing it has formed part of a project financed by the American Social Science Research Council.

SOURCE: From "The Nayars and the Definition of Marriage," by E. Gough in *Journal of the Royal Anthropological Institute, 89,* 1959, pp. 23–34. Copyright © 1959 by the Royal Anthropological Institute of Great Britain and Ireland. Reprinted by permission.

legal marriage between a man and a woman. Few therefore would question Evans-Pritchard's logic in calling this union a marriage.

The *Notes and Queries* definition contains two criteria: that marriage is a union between one man and one woman, and that it establishes the legitimacy of children. Nuer woman-marriage does not conform to the first criterion but it does to the second. At this point the problem therefore becomes: is a definition feasible which would insist only on the second criterion, that of legitimizing children?

In Europe,[2] Dr. Edmund Leach initiated the most recent chapter in this discussion (Leach 1955), and rather than review its whole history it is pertinent for me to take up the argument where he and others have left it. In effect, Dr. Leach answered 'no' to the question posed above. He argued not only against the vagueness of the phrase 'legitimate offspring' but also against any use of potential legal paternity as a universal criterion of marriage. He concluded in fact that no definition could be found which would apply to all the institutions which ethnographers commonly refer to as marriage. Instead he named ten classes of rights[3] which frequently occur in connection with what we loosely term

marriage, added that 'one might perhaps considerably extend this list,' and seemed to conclude that since no single one of these rights is invariably established by marriage in every known society, we ought to feel free to call 'marriage' any institution which fulfills any one or more of the selected criteria.

There is, surely, a quite simple logical flaw in this argument. For it would mean in effect that every ethnographer might extend at will Dr. Leach's list of marital rights, and in short define marriage in any way he pleased. This may be legitimate in describing a single society. But I would argue that for purposes of cross-cultural comparison, we do need a single, parsimonious definition, simply in order to isolate the phenomenon we wish to study.

In support of his argument against using the legitimizing of children as a universal criterion of marriage, Dr. Leach cited the Nayar case. On the basis of two of my papers on the Nayars (Gough 1952, 1955a), he stated that the Nayars traditionally had 'no marriage in the strict (i.e. *Notes and Queries*) sense of the term but only a "relationship of perpetual affinity" between linked lineages (Gough 1955a). The woman's children, however they might be begotten, were simply recruits to the woman's own matrilineage.' He stated further, 'The notion of fatherhood is lacking. The child uses a term of address meaning "lord" or "leader" towards *all* its mother's lovers, but the use of this term does not carry with it any connotation of paternity, either legal or biological. On the other hand the notion of affinity is present, as evidenced by the fact that a woman must observe pollution at her ritual husband's death (Gough 1955a).' Later Dr. Leach concludes that 'among the matrilineal matrilocal Nayar, as we have seen, right J (to establish a socially significant "relationship of affinity" between the husband and his wife's brothers) is the only marriage characteristic that is present at all' (Leach 1955, p. 183).

This paper has two objectives. It will begin by analyzing traditional Nayar marital institutions and thereby showing that in fact the notion of

---

[2]In America Miss Alisa S. Lourié, Douglass College, Rutgers University, has recently worked on this problem, and I have been stimulated by correspondence with her and by reading an unpublished paper of hers, *Concepts in Family Sociology*. In this paper Miss Lourié formulates a definition of marriage which is narrower than mine, but when her work is published readers will see that I was helped toward my definition by her analysis. I have also profited much from discussions with my husband, David F. Aberle.

[3]A. To establish the legal father of a woman's children.
  B. To establish the legal mother of a man's children.
  C. To give the husband a monopoly in the wife's sexuality.
  D. To give the wife a monopoly in the husband's sexuality.
  E. To give the husband partial or monopolistic rights to the wife's domestic and other labour services.
  F. To give the wife partial or monopolistic rights to the husband's labour services.
  G. To give the husband partial or total rights over property belonging or potentially accruing to the wife.
  H. To give the wife partial or total rights over property belonging or potentially accruing to the husband.
  I. To establish a joint fund of property—a partnership—for the benefit of the children of the marriage.
  J. To establish a socially significant 'relationship of affinity' between the husband and his wife's brothers. (Leach 1955, p. 183.)

fatherhood is not lacking and that marriage does serve to establish the legitimacy of children. My analysis will, I hope, not only dispose of a misinterpretation on Dr. Leach's part, but will in general clarify what has always proved a crucial but difficult borderline case for theorists of kinship. The paper will conclude with a new definition of marriage which will again make the status of children born to various types of union critical for decisions as to which of these unions constitute marriage. The ultimate aim is not of course to re-define marriage in a dogmatic way to suit a particular case, for definitions are tools of classification and not aims of research. The aim is to show that there *is* a common element not only in the institutions anthropologists have confidently labelled 'marriage' by the *Notes and Queries* definition, but also in some unusual cases to which that definition does not apply. Whether we call the element 'marriage' does not much matter provided it is made explicit, but it would probably be convenient to do so.

NAYAR MARRIAGE IN CENTRAL KERALA

This account will refer to Nayars in the former kingdoms of Calicut, Walluvanad, and Cochin in the centre of the Malabar Coast or Kerala. In the northernmost kingdoms (Kolattunad, Kottayam) and probably also in the southernmost kingdom of Travancore, Nayar residence appears to have been avunculocal even before the period of British rule, marriage was optionally polygynous but not polyandrous, and individual men appear to have had definite rights in and obligations to their children. Full information is not available for these northernmost and southernmost kingdoms in the pre-British period. But it seems probable that in the northern kingdoms at least, even the *Notes and Queries* definition of marriage was applicable to the Nayars. It was certainly applicable in the latter half of the nineteenth century for which I have accounts from informants.

My account of marriage in the central king-

doms is a reconstruction of a state of affairs which appears to have been general before 1792 when the British assumed government of the Coast. As I have shown elsewhere (Gough 1952) Nayar kinship was slowly modified in the nineteenth century and more rapidly in the twentieth. But in remote villages the traditional institutions persisted until towards the end of the nineteenth century and were remembered by a few of my older informants. Their reports are not contradicted and are substantially corroborated by writings of Arab and European travellers of the fifteenth to eighteenth centuries.

In this account I shall use the terms 'marriage,' 'husband' and 'wife' without definition. My reasons for doing so will appear later.

In each of the three central kingdoms the Nayar caste was divided into a number of ranked subdivisions characterized by different political functions. Chief of these were (a) the royal lineage, (b) the lineages of chiefs of districts, (c) the lineages of Nayar village headmen and (d) several sub-castes of commoner Nayars. Each of these last either served one of the categories (a) to (c) or else served patrilineal landlord families of Nambudiri Brahmans. I shall deal first with the commoner Nayars of category (d).

There were present in each village some four to seven exogamous matrilineages of a single sub-caste of commoner Nayars. These owed allegiance to the family of the head of the village, which might be a patrilineal Nambudiri family, a Nayar village headman's matrilineage, a branch of the lineage of the chief of the district, or a branch of the royal lineage. The commoners held land on a hereditary feudal-type tenure from the headman's lineage and, in turn, had authority over the village's lower castes of cultivators, artisans, and agricultural serfs. Each retainer lineage tended to comprise some four to eight property-owning units which I call property-groups. The property-group formed a segment of the total lineage and was usually composed of a group of brothers and sisters together with the children and daughters' children of the sisters. The members owned or leased property in common, lived in one house, and were under the legal guardianship of the oldest male (*kāranavan*) of the group. Both the property-group and the lineage were called *taravād*.

Nayar men trained as professional soldiers in village gymnasia, and for part of each year they tended to be absent from the village in wars against neighbouring kingdoms or for military exercises at the capitals. Only the *kāranavan,* the women and the children of the property-group remained permanently in their ancestral homes.

The Nayars of one village or of two adjacent villages formed a neighbourhood group (*kara* or *tara*) of some six to ten lineages. Each lineage was linked by hereditary ties of ceremonial co-operation with two or three other lineages of the neighbourhood. These linkages were reciprocal but not exclusive, so that a chain of relationships linked all the lineages of the neighbourhood. The lineages linked to one's own were called *enangar;* the total neighbourhood group, the *enangu.* At least one man and one woman of each linked lineage must be invited to the house of a property-group for the life-crisis rites of its members. Its linked lineages were also concerned if some member of a lineage committed a breach of the religious law of the caste. It was their duty at once to break off relations with the offending lineage and to call a neighbourhood assembly to judge and punish the offence. Its linked lineages thus represented the neighbourhood group as a whole to the offending lineage and were special guardians of its morality. Sometimes in small neighbourhoods the commoner Nayar lineages were all *enangar* to each other, but in larger neighbourhoods this was not feasible, for the heads of property-groups would have had too many ceremonial obligations to fulfil.

The linked lineages played their most important role at the pre-puberty marriage rites (*tālikettukalyānam*) of girls (Gough 1955b). At a convenient time every few years, a lineage held a grand ceremony at which all its girls who had not attained puberty, aged about seven to twelve, were on one day ritually married by men drawn from their linked lineages. The ritual bridegrooms were selected in advance on the advice of the village astrologer at a meeting of the neighbourhood assembly. On the day fixed they came in procession to the oldest ancestral house of the host lineage. There, after various ceremonies, each tied a gold ornament (*tāli*) round the neck of his ritual bride. The girls had for three days previously been secluded in an inner room of the house and caused to observe taboos as if they had menstruated. After the *tāli*-tying each couple was secluded in private for three days. I was told that traditionally, if the girl was nearing puberty, sexual relations might take place. This custom began to be omitted in the late nineteenth century, but from some of the literature it appears to have been essential in the sixteenth and seventeenth centuries. At the end of the period of seclusion each couple was purified from the pollution of cohabitation by a ritual bath. In Calicut and Walluvanad each couple in public then tore in two the loin-cloth previously worn by the girl during the 'cohabitation' period, as a token of separation. This rite appears to have been omitted in Cochin. In all three kingdoms however, the ritual husbands left the house after the four days of ceremonies and had no further obligations to their brides. A bride in turn had only one further obligation to her ritual husband: at his death, she and all her children, by whatever biological father, must observe death-pollution for him. Death-pollution was otherwise observed only for matrilineal kin. In Cochin, even if their mother's ritual husband never visited his wife again, her children must refer to him by the kinship term *appan.* Children in the lower, patrilineal castes of this area used this word to refer to the legal father, who was presumed also to be the biological father. In Walluvanad and Calicut I did not hear of this verbal usage and do not know by what term, if any, Nayar children referred to their mother's ritual husband.

The pre-puberty *tāli*-rite was essential for a girl. If she menstruated before it had been performed, she should in theory be expelled from her lineage and caste. In fact, however, my informants told me that in such a case the girl's family would conceal the fact of her maturity until after the rite had been performed. But it was a grave sin to do so and one which would never be publicly admitted.

The *tāli*-rite marked various changes in the social position of a girl. First, it brought her to social maturity. She was now thought to be at least ritually endowed with sexual and procreative functions and was thenceforward accorded the status of a woman. After the rite people addressed her in public by the respectful title *amma* meaning 'mother,' and she might take part in the rites of adult women. Second, after the *tāli*-rite a girl must observe all the rules of etiquette associated with incest prohibitions in relation to men of her lineage. She might not touch them, might not sit in their presence, might not speak first to them and might not be alone in a room with one of them. Third, after the *tāli*-rite and as soon as she became old enough (i.e., shortly before or after puberty), a girl received as visiting husbands a number of men in her subcaste from outside her lineage, usually but not necessarily from her neighbourhood. In addition she might be visited by any Nayar of the higher sub-castes of village headmen, chiefs or royalty, or by a Nambudiri Brahman. All of these relationships were called *sambandham*. Among commoner Nayar women, however, the great majority of unions were with men of commoner sub-caste.

Relations between any Nayar women and a man of *lower* Nayar sub-caste, or between any Nayar woman and a man of one of the lower, non-Nayar castes, were strictly prohibited. If a woman was found guilty of such a relationship her lineage's *enangar* carried the matter to the neighbourhood assembly. This temporarily excommunicated the woman's property-group until justice had been done. In the nineteenth century and early this century the property-group was re-accepted into caste only after its *kāranavan* had dismissed the woman from her household and caste, never to return. In pre-British times a woman so dismissed became the property of the king or chief and might be sold into slavery with foreign traders. Alternatively, however, the men of her property-group had the right, sometimes exercised, to kill both the woman and her lover and thus preserve the good name of their lineage.

After the ritual marriage the bridegroom need have no further contact with his ritual wife. If both parties were willing, however, he might enter into a sexual relationship with his ritual bride about the time of her puberty. But he had no priority over other men of the neighbourhood group. There is some uncertainty as to the number of visiting husbands a woman might have at one time. Writers of the sixteenth and seventeenth centuries report that a woman usually had some three to eight regular husbands but might receive other men of her own or a higher caste at will. Hamilton in 1727 stated that a woman might have as husbands 'twelve but no more at one time' (Hamilton 1727 I, p. 310). As late as 1807 Buchanan reported that Nayar women vied with each other as to the number of lovers they could obtain (Buchanan 1807 I, p. 411). A few of my older informants could remember women who had had three or four current husbands, although plural unions were being frowned upon and had almost died out by the end of the last century. There appears to have been no limit to the number of wives of appropriate sub-caste whom a Nayar might visit concurrently. It seems, therefore, that a woman customarily had a small but not a fixed number of husbands from within her neighbourhood, that relationships with these men might be of long standing, but that the woman was also free to receive casual visitors of appropriate sub-caste who passed through her neighbourhood in the course of military operations.

A husband visited his wife after supper at night and left before breakfast next morning. He placed his weapons at the door of his wife's room and if others came later they were free to sleep on the verandah of the woman's house. Either party to a union might terminate it at any time without formality. A passing guest recompensed a woman with a small cash gift at each visit. But a more regular husband from within the neighbourhood had certain customary obligations. At the start of the union it was common although not essential for him to present the woman with a cloth of the kind worn as a skirt. Later he was expected to make small personal gifts to her at the three main festivals of the year. These gifts included a loin-cloth, betel-leaves and areca-nuts for chewing, hair-oil and bathing-oil, and certain vegetables. Failure on the part of a husband to make such a gift was a tacit sign that he had ended the relationship. Most important, however, when a woman became pregnant it was essential for one or more men of appropriate sub-caste to acknowledge probable paternity. This they did by providing a fee of a cloth and some vegetables to the low caste midwife who attended the woman in childbirth. If no man of suitable caste would consent to make this gift, it was assumed that the woman had had relations with a man of lower caste or with a Christian or a Muslim. She must then be either expelled from her lineage and caste or killed by her matrilineal kinsmen. I am uncertain of the precise fate of the child in such a case, but there is no doubt at all that he could not be accepted as a member of his lineage and caste. I do not know whether he was killed or became a slave; almost certainly, he must have shared the fate of his mother. Even as late as 1949, over a hundred and fifty years after the establishment of British rule, a Nayar girl who became pregnant before the modern marriage ceremony was regarded as acting within the canons of traditional religious law if she could simply find a Nayar of suitable sub-caste to pay her delivery expenses. But if no Nayar would consent to this she ran the danger of total ostracism, with her child, by the village community. I heard of several cases in which such a girl was driven from her home by her *kāranavan* at the command of the sub-caste assembly. Her natal kinsmen then performed funeral rites for her as if she had died. In each case the girl took refuge in a town before or shortly after her child was born.

Although he made regular gifts to her at festivals, in no sense of the term did a man maintain his wife. Her food and regular clothing she obtained from her matrilineal group. The gifts of a woman's husbands were personal luxuries which pertained to her role as a sexual partner—extra clothing, articles of toilet, betel, and areca-nut the giving of which is associated with courtship, and the expenses of the actual delivery, not, be it noted, of the maintenance of either mother or child. The gifts continued to be made at festivals only while the relationship lasted. No man had obligations to a wife of the past.

In these circumstances the exact biological fatherhood of a child was often uncertain, although, of course, paternity was presumed to lie with the man or among the men who had paid the delivery expenses. But even when biological paternity was known with reasonable certainty, the genitor had no economic, social, legal, or ritual rights in nor obligations to his children after he had once paid the fees of their births. Their guardianship, care and discipline were entirely the concern of their matrilineal kinsfolk headed by their *kāranavan*. All the children of a woman called all her current husbands by the Sanskrit word *acchan* meaning 'lord.' They did not extend kinship terms at all to the matrilineal kin of these men. Neither the wife nor her children observed pollution at the death of a visiting husband who was not also the ritual husband of the wife.

In most matrilineal systems with settled agriculture and localized matrilineal groups, durable links are provided between these groups by the interpersonal relationships of marriage, affinity and fatherhood. The husbands, affines, fathers, and patrilateral kin of members of the matrilineal group have customary obligations to and rights in them which over time serve to mitigate conflicts between the separate matrilineal groups. The Nayars had no such durable institutionalized interpersonal links. This does not mean that men did not sometimes form strong emotional attachments to particular wives and their children. My information indicates that they did. I know for example that if a man showed particular fondness for a wife, his wife's matrilineal kin were likely to suspect the husband's matrilineal kin of hiring sorcerers against them. For the husband's matrilineal kin would be likely to fear that the husband might secretly convey to his wife gifts and cash which belonged rightfully to his matrilineal kin. This suspicion was especially rife if the husband was a *kāranavan* who controlled extensive property. Informal emotional attachments did therefore exist between individuals of different lineages. But what I wish to indicate is that among the Nayars, these interpersonal affinal and patrilateral links were not invested with customary legal, economic, or ceremonial functions of a kind which would periodically bring members of different lineages together in mandatory forms of co-operation. Four special kinship terms did apparently exist for use in relation to affines acquired through the *sambandham* relationship, although, as I have said, there were no patrilateral terms for kin other than the mother's husbands. All men and women currently engaged in *sambandham* unions with members of ego's property group, and all members of the property-groups of these individuals, were collectively referred to as *bandhukkal* ('joined ones'). A current wife of ego's mother's brother was addressed and referred to as *ammāyi,* and a wife of the elder brother as *jyeshtati amma* (lit. 'elder-sister-mother'). Finally, the own brother and the *sambandham* husband of a woman employed the reciprocal term *aliyan* to refer to each other but used no term of address. All the current *bandhukkal* of a property-group were invited to household feasts, but as individual affines they had no ceremonial or economic obligations and were not obliged to attend. As representatives of *enangar* lineages, however, some of these same individuals might be obliged to attend feasts and to fulfil ceremonial obligations *as enangar.* But as particular affines they had no obligations. In place therefore, of institutionalized interpersonal patrilateral and affinal links, the Nayars had the hereditary institution of linked lineages.

Whether or not, at a particular time, sexual relationships existed between individuals of linked lineages, the linked lineages must fulfil their obligations at household ceremonies and give neighbourly help in such emergencies as birth and death. In the patrilineal and double unilineal castes of Kerala precisely the same obligations are fulfilled by the matrilateral kin and affines of individual members of the patrilineal group. The linked lineages of the Nayars must therefore, I think, be regarded as having a relationship of 'perpetual affinity,' which carried the more normal functions of affinity and persisted through the making and breaking of individual sexual ties.

In view of these facts, it is convenient to mention here that Dr. Leach's statement that Nayar marriage served 'to establish a socially significant relationship between the husband and his wife's brothers' is not, strictly speaking, correct. The *sambandham* union did not establish 'a socially significant relationship' between brothers-in-law, for in spite of the reciprocal kinship term these persons had no institutionalized obligations to one another by virtue of the particular *sambandham* tie. Further, the *tāli*-rite did not *establish* a relationship between the ritual husband and the brothers of his ritual bride. The ceremony set up no special obligations between these persons; it was merely that their lineages were, hereditarily, *enangar,* both before and after any particular *tāli*-rite. What the rite did *establish* was a ritual relationship between the *tāli*-tier and his ritual bride, and, as I shall try to show later, a relationship of group-marriage between the bride and all men of her sub-caste outside her lineage. But a particular *tāli*-rite in no way modified the hereditary relationships between male *enangar*. It is for this reason that I call the *enangar* relationship one of 'perpetual affinity' *between lineages,* which, though it carried the ceremonial functions of affinity, persisted irrespective of particular *sambandhams* and *tāli*-rites.

The Nayars of this area were thus highly unusual. For they had a kinship system in which the elementary family of father, mother and children was not institutionalized as a legal, productive, distributive, residential, socializing or consumption unit. Until recent years, some writers have thought that at least as a unit for some degree of co-operation in economic production and distribution, the elementary family was universal. This view has been put forward most forcibly by Murdock (Murdock 1949, chapter I). Radcliffe-Brown, however, was one of the earliest anthropologists to observe that if the written accounts of the Nayars were accurate, the elementary family was not institutionalized among them.[4] My research corroborates his findings.

I turn briefly to marital institutions among the higher Nayar sub-castes of village headmen, district chiefs, and royalty. At various times during the pre-British period these lineages were accorded political office and set themselves up as of higher ritual rank than the commoner Nayars. The ritual ranking between these major aristocratic sub-divisions was fairly stable, but the mutual ranking of lineages within each sub-division was in dispute. Most village headmen acknowledged the ritual superiority of district chiefs, and most chiefs, of the royal lineage. But some village headmen disputed among themselves for ritual precedence and so did many chiefs. As a result, each of these aristocratic lineages tended to set itself up as a separate sub-caste, acknowledging ritual superiors and inferiors but acknowledging no peers. In the course of time, moreover, following the vicissitudes of political fortune, such lineages could rise or fall in the ritual hierarchy. It was in these lineages therefore that hypergamous unions became most highly institutionalized, for most of these lineages refused to exchange spouses on equal terms. Instead, most of them married all their women upwards and all their men downwards. Women of village headman's lineage entered *sambandham* unions with chiefly, royal, or

[4]Radcliffe-Brown expressed this view most recently and fully in his Introduction to *African Systems of Kinship and Marriage* (1950, pp. 73 seq.).

Nambudiri Brahman men. Men of these lineages had unions with commoner Nayar women. Chiefly women had unions with royals 'children.' These fall into two categories: those of the *tāli*-rite and those of the *sambandham* union. In relations between spouses of the *tāli*-rite, the important rights are those of the woman. The ritual husband had, it is true, apparently at one time the right to deflower his bride. But the accounts of many writers indicate that this right was not eagerly sought, that in fact it was viewed with repugnance and performed with reluctance. The ritual husband also had the right that his ritual wife should mourn his death. But we may assume that this right had more significance for the wife than for the husband, for it was not attended by offerings to the departed spirit. These could be performed only by matrilineal kin. The ritual bride's rights were complementary to her husband's, but for her they were of supreme importance. She had, first, the right to *have* a ritual husband of her own or a superior sub-caste before she attained maturity. Her life depended on this, for if she was not ritually married before puberty she was liable to excommunication and might possibly be put to death. She held this claim against her sub-caste as a whole exclusive of her lineage, or (in the case of aristocratic lineages) against a higher sub-caste. This group must, through the institution of the linked lineages, provide her with a ritual husband of correct rank and thus bring her to maturity in honour instead of in shame. It was the duty of her lineage kinsmen to see to it that some representative from their linked lineages fulfilled this right. The ritual wife's second right was that of observing pollution at the death of her ritual husband. I interpret this as a mark of proof that she had once been married in the correct manner and that this ritual relationship had retained significance for *her* throughout her ritual husband's life.

The *tāli*-tier had no rights in his ritual wife's children except that they should observe pollution at his death. From the child's point of view, however, his mother's ritual husband must have been a figure of great symbolic significance. For a child whose mother had no ritual husband could not acquire membership in his caste and lineage at all. The birth of a child before his mother's *tāli*-rite was absolutely forbidden and, in the nature of the case, can scarcely ever have happened. If it did occur, mother and child must certainly have been expelled and were most probably killed. The child's observance of pollution for his mother's ritual husband—like the use of the kinship term *appan* in Cochin—was a formal recognition that, for ritual purposes, he had been 'fathered' by a man of appropriate caste.

Turning to the *sambandham* union, it seems clear that the husband had no exclusive rights in his wife. He had only, in common with other men, sexual privileges which the wife might withdraw at any time. Again it is the wife's rights which are important. The wife had the right to gifts from her husband at festivals, gifts of little economic value but of high prestige value, for they established her as a woman well-favoured by men. But most significant was the woman's right to have her delivery expenses paid by one or more husbands of appropriate caste, that is, to have it openly acknowledged that her child had as biological father a man of required ritual rank. Her matrilineal kinsmen could if necessary press for the fulfillment of this right in a public assembly of the neighbourhood: in cases of doubtful paternity any man who had been currently visiting the woman could be forced by the assembly to pay her delivery expenses. But if no man of appropriate rank could be cited as potential father, woman and child were expelled from their lineage and caste.

The *sambandham* father had no rights in his wife's children. Here again, however, the child had one right in his possible biological fathers: that one or more of them should pay the expenses associated with his birth, and thus entitle him to enter the world as a member of his lineage and caste.

It is clear therefore that although the elementary family of one father, one mother and their children was not institutionalized as a legal, residential, or economic unit, and although individual men had no significant rights in their particular wives or children, the Nayars did institutionalize the concepts of marriage and of paternity, and gave ritual and legal recognition to both. It is here that I must contradict Dr. Leach's interpretation of the situation, for it is not true that 'the notion of fatherhood is lacking' nor is it true that 'a woman's children, however they might be begotten, were simply recruits to the woman's matrilineage' (Leach 1955, p. 183). For unless his mother was ritually married by a man of appropriate caste and, unless his biological paternity was vouched for by one or more men[5] of appropriate caste, a child could never enter his caste or lineage at all. As I pointed out in both the papers quoted by Dr. Leach, the Nayars were aware of the physiological function of the male in procreation and attached significance to it, for they expected a child to look like his genitor. Like all the higher Hindu castes of India, they based their belief in the moral rightness of the caste system in part upon a racist ideology which involved the inheritance of physical, intellectual, and moral qualities by a child from both of its natural parents, and which held that the higher castes were, by virtue of their heredity, superior to the lower castes. It was ostensibly for this reason that the Nayars forbade with horror sexual contacts between a Nayar woman and a man of lower caste, and that they expelled or put to death women guilty of such contacts. This racist ideology also provided a motive for hypergamous unions, for Nayars of aristocratic lineages boasted of the superior qualities they derived from royal and Brahmanical fatherhood.

Moreover, although individual men had no significant customary rights in their wives and children, marriage and paternity were probably

---

[5] I do not know whether the Nayars believed it possible for two or more men to contribute to the formation of one embryo. I think it possible that they did, for I found this belief among villagers of the Tamil country. Among these castes it formed part of a belief that several acts of intercourse are necessary to 'feed' the embryo and assist it to grow.

significant factors in political integration. For hypergamous unions bound together the higher sub-castes of the political and religious hierarchies. Multiple sexual ties, as well as the *enangar* relationship, linked office-bearing lineages to each other and to their retainers in a complicated manner. And Nayar men phrased their loyalty to higher ranking military leaders, rulers, and Brahmans in terms of a debt owed to benevolent paternal figures whose forebears had collectively fathered them and whose blood they were proud to share. The generalized concept of fatherhood thus commanded the Nayar soldier's allegiance to his wider caste unit, to the rulers of his village, chiefdom, and kingdom and to his religious authorities. It was associated with tender loyalty and with fortitude in war.

I cannot entirely blame Dr. Leach for underestimating the significance of Nayar paternity on the basis of his reading of my earlier papers. For in those papers I was concerned to emphasize the lack of rights of individual men in their spouses and children. It is true that in 1952 I wrote: 'Marriage . . . was the slenderest of ties, while as a social concept fatherhood scarcely existed' (Gough 1952, p. 73). I had not then realized the fundamental necessity to a Nayar of having both a ritual and a biological father of appropriate caste. Moreover I myself confused the issue by referring to the *sambandham* partners as 'husbands' and 'wives' in my first paper (Gough 1952) and as 'lovers' and 'mistresses' in my second (Gough 1955a). For it was not until some time after I read Dr. Leach's paper that I decided to classify Nayar unions unequivocally as marriage and arrived at a definition of marriage which would include the Nayar case. In my own defence I must, however, note that in my paper of 1955 I mentioned that children must observe death pollution for their mother's ritual husband, and that in Cochin they used the kinship term *appan* for this ritual father. In both papers quoted by Dr. Leach, finally, I noted that sexual relations were forbidden between a Nayar woman and a man of lower caste or sub-caste, and that the

current *sambandham* husbands of a woman must pay her delivery expenses.

I regard Nayar unions as a form of marriage for two reasons. One is that although plural unions were customary, mating was not promiscuous. Sexual relations were forbidden between members of the same lineage on pain of death. It was also forbidden for two men of the same property-group wittingly to have relations with one woman, or for two women of the same property-group to have relations with one man. (This rule of course automatically excluded relations between a man and his biological daughter.) Further, relations were absolutely prohibited between a Nayar woman and a man of lower sub-caste or caste. These prohibitions are directly connected with my second and more important reason for regarding these unions as marriage, namely that the concept of legally established paternity *was* of fundamental significance in establishing a child as a member of his lineage and caste.

Granted that Nayar unions constituted a form of marriage, we must I think classify them as a clear case of group-marriage. This was the interpretation to which I inclined in 1952 (Gough 1952, p. 73) and it is, I now think, the only interpretation which makes sense of the descriptive material I have presented. The *tāli*-rite, as I see it, initiated for each individual Nayar girl a state of marriage to a collectivity of men of appropriate caste. First, the rite ceremonially endowed the girl with sexual and procreative functions. (The mock menstrual seclusion before the rite is relevant to this, as is the actual defloration.) Second, the woman's natal kinsmen surrendered the newly acquired rights in her sexuality, though not in her procreative functions, to a male representative from outside her lineage. This appears in that rules of etiquette associated with incest prohibitions came into force from this date. Third, rights in the woman's sexuality were received by her *enangan* as representative of the men of his sub-caste as a whole. This appears in that the individual *enangan*, as a special sexual partner, was dismissed at the end of the ceremonies and might approach the woman again only as one among a series of equal husbands. In the commoner sub-castes the *enangan* was of the same sub-caste as the woman, and through him as representative sexual rights in the woman were conferred on all men of her sub-caste as a collectivity. They were also in fact extended to any man of higher sub-caste who might favour her with his attentions. In aristocratic lineages the ritual husband was of a sub-caste higher than the woman's, and through him, as representative, sexual rights in the woman were conferred upon all men of higher sub-caste as a collectivity. Fourth, the *tāli*-rite, by providing the woman with a ritual husband who (in my view) symbolized all the men of his sub-caste with whom the woman might later have relationships, also provided her children with a ritual father who symbolized the correctness of their paternity. The children acknowledged their debt to him by mourning at his death.

The later *sambandham* unions, by this interpretation, involved the claiming of sexual privileges by men all of whom were potential husbands by virtue of their membership in a sub-caste. The husbands had, however, no individually exclusive rights and could be dismissed at the woman's wish. Their duties as members of their caste were to provide the woman and her lineage with children and to acknowledge their potential biological paternity through birth-payments which legitimized the woman's child.

THE DEFINITION OF MARRIAGE

I have called the Nayar unions marriage because they involved the concept of legal paternity. It is clear however that such a form of group marriage will not fit the *Notes and Queries* definition of 'a union between *a* man and *a* woman such that children born to the woman are recognized legitimate offspring of both parents' (my italics). For legitimacy in the case of the Nayar child required both a ritual father and a 'legalized genitor' of appropriate rank, and indeed a child

might have more than one 'legal genitor' if two or more men had jointly paid the expenses of his birth.

As a tentative move toward a new definition which will have cross-cultural validity and will fit the Nayar and several other unusual cases, I suggest the following: 'Marriage is a relationship established between a woman and one or more other persons, which provides that a child born to the woman under circumstances not prohibited by the rules of the relationship, is accorded full birth-status rights common to normal members of his society or social stratum.'

A few footnotes to this definition may help to vindicate its inevitably clumsy phraseology. 'One or more persons' (in place of 'a man') will bring into the definition both group-marriage of the Nayar type and also true fraternal polyandry.[6] It also brings within the definition such unusual types as woman-marriage-to-a-woman. 'Under circumstances not prohibited by the rules of the relationship' would bring into the definition various problematic cases. It is possible for example that there are patrilineal societies in which a husband may legally repudiate a child illicitly begotten upon his wife by another man, without divorcing the wife herself. In this case the previous establishment of the marriage would *not* ensure full birth-status rights to the child, for the rules of the marriage relationship would have been broken through the circumstances which led to his birth. 'Full birth-status rights common to all normal members . . . ' is a compressed reference to all the social relationships, property-rights, etc. which a child acquires at birth by virtue of his legitimacy, whether through the father or through the mother. For patrilineal societies the phrase 'full birth-status rights' will include the rights which a child acquires in his *pater* as a person and in his *pater*'s

---

[6]I agree with Dr. Leach that the Iravas of Central Kerala had true fraternal polyandry. My own enquiries produced evidence supporting Aiyappan's view that the brothers shared equally both sexual rights in the woman and also legal paternity of the children, in the same manner in which they were co-owners of the ancestral property. The eldest living brother at any given time was simply the legal representative of this corporation.

group. It will include, that is to say, the legitimization of fatherhood, or more precisely, of 'father-sonhood.' The phrase is, however, broader than any concept of specific rights in a particular father. It will therefore take care of a case like the Nayar in which all rights are acquired *through* the mother but in which a relationship must be established between the mother and one or more other persons in order for these matrilineal rights to be ratified. Such a process may be called the legitimization of motherhood, or more precisely of 'mother-sonhood.' Moreover 'full birth-status rights' is, I think, not only broader but more precise than 'recognized legitimate offspring,' to the vagueness of which Dr. Leach took exception. The inclusion of 'society or social stratum' makes allowances for class or caste systems in which birth-status rights vary between strata. The case of the Nayars, who are a matrilineal caste in a predominantly patrilineal society, is an obvious example of this.

It should also perhaps be pointed out that this definition does not state that full birth-status rights cannot be acquired by a child except through the marriage of its mother, but only that marriage provides for the acquisition of these rights. The definition does not therefore exclude societies like the Nuer in which a man may legitimize the child of an unmarried woman upon payment of a legitimization fee, without becoming married to the mother (Evans-Pritchard 1951, pp. 21, 26).

Prince Peter has objected to the *Notes and Queries* definition and, by implication, to any definition which would make the legitimization of children through the mother's relationship to another party the distinctive characteristic of marriage (1956, 46). His reason for objecting is that in some societies like the Toda, 'marriage and legitimacy of the children can be looked upon as two different and separate concepts, and it may be necessary to go through a ceremony of legitimization of the offspring (the Toda *pursütpimi* ceremony) in order to establish who is the legal father, because marriage rites are insufficient in themselves to do this.'

However, it seems from Rivers' account that precisely what distinguishes the Toda institution which Prince Peter translates as 'marriage' (*mokh-vatt*) from that which he translates as 'concubinage' (*mokhthoditi*) (1957, 35), is that a 'husband' holds the right to legitimize some or all of his 'wife's' children by the *pursütpimi* ceremony, whereas a lover in the *mokhthoditi* union, being of a different endogamous group from the woman, does not hold this right (Rivers 1909, p. 526). A husband acquires the right to perform the *pursütpimi* ceremony, it seems, by virtue of arranged marriage to an infant or through payment of cattle to a former husband or to a group of former husbands of the wife. The Toda marriage union at its inception does therefore provide that a child born to the woman (under circumstances not prohibited by the rules of the relationship) *must be* legitimized before his birth; the *pursütpimi* ceremony confirms his legitimacy by attaching him to a particular father and giving him rights in the father's patrilineal group. In the Toda case again therefore the concept of legal paternity is *the* distinguishing characteristic of marriage, even though the individual husband, because of polyandry, may be permitted to legitimize only some and not all of the children born to his wife. The Toda case therefore fits my definition,[7] whether we regard the *pursütpimi* ceremony as the final one of a sequence of marriage rites, or as a legitimizing act which, under circumstances not prohibited by the rules of the relationship, one or another of the woman's husbands is legally obliged to fulfil.

I do not argue that all societies must necessarily be found to have marriage by my definition. There may yet turn out to be whole societies—or more probably whole social strata—in which children acquire no birth-status rights except through their mother, by the simple fact of birth.

[7]I agree with Dr. Fischer that Prince Peter's definition of marriage is a tautology and so of no assistance (1956, 92). All that Prince Peter's second note shows (1957, 35) is that several peoples of his acquaintance have different terms for different kinds of relationships between men and women. But unless we approach these with some guiding concepts of our own in mind, we cannot decide which of them to translate as 'marriage' and which as 'concubinage.'

It is possible for example that some slave populations do not have marriage in this sense of the term. What I do wish to suggest however is that for most if not all the societies for which we now have information, including the Nayar, marriage as I have defined it is a significant relationship, distinguished by the people themselves from all other kinds of relationships. My definition should therefore enable us to isolate marriage as a cross-cultural phenomenon, and from there to proceed to the more exciting task: that of investigating the differential circumstances under which marriage becomes invested with various other kinds of rights and obligations. Some of the most important of these Dr. Leach has already listed for us.

REFERENCES

BUCHANAN, FRANCIS (HAMILTON) 1807. *A Journey from Madras through Mysore, Canara and Malabar.* 3 vols. London.

EVANS-PRITCHARD, E. E. 1951. *Kinship and Marriage among the Nuer.* Oxford.

FISCHER, H. TH. 1956. For a New Definition of Marriage. MAN, 1956, 92.

GOUGH, E. KATHLEEN 1952. Changing Kinship Usages in the Setting of Political and Economic Change among the Nayars of Malabar. J. R. ANTHROP. INST. **82,** pp. 71–87.

GOUGH, E. KATHLEEN 1955a. The Traditional Lineage and Kinship System of the Nayars. [Unpublished manuscript in the Haddon Library, Cambridge.]

GOUGH, E. KATHLEEN 1955b. Female Initiation Rites on the Malabar Coast, J. R. ANTHROP. INST. **85,** pp. 45–80.

HAMILTON, ALEXANDER 1727. *A New Account of the East Indies,* 2 vols. Edinburgh.

LEACH, E. R. 1955. Polyandry, Inheritance, and the Definition of Marriage. MAN, 1955, 199.

LOURIÉ, ALISA S. 1957. 'Concepts in Family Sociology.' 1957. [Unpublished manuscript kindly made available to this author.]

MURDOCK, G. P. 1949. *Social Structure.* New York.

Notes and Queries in Anthropology 1951. 6th ed. London.

H.R.H. PRINCE PETER OF GREECE AND DENMARK For a New Definition of Marriage. MAN, 1956, 46; 1957, 35.

RADCLIFFE-BROWN, A. R. & FORDE, D. (eds.) 1950. *African Systems of Kinship and Marriage.* Oxford.

RIVERS, W. H. R. 1906. *The Todas.* London.

15

Causes of Polygyny: Ecology, Economy, Kinship, and Warfare

Douglas R. White / Michael L. Burton

We discuss and test competing explanations for polygyny based on household economics, male-centered kin groups, warfare, and environmental characteristics. Data consisted of codes for 142 societies from the Standard Cross-Cultureal Sample, including new codes for polygyny and environmental characteristics. An explanatory model is tested for the worldwide sample using regression analysis, and then replicated with regional samples. We obtain convergent results with two different measures of polygyny, cultural rules for men's marriages and the percentage of women married polygynously. We conclude that the best predictors of polygyny are fraternal interest groups, warfare for capture of women, absence of constraints on expansion into new lands, and environmental quality and homogeneity.

Nothing could be more central to the anthropological tradition than the study of kinship, marriage, and gender. Within this domain, variations in the frequency and form of polygyny play a critical and poorly understood role. We can readily disprove simplistic hypotheses about polygyny, such as the belief that it exists mainly to satisfy male sexual appetites, but developing a comprehensive model of polygyny has proved elusive. In this article we present a model of general polygyny that improves upon existing explanations and replicates across world regions.

General polygyny, our dependent variable, requires access to large numbers of potential wives, something which is difficult to effect through wives' kin networks, Hence, general polygyny tends to be nonsororal. In its most extreme form, general polygyny falls into a pattern where all men aspire to marry polygynously,

Douglas R. White is Professor, School of Social Sciences, University of California, Irvine, CA 92717. Michael L. Burton is Professor, School of Social Sciences, University of California, Irvine, CA.

Source: From "Causes of Polygyny: Ecology, Economy, Kinship, and Warfare" by D. White and M. Burton, *American Anthropologist, 90:4*, December, 1988. Copyright © 1988 by American Anthropological Association. Reprinted by permission. Not for further reproduction.

where most men succeed with age, and where success increases the chance of future success (Spencer 1980). It is associated with separate residences for co-wives, and with a pattern of aloofness between husbands and wives (Whiting and Whiting 1975).

Nineteenth-century evolutionary theorists thought polygyny occurred in the middle stages of societal evolution. For example, Engels posited three evolutionary stages: group marriage, polygynous marriage, and monogamy. He saw monogamy as developing with civilization and social classes (Engels 1972 [1884]:129) and coinciding with a decline in female status. Engels's notion that polygyny occurs mainly in the middle ranges of societal complexity is supported by cross-cultural research (Martin and Voorhies 1975; Blumberg and Winch 1972; Osmond 1965). Although useful for generating hypotheses, these kinds of evolutionary studies do not constitute explanations, since they do not identify the processes that cause polygyny to be most common in middle-level food-producing societies.

Sociobiologists view polygyny as a reproductive strategy by which men maximize the number of their offspring but minimize investment in each child, called the r-strategy (Alexander et al. 1979; Alvard 1986; Chagnon 1979; Hartung 1982). These analyses suggest that polygyny has more reproductive benefits for men than for women, and in so doing direct our attention to social circumstances that favor men in reproductive decision making. The male-centered view is qualified by Hartung (1982), who notes that polygyny allows women to have large numbers of grandchildren, provided they have sons. Hence, mothers will form alliances with their sons to favor the allocation of additional wives to their sons rather than to their husbands (Hartung 1982:5).

While describing the parameters of reproductive decisions within polygynous societies, sociobiologists tell us relatively little about cross-societal variations in the rate of polygyny. For these explanations we must turn to the cross-cultural literature, which emphasizes the roles of economics and warfare.

ECONOMIC EXPLANATIONS FOR POLYGYNY

We find two kinds of economic explanations for polygyny, one based on household economics, and a second based on the degree of agriculture intensification. Three studies (Boserup 1970; Goody 1976; Burton and Reitz 1981) link the two explanations.

Explanations for polygyny based on household economics see polygyny as a consequence of rational choices made by household members. Grossbard (1976, 1980, 1984) develops a formal economic model of polygyny based on Becker's (1981) work and tests it with Nigerian data (Cohen 1971; Steckle and Lewanyk 1973). Grossbard's model focuses on the supply and demand for, and trade-offs among, the gender-specific types of household and wage labor. Defining income to include both cash and imputed value, Grossbard posits that married men are able to benefit from female income through family labor, but not from female income through wage labor. Hence, the benefit to men and women from marriage will depend upon the relative quantities of female income from family versus wage labor. Grossbard derives several hypotheses, including:

1. As the value of women's subsistence contributions ("domestic income") increases, polygyny becomes more likely, since the income that men gain from marriage increases.
2. As women's wage opportunities outside the domestic domain increase, polygyny decreases.
3. As inequality among men increases, polygyny increases, since women will choose to marry wealthy men who already have several wives. Further, wealthier men will be more likely to choose polygynous marriages.
4. Homogamy decreases the incidence of polygyny by limiting the possibilities for polygynous marriages.
5. As the sex ratio decreases, polygyny will increase.
6. If there are economies of scale in polygynous households, polygyny is more likely.

Grossbard's first hypothesis appears frequently in the cross-cultural literature. Heath (1958) hypothesizes that polygyny and bride price will both increase with women's economic contributions, and finds modest positive correlations to support his hypotheses. Osmond (1965) obtains a positive correlation between female economic contributions and polygyny only for the societies without plow agriculture, whereas Burton and Rietz (1981) find a positive relationship between polygyny and female contributions to crop tending, when controlling for the presence of plow agriculture. Lee (1979) finds a positive correlation between polygyny and female subsistence contributions for agricultural and gathering societies, and a negative correlation between these two variables for fishing, hunting, or herding societies. Finally, Ember (1984) finds no relationship between total female subsistence contributions and polygyny. These studies paint a mixed picture of the relationship between female subsistence contributions and polygyny, suggesting that it may be valid only for agricultural and gathering societies.

The household economics model is intriguing, but it cannot address the larger political, economic, or ecological factors that affect polygyny. Even Grossbard's model begs for understanding of the exogenous causes of variations in its independent variables—the sex ratio, homogamy, social inequality among men, and female domestic income. The literature on agricultural intensification, though limited to agrarian societies, may offer more fruitful hypotheses about cross-societal variations. This literature seeks to explain the very low frequency of polygyny in plow-farming societies. Both Goody (1976) and Burton and Reitz (1981) show that this is not simply due to low female subsistence contributions in plow farming.

Goody (1973) argues against the female contributions hypothesis. He notes Dorjahn's (1959) comparison of East and West Africa, showing higher female agricultural contributions in East Africa and higher polygyny rates in West Africa, especially in the West African savannah, where one finds especially high male agricultural contributions. Goody says, "The reason behind polygy-

ny are sexual and reproductive rather than economic and productive" (1973:189), arguing that men marry polygynously to maximize their fertility and to obtain large households containing many young dependent males.

In *Production and Reproduction* (1976) Goody hypothesizes that plow agriculture, economic differentiation, and a complex polity act to produce bilateral inheritance and/or dowry, two social institutions that transmit part of a man's property to his daughters, either when he dies or when they marry. Goody claims that this mode of property transmission requires the husband's estate to be matched with the wife's estate, and that it would be difficult for a man to make more than one of these arrangements, so that polygyny will be infrequent. Hence, Goody foreshadows Grossbard's hypothesis about the relationship between homogamy and monogamy. He tests his model cross-culturally, finding empirical support for it with a path analysis.

Boserup (1970) explains the lack of polygyny in plow-farming societies in terms of access to land, saying that polygyny occurs in long-fallow agricultural societies with communal land tenure and land available for expansion, where "an additional wife is an additional economic asset which helps the family to expand its production" (1970:38). This view also appears in Goldschmidt and Kunkel, who say that "polygyny is advantageous where two conditions prevail: (1) the women do the bulk of the farm work and (2) land can be readily obtained for successive wives" (1971:1061).

Both Goody and Boserup focus on the acquisition and transmission of land, with Boserup emphasizing expansion into new lands in polygynous societies, and Goody emphasizing the inheritance of scarce land in monogamous societies. It will prove useful to generalize this thinking beyond agricultural societies by expanding the scope of the theory to include resources other than land.

A weakness of the economic theories of polygyny is their failure to specify demographic mechanisms by which polygynous societies have more wives than husbands. Explanations for polygyny based on warfare suggest some of these mechanisms. Before we discuss warfare it will be useful to discuss in some detail the demographic processes that affect the ratio of wives to husbands.

THE DEMOGRAPHIC PERSPECTIVE

Several demographic processes produce larger numbers of married women than married men. These processes may affect the adult sex ratio or the relative proportions of adult males and adult females who are married. Both endogenous and exogenous processes can affect the adult sex ratio. Possible endogenous processes include an effect of polygyny upon the natal sex ratio (Whiting 1977), and higher male mortality from disease, warfare, or dangerous occupations such as hunting, ocean fishing, or male labor migration (Dorjahn 1959). High male mortality may explain in part the increase in polygyny with male contributions to hunting, fishing, and herding (Lee 1979).

Exogenous processes include male labor migration, capturing women, and moving women at marriage with payment of bridewealth. Of these, we think capture of women is an especially important variable; many early ethnographies describe capture of women in warfare, along with marriage of the captives. We assume that there is intraregional variation in polygyny rates, and that this variation may be related to variations in the rate of taking captives (Dow 1983).

The proportions of adults who are married will be affected by the ease of divorce and remarriage, and by the sex difference in age of first marriage. The difference between mean male and female marriage ages can be as much as ten years, and can have a large effect on the ratio of wives to husbands. This variable is emphasized by Dorjahn (1959). Witkowski (1975) and Ember (1984) find significant relationships between polygyny and delayed marriage for males. Delayed marriage for men is often associated with the presence of a class of warriors; hence, this custom is correlated with warfare.

High male mortality from warfare, disease, or dangerous occupations will magnify the effect of differences in marriage age by reducing the cohort of older men relative to the cohort of younger wives. An expanding population also will interact with age differences at marriage, by increasing the cohort of younger wives relative to the cohort of older married men. The interaction of age differences at marriages, differential mortality, and an expanding population can easily produce an average of more than two wives per husband. It is this interaction effect that makes the difference in marriage age an especially powerful mechanism affecting polygyny.

WARFARE AND POLYGYNY

Murdock (1949) sees polygyny as based on high female contributions to subsistence, and as part of a complex that includes "movable property in herds, slaves, or other valuables" (1949:205), patrilocal or avunculocal residence, and warfare. Of war, Murdock says that it "enhances men's influence and brings them captive (and hence patrilocal) wives and plunder wherewith to buy other women" (1949:207).

Ember (1947) hypothesizes that polygyny is a consequence of high male mortality in warfare, which reduces the sex ratio. In a second article Ember (1984) tests the hypothesis that polygyny is associated with a delayed age for marriage of males, male mortality in warfare, and internal warfare. In both studies Ember finds empirical support of his hypotheses. Dow (1983), however, finds the demographic evidence on male mortality in warfare in relation to the adult sex ratio to be equivocal.

Dorjahn (1959) says African warfare emphasized taking captives, rather than killing the enemy. Kelly's discussion of Nuer warfare provides an interesting perspective on this phenomenon. In Nuer warfare the main casualties were younger men and older women, with male and female mortality being almost equal. Younger women and children were captured. Female captives were valued because they could be used to generate bridewealth when they were married to other Nuer, whereas captive boys were adopted into the lineage of their captor and would require bridewealth payment when they married. Consequently, few males were taken captive (Kelly 1985:56–57).

It is possible that male and female mortality in warfare are highly correlated and that both are associated with the taking of captives. If so, then Ember's relationship between male mortality and the sex ratio may be spurious, with the stronger relationship being that between mortality in warfare and the taking of captives. We will test these alternative hypotheses in the study that forms the core of this article.

Warfare may include plunder of resources rather than capture of women; in many cases, plunder may be transformed into the means of bridewealth payment. A community that is richer than its neighbors can easily take more wives than it gives and if it is a militarily dominant community, it may be able to steal the means of bride price payment, hence indirectly obtaining surplus wives from its neighbors, in addition to directly capturing wives. Hence, the position of a society in a local political network may have a strong effect on its adult sex ratio.

POLYGYNY AND THE ENVIRONMENT

With high rates of general polygyny, it becomes important for men to have access to the resources needed for support of large polygynous families. The need for access to resources will be even greater if there is rapid population growth. Polygyny will be constrained by any factor that constrains access to resources, including dependence upon a single plot of farm land (Boserup 1970), or dependence upon a single lagoon or river for fishing. Expansion into new territory through success in war, or through migration to unoccupied lands, will increase access to resources, and facilitate polygyny.

Ease of acquisition of new lands will be affect-

ed by environmental characteristics. A high-quality environment will provide more resources. A homogeneous environment will make movement to new territories easier, first because it poses fewer physical barriers to migration, and second because it will be easier to adapt to an environment similar to the previous environment.

Verdon (1983) compares two Ewe communities, a forest zone community with lower rates of polygyny and a savannah community with higher rates of polygyny. Verdon argues that higher levels of polygyny in the savannah community are associated with fissioning and migration to new communities. In the forest community, there is no level of sovereignty higher than the village, whereas the savannah communities are integrated at a regional level; hence, forest zone migrants lose their clan memberships and political rights, whereas savannah zone migrants maintain those rights. Verdon postulates general differences between forest and savannah adaptations in rates of polygyny, saying "Savannah environments may then be intrinsically more conducive to polygyny" (1983:20). This conjecture is supported by White, Burton, and Dow's (1981) study, which finds the highest levels of African polygyny occurring in the savannah region. We think the high rates of polygyny in the African savannah are due to the facilitating effect of this homogeneous, high-quality environment.

A MULTIVARIATE MODEL OF GENERAL POLYGYNY

Following the reasoning above, we hypothesize that the incidence of general polygyny will be a function of variables that (1) affect the flow of women across community boundaries, (2) facilitate societal expansion, or (3) constrain societal expansion.

1. The flow of women across community boundaries, in turn, is affected by at least three factors:

a. *Male-centered residence with bridewealth,* sometimes called fraternal interest groups. Residence patterns (patrilocal, virilocal, or avunculocal) that aggregate related males within the same community make it easier to import women from other communities. Bride price provides a motive for the movement of women at marriage, and also allows men to transform wealth into wives or, at the class level, wealth inequality into marriage inequality. Furthermore, bride price provides a motive for marrying women early, so as to collect bride price early, and for delaying the age of marriage of men, so as to delay the bride price payment, thereby increasing the difference in marriage ages (Boserup 1970:44). Hence, we hypothesize that fraternal interest groups will have a positive effect upon polygyny.

b. *Warfare with plunder or marriage of captive women.* Capture of women reduces the adult sex ratio, making higher rates of polygyny possible; plunder of such resources as cattle provides an exchangeable resource for marriage transactions. Further, warfare with plunder will increase wealth differentiation among men. Given Grossbard's prediction that social differentiation among men will be associated with higher levels of polygyny, plunder should cause increasing polygyny even in the absence of the capture of wives. Since the capture of wives may decrease social differentiation by allowing younger warriors to obtain wives without paying bridewealth, the two variables may have different effects on polygyny.

Cross-culturally it appears that marriage of captives is usually accompanied by warfare for plunder. It is possible, however, to have marriage of captives without plunder. An example is the Tallensi. Fortes (1967 [1945]:239), describing Tallensi warfare, says that it was prohibited to kill enemy women or children, or to "carry off any of the enemy's posses-

sions." In a second account Fortes (1949:83) says that "it is permissible, nay, commendable, to abduct the wife of a member of a distant, unrelated clan," and describes this kind of wife-stealing as a cause of warfare.[1]

c. *A small population.* A smaller total population allows external warfare with capture of wives to have greater proportional effects on the rates of polygyny. We hypothesize an interaction between population size and marriage of captives, so that a small population enhances the effect of marrying captives upon polygyny.

2. As discussed above, we hypothesize that environmental quality and homogeneity will facilitate societal expansion. High-quality environments will provide more resources for the support of large polygynous families; homogeneous environments facilitate migration and adaptation to new territories. The quality of an environment tends to decrease with cold or aridity, so that dry polar regions are lowest on environmental quality, and moist tropical regions highest. Grasslands are among the most homogeneous environments; mountains and rain forests among the most heterogeneous.

We see environmental quality as interacting with environmental homogeneity to generate the optimal conditions for general polygyny. We hypothesize that tropical savannah—a homogeneous and high-quality environment—will have a positive effect on polygyny. We further hypothesize that three low-quality or heterogeneous environments—highlands, desert, and polar environments—will have negative effects on polygyny.

In theory, high female subsistence contributions may facilitate expansion by making it easier for the polygynous household to support itself. However, the empirical studies suggest that the relationship between female subsistence contributions and polygyny is valid

---

[1]The Tallensi are coded by Wheeler as lacking warfare for captives or plunder (although they lack plunder only); we code them as marrying captives but lacking warfare for plunder.

mainly for agricultural societies. Accordingly, we hypothesize a positive effect of female agricultural contributions upon polygyny.

3. Circumstances that inhibit migration will also inhibit polygyny. *Plow agriculture* ties a household to a particular piece of land and makes acquisition of new land expensive. *Fishing* has a similar effect to the extent that it is dependent upon controlling access to particular rivers, lakes, or lagoons. Finally, residence on a *small island* limits the land available for cultivation, and makes migration difficult. We hypothesize that these will all have negative effects upon polygyny.

DEFINITION OF VARIABLES

We test our hypotheses on data coded for the Standard Cross-Cultural Sample (Murdock and White 1969), using multiple regression analysis. Following are definitions of our variables, with their abbreviations.

POLYGYNY

We use three measures of the incidence of polygyny. The first is a new code that measures the cultural rules for men's marriages (White 1988). It has five categories, ordered in terms of increasing involvement of larger classes of men with polygynous marriage:

Cultural Rule of Polygyny
1 = Monogamy prescribed
2 = Monogamy preferred, but exceptional cases of polygyny
3 = Polygyny for leaders or achievers (e.g., hunters, shamans)
4 = Polygyny limited to a general social class of men, and generally not attainable by others
5 = Polygyny preferred by most men, and attained by most men of sufficient years or wealth

Our other two measures of polygyny pertain to behaviors rather than cultural rules: to the percentages of males and females who are married polygynously. These are based on codes developed by John Whiting, who coded 60 Standard Sample societies for these two variables. These have been cross-checked for reliabilities, and extended to an additional 88 societies (White 1988). Together, the three measures are intended to provide convergent measures of polygyny. The correlation between the two frequency measures is .97, and the correlations of the cultural rules measure with the male and female frequency measures are .76 and .81, respectively. Hence, the three measures appear to be measuring the same construct. We use the logs of the frequency variables in our statistical analyses.

FRATERNAL INTEREST GROUPS

We define fraternal interest groups as the interaction of male-centered residence with bridewealth payments (Paige and Paige 1981). Both codes are from the *Ethnographic Atlas* (Murdock 1967):

Degree of Male-Centered Residence
3 = Patrilocal
2 = Virilocal or avunculocal
1 = Matrilocal, neolocal, or bilocal
Bridewealth
3 = Bridewealth
2 = Token bride price, brideservice, gift exchange, sister exchange, or no exchange
1 = Dowry

The scale is computed by multiplying the residence score by the bridewealth score.

WARFARE

The variable measuring warfare for plunder or for captives is taken from Wheeler's (1974) cross-cultural study of warfare. This and the following variable, following Otterbein (1970) and Ember (1974), code for warfare within 50 years of the focal date of ethnographic observation.

War for Plunder or Captives
2 = Present
1 = Absent

A second variable measures the marriage of captive women, and is a new code (White 1988). Marriage of captive women includes concubinage, in cases where the children of the union are legitimate, and adoption of captive females if they later become wives of the society's men. In many cases the captive has slave status; usually she or her children attain freedom as a consequence of the marriage (Patterson 1982:228–230).

Marriage of Captive Women
2 = Present
1 = Absent

From these two variables we compute a third variable to measure plunder in the absence of marriage of captive women:

Plunder Without Marriage of Captives
2 = Present
1 = Absent

SMALLNESS OF POPULATION

This variable has eight categories that are inversely proportional to the log of population size. This variable will appear in our model in an interaction with marriage of captives, following the reasoning above to the effect that a small population magnifies the effect of marriage of captives upon the adult sex ratio.

ENVIRONMENTAL CHARACTERISTICS

Climate zone is coded by White, Whiting, and Burton (1986) from Goode's *World Atlas* (Espenshade 1986), and is cross-checked against Whiting, Sodergren, and Stigler's (1982) data on temperature and rainfall. Six major zones are distinguished and recorded into three categories, according to our notions of environmental homogeneity and quality.

Climate Zone
3 = Tropical savannah
2 = Tropical rain forest or humid temperate
1 = Tropical highlands, desert, or polar

SMALL ISLAND

This variable is coded by the authors, and is 1 for residence on an island smaller than 2,500 km²; zero otherwise.

SUBSISTENCE VARIABLES

Codes for the presence of the plow are from the *Ethnographic Atlas* (Murdock 1967):

Plow
1 = Plow present
0 = Plow absent

Codes for the contribution of fishing to subsistence are computed by averaging a nine-point scale from the *Ethnographic Atlas* and a five-point scale from Murdock and Morrow (1970).

Female Contribution to Subsistence is measured by three sets of raters: Murdock and Wilson (1972), Barry and Schlegel (1982), and Whyte (1978). We found correlations ranging from .51 to .64 among these three scales, and computed an aggregate index from them.

Female Contributions to Agriculture is coded zero for societies that lack agriculture, and coded on a five-point scale from the *Ethnographic Atlas* for societies that have agriculture.

ZERO-ORDER RELATIONSHIPS

Correlations among the major variables used in our model are shown in Table 15-1. The strongest zero-order correlates of polygyny are fraternal interest groups, marriage of captives, the presence of the plow, and female subsistence contributions.

Table 15-2 is a cross-tabulation of climate zone with the five-point polygyny scale. Here we see that the three forms of polygyny have different distributions. While general polygyny is most frequently found in the tropical savannah, class-based polygyny is most frequently found in the temperate or rain forest zones, and polygyny for leaders is found most frequently in zones other than the tropical savannah.

REGRESSION ANALYSES: TESTS OF THE HYPOTHESES

The regression analyses involve two measures of the dependent variable (cultural basis of men's marriages and percentage of female polygyny), and replication within three regions: Western Old World (Europe and Africa), Eastern Old World (Asia and Oceania), and the Americas. The purpose of the regional replication is to test for the presence of unique historical events or processes not accounted for by our model (White, Burton, and Dow 1981; Burton and White 1984). The regressions for the regional replications involve a relatively small ratio of cases to variables; hence, they have less statistical stability than the overall model, and we cannot expect every variable to replicate perfectly. Rather, we look for an overall consistency in the pattern of results.

Table 15-3 shows the regressions using cultural rules for men's marriages as the dependent variable. All predictions are confirmed except for the effect of residence on a small island. Using stepwise regression we find the strongest predictors of polygyny to be marriage of captives, fraternal interest groups, and the plow, in that order, with

TABLE 15-1   Pearson correlation matrix.

	Cultural rules scale	% female polygyny	% male polygyny	Fraternal interest groups	Marry captives
% Female polygyny	0.885	1.000			
% Male polygyny	0.880	0.983	1.000		
Frat. int. grp.	0.361	0.251	0.263	1.000	
Marry captives	0.503	0.373	0.381	0.244	1.000
War for plunder	0.023	0.015	0.048	−0.024	−0.510
War mortality	0.287	0.140	0.129	0.198	0.347
Plow	−0.355	−0.342	−0.352	0.128	−0.290
Fishing	−0.150	−0.224	−0.208	−0.254	0.011
Small island	−0.101	−0.228	−0.199	−0.085	−0.016
Climate zone	0.281	0.266	0.246	0.017	0.163
Fem. subs. cont.	0.294	0.301	0.307	0.111	0.135
Fem. ag. cont.	0.238	0.174	0.171	0.026	0.156
Small population	0.109	0.200	0.220	−0.262	−0.022
	War for plunder	War mortality	Plow	Fishing	Small island
War mortality	0.026	1.000			
Plow	−0.006	−0.024	1.000		
Fishing	0.089	0.036	−0.261	1.000	
Small island	−0.017	−0.007	−0.168	0.424	1.000
Climate zone	−0.144	−0.128	−0.142	−0.039	0.018
Fem. subs. cont.	−0.106	−0.229	−0.258	−0.081	0.059
Fem. ag. cont.	−0.051	−0.106	−0.038	−0.118	0.066
Small population	0.101	−0.073	−0.586	0.366	0.178
	Climate zone	Fem. subs. cont.	Fem. ag. cont.	Small pop.	
Fem. subs. cont.	0.207	1.000			
Fem. ag. cont.	0.313	0.490	1.000		
Small population	−0.099	0.041	−0.154	1.000	

these three variables accounting for 42% of the variance in polygyny. Consistent with previous research, the female agricultural contributions variable has a statistically significant effect upon polygyny, and accounts for as much variance in polygyny as the more global female contributions scale.

The model replicates on each variable at the .10 level with two exceptions: the climate zone variable replicates only within the West and the female agricultural contributions variable replicates only within the East. All regression coefficients are in the predicted direction. Overall, the extent to which this model replicates across regions is impressive, given the marked differences between these regions in the relative frequencies of polygyny and the independent variables. For example, general polygyny, fraternal interest groups, and tropical savannah are much more common in the West; in the East, small islands are present and general polygyny is underrepresented; and in the Americas the plow and fraternal interest groups are rare, but high dependence on fishing is much more common than in the other regions.

A further test of the replication of this model is provided by using as the dependent variable the two measures of the percentage of polygyny. Regression results for these two measures are

TABLE 15-2 Cross-tabulation of polygyny with climate zone.

	Polar or desert highlands	Temperate or tropical rainforest	Tropical savannah
Monogamous	9	15	1
Mainly monogamous	10	18	7
Polygyny for leaders	18	20	7
Class-based polygyny	7	19	4
General polygyny	7	15	23

Chi-squared = 31.6, d.f. = 8, $p < .001$

TABLE 15-3 Predictors of cultural rules for polygyny scale.[2]

	World		Western Old World		Eastern Old World		Americas	
	Beta	p	Beta	p	Beta	p	Beta	p
Fraternal interest groups	.166	.001	.184	.004	.163	.003	.259	.026
Marriage of captives × small population	.264	.001	.278	.075	.279	.002	.231	.003
War for plunder	.794	.001	1.099	.025	.685	.047	.687	.069
Plow	−1.282	.001	−.907	.018	−.983	.009	−2.053	.029
Fishing	−.213	.002	−.358	.050	−.283	.033	−.183	.087
Small island	−.362	n.s.	—	—	.084	n.s.	—	—
Climate zone	.388	.001	.674	.002	.316	.188	.246	n.s.
Female contributions to agriculture	.118	.029	.112	n.s.	.202	.055	.115	n.s.
	$R^2 = .59$		$R^2 = .75$		$R^2 = .59$		$R^2 = .38$	
	$N = 142$		$N = 45$		$N = 46$		$N = 51$	

[2]The second variable is an interaction term, marriage of captives multiplied by smallness of population. Using marriage of captives alone produces a similar but weaker relationship. In all regressions we use unstandardized regression coefficients so as to be able to compare regression coefficients across regions.

very similar, so we present results in Table 15-4 for only one of these variables: percentage of females polygynously married. These regressions are similar to the first set. However, we find that residence on a small island has a strong negative effect on the frequency of polygyny, even though it did not affect men's marriage rules. A second difference from the prior analysis is the weaker replication of the two warfare variables.

The two sets of regression equations give remarkably convergent results, with the highest replication across regions and measures for the effects of fraternal interest groups, the plow, and dependence on fishing. The effects of the warfare variables, climate zone, and female contributions to agriculture show weaker replication.[3]

The two kinds of measures of polygyny provide a contrast between cultural rules and frequencies of behavior. It seems plausible to hypothesize that social structural variables, which measure

[3]We computed the regression models with network autocorrelation analysis (Dow et al. 1984) as a test for Galton's problem, and found no residual autocorrelation. We are grateful to Karl Reitz for assistance with this analysis. Since our dependent variable is ordinal, we replicated the model with a logit analysis, finding no differences from the ordinary least squares analysis. All models were tested for multicollinearity. Only the equations for the Western Old World show enough multicollinearity to be of concern; these equations are less stable than the others.

cultural institutions, would play a larger role in explaining the cultural rules scale, and that economic and ecological variables, which measure material processes and constraints, would play a larger role in accounting for the frequencies measures. We tested this hypothesis by comparing the variance accounted for solely by the social structure variables (warfare for plunder, marriage of captives, and fraternal interest groups) with variance accounted for solely by the ecological and economic variables (plow, dependence on fishing, small island, climate zone, and female contribution to agriculture). The social structural variables account for 35% of the variance in the cultural rules scale, whereas ecological and economic variables account for 26% of the variance in that scale. Hence, social structural variables are a better predictor of the cultural rules than are the economic and ecological variables. By way of contrast, the social structural variables account for only 19% of the variance in the frequencies of women's polygynous marriages, whereas the economic and ecological variables account for 27% of the variance in that measure. Hence, men's marriage rules are determined primarily by fraternal interest groups and warfare; frequency of polygyny is determined primarily by economy and ecology.

TABLE 15-4   Predictors of percent of women in polygynous marriages.

	World		Western Old World		Eastern Old World		Americas	
	Beta	p	Beta	p	Beta	p	Beta	p
Fraternal interest groups	.120	.002	.141	.029	.180	.006	.300	.041
Marriage of captives × small population	.151	.015	−.128	n.s.	.070	.508	.188	.061
War for plunder	.533	.039	1.080	.027	.415	n.s.	.433	n.s.
Plow	−1.424	.001	−1.712	.001	−1.165	.016	−2.748	.019
Fishing	−.250	.005	−.721	.001	−.321	.045	−.143	.325
Small island	−.933	.013	—	—	−.460	n.s.	—	—
Climate zone	.415	.007	.885	.001	.268	n.s.	.251	n.s.
Female contributions to agriculture	.108	.114	.334	.018	.054	n.s.	.109	n.s.
	$R^2 = .47$		$R^2 = .77$		$R^2 = .46$		$R^2 = .32$	
	$N = 123$		$N = 38$		$N = 43$		$N = 42$	

ALTERNATIVE WARFARE EXPLANATIONS

Earlier we described Ember's competing hypothesis to the effect that polygyny is due to male mortality in warfare. We can test this hypothesis using Ember's codes. Doing so reduces the sample size for the regression to 58 cases. In a model without the captives or plunder variables, but with the male mortality variable and other significant independent variables, male mortality shows a significant positive effect on polygyny. However, the R-squared for this model is much lower (.35) than the R-squared for our model, and controlling for marriage of captives causes male mortality to drop out of the model. Other warfare variables, such as internal war and external war, are also deleted from the model when warfare for plunder and marriage of captives are controlled.

EFFECTS OF DATA QUALITY

Several of our variables have been coded in two or more studies, allowing for computation of reliabilities. These reliabilities are plow (.89), dependence on fish (.86), female contributions to subsistence (.57), polygyny (.85), residence (.80), and bridewealth (.54). When bridewealth is multiplied by residence, the resulting variable, fraternal interest groups, has a reliability of .78. For the economic or subsistence variables (plow, fish, female labor contributions, agriculture) we have used averaged or combined ratings from the several coders. For social structural variables (polygyny, residence, bridewealth) we have used the more authoritative sources.

No reliabilities are as yet available on the entire sample for the warfare or climate codes. Our independent ratings of 20 cases of marriage of women captives showed an agreement of $r = .92$. We can get some idea of the convergence of Wheeler's code and our code for mar-

riage of captives by cross-tabulating the two. There are 131 cases where the two codes are consistent with each other, and only seven discrepant cases, in each of which we have coded marriage of captives as present while Wheeler (1974) codes warfare for plunder or captives as absent.

The higher the reliability of the data, especially for the independent variable, the more variance we might expect to explain with our model. Given reliabilities that are in the range of .85, the ability of the model to account for nearly 60% of the variance in polygyny is impressive.

A second source of potential error is bias in the judgments of informants, ethnographers, or coders (Naroll 1962). We tested 14 data quality variables from Rohner, Berg, and Rohner (1982) and Whyte (1985). Three variables proved significant—high language fluency, length of fieldwork, and non-American nationality—but they account for little variance. Of these, non-American nationality has the strongest effect. Since lower rates of polygyny are more typical of the North American and Oceanic areas in which American ethnographers have tended to work, the finding may indicate a regional effect rather than a source of systematic bias.

IMPLICATIONS FOR COMPARATIVE RESEARCH

This project offers two important guidelines for conducting cross-cultural research. The first is the importance of doing a detailed analysis of intrasocietal processes before engaging in cross-cultural hypotheses testing. In this case, that analysis involved a careful look at the demographic processes involved in polygyny. That analysis pointed the way toward possible variables to test cross-culturally. The second guideline concerns the importance of viewing social institutions in a regional context. Societies that engage in plunder of resources or capture of women take people or resources away from others. A given society's high polygyny rate thus would entail lower polygyny rates for less militarily dominant neighbors. Our model predicts high and low polygyny patterns at respective ends of the scale of military dominance, but it also predicts that regions would tend to be heterogeneous in this regard, with the more successful societies expanding at the expense of the weaker.

IMPLICATIONS FOR THEORIES OF POLYGYNY

Our analysis provides strong support for four interrelated views of polygyny: that polygyny is an expansionist strategy, favored by homogeneous and high-quality environment; that polygyny is associated with warfare for plunder and/or female captives; that polygyny is associated with the presence of fraternal interest groups; and that polygyny is constrained by the presence of the plow or by high dependence upon fishing. We find weaker support for two other variables: female contributions to agriculture and residence on small islands.

Use of two different kinds of measures of polygyny has allowed us to distinguish between predictors of two different kinds of measures of polygyny: rules for men's marriages and frequencies. The social structural variables (warfare and fraternal interest groups) are better predictors of the rules for polygynous marriages, whereas the economic and ecological variables are better predictors of the frequencies of polygyny. Despite these differences in the strength of relationships, both kinds of predictors have statistically significant effects on either measure of polygyny.

A multivariate model allows one to assess the relative importance of competing explanatory hypotheses. In formulating our explanatory model, we tested several alternative hypotheses that we have not reported here because they were eliminated in competition with the model we have presented. Internal warfare was included in our model at one point, but was later dropped because warfare for plunder or captives was a more powerful and correlated predictor. We also tested several measures of social stratification, including slavery and presence of the state, which were dropped when we controlled for warfare.

Our analysis contrasts two alternative views of polygyny that have quite different implications for thinking about gender. The economic model of polygyny views it as having benign effects on the status of women. In that view, polygyny exists in societies where women make high subsistence contributions, particularly to agriculture. They choose polygynous marriages because it is to their own economic advantage to do so. Polygyny can be seen as part of a complex of social institutions that includes high rates of participation in marketing and even politics, as was the case in some West African societies. Our findings provide some support for this model, but give stronger support to a model wherein polygyny is seen as associated with the expansion of male-oriented kin groups through favorable environments, facilitated by capture of women or bridewealth via warfare. Following this analysis, it is difficult to see polygyny as having benign effects upon the lives of all women. Rather, polygyny produces benefits for senior wives, who have sons and can mobilize the labor of junior wives and children (Hartung 1982); it has negative effects on women who become slaves, captives, or junior wives, or who do not have sons. While women as well as men may seek greater advantage from polygyny, its main effect is to stratify women as well as men.

We conclude by mentioning two limitations of the current analysis. The first limitation is the absence of measures of social processes that are affected by the world system. Most notable of these would be male labor migration. High levels of male labor migration skew the sex ratio in a society, and may provide continued support for polygyny in the absence of our predictor variables. This phenomenon may explain the maintenance of polygyny in many societies after warfare ceased.

The second limitation is that the model has greater predictive power for the Old World than for the New World. We think New World polygyny often takes a different form from the pattern of general polygyny described herein. With general polygyny co-wives tend not to be related to each other and to live in separate houses. Much of New World polygyny appears to be of a different pattern, in which wives tend to be related to each other and to live in the same house. Explaining this kind of polygyny would require a different model (Whiting 1986).

NOTES

Acknowledgments. Research for this article was supported by BNS grants 8023904, 8304782, and 8507685 from the National Science Foundation and from the UCI Committee on Research. We acknowledge the comments of Duran Bell, Ronald Cohen, Elizabeth Colson, James Dow, Dwight Read, Karl Reitz, and Beatrice Whiting, and the assistance of Candice Bradley and Carmella Moore. We are especially indebted to John Whiting for numerous discussions about polygyny.

REFERENCES

ALEXANDER, R. D., J. HOOGLAND, R. HOWARD, K. NOONAN, AND P. SHERMAN 1979 Sexual Dimorphisms and Breedings Systems in Pinnipeds, Ungulates, Primates and Humans. *In* Evolutionary Biology and Human Social Behavior: An Anthropological Perspective. N. Chagnon and W. Irons, eds. Pp. 402–435. North Scituate, MA: Duxbury Press.

ALVARD, MICHAEL S. 1986 Polygyny as a Human Female Reproductive Strategy. Haliska'i: UNM Contributions to Anthropology 5:42–56.

BARRY, HERBERT, AND ALICE SCHLEGEL 1982 Cross-Cultural Codes on Contributions by Women to Subsistence. Ethnology 21:165–188.

BECKER, GARY 1981 A Treatise on the Family. Cambridge, MA: Harvard University Press.

BLUMBERG, RAE L., AND ROBERT F. WINCH 1972 Societal Complexity and Familial Complexity: Evidence for the Curvilinear Hypothesis. American Journal of Sociology 77:898–920.

BOSERUP, ESTER 1970 Woman's Role in Economic Development. New York: St. Martin's Press.

BURTON, MICHAEL L., AND KARL P. REITZ 1981 The Plow, Female Contribution to Agricultural Subsistence, and Polygyny. Behavior Science Research 16:275–305.

BURTON, MICHAEL L., AND DOUGLAS R. WHITE 1984 Sexual Division of Labor in Agriculture. American Anthropologist 86:568–583.

CHAGNON, N. 1979 Is Reproductive Success Equal in Egalitarian Society? *In* Evolutionary Biology and Human Social Behaviors: An Anthropological Perspective. N. Chagnon and W. Irons, eds. Pp. 374–401. North Scituate, MA: Duxbury Press.

COHEN, R. 1971 Dominance and Defiance. Washington: American Anthropological Association.

DORJAHN, VERNON R. 1959 The Factor of Polygyny in African Demography. *In* Continuity and Change in African Cultures. William R. Bascom and Melville J. Herskovits, eds. Pp. 87–112. Chicago: University of Chicago Press.

DOW, JAMES 1983 Woman Capture as a Motivation for Welfare. *In* Rethinking Human Adaptation: Biological and Cultural Models. R. Dyson-Hudson and M. A. Little, eds. Pp. 97–115. Boulder: Westview.

DOW, MALCOLM M., M. L. BURTON, D. R. WHITE, AND K. P. REITZ 1984 Galton's Problem as Network Autocorrelation. American Ethnologist 11: 754–770.

EMBER, MELVIN 1974 Warfare, Sex Ratio, and Polygyny. Ethnology 13:197–206. 1984 Alternative Predictors of Polygyny. Behavior Science Research 19:1–23.

ENGELS, FREDERICK 1972 [1884] The Origin of the Family, Private Property and the State. Eleanor B. Leacock, ed. New York: International Publishers.

ESPENSHADE, EDWIN B., JR., ED. 1986 Goode's World Atlas. 17th edition. Chicago: Rand McNally.

FORTES, MEYER 1949 The Web of Kinship among the Tallensi. London: Oxford University Press. 1967 [1945] The Dynamics of Clanship among the Tallensi. Oosterhout, The Netherlands: Anthropological Publications. (Originally published by Oxford University Press).

GOLDSCHMIDT, WALTER, AND EVALYN J. KUNKEL 1971 The Structure of the Peasant Family. American Anthropologist 73:1058–1076.

GOODY, JACK 1973 Polygyny, Economy and the Role of Women. *In* The Character of Kinship. Jack Goody, ed. Pp. 175–190. London: Cambridge University Press. 1976 Production and Reproduction. London: Cambridge University Press.

GROSSBARD, AMYRA S. 1976 An Economic Analysis of Polygyny: The Case of Maiduguri. Current Anthropology 17:701–707. 1980 The Economics of Polygamy. *In* Research in Population Economics, Vol. 2. J. L. Simon and J. DaVanzo, eds. Pp. 321–350. Greenwich, CT:JAI Press. 1984 A Theory of Allocation of Time in Markets for Labour and Marriage. The Economic Journal 94:863–882.

HARTUNG, J. 1982 Polygyny and the Inheritance of Wealth. Current Anthropology 23:1–12.

HEATH, DWIGHT B. 1958 Sexual Division of Labor and Cross-Cultural Research. Social Forces 37:77–79.

KELLY, RAYMOND C. 1985 The Nuer Conquest: The Structure and Development of an Expansionist System. Ann Arbor: University of Michigan Press.

LEE, GARY R. 1979 Marital Structure and Economic Systems. Journal of Marriage and the Family 41:701–713.

MARTIN, M. KAY, AND BARBARA VOORHIES 1975 Female of the Species. New York: Columbia University Press.

MURDOCK, GEORGE P. 1949 Social Structure. New York: Macmillan. 1967 Ethnographic Atlas. Ethnology 9:122–225.

MURDOCK, GEORGE P., AND DIANA O. MORROW 1970 Subsistence Economy and Supportive Practices: Cross-Cultural Codes 1. Ethnology 9:302–330.

MURDOCK, GEORGE P., AND DOUGLAS R. WHITE 1969 Standard Cross-Cultural Sample. Ethnology 8:329–369.

MURDOCK, GEORGE P., AND SUZANNE F. WILSON 1972 Settlement Patterns and Community Organization: Cross-Cultural Codes 3. Ethnology 11:254–295.

NAROLL, RAOUL 1962 Data Quality Control. New York: Free Press.

OSMOND, MARIE W. 1965 Toward Monogamy: A Cross-Cultural Study of Correlates of Type of Marriage. Social Forces 44:6–16.

OTTERBEIN, KEITH 1970 The Evolution of War. Pittsburgh: University of Pittsburgh Press.

PAIGE, K. E., AND J. M. PAIGE 1981 The Politics of Reproductive Ritual. Berkeley: University of California Press.

PATTERSON, ORLANDO 1982 Slavery and Social Death: A Comparative Study. Cambridge: Harvard University Press.

ROHNER, RONALD P., D. SCOTT BERG, AND EVELYN C. ROHNER 1982 Data Quality Control in the Standard Cross-Cultural Sample: Cross-Cultural Codes. Ethnology 21:359–369.

SPENCER, PAUL 1980 Polygyny as a Measure of Social Differentiation in Africa. *In* Numerical Techniques in Social Anthropology. J. Clyde Mitchell, ed. Philadelphia: ISHI Press.

STECKLE, J., AND L. EWANYK 1973 A Consumer Preference Study in Grain Utilization. Preliminary report, Ministry of National Resources, North Eastern State, Nigeria.

VERDON, MICHEL 1983 Polygyny, Descent, and Local Fission: A Comparative Hypothesis. Journal of Comparative Family Studies 14:1–22.

WHEELER, VALERIE 1974 Drums and Guns: A Cross-Cultural Study of the Nature of War. Ph.D. dissertation, Department of Anthropology, University of Oregon.

WHITE, DOUGLAS, R. 1988 Rethinking Polygyny: Co-Wives, Codes, and Cultural Systems. Current Anthropology 29:529–572.

WHITE, DOUGLAS R., MICHAEL L. BURTON, AND MALCOLM M. DOW 1981 Sexual Division of Labor in African Agriculture. American Anthropologist 83:824–849.

WHITE, DOUGLAS R., JOHN W. M. WHITING, AND MICHAEL L. BURTON 1986 Climate and Subsistence Codes. World Cultures 2(2).

WHITING, J. W. M. 1977 Paper presented at meetings of Society for Cross-Cultural Research, East Lansing, Michigan. 1986 Play it Again Sam: A New Paradigm for Cross-Cultural Research. Paper presented at meetings of Society for Cross-Cultural Research, San Diego, California.

WHITING, JOHN W. M., JOHN A. SODERGREN, AND STEPHEN M. STIGLER 1982 Winter Temperature as a Constraint to the Migration of Preindustrial Peoples. American Anthropologist 84:279–298.

WHITING, JOHN W. M., AND BEATRICE B. WHITING 1975 Aloofness and Intimacy of Husbands and Wives: A Cross-Cultural Study. Ethos 6:183–207.

WHYTE, M. 1978 Cross-Cultural Codes Dealing with the Relative Status of Women. Ethnology 17:211–237. 1985 Independent Variables for Testing Hypotheses on the Status of Women. World Cultures 1(4).

WITKOWSKI, S. 1975 Polygyny, Age of Marriage, and Female Status. Paper presented at meetings of American Anthropological Association, San Francisco, CA.

VI

SEX AND THE UNIVERSAL TABOO: INCEST

INTRODUCTION

Few questions have engaged anthropologists as thoroughly as has that of the origins of the incest taboo. Many theorists have argued for social explanations (such as Edward B. Tylor's "marry out or die out") and the need for groups to form alliances with one another through exogamy and the exchange of women. Other theorists have proposed psychological explanations (for example, Edward A. Westermarck's "familiarity breeds contempt") to account for the apparent "natural aversion" toward marrying and mating expressed by those who are reared together. More recently, sociobiologists have attempted to explain the in-

cest taboo in terms of the individual's concern for reproductive success.

A proponent of the sociobiological approach, Joseph Shepher (1983) assumes that incest has undergone an evolutionary process. He discusses the costs and benefits of inbreeding and concludes that certain forms of inbreeding are desirable. He believes that incest rules function primarily to prevent inbreeding between relatives who share 50% or more of their genes. For such individuals, the costs of inbreeding normally outweigh any benefits.

The readings in this section cover both the major biosocial and cultural explanations for the universality of the incest taboo. In assessing the arguments of these authors, one might do well to ask whether or not parent/child incest and brother/sister (or sibling) incest are distinct phenomena. It may be that they are only classified as equivalent because they both involve family members.

Readers also should be aware that, just as marriage and mating are not necessarily the same, incest and sexual abuse are not absolutely equivalent—even if the sexual abuse is perpetrated by a father or brother. This distinction is especially important from the sociobiological perspective, which is concerned primarily with the production of offspring with similar genetic composition.

Robin Fox attempts to reconcile the positions of Freud and Westermarck on the incest taboo. According to Fox's theory of equilibration (the ability to make socially tempered judgments), individuals are faced with the dilemma of striving to compete with their elders while realizing that they also want to become the elders. With regard to reproduction, kinship and initiation ceremonies are the social expression of the taming and socializing of these emotions.

Arthur P. Wolf describes an unusual practice in traditional Hokkien-speaking Chinese families, whereby families adopt a female child to raise as the future bride of a biological son. Wolf argues that this overcomes the problem of an adult female "intruder" entering the family upon the marriage of a son. At the same time, it creates the potential problem of boys and girls who are reared together having an aversion to marrying and to mating. Data on this institution of *simpua* marriage, as described by Wolf, seem to support Westermarck's "familiarity breeds contempt" position.

Claude Lévi-Strauss argues that incest is "less a rule prohibiting marriage with the mother, sister or daughter, than a rule obliging that the mother, sister or daughter be given to others." Thus the taboo's purpose is alliance insurance. The French structuralist's perspective holds that the incest taboo is cultural in origin. Indeed, it represents, in a sense, the origin of culture.

REFERENCES

SHEPHER, JOSEPH. (1983). *Incest: A Biosocial View.* New York: Academic Press.

SUGGESTED READINGS

COHEN, YEHUDI. (1978). The Disappearance of the Incest Taboo. *Human Nature, 1:*72–78.

HÉRITIER, FRANCOISE. (1982). The Symbolics of Incest and Its Prohibition. In Michel Izard and Pierre Smith (Eds.), *Between Belief and Transgression: Structural Essays in Religion, History, and Myth* (pp. 152–179). Chicago: University of Chicago Press.

LEAVITT, GREGORY C. (1989). Disappearance of the Incest Taboo: A Cross-Cultural Test of General Evolutionary Hypotheses. *American Anthropologist, 91:*1:116–131.

LEAVITT, GREGORY C. (1990). Sociobiological Explanations of Incest Avoidance: A Critical Review of Evidential Claims. *American Anthropologist, 92:*4:971–993.

WAGNER, ROY. (1972). Incest and Identity: A Critique and Theory on the Subject of Exogamy and Incest Prohibition. *Man, 7:*601–613.

YOUNG, FRANK W. (1967). Incest Taboos and Social Solidarity. *American Journal of Sociology, 72:*589–600.

16

THE LAMP AT THE
END OF THE TUNNEL

ROBIN FOX

To complete the picture, then, it is necessary to keep the promise to look closely at our reactions to sex with close kin in the light of this equilibrational theory. It is best to start with Freud's own insistence that incest prohibitions are directed primarily against the young male, since apart from anything else, it is absolutely true. It is a natural outcome of the young male being torn in two directions: He (or his phyletic memory) wants on the one hand to displace the old man or men and have free access to the women; on the other hand, he too is going to be an older male, and at the same time, therefore, he wants to *be* the old man. Kinship and initiation ceremonies are the social expression of the taming of these emotions and the socializing of them. But these two sets of social institutions are not free creations of the intellect. The brain is geared, wired, or what have you, to produce them in some form or other, since it is itself the product of the forces they represent. The brain faithfully reproduces a version of what produced it in the first place—or rather produced it over many millions of years of primate and hominid evolution. This is what Freud was so gallantly struggling to say, and given the hindsight we have

SOURCE: From *The Red Lamp of Incest: An Enquiry into the Origins of Mind and Society* by R. Fox. Copyright © 1983 by University of Notre Dame Press. Reprinted by permission of the publisher.

today, I like to think this is how he would say it if he were alive now. In some sense, then, we do reproduce the evolutionary drama of the primal horde. But exogamy and initiation are truer exemplars of this than incest taboos with all their variability.

As we said, we probably would not commit much incest anyway, either for the demographic reasons we explored in chapter one or for the many reasons mammals avoid incest, as pointed out by Bischof. During the intensification stage, however, the normal mechanisms were strained. This is the context in which we must look at our current reactions to incest. The young male meets his first trial of equilibration with those older males and females that he finds himself among and who are defined as having power over him (males) or being forbidden to him (females). In the evolutionary context, such women as "mother" and "sister" would both be females controlled by older males. The effective older male might be "father" but it might just as likely be "mother's brother"—which is why there is no problem of interpretation of matrilineal societies. It is only if we are sold on the nuclear family as a biological human universal that the problem arises. If we see it as a universal problem of old males versus young males, then there is no problem. The young males will, as Auden said, "kill their mother's brothers/In their dreams" if the maternal uncles are the present stimulus to the atavistic memories. But they will only do it in their dreams. This is what equilibration is about—the whole secret of the wiring of the brain-hormonal system. The young male goes into an inhibitory reaction against his own hostile impulses: or rather, he is easily triggered into doing so because he is easily made guilty about them. The mechanism may not be used—but it is there and ready. The relationship can, in fact, be friendly and co-operative, but the mechanism is there in case it isn't. The young male may not even know the nature of his feelings about the women. The reality may be his hostility to the elders.

As we saw in the sibling chapter, the mechanism will only be needed if natural avoidance of the sister has not been learned. Natural avoidance is there as a possibility with all its vicissitudes, but should it not be learned, should the young males indeed "turn their sisters into wives" even in their dreams, then the mechanism is there to step in—the guilt and inhibition are easily provoked. For the sister is either a "daughter" or a "niece" and thus in some older male's charge. But what of the "daughter"? By the time there is a daughter, the young male has become an older male himself with all the responsibilities of maintaining the kinship system. True, the daughter (unless this is a matrilineal society) is a "female under his control," but he has by now used his equilibrational powers to the full in learning that "own" women are means of exchange and alliance. Again, we must be consistent. There is technically no reason why he should not have sex with her and then marry her off. This is the commonest form of incest it seems on a worldwide basis, and it accords with our theory that it should be. But other inhibitions can exist, and a mature male has the fully developed equilibrational powers of an adult brain to call into play. In many cases—and we must keep in mind that our society's demography is unusual—she will already have been pledged and delivered as a wife to someone else by the time she is sexually mature. We keep young adults as children much longer than is the norm for human society, which is why societies like ours may have more problems with father-daughter incest. But not only that. It may be just as difficult to make over the protective feelings felt toward the daughter after a period of long nurture from childhood into sexual feelings. In the same way, it is difficult to make over the asexual brother-sister feelings in cases where natural avoidance has occurred. Very generalized bonds of this kind—very diffuse bonds, that is—seem hard to convert into something radically different. (Fathers and sons do not seem to work well as partners, nor old teachers and pupils as colleagues either.) But there is no question that with the father and daughter there is much more room for variability. It is here however that I would see Lévi-Strauss's argument at its strongest. The daughter has been reared for all those years as a potential wife for *another man*. This must have a powerful effect in restraining the father, and the ancient mechanisms of equilibrational inhibition will be brought into powerful play here, with the fact of exogamy itself as a stimulant to restraint.

As to "mother," we have already seen that she is ruled out, as Goody saw, because she is under the control of another man—and a man who is the focus of the whole weight of the equilibrational process at that. But she is also the mother who has nursed and suckled the boy. This is a powerful bodily relationship, and if natural avoidance can operate as a result of close body contact in siblings, why not in the case of mother and son? Suckling responses in the mother are strongly sexual as we now know and can admit.[1] (In many societies, mothers stimulate the genitals of their baby sons to calm them.) To use Earl Count's memorable phrase, the experiences of the lactation period "reverberate" throughout the males' life.[2] Add to this the age difference and that the mother is someone else's wife, and the cards are heavily stacked against the son's chances.[3]

The process weighs heavily on the young males and later becomes a problem for the old ones. What of the females? Here we are on less

sure grounds, and since the males tend to make the rules, we hear less of the female case. But I suspect that the equilibrational process is not so strong in females as in males, because the conflicts are not as great and hence the reactions less charged. I doubt that unless it is severely inculcated, there is much guilt in female feelings about sex with brothers and fathers. If there has developed a natural avoidance with the brother, then there will be few sexual feelings, of course; the same may be true between mothers and sons. There is unlikely to be so strong an avoidance between fathers and daughters, and in this case where there is most incest, there is also perhaps least guilt—least inhibition—on the part of the girl. It is hard to say, but some observers believe that even where the relationship is socially tabooed, a girl can enter it without guilt or psychological damage, which often follows only on discovery when she learns of the shame attached or is treated as a "problem" by social workers, psychiatrists, and the law. Evidence is thin, but theoretically, we would not expect as much inner conflict with the young female as with the young male.[4]

If, then, we put the problem of incest motivations in the context of the equilibrational process, we can see how the various relationships and the varying motivations make more sense than if we look at them as products of the nuclear family. Even if there were no nuclear family, there would still be older males controlling the women. The nuclear family, where it exists, simply concentrates all this turmoil onto the little groups of actors who must play out the equilibrational drama amongst themselves first and in the wider society later. Nor does it do us much good to concentrate on taboos and injunctions and sanctions generally, for the reasons advanced in chapter one. These, too, are highly variable. The red lamp glimmers in our heads and hormones if anywhere, not in our laws. We have allowed incest, even encouraged it, but this is consonant with the theory. It will depend on

[1] A. Rossi, "A Biosocial Perspective on Parenting, *Daedalus,* 106 (1977): 1:31.
[2] Earl W. Count, "The Lactation Complex: A Phylogenetic Consideration of the Mammalian Mother-Child Symbiosis, with Special Reference to Man," *Homo* 18 (1) (1967): 38–54; idem, "The Biological Basis of Human Sociality," *American Anthropologist* 60 (1958): 1049–85.
[3] I am not implying that there can *never* be incestuous attraction between mother and son nor that a great deal of psychic energy does not go into the suppression or conversion of such attractions. But it is the very *incompatibility* of such thoughts with the "reverberations" of the nurturing experience that cause the anxiety where it occurs. This comes out acutely in the "madonna/whore" contrast on the one hand, and the "suppressed archetype" of the "mother-lover" on the other, as exemplified by the figure of Aphrodite. It is significant that while all kinds of simpleminded rantings make headlines in anthropology today, Paul Friedrich's exquisite study *The Meaning of Aphrodite* (Chicago: Chicago University Press, 1978) has gone totally unnoticed.

[4] See a sensible review of some current literature by James W. Ramey, "Dealing with the Last Taboo," *SIECUS Report* 7 (5) (1979).

how we juggle the categories of marriageable and unmarriageable, and who we decide has power over whom. There is no automatic universal horror. Sometimes, groups decide to do the reverse of exogamy and *not* to exchange women (castes, for example), and this can be carried all the way to marriage with the sibling or the daughter. It is rare, but it happens. What the equilibrational wiring does is make it easy to prevent it happening, and most circumstances conspire to ensure that in most cases, where natural avoidance is not working, the equilibrational process will step in and do its work. By and large, incest will not happen, regardless of the laws of exogamy, the rules of marriage. Exogamy is certainly not necessary to guard against incest—it might or might not have that effect. But then neither is the incest taboo, so called. Simply to forbid it is not enough. The two processes of natural aversion and inhibition under equilibrational pressure will do it.

The taboos, the red lamp that has gleamed so temptingly for all those students of human nature, are perhaps best regarded as expressions of anxiety in circumstances when incest wishes have been provoked in the face of either a motivation of avoidance or of inhibition. We do make it difficult for ourselves, but that is the human way. It is why we are more interesting than animals. It is why we have taboos at all. It is all the work of the mind, and if the process I am describing here has produced the brain, and if the brain is the organ of mind (as the legs are the organ of walking or the genitals of sex), then this process must have produced the mind, which produces totems and taboos among other things. Is it again producing what produced it? And is this the link between incest, totemism, taboo, and exogamy that has eluded us so far? If so, the fading gleams from the red lamp may illumine the darkest corner of all: the nature of the human mind.

Adopt a Daughter-in-Law, Marry a Sister: A Chinese Solution to the Problem of the Incest Taboo

Arthur P. Wolf

In stressing the social advantages of the familial incest taboo, most explanations of the taboo ignore the fact that it makes marriage the enemy of the family. The stranger intruded by marriage often poses a threat to existing domestic relationships. The Chinese solution to this problem is to circumvent the taboo by adopting female children who are raised as wives for their foster parents' sons. The family choosing this form of marriage sacrifices prestige and dependable affinal ties, but by socializing their own daughters-in-law they preserve domestic harmony. The fact that many Chinese arrange marriages within the family as a means of preserving the family suggests that widely accepted explanations of the incest taboo exaggerate the dangers of incest and ignore the dangers of the taboo.

Although the general character of the Chinese family has been known to the West for several generations, the variety of Chinese family forms is such as to always provide the newcomer with a few surprises. My favorite example occurs in C. F. Gordon-Cumming's account of her visit to the city of Foochow in 1879. A missionary lady of the author's acquaintance had recently returned from a trip to a Christian school in a nearby village. "Particularly attracted by a bright little fellow, about eight years of age, who for some months had refused to worship the vil-lage idols, and who repeated various Christian hymns with much feeling," the lady noted that "the little chap carried in his arms a wee baby girl." In an attempt to strike up a conversation with the boy she "naturally asked if it was his sister, whereupon he looked shy, and did not answer, but his brother volunteered the infor-mation, 'She is his wife!'" (1884:195).

The girl was in fact a *t'ung-yang-hsi,* a "daughter-in-law raised from childhood," or what Hokkien speakers call a *sim-pua,* a "little daughter-in-law." The institution was first described in

Source: From "Adopt a Daughter-in-Law, Marry a Sister: A Chinese Solution to the Problem of the Incest Taboo" by A. Wolf in *American Anthropologist,* 70:5, 1968, pp. 864–874. Copyright © 1968 by American Anthropological Association. Reprinted by permission. Not for further reproduction.

217

English by another nineteenth century visitor to Foochow, the Reverend Justus Doolittle.

> When a girl is born in a poor family, which it feels unable or is unwilling to rear, she is often given away or sold when but a few weeks or months old, or one or two years old, to be the future wife of a son in the family of a friend or relative which has a little son not betrothed in marriage. . . . The girl is called a 'little bride' and is taken home, and brought up in the family together with her future husband. When of marriageable age, and the family can afford the little additional expense, she is married to her affianced on a fortunate day, which has been selected by a fortune-teller. Friends are invited and a feast is made. No bridal cakes are distributed among her relatives, and no red bridal chair is used, because she is living in the family of her husband [1865:98].

The slight attention paid to this form of marriage in general books on the Chinese family creates the impression that such marriages are rare. This may be true of the North China Plain, Manchuria, and the Shantung Peninsula, but it is certainly not true of the lower Yangtze delta, the southeastern hills, and the Hokkien-speaking areas of Fukien and Taiwan. An article printed in a number of provincial newspapers tells us that 16,454 t'ung-yang-hsi were "freed" in Kiangsi province in the first two years following the promulgation of new marriage laws in May of 1950. The same article complains that despite this progress marriages involving t'ung-yang-hsi "have not been fully abolished." "Of all the women in the 2nd *ch'u*, Yungchun *hsien*, in Fukien province, twenty percent were found to be t'ung-yang-hsi" (Hopei Jihpao, Feb. 1, 1953). A second widely printed article appearing a week later (Hopei Jihpao, Feb. 9, 1953) repeats this complaint and again notes the persistence of "such barbarous and backward feudal practices as the keeping of t'ung-yang-hsi and teng-lang-hsi."[1] "Of all the women in Pingho hsien in Fukien, seventy

percent are or have been t'ung-yang-hsi, while in nine ch'u in Chenping hsien in Honan province, there are still more than 2,000 unmarried t'ung-yang-hsi."

J. Lossing Buck's famous rural surveys report much lower frequencies of t'ung-yang-hsi in China in the 1930s, but Buck's questionnaire did not ask informants if they were raising a wife for one of their sons (1937 Statistics: 443–463). The unexpectedly large proportion of males in the ages five to fifteen indicates that many families were raising a t'ung-yang-hsi but simply did not mention the fact.[2] Studies by Chinese and Japanese scholars who were aware of the institution report finding large numbers of t'ung-yang-hsi in communities on the Yangtze delta and in South China. The most reliable of these are Fei Hsiao-tung's 1936 study of the village of Kaihsienkung in southern Kiangsu; C. M. Chiao's 1931–1935 study of the population of the Hsiaochi registration district in central Kiangsu; Feng Tzu-kang's 1933 survey of Lanhsi hsien in central Chekiang; Michiyoshi Kajiwara's 1934 investigation of the household registers of nine villages in northern Taiwan; and Uzuru Okada's 1936 survey of the Shihlin district, also in northern Taiwan. At the time of Fei's study 95 of Kaihsienkung's 244 unmarried girls were *siaosiv* (the equivalent of t'ung-yang-hsi and sim-pua) (1939:54); Chiao's data indicate that approximately one-fourth of all the brides marrying into Hsiaochi came as t'ung-yang-hsi (1938:60–61)[3];

---

[1]Like the t'ung-yang-hsi and the sim-pua, a teng-lang-hsi enters her future husband's household as a child. The difference is that she is adopted in anticipation of the birth of her husband: literally, a teng-lang-hsi is "a bride waiting for a groom." If a family takes a teng-lang-hsi and does not later produce a boy for her to marry, they either allow the girl to marry out of her foster family, or, more commonly, use her to acquire a son-in-law by way of an uxorilocal marriage.

[2]In his report of the 1922–1925 survey Buck writes:

> In this study for the first two decades the ratio of males to females is 123.4 for the 0–9 age group, and 118.3 for the 10–19 group. The ratio by five-year groups shows much variation and reaches 143 for the years 5–9. The reason for this high ratio in comparison with that of 106 for the age group 0–4 and with that of 119.5 for the age group of 10–14 is not clear (1930:343–345).

And then in a summary of the 1929–1931 survey we find this comment (1937:376): "The relatively small number of females at ages under 20 . . . also suggests an under-enumeration of females. It is difficult on other terms to explain the marked leveling of the curve between the 10 to 19 and 20 to 29 age groups." My suggestion is that the missing girls are t'ung-yang-hsi. They leave the population of "daughters" at an early age and return after puberty as "wives."

[3]Chiao writes:

> More females than males were found among immigrants during the first and second years [of the study] and a few more during the fourth year. This is due to the fact that all the women from outside

the 538 families in Feng's sample included 97 who were raising a son's wife (1935:54); the household registers studied by Kajiwara listed 208 sim-pua in a total of 839 families (1941: 180–183); and in a survey of only 148 households Uzuru Okada reports finding a total of 137 sim-pua (1949:8).

The fact that t'ung-yang-hsi were so common in some areas of China as late as thirty years ago argues for an even higher frequency fifty to sixty years ago. This form of marriage assumes strong parents, and by the 1930s Chinese parents had lost a great deal of their authority. Imported ideas of conjugal relations and a changing economy provided their children with an example of marital independence and the means of achieving it. There were probably many parents in the 1930s and after who considered raising a wife for one of their sons but rejected the idea because of the difficulties encountered by a friend or relative. A couple raised in the same household as intimately as brother and sister find the prospect of sexual intercourse with each other "embarrassing" and "uninteresting" and are reluctant to marry (Wolf 1966).[4] So long as the groom's parents wield the very considerable authority granted Chinese parents, they can override the couple's reluctance and "push them together," but as soon as parental authority begins to deteriorate, the younger

who were married to a man in Hsiao Chi were counted as immigrants. In China, after marriage, a woman almost always lives in her husband's community. . . . The large proportion of female immigrants at ages 15–24 is due to those newly-married people from outside. In Hsiao Chi community the rearing of a fiancée for the son or for the grandson is practiced and especially in recent years because of the falling prices of farm products. Most girls under 14 who have come to the area came under these conditions [1938:60].

I have therefore taken the relative number of female immigrants in these two groups as a rough indication of the relative frequency of the two forms of patrilocal marriage. There were 377 immigrants between 15 and 24 years of age, and 122 under 14 years of age: thus approximately one-fourth of all brides entering the community came as t'ung-yang-hsi.

[4]I have since discovered that I was not the first to see the implications of this situation for Westermarck's explanation of the incest taboo. In 1943 Tai Yen-Hui wrote: "Westermarck says that when people are acquainted too closely they become sexually indifferent. He therefore emphasized the need for marriage outside of the family. It is possible that there may be feelings of disgust or coolness between a *sim-pua* and her intended husband" (1943:3).

generation revolts and insists on marriages outside of the family. The inevitable result is decline in the frequency of t'ung-yang-hsi. As one of my informants on Taiwan explained when I asked him why he had not adopted a wife for his son, "There is no point in raising another daughter if she won't marry your son."

One estimation of the frequency of t'ung-yang-hsi in late traditional China occurs in the Reverend George MacKay's account of his years as a missionary in Taiwan. After describing the various ways in which a family can obtain a daughter-in-law, MacKay writes: "The most common method is for the parents to purchase a young girl and bring her up in their own homes to be a wife for their son" (1895:120). While it would be easy to pass off MacKay's observation as uninformed or exaggerated, the fact is that his estimation is entirely accurate for the area of the island with which he was familiar. This past summer I obtained the Japanese household registration records for two districts known to MacKay and am now in the process of analyzing these for the years 1905–1925. This work is not far enough along to report the results in any detail, but it is obvious that raising the girl from childhood was the most popular way of acquiring a daughter-in-law. At least forty percent of all marriages involved a woman raised as a member of her husband's family, and many men who married a woman raised elsewhere were originally matched with a sim-pua who died as a child.

There is no evidence of comparable quality for the China mainland prior to the survey conducted in the 1920s and 1930s, but such evidence as there is makes the t'ung-yang-hsi a prominent feature of the Chinese social landscape. After describing a number of instances of such marriages among his converts and the employees of the American Mission Board in Foochow, Doolittle notes that "this way of disposing of girls is quite common among the poor, whether living in the city or in the country" (1865: 2:205). The medical missionary William Lockhart tells us that the many children deposited in the Shanghai Foundling Hospital were "taken by various families to be brought up as domestics or artificers of various kinds, or in other instances adopted as children; the boys as heirs where there are no sons, the girls as the future wives of the sons or grandsons of the family" (1861:26). Mrs. Mary Bryson also seems to regard the practice of raising a son's wife as commonplace. In her account of life as a missionary in Wuchang in southern Hupeh, she remarks, " 'Is that your daughter?', I have sometimes asked a Chinese woman, as I have seen a little girl sitting by her side. 'No, she is betrothed to my son', is a frequent reply, as she looks away to a small boy playing merrily, with his thoughts more exercised by the making of mud-pies than anything else" (1885:65).

The popularity of this form of marriage is evident in every facet of the traditional culture. Many folksongs recall the tragedy or the humor in the lives of t'ung-yang-hsi and teng-lang-hsi (Chen 1943:38–39), and their behavior is commonly taken as a point of reference in proverbs and popular expressions (Wu 1943:36–37). Litigation involving the rights and obligations of t'ung-yang-hsi is preserved in such compilations of legal precedents as the *Hsing-an Hui-lan* and the *Hsü-tsêng Hsing-an Hui-lan* (Chu 1843 and 1840). The fact that the institution is not mentioned in the legal code of the last dynasty (the *Ta Ching Lü Li*) says more about elite attitudes toward the practice than about its place in Chinese family life. When the government undertook a survey of customary law as the first step towards working out a civil code on the Western model, the results revealed the presence of t'ung-yang-hsi in every corner of the empire.[5] Officials in many localities devoted large sections of their reports to the relevant legal and ritual details, and many wrote as though this were a most common way of obtaining a daughter-in-law. The most striking statement occurs in the introduction to the report from Kiangsi. With reference to Anlan, a term

used to refer to the southern half of the province, the report tells us that "not more than one or two of every ten" brides enter their future husband's households as adults. "Five or six of every ten" come as t'ung-yang-hsi and "three or four of every ten" as teng-lang-hsi (Ministry of Justice 1930:1501–1502).

Perhaps the reason many Western scholars have ignored the practice of raising a son's wife is that the Chinese themselves disparage the practice and often disclaim it entirely. If you ask a Chinese informant to describe marriage practices in his area of the country, he will always talk about those forms of marriage in which the bride enters her husband's family as a young adult. While customary law throughout the country recognizes the legality of adopting a daughter-in-law, the mores of the society condemn such marriages as vulgar and inferior. In official writings those marriages that bring the bride into her husband's house as a child are termed *hsiao-hun*, "small marriages" or "minor marriages"; those in which the bride joins her husband's family as a young adult are *ta-hun*, "large marriages" or "major marriages." In translation the terms suggest the relative ages of the two kinds of brides, but this is not the implication of the Chinese. The major form of marriage, or what I have previously termed the "grand marriage," is "major" because it is the culturally preferred form of marriage, the right and proper way of acquiring a daughter-in-law. The minor form of marriage is "minor" not because the bride is a minor, but because it is socially despised.[6]

The minor form of marriage is also recognized as having social disadvantages of another kind. Where the transfer of a bride as a young adult

<hr/>

[5]This report was published in 1930 by the Ministry of Justice under the title *Min-shang-shih Hsi-kuan Tiao-ch'a Pao-kao-lu.* For a description and evaluation see François Théry (1948: 368–371). A Xerox copy of the original Chinese document is available in Cornell University's Wason Collection.

[6]In my first article on this subject (Wolf 1966) I refer to marriages involving an adult bride as "grand marriages" and those involving a t'ung-yang-hsi or teng-lang-hsi as "alternative patrilocal marriages." I have abandoned these terms because the second is clumsy and the first conflicts with Freedman's use of the term "grand" to refer to a type of Chinese family (1966:49). The terms "minor" and "major" are preferable because they suggest both the relative ages of the two kinds of brides and the relative social standing of the two forms of marriage.

creates strong bonds between her natal family and her husband's family, the affinal ties of the parties to a marriage of the minor type are "very loose, and in some cases entirely eliminated" (Fei 1939:54).[7] On Taiwan the members of the two families greet one another with the appropriate kinship terms if they should happen to meet in the train station or in the market, but they do not invite one another to annual festivals and do not regard themselves as having any responsibility for one another's welfare. As one of my informants in Hsiachichou put it, "They sometimes talk as though they were related, but they know that they aren't really related."

By choosing the minor form of marriage a family loses prestige and the advantages of affinal alliances. Why then do so many families choose this form of marriage? Part of the answer is the expense of the major form of marriage. As Mao Tse-tung observes in his now famous *Nung-ts'un Tiao-ch'a*, "a poor man who doesn't have a tung-yang-hsi must be satisfied with an old woman" (1949:45). The costs of marrying a young woman in the major fashion are prohibitive. The family must retain a go-between to find the right girl and negotiate the arrangements; they must pay the girl's family a substantial bride price "to thank them for raising her"; and the girl herself will expect gifts of at least three items of gold jewelry. The family should distribute red cakes to all of their relatives and friends to announce the "happy occasion," and then on the wedding day they must hire a chair and bearers to convey the bride to her new home. It can cost a family a small fortune just to get the girl as far as their threshold and another fortune to conduct a proper wedding. A wedding of this type is defined as a festive event, and all friends, relatives, and neighbors expect to be invited. The small gifts of cash they present upon arrival do not begin to pay for the food they eat and the wine they drink. On Taiwan the average farm family spends a minimum of six month's gross income on a marriage of this type,

and families "who care about face" spend as much as a year or even two year's income.

A family can economize by bargaining hard on the bride price and by limiting the number of wedding guests, but the social costs of such economy are very high. The prestige gained by the major form of marriage is more than offset by the disgrace of not carrying out a marriage of this type in the proper fashion. The safest course for a poor family is to adopt a girl and raise her as a daughter-in-law. The bride price for a t'ung-yang-hsi is never more than a token amount, and there is no need to spend more than a few dollars on the wedding of a girl who is already a member of the family. The event is a domestic matter that does not require public display. The one major expense of the minor form of marriage is that of raising the girl, but this expense can be spread over a number of years and does not require a large amount of cash. What most families do is to give away their own female children and adopt girls who are raised as wives for their sons. One family in Hsiachichou saved the costs of six dowries and six bride prices by giving away all six of their daughters and adopting in their places six wives for their six sons.[8]

The desire to economize is one motive for choosing to raise a son's wife, but it is not the only motive or even the most important motive. Contrary to Fei Hsiao-tung's widely accepted analysis, the minor form of marriage is not economically advantageous (1939:54–55). It is only cheaper. The loss of affinal ties narrows the circle of people a family can depend on in times of financial crisis and also contracts the field of social support they can organize for economic ventures. As Fei himself observes in discussing the economic advantages of a wide net of kinship ties, "In this connection, we can see that institutions such as the *siaosiv*, which diminish the kinship circle, will in the long run produce unfavorable economic consequences" (1939:269). The

---

[7]Arthur H. Smith also observes that "in some instances the relations with the family of the girl are wholly broken off, when she is taken for a 'rearing marriage'" (1899:260).

[8]Hsiachichou is a small Hokkien-speaking community located on the southwestern edge of the Taipei basin in northern Taiwan. This is the site of my own fieldwork and the source of most of the data reported in my previous paper (Wolf 1966).

price of these advantages is the bride price required by the major form of marriage, but we must remember that no family chooses the minor form of marriage as a last resort because they cannot raise a bride price. The decision between the two forms of marriage is always made ten to twenty years before the bride price is due. The impoverished may despair of raising the money by the time their son is old enough to marry, but this is not the reason most families adopt a daughter-in-law. If it were, there would not be so many marriages of this type. Only the hopelessly poor would give up the advantages of affinal ties and the prestige of the major marriage for no other reason than a fear of being unable to collect a bride price in fifteen years.

That there are better reasons for choosing the minor form of marriage is evident in the fact that many wealthy families raise their sons' wives. Three of the most affluent families I knew on Taiwan had chosen the minor form of marriage for their sons, and they were not exceptional or even unusual. The 148 families inclued in Okada's 1936 survey enjoyed incomes three times the average for all households in the Shihlin district (1949:3). They could easily afford the expenses of the major form of marriage, but in fact many of them chose to raise their sons' wives. Okada asked each family how they had married their daughters and how they had obtained their wives and daughters-in-law. Of a total of 388 women marrying into these families 179 had come as sim-pua, and of a total of 387 marrying out, 291 had left as sim-pua (1949:15–16). The two wealthiest families in Okada's sample had annual incomes of Y30,000 and Y11,000 as against a district average of only Y428. The former consisted of the head of the family and his wife and two sons, their wives and the wives of two deceased sons, the sons' two concubines, thirteen grandchildren, the wives of nine grandsons and the sim-pua of another, ten great-grandchildren, and sim-pua for four great grandsons; the latter included the head and his wife and three sons, one son's wife and another's sim-pua, an adopted daughter,

two grandchildren, the head's mother and her younger son, this man's wife and a deceased brother's wife, their two sons and two daughters, a sim-pua for one of these boys, the head's uncle and his wife, their two daughters, their two sons, and one's wife and the other's sim-pua (1949:166).

Men who can afford concubines do not raise their sons' wives to save money. The money saved is not worth the loss of prestige and useful affinal ties. The fact is that many wealthy families who choose the minor form of marriage do not take advantage of the opportunity for economy. In his valuable little book on family life in Wanhua, the old section of Taipei City, Toshio Ikeda notes that "polite families" return a sim-pua to her natal home a few days before her wedding. They then send the girl's family gifts, hire a red sedan chair, and bring the bride back with all of the fanfare of a marriage of the major type (1944:202–203). This is not an economical arrangement. While the groom's family does save the bride price asked for a nubile woman, they have to bear both the expenses of raising a girl and the costs of an expensive wedding. By demonstrating their ability to afford a wedding of the major type the family does offset the loss of prestige associated with raising a son's wife, but why should they go to all of the trouble and expense of raising a daughter-in-law when they can afford to wait and take an adult bride for their son?

A clue to the answer occurs in the engagement that commits two families to a marriage of the major type. On Taiwan this ceremony takes place in the bride's home with the bride and her future mother-in-law as the central actors. The girl sits on a stool in front of her family's ancestral altar, facing the open door of the hall, a position symbolizing her imminent departure as a member of the household. The simple act of the mother-in-law's slipping a gold ring on the younger woman's finger completes the legal action of the ceremony, but the legal action does not exhaust the significance of the event. It is said that if the mother-in-law manages to push the ring past the girl's knuckle, she will be able to dominate her as a daughter-in-law, while, if she fails, the girl will be able to maintain a certain independence of the older woman in her new home. The result is often a tense if brief struggle at the very moment the two women enter into a relationship of mother-in-law and daughter-in-law. The occasion is a peculiarly apt one for it both completes the legal arrangements for the marriage and dramatizes the consequences.

The Chinese view of what can be expected of the two women brought together by a marriage of the major type is also evident on the day of the wedding. As the bride leaves her parental home, crying bitterly, her sisters call after her, "May you soon bear a son, and may you soon become a mother-in-law yourself." Upon arrival at the groom's home the go-between warns the bride not to step on the threshold as she enters the house. "It's like stepping on your mother-in-law's head." After entering the house the girl is lead to the bridal chamber where she finds on the bed strips of cloth the mother-in-law uses to bind her feet. The mother-in-law herself avoids entering the bridal chamber for a few days before the wedding "so the daughter-in-law will be afraid and obey her" (Ikeda 1944:148). But she does have her foot-bindings on the bed to remind the bride of what is expected of her in her new home. She must submit to her mother-in-law as the foot submits to the pressure of the binding (Ikeda 1944:147–148). As Chinese women bound their feet so tight as to bend and break the bones, this is a forceful symbolic injunction.

It would be incorrect to represent the relationship created by the major form of marriage as one of inevitable conflict, but it is not too much to affirm that this is the normal consequence. My field notes from Hsiachichou include references to quarrels between every mother-in-law and daughter-in-law living in the village at the time of my study. So nearly universal is the conflict between the two women that the villagers themselves regard a harmonious relationship as extraordinary. When one village woman praised

her new daughter-in-law repeatedly the situation was so widely discussed that references to the matter appear again and again in my notes over a period of several months. At first the tone of the village response was one of knowing amusement, everyone confidently implying that it would not last more than a few weeks. When the usual change for the worse did not take place quite as soon as expected, this attitude gradually gave way to resentment and even irritation. Several women felt that the mother-in-law in question was causing everyone trouble by praising her daughter-in-law. As one of them explained, "She just goes around telling everyone how good her daughter-in-law is and this makes a lot of trouble. It makes others angry at their own daughters-in-law just to hear it." The eventual deterioration of the relationship was greeted by the family's relatives and neighbors with satisfaction and relief.

The topics of daily bickering among the women of a household create the impression that the source of the conflict between mother-in-law and daughter-in-law is domestic responsibility. The older woman accuses the younger of "not even knowing how to cook rice," of pocketing some of the money she is given to buy food in the market, of being lazy and incompetent, in short, "of wanting to eat her rice off the top of the pan." The daughter-in-law complains that her husband's mother is "a hot pepper who really knows how to scold," that she is stingy and "won't even give me five cents to buy candy for my children," generally accusing the older woman of being unfair and unreasonable. The domestic arrangements of a Chinese family do create ample opportunities for conflict between a woman and her sons' wives, but the family's domestic affairs are only the topics of their struggle, not its source. The source of the tension between mother-in-law and daughter-in-law is a competition for the loyalty and affection of the young man who is the older woman's son and the younger woman's husband.

The Chinese ideal of a distant and unemotional relationship between husband and wife recognizes the danger of a mother's jealousy. A man should never display any affection for his wife outside of the privacy of their bedroom, and so far as possible he should avoid even speaking to her except to give orders. Unfortunately for the harmony of those families that choose the major form of marriage, this social device does not prevent the mother's resenting her daughter-in-law's role as a wife. A woman's son is too important in Chinese society for her to accept an intimacy from which she is excluded. Mothers do resent a son's relationship with his wife and express this resentment by abusing their authority over the daughter-in-law. Criticized, scolded, and not uncommonly beaten by her husband's mother, the daughter-in-law responds in the only way she can. She tries to win over her husband in the hope of talking him into leaving the extended family, thereby freeing her forever of her mother-in-law. This tactic naturally serves to confirm the worst of the older woman's fears and justifies her hatred of the daughter-in-law. The result is a conflagration fed on its own flames. The more resentful and jealous the mother-in-law, the more she tyrannizes her son's wife; the more she is victimized, the harder the girl works to pry her husband out of his natal family, an effort that only serves to intensify the older woman's fears and escalate the conflict.

In their daily encounters both women express themselves in the rhetoric of the kitchen, but in crises the real cause of their conflict comes to the fore. When an elderly mother in Hsiachichou seemed in danger of being overwhelmed by a particularly aggressive daughter-in-law, her complaint was not that the daughter-in-law was lazy or incompetent, but that "my daughter-in-law is trying to steal my son away from me." She told her son, "I'll go kill myself, and then the two of you can be alone and not be bothered with a mother." In this case the son responded handsomely, assuring his mother that he would rather send his wife away than cause his mother anxiety. In his own words, "How can I let you do that? If she isn't good to you, then I'll send her back to her family. How can I let you kill yourself?" Such a response naturally encourages a

mother and temporarily calms her fears, but there is always the danger that someday the daughter-in-law will alienate her son. To bear sons is a woman's first great trial in life; to maintain their loyalty and affection is the second and more difficult trial. As one village mother put it to me, "You raise your children and then when they grow up they are always someone else's. Your daughter belongs to her husband, and your son belongs to his wife. Especially those men who always listen to what their wives say. If you say more than two words to your daughter-in-law, they'll get mad and move out of the family. 'You can give birth to a son's body, but you can never know a son's heart.' "

The Chinese are well aware of this conflict and do what they can to minimize its intensity. Although Chinese villages are not exogamous in the jural sense, daughters-in-law are seldom taken from within the same community. The explanation of my informants in Hsiachichou is that this would exacerbate the conflict between mother-in-law and daughter-in-law by giving the younger woman natural allies close at hand. "Every time someone said a word to her she would run home and say something to her parents." And this is also the reason Chinese families seldom take a daughter-in-law from a family whose social status is higher than their own. The bride's family must always be of approximately the same social status or of a lower status. "A girl from a rich family wouldn't know how to work and she wouldn't know the worth of money. She would always be saying something to her mother-in-law, and this would cause everyone a lot of trouble."

While these strategies may help preserve the family by strengthening the mother-in-law's position, they do not solve the problems created by the intrusion of a strange young woman into the family circle. The girl's intimate relationship with her husband inevitably arouses his mother's jealousy and sets in motion a volatile triangle of strife. The only solution is the one suggested by the Chinese ideal of a family in which the daughter-in-law accepts her mother-in-law as a mother and the son puts the welfare of his parents before those of his wife. In such an ideal family the daughter-in-law turns to her mother-in-law before she complains to her husband, and the husband refuses to advocate his wife's interests when they run counter to those of his parents. The threat marriage poses to the Chinese family is thus removed by creating a household in which intergenerational ties take precedence over conjugal ties. The mother-in-law does not abuse her authority because she has nothing to fear from her son's wife, and the wife does not make exclusive claims on her husband because she has no need to pry him away from his parents.

It is the minor rather than the major form of marriage that comes closest to achieving this ideal. Raised from early childhood as a member of her future husband's family, the daughter-in-law does accept his parents as her own parents. She is first a daughter and only later and secondarily a daughter-in-law and a wife. The strain of shared domestic responsibility does sometimes cause conflict with her mother-in-law, but the intensity of these encounters remains low because they do not involve the husband. The mother-in-law can hardly feel jealous of her son's relationship with a girl whom she has raised as a daughter, and the daughter-in-law does not arouse her mother-in-law by trying to turn her son against her. The sexual aversion created by the couple's intimate childhood association separates them as husband and wife and precludes the development of an exclusive conjugal bond. The girl is more likely to seek her mother-in-law as an ally against her husband than she is to try to turn her husband against his mother. The effect of the minor form of marriage is to drive a wedge between husband and wife and thereby take the strain off the bonds between the generations.

While the average man in a village like Hsiachichou is not aware of the dynamics of the minor form of marriage, he is very much aware of their practical consequences for the family. Asked why they had chosen to raise a wife for one of their sons, or what they saw as the advantages of the minor form of marriage, many of my informants spoke of these marriages as "less troublesome." "A girl you raise yourself will listen to what you say and not start trouble," or "The advantage is that a girl you adopt won't always be saying things to your son." One elderly informant who had raised wives for two of her three sons put it this way: "It is always better for a boy to marry an adopted daughter than to marry a girl from another family. This is because you can get to know an adopted daughter's disposition better and can correct her without causing a lot of trouble. A girl from another family will always get mad when you try to correct her, and then she will say things to her husband and make trouble between him and his parents."

My own observations of families created by the minor form of marriage bear out this view, and yet I am still surprised by the fact that home-raised daughters-in-law are less troublesome. Abuse of these girls by their foster families is so common that the sim-pua has become a symbol of the life of misery (Wu 1943:36–37). When a child falls down and hurts herself, her mother picks her up, singing, "Oh, oh, crying like a sim-pua," or, if a child appears angry and sullen, the mother says, "Oh, look, a sim-pua face." So many families assign every dirty, unpleasant task to their future son's wife that people in Hsiachichou made a point of telling me that "we don't mistreat our adopted daughter." Before I had been in the village long enough to know better, I asked a woman who had been raised as a sim-pua if this were really true. She answered, "You walk around here all day talking to people. Can't you see? Haven't you heard people say that it is better to be a poor man's daughter than a rich man's sim-pua?"

Where one would expect this treatment to give rise to an explosive resentment, the fact is that it seems to be an entirely successful way of training daughters-in-law. Sim-pua are noted for being "clever" and "sullen," not "obstinate" and "quarrelsome." "They are the kind of people who watch other people's faces." The only resentment most girls express is directed towards their natal families for giving them away rather than towards their foster families for maltreatment. One former sim-pua explained her attitude this way, "You know it was very funny when I was a child. My foster mother was beating me up all the time, but whenever I heard someone from my natal home coming to take me back for a visit I was scared and ran and hid in the toilet. Everyone would run and try to drag me out, but I wouldn't come out. The thought of going back to my natal home was like having a piece of my flesh cut off." When another sim-pua refused to marry her foster brother, her mother-in-law asked the girl's mother to try to talk her into changing her mind. "But it didn't work. I hated her much more than I hated my foster mother. I could never get used to the idea of having two mothers. I used to think, 'Everybody else has only one mother. Why should I have two mothers?' I knew she was my real mother, but I would make myself think, 'This other woman (her foster mother) is my real mother; she isn't my mother.'"

When life becomes intolerable for a woman who has entered her husband's family by way of the major form of marriage, she visits her natal home and complains to her parents. Although it is unusual for the parents to do anything more than to comfort her, she does at least have some external emotional support. That the sim-pua does not express her bitterness towards her foster parents is probably because they are her only parents. Many girls do not even know their real parents, and many of those who do cannot regard them as parents. The one advantage of the sim-pua's situation is that she is not a stranger in her husband's village, but this cannot be used to advantage against her foster parents. While public opinion is only amused at the sight of an adult bride railing against her mother-in-law, it would not tolerate a sim-pua's expressing the same sentiments. Whatever her jural status in the family, a sim-pua is still her mother-in-law's daughter. For her to criticize her parents-in-law would constitute a breach of filial piety. More often treated like a servant than like a daughter,

a sim-pua has no choice but to accept her status as a daughter and behave like a good daughter-in-law.

While this description of the consequences of the two forms of marriage is based on my own fieldwork in Taiwan, the differences between the two are not a function of conditions peculiar to this one area of China. The same contrasts are drawn by Fei Hsiao-tung in his account of the village of Kaihsienkung in southern Kiangsu. Of the mother-in-law and daughter-in-law brought together by the major form of marriage, Fei writes:

> It comes to be taken more or less for granted that the mother-in-law is a potential enemy of the daughter-in-law. Friction between them is taken as usual and harmony as worthy of special praise. Anyone who has listened to gossips among the elder women, will confirm this statement. They are never tired of cursing their daughters-in-law [1939:48].

In contrast, Fei finds that

> the girl brought up from an early age by her future mother-in-law, becomes . . . very closely attached to the latter and feels towards her just like a daughter, especially in those frequent cases where there is no daughter. Even those who are badly treated by the future mother-in-law become used to their position and do not thus experience a crisis after marriage. Thus the conflict between the mother-in-law and the daughter-in-law is often not so acute, even if not entirely avoided [1939:54].

Although a few impoverished families may choose the minor form of marriage because they despair of ever raising a bride price, this does not explain the popularity of this type of marriage. Many families who could raise the money by the time their sons were old enough to marry do not make the effort, and many of those who can easily afford a bride price prefer to raise their sons' wives. The real purpose of the minor form of marriage is not to save money but to preserve the family. Aware of the conflict created by the major marriage and fearing the loss of their sons as a result of this conflict, many families choose the minor form of marriage as a means of promoting domestic harmony. They know that this choice sacrifices useful affinal ties and the prestige associated with the major marriage, but they are more concerned with retaining the loyalty of their sons. As one of my informants explained, "In China no one asks how much land you have. Here people ask you how many sons you have. You can work when you are young, but when you are old you have to have children to support you."

While the Chinese themselves do not see their situation in this perspective, it is obvious that the real source of their difficulty is the incest taboo. By forcing families to take a daughter-in-law from the outside, the taboo makes marriage a threat to the family. The girl intruded into the family circle cannot be absorbed without disrupting intergenerational ties. The only solution is to circumvent the taboo by adopting the girl as a child and raising her as a member of her future husband's household. This maneuver satisfies the formal requirements of the incest taboo and also avoids its dangerous consequences. The one problem is that the aversion that makes this solution successful also creates resistance to marriage on the part of the adopted daughter and her intended husband. As long as the groom's parents command all of their authority as parents, they can override this resistance and force the couple to consummate the arrangement. But as soon as changing conditions give the young couple a voice in the matter of their marriage, this solution to the problem of the incest taboo fails. To follow Malinowski's example of "a terse, if somewhat crude formula," we might say that the goal of many Chinese families is to substitute daughters for daughters-in-law; the difficulty is that brothers don't like to marry their sisters.

This example is interesting for the challenge it poses to most sociological explanations of the familial incest taboo. Beginning with the assumption that men are naturally inclined to mate and marry within the family, the most widely accepted of these explanations argue that the taboo is necessary to achieve the advantages of marriage outside of the family. This may be true of societies in which marriage creates new families, but it is not always true of those in which marriage recruits to existing families. While taking a daughter-in-law from another family does have the advantage of creating dependable affinal ties, it has the marked disadvantage of intruding a stranger into the family circle. The only solution is to ignore the spirit of the law and raise daughters-in-law as daughters, but this is not feasible in most societies. Contrary to the initial assumption of the sociological explanations, men and women who are raised from childhood as members of the same family are not inclined to mate and marry. The problem of the incest taboo is how to overcome this aversion and thereby avoid the necessity of taking husbands and wives from outside. The reason the Chinese are the only known human society to have solved this problem may be because they are one of the few societies in which parents have absolute authority over their adult offspring.[9]

[9] I have argued that the minor form of marriage creates sexual aversion on the part of the married couple and promotes domestic harmony by removing the mother-in-law/daughter-in-law conflict. If these statements are true, women who marry a childhood housemate should bear fewer children than those who marry in the major fashion, and families in which two or more sons marry sim-pua should survive longer as joint households than those in which brothers marry women who enter the home as young adults. I am now analyzing household registration records from Taiwan to test these two hypotheses. The results of these tests will form the basis of two further papers on the minor form of marriage and its implications.

REFERENCES

BRYSON, MARY ISABELLA
    1885 Child life in Chinese homes. London, The Religious Tract Society.
BUCK, JOHN LOSSING
    1930 Chinese farm economy. Chicago, The University of Chicago Press.
    1937 Land utilization in China. 3 Vols. Nanking, University of Nanking.

CHEN, SHAO-HSING
  1943 T'ung-yang-hsi. Minzoku, Taiwan 3 (11):38–39.
CHIAO, C. M., WARREN S. THOMPSON, AND D. T. CHEN
  1938 An experiment in the registration of vital statistics in China. Oxford, Ohio, Scripps Foundation for Research in Population Problems.
CHU, CH'ING-CH'I, COMP.
  1834 Hsing-an hui-lan. A collection of more than 5000 judicial cases covering the period 1736–1833.
  1840 Hsü-tsêng hsing-an hui-lan. A collection of an additional 1670 cases covering the period 1833–1838.
DOOLITTLE, JUSTUS
  1865 Social life of the Chinese. 2 vols. New York, Harper and Brothers.
FEI, HSIAO-TUNG
  1939 Peasant life in China. New York, E. P. Dutton and Company.
FENG, TZU-KANG
  1935 Lanhsi nung-ts'un tiao-ch'a (A rural survey in Lanhsi, Chekiang). Hangchow, Department of Agriculture, University of Chekiang.
FREEDMAN, MAURICE
  1966 Chinese lineage and society. London, The Athlone Press.
GORDON-CUMMING, C. F.
  1884 Wanderings in China. 2 vols. Edinburgh and London, William Blackwood and Sons.
HOPEI JIHPAO (HOPEI DAILY)
  1953a Ch'üan-kuo kuan-shih hun-yin-fa kung-tso chi-pu p'ing-hêng (Implementation of marriage law in different parts of the country uneven). February 1.
  1953b Fêng-chien hun-yin shih-tu jêng-jan yen-chung ts'un-tsai (Feudal marriage customs still survive). February 9.

IKEDA, TOSHIO
  1944 Taiwan no katei seikatsu (Home life in Taiwan). Taipei, Tōto Shoseki.
KAJIWARA, MICHIYOSHI
  1941 Taiwan nōmin seikatsu kō (Peasant life in Taiwan). Taipei, Ogata Takezō.
LOCKHART, WILLIAM
  1861 Medical missionary in China. London, Hurst and Blackett.
MACKAY, GEORGE LESLIE
  1895 From far Formosa. New York, Chicago, and Toronto, Fleming H. Revell Company.
MAO, TSE-TUNG
  1949 Nung-ts'un tiao-ch'a (Rural suveys). Shanghai, Chieh-fang-she.
MINISTRY OF JUSTICE, REPUBLIC OF CHINA
  1930 Min-shang-shih hsi-kuan tiao-ch'a pao-kao-lu (Report of a survey of customary law in civil and commercial affairs). Nan-king.
OKADA, UZURU
  1949 Kiso shakai (Elementary groups of society). Tokyo, Kōbundō.
SMITH, ARTHUR H.
  1899 Village life in China. New York, Chicago, Toronto, Fleming H. Revell Company.
TAI, YEN-HUI
  1943 Sim-pua zakkō (Notes on sim-pua). Minzoku, Taiwan 3 (11):2–4.
THÉRY, FRANÇOIS
  1948 Les coutumes chinoises relatives au marriage. Bulletin de l'Université l'Aurore 9(36):368–371.
WOLF, ARTHUR P.
  1966 Childhood association, sexual attraction, and the incest taboo: a Chinese case. American Anthropologist 68:883–898.
WU, HSIN-YUNG
  1943 Sim-pua lei (Poor sim-pua). Minzoku, Taiwan 3(11):36–37.

18

THE INCEST PROHIBITION*

CLAUDE LÉVI-STRAUSS

II

The prohibition of incest is less a rule prohibiting marriage with the mother, sister or daughter, than a rule obliging the mother, sister or daughter to be given to others. It is the supreme rule of the gift, and it is clearly this aspect, too often unrecognized, which allows its nature to be understood. All the errors in interpreting the prohibition of incest arise from a tendency to see marriage as a discontinuous process which derives its own limits and possibilities from within itself in each individual case.

Thus it is that the reasons why marriage with the mother, daughter or sister can be prevented are sought in a quality intrinsic to these women. One is therefore drawn infallibly towards biological considerations, since it is only from a biological, certainly not a social, point of view that motherhood, sisterhood or daughterhood are properties of the individuals considered. However, from a social viewpoint, these terms cannot be regarded as defining isolated individuals, but relationships between these individuals and

*Editor's note: Part I including footnotes 1–3 are not included here.

SOURCE: From *The Elementary Structures of Kinship,* by Lévi-Strauss, pp. 481–490. Copyright © 1969 by Beacon Press. Reprinted by permission.

everyone else. Motherhood is not only a mother's relationship to her children, but her relationship to other members of the group, not as a mother, but as a sister, wife, cousin or simply a stranger as far as kinship is concerned. It is the same for all family relationships, which are defined not only by the individuals they involve, but also by all those they exclude. This is true to the extent that observers have often been struck by the impossibility for natives of conceiving a neutral relationship, or more exactly, no relationship. We have the feeling—which, moreover, is illusory—that the absence of definite kinship gives rise to such a state in our consciousness. But the supposition that this might be the case in primitive thought does not stand up to examination. Every family relationship defines a certain group of rights and duties, while the lack of family relationship does not define anything; it defines enmity:

> If you wish to live among the Nuer you must do so on their terms, which means that you must treat them as a kind of kinsman and they will then treat you as a kind of kinsman. Rights, privileges and obligations are determined by kinship. Either a man is a kinsman, actually or by fiction, or he is a person to whom you have no reciprocal obligations and whom you treat as a potential enemy.[4]

The Australian aboriginal group is defined in exactly the same terms:

> When a stranger comes to a camp that he has never visited before, he does not enter the camp, but remains at some distance. A few of the older men, after a while, approach him, and the first thing they proceed to do is to find out who the stranger is. The commonest question that is put to him is "Who is you *maeli* (father's father)?" The discussion proceeds on genealogical lines until all parties are satisfied of the exact relation of the stranger to each of the natives present in the camp. When this point is reached, the stranger can be admitted to the camp, and the different men and women are pointed out to him and their relation to him defined . . . If I am a blackfellow and meet another blackfellow that other

must be either my relative or my enemy. If he is my enemy I shall take the first opportunity of killing him, for fear he will kill me. This, before the white man came, was the aboriginal view of one's duty towards one's neighbour . . . [5]

Through their striking parallelism, these two examples merely confirm a universal situation:

> Throughout a considerable period, and in a large number of societies, men met in a curious frame of mind, with exaggerated fear and an equally exaggerated generosity which appear stupid in no one's eyes but our own. In all the societies which immediately preceded our own and which still surround us, and even in many usages of popular morality, there is no middle path. There is either complete trust or complete mistrust. One lays down one's arms, renounces magic, and gives everything away, from casual hospitality to one's daughter or one's property.[6]

There is no barbarism or, properly speaking, even archaism in this attitude. It merely represents the systematization, pushed to the limit, of characteristics inherent in social relationships.

No relationship can be arbitrarily isolated from all other relationships. It is likewise impossible to remain on this or that side of the world of relationships. The social environment should not be conceived of as an empty framework within which beings and things can be linked, or simply juxtaposed. It is inseparable from the things which people it. Together they constitute a field of gravitation in which the weights and distances form a co-ordinated whole, and in which a change in any element produces a change in the total equilibrium of the system. We have given a partial illustration at least of this principle in our analysis of cross-cousin marriage. However, it can be seen how its field of application must be extended to all the rules of kinship, and above all, to that universal and fundamental rule, the prohibition of incest. Every kinship system (and no human society is without one) has a total character, and it is because of this that the mother, sister, and daughter are perpetually coupled, as it were, with ele-

[4]Evans-Pritchard, 1940, p. 183.

[5]Radcliffe-Brown, 1913, p. 151.
[6]Mauss, 1925, p. 138.

ments of the system which, in relation to them, are neither son, nor brother, nor father, because the latter are themselves coupled with other women, or other classes of women, or feminine elements defined by a relationship of a different order. Because marriage is exchange, because marriage is the archetype of exchange, the analysis of exchange can help in the understanding of the solidarity which unites the gift and the counter-gift, and one marriage with other marriages.

It is true that Seligman disputes that the woman is the sole or predominant instrument of the alliance. She cites the institution of blood brotherhood, as expressed by the *henamo* relationship among the natives of New Guinea.[7] The establishment of blood-brotherhood does indeed create a bond of alliance between individuals, but by making them brothers it entails a prohibition on marriage with the sister. It is far from our mind to claim that the exchange or gift of women is the only way to establish an alliance in primitive societies. We have shown elsewhere how, among certain native groups of Brazil, the community could be expressed by the terms for 'brother-in-law' and 'brother.' The brother-in-law is ally, collaborator and friend; it is the term given to adult males belonging to the band with which an alliance has been contracted. In the same band, the potential brother-in-law, i.e., the cross-cousin, is the one with whom, as an adolescent, one indulges in homosexual activities which will always leave their mark in the mutually affectionate behaviour of the adults.[8] However, as well as the brother-in-law relationship, the Nambikwara also rely on the notion of brotherhood: 'Savage, you are no longer my brother!' is the cry uttered during a quarrel with a non-kinsman. Furthermore, objects found in a series, such as hut posts, the pipes of a Pan-pipe, etc., are said to be 'brothers,' or are called 'others,' in their respective relationships, a terminological detail which is worth comparing with Montaigne's observation that the Brazilian Indi-

ans whom he met at Rouen called men the 'halves' of one another, just as we say 'our fellow men.'[9] However, the whole difference between the two types of bond can also be seen, a sufficiently clear definition being that one of them expresses a mechanical solidarity (brother), while the other involves an organic solidarity (brother-in-law, or god-father). Brothers are closely related to one another, but they are so in terms of their similarity, as are the posts or the reeds of the Pan-pipe. By contrast, brothers-in-law are solidary because they complement each other and have a functional efficacy for one another, whether they play the rôle of the opposite sex in the erotic games of childhood, or whether their masculine alliance as adults is confirmed by each providing the other with what he does not have—a wife—through their simultaneous renunciation of what they both do have—a sister. The first form of solidarity adds nothing and unites nothing; it is based upon a cultural limit, satisfied by the reproduction of a type of connexion the model for which is provided by nature. The other brings about an integration of the group on a new plane.

Linton's observation on blood-brotherhood in the Marquesas helps to place the two institutions (blood-brotherhood and intermarriage) in their reciprocal perspectives. Blood-brothers are called *enoa*: 'When one was *enoa* with a man, one had equal rights to his property and stood in the same relation to his relatives as he did.'[10] However, it emerges very clearly from the context that the *enoa* system is merely an individual solution acting as a substitute, while the real and effective solution of the relations between the groups, i.e., the collective and organic solution of intermarriages, with the consequent fusion of the tribes, is made impossible by the international situation. Although vendettas may be in progress, the institution of *enoa,* a purely individual affair, is able to ensure a minimum of liaison and collaboration, even when marriage, which is a group affair, cannot be contracted.

[7]B. Z. Seligman, 1935, pp. 75–93.
[8]Lévi-Strauss, 1948a.

[9]Montaigne, 1962, vol. I, ch. XXXI ('Des Cannibales').
[10]Linton, 1945, p. 149.

Native theory confirms our conception even more directly. Mead's Arapesh informants had difficulty at first in answering her questions on possible infringements of the marriage prohibitions. However, when they eventually did express a comment the source of the misunderstanding was clearly revealed: they do not conceive of the prohibition as such, i.e., in its negative aspect; the prohibition is merely the reverse or counterpart of a positive obligation, which alone is present and active in the consciousness. Does a man ever sleep with his sister? The question is absurd. Certainly not, they reply: 'No, we don't sleep with our sisters. We give our sisters to other men, and other men give us their sisters.'[11] The ethnographer pressed the point, asking what they would think or say if, through some impossibility, this eventuality managed to occur. Informants had difficulty placing themselves in this situation, for it was scarcely conceivable: 'What, you would like to marry your sister! What is the matter with you anyway? Don't you want a brother-in-law? Don't you realize that if you marry another man's sister and another man marries your sister, you will have at least two brothers-in-law, while if you marry your own sister you will have none? With whom will you hunt, with whom will you garden, whom will you go to visit?'[12]

Doubtless, this is all a little suspect, because it was provoked, but the native aphorisms collected by Mead, and quoted as the motto to the first part of this work, were not provoked, and their meaning is the same. Other evidence corroborates the same thesis. For the Chukchee, a 'bad family' is defined as an isolated family, 'brotherless and cousinless.'[13] Moreover, the necessity to provoke the comment (the content of which, in any case, is spontaneous), and the difficulty in obtaining it, reveal the misunderstanding inherent in the problem of marriage prohibitions. The latter are prohibitions only secondarily and derivatively. Rather than a pro-

hibition on a certain category of persons, they are a prescription directed towards another category. In this regard, how much more penetrating is native theory than are so many modern commentaries! There is nothing in the sister, mother, or daughter which disqualifies them as such. Incest is socially absurd before it is morally culpable. The incredulous exclamation from the informant: 'So you do not want to have a brother-in-law?' provides the veritable golden rule for the state of society.

III

There is thus no possible solution to the problem of incest within the biological family, even supposing this family to be already in a cultural context which imposes its specific demands upon it. The cultural context does not consist of a collection of abstract conditions. It results from a very simple fact which expresses it entirely, namely, that the biological family is no longer alone, and that it must ally itself with other families in order to endure. Malinowski supported a different idea, namely, that the prohibition of incest results from an internal contradiction, within the biological family, between mutually incompatible feelings, such as the emotions attached to sexual relationships and parental love, or 'the sentiments which form naturally between brothers and sisters.'[14] These sentiments nevertheless only become incompatible because of the cultural rôle which the biological family is called upon to play. The man should teach his children, and this social vocation, practised naturally within the family group, is irremediably compromised if emotions of another type develop and upset the discipline indispensable to the maintenance of a stable order between the generations: 'Incest would mean the upsetting of age distinctions, the mixing up of generations, the disorganization of sentiments and a violent exchange of rôles at a time when the family is the

[11]Mead, 1935, p. 84.
[12]loc. cit.
[13]Borgoras, 1904–9, p. 542.

[14]Malinowski, 1934, p. lxvi.

most important educational medium. No society could exist under such conditions.'[15]

It is unfortunate for this thesis that there is practically no primitive society which does not flagrantly contradict it on every point. The primitive family fulfils its educative function sooner than ours, and from puberty onwards—and often even before—it transfers the charge of adolescents to the group, with the handing over of their preparation to bachelor houses or initiation groups. Initiation rituals confirm this emancipation of the young man or girl from the family cell and their definitive incorporation within the social group. To achieve this end, these rituals rely on precisely the processes which Malinowski cites as a possibility solely in order to expose their mortal dangers, viz., affective disorganization and the violent exchange of rôles, sometimes going as far as the practice, on the initiate's very person, of most unfamilial usages by near relatives. Finally, different types of classificatory system are very little concerned to maintain a clear distinction between ages and generations. However, it is just as difficult for a Hopi child to learn to call an old man 'my son,' or any other assimilation of the same order, as it would be for one of ours.[16] The supposedly disastrous situation that Malinowski depicts in order to justify the prohibition of incest, is on the whole, no more than a very banal picture of any society, envisaged from another point of view than its own.

This naïve egocentrism is so far from being new or original that Durkheim made a decisive criticism of it years before Malinowski gave it a temporary revival in popularity. Incestuous relationships only appear contradictory to family sentiments because we have conceived of the latter as irreducibly excluding the former. But if a long and ancient tradition allowed men to marry their near relatives, our conception of marriage would be quite different. Sexual life would not have become what it is. It would have a less personal character, and would leave less room for the free play of the imagination, dreams and the spontaneities of desire. Sexual feeling would be tempered and deadened, but by this very fact it would compare closely with domestic feelings, with which it would have no difficulty in being reconciled. To conclude this paraphrase with a quotation: 'Certainly, the question does not pose itself once it is assumed that incest is prohibited; for the conjugal order, being henceforth outside the domestic order, must necessarily develop in a divergent direction. This prohibition clearly cannot be explained in terms of ideas which obviously derive from it.'[17]

Must we not go even further? On the very occasion of marriage, numerous societies practise the confusion of generations, the mingling of ages, the reversal of rôles, and the identification of what we regard as incompatible relationships. As these customs seem to such societies to be in perfect harmony with a prohibition of incest, sometimes conceived of very rigorously, it can be concluded, on the one hand, that none of these practices is exclusive of family life, and, on the other hand, that the prohibition must be defined by different characteristics, common to it throughout its multiple modalities. Among the Chukchee, for example:

> the age of women thus exchanged is hardly considered at all. For instance, on the Oloi River, a man named QI'mIqai married his young son five years old to a girl of twenty. In exchange he gave his niece, who was twelve years of age, and she was married to a young man more than twenty years old. The wife of the boy acted as his nurse, fed him with her own hands and put him to sleep.[18]

The writer also cites the case of a woman who, married to a two-year old baby and having a child by 'a marriage companion,' i.e., an official and temporary lover, shared her attentions between the two babies: 'When she was nursing her own child, she also nursed her infant husband . . . In this case the husband also readily took the breast of his wife. When I asked for the reason of the wife's conduct, the Chukchee replied,

[15]ibid. 1927, p. 251.
[16]Simmons, 1942, p. 68.

[17]Durkheim, 1898, p. 63.
[18]Bogoras, 1904–9, p. 578.

"Who knows? Perhaps it is a kind of incantation to insure the love of her young husband in the future."[19] At all events, it is certain that these apparently inconceivable unions are compatible with a highly romantic folklore, full of devouring passions, Prince Charmings and Sleeping Beauties, shy heroines and triumphant loves.[20] We know of similar facts in South America.[21]

However unusual these examples may appear, they are not unique, and Egyptian-style incest probably represents only the limit. They have their parallel among the Arapesh in New Guinea, among whom infant betrothals are frequent, the two children growing up as brother and sister. But this time the age difference is on the side of the husband:

> An Arapesh boy grows his wife. As a father's claim to his child is not that he has begotten it but rather that he has fed it, so also a man's claim to his wife's attention and devotion is not that he has paid a bride-price for her, or that she is legally his property, but that he has actually contributed the food which has become flesh and bone of her body.[22]

Here again, this type of apparently abnormal relationship provides the psychological model for regular marriage: 'The whole organization of society is based upon the analogy between children and wives as representing a group who are younger, less responsible, than the men, and therefore to be guided. Wives by definition stand in this child-relationship . . . to all of the older men of the clan into which they marry.'[23]

Likewise, among the Tapirapé of central Brazil, depopulation has brought about a system of marriage with young girls. The 'husband' lives with his parents-in-law and the 'wife's' mother is responsible for woman's work.[24] The Mohave husband carries the little girl that he has married on his shoulders, busies himself with household duties, and generally speaking acts both as husband and *in loco parentis*. The Mohave comment upon the situation cynically, and ask, sometimes even when the person concerned is present, whether he has married his own daughter: ' "Whom are you carrying around on your back? Is that your daughter?" they ask him. When such marriages break up, the husband often has a manic attack.'[25]

I myself have been present, among the Tupi-Cawahib of the upper Madeira, in central Brazil, at the betrothal of a man about thirty years old with a scarcely two-year-old baby, still in its mother's arms. Nothing was more touching than the excitement with which the future husband followed the childish frolics of his little fiancée. He did not tire of admiring her, and of sharing his feelings with the onlookers. For some years his thoughts would be filled with the prospect of setting up house. He would feel strengthened by the certainty, growing alongside him in strength and beauty, of one day escaping the curse of bachelorhood. Henceforth, his budding tenderness is expressed in innocent gifts. According to our standards, this love is torn between three irreducible categories, viz., paternal, fraternal, and marital, but in an appropriate context it reveals no element of disquiet or defect, endangering the future welfare of the couple, let alone the whole social order.

We must decide against Malinowski and those of his followers who vainly attempt to support an outmoded position,[26] in favour of those, like Fortune and Williams, who, following Tylor, found the origin of the incest prohibition in its positive implications.[27] As one observer rightly puts it: 'An incestuous couple as well as a stingy family automatically detaches itself from the give-and-take pattern of tribal existence; it is a foreign body—or at least an inactive one—in the body social.'[28]

[19]loc. cit.
[20]ibid. pp. 578–83.
[21]Means, 1931, p. 360.
[22]Mead, 1935, p. 80.
[23]Mead, 1935, pp. 80–1.
[24]Wagley, 1940, p. 12.

[25]Devereux, 1939, p. 519.
[26]Seligman, 1931–2, pp. 250–76.
[27]Fortune, 1932, pp. 620–2; Williams, 1936, p. 169; Tylor, 1889.
[28]Devereux, 1939, p. 529.

No marriage can thus be isolated from all the other marriages, past or future, which have occurred or which will occur within the group. Each marriage is the end of a movement which, as soon as this point has been reached, should be reversed and develop in a new direction. If the movement ceases, the whole system or reciprocity will be disturbed. Since marriage is the condition upon which reciprocity is realized, it follows that marriage constantly ventures the existence of reciprocity. What would happen if a wife were received without a daughter or a sister begin given? This risk must be taken, however, if society is to survive. To safeguard the social perpetuity of alliance, one must compromise oneself with the chances of descent (i.e., in short, with man's biological substructure). However, the social recognition of marriage (i.e., the transformation of the sexual encounter, with its basis in promiscuity, into a contract, ceremony or sacrament) is always an anxious venture, and we can understand how it is that society should have attempted to provide against the risks involved by the continual and almost maniacal imposition of its mark. The Hehe, say Brown, practise cross-cousin marriage, but not without hesitation, for if cross-cousin marriage allows the clan-line to be maintained, it risks it in the case of a bad marriage, and informants report: 'Thus some forbid their children to marry a cousin.'[29] The ambivalent attitude of the Hehe towards a special form of marriage is the preeminent social attitude towards marriage in any of its forms. By recognizing and sanctioning the union of the sexes and reproduction, society influences the natural order, but at the same time it gives the natural order its chance, and one might say of any culture of the world what an observer has noted of one of them: 'Perhaps the most fundamental religious conception relates to the difference between the sexes. Each sex is perfectly all right in its own way, but contact is fraught with danger for both.'[30]

[29]Brown, 1934, p. 28.
[30]Hogbin, 1935, p. 330.

Marriage is thus a dramatic encounter between nature and culture, between alliance and kinship. 'Who has given the bride?' chants the Hindu hymn of marriage: 'To whom then is she given? It is love that has given her; it is to love that she has been given. Love has given; love has received. Love has filled the ocean. With love I accept her. Love! let her be yours.'[31] Thus, marriage is an arbitration between two loves, parental and conjugal. Nevertheless, they are both forms of love, and the instant the marriage takes place, considered in isolation, the two meet and merge; 'love has filled the ocean.' Their meeting is doubtless merely a prelude to their substitution for one another, the performance of a sort of *chassé-croisé*. But to intercross they must at least momentarily be joined, and it is this which in all social thought makes marriage a sacred mystery. At this moment, all marriage verges on incest. More than that, it is incest, at least social incest, if it is true that incest, in the broadest sense of the word, consists in obtaining by oneself, and for oneself, instead of by another, and for another.

However, since one must yield to nature in order that the species may perpetuate itself, and concomitantly for social alliance to endure, the very least one must do is to deny it while yielding to it, and to accompany the gesture made towards it with one restricting it. This compromise between nature and culture comes about in two ways, since there are two cases, one in which nature must be introduced, since society can do everything, the other in which nature must be excluded, since it rules from the first—before descent and its assertion of the unilineal principle, and before alliance, with its establishment of prohibited degrees.

[31]Banerjee, 1896, p. 91. As to marriage considered as bordering upon incest, compare the following, written in a completely different spirit: 'Profound sentiment [between husband and wife] would have seemed odd and even "ridiculous," in any event unbecoming; it would have been as unacceptable as an earnest "aside" in the general current of light conversation. Each has a duty to all, and for a couple to entertain each other is isolation; in company there exists no right of the *tête-à-tête.*" (Taine, 1876, p. 133.)

REFERENCES

BANERJEE, G. N. *The Hindu Law of Marriage and Stridhana.* Calcutta, 1896.

BEST, E. *The Maori.* 2 vols. Wellington, 1924.

—— 'The Whare Kohanga (the "Nest House") and Its Lore.' *Dominion Museum Bulletin,* no. 13, pp. 1–72. 1929.

BOGORAS, W. 'The Chukchee.' *Memoirs of the American Museum of Natural History,* no. 11, pp. 1–733. 1904–9.

BROWN, G. G. 'Hehe Cross-Cousin Marriage.' *Essays Presented to C. G. Seligman,* ed. E. E. Evans-Pritchard *et al.* London, 1934.

DEVEREUX, G. 'The Social and Cultural Implications of Incest among the Mohave Indians.' *Psychoanalytic Quarterly,* vol. VIII, pp. 510–33. 1939.

DURKHEIM, D. 'La Prohibition de l'inceste et ses origines.' *Année sociologique,* vol. I, pp. 1–70. 1898.

EVANS-PRITCHARD, E. E., *The Nuer.* Oxford, 1940.

FORTUNE, R. F. *Sorcerers of Dobu.* London, 1932.

HOGBIN, H. I. 'Native Culture in Wogeo: Report of Field Work in New Guinea.' *Oceania,* vol. V, pp. 308–37. 1935.

LÉVI-STRAUSS, C. *La Vie familiale et sociale des Indiens Nambikwara.* Paris, 1948a.

LINTON, R. 'Marquesan Culture.' *The Individual and His Society,* ed. A. Kardiner. New York, 1945.

MALINOWSKI, B. *Sex and Repression in Savage Society.* London, 1927.

—— 'Introduction' to H. I. Hogbin, *Law and Order in Polynesia.* London, 1934.

MAUSS, M. 'Essai sur le don: Forme et raison de l'échange dans les sociétés archaïques.' *Année sociologique,* n.s., vol. I, pp. 30–186. 1925.

MEAD, M. *Sex and Temperament in Three Primitive Societies.* New York, 1935.

MEANS, P. A. *Ancient Civilizations of the Andes.* New York, 1931.

MONTAIGNE, M. DE. *Essais.* 2 vols. Paris, 1962.

RADCLIFFE-BROWN, A. R. 'Three Tribes of Western Australia.' *Journal of the Royal Anthropological Institute,* vol. XLIII, pp. 143–70. 1913.

SELIGMAN, B. Z. 'The Incest Barrier: Its Rôle in Social Organization.' *British Journal of Psychology,* vol. XXII, pp. 250–76. 1931–2.

—— 'The Incest Taboo as a Social Regulation.' *The Sociological Review,* vol. XXVII, pp. 75–93. 1935.

SIMMONS, L. W. (ed.). *Sun Chief.* New Haven, 1942.

TAINE, H. A. *Les Origines de la France contemporaine.* London, 1876.

TYLOR, E. B. 'On a Method of Investigating the Development of Institutions: Applied to Laws of Marriage and Descent.' *Journal of the Anthropological Institute,* vol. XVIII, pp. 245–72. 1889.

WAGLEY, C. 'The Effects of Depopulation upon Social Organization as Illustrated by the Tapirapé Indians.' *Transactions of the New York Academy of Sciences,* series 2, vol. III, pp. 12–16. 1940.

WILLIAMS, F. E. *Papuans of the Trans-Fly.* Oxford, 1936.

VII

SEX AND THE
NATURE OF THE SACRED

INTRODUCTION

The near-universal association of religion with sex is intriguing, for it raises many questions. Is this association owing primarily to an effort to control reproduction? Do humans perceive a similarity between religious and sexual ecstasy and bliss? Why is celibacy considered an ideal state for priests and ascetics in many cultures, whereas other cultures promote ceremonial sex as an important ritual element? Why do all cultures reinforce their particular variant of the incest taboo by reference to myth and supernatural sanctions? Why are the ideals of sexual behavior, as well as the limits of acceptability, so often imbedded in mythology? In short, how are we to understand this relationship between the sacred and the sexual?

Extending the work of Emile Durkheim, Victor Turner (1967, 1971) realized that those times and places that lay between the boundaries of normal categories (those that are liminal) are most clearly associated with the supernatural. Or, as Mary Douglas (1966) has noted, things that do not conform to the natural categories of a culture, if not worshipped, are abhorred. In short, any thing or any individual that transcends the bounds of the normal has power.

The ethnographic literature is replete with examples illustrating these points. Religious festivals are times set apart from the ordinary, where

237

extraordinary behaviors condoned by the supernatural may serve to reinforce the normal. And those individuals, whether contemporary or mythical, who exhibit traits from opposing categories (such as male and female) are similarly set apart, either to be abhorred or revered for the power such transcendence provides.

This section discusses the ways in which magico-religious beliefs control and/or promote sexual interaction. Ethnographic accounts show a continuum of beliefs, from validating only limited marital sexual interaction to the use of sexual interaction as a form of worship.

John C. Messenger describes the sexual repression by the Irish on the island of Inis Beag. Religious beliefs in Inis Beag limit sexual expression to marriage and to procreative sex, whereas sexual renunciation is identified with virtue and distinction. Messenger's analysis emphasizes the role of the Oedipus complex on Irish character, and the article presents a wealth of cultural data in support of his argument.

Alice B. Kehoe describes a practice involving sexual intimacy as a means of transferring spiritual power. Among Northern Plains Indians, sexual intercourse by a sacred couple during religious ceremonies was a means of renewing the life of the group. According to Kehoe, the partic-

ular manifestation of this cultural trait and its meaning within a tribe reflected variations in kinship structure.

Donald R. Tuck describes the role of sexual interaction as a pathway to the divine in Santal worship. The Sohrae harvest festival serves to alleviate marital tension, celebrate fertility, and promote love within the context of sexual pleasure for all ages of the society. Extramarital and premarital liaisons are encouraged during the festival, although incest taboos, including those prohibiting interclan and subclan sexual relations, remain in force.

As described by Serena Nanda, the *hijras* of India are males who exhibit extreme cross-gender behavior and form a religious community associated with the Mother Goddess Bahuchara Mata. The *hijra* (eunuch/transvestite) is an institutionalized third gender role rooted in Indian mythology. As emasculated males who adopt female dress and behaviors, *hijras* express the confrontation of femaleness and maleness as polar opposites. Traditionally, they support themselves through religious performances at births, weddings, and festivals. The article discusses the tensions between the ascetic ideal and real sexual aspects of the role.

REFERENCES

DOUGLAS, MARY. (1966). *Purity and Danger.* London: Routledge and Kegan Paul.

TURNER, VICTOR W. (1967). *The Forest of Symbols.* Ithaca, NY: Cornell University Press.

TURNER, VICTOR W. (1971). *The Ritual Process.* Chicago: Aldine.

SUGGESTED READINGS

BRADFORD, NICHOLAS J. (1983). Transgenderism and the Cult of Yellamma: Heat, Sex, and Sickness in South Indian Ritual. *Journal of Anthropological Research, 39*:3:307–322.

CATLIN, GEORGE. (1967). *O-Kee-Pa: A Religious Ceremony and Other Customs of the Mandans.* Edited

and with an Introduction by John C. Ewers. (Centennial Edition.) New Haven: Yale University Press.

LANCASTER, D. GORDON, AND W. V. BRELSFORD. (1950). Hymen and Semen Ritual among the

Chewa. *International Journal of Sexology, 3*:4:219–223.

PAIGE, KAREN E., AND JEFFREY M. PAIGE. (1981). *The Politics of Reproductive Ritual.* Berkeley: University of California Press.

SCOTT, GEORGE RYLEY. (1966). *Phallic Worship: A History of Sex and Sex Rites in Relation to the Religions of All Races from Antiquity to the Present Day.* London: Luxor Press Ltd. (Originally published in 1941.)

WILLIAMS, WALTER L. (1986). *The Spirit and the Flesh: Sexual Diversity in American Indian Culture.* Boston: Beacon.

19

SEX AND REPRESSION IN AN IRISH FOLK COMMUNITY

JOHN C. MESSENGER*

In this chapter I will discuss sexual repression—its manifestations in behavior and beliefs, its causes, its inculcation, and its broader historical and cultural implications—in a small island community of the Gaeltacht that I will call Inis Beag.[1] My wife and I conducted ethnographic research there for nineteen months, between 1958 and 1966, which included a one-year stay and eight other visits of from one to seven weeks—at Christmas or during the summer. Ours is the only holistic ethnographic study of this community, although archeologists, linguists, philologists, folklorists, geographers, anthropometricians, and other scientists have undertaken research there for over a century. We collected a large body of culture and personality data on three other Irish islands for the purposes of making comparisons and testing hypotheses concerning culture and personality concomitants of island living. Inis Beag is ideally suited to ethnographic and folklore research in that its population possesses a tradition which is less

*A grant from the Indiana University Ford International Program enabled me to write this chapter.

[1] For other reports on Inis Beag, consult Messenger 1962, 1968, and 1969.

SOURCE: "Sex and Repression in an Irish Folk Community" from *Human Sexual Behavior* by Donald S. Marshall and Robert C. Suggs. Copyright © 1971 by the Institute for Sex Research, Inc. Reprinted by permission of Basic Books, a division of HarperCollins Publishers, Inc.

acculturated than that of any other local Irish group.

According to anthropological definition (Lewis 1960: 1–2), the islanders qualify as folk people in almost every respect. The community has maintained its stability for at least 200 years; there is a strong bond between the peasants and their land, and agriculture provides them with the major source of their livelihood; production is mainly for subsistence and is carried on with a simple technology, using the digging stick, spade, and scythe as primary implements; the island folk participate in a money economy, but barter still persists; a low standard of living prevails, and the birth rate is high; the family is of central importance, and marriage figures prominently as a provision of economic welfare; the island is integrated into the country and national governments and is subject to their laws; the people have long been exposed to urban influences and have borrowed cultural forms from other rural areas on the mainland, integrating them into a relatively stable system; and, finally, the experience of living under English rule for centuries has created in the islanders an attitude of dependence on—yet hostility toward—government which continues to this day. The only conditions in Inis Beag which run counter to those found in most other peasant communities are low death and illiteracy rates and bilateral, rather than unilineal, descent (although inheritance is patrilineal).

Inis Beag culture also characterizes people of nearby islands, and the traditions of the several together might be regarded as forming a subculture of the total Irish system. Many island customs are shared with rural peasants on the mainland (where numerous regional subcultures exist), and some are part of a broader European matrix. The island has experienced considerable cultural change since the establishment of the Congested Districts Board (forerunner of the Gaeltacht) in 1891 and the growth of tourism in this century. But conditions there still approximate those which must have prevailed two generations ago, and earlier, throughout this region of peasant Ireland.

Inis Beag has a population of approximately 350 persons living in seventy-one "cottages" distributed among four settlements, called "villages." Bordering a "strand" and a large tract of common land on the northeastern side of the island are a series of limestone terraces, separated by water-bearing shales and faced by small cliffs, on which the villages are situated. Most of the arable land is found on this side, where the shales have been broken down by weathering and alien soils deposited by wind and by ice of the Weichsel glacier. Over many generations, the islanders have deepened these soils and created new soils on rock surfaces by adding seaweed, sand, and human manure. On the southwestern side of Inis Beag, known as the "back of the island," limestone pavements slope rather evenly, almost as the gentle dip of the strata, from the crest of the highest terrace to the sea a mile away. The bared surfaces are intersected in all directions by crevices, which contain a large portion of the natural flora—herbs and shrubs—of the island. Stone fences delimit many hundreds of plots which compose most of the two-square-mile land surface of Inis Beag.

The island boasts a post office with radio-telephone facilities, a "national school" in which three teachers instruct ninety pupils in the seven "standards," two provision shops with attached "pubs," a former coast guard station now housing the nurse and a knitting industry which employs local girls, a lighthouse, and a chapel served by a curate who resides nearby. Inis Beag lacks electricity and running water, and the only vehicles are several ass-drawn carts which are able to travel the narrow, fence-bordered trails. A small "steamer" carrying supplies, passengers, and mail to and from a mainland port visits the island at least once each week. That Inis Beag has experienced far less cultural change than other island communities of Ireland is largely due to the fact that, in absence of a deep water quay, the steamer has had to stand off the strand and be met by "canoes." Most of the tourists who come to the island stay only for the hours that the steamer is anchored and go ashore mainly for the thrill of riding in the canoes, which the island men row with consummate skill. Insofar as I can discover, the inhabitants of Inis Beag are less prone to visit the mainland than are the peoples of other Irish islands.

INIS BEAG HISTORY AND CULTURE[2]

The prehistory and history of Inis Beag are recorded dramatically in a multitude of monuments and artifacts of stone and metal, including Neolithic axe-heads and kitchen middens, Copper-Bronze Age gallery grave tombs and burial mounds of earth and stone, an Iron Age promontory fort, and medieval Christian monasteries, churches, cemeteries, stone houses, and a sacred well, as well as a three-story tower house built by the political overlords of the island. Irish nativists claim that the contemporary folk are lineal descendants of ancient, once civilized Celts. But local legend, historical evidence, and genealogical data collected by my wife and me indicate that the present population is descended from immigrants who came to the island from many parts of Ireland following the Cromwellian incursion of the seventeenth century. The islanders still express bitterness over conditions of poverty and servitude experienced by their ancestors during the 300 years that they lived under absentee Anglo-Irish landlords. All of the excesses of foreign domination suffered by mainland peasants were suffered by the inhabitants of Inis Beag, but were aggravated by the ordinary hardships of island living. Little was known about events in Inis Beag during the eighteenth and early nineteenth centuries until the island was visited by archeologists and publicized in their scientific writings. The surrounding area of the mainland was very much isolated and seldom visited at that time, although trading between Inis Beag and nearby communities

was carried on, and passing ships sometimes called at the island.

Agricultural pursuits have always dominated the subsistence economy of Inis Beag. Most householders own land on which they grow potatoes and other vegetables, grass, and sometimes rye and sally rods and where they pasture cattle, sheep, goats, asses, and horses. The back of the island, behind the communities, is divided into four strips, and each landowner possesses numerous plots located along the "quarter" on which his village fronts. The average combined holding is sixteen acres, and almost 50 percent of the land is composed of arable indigenous and manufactured soils. Potatoes are the staple crop, and they are supplemented by various other vegetables, milk from cattle and goats, meat from island sheep, fish, eggs, and other foods, many of which are imported and sold in the shops. Rye is grown for thatching, and sally rods are used to weave several types of containers. Other subsistence activities (which also provide income for some folk) are knitting, weaving, crocheting, tailoring, and sandal making.

A slowly expanding cash economy features the export of cattle and sheep fattened on the island and of surplus potatoes and fish, the collection of seaweed for extraction of iodine at a mainland factory, the keeping of tourists in private homes, and the manufacturing of craft objects for sale to visitors and for export. At the turn of the century, fishing from canoes—with nets and lines often many miles out in the ocean—was an important subsistence and income activity. A few islanders who owned little or no land lived primarily by fishing and kelp-making. But over the past few decades, fish have become less plentiful and the weather more inclement, especially during winter months; less than a dozen crews now fish regularly, and most fish are consumed locally rather than exported. Government subsidies of many sorts and remittances from relatives who have emigrated supplement the cash economy. The government further aids the islanders by not collecting "rates" and by setting low rents on land. Income information is as difficult to come by as

---

[2]The culture described herein is that of 1959–1960 and excludes important changes which have occurred since then, such as those resulting from the introduction of television, a summer language school for pupils from the mainland, and free secondary education.

data on sex, disputes, and pagan religious retentions; since the people do not wish to jeopardize their unemployment benefits (most of them receive the "dole") and old age pensions and fear taxation in the future, they are secretive about sources and amounts of income.

More important than the formal political structure of Inis Beag are the local informal system and social control techniques of gossip, ridicule, satire, and the like. Crime is rare in Inis Beag, and there are no "guards" stationed there. The island is seldom visited by politicians, and many inhabitants are either apathetic or antagonistic toward the county and national governments. Those asked to account for their antigovernment attitude cite widespread nepotism and corruption among officials, the slight differences between the platforms of the two major parties, and "foolish" government schemes in Inis Beag—usually instituted without consulting the islanders. Government aid is sought and even expected as a "right," but it is seldom considered adequate. Taxation in any form, especially of tobacco and stout, is bitterly opposed.

The informal political system is dominated by the curate, the "headmaster" of the national school, and a self-appointed local "king." In the past, the amount of influence exerted by curates has varied; some have been concerned mostly with fulfilling spiritual responsibilities, while others have attacked by sermon, threat, and even physical action such activities as courting, dancing, visiting, gossiping, and drinking spirits. Anticlerical sentiment (seldom manifested in overt acts) is as strong as, or stronger than, its antigovernment counterpart. The clergy are said to interfere too much in secular affairs, to live too "comfortably," to be absent from the island too often, and to act overly aloof and supercilious. The most outspoken anticlerics assert that curates have employed informers, allocated indulgences, withheld the sacraments, and placed curses ("reading the Bible at") in their efforts to regulate the secular life of Inis Beag. The headmaster, appointed and rigidly supervised by the parish priest and curate, presides over social

events and serves as an adviser to the islanders in many matters, in addition to carrying out his official duties.

Inis Beag lacks a class system, and the status symbols which affect human relationships are few. There is, in fact, little difference in the style of life between the most and the lest prosperous of the islanders. The web of kinship rather than the possession of status attributes, for the most part, determines who will interact with whom and in what manner. Land and money are the principal symbols, with formal education and influential relatives (particularly priests, nuns, and teachers), on the mainland and abroad, becoming more important. Two generations ago, strength, courage, economic skills, and musical and story-telling abilities were highly regarded as well, but acculturation has lessened their significance.

Although there are fifty-nine nuclear families, only thirteen surnames exist today. There is much inbreeding, as might be expected, and the church carefully checks the genealogies of prospective spouses to ascertain their degree of consanguinity. Courtship is almost nonexistent, and most marriages are arranged with little concern for the desires of the young people involved. Late marriage and celibacy are as prevalent in Inis Beag as elsewhere in Ireland. The average marriage age for men is thirty-six and for women twenty-five, and 29 percent of those persons eligible for marriage are single.[3] The functions of the family are mainly economic and reproductive, and conjugal love is extremely rare. A sharp dichotomy exists between the sexes; both before and after marriage men interact mostly with

[3]Twenty-nine percent of those islanders of marriageable age are single. This rises to a high of 37 percent among first and second generation Inis Beag emigrants, indicating the actions of more than just economic causes. Irish scholars, for obvious reasons, tend to stress economic and other (climate, race, English oppression, the famine, loss of the Irish tongue, etc.) monistic causes in their analyses of culture and personality phenomena. Inadequate statistics for second and third generation migrants from Inis Beag suggest that the celibacy rate lowers markedly only when descendants of immigrants dissociate themselves from Irish ethnic communities and Irish-American priests. Ethnographic research is sorely needed among Irish of several generations in the countries to which they have migrated to probe this and other phenomena.

men and women with women. The average family has seven offspring, and many women are unhappy about being forced by the unauthorized decree of local priests to produce as many children as possible. They feel that the constant bearing and rearing of offspring increase their work, restrict their freedom, and perpetuate the poverty of their families. Jealousy of the greater freedom of men is commonly expressed by women who have many young children. Mothers bestow a considerable amount of attention and affection on their offspring, especially on their sons. However, tensions between fathers and sons which develop in childhood often flare into scarcely repressed hostility later on, particularly in those families where competition for the inheritance of property is engendered among siblings by the fathers' attempts to ensure favored treatment in old age.

Men are far more active socially than are women. The latter are restricted by custom mostly to visiting, attending parties during the winter, and participating in church-associated activities. Many women leave their cottages only to attend mass, wakes, and funerals or to make infrequent calls on relatives; my wife and I talked with some elderly women who had not visited other villages or walked to the back of the island for thirty or more years. Men not only attend parties with their womenfolk but go to dances during the summer, frequent the pubs, play cards almost nightly during November and December (the period when once people congregated to hear storytellers), visit the homes of kin and friends or meet along the trails at night, and range the entire island and the sea about it in their economic pursuits. Before the age of benevolent government, women shared many economic tasks with men, such as collecting seaweed, baiting lines, and gutting fish. But now they tend to household chores and only milk cows and perform some of the lighter farming jobs with their fathers and husbands.

The island folk are devout Catholics, despite the fact that they are critical of their priests and hold pagan religious beliefs. Youth of Inis Beag

overtly disallow the existence of other than church-approved supernatural entities. However, their elders cling to traditional pagan beliefs and practices (many of which are Druidic in origin) about which they are extremely secretive for fear of being ridiculed by outsiders and their more skeptical neighbors. The non-Christian array of spiritual beings includes various spirits and demons, ghosts, witches, phantom ships, and animals and material objects possessing human attributes and volitions. Prominent among the spirits thought to inhabit Inis Beag are the trooping and solitary fairies, sea creatures, mermaids, and the banshee. The most formidable of the demons is a pooka which lives in a Bronze Age burial mound and roams the strand and common land at night altering its shape and size at will; during the day it will twist the limbs of unwary persons who choose the hill for a resting place. Ghosts, called "shades," are frequently seen after dark performing economic tasks. They are thought to be doing penance in purgatory, which embraces the earth as well as a spiritual locus; this is one example of the many reinterpretations of Christian and pagan belief effected by the islanders. The only form of witchcraft practiced today is the casting of the evil eye. At least three persons, suitably ostracized, are believed to be able to perpetrate evil by the act of complimenting their victims. Other religious retentions found in Inis Beag are a multitude of taboos, divination through the seeking of omens, magical charms and incantations of a protective nature, and an emphasis on "natural" foods, folk medicines, and other products impinging on the human body.

It is believed by many people in Ireland that the Catholicism of the islanders embodies an ideal unattained on the mainland, where the faith is thought to set an example for the world. In fact, the worship of the folk is obsessively oriented toward salvation in the next world, with a corresponding preoccupation with sin in this world; there is a resemblance to polytheism in the manner in which they relate to the Blessed Virgin and Irish saints; Christian as well as pagan rituals and religious artifacts are often employed to serve magical ends; and many beliefs that they hold to be orthodox Catholic are in reality idiosyncratic to Inis Beag or Ireland. Christian morality in its "outward" manifestations is realized to a remarkable degree. This can be attributed, in part, to the emphasis placed on good works as a means of gaining salvation; but, more importantly, it results from the already-mentioned techniques of social control exercised by the clergy, based on an overwhelming fear of damnation.

RESEARCH PROCEDURES

The most active researchers in Inis Beag have been folklorists. Although ethnology as a discipline is not represented in the national universities and elsewhere in the Republic, folklore in the European humanistic tradition is strongly developed. The deliberate recording of the immense body of Irish folklore, folk beliefs, and folk customs began in the early part of the last century, was spurred by nativism—of which the Gaelic Revival was the main strand, and was institutionalized in the Republic with the formation of, first, the Folklore of Ireland Society in 1926, then the Irish Folklore Institute in 1930, and, finally, the Irish Folklore Commission in 1936 (Delargy 1957). For many years, commission collectors have visited Inis Beag, recording mostly the verbal art and material traits—with their associated behavior—of the island folk. They have not attempted to describe and analyze functionally and dynamically the total culture of the island; their visits have been brief and intermittent; they have depended on a limited sample of respondents; and most of their queries have been guided by Sean O'Suillaebhain's *A Handbook of Irish Folklore,* which does not contain numerous categories of significance to anthropologists.

My wife and I devoted most of our research to documenting the contemporary culture of Inis Beag: its economic, political, social, religious,

esthetic, and recreational aspects. We also described formal and informal education and the personality traits formed by it, reconstructed Inis Beag history of the past century by examining historical materials of many types and probing the memories of aged island respondents, and recorded cultural change in process over an eight-year period. The standard ethnographic research techniques that we employed include guided and open-ended interviews, external and participant observation, collection of life histories, cross-checking, photography, and phonography. The sample for much of our data was the total universe of 350 inhabitants.

It is extremely difficult to obtain information in Inis Beag about such matters as amounts and sources of income, disputes, pagan religious retentions and reinterpretations, and sex. This brief list might be increased by at least threefold and gives rise to a consideration of the problems associated with obtaining reliable data from the Irish in general and the islanders in particular. Honor Tracy, in the first chapter (aptly entitled "Forebodings") of her book, *Mind You I've Said Nothing,* humorously presents one of the shortest, yet most discerning analyses of Irish national character yet written by a novelist and predicts the various reactions that her volume will evoke in Irish readers.[4] She concludes with the following remarks about the difficulties surrounding fact finding in Ireland:

> This question of fact was another of the spectres hovering in my path. In every book there should be a fact here and there or the writer is charged with aimless frivolity. But facts in Ireland are very peculiar things. They are rarely allowed to spoil the sweep and low of conversation: the

[4]These reactions appear to be institutionalized, as my writings and conversational remarks have also evoked them. Two additional responses that I have encountered are: my conclusions are invalidated because I failed to consult certain "source materials" written in Gaelic, and my inferior writing style precludes serious consideration of my findings. I take pains to explain, usually in vain, the many methods of fieldwork utilized by ethnographers to Irish persons who are critical of my data and who invariably use the phrase, "You can't trust what an Irishman tells you." On a rare occasion, one listener to my lengthy explanation said, "Ah, you're cuter than we are"—a compliment indeed!

crabbing effect they have on good talk is eliminated almost entirely. I do not believe myself that the Irishman conveniently ignores their existence, as sometimes is said, so much as that he is blithely unaware of it. He soars above their uninviting surfaces on the wing of his fancy. Who then would answer my questions truthfully, who would supply me with that modicum of sober and accurate information required to give my book a serious air? No one, as far as I know. And if facts are elusive and shadowy things in Ireland, opinions are more so. An Irishman, sober, will say not what he thinks but what he believes you would like him to think; he is a man of honeyed words, anxious to flatter and soothe, cajole and caress. When he has taken a jar or two . . . he will say whatever he judges will give the greatest offence. In neither case does he reveal his own true thoughts if, to be sure, he has any. He would be in dread lest you quoted him and the story went round and he got the name of a bold outspoken fellow, which might be bad for business. And then again so many Irishmen find an innocent glee in misleading and deceiving for its own sake. Obfuscation is the rule, and while it may seem a little foolish at times, there is no doubt that it makes for a great deal of fun. It cultivates too a sharpness of ear, a feeling for half-tones and shades and subtleties, and a wary alertness that would be worth its weight in gold should one ever be lost in a jungle (Tracy 1953: 20–21).

I will not concern myself with the various cultural and psychological causes accounting for this state of affairs, which would require an essay equal in length to this one. Suffice it to say, the quotation in considerable measure applies to interviewing in Inis Beag, where my wife and I took great pains to disentangle real from ideal culture by substantiating interview data with observation, wherever possible. The existence of the conditions depicted by Tracy, as well as the numerous cultural practices shrouded in secrecy, led us to return to the island several times after 1960 before attempting an ethnography, to emphasize various modes of participant observation in order to gain added rapport, to devise ad hoc research methods of an unorthodox nature,[5] to "hone" our orthodox

tools and employ cross-checking techniques at every stage of our research, and to cultivate that "sharpness of ear . . . feeling for half-tones and shades and subtleties, and . . . wary alertness" which characterize ethnographic endeavor as an art as well as an epistemology.

The use by the folk of "wings of fancy," "honeyed words," and "obfuscations"—popularly known as "blarney"—reflects a long tradition of verbal skill. It is a vital component of Irish and Inis Beag "charm," which often is a product of a delicately poised set of defense mechanisms; beneath it can lie feelings of inferiority and dislike, envy, and jealousy of others. Blarney can very effectively serve to shield genuine thoughts and feelings and thus protect the ego. Irish folklore and literature also reflect this tradition of verbal skill, and it is probably expressed most formidably in James Joyce's *Ulysses* and *Finnegans Wake*. (At least one folklorist has collected "Joycean utterances" from Irish peasants.)

Most of our information came from observation and unguided interviews. It proved impossible to take field notes openly, except when collecting innocuous data—such as the number of livestock owned by each householder—from a few particular persons. Thus, we were forced to limit our visits to less than two hours, after which we immediately transcribed what our combined memories could resuscitate. Despite frequent explanations of our presence in Inis Beag, which were candid and truthful, it was thought by the islanders that I was interested only in archeological sites and oral literature, and that my wife was not a trained and experienced co-worker; this, obviously, reflects their previous experiences with scientists and their conception of the position of women in society. Their inability to evaluate adequately our intentions proved to be a research boon. For once "accepted" (a relative term, since no outsider is

---

[5]Departures from methodological orthodoxy were our use, as projective devices, of literary works and a ballad that I composed. Islanders read at our request books about Inis Beag, and we recorded and analyzed their responses. The ballad that I wrote, now embedded in the local verbal art tradition, is based on a shipwreck and rescue that we witnessed, and a series of fascinating events which ensued during the following months. The manner of its composition, the alteration of it by Inis Beag singers after it was written, and the circumstances surrounding its public presentation by various balladiers before differing audiences gave us invaluable ethnographic insights.

ever accepted) after many months in the island, we were allowed to listen to and participate in conversations and activities from which we would otherwise have been excluded.

Our data on sex came from my involvement as a participant-observer in personal and often intimate conversations with men and my wife's counseling of women who were bothered by such matters as explaining and coping with menstruation, menopause, mental illness, the sexual curiosity of their children, and "excessive" sexual demands of their spouses. Our sexual knowledge and sympathy coupled with their needs and inquisitiveness gave rise to a "counselor-client" relationship between many of the folk and ourselves. They came to speak freely, albeit indirectly at times, with each of us about this sphere of behavior which arouses so much anxiety and fear. I must mention that the relationship arose partly out of our desire to alleviate distress and not solely to collect information. We had performed the same role seven years earlier among primitive Nigerians, and for similar reasons. However, the Africans were uninhibited, talked freely with us about sex, and were not offended by what we subsequently wrote.

Another important source of information on sex was the island nurses, who supplied us with accounts of their own observations over an eight-year period and gave us access to pertinent medical records. My wife and I believe that our information is, for the most part, reliable, but that some of it may well be erroneous. This report will, we are afraid, offend and alienate some of our Inis Beag friends, for whom we hold deep affection; they do not comprehend the aims and values of anthropology and may regard our reporting of sexual beliefs and behavior as a breach of friendship and trust. Certainly our findings will be denied by many Irish readers.

More than any other type of research, culture and personality investigations are needed in Ireland today. Social and cultural anthropologists, rural sociologists, folklorists, and geographers in small numbers have managed to describe and analyze the major sociocultural forms of the Irish folk, but personality generalizations, by and large, have been the by-products of research into other areas and have tended to be impressionistic. Some of the most penetrating studies of Irish character have been made "at a distance" and through the analysis of projective systems and narrow units of culture, such as drinking patterns (Bales 1962). Some Irish writers—"intuitive anthropologists" I call them—also have had insightful things to say about Irish character (usually at a distance too, from church and state). What is sorely needed is a holistic community study done by a culture and personality specialist—a person skilled not only in ethnography, social psychology, and psychiatry (and able to administer projective tests), but well versed in Irish history, literature, and contemporary affairs as well.

SEXUAL REPRESSIONS: ITS MANIFESTATIONS

Both lack of sexual knowledge and misconceptions about sex among adults combine to brand Inis Beag as one of the most sexually naive of the world's societies. Sex never is discussed in the home when children are about; only three mothers admitted giving advice, briefly and incompletely, to their daughters. We were told that boys are better advised than girls, but that the former learn about sex informally from older boys and men and from observing animals. Most respondents who were questioned about sexual instructions given to youths expressed the belief that "after marriage nature takes its course," thus negating the need for anxiety-creating and embarrassing personal confrontation of parents and offspring. We were unable to discover any cases of childlessness based on sexual ignorance of spouses, as reported from other regions of peasant Ireland. Also, we were unable to discover knowledge of the sexual categories utilized by researchers in sex: insertion of tongue while kissing, male mouth on female breast, female hand on penis, cunnilingus, fellatio, femoral coitus, anal coitus, extramarital coitus, manifest homosexuality, sexual contact with animals, fetishism, and sado-masochistic behavior. Some of these activities may be practiced by particular individuals and couples; however, without a doubt they are deviant forms in Inis Beag, about which information is difficult to come by.

Menstruation and menopause arouse profound misgivings among women of the island, because few of them comprehend their physiological significance. My wife was called on to explain these processes more than any other phenomena related to sex. When they reach puberty, most girls are unprepared for the first menstrual flow and find the experience a traumatic one—especially when their mothers are unable to provide a satisfactory explanation for it. And it is commonly believed that the menopause can induce "madness"; in order to ward off this condition, some women have retired from life in their mid-forties and, in a few cases, have confined themselves to bed until death, years later. Others have so retired as a result of depressive and masochistic states. Yet the harbingers of "insanity" are simply the physical symptoms announcing the onset of menopause. In Inis Beag, these include severe headaches, hot flashes, faintness in crowds and enclosed places, and severe anxiety. Mental illness is also held to be inherited or caused by inbreeding (or by the Devil, by God punishing a sinner, or by malignant pagan beings) and stigmatizes the family of the afflicted. One old man came close to revealing what is probably the major cause of neuroses and psychoses in Ireland, when he explained the incarceration of an Inis Beag curate in a mental institution for clerics as caused by his constant association with a pretty housekeeper, who "drove him mad from frustration." This elder advocated that only plain-appearing older women (who would not "gab" to "our man") be chosen for the task. Earlier, according to island opinion, the same priest had caused to be committed to the "madhouse" a local man who pub-

licly challenged certain of his actions. The unfortunate man was released six months later, as per law, since he was not mentally ill.

Sexual misconceptions are myriad in Inis Beag. The islanders share with most Western peoples the belief that men by nature are far more libidinous than women. The latter have been taught by some curates and in the home that sexual relations with their husbands are a "duty" which must be "endured," for to refuse coitus is a mortal sin. A frequently encountered assertion affixes the guilt for male sexual strivings on the enormous intake of potatoes of the Inis Beag male. (In Nigeria, among the people whom my wife and I studied, women are thought to be more sexually disposed than men and are the repositories of sexual knowledge; it is they who initiate coitus and so pose a threat to their spouses. Nigerian men place the blame on clitoridectomy performed just prior to marriage.) Asked to compare the sexual proclivities of Inis Beag men and women, one mother of nine said, "Men can wait a long time before wanting 'it,' but we can wait a lot longer." There is much evidence to indicate that the female orgasm is unknown—or at least doubted, or considered a deviant response. One middle-aged bachelor, who considers himself wise in the ways of the outside world and has a reputation for making love to willing tourists, described one girl's violent bodily reactions to his fondling and asked for an explanation; when told the "facts of life" of what obviously was an orgasm, he admitted not realizing that women also could achieve a climax, although he was aware that some of them apparently enjoyed kissing and being handled.

Inis Beag men feel that sexual intercourse is debilitating, a common belief in primitive and folk societies. They will desist from sex the night before they are to perform a job which will require the expenditure of great energy. Women are not approached sexually during menstruation or for months after childbirth, since they are considered "dangerous" to the male at these times. Returned "Yanks" have been denounced from the pulpit for describing American sexual practices to island youths, and such "pornographic" magazines as *Time* and *Life,* mailed by kin from abroad, have aroused curates to spirited sermon and instruction.

The separation of the sexes, started within the family, is augmented by separation in almost all segments of adolescent and adult activity. Boys and girls are separated to some extent in classrooms, and completely in recess play and movement to and from school. During church services, there is a further separation of adult men and women, as well as boys and girls, and each of the four groups leaves the chapel in its turn. The pubs are frequented only by men or by women tourists and female teachers who have spent several years on the mainland while training and thus are "set apart" (and, of course, by inquisitive female ethnographers). Women occasionally visit the shops to procure groceries, but it is more common for them to send their children to do so, since supplies and drinks are proffered across the same counter, and men are usually to be found on the premises. Even on the strand during summer months, male tourists tend to bathe at one end and women at the other. Some swimmers "daringly" change into bathing suits there, under towels and dresses—a custom practiced elsewhere in Ireland which has overtones of sexual catharsis.

It is often asserted that the major "escape valve" of sexual frustration among single persons in Ireland is masturbation; frustration-aggression theorists, however, would stress the ubiquity of drinking, alcoholism, disputes, and pugnacity as alternative outlets. Pugnacity can also be linked to the widespread problem of male identity. Our study revealed that male masturbation in Inis Beag seems to be common, premarital coitus unknown, and marital copulation limited as to foreplay and the manner of consummation. My wife and I never witnessed courting—"walking out"—in the island. Elders proudly insist that it does not occur, but male youths admit to it in rumor. The claims of young men focus on "petting" with tourists and a few

local girls, whom the "bolder" of them kiss and fondle outside of their clothing. Island girls, it is held by their "lovers," do not confess these sins because they fail to experience pleasure from the contact. The male perpetrators also shun the confessional because of their fear of the priest.

We were unable to determine the frequency of marital coitus. A considerable amount of evidence indicates that privacy in the act is stressed and that foreplay is limited to kissing and rough fondling of the lower body, especially the buttocks. Sexual activity invariably is initiated by the husband. Only the male superior position is employed; intercourse takes place with underclothes not removed; and orgasm, for the man, is achieved quickly, almost immediately after which he falls asleep. (I must stress the provisional nature of these data, for they are based on a limited sample of respondents and relate to that area of sexual behavior least freely discussed.)

Many kinds of behavior disassociated from sex in other societies, such as nudity and physiological evacuation, are considered sexual in Inis Beag. Nudity is abhorred by the islanders, and the consequences of this attitude are numerous and significant for health and survival. Only infants have their entire bodies sponged once a week, on Saturday night; children, adolescents, and adults, on the same night, wash only their faces, necks, lower arms, hands, lower legs, and feet. Several times my wife and I created intense embarrassment by entering a room in which a man had just finished his weekly ablutions and was barefooted; once when this occurred, the man hurriedly pulled on his stockings and said with obvious relief, "Sure, it's good to get your clothes on again." Clothing always is changed in private, sometimes within the secrecy of the bedcovers, and it is usual for the islanders to sleep in their underclothes.

Despite the fact that Inis Beag men spend much of their time at sea in their canoes, as far as we could determine none of them can swim. Four rationales are given for this deficiency: the men are confident that nothing will happen to them, because they are excellent seamen and weather forecasters; a man who cannot swim will be more careful; it is best to drown immediately when a canoe capsizes far out in the ocean rather than swim futilely for minutes or even hours, thus prolonging the agony; and, finally, "When death is on a man, he can't be saved." The truth of the matter is that they have never dared to bare their bodies in order to learn the skill. Some women claim to have "bathed" at the back of the island during the heat of summer, but this means wading in small pools with skirts held knee-high, in complete privacy. Even the nudity of household pets can arouse anxiety, particularly when they are sexually aroused during time of heat. In some homes, dogs are whipped for licking their genitals and soon learn to indulge in this practice outdoors. My wife, who can perform Irish step-dances and sing many of the popular folk songs, was once requested to sing a seldom-heard American Western ballad; she chose "The Lavendar Cowboy," who "had only two hairs on his chest." The audience response was perfunctory and, needless to say, she never again was "called out" to sing that particular song.

The drowning of seamen, who might have saved themselves had they been able to swim, is not the only result of the sexual symbolism of nudity; men who were unwilling to face the nurse when ill, because it might have meant baring their bodies to her, were beyond help when finally treated. While my wife and I were on the island, a nurse was assaulted by the mother of a young man for diagnosing his illness and bathing his chest in the mother's absence. (In this case, Oedipal and sexual attitudes probably were at work in tandem.)

It must be pointed out that nudity is also shunned for "health" reasons, for another obtrusive Inis Beag character trait is hypochondria. In some cases, however, it is hard to determine whether concern with modesty or health is dominant in a particular behavioral response. Fear of colds and influenza is foremost among health concerns; rheumatism and related muscular joint ailments, migraine headaches and other psychosomatic disorders, tooth decay, indigestion ("nervous stomach"), and hypermetropia are other widespread pathologies which cause worry among the folk—not to mention those of supernatural origin.

Secrecy surrounds the acts of urination and defecation. The evacuation of infants before siblings and strangers is discouraged, and animals that discharge in the house are driven out. Chickens that habitually "dirty" their nests while setting are soon killed and eaten. Although some women drink spirits privately, they seldom do so at parties. In part this is because of the embarrassment involved in visiting the outside toilet with men in the "street" looking on. One of the most carefully guarded secrets of Inis Beag, unreported in the many works describing island culture, is the use of human manure mixed with sand as a fertilizer. We were on the island eight months before we discovered that compost is not "street drippings" and "scraw," but decomposed feces. With "turf" becoming more difficult to procure from the mainland, some islanders have taken to importing coal and processed peat and burning cattle dung. The dung is prepared for use in difficult-to-reach plots at the back of the island when tourists are few in number; it is burned covertly because of the overtones of sex and poverty. Another custom that my wife and I learned of late in our research, due to the secrecy surrounding it, concerns the thickening of wool; men are required to urinate in a container and tread the wool therein with their bare feet.

Other major manifestations of sexual repression in Inis Beag are the lack of a "dirty joke" tradition (at least as the term is understood by ethnologists and folklorists) and the style of dancing, which allows little bodily contact among participants. I have heard men use various verbal devices—innuendoes, puns, and asides—that they believed bore sexual connotations; relatively speaking, they were pallid. In the song that I composed, one line of a verse refers to an island bachelor arising late in the day after "dreaming perhaps of a beautiful mate"; this is regarded as a highly suggestive phrase, and I have seen it redden cheeks and lower glances in a pub. Both step- and set-dancing are practiced in Inis Beag, although the former type is dying out. This rigid-body dancing, from which sex is removed by shifting attention below the hips, appears to have originated in Ireland during the early nineteenth century. The set patterns keep partners separated most of the time; but, even so, some girls refuse to dance, because it involves touching a boy. Inis Beag men, while watching a woman step-dance, stare fixedly at her feet, and they take pains to appear indifferent when crowding at a party necessitates holding women on their laps and rubbing against them when moving from room to room. But they are extremely sensitive, nevertheless, to the entire body of the dancer and to these casual contacts, as are the women. Their covert emotional reactions (which become overt as much drink is taken) are a form of catharsis.

SEXUAL REPRESSION: ITS HISTORICAL CAUSES

Analysts of Irish character have put forth various hypotheses to account for sexual repression, ranging from the sophisticated to the absurd. The former can be classified under three rubrics: historical (e.g., the influence of ascetic monasticism, Augustinianism, and Jansenism), sociocultural (e.g., the Oedipus complex in the Irish family and male solidarity), and psychological (e.g., masochism). Beyond serious scientific consideration are such hypotheses as the loss of the Irish tongue, lack of a Catholic aristocracy, fear of Protestant libertinism, and the ever-appealed-to factors of race, climate, and the famine. In the following paragraphs, I will quote excerpts from Irish authors and from critical observers of the Irish scene, including social scientists, rather than dissect their views myself.

Paul Blanshard, in his polemical but insightful (and, in my estimation, often understated) work, *The Irish and Catholic Power,* says that "whatever the explanation, the total sexual expression of the Irish people is much less than it is in other countries, and that the Catholic crusade against normal sexual life has actually created a nation of men and women who try to drown their fundamental instincts." In attempting to account for sexual repression on such a scale, he writes:

> Ireland was . . . one of the world's most ascetic countries, and the monastic ideal has undoubtedly left a deep mark on the Irish mind. Although Irish priests were permitted to have wives as late as the eighth century, sexual renunciation came to be identified with virtue and distinction in the community, and thousands of the best men and women lived apart from each other. Kevin Devlin in his *Christus Rex* article on "Single and Selfish" . . . says of the ancient Irish that "when they 'fell in love with Christianity' . . . they took to the ideal of virginity with a Pauline enthusiasm unknown elsewhere. St. Patrick himself noted this with an inflection of surprise in the *Confessions* . . ." (Blanshard 1954: 160–161).

Several Irish scholars since 1955 have expressed the opinion in personal conversations that the rapidity of Irish conversion to monasticism in the early medieval period can be attributed, in large measure, to masochism. This ancient character trait is most evident in the projective system of early Irish verbal art, if one discounts the possibility of widespread distortion through the actions of Celtic defense mechanisms and later revisionists.

In a recent book, the impact of Augustinianism at this time and in the centuries to come is examined by Fr. Alexander Humphreys. He says in *New Dubliners:*

> The specific doctrinal tradition to which Ireland and the Irish countryman in particular has fallen heir is the Augustinian. . . . [It] lays relatively greater emphasis on the weakness and evil to which human nature is prone as the result of original sin. By the same token, it attributes relatively less efficacy to natural knowledge and human action and relatively more validity to God's revelation and more power to the action of God's grace. . . . [The] Irish countryman has

acquired a more than average distrust of native human reason. As a Catholic he cannot and does not deny the validity of rational thought, but he tends to be quite suspicious of the pride of the mind and so wary of ultimate rationalism that he shies away from reasoned discussions of high truths. . . . The tradition he inherits tends toward a certain historical and theological positivism in regard to the major truths and values of life, and, together with other historical factors, has led him to an intensified reliance upon the teaching power of the Church as voiced by the clergy. At the same time, while appreciating the need for positive good works, he is inclined to place relatively greater emphasis on those which are directly concerned with obtaining grace and relatively lesser store by simple ethical behaviour. And finally, although he is certain that man's bodily nature with its emotions is at root good, he is rather more suspicious of it and deals with it somewhat more severely. As a result he inclines to a jaundiced view of sex and a generally ascetic outlook which places a high premium upon continence, penance and, in most spheres of life, on abstemiousness (Humphreys 1966: 25–26).

Humphreys further points out that "the effects of the religious tradition of the Irish, let alone of the countryman, upon the social behavior and attitudes of the people has never been systematically studied from a sociological point of view." He notes that the classic study, *Family and Community in Ireland,* by Conrad Arensberg and Solon Kimball, based on research done over thirty years ago, "leaves the matter virtually untouched," and "attributes the countryman's attitude towards sex almost exclusively to the structure of life in the rural community."

Granted the profound influence social structure has on such a basic matter, a purely structural-functional analysis is hard put to explain adequately the quite ascetic sexual morality of the Irish countryside. . . . [An] attitude similar to that of the countryman is far from uncommon in a city such as Dublin—and among New Dubliners and Old Dubliners to boot—whose social structure differs so radically from that of the countryside. Structural-functional explanations of attitudes do hold up to a point. But worldviews and their ethical consequences also have their special effect (Humphreys 1966: 24–27).

Monasticism and Augustinianism certainly "set the stage" for later Jansenism, although all three probably are connected with basic Irish culture and personality traits of long standing.

Jansenism is succinctly placed in its historical context in Ireland by Joe McCarthy.

Like most everything in Ireland, the severe strictness of the old-time Catholic clergymen was rooted in historical events of the country's past. During the dark era of the anti-Catholic Penal Laws in the 18th Century, young Irishmen had to study for the priesthood on the Continent. In the early 1790's, the British Government became alarmed by the rise of Theobald Wolfe Tone's Irish Protestant revolutionary movement and made hurried bids of appeasement to Irish Catholics in an effort to win their loyalty. One of these conciliatory moves was the establishment of the Catholic theological seminary at Maynooth in 1795. Perhaps not entirely by accident, the faculty of the new college was staffed by refugees from the French Revolution, promonarchy theologians who hated Tone's republican ideas. Most of these theologians had been influenced by Jansenism—the rigid and gloomy doctrine, denounced as Calvinistic by the Jesuits, that man is a helplessly doomed being who must endure punishing soul-searching and rigorous penances to prove his love of God. Mere faith and constant church-going . . . are not enough to win salvation. . . . Thanks to the influence of the French theologians at Maynooth, most of the Irish Catholic hierarchy sided with the British against Tone in the rebellion of 1798, and supported Prime Minister William Pitt's Act of Union. Their forbidding and stern Jansenist theory strongly flavored Irish Catholicism until it was finally officially discouraged in the middle of the 19th Century. The last vestiges of the doctrine have long since disappeared from Irish Catholicism, but the unusual devotion of the Irish people today to physically punishing religious pilgrimages possibly could be traced in part back to the old teaching of Maynooth that love of God must be demonstrated by harder acts than receiving the sacraments and going to daily Mass (McCarthy 1964: 78).

Our research reveals that in some areas of Ireland "the last vestiges of the doctrine" are still associated with Irish Catholicism. In fact, one Dublin social scientist with whom I correspond asserts that Jansenism as manifested in sexual repression probably reached its zenith in the 1930s and has gradually been dying out since then. However, it is still very apparent, even among "emancipated" Dubliners of the middle and upper classes.

A much harsher evaluation of Jansenism, again in an historical context, is found in Bryan McMahon's chapter in *The Vanishing Irish,* edited by Fr. John O'Brien, a collection which also includes pertinent essays by Arland Ussher and the editor himself. McMahon says:

> Associated with the heresy of Jansenism were the principles of an exaggerated moral and disciplinary rigorism under the pretext of a return to the primitive Church. The Celtic spirit, despite or rather because of is essential volatility . . . would appear to me to provide an ideal field for the culture of Jansenism. The penances of the early Celtic monks were severity itself. . . . Today, when the idea of physical penance would appear to be repugnant to the entire world, such laudable manifestations of physical denial as the exercises of Lough Derg and Croagh Patrick are beacons amid the darkness. But the danger is that by a flaw in the Celtic nature we are apt to be led by overcompensation into penitential excesses; then it is that the traits of Jansenism are there to fill lacunae in our nature. Significant in this context is the presence of four refugee doctors of the Sorbonne on the staff of Maynooth College in its early and formative years. [Their] teachings . . . cannot but have in some measure colored . . . the whole course of Irish seminary life and consequently the whole body of Irish lay thought (O'Brien 1953: 215–216).

Might not the "volatile nature" of the "Celtic spirit" and the "flaw in the Celtic nature" whose "lacunae" Jansenism fills be persistent masochism? Ussher addresses his remarks more directly to the sexual implications of Jansenism.

> Certainly the puritanic bias of the Church in Ireland surprises visitors from other Catholic communities. It is often said that Irish schools and seminaries in the last century were infected with the remnants of Jansenism. . . . The dismal fact remains that Irishmen tend to regard procreation as a shameful necessity, and Irish girls grow up to think of sex as something dark, cold,

and forbidding. Statistics are scarcely available, but it seems to me that the word "dirty" is used in modern Ireland in one sense only, namely, to cover every manifestation, even the most natural, of sex passion. . . . Irish married couples seldom give the impression of being biologically satisfied or even awakened; and if they are not, it may partly account for the slovenly, listless, don't care rather than devil-may-care quality of Irish life—the "spit" but never the "polish" (O'Brien 1953: 161–162).

It is interesting to note that Ussher, an Irishman, uses the word "puritanic." I have been severely criticized by Irish readers for using it in this and previous works, since it refers to an English religious movement as well as Cromwell's party.

The editor presents an equally down-to-earth pronouncement of the effects of Jansenism.

> Here Father Murphy has singled out a factor of enormous importance in explaining the grotesque proportion of bachelors and spinsters among the Irish: the typical Irish attitude toward marriage, which, as he and many other priests have suggested, would seem to have an underlying touch of Jansenism. That attitude looks upon marriage and sex as rather regrettable necessities in the propagation of the race: it would have been much better if God had arranged for offspring in some other way. Irish parents shy away from the distasteful task of lifting the veil upon this earthy, unappetizing, and somewhat unclean subject (O'Brien 1953: 105).

The plea for a less "distasteful" manner of reproduction was actually voiced by several Inis Beag women; and most island parents do not lift the "veil," in part because of their own ignorance of sexual matters.

The impact of the Oedipus complex on Irish character has been explored by cultural analysts and writers almost from the time Freud first conceptualized the phenomenon. Indeed, Freud might have been describing Ireland rather than a particular class in Austria at the turn of the century (just as Marx might have had Ireland in mind when positing religion as the opiate of the oppressed masses). Two recent controversial novels use the Oedipus complex as a focus. *Michael Joe,* by William Murray, examines the role of the emasculating Irish mother, and John McGahern, in *The Dark,* probes the conflict between father and son so characteristic of Irish society.

One of the most penetrating studies of this sociocultural configuration, which has such momentous psychological consequences, is that of Marvin Opler and Jerome Singer, conducted among first, second, and third generation Irish male schizophrenic patients in New York hospitals. The intent of these social scientists was to determine how psychotic syndromes are culturally patterned. For a year they observed their respondents to obtain total psychiatric, anthropological, and psychological profiles. Their observations included ward scrutiny, interviews, the collection of life histories and case histories, and the administration of thirteen tests, among them the Rorschach, Thematic Apperception, Sentence Completion, and Porteus Maze. The investigators conclude that there is a continuity of Irish (and Italian) culture and personality forms among immigrants for at least three generations; their psychological findings are buttressed by research data collected in Irish and English mental institutions. My wife and I visited one of these hospitals and interviewed several Irish psychiatrists both there and in America. Our own conclusions support many of those reported by Opler, Singer, and the psychiatrists interviewed.[6] Opler and Singer have the following to say about the Oedipus complex in Ireland:

> Normative cultural standards led to the hypothesis that the central female figure in the Irish family, the mother, could instil primary anxiety and fear toward female figures. . . . This hypothesis grew out of anthropological observations that the central figure in Irish families is more likely to be a controlling figure on the distaff side, while fathers, especially in straitened economic circumstances, are frequently by contrast shadowy

and evanescent. . . . An Irish male patient beset with anxiety and fear of female figures early in life, and lacking possibilities of firm male identification with a father, would later experience the sexual repressions and socio-religious definitions of marriage and sexuality for which his culture, with its high celibacy rates, protracted engagements, and sin-guilt emphases, is justly famous. . . . All this spells a final anxious and fearful lack of positive sexual identification, varying in a continuum from repressed and latent homosexual balances through to added displacements and distortions that are either pallid asexuality or fearful and bizarre misidentifications. Since the culture does not condone sexual expression or postpones and then rigidly defines it in marriage . . . latent homosexual balances [were hypothesized] for this group, no overtly sought interpersonal manifestations, and a facade of asexual misogyny varied only by the most personalized and bizarre female identifications. . . . [The] basic personality has stamped into it such feelings as male inadequacy, the masculine protest, hostility toward females, and the kind of latent homosexual feelings which produce a further sense of sin and guilt (Opler and Singer 1956: 15–18).

Among the seven diagnostic variables utilized by the researchers, the Irish patients ranked highest in the "Sin, Sex, and Guilt Ideology" (93 percent of the sample) and "Homosexuality Types" (90 percent of the sample latent, none overt) categories.

Complementing the Oedipus complex in the etiology of sexual puritanism is male solidarity. It has a long history in Ireland—revealed in legend and modern literature alike—and is instrumental in delaying marriage and making for marital maladjustment. Freudian psychologists see it as one of the many possible by-products of the "universal" Oedipus complex—"male inadequacy, the masculine protest, hostility toward females, and . . . latent homosexual feelings"; but many anthropologists (especially structural-functionalists) analyze it as a sociocultural phenomenon, for it is found in societies in which the Oedipal configuration appears not to exist. Elizabeth Coxhead, in discussing Lady Gregory's play, *Grania,* alludes to the tragic plight of most Irish women, past and present.

[6]Irish psychiatrists in that country, England, and America are often reticent about discussing sex. Psychiatric theory in Ireland is modified by Catholic dogma, and specialists are influenced in writings, therapy, and discussions by subtle religious and political forces, as well as by their own character structure shaped by the Irish milieu. One psychologist, well acquainted with psychiatry in Ireland, dubbed much of it "Freud with clothes on."

Grania is . . . a play in which a woman is ousted from an emotional relationship between two men. The "love" is that of man for man, of brother for brother; it is loyalty to the warrior band, and a corresponding resentment of the woman who takes away the warrior's freedom, makes trouble with his comrades, distracts him from his purpose in life. It is an attitude which filters through the play as light filters through crystal; which runs through the heroic Irish sagas. . . . Its continuing validity was borne out by all Lady Gregory had observed in the world around her, the world of the "loveless Irishman," the peasant society which relegated women to serfdom, the middle-class intellectual society which left them only donkey-work. . . . Such a view of the Irishwoman's role, of her relegation to insignificance and her resentment under it, is not exclusively feminine. It is abundantly confirmed by Synge. His heroines . . . are creatures caged and raging, given no scope for their powers, condemned to love men who are poor things beside them and do not really care for them at all. O'Casey's Juno offers further positive support, and on the negative side, so to speak, are the quantities of second-rate Irish plays and stories that have for their mainspring a panic dislike of women, invariably represented as shrews, hussies, and Aunt Sallies at whom anything can be thrown. A woman has only to put her nose into a saloon bar . . . to realise that Almhuin is with us still (Coxhead 1961: 145–146).

In concluding this section, I would like to mention briefly an ingenious hypothesis of the cause of sexual repression in Ireland, presented by Sean de Freine in *The Great Silence*. His book is the most "convincing" expression to date of what linguists (outside of Ireland) term "language determinism," a monism still popular in that country a century after the advent of the Irish nativistic movement. Displaying a lack of knowledge both of contemporary linguistic theory and of sexual ethics in the "heart of the Gaeltacht," de Freine says:

> The Irish are often accused of a Jansenist approach to sex, which is supposed to date from the French influence in the Irish Church in and just after the penal times. But this attitude did not exist in Irish Ireland and does not exist in the Gaeltacht today. It would seem as though, when English spread throughout the country, it was

> English Puritanism and not French Jansenism, which brought about the change. For example, certain English words with prudish connotations were accepted, with their connotations, by the Irish, while their equivalents in Irish have no such nuances. In its English setting Puritanism was kept in reasonable check by the other native traditions: In Ireland, as the old culture died, there were no such natural checks to contain it (de Freine 1965: 164).

Space does not permit me to consider other causal factors listed earlier which are equally untenable.

SEXUAL REPRESSION: ITS INCULCATION

The inculcation of sexual puritanism in Inis Beag must be examined in four contexts: the role of the curate, the influence of visiting missions, enculturation in the home, and what I will term "secular social control"—the behavioral regulations imposed on themselves by Inis Beag adolescents and adults. It is through these agencies that Jansenism, masochism, the Oedipus complex, male solidarity, and other inextricably linked factors shape the severe sexual repression which gives rise to the cultural manifestations discussed in the last section of the chapter.

Priests of Jansenist persuasion have had subtle means of repressing the sexual instincts of the islanders in addition to the more extreme methods of controlling behavior—"clerical social control," such as employing informers, allocating indulgences, and refusing the sacraments to, and placing curses on, miscreants. Through sermons and informal classroom talks, the pulpit and the national school have served as effective vehicles of church discipline. The talks are especially telling, since they take advantage of the personality malleability of the formative years. The adult Irish person is rare who, although anticlerical, and even agnostic or atheistic, can transcend these early enculturative experiences, particularly in times of social crisis or personality disorganization. Erring islanders have often been sought out by priests and talked to privately after their ways have become known through gossip, informers, or the confessional. Some curates have suppressed courting, dancing, visiting, and other behavior either directly or "indirectly" (widely interpreted in Ireland) sexual in nature by physical action: that is, roaming the trails and fields at night seeking out young lovers and halting dancing by their threatening presence. This outward form of intrusion into island affairs is resented by most folk, as is the inward intrusion through priestly remonstrances; they question the right of the young, virginal, inexperienced, and sexually unknowledgeable curates to give advice in this sphere.

Church influence is also exerted through missions which visit Inis Beag every three to five years. On these occasions, two Redemptorist priests (occasionally Franciscans, Dominicans, or Passionists) spend a week on the island, where they conduct mass each morning and deliver long sermons in the chapel every afternoon or early evening. Everyone, even old people and mothers with young infants, is urged to attend to receive the "blessings of the mission." To some, this means shortening the time in purgatory for themselves or a deceased relative (an indulgence used to enforce church discipline). To others, absence carries with it the penalty of damnation, just as viewing an eel or small fish in the sacred well, appropriated from the Druids, promises salvation in an equally magical fashion. A mission usually has a theme, the variations of which are explored with high emotion and eloquence by the visiting clerics in their exhortations. The most common theme is "controlling one's passions," but two others have often been addressed in the missionizing effort: abstaining from intoxicating drink and maintaining the faith as an emigrant. Collections are made by children to support the endeavor, and a list of contributors and their respective donations is displayed publicly. This technique of social control is also used by the curate at the several yearly offerings. A mission creates an emotionally charged atmosphere on the island, which continues for weeks after the departure of the clerics.

The seeds of repression are planted early in childhood by parents and kin through instruction supplemented by rewards and punishments, conscious imitation, and unconscious internalization. Although mothers bestow considerable affection and attention on their offspring, especially on their sons, physical love as manifested in intimate handling and kissing is rare in Inis Beag. Even breast feeding is uncommon because of its sexual connotation, and verbal affection comes to replace contact affection by late infancy. Any form of direct or indirect sexual expression—such as masturbation, mutual exploration of bodies, use of either standard or slang words relating to sex, and open urination and defecation—is severely punished by word or deed. Care is taken to cover the bodies of infants in the presence of siblings and outsiders, and sex is never discussed before children. Several times my wife inadvertently inquired as to whether particular women were pregnant, using that word before youths, only to be "hushed" or to have the conversation postponed until the young people could be herded outside. The adults were so embarrassed by the term that they found it difficult to communicate with her after the children had departed. She once aroused stupefaction among men on the strand when she attempted unsuccessfully to identify the gender of a bullock about to be shipped off.

It is in the home that the separation of sexes, so characteristic of Inis Beag life, is inaugurated among siblings in early childhood. Boys and girls in the family remain apart not only when interacting with the parent of the same sex at work, but when playing in and near the cottage and traveling to and from school. Parents and their older offspring read popular religious journals, found in most homes, many of the articles in which deal with sexual morality of the Irish Catholic variety.

One sociologist (Berger 1963: 66–92) classifies social control methods as those which involve physical violence or its threat (e.g., political and legal sanctions), those which result in economic pressures (e.g., occupation and market place relations), and, finally, those which govern our "morality, custom, and manners" (e.g., persuasion, ridicule, and gossip). I will not consider political and economic manipulation; more significant are other techniques that I have labelled secular social control. Inis Beag, as much as any human community, is characterized by gossip, ridicule, and opprobrium. Influenced by nativism, primitivism, and structural-functional theory, writers and social scientists have painted a distorted picture of culture and personality equilibrium among Irish peasants. Actually, the folk are neither glorified Celts nor "noble savages," and dysfunctional sociocultural forms, mental aberrations (neuroses, psychoses, and psychosomatic disorders), and exaggerated defense postures abound.

Inis Beag people are ambivalent about gossip; they welcome every opportunity to engage in it, yet detest the practice when they are its victims. When asked to cite the major deficiencies of their way of life, islanders usually place the prevalence of malicious gossiping near the top of their list. Boys and men hide themselves in the darkness or behind fences to overhear the conversations of passersby; they maintain close scrutiny of visitors during the summer, both day and night, in order to discover them in "compromising" situations. Parties are organized at the last moment and persons will leave the island without any previous announcement—often to emigrate or enter the hospital or join a religious order—in order to circumvent gossip. Rumors run rife in Inis Beag, especially when they concern, for example, the "nude" sun bathing of a visiting actress (bared shoulders and lower thighs) or the "attack" on a Dublin girl late at night by an island youth (an effort to hold her hand while under the influence of stout). Over a dozen efforts on our part to determine the truth behind the most pernicious rumors of this genre revealed sexual fantasy at their core in every case.

The force most responsible for limiting the potential social activities of women—which would make their lot much easier and possibly stem the tide of emigration—is the fear of gossip: "If I went for a walk, they'd wonder why I wasn't home tending my chores." Even couples who might otherwise disregard religious teachings and the wrath of the priest do not court, because it might be observed and reported through gossip to the entire population.[7] An islander must carefully regulate his own words and actions in the presence of others so that the fires of factionalism are not ignited. Equally feared are informers of the curate and relatives or close friends of persons in an audience who might be offended by a heedless remark brought to their attention by the listeners.

It is sometimes heard in Ireland, from those aware of, and willing to admit, the fact, that the inability of most Irish to "share themselves" with one another, even husbands and wives, is a heritage of the fear of gossip—a fear that one's intimate revelations will become common knowledge and lead to censure and "loss of face." A more likely explanation, according to those of Freudian bent, is the Oedipus configuration, which numbers among its many effects the following: the prevalence of romantic attachments and the rarity of conjugal love; the lack of sexual foreplay, marked by little or no concern with the female breast; the brevity of the coital act and the frequent spurning of the woman following it; the need to degrade the woman in the sexual encounter and the belief that the "good" woman does not like sex, and, conversely, that the sexually disposed woman is by virtue of the fact "bad." All of these widely reported phenomena bespeak the overwhelming influence of the mother image.

Ridicule and opprobrium, as well as satire in song and tale, are effective control mechanisms in light of the emphasis placed by Inis Beag folk on saving face. Most islanders could not believe that I was author of the ballad referred to in

[7]The fear of being observed, as well as repression, may account for the apparent lack of sexual contact with animals. This practice may be common among mainland peasants, if one is willing to accept as evidence the existence of a genre of dirty jokes popular there, and hearsay among certain scholars concerning confessional materials.

footnote 5 because several stanzas attack my character; they find it difficult to conceive of anyone publicly proclaiming their own faults, under any circumstances. Opinions, once formed, are clung to tenaciously, even in light of obviating circumstances, since to alter them would be an admittance that they were ill advised in the first instance. The folk pride themselves on being able to judge a stranger's character immediately on meeting him, and this initial impression is rarely modified no matter how long their interaction continues. A seldom revealed tradition of satirical balladry exists in Inis Beag, but its employment is infrequent and then calculated according to singer and audience so as not to offend directly. Apprehensiveness and anxiety about real and imagined ego assaults by others are dominant personality traits of the islanders.

HISTORICAL AND CULTURAL IMPLICATIONS

I have already touched tangentially on some of the historical and broad cultural implications of sexual puritanism, in Ireland as well as Inis Beag. In this final section I will examine the perennially addressed phenomena of late marriage, celibacy, and emigration, in their island setting, with special reference to the factor of sexual repression.

In a population of 350, 116 persons are married, 13 are widows, 3 are widowers, and 33 males over twenty-three years of age and 21 females over seventeen are single. Since marriage occurs between twenty-four and forty-five for men and eighteen and thirty-two for women, on the basis of past statistics, only 18 men and 9 women are eligible for marriage. As mentioned earlier, the average marriage age for males is thirty-six and for females twenty-five. My wife and I isolated almost two dozen interrelated causes of late marriage and the prevalence of

bachelor and spinsterhood. The most emphasized cause in Ireland is the pattern of inheritance: one son, usually the eldest, must wait until the father is ready to pass on his patrimony and his own siblings have married or emigrated. In an attempt to alleviate the situation somewhat, a law today requires that to receive the "old-age" (pension) a man at seventy must will his property to a son, or other appropriate person. This cause is important in Inis Beag, although primogeniture is not so well defined (of those sons inheriting property, 47 percent are first born, 42 percent second, 8 percent third, and 3 percent fourth and later). Inis Beag fathers are loath to surrender their land and control of the household to their sons and will often play off the sons, one against another, in order to achieve favored treatment for their wives and themselves in their waning years. Occasionally this procedure "backfires": the sons, acting in concert, emigrate together, and an increasing amount of land lies idle because of this.

Equally loath to disturb the family status quo, island mothers will resist incoming daughters-in-law, who threaten not only their commanding position but the loss of their sons' affection. Mothers whom we have interviewed in Inis Beag and elsewhere in Ireland display the extreme of Oedipal attachment when they rejoice in their sons' decision to join the priesthood; not only are spiritual blessings and prestige brought to the family as a result, but their sons are at last removed from potential wives. Yet the Inis Beag man who wants to marry and is prevented from doing so by domineering and jealous parents is the subject of much gossip. Outwardly, at least, his plight is considered a "shame."

To the man in his late twenties and thirties who is secure in his home and has established regularized patterns of conduct (and has a mother who acts in most ways as a wife surrogate), the general responsibilities of marriage, and specifically its sexual responsibility, are factors militating against his seeking a spouse. Some men who have land, the consent of their parents, and willing "sweethearts" will balk at a match because they are too happy "running with the lads," and if persuaded to marry, they will try to retain as much of their bachelor role as possible within marriage. It was hinted to my wife and me on several occasions that particular island celibates almost married several times in succession, only to find the sexual commitment too difficult to make at the last moment.

Three other causes of late marriage and the single estate in Inis Beag must be mentioned. Girls are more dissatisfied with their future lot than are boys and men and are emigrating at ever younger ages, thus sharply reducing the number of eligible females. During the 1950–1959 period, the average age at which girls emigrate dropped below twenty-one years. Each year more of them attend schools on the mainland and thus are more exposed to stimuli which promote emigration. Mothers are puzzled at the increasing exodus of their daughters, since women today have a far easier time than they did a generation or two ago; but some are glad to see them escape the drudgery and boredom of island existence. Since late marriage has been a persistent phenomenon in Ireland since the great famine, it has become institutionalized and serves as an expectation for young people. We heard Inis Beag adults assert that marriage should be postponed to conform to island mores; this usually was buttressed by a rationale of males not having "enough sense" to marry until they are nearly forty years of age. Reflected in this rationale is the male age-grading conceptualized by the folk: a man is a "boy" or "lad" until forty, an adult until sixty, middle-aged until eighty, and aged after that (exhilarating to the American anthropologist approaching forty who comes from a society obsessed with the "cult of youth"). A final cause, often articulated by the islanders, is the fact that divorce is impossible in Ireland, therefore the choice of a spouse must be well considered. It appears, however, that this argument is usually used as a rationalization for late marriage, when

other causal factors are, in reality, responsible—certainly when "considering" covers two or more decades!

The population of Inis Beag has dropped from a high of 532 persons in 1861 (up 76 from the prefamine census a decade earlier) to 497 in 1881, 483 in 1901, 409 in 1926, 376 in 1956, and 350 when my wife and I were there two years later. Today, there is grave concern over the future of the island, and some folk hold that within another generation or two Inis Beag will have gone the way of the Blasket Islands. Although my wife and I isolated almost two dozen causes for the phenomena of late marriage and celibacy, over thirty interrelated causes pertain to emigration (many of those at work in the marital sphere also stimulate emigration). Once again, I will address only the principal causes and stress the role of sexual repression, dealing first with internal factors and then external ones promoting emigration.

Among internal causes, the previously considered inheritance pattern, parents who want to maintain the family status quo for various reasons, and the girls' and young women's increasing dissatisfaction with their lot figure as prominently in the emigration picture as the marital. Some Inis Beag men claim that the reason male youths are leaving the island is economic depression, caused by the collapse of kelp-making and the fishing industry. But this cause is untenable when one examines the increase in government subsidies, remittances from relatives abroad, and taxation and land rental policies; these have far more than made up for the loss of previous revenue. Real income has increased substantially, despite recent inflation, and young men are very much aware of this fact. Just as late marriage has become institutionalized over the past century, so has emigration since the first large-scale migration of islanders in 1822. Emigration is a way of life, which will stimulate some folk to leave in spite of other conditions which might lead an observer to advise their remaining.

By far the most important reason for Inis Beag's long dwindling population is the total cultural impact of sexual puritanism and the secular "excesses" of the clergy. Blanshard writes, "When all the reasons for a flight from Ireland have been mentioned, there still remains a suspicion that Irish young people are leaving their nation largely because it is a poor place in which to be happy and free. Have the priests created a civilization in which the chief values of youth and love are subordinate to Catholic discipline?" (Blanshard 1954: 154). What "remains a suspicion" to Blanshard is fully confirmed by a wealth of data from Inis Beag, only limited amounts of which have been reported in this chapter. Even though sexual repression and fear of the clergy prevent the folk from being outspoken in this matter, it is constantly broached among themselves.

Paramount among external factors stimulating emigration are prosperity on the mainland and abroad, the impact of the mass media of communication, the increasing number of tourists visiting Inis Beag, the return of former emigrants, and the fact that, with an increase in incomes and scholarship funds, more island children are going to the mainland for their schooling each year. America has been a land of freedom and prosperity to the Irish since before the famine, and, until the Second World War, most islanders migrated there never to return. But the growth of prosperity in England following 1946 shifted the stream of emigration in that direction, for not only were jobs plentiful across the Irish Sea, but large, viable ethnic communities served by Irish clergy had sprung up in big cities. And it was possible to visit Ireland frequently, as the distance and cost are slight compared to a journey across the Atlantic. It is common for youths vacationing in Inis Beag from England to talk others into returning with them. The latter declare that they will soon come back to the island to settle permanently, hopefully with "great riches," but they seldom return. Since the war, a number of "Yanks" have also

returned home, and their stories of life in America make the youthful islanders restive. Tourists who remain for weeks and months in Inis Beag and come to know many folk also sow the seeds of discontent.

Television was introduced into Inis Beag during 1963, and the two sets now installed always have ready and willing audiences. Almost every cottage has a radio, and, although the islanders seldom read books, a wide assortment of domestic and foreign magazines and newspapers find their way into most homes. These mass media also are an emancipating force making for restiveness and discontent, as they allow the islanders to glimpse behind the "lace curtain" at what appears to be a happier and freer world. Television and radio programs are censored, but, even so, the morality expressed in them—especially the sex and violence drenched American ones—presents a striking contrast to locally conceived moral precepts. A censor from Inis Beag would most certainly create more discontinuities in films with his shears than do his much maligned "secularized" colleagues in Dublin.

Most of what I have written in this essay is to be found expressed in the works of such older Irish writers as James Joyce, Sean O'Casey, Austin Clarke, and Patrick Kavanaugh, and such younger ones as William Murray, John McGahern, Edna O'Brien, John Broderick, Brian Moore, and Benedict Kiely. Irish reviewers of the writings of the younger authors often criticize them for portraying an Ireland of the distant past. But, although conditions there are changing quite rapidly, sexual repression is still a force active enough to command the attention of creative artists and social scientists.[8] The subtle influences of nationalism, religion, and sexual puritanism were very apparent in the revi-

---

[8] I am confident that one of the major "lines of attack" on my ethnography by Irish nativist reviewers will be that the community described is atypical and conditions in urbanized Ireland no longer bear any resemblance to those in Inis Beag. Since 1957, I have been much criticized by African elitists for describing in my writings a primitive culture which they claim is no longer characteristic of that developing continent.

sions suggested by most of the twenty-six "unbiased" scholars of Irish descent—in Ireland, England, and America—to whom I submitted the first version of this article for comment.

REFERENCES

ARENSBERG, C. M. AND KIMBALL, S. T. 1968. *Family Community in Ireland.* Cambridge: Harvard University Press.

BALES, R. F. 1962. "Attitudes Toward Drinking in the Irish Culture." In *Society, Culture, and Drinking Patterns,* eds. David J. Pittman and Charles R. Snyder, pp. 157–187. New York: John Wiley and Sons, Inc.

BERGER, P. L. 1963. *Invitation to Sociology: A Humanistic Perspective.* Garden City: Anchor Books.

BLANSHARD, P. 1954. *The Irish and Catholic Power.* London: Derek Verschoyle.

COXHEAD, E. 1961. *Lady Gregory.* London: MacMillan and Co., Ltd.

DE FREINE, S. 1965. *The Great Silence.* Dublin: Foilseachain Naisiunta Teoranta.

DELARGY, J. H. 1957. "Folklore." In *A View of Ireland,* eds. James Meenan and David A. Webb, pp. 178–187. Dublin: Hely's Limited.

HUMPHREYS, FR. A. J. 1966. *New Dubliners.* New York: Fordham University Press.

LEWIS, O. 1960. *Tepoztlan: Village in Mexico.* New York: Holt, Rinehart and Winston, Inc.

MCCARTHY, J. 1964. *Ireland.* New York: Time Incorporated.

MCGAHERN, J. 1965. *The Dark.* London: Faber and Faber.

MESSENGER, J. C.
  1962. "A Critical Reexamination of the Concept of Spirits." *American Anthropologist,* 64, No. 2: 267–272.
  1968. "Types and Causes of Disputes in an Irish Community." *Eire-Ireland,* 3, No. 3: 27–37.
  1969. *Inis Beag: Isle of Ireland.* New York: Holt, Rinehart and Winston, Inc.

MURRAY, W. C. 1965. *Michael Joe.* New York: Appleton-Century.

O'BRIEN, FR. J. A., ED. 1953. *The Vanishing Irish.* New York: McGraw-Hill Book Company.

OPLER, M. K. AND SINGER, J. L. 1956. "Ethnic Differences in Behavior and Psychopathology: Italian and Irish." *The International Journal of Social Psychiatry,* 2, No. 1: 11–23.

O'SUILLEABHAIN, S. 1963. *A Handbook of Irish Folklore.* Hatboro: Folklore Associates, Inc.

TRACY, H. 1953. *Mind You I've Said Nothing.* London: Methuen and Co., Ltd.

20

THE FUNCTION OF CEREMONIAL SEXUAL INTERCOURSE AMONG THE NORTHERN PLAINS INDIANS

ALICE B. KEHOE

Sexual intimacy as a means of transferring spiritual power appears to have been a Mandan-Hidatsa ceremonial trait borrowed by three Algonkian Plains tribes as part of the graded men's societies complex. The Algonkian tribes modified the rite, which in the village tribes emphasized the role of father's clan. The Arapaho emphasized the cosmic symbolism of the rite, the Atsina made it a test of self-discipline, and the Blackfoot stressed the dangerous power commanded by those who performed it. These modifications parallel the differences in kinship structure between village and nomadic Plains tribes discussed by Eggan.

It is well known that among the northern Plains tribes, power could be transferred from one man to another upon the presentation of a suitable honorarium. It is not so well known that several northern Plains tribes also recognized the transfer of power from one man to another through a woman as intermediary, with sexual intimacy the channel of transfer. Such transfer seems to have been an integral aspect of Mandan ceremonialism, to have diffused from the Mandan or Hidatsa to the three Algonkian-speaking northern Plains tribes with graded men's societies and to the Cheyenne, and to

have acquired peculiar significance in the Algonkian tribes, which did not otherwise respect extra-marital intimacy.

Lowie outlined the distribution and associations of transfer of power through sexual intimacy in his synthesis of Plains Indian age-societies (1916). He points out (1916:884) that the graded men's societies, found among the Mandan, Hidatsa, Arapaho, Atsina ("Gros Ventres"), and Blackfoot, differ from the ungraded societies of other Plains tribes in requiring "two conditions for entrance, . . . age and purchase." "The features common to all five systems were

SOURCE: From "The Function of Ceremonial Intercourse Among the Northern Plains Indians" by A. Kehoe in *Plains Anthropologist, 15:*48, 1970, pp. 99–103. Copyright © 1970 by Plains Anthropological Society. Reprinted by permission.

these: In each tribe the societies were graded in a series, the difference in grade corresponding to a difference in age. Except for the very young and the very old, practically every male member of the tribe belonged to one of the societies. Age was nowhere the sole condition of joining; either membership itself or the requisite emblems and instructions had to be bought, and this purchase . . . was normally collective rather than individual. As part of the purchase price, the buyer ceremonially surrenders his wife to an older man in some, at least, of the societies of each tribe. In every case the function of a tribal police during the hunt is associated either with the entire system or with one of the societies in the series. Finally, in every one of the five tribes a woman's organization connected with the buffalo is associated with the series" (Lowie 1916:919). Partly on the basis of ceremonial wife surrender being less strongly developed in the Algonkian tribes (Lowie 1916:949), Lowie concludes (1916:951) that graded men's societies originated with the Mandan and Hidatsa.

Mandan belief in the possibility of power transference through sexual intercourse was notorious in the fur-trade era (Bowers 1965:462–3; Bruner 1961:232; Newman 1950:259, quoting David Thompson). As Newman suggests in his review of the question whether there were blond Mandan, the amount of genetic transfer that could have accompanied the desired power transference might have significantly affected the Mandan gene pool. Both Lowie (1913, 1917) and Bowers (1950), as Lewis and Clark and Maximilian much earlier, describe the Mandan and Hidatsa custom of a man desiring power offering his wife to an older man of recognized power, who was felt to confer a favor upon the younger man by transmitting some power through the woman. The custom was not confined to the transfer of membership in societies, but was a method generally used by younger men wishing to obtain spiritual aid. The custom was compatible with the display of obvious fertility symbols in major ceremonials (Bowers 1950:284, 317–8) in which both symbolic and actual intercourse between married women and the men from whom their husbands wished power were believed to reenact intercourse with the life-giving bison, ensuring a happy and prosperous life for the married pairs (Bowers 1950:336).

For the Mandan, symbolic intercourse with the bison ("Walking With the Buffaloes") represented the origin and essence of human society. Okipa ceremony myths claimed that the ceremony's Buffalo Dance was one of the most ancient Mandan rituals, practised at a period when the people had not yet developed tools, complex social organization, or the many later ceremonials. The Buffalo Dance, and accompanying Okipa rites, was believed to bring abundant bison herds and prosperity to the villages (Bowers 1950:117–22). Intercourse between a respectable matron and a man of power drew to the woman, and her marital partner, some of the power flowing from the primal bison; this concept was clearly demonstrated in the bison-calling ceremonies, in which women made the motion of physically pulling the power from a bundle-owner into their own bodies (Bowers 1950:336–7).

The Hidatsa paralleled the Mandan in their use of sexual intercourse for the transfer of power. Lowie's data on the Hidatsa emphasize a feature of this ceremonialism that adds another dimension to the rite: the singling-out of father's clansmen as sources of spiritual power. Among this matrilineally organized people, the inheritance of bundles from father to son (Lowie 1917:40; Bowers 1965:107–9) constitutes a system of "double descent" reminiscent of that of the Ashanti. Purchasers of membership in the graded men's societies were expected to select a father's clansman to act as sponsoring ceremonial "father" (Lowie 1917:40), required to have intercourse with the purchaser's wife (Lowie 1913:228). Father's clansmen might be requested to transfer power through the son's wife even outside purchase rituals (Lowie 1913:229). Relinquishing a wife to a father's clansman reinforced the special position of the father's clan as the proper source of religious knowledge and consequent spiritual power. A man received his physical being by the act of intercourse between his father and his mother, then his adult life was strengthened and enhanced by intercourse between his "fathers," in the extended sense of father's clansmen, and the woman who filled the role of mother in the lodge he established upon reaching maturity. The bison bulls begat life, re-enactment of their intercourse with human "daughters-in-law" supposedly being followed by the regeneration and attraction of the bison herds. Alloting the role of bison bull to a father's clansmen underscored the importance of the male begetter in the maintenance of Hidatsa life, and would tend to prevent the ordinary dominance of the mother's clan, in this matrilineal society, from obscuring the father's crucial position. The social unity of the tribe was thus furthered by the involvement of fathers' clans in many of the most meaningful acts of men's lives.

Power transfer through intercourse is more restricted, more covert, and more titilating among the Algonkian-speaking tribes than among Mandan and Hidatsa. Lacunae in the published data of some of the older ethnographers implies a circumspection regarding this trait on the part of either these ethnographers or their informants; lack of mention of sexual transfer is no proof of its absence. For example, Flannery (1957:296–7) records sexual intercourse during the transfer of doctoring power from an Atsina man to a woman, and in the transfer of love medicine. While Flannery suggests that sexual contact, "validated" the acquisition of love medicine, her following remark, "If the transferrer were a woman, one of her adult male kin might be chosen by her to have sexual intercourse with the woman transferee" (Flannery 1957:297) shows that at least for love medicine, intercourse was probably the actual channel of transfer. Kroeber's ethnography of the Atsina described love medicine obtained from a vision during a fasting vigil, and said its use could be transferred by the male owner "to young men for two horses" (Kroeber 1908:224). Kroeber does not mention sexual transfer. Whatever the source of Kroeber's

omission, it is clear that sexual transfer of power was an integral, fundamental part of Mandan and Hidatsa ceremonialism, but was less general and less comfortably accepted (Flannery 1957:297) among the Algonkian-speakers.

Dorsey's account of sexual intercourse in the Arapaho Sun Dance rites is especially useful in an evaluation of the feature. "Concerning the subject under discussion . . . , great difference of opinion evidently exists among the Arapaho as a tribe," Dorsey wrote (1903:172). "In former times" (Dorsey 1903:173) the man who sponsored the Sun Dance sent his wife out twice with the elder, former Sun Dance sponsor who transferred the power to make the Dance. The elder man was said to be the ceremonial "grandfather," of the sponsor. The Transferrer, as Dorsey terms the "grandfather," would go out alone with the sponsor's wife about midnight, after having a call made to the camp at large requesting everyone to remain quietly in their tipis. With his ceremonial pipe, the Transferrer prayed, offering the naked woman to a number of supernatural beings; then the man had intercourse with the woman, conveying a medicinal root from his mouth to hers during the act. The woman handed this root to her husband, the sponsor, upon her return to the ceremonial tipi (Dorsey 1903:173). When Dorsey himself sneaked out of the tipi to spy on what actually took place between the Transferrer and the sponsor's wife, no intercourse occurred, the woman merely briefly exposing herself to the moon while the man prayed. The sponsor received pieces of the root from both his wife and his "grandfather," using mouth-to-mouth contact for each transfer (Dorsey 1903:174–6).

Arapaho symbolism for the ritual involving the Transferrer and the sponsor's wife reflects Mandan and Hidatsa concepts: the "grandfather" personified a heavenly body (the sun, according to Dorsey's Oklahoma informants; the moon, according to a Northern Arapaho priest who further identified the moon with the bison). The place of intercourse symbolized a bison wallow. The transferred root represented seed from which the tribe will grow. The Oklahoma Arapaho added that the ceremonial "straight-pipe is the penis or root of man" (Dorsey 1903:176–8). It is obvious from Dorsey's surreptitious checking that the symbolism of the fertility ritual was more important than its physical aspects, or to phrase it another way, that the ritual was more reenactment of myth than transfer of power.

The Cheyenne Sun Dance includes a rite similar to that of the Arapaho, but even more restrained. When the Cheyenne Chief Priest is required to have physical contact with the sponsor's wife, the Priest and the woman remain together under a single bison robe which also serves to confine the sweetgrass smoke ensuring the religious meaning of the act (Dorsey 1905: 130–1). Cheyenne men's societies were not graded, were joined by invitation rather than by purchase, and did not involve pairing of the new member's wife with an elder.

Atsina did not include a rite between transferrer and sponsor's wife in their Sun Dance, but four Atsina men's societies invoked a similar relationship between society members' wives and the members' ceremonial "grandfathers," elder instructors. The Atsina societies' rite is remarkably like both the Arapaho Sun Dance rite and the rites of two of the Arapaho men's societies, as Kroeber (1908:244) noted. For the Crazy, Kit-Fox, Dog, and Soldiers' (Nanannahanwu) ceremonies of the Atsina, and the Crazy and Dog societies, as well as the Sun Dance, of the Arapaho, the "grandson's" wife went out during the nights of the ceremony with the "grandfather" who prayed with a pipe that the Above-Persons should bless the woman. Then the "grandfather" had to give the woman, who lay exposed upon her robe, a medicinal root. Flannery's, as well as Kroeber's, Atsina informants explicitly stated that the "grandfather" was *not* supposed to indulge in coitus with the "granddaughter," but to pass the root from his mouth to hers without violating her chastity. The Atsina rite was conceived as a test of the self-discipline of "grandfather," "granddaughter," and "grandson" (who realized that the couple might not be able to restrain their desire, but who was not supposed to

show jealousy) (Flannery 1957:214–5). The difficulty of the test was heightened by the practice of having the "grandfather" paint the nude bodies of both his "grandchildren" each morning before the day's ceremonies commenced.

Shifting the emphasis in the relationship between "grandfather" and "grandson's" wife from transfer of power to test of self-discipline is entirely consonant with the general pattern of differences between Mandan and Hidatsa, on the one hand, and the nomadic Algonkian tribes, on the other. Eggan has discussed (esp. 1966 Ch. III) the concern of the clan-organized village tribes with the orderly vertical transmission of property rights, in contrast to the need of the nomadic tribes for maximum flexibility of cooperating units. The problem of the nomadic tribes of the historic Plains was to find means of unifying the rallied segments without imposing extended periods of communal living. Northern Plains Algonkians found a solution by organizing all ablebodied men into fraternal societies whose rituals stressed self-discipline to further common goals. The Atsina "test" perfectly exemplifies the abnegation of selfish desires for the better realization of the group's prosperity.

The Blackfoot, most distant from the Missouri village tribes, have the most attenuated utilization of sexual transfer. They employ the rite only in the purchase of membership in the Horn Society of the Blood tribe. Wissler (1913:410–8) gives a very complete description of the purchase, recorded from a Blood woman participant. The Horns selected the men to whom they wished to sell their membership after the expiration of the ideal four-year period of ownership. The elected are forced, regardless of their wishes, to come to the tipi in which the secret ceremonies of transfer are to take place. In the first section of the ceremonies, the new members and their wives are painted and given new clothing and regalia, the wives of the sellers caring for the new members' wives in privacy. The new members dance with their new insignia. Then the second part of the ceremonies begins with a crier ordering the people of the camp to remain quiet inside their tipis until the Horns have completed their secret rites. Each new member's wife covers herself only by a robe and goes, carrying a pipe, to the tipi of her husband's ceremonial "father," the older Horn who is selling him the membership. After smoking the pipe beside the woman in the tipi, the "father" takes her a suitable distance outside, she lies down, and the "father" again prays with the pipe. At the culmination of the prayer, the "father" touches his penis to the woman's vulva. The rite is continued past this point only if the woman is known to be virtuous and her husband is a worthy man. If such is the opinion of the "father," he next bends his forefinger into the shape of a horn, bellows like a bison bull, and finally has coitus with the woman, transferring a piece of prairie turnip from his mouth to hers during the act. Each woman must lie quietly and fast for a day after she returns to her husband in the Horn tipi. Her "father" ends the rite, and the fast, by painting her, one pattern indicating performance of only the first half of the ritual, another pattern indicating completion of the entire ritual and, therefore, honor to the woman and her husband.

Several aspects of Blackfoot culture color this Horn ritual. First, chastity was highly regarded (Wissler 1911:8–11). Only a woman who had never indulged in adultery could pray to the sun for help and could participate in the prestigious Cutting of the (Bison) Tongues ceremony of the Sun Dance (Wissler 1918:234–40). An adulteress might be punished by death, mutilation, or gang-rape by the members of her husband's society. Virtuous women would publicly proclaim their chastity by coming forward to claim the right to help cut up the perfect bison tongues used in the Sun Dance. A woman's announcement often included naming the men whose attempts at seduction she had repulsed. Wissler states (1918:240), "great presence of mind and will power" were assumed to have been required for the preservation of the woman's virtue. The steadfast, disciplined character demonstrated by an unsullied woman was comparable to the firm courage of a warrior, and indeed, the women

proclaimed their chastity in the manner of men recounting their coups. Thus, in the normal course of Blackfoot life, no good and ambitious woman lies with a man not her husband; but the powerful Horns acknowledge a woman's virtue inversely, by admitting her to intercourse with another man.

A second aspect of the Horn ceremony to be noted is the imagery of the bison bulls. Wissler's informants (1913:418) explained this by saying that the early 20th-century Horn society had incorporated a formerly distinct Bull society, the oldest and most respected of the graded Blackfoot societies. Proof of this merging comes not only in the Horns' bull imitation, but also in the Horns' use of the Blackfoot stand-up ("boss-ribs") feather bonnet, generally considered the insignia of the Bulls. A relationship between the Horn society rite and the bison fertility ceremonies of the tribes to the east is therefore likely.

Third to be noted is the awesome power of the Blood Horns. They are said to know magic formulae that enable them to kill (men or bison). They pass with impunity in front of medicine-pipe owners who would ordinarily expect to take precedence (Wissler 1913:416). Blood Indians would swear oaths in court "by the Horns" (Wissler 1913:411). The fear inspired by this society sets it apart from other Blackfoot societies.

Taking these several aspects in conjunction, it is apparent that the rite of sexual contact between ceremonial "father" and "son's" wife in the transfer of Horn power emphasized by its deviance from general Blackfoot rituals the peculiar, fearful nature of Horn membership. The Horn rite flaunts Blackfoot propriety and imbues its performers with an aura of potential evil unanswerable to ordinary mortals. The form of the bison fertility ritual is retained by the Blackfoot, but it has ceased to signify the physical transfer of power, or even a test of strength; it has become a frightening demonstration of the power that can be wielded by the comrades of the Horn.

Lowie discussed the distribution of traits associated with the graded men's societies in terms of their diffusion from tribe to tribe on the northern Plains. His conclusions on the history of the traits are not challenged here, for this recapitulation supports the probability that the form and symbolism of the rite were borrowed by one tribe from another. This scrutiny has suggested that interesting changes in function occurred in the course of the borrowings: a rather obvious fertility ritual used by the Mandan and Hidatsa to uphold the lineal structure of their villages was modified by the nomadic tribes to emphasize the value of self-discipline in the pursuit of tribal goals, among the strongly individualistic Blackfoot becoming perverted into an instrument of clique power. Linton's famous distinction between form and function is beautifully illustrated by the several uses of this interesting ritual.

Acknowledgement: I wish to thank Mary Jo Amatruda, of Marquette University's Department of Classical Languages, for her translation of the Latin passages in Wissler's (1913) description of the Horn Society ritual.

REFERENCES

BOWERS, A. W.
  1950. *Mandan Social and Ceremonial Organization.* The University of Chicago Press, Chicago.
  1965. Hidatsa Social and Ceremonial Organization. *Bureau of American Ethnology, Bulletin* 194. Smithsonian Institution, Washington.
BRUNER, E. M. 1961. Mandan. *Perspectives in American Indian Culture Change,* edited by E. H. Spicer, pp. 187–277. The University of Chicago Press, Chicago.
DORSEY, G. A.
  1903. The Arapaho Sun Dance: The Ceremony of the Offerings Lodge. *Field Columbian Museum Publication 75, Anthropological Series,* Vol. IV. Chicago.
  1905. The Cheyenne. II, The Sun Dance. *Field Columbian Museum Publication* 103, *Anthropological Series,* Vol. IX, No. 2. Chicago.
EGGAN, FRED. 1966. *The American Indian.* Aldine Publishing Company, Chicago.
FLANNERY, R. 1957. The Gros Ventres of Montana: Part II, Religion. *The Catholic University of America Anthropological Papers,* Vol. I, Part IV. New York.
KROEBER, A. L. 1908. Ethnology of the Gros Ventre. *American Museum of Natural History Anthropological Papers,* Vol. I, Part IV. New York.
LOWIE, R. H.
  1913. Societies of the Crow, Hidatsa and Mandan Indians. *American Museum of Natural History Anthropological Papers,* Vol. XI, Part III. New York.
  1916. Plains Indian Age-Societies: Historical and Comparative Summary. *American Museum of Natural History Anthropological Papers,* Vol. XI, Part XIII. New York.
  1917. Notes on the Social Organization and Customs of the Mandan, Hidatsa, and Crow Indians. *American Museum of Natural History Anthropological Papers,* Vol. XXI, Part I. New York.
NEWMAN, M. T. 1950. The Blond Mandan: A Critical Review of an Old Problem. *Southwestern Journal of Anthropology,* Vol. 6, pp. 255–272. Albuquerque.
WISSLER, C.
  1911. The Social Life of the Blackfoot Indians. *American Museum of Natural History Anthropological Papers,* Vol. VII, Part I. New York.
  1913. Societies and Dance Associations of the Blackfoot Indians. *American Museum of Natural History Anthropological Papers,* Vol. XI, Part IV. New York.
  1918. The Sun Dance of the Blackfoot Indians. *American Museum of Natural History Anthropological Papers,* Vol. XVI, Part III. New York.

21

SANTAL RELIGION: SELF-IDENTIFICATION AND SOCIALIZATION IN THE SOHRAE-HARVEST FESTIVAL

DONALD R. TUCK

This paper will attempt to understand several aspects of religion as expressed verbally and symbolically in social forms which give meaning and identity to tribal Santals. Its thesis is that a more productive method for studying tribal religion is to study religion not as belief abstractions, but practices which are symbols of their beliefs in communal settings. The Santals in other words, know who they are because their complex and varied lives are given meanings as they are lived within the context of the social framework. Thus, religion must be studied as practices, beliefs and symbols of meaning in their social settings.

Santal beliefs are symbolized and manifested in festivals correlated to the calendrical cycle of agriculture, the social-structure of their villages and the recurring rites of passage. The festival chosen for this paper is the Harvest Festival. (The Flower Festival and the Annual Hunt as well as the rites of passage, initiation, marriage, and death might also be discussed for an understanding of the Santal and the Santali religious society.) The festival symbolizes Santal beliefs and affords enough variety for the individual to learn his own identity as he develops as a person, simultaneously as a part of the endogamous tribal society.

Modern Santals who are searching their traditions in view of their own identity will use the word d*horom* for their religion. The word has obvious Sanskrit derivation (*dharma*), and is also found in the Oriya language (*dhorom*) where it is roughly equated by Orans as reli-

DR. DONALD R. TUCK, is Associate Professor Dept. of Philosophy and Religion, Western Kentucky University, Bowling Green, Kentucky 42101 U.S.A.

SOURCE: From "Santal Religion" by D. Tuck, in *Man in India, 56,* 1976, p. 215–236. Copyright © 1976 by Man in India Office. Reprinted by permission.

268

gion.[1] Culshaw translates it as "the right way to live."[2] A folk song translated by Mukherjea catches this idea:[3]

> The straight road is narrow, O Nupal!
> We must not walk carelessly, O Nupal!
> To its right and left are fences of thorns, O Nupal!
> By chance thorns may prick us.

Orans relates a conversation with a Santal, whom he describes as a somewhat naive industrial worker, although a member of the Legislative Assembly who used *Sarna Dhorom* to describe his religion. (*Sarna* is the Munda tribal word for "Sacred Grove"; the Santali idea is expressed by jaher.[4]) Santal religion expresses itself in community with the use of rice-beer, central locus at the Sacred Grove and the eating of beef as distinguishing characteristics.

The Santals are primarily a tribe of settled agriculturalists, who engage in some collecting, fishing and hunting to supplement their living or to maintain themselves in adverse climatic-agricultural times.

The post world wars years have brought various new opportunities as well as social tensions for Santals who have migrated to nearby cities or settled at the tea plantations for employment. In those circumstances, Santals are removed from their village securities and are undergoing interactions with other ethnic groups.[5]

According to the Indian census of 1961, Santals number over three million persons—one of the largest, if not the most populous tribe in India. The greatest concentration of Santals Parganas on the eastern edge of the Chota Nagpur plateau, in Bihar. Santals also live in northern Orissa, West Bengal and Tripura.

RELIGIOUS DIMENSIONS TO FESTIVALS

Prior to a discussion of the religious dimensions of the festivals, it will be necessary to understand the Santal village and its religio-social stratification. A Santal village usually consists of ten to thirty-five families. Each family has a home of one or more rooms with auxiliary sheds for cattle, pigs, and fowl. The rooms encircle a courtyard. The most used entrance opens on to the main street, but the living areas are separated from the street areas.

Religious activities of varying intensity and importance are held at three centers within the village. First, family and individual identity is exercised in a small space in one corner of the principal room of the house; this space is cut off from the rest of the rooms by a low wall. This is the *bhitar,* the "inside" altar. Here sacrifices of rice-beer and food are offered along with verbal petitions to the spirits of dead ancestors and family deities. The worship is lead by the household head in cooperation with the male members. Secondly, there is a dwelling opposite the village headman's (*manjhi*) home called the "abode of the spirits of the village" (*manjhithan*). Here the central deity, the spirit of the founding father (*manjhi-Haram*) and other village deities are worshipped, placated and enlisted for village concerns. Finally, there is the sacred grove (*jaherthan*) at the end of the main street, but within the boundary of the village. It consists of a cluster of tall trees, which were a part of the original forest before the area was cleared for the village. In it there are several huts which have been built in the past for village festivals. This grove contains symbolic manifestations of the village deities, e.g. specific trees and stones are symbolizations of the village deities and, as will be

[1] Orans, Martin, *The Santal: A Tribe in Search of a Great Tradition.* Detroit: Wayne State University Press, 1965:106.

[2] Culshaw, W. J., *Tribal Heritage: A Study of the Santals.* London: Lutterworth Press, 1948:101, n. 2; cf. p. 66. Myth of first couples search for *dhorom*.

[3] Mukherjea, C., *The Santals,* Calcutta: A Mukherjee, 1962:365.

[4] Orans, *op. cit.,* p. 106.

[5] This is the subject of Oran's book, in which he interprets some of the contributing as well as destructive aspects of this acculturation.

discussed later, the huts house human-deity surrogates during certain festive activities.

A Santal village (ato) consists of several patrilineal kin-groups, which are organized as a social unit. The chief officers, the Headman (Manhi) and the Priest (naeke) are members of the founding lineage and through their control of authority, wealth and prestige, they cooperatively guide the village life. They are assisted by a village council which is usually hereditary, though in the case of incompetence or selfishness is elected by village representatives.

Our concern is with the religious leaders in the village. Assistant to the Headman is the Moral Guardian (ojgmanjhi) of village sexual behaviour. He arranges the communal feasts and by his wit or use of social force controls the moral patterns of the young and older aggressive villagers. The community shares in his joys as well as his sorrows.

The most important village religious leader is the village Priest (naeke). As a member of the founding lineage, he is both propertied and wealthy; his land holdings are rent free. He is responsible for the annual observances which honour the tribal deities of the Santals and the performance of which accrue to his own and the public good. For services rendered the Priest receives his financial rewards. His greatest authority, however, is imputed to him by the spirits (bonga). Thus, he is a man who in a sense is set apart from, but is at the same time a part of the village life. His religious identity is established and manifested through bonga possession (rum). Through him the wants of the spirits are revealed, and comfort, fellowship and warnings are conveyed to the people through his temporary possession. (The people correlate possession with characteristics similar to but not the same as madness.) In order to perform his services, he temporarily separates himself from village norms, e.g. he sleeps on the floor instead of a string-bed, refrains from sexual contact with his wife, and fasts until his religio-social duties are fulfilled.

He is assisted by the Associate Priest (Kudam-naeke) whose duties include the ceremonial worship of these spirits (bonga), as well as the guardians and personifications of the boundaries and outskirts of the village. During the village festivals, the Associate Priest offers to the spirits under his control drops of blood, which have been extracted from his own arm. Benefits and protection against the actions of the boundary bonga are under his religious jurisdiction.

Two other religious leaders function to handle special concerns at the sub-village level of the Santal. The ojha guru[6] is a Medicine Man who handles disease and calamities which are discerned to be caused by the immediate intervention of supernatural beings or the mediated magical powers of men. By divination he ascertains the causes, and prescribes the cure for the misfortune. He also can by means of temporary possession have direct communication with the spirits involved; by means of his powers of sacrifice, medicine, word and sound, he can neutralize maleficent, supernatural interferences. Human interferences (black magic) are nullified by charms and armulets which are backed up by his powers of social control. The jan guru[7] is the Santal diviner of witches. He has received his powers through dreams or visions, and exercises these authorities to ascertain which women are witches, who have allied with the spirits to cause harm to smaller sections of the village, e.g., a family is harassed through an individual female witch, and the jan guru is hired to discover the witch.

Finally, the leaders of the annual hunting expedition (sendra) is the Hunting Priest (dihri). He is elected to this office because he knows the appropriate knowledge—the sacrifices and powerful word symbols—both to insure hunting success and to avoid physical harm during the hunt.

[6]Biswas, P. C. *San als of the Santal Parganas.* Delhi: Bharatiya Adimjati Sevak Sangh, 1956: 121ff points out that *ojha* is a Hindi-Sanskrit word, and cites P. O. Bodding who postulates exorcism as a religious exercise borrowed from their neighbours. Spirits invoked by the *ojha* have some Hindu correlates, and seem to suggest interaction with that community.

[7]Biswas: 132, draws the etymological parallel to the Hindi-Sanskrit word which is interpreted as "Knower by revelation (*jhana).*"

By divination, he ascertains the names of those who are threatened with injury during the hunt, and either advises them not to go or makes the appropriate sacrifices to avert the foreknown mishap and allows the man to go on this important event in the Santal year.

Let us turn our attention to some of the religious meanings of a calendrical festival; The Harvest Festival (*Sohrae*).

The academic study of primitive or tribal religions has suffered from two extreme types of approaches: it has been either so descriptive in detail (contextual) or normative (theological) to the extreme that the people involved are portrayed as certainly bored with such a life, because it seems drab and mundane to the scholar who writes about it. Another approach to the understanding of religious people is to see them as expressive, i.e., their lives express their pleasure with themselves and their social surroundings in spite of negative influences, events and threats to their identity-equilibrium. The Santal enjoy life and express themselves in festivals which give and sustain meaning and wholeness.

The Santal have a word which expresses this pleasure—*raska*. *Raska* is the expression of the Santal good life. Its festive communication includes public-mixed dancing, singing, recreation, music, festive eating, and drinking rice-beer. Such expressions have subtle and implicit sexual nuances and in context include explicit sexual activities. Many of *raska* pleasures transmit truth elements from their historical-meaningful myths, e.g. the drinking of rice-beer enabled their ancestors to overcome their bashfulness and to engage in sexual intercourse, subsequently enjoyed as the paradigm for tribal life.[8]

Martin Orans has recorded a Santal song which illustrates *raska* in its social setting.[9]

> Oh, flower friend (phul, a ritual friendship which is celebrated formally)
> I am thirsty and I am hungry;

But hearing the sound of the drums under the canopy (chamda, a wedding canopy)
My thirst and hunger are banished.

One of the largest tribal groups in India, the Santals are non-Hindu, and descend from pre-Dravidian ancestors; they lack caste distinctions. Their political authority is relaxed enough to allow the people a degree of interaction with tribal law and order to the extent that it tolerates humour and ridicule, but at the same time maintains social institutions of control. Its patrilineal kinship system allows its women to express a degree of independence, as well as to prove their integration into the society. When its villagers are on their annual hunt, they adjudicate grievances, foster inter-communal ties, hunt cooperatively, and enjoy entertainment within an all-male audience; songs, dances, jokes and discussions during the hunt are male oriented, and not meant for mixed audiences as they might be at home.

Non-Santal religious leaders, who have come among them armed with a conservative oriented and puritan work ethic, reform, productions and discipline have condemned the Santal as "fun-loving." European and American Christian missionaries as well as modern Indian reform groups upon contact with the Santal have decided that the Santal "pleasures" must cease to be a part of the lives of their converts. Santals who have observed these converts to American, mainly Baptist-Methodist missionary Christianity have decided that Christians do not enjoy life very much.[10] The Brahmo-Samaj ambassadors of change have insisted that their Hinduized Santals convert to a new religion purified of these excesses.

The mixed public dancing at the village festivals are regarded by Vaisnava Hindus as orgies, and the drinking of rice-beer is forbidden for Santali-Hindu converts. Sacrifices of cattle and the eating of beef have sometimes had to be forcibly halted by neighbouring Hindu authorities. Such force could have caused a crisis in meaning

---

[8]For the earliest western transcription of the "Ancestor's Story" see Skrefsrud, L. O., *Traditions and Institutions of the Santals,* Oslo: Oslo Etnografiske Museum, 1942: 3ff.
[9]Orans, *op. cit.,* p. 8.

[10]Culshaw, *op. cit.,* p. 168.

for the Santal festivals, but Santali leadership has substituted fowl and other sacrifices (more on this below) to assuage their objecting neighbour and to revitalize truth concerns in their festive practices.

The Santal insiders, however, view life quite differently than their recently arrived, ostensibly morally superior religious neighbours. To them, the right way to live (*dhorom* the word usually used for religion) includes (*raska)* the pleasures derived from dancing, singing, musical performing, drinking, feasting, joking, playing and at times sexual activity. The cycle of the agricultural-work year is enlivened by festivals (*porob),* which, with their myth, ceremony and social interaction, give and enhance meanings to their complex and varied lives.

SOHRAE-HARVEST FESTIVAL

The Sohrae festival occurs during the Bengali month Pous comparable to the western calendar months December-January. In Santali India the months from June until the harvest have been time of scarcity and hunger. When the good harvests of rice have been reaped, there is ample food and work is at a standstill; a festival of abundance is celebrated with joy and abandon for 3–6 days.[11]

At least three days before the festival, parties of women hunt for and collect the forest roots necessary for fermenting the rice-beer (*handi),* which is made in every Santal home and which is a necessity for all festive celebrations of religious observances. The ferment from these roots called "medicine of medicines" (*ranu ran)* produces rice-beer in three days. Since the Santal have little means to store it, it is made fresh for each occasion. Out of their myths[12] comes the justification

for rice-beer, and Santals not only accept it on that basis, but wonder why anyone would want to live without it's beneficial pleasure. Since it is an indispensable offering to the spirits, Santals who have converted to outside religions and have abandoned its production and use are charged by the men (*hor),* their own identifying label, with being the cause of imbalanced relations between the Santals and the spirits.

In order to catch the interpenetration of religious discipline and expressive pleasure, we will focus primarily upon the behavior of the priests and the villagers during the Sohrae Festival.

One of the functions of Sohrae is the celebration of past fertility and sexual stability. The harvest has been gathered, it is a time to renew familial connections. Married daughters return with their families to the village of their parents. For that time and that place sexual conduct within the disciplined social restraints of clan and subclan regulations is deliberately relaxed. Newlyweds meet and renew some former loves; maturer married partners engage in extramarital relations. The outlet of such behaviour saves many otherwise precariously balanced marriages from disgrace and divorce. As Archer says, "Sohrae adds excitement to the marital state. It injects variety into the conjugal routine and by doing so buttresses everyday fidelity."[13]

The anticipation of Sohrae's pleasures can be sampled in Santal songs and dance. The dance is a non-verbal symbol, the descriptive dimensions of which are limited but the lyrics of the songs, if they are imagined in the social context can give us a hint of the Santal enjoyment of Sohrae.

A daughter anticipates her return to her parental village and sings:[14]

> Come husband
> Hold the horse
> Come to my father's

---

[11]While their Saivite neighbours celebrate the joyful Kali *puja* and their lectionary oriented Christians have celebrated the birth of Christ, the Santals' festival accentuates joyful pleasure.

[12]There are numerous versions of these myths, because specific Santals have only fragments of them. The chief Santali spirit (*bonga),* Maran Buru, Thakur's principal assistant, instructed Pilcu Haram and Pilcu Budhi, the first Santal couple, how to make rice-beer. Because they were

brother and sister, they were ashamed to have sexual intercourse. But drunk on beer they coupled and out of their union were born seven sons and seven daughters who mated likewise and populated the land of "men." Skrefsrud, *op. cit.,* p. 3ff.

[13]Archer, W. G. *Hill of Futes.* Pittsburgh: University of Pittsburgh, 1974:197.

[14]Ibid., Song 260, p. 197.

If you want rice-beer
You will have rice-beer
If you want meat
They will give it to you
Come to my father's.

During the Sohrae celebrations, the women sing trysting songs of pleasurable love.[15]

Sit down, stand up
O friends we have no food or drink
But in the eyes' meeting there is pleasure.
On the Headman's smooth verandah
I was grinding *Kode* (a millet), boy
But when I saw and heard you
How my body trembled.
Mother, father
The drums sound in the village
And like a lotus leaf in water
My body trembles as I hear them.

It is the Santal myths which give the festival its name and form. In one version of the myth,[16] Sohrae is the eldest daughter of the first Santal couple. After her birth, Pilcu Budhi gave birth to seven younger daughters and seven sons. One day, the girls were gathering fruit; the boys not recognizing their sisters made advances and lead the consenting girls off for sexual enjoyment (and legally as yet non-censored incest). Since Sohrae was the eldest, she had climbed to the top of the tree. Each brother enticed his own comparably aged sister, but by the time the seventh girl had left, there was no suitor left for Sohrae. Sympathizing with her lack of a mate, the others promised her that an annual festival at which a "virgin thing" would be offered would be a memorial to her. Subsequently, the festival has been called by her name, has had an emphasis upon sexual pleasures and marriage stability with warnings against incest. The egg "the virgin thing" has been offered since the mythical time (more about this later when we consider the priestly part and the disciplined aspect of his activities as he interacts with the villagers).

On the first day of the festival the village Headman addresses the Santal with mythical references and meanings. He welcomes the "el-

der sister" (festival) and inaugurates the festivities of enjoyment. He cautions the people against interclan and subclan prohibited sexual relations and warns them explicitly against incest. Yet within these social obligations to their corporate groups, he encourages them to enjoy the Santal way of life during the festival and says, "If you see anything, say nothing."[17] The first day is concluded with dancing, trysting, and singing during which the women sing.[18]

Elder sister, elder sister.
Go out, O eldest sister.
The festival like an elephant has come.
How shall we welcome it?
How shall we receive it?
Sister, O eldest sister
How shall we bring it in?
With a glad heart
And a sound of joy
We shall open our heart's door
And take it to our hearts.

During the festivities of the first day the youth and younger minded adults of both sexes come to the home of the *Jogmanji,* the Moral Guardian of youth behaviour, and ask him to relax the normal day-to-day sexual restraints for the period of the festival. The guardian of normal Santal morals shuts his eyes to permissible encounters during these few days with the understanding that these outlets will bring overall health to those under his jurisdiction, and that they fortify the interdependence of the sexes and foster mutual respect for the norms of other times when he must maintain standard Santal moral behaviour.[19]

The second day's pleasurable activities are opened and enhanced by male and female dances and songs. The male songs emphasize male and female interdependency as males don female attire and dance and sing intermingled with the men. Their songs emphasize mythical themes and festive celebrations.[20]

[15]Ibid., Song 278 and 289, p. 204f.
[16]Ibid., p. 198.9.

[17]Ibid., p. 200.
[18]Ibid., Song 266, p. 202.
[19]Culshaw, *op. cit.,* p. 111.
[20]Ibid., Song 268, p. 202; Song 273, p. 203.

Beat the sticks
Crash the sticks
Knock the sticks
All of us know
We are the sons
of Pilcu Haram
In the field of sugar cane
The jackal went
No it is not a jackal
But boys who saw some girls.

The festivities, then, celebrate sexual balance and mutual married health by praising marriage fidelity as the normal Santal good life. During the dances, pairs of dancers symbolize married couples, and song and dance propose longevity to the married state.[21]

It is due to the Santal conception that the good life for the most part must be disciplined, although enjoyed in periodic release, that sexual institutions are honoured, understood and maintained. Among them, the stability of marriage itself can be mocked and brides and bridegrooms kidded. In such a way children learn the enjoyment of the married state, as well as the seriousness concerned with family and linear kin obligations. Such an education is learned in an atmosphere of joking relaxation, in which fun is modest among mixed groups and sport is disciplined by social norms. In this way, Santal individuals know who they are and how they are a part of a social fabric of identification. Sohrae is the festive context for expressive religious concerns. It is a fitting conclusion that as boys engage in competitive sports, the girls sing and dance wistfully entreating "the elder sister" to return.[22]

Elder sister
I will catch it by the hand
I will pull it by the leg
The festival like an elephant
Is going away.
Sohrae, Sohrae
It was good while you were here
It was different while you stayed
Come again in time
Joy, do not cry

21Ibid., p. 204, Outsiders have often missed this functional purpose.
22Ibid., Song 298–299, pp. 212–213.

Joy, do not mourn
On the due day come back.

The respectful relationship between the unmarried men and girls and the *Jogmanjhi,* Moral Guardian, is again emphasized at the end of the festival. In order to symbolize their mutual regard, the unmarried sleep that night in the house of the *Jogmanjhi.* The license has ended, the regulations are again to be enforced; both youth and restraining authority figure are in agreement and mutually respectful.

The compound motifs of the Sohrae festival are the alleviation of marriage tension, the celebration of fertility, and the educational understanding of love within the context of sexual pleasure for all ages of the society. Such Santal expressions of social religion are not orgies, but are pleasurable reliefs to normal human tensions, enjoyed in order to protect the society from overprotective moral enforcement or the breakdown of marriage and family norms.

THE PRIESTLY EXPRESSION

The village priest (*naeke*) is like the Headman, a descendant of the founding or major lineage of the community. Together the priest and headman work for the spiritual and physical well-being of the people. The *naeke's* sphere of influence often overlaps or even coincides with those of the other village officials, consequently, a close, cooperative relationship is maintained so that the religious dimension of the festivals is not separated from their social meanings.

In order to purify himself for the Sohrae, the *naeke* separates himself not specifically but functionally from the people in order to perform the duties required of him. He interrupts his normal, everyday routine. Whereas the villagers may sleep on their string beds, during the festival he sleeps on the floor. Such preparation though seemingly incidental ready him for the specific duties which only he can perform.

Before noon of the first day, he has bathed,

and accompanied by the *kudam naeke,* his assistant or the back-up priest, he purifies with a cowdung-mixture an area sacralized for the sacrifices to the village spirits. Circles and squares are drawn with rice flour on the purified space and the sacrificial fowls, rice and salt, which have been collected by the *godet* Messenger of the Headman, are put within these diagrams. The birds feed on the rice while the priest puts vermillion on their heads, wings and legs. White (to Maran Buru bonga) and brown (to Joher-era bonga) fowls are decapitated and their blood mixed with the rice within the circle. During the offering, the *naeke* addresses the village (*bongas*) spirits. The sacrifice of the fowls symbolizes again the male-female sexual unity and harmony necessary for the maintenance of everyday life among the Santal. The community and spirits interact and develop through the intermediacy of the priest.

Although the Santal have vague ideas of an ultimate, invisible and abstract deity, whom they call by many names (Sin Bonga, Dhorom, Thakur,[23] Cando, among others) and about whom a few elderly know some myths in the life concerns of the Santal, Thakur receives little recognition by the villagers and even less direct relationship is maintained with Thakur by the Santal religious functionaries. Most often he is, if addressed at all, considered to be one of the *bonga*.

The (*bonga*) spirits, on the other hand, have direct daily relationship with the Santal. They are the cause of both good and bad effects in the Santal life. Because Santal spirits are more than abstractions, they are manifested in time and place. The Santal believe that the varied effects necessitate several categories of *bonga*. It is the religious leaders on the different levels of village life who are able to detect them, to ascertain their wishes and to enlist their support for the overall cohesion and health of the community.

The village *bonga* also make themselves known to and are the primary concern of the priest-*naeke*. They are the focus of attention at

all major village festivals and affect Sohrae. Although there are differences as to number and slight variations as to function among the Santal groups, we will discuss five bonga (village spirits which are known and worshipped by most Santals). Sometimes they are called the National Bonga.

The primary village *bonga* is Maran Buru,[24] (the Great Mountain), who is the chief or leader of the spirits and is associated with the hills and mountains. In the myths, Maran Buru is anthropomorphized as Thakur's male assistant who maintained contact with the Santal and guided them as they developed the right way of life. He is otherwise symbolized by the Santal in the form of a *sal* tree and a small stone which are located in the Sacred grove (*Jahirthan*). At sacrifices he is offered a white fowl.[25] He can possess (*rum*) a man especially designated as his medium and is associated with the battle-axe (these ideas are especially prominent in another festival, *Baha* festival). Maran Buru is loved and regarded as a gentle grandfather figure from whom the Santal receive instructions in and the enjoyment of sex as well as the making of festive rice-beer; he is the establisher of the interdependence of *bonga* and the Santal, and the founder of Sacred grove worship which maintains the balanced and morally good relationship between the spirits and Santal life. At Sohrae, the priest offers a white fowl accompanied by respectful address to Maran Buru.[26]

Jaher-era (Lady of the Grove) is conceptualized as a feminine *bonga,* often idealized as femininity or the female counterpart of Maran Buru. The Santal symbolize her too as a *sal* tree and a stone localized in the Sacred grove. Her proper offerings include the brown/red hen[27] offered by the priest at Sohrae. At the Baha-Flower she posseses a man who dresses in feminine

---

[23]Bengali for "one who is worthy of worship." Culshaw, *op. cit.,* p. 90.

[24]Lita and Sikhar are other names for Maran Buru. Note the association of the axe, hunting, the rainbow, and mountain lands with Lita. Mukherjea. *op. cit.,* p. 228, 258, 276; Skrefsrud, *op. cit.,* p. 132.

[25]Mukherjea, *op. cit.,* p. 275.

[26]Skrefsrud, *op. cit.,* p. 169.

[27]Ibid.

attire and her symbolic ornaments are a necklace, bangles, a flower basket and broom.

The third bonga is closely associated with Jaher-era and with the *sal* tree and the stones in the Sacred grove. Its tree representation stands in a row with Maran Buru and Jaher-era and its stone symbol is at the base of the tree in the cowdung purified area. It is a composite unit variously called Moreka (The five), conceived as a male or males, Tureko (The Six), a female or females, or as the composite Moreko-Tureko (The Five-Six), both male and female. Mukherjea[28] has translated a devotional song sung by men and women antiphonally which illustrates Santal beliefs about Moreko-Tureko:

Men: The five are five brothers.
Women: O, the six goddesses are six sisters
(He names them in a footnote and notes also that they are the wives of Moreka)
Men: The five beat on broad *demba* (musical instruments)
Women: O, the six goddesses blow on horns.

These three *bongas* are of slightly superior status, though the remaining two are also major spirits concerned with the life of Santals.

Gosae-era[29] is a female *bonga,* also represented in the Sacred grove by a *Mowah* tree, at the foot of which is a stone symbol of her, and she is often associated with the Five-Six *bonga.*

The last *bonga* of major concern for the life of the Santal is Pargana Bonga, whose symbolic representation in the Sacred grove is an Ashan tree with a stone at its base. This *bonga* is the symbolized spirit form of the *parganait,* the special institution in which a group of villages (10–12) join for mutual concerns, e.g. festive ceremonies, and judicial questions. It gives a religious dimension to inter-village issues. The *parganait* is ruled by a headman (*pargana),* who is elected by the separate villages and is respected for his leadership which makes him the spokesman for the group.

These are the most important spirits of the village, and to whom the Priest addresses his words and mediated actions. When these spirits are satisfied, the individual Santal experiences wholeness in his own identity and in the social context of Santal festive and everyday village life.

The *bonga* relate themselves to Santal only. Thus, neighbouring religious communities are not under their care; Hindu, Christian, British or Muslim life is not their concern, either punitively or beneficially. The overseeing of Santal life by the *bongas* means that they are intimately involved in Santal welfare and moral behaviour. Sometimes such concern necessitates sudden, negative, corrective measures. Otherwise, they afford continued protection and pleasant disposal toward the villagers in order to keep life both balanced and enjoyable. At Sohrae, animals are sacrificed to honour and ensure *bonga* benevolence. To ensure both safety and health, after the priest has sacrificed to the major *bongas,* his assistant (*kudam naeke*) offers fowls to the *bongas* resident on the outskirts of the village, while village heads make appropriate offerings to the *bongas* of hearth and family. Such coordinated sacrificial safety is accompanied by feasting and rice-beer drinking. Religion is not separate from society, but coordinated with other village leadership and always on behalf of the Santal.

VILLAGERS' EXPRESSIONS

The pleasures of Santal life are mutilated by the written medium, i.e., a translation of a poem song, and need to be embodied with sound and movement to experience more meaningful levels of Santal life. In an attempt to fill in for this verbal deficiency, a verbal explanation of their song, dance, and musical context will try to amplify their festive atmosphere.

Both sexes and all ages of Santals participate in the various village songs, dances, and pantomimes accompanied by their musical instruments. Such festive expressions connect the wisdom and practices of the *bongas* to the adult

[28]C. L. Mukherjea on the Mayurbhanj Santal, *op. cit.,* p. 364. Various myths show how diverse is this *bonga's* existence: compare Archer, *op. cit.,* p. 28-9.
[29]Cf. Gasain, Hindu for "Pious One"; Biswas *op. cit.,* p. 137f.

Santal life and aid the younger members of the society in their transition from a child to an active participant in everyday mature responsibilities and enjoyments. As the individual Santal dances, sings, and acts during the festivals, he does so aesthetically and learns via poetry and prose his or her part in the integral workings of adult life.

These Santal festive expressions are learned by direct participation from the earliest age of childhood. At Sohrae, the songs are modest and indirect allusions are made to sexual matters. Ribald songs are not sung at Sohrae, and the songs of everyday life make their point without descending to baudy exposure.

The songs (*Seren*) are metaphorical; they are of common village life and need extended comments, when they are translated without Santal cultural norms, for example:[30]

In the upper village
The tiger eats
In the lower village
The oriole sings.

To Santals, the tiger is a male who is seeking adult adventure, and the oriole is a female whose contemplation breaks forth into song in the hope that she will meet, enjoy and be satisfied by the sensuous hunger of her pursuing lover.

While this and other Sohrae songs are being sung to suggest what is being experienced by males and females who are meeting in trysting places, where secret longings are being satisfied, in the open areas of the village the men and women dance, mime and enjoy the musical festive atmosphere.

The second day of Sohrae is filled with dancing (*enec*). In front of the Headman's house, the men do their steps and clap moving in a semicircular row (*danta*). Then the choreography changes to a line which moves outward and returns (*gunjar*). Then, the men circle with their left arms outstretched (*matwar mucet kher*). As they dance, they sing, ending their compositions with a shrill "O-ho-ho-ho-ho."

[30]Archer, *op. cit.,* p. 108.

At the conclusion of the male dances, one calls out "and now boys, take your sticks and go to the cows"—a direct reference to a sexual function and some of the adult activities of Sohrae.[31]

When the men tire, the women replace them and take the village celebrations away from the headman's house to the streets. Their dances are of another mood and their songs are more feminine oriented.

During these song-dances, the poetry and actions both fortify and mime the actions of men and women, as they learn to love and live with one another. The problems associated with marriage—cohabitation and adjustment—are mocked so that their seriousness may be examined festively. Adults, who clench these behaviour patterns within their fists of jealousy, are urged to relax and see that there are alternative means for settling confusions and disputes. Standards of beauty, winsomeness and attractiveness are projected publically, so that each sex and age can appreciate one another more.[32]

On the drum
My former friend is playing
And like a plaintain shoot
He sways and bends
On the flute
My present friend is playing
And his body swings
Like trim bamboos.

An adolescent, young married or even maturer woman sees such male friends, she hears their musical and poetic talents expressed, she fancies fulfilling experiences and adjusts even better to Santal social norms. Through the experiences of song and dance, she dreams and tastes of love anew.

The demonstrations are not meant to destroy but, on the contrary, to discipline life. Imagine the young man at Sohrae, whose senses are filled by sound, sight, smell, taste, touch and thought as the following song is performed:[33]

[31]Archer, *op. cit.,* p. 204.
[32]Archer, *op. cit.,* p. 118.
[33]Archer, *op. cit.,* p. 107.

You are walking in the village street
You are strolling up and down.
To the right and left of you are marigolds (girls)
But do not take them in your eyes (coitus)

Sohrae would be destructive for the youth, if love became rape. Prudence is the advice of the community, and responsible behaviour is admonished, because today's lover is to be tomorrow's friend.

The festival is not a "now" only experience for the Santal and their songs and dances remind them that life is coupled with death. Here seems to be the balance that Sohrae offers educatively for the people, for in the midst of the action of life they sing:[34]

O my love
The life of man
Is only a gourd of water
Let it leak only a little
And all is gone

This is not morbidity, but a proper perspective, which a religious ceremony must stress as it emphasizes the relationships between men and *bonga,* men and women, individual and society, and the older and the younger members of the community.

As the dancers move and sing at Sohrae, the drummers, fiddlers and flutists demonstrate their talents. The *tum dak* drum consists of a clay cylinder, is struck by the hands and gives rhythm to the song and dance. The *tamak* is a hide-covered bowl which is beaten by sticks and adds depth to the sound.

The flute carries the melody, but the flutist and the flute are highly suggestive and become synonyms that bridge language and non-verbal meanings. Many Sohrae songs mention the flute and from them we catch some of their complex meanings.[35]

Beyond the mountain
The ring dove is cooing (girl)
Under the mountain
The boys are with the cattle
With a flute they struck the dove (coitus)
O my friend, go slowly
Very slowly.

The call of the flute is irresistible, necessitates prudence and conjures up for the mind the experience of love's paradox and wholeness:[36]

Darling
Play your flute on the mountain
I will hear you at the spring
If I leave my pot, the men will see me
If I stay away, my love will scold me.

Song, dance and musical instruments give levels of meaning to the festive air of Sohrae that verbal descriptions cannot exhaust, but one final dimension must be added—pantomime (*golwari*). The women gesture a variety of these movements of body and limbs as they "plant and reap the rice," "greet" one another with folded hands and lowered heads, "catch fish" or "pick flowers."[37]

Such motions display their body parts and suggest meanings symbolized in the Sohrae celebrations much to the pleasure of attendant males.

We have tried to give a fuller context to the Sohrae festival than that of more verbal description. The life of the Santal is exciting, disciplined and satisfying. In their play, they exercise religious concerns. Religion is not apart from their lives, but is a dimension of disciplined enjoyment that colours other aspects of the living whole. It is never far away or separated from life either intellectually or practically in the experience of being a Santal. Pleasure means more to them as a living experience than its English equivalent can but suggest.

[34]Archer, *op. cit.,* p. 326.
[35]Archer, *op. cit.,* p. 69.

[36]Archer, 126; cf. p. 141 where the flute is addressed as the bridegroom to be.
[37]Archer, *op. cit.,* p. 70 ff.

22

THE HIJRAS OF INDIA: CULTURAL AND INDIVIDUAL DIMENSIONS OF AN INSTITUTIONALIZED THIRD GENDER ROLE

SERENA NANDA

The hijra (eunuch/transvestite) is an institutionalized third gender role in India. Hijra are neither male nor female, but contain elements of both. As devotees of the Mother Goddess Bahuchara Mata, their sacred powers are contingent upon their asexuality. In reality, however, many hijras are prostitutes. This sexual activity undermines their culturally valued sacred role. This paper discusses religious meanings of the hijra role, as well as the ways in which individuals and the community deal with the conflicts engendered by their sexual activity.

The hijra, an institutionalized third gender role in India, is "neither male nor female," containing elements of both. The hijra are commonly believed by the larger society to be intersexed, impotent men, who undergo emasculation in which all or part of the genitals are removed. They adopt female dress and some other aspects of female behavior. Hijras traditionally earn their living by collecting alms and receiving payment for performances at weddings, births and festivals. The central feature of their culture is their devotion to Bahuchara Mata, one of the many Mother Goddesses worshipped all over India, for whom emasculation is carried out. This identification with the Mother Goddess is the source both of the hijras' claim for their special place in Indian society and the traditional belief in their power to curse or confer blessings on male infants.

For their assistance is developing the ideas in this paper, grateful acknowledgement is made to Joseph Carrier, David Greenberg, A.M. Shah, Rajni Chopra, Evelyn Blackwood, John Money, the participants of the Columbia University Seminar on the Indian Self, and most especially, Owen Lynch and Alan Roland. I am also grateful to Mrs. Banu Vasudevan, Bharati Gowda, and Shiv Ram Apte, as well as my friends among the hijras, without whom this paper could not have been written.

SERENA NANDA, is Professor of Anthropology at John Jay College of Criminal Justice (CUNY).
SOURCE: From "The Hijaras of India" by S. Nanda in the *Journal of Homosexuality 11 (3/4)*, 1985, pp. 35–54. Copyright © 1986 by The Haworth Press. Reprinted by permission.

The census of India does not enumerate hijras separately so their exact numbers are unknown. Estimates quoted in the press range from 50,000 (*India Today,* 1982) to 500,000 (*Tribune,* 1983). Hijras live predominantly in the cities of North India, where they find the greatest opportunity to perform their traditional roles, but small groups of hijras are found all over India, in the south as well as the north. Seven "houses," or subgroups, comprise the hijra community; each of these has a guru or leader, all of whom live in Bombay. The houses have equal status, but one, Laskarwallah, has the special function of mediating disputes which arise among the others. Each house has its own history, as well as rules particular to it. For example, members of a particular house are not allowed to wear certain colors. Hijra houses appear to be patterned after the *gharanas* (literally, houses), or family lineages among classical musicians, each of which is identified with its own particular musical style. Though the culturally distinct features of the hijra houses have almost vanished, the structural feature remains.[1]

The most significant relationship in the hijra community is that of the *guru* (master, teacher) and *chela* (disciple). When an individual decides to (formally) join the hijra community, he is taken to Bombay to visit one of the seven major gurus, usually the guru of the person who has brought him there. At the initiation ritual, the guru gives the novice a new, female name. The novice vows to obey the guru and the rules of the community. The guru then presents the new chela with some gifts.

The chela, or more likely, someone on her behalf, pays an initiation fee and the guru writes the chela's name in her record book. This guru-chela relationship is a lifelong bond of reciprocity in which the guru is obligated to help the chela and the chela is obligated to be loyal and obedient to the guru.[2] Hijras live together in communes gen-

erally of about 5 to 15 members, and the heads of these local groups are also called guru. Hijras make no distinctions within their community based on caste origin or religion, although in some parts of India, Gujerat, for example, Muslim and Hindu hijras reportedly live apart (Salunkhe, 1976). In Bombay, Delhi, Chandigarh and Bangalore, hijras of Muslim, Christian, and Hindu origin live in the same houses.

In addition to the hierarchical guru-chela relationship, there is fictive kinship by which hijras relate to each other. Rituals exist for "taking a daughter" and the "daughters" of one "mother" consider themselves "sisters" and relate on a reciprocal, affectionate basis. Other fictive kinship relations, such as "grandmother" or "mother's sister" (aunt) are the basis of warm and reciprocal regard. Fictive kin exchange small amounts of money, clothing, jewelry and sweets to formalize their relationship. Such relationships connect hijras all over India, and there is a constant movement of individuals who visit their gurus and fictive kin in different cities. Various annual gatherings, both religious and secular, attract thousands of hijras from all over India.[3]

The extant literature on the hijras is scant, confusing, misleading, contradictory, and judgmental. With few exceptions (Salunkhe, 1976; Sinha, 1967) it lacks a basis in fieldwork or intensive interviewing. A major dispute in that literature has been whether or not the hijra role encompasses homosexuality.

In my view, the essential cultural aspect of the hijra role is its asexual nature. Yet, empirical evidence also indicates that many hijras do engage in homosexual activity. This difference between the cultural ideal and the real behavior causes a certain amount of conflict within the community. The present paper, based on a year's fieldwork among hijra communes in various parts of India, examines both the cultural ideal of asexuality and the behavioral dimension

---

[1]I would like to thank Veena Oldenburg for calling this to my attention. A similar pattern exists among the courtesans in North India (Oldenburg, 1984).

[2]Alan Roland (1982) has insightfully examined some of the emotional and psychological aspects of hierarchy within the Hindu joint family, and many of his conclusions could well be applied to the hijra hierarchy.

[3]Some of these religious occasions are participated in by non-hijras as well, while others celebrate events specific to the hijra community, such as the anniversary of the deaths of important gurus.

of homosexuality, and how the conflict is experienced and handled within the community.

CULTURAL DIMENSIONS OF THE HIJRA ROLE
HIJRAS AS NEITHER MAN NOR WOMAN

A commonly told story among hijras, which conceptualizes them as a separate, third gender, connects them to the Hindu epic, the *Ramayana:*

> In the time of the Ramayana, Ram . . . had to leave Ayodhya (his native city) and go into the forest for 14 years. As he was going, the whole city followed him because they loved him so. As Ram came to . . . the edge of the forest, he turned to the people and said, "Ladies and gents, please wipe your tears and go away." But these people who were not men and not women did not know what to do. So they stayed there because Ram did not ask them to go. They remained there 14 years and snake hills grew around them. When Ram returned from Lanka, he found many snake hills. Not knowing why they were there he removed them and found so many people with long beards and long nails, all meditating. And so they were blessed by Ram. And that is why we hijras are so respected in Ayodhya.

Individual hijras also speak of themselves as being "separate," being "neither man nor woman," being "born as men, but not men," or being "not perfect men." Hijras are most clearly "not men" in relation to their claimed inability and lack of desire to engage in the sexual act as men with women, a consequence of their claimed biological intersexuality and their subsequent castration. Thus, hijras are unable to reproduce children, especially sons, an essential element in the Hindu concept of the normal, masculine role for males.

But if hijras are "not men," neither are they women, in spite of several aspects of feminine behavior associated with the role. These behaviors include dressing as women, wearing their hair long, plucking (rather than shaving) their facial hair, adopting feminine mannerisms, tak-

ing on women's names, and using female kinship terms and a special, feminized vocabulary. Hijras also identify with a female goddess or as wives of certain male deities in ritual contexts. They claim seating reserved for "ladies only" in public conveyances. On one occasion, they demanded to be counted as women in the census.[4]

Although their role requires hijras to dress like women, few make any real attempt to imitate or to "pass" as women. Their female dress and mannerisms are exaggerated to the point of caricature, expressing sexual overtones that would be considered inappropriate for ordinary women in their roles as daughters, wives, and mothers. Hijra performances are burlesques of female behavior. Much of the comedy of their behavior derives from the incongruities between their behavior and that of traditional women. They use coarse and abusive speech and gestures in opposition to the Hindu ideal of demure and restrained femininity. Further, it is not at all uncommon to see hijras in female clothing sporting several days growth of beard, or exposing hairy, muscular arms. The ultimate sanction of hijras to an abusive or unresponsive public is to lift their skirts and expose the mutilated genitals. The implicit threat of this shameless, and thoroughly unfeminine, behavior is enough to make most people give them a few cents so they will go away. Most centrally, as hijras themselves acknowledge, they are not born as women, and cannot reproduce. Their impotence and barrenness, due to a deficient or absent male organ, ultimately precludes their being considered fully male; yet their lack of female reproductive organs or female sexual organs precludes their being considered fully female.

Indian belief and the hijra's own claims commonly attribute the impotence of the hijra as male to a hermaphroditic morphology and physiology. Many informants insisted "I was born this way," implying hermaphroditism; such a condition is the standard reason given for joining the community. Only one of 30 informants,

---

[4]More recently, hijras have been issued ration cards for food in New Delhi, but must apply only under the male names.

however, was probably born intersexed. Her words clearly indicate how central this status is to the hijra role, and make explicit that hijras are not males because they have no male reproductive organ:

> From my childhood I am like this. From birth my organ was very small. My mother tried taking me to doctors and all but the doctors said, "No, it won't grow, your child is not a man and not a woman, this is God's gift and all . . ." From that time my mother would dress me in girl's clothes. But then she saw it was no use. So she sent me to live with the hijras. I am a real hijra, not like those others who are converts; they are men and can have children, so they have the (emasculation) operation, but I was born this way. (Field notes, 1981–2)

Hijra Impotence and Creative Asceticism

If, in Indian reality, the impotent male is considered useless as a man because he is unable to procreate, in Indian mythology, impotence can be transformed into generativity through the ideal of *tapasya,* or the practice of asceticism. *Tapas,* the power that results from ascetic practices and sexual abstinence, becomes an essential feature in the process of creation. Ascetics appear throughout Hindu mythology in procreative roles. In one version of the Hindu creation myth, Siva carries out an extreme, but legitimate form of tapasya, that of self-castration. Because the act of creation he was about to undertake had already been accomplished by Brahma, Siva breaks off his linga (phallus), saying, "there is no use for this linga . . ." and throws it into the earth. His act results in the fertility cult of linga-worship, which expresses the paradoxical theme of creative asceticism (O'Flaherty, 1973). This theme provides one explanation of the positive role given the hijras in Indian society. Born intersexed and impotent, unable themselves to reproduce, hijras can, through the emasculation operation, transform their liability into a source of creative power which enables them to confer blessings of fertility on others.

The link between the Hindu theme of creative asceticism and the role and power of the hijras is explicitly articulated in the myths connecting them to their major point of religious identification—their worship of Bahuchara Mata, and her requirement that they undergo emasculation. Bahuchara was a pretty, young maiden in a party of travelers passing through the forest in Gujerat. The party was attacked by thieves, and, fearing they would outrage her modesty, Bahuchara drew her dagger and cut off her breast, offering it to the outlaws in place of her body. This act, and her ensuing death, led to Bahuchara's deification and the practice of self-mutilation and sexual abstinence by her devotees to secure her favor.

Bahuchara has a special connection to the hijras because they are impotent men who undergo emasculation. This connection derives special significance from the story of King Baria of Gujerat. Baria was a devout follower of Bahucharaji, but was unhappy because he had no son. Through the goddess' favor a son, Jetho, was born to him. The son, however, was impotent. The King, out of respect to the goddess, set him apart for her service. Bahucharaji appeared to Jetho in a dream and told him to cut off his genitalia and dress himself as a woman, which he did. This practice has been followed by all who join the hijra cult (Mehta, 1945–1946).

Emasculation is the *dharm* (caste duty) of the hijras, and the chief source of their uniqueness. The hijras carry it out in a ritual context, in which the client sits in front of a picture of the goddess Bahuchara and repeats her name while the operation is being performed. A person who survives the operation becomes one of Bahuchara Mata's favorites, serving as a vehicle of her power through their symbolic rebirth. While the most popular image of Bahuchara is that of the goddess riding on a cock, Shah (1961) suggests that her original form of worship was the *yantra,* a conventional symbol for the vulva. A relation between this representation of the goddess and emasculation may exist: emasculation certainly brings the hijra devotee into a closer identification with the female object of devotion.

Identification of the hijras with Bahuchara specifically and through her, with the creative powers of the Mother Goddess worshipped in many different forms in India, is clearly related to their major cultural function, that of performing at homes where a male child has been born. During these performances the hijras, using sexual innuendos, inspect the genitals of the infant whom they hold in their arms as they dance. The hijras confer fertility, prosperity, and health on the infant and family.

At both weddings and births, hijras hold the power to bless and to curse, and families regard them ambivalently. They have both auspicious functions and inauspicious potential. In regard to the latter, charms are used during pregnancy against eunuchs, both to protect against stillbirth, and a transformation of the embryo from male to female. Hiltebeitel (1980) suggests that the presence of eunuchs at birth and weddings:

> marks the ambiguity of those moments when the nondifferentiation of male and female is most filled with uncertainty and promise—in the mystery that surrounds the sexual identity of the still unborn child and on that [occasion] which anticipates the re-union of male and female in marital sex. (p. 168)

Thus, it is fitting that the eunuch-transvestites, themselves characterized by sexual ambiguity, have ritual functions at moments that involve sexual ambiguity.

The eunuch-transvestite role of the hijras links them not only to the Mother Goddess, but also to Siva, through their identification with Arjuna, the hero of the Mahabharata. One origin myth of the hijras is the story of Arjuna's exile. He lives incognito for one year as part of the price he must pay for losing a game of dice, and also for rejecting the advances of one of the celestial nymphs. Arjuna decides to hide himself in the guise of a eunuch-transvestite, wearing bangles made of white conch, braiding his hair like a woman, clothing himself in female attire, and serving the ladies of the King's court (Rajagopalachari, 1980). Some hijras say that whoever is born on Arjuna's day, no matter where in the world, will become a hijra. Hiltebeitel (1980) makes a persuasive case for the identification of Arjuna with Siva, especially in his singer/dancer/eunuch/transvestite role.

The theme of the eunuch state is elaborated in a number of ways in the Mahabharata, and it is Arjuna who is the theme's central character. Arjuna, in the disguise of eunuch-transvestite, participates in weddings and births, and thus provides a further legitimatization for the ritual contexts in which the hijras perform. At one point, for example, Arjuna in this disguise helps prepare the King's daughter for her marriage and her future role as mother-to-be. In doing this, he refuses to marry the princess himself, thus renouncing not only his sovereignty, but also the issue of an heir. His feigned impotence paves the way for the birth of the princess' child, just as the presence of the impotent hijras at the home of a male child paves the way for the child's fertility and the continuation of the family line.

This evidence suggests that intersexuality, impotence, emasculation and transvestism are all variously believed to be part of the hijra role, accounting for their inability to reproduce and the lack of desire (or the renunciation of the desire) to do so. In any event, sexual abstinence, which Hindu mythology associates with the powers of the ascetic, is in fact, the very source of the hijras' powers. The hijras themselves recognize this connection: They frequently refer to themselves as *sannyasin*, the person who renounces his role in society for the life of a holy wanderer and begger. This vocation requires renunciation of material possessions, the duties of caste, the life of the householder and family man, and, most particularly, the renunciation of sexual desire (*kama*). In claiming this vocation, hijras point out how they have abandoned their families, live in material poverty, live off the charity of others, and "do not have sexual desires as other men do."

Hijras understand that their "other-worldliness" brings them respect in society, and that if they do not live up to these ideals, they will damage that respect. But just as Hindu mythology contains many stories of ascetics who renounce desire but nevertheless are moved by desire to engage in sexual acts, so, too, the hijra community experiences the tension between their religious, ascetic ideal and the reality of the individual human's desire and sensuality.

INDIVIDUAL DIMENSIONS OF THE HIJRA ROLE

HIJRAS AS HOMOSEXUALS

The remainder of this paper focuses on the sexual activities of hijras, and the ways in which the community experiences the conflict between the real and the ideal.

A widespread belief in India is that hijras are intersexed persons claimed or kidnapped by the hijra community as infants. No investigator has found evidence to support this belief. Given the large and complex society of India, the hijra community attracts different kinds of persons, most of whom join voluntarily as teenagers or adults. It appears to be a magnet for persons with a wide range of cross-gender characteristics arising from either a psychological or organic condition (Money & Wiedeking, 1980). The hijra role accommodates different personalities, sexual needs, and gender identities without completely losing its cultural meaning.

While the core of the positive meaning attached to the hijra role is linked to the negation of sexual desire, the reality is that many hijras do, in fact, engage in sexual activities. Because sexual behavior is contrary to the definition of the role such activity causes conflict for both the individuals and the community. Individual hijras deal with the conflict in different ways, while the community as a whole resorts to various mechanisms of social control.

Though it is clear from the literature that some hijras engage in homosexual activity, there has been controversy over the centrality of this activity in the institutionalization of the role in India.[5] In his psychoanalytical study of high castes in a village in Rajasthan, Carstairs (1957) asserted that the hijra role is primarily a form of institutionalized homosexuality that developed in response to tendencies toward latent homosexuality in the Indian national character. Morris Opler (1960) contested both Carstairs' evaluation of Indian character and his assertion that hijras are primarily conceptualized as homosexuals or that they engaged in any sexual activity.

Opler argued that the cultural definition of their role in Indian society was only one of performers. Sinha (1967), who worked in Lucknow in North India, acknowledged their performing role, but treated hijras primarily as homosexuals who join the community specifically to satisfy their sexual desires. Lynton and Rajan (1974), who interviewed hijras in Hyderabad, indicate that a period of homosexual activity, involving solicitation in public, sometimes precedes a decision to join the hijras. Their informants led them to believe, however, that sexual activity is prohibited by hijra rules and that these are strictly enforced by the community elders. Freeman (1979), who did fieldwork in Orissa at the southern edge of North Indian culture, discusses hijras as transvestite prostitutes and hardly mentions their ritual roles.

My own data (Nanda, 1984), gathered through fieldwork in Bangalore and Bombay, and in several North Indian cities, confirm beyond doubt that, however deviant it may be regarded within the hijra community, hijras in contemporary India extensively engage in sexual relations with men. This phenomenon is not entirely modern: 19th-century accounts (Bhimbhai, 1901; Faridi, 1899) claim that hijras were known to kidnap small boys for the purposes of sodomy or prostitution. Such allegations still find their way into the contemporary popular press (*India Today,* 1982).

Although hijras attribute their increased prostitution to declining opportunities to earn a living in their traditional manner, eunuch-

[5]A more detailed description of this literature is found in Nanda (1984) and Nanda (in press).

transvestites in Hindu classical literature also had the reputation of engaging in homosexual activity. The classic Hindu manual of love, the *Kamasutra,* specifically outlines sexual practices that were considered appropriate for eunuch-transvestites to perform with male partners (Burton, 1962).[6] Classical Hinduism taught that there was a "third sex," divided into various categories, two of which were castrated men, eunuchs, and hermaphrodites, who wore false breasts, and imitated the voice, gestures, dress and temperaments of women. These types shared the major function of providing alternative techniques of sexual gratification (Bullough, 1976). In contemporary India, concepts of eunuch, transvestite and male homosexual are not distinct, and the hijras are considered all of these at once (O'Flaherty, 1980).

The term hijra, however, which is of Urdu origin and the masculine gender, has the primary meaning of hermaphrodite. It is usually translated as eunuch, never as homosexual. Even Carstairs' informants, among whom the homosexuality of the hijras was well known, defined them as either drum players at the birth of male children, or eunuchs, whose duty was to undergo castration. In parts of North India, the term for effeminate males who play the passive role in homosexual relations is *zenanas* (women); by becoming a hijra, one removes oneself from this category (see also Lynton & Rajan, 1974). Furthermore, a covert homosexual subculture exists in some of the larger cities in North India (Anderson, 1977), but persons who participate in it are not called hijras. In fact, as in other cultures (Carrier, 1980; Wikan, 1977) men who play the insertor role in sexual activities between men have no linguistically or sociologically distinguished role. Unlike western cultures, in India sexual object choice alone does not define gender. In some South Indian regional languages,

the names by which hijras are called, such as *kojja* in Telegu (Anderson, 1977) or *potee* in Tamil, are, unlike the term *hijra,* epithets used derogatorily to mean a cowardly or feminine male or homosexual. This linguistic difference, however, is consistent with the fact that in South India the hijras do not have the cultural role which they do in North India.

According to my research, homosexual activity is widespread among hijras, and teenage homosexual activity figures significantly in the lives of many individuals who join the community. As Sinha's interviews also indicate (1967), those hijras who engage in homosexual activity share particular life patterns before joining the community. Typically such individuals liked during childhood to dress in feminine clothes, play with girls, do traditionally female work, and avoid the company of boys in rough play. In lower class families, the boy's effeminancy is both ridiculed and encouraged by his peers, who may persuade him to play the insertee role for them, possibly with some slight monetary consideration. At this stage the boy lives with his family, though in an increasingly tense atmosphere. He thinks of himself as a male and wears male clothing, at least in public. As his interest in homosexual activity increases, and his relations with his family become more strained, he may leave home. In most cases their families make serious attempts to inhibit their feminine activity with scoldings, surveillance, restrictions, and beatings, so that the boy finally has no choice but to leave.[7]

There are two modes of sexual relations

---

[6]"Mouth Congress" is considered the appropriate sexual activity for eunuchs disguised as women, in the Kama Sutra. An Editor's note (Burton, 1962, p. 124) suggests that this practice is no longer common in India, and is perhaps being replaced by sodomy, which has been introduced since the Muslim period.

[7]Social class factors are relevant here. Boys who are born with indeterminate sex organs (I came across three such cases by hearsay) to upper middle class families would not be likely to join the hijras. In two of these cases the men in question were adults; one had been sent abroad to develop his career in science with the expectation that he would not marry, but at least would have the satisfaction of a successful and prestigious career. The other was married by his parents to a girl who, it was known, could not have children. The third is still a toddler and is being brought up as a boy. I also had the opportunity to interview a middle-aged, middle-class man who was desperately trying to find a doctor to perform the transsexual operation on him in a hospital. He chose not to join the hijras because of their "reputation" but envied them their group life and their ability to live openly as women.

among hijras. One is casual prostitution, the exchange of sexual favors with different men for a fixed sum of money, and the other is "having a husband." Hijras do not characterize their male sexual partners as homosexuals; they quite explicitly distinguish them as being different than homosexuals. One hijra, Shakuntala, characterizes the customers in the following way:

these men . . . are married or unmarried, they may be the father of many children. Those who come to us, they have no desire to go to a man . . . they come to us for the sake of going to a girl. They prefer us to their wives . . . each one's tastes differ among people. . . . It is God's way; because we have to make a living, he made people like this so we can earn. (Field notes, 1981–2)

Shakuntala clearly expressed a feminine gender identity and was, in fact, the person who came closest to what would be called in the west a transsexual; that is, experiencing himself as a "female trapped in a male body." She remembered having felt that she was a female since childhood, liking to dress in female clothing, doing woman's work inside the house and playing with girls rather than boys. She was introduced to homosexual activity in her teens, which she claims "spoiled" her for the normal, heterosexual male role. She has a very maternal, nurturing temperament, and emphasizes the maternal aspect of the guru role to her young chelas.[8] She is currently involved in a long-term, monogamous relationship with a young man who lives in her neighborhood and whom she hopes will "marry" her. She underwent the emasculation operation because she wanted "to become more beautiful, like a woman." She was the only hijra interviewed who was taking hormones "to develop a more feminine figure." She always dressed as a woman and was very convincing in a feminine role, not exhibiting the more flamboyant mannerisms and gestures of the typical hijra. Because of her strong attachment to her

present boyfriend, she is sometimes criticized by her hijra friends:

Those people, like Shakuntala, with husband fever, they are mad over their husbands, even to the point of suicide. If that fellow even talks to a[nother] girl, immediately they'll fight with him. If he is out at night, even if it is three o'clock in the morning, they'll go in search of him. They won't even sleep till he returns. (Field notes, 1981–2)

This devotion to one man is seen as typical of Shakuntala's extremely feminine identification.

Not all hijras who engage in sexual relations with other men express such complete feminine identification. One hijra, for example, explained the attraction of men to hijras on different grounds:

See, there is a proverb, "for a normal lady [prostitute] it is four annas and for a hijra it is twelve annas." These men, they come to us to have pleasure on their own terms. They may want to kiss us or do so many things. For instance, the customer will ask us to lift the legs (from a position lying on her back) so that they can do it through the anus. We allow them to do it by the back [anal intercourse], but not very often. (Field notes, 1981–2).

This statement suggests that the attraction of the hijras is that they will engage in forms of sexual behavior in which Indian women will normally not engage. Several of my non-hijra male informants confirmed this view.

Having a husband is the preferred alternative for those hijras who engage in sexual relations. Many of my informants have, or recently had, a relatively permanent attachment to one man whom they referred to as their husband. They maintain warm and affectionate, as well as sexually satisfying and economically reciprocal, relationships with these men, with whom they live, sometimes alone, or sometimes with several other hijras. Lalitha, a very feminine looking hijra in her middle thirties, has had the same husband for nine years. He used to come for prostitution to the hijra commune in which Lalitha lived and then they lived together in a small house until he

---

[8]Gurus are sometimes considered like mothers, sometimes like fathers, and sometimes like husbands. Their female aspect is related to the nurturing and care and concern they have for their chelas; the male aspect refers more to the authority they have over their chelas and the obedience and loyalty that is due them.

Shakuntala (left), who expresses a complete feminine identity, emphasizes the maternal aspect of her chelas, one of whom she is pictured with here. Photo by Serena Nanda.

got married. Now Lalitha has moved back with the hijras, where she cooks their meals in return for free food and lodging, but she still maintains her relationship with her "husband":

> My husband is a Christian. He works in a ciga-
> rette factory and earns 1000 rupees a month. He
> is married to [another] woman and has got four
> children. I encouraged him to get married and
> even his wife and children are nice to me. His
> children call me *chitti* [mother's sister] and even
> his wife's parents know about me and don't say
> anything. He gives me saris and flowers and
> whenever I ask for money he never says no.

When he needs money, I would give him also.
(Field notes, 1981–2).

Hijras who have husbands do not break their ties with the hijra community, although sometimes their husbands urge them to do so. Sushila, an attractive, assertive, and ambitious hijra in her early thirties has a husband who is a driver for a national corporation headquarters and earns 600 rupees a month. She continues to be very active in the local hijra community, however, and even refuses to give up practicing prostitution in spite of her husband's objections:

My husband tells me, "I earn enough money. Why do you go for prostitution?" I tell him, "You are here with me today. What surety is there you will be with me forever? I came to you from prostitution, and if you leave me, I'll have to go back to it. Then all those other hijras will say, 'Oh, she lived as a wife and now look at her fate, she has come back to prostitution.' " So I tell him, "don't put any restrictions on me; now they all think of me as someone nice, but when I go back to prostitution, they will put me to shame." If he gives me too much back talk, I give him good whacks. (Field notes, 1981–2)

Sushila is saving the money she makes from prostitution and from that her husband gives her so that she can buy a business, probably a bathhouse for working class men. In Bangalore, bathhouses are commonly run by hijras.

Although many hijras complain that it is hard for them to save money, some have a good business sense and have invested in jewelry and property so that they can be relatively independent financially in their old age. For hijras who are not particularly talented singers and dancers, or who live in cities where their ritual performances are not in demand, prostitution provides an adequate way of earning a living. It is a demanding and even occasionally dangerous profession, however, because some customers turn out to be "rowdies." Although a hijra living in a commune has to pay 50% of her fees from prostitution to her household head, few of the younger hijra prostitutes can afford their own place; and living with others provides a certain amount of protection from rough customers and the police. In spite of the resentment and constant complaints by younger hijra prostitutes that they are exploited by their elders, they are extremely reluctant to live on their own.

Hijra Sexuality as a Source of Conflict

The attraction that the hijra role holds for some individuals is the opportunity to engage in sexual relations with men, while enjoying the sociability and relative security of an organized community; these advantages are apparent in contrast to the insecurity and harassment experienced by the effeminate homosexual living on his own. But, whether with husbands or customers, sexual relations run counter to the cultural definitions of the hijra role, and are a source of conflict within the community. Hijra elders attempt to maintain control over those who would "spoil" the hijras' reputation by engaging in sexual activity.

Hijras are well aware that they have only a tenuous hold on respectability in Indian society, and that this respectability is compromised by even covertly engaging in sexual relations. Ascetics have always been regarded with skepticism and ambivalence in Indian society. While paying lip service to the ascetic, conventional Hinduism maintained a very real hostility to it. It classed the non-Vedic ascetic with the dregs of society, "such as incendiaries, poisoners, pimps, spies, adulterers, abortionists, atheists and drunkards"; these fringe members of society found their most respectable status among the Siva sects (O'Flaherty, 1973, p. 67). This ambivalence toward ascetics accurately describes the response of Indian society to the hijra as well, who are also, not coincidentally, worshippers of Siva. In addition, the notion of the false ascetic (those who pretend to be ascetics in order to satisfy their lust) abounds in Hindu mythology. This contradictory attitude, a high regard for asceticism coupled with disdain for those who practice it, characterizes contemporary as well as classical India. Even those families who allow the hijras to perform at births and weddings ridicule the notion that they have any real power.

Indian audiences express their ambivalence toward the hijras by challenging the authenticity of hijra performers. The hijras' emasculation distinguishes them from *zenanas,* or practicing effeminate homosexuals, who do not have the religious powers ascribed to the hijras, but who sometimes impersonate them in order to earn a living. Thus, hijras state that emasculation is necessary because, when they are performing or asking for alms, people may challenge them. If their genitals have not been removed, they will be reviled and driven away as imposters. Hijra elders themselves constantly deride those "men who are men and can have children" and join their community only to make a living from it, or to enjoy sexual relations with men. The parallel between such "fake" hijras and the false ascetics is clear.

Hijras consider sexual activity offensive to the hijra goddess, Bahuchara Mata. Upon initiation into the community, the novice vows to abstain from sexual relations or to marry. Hijra elders claim that all hijra houses lock their doors by nine o'clock at night, implying that no sexual activities occur there. In the cities where hijra culture is strongest, hijras who practice prostitution are not permitted to live with hijras who earn their living by traditional ritual performances. Those who live in these respectable or "family" houses are carefully watched to see that they do not have contact with men. In areas more peripheral to the core of hijra culture, including most of South India, prostitutes do live in houses with traditional hijra performers, and may, in fact, engage in such performances themselves whenever they have an opportunity to do so.

Sexually active hijras usually assert that all hijras join the community so that they can engage in sexual relations with men. As Sita, a particularly candid informant, said:

> Why else would we wear saris? Those who you see who are aged now, when they were young they were just like me. Now they say they haven't got the sexual feeling and they talk only of God and all, but I tell you, that is all nonsense. In their younger days, they also did this prostitution and it is only for the sexual feeling that we join. (Field notes, 1981–2)

The hijras who most vehemently denied having sexual relations with men were almost always over 40. It appears that as they get older, hijras give up sexual activity. Such change over the life cycle parallels that in India generally; in the Hindu cultural ideal, women whose sons are married are expected to give up sexual activity. In

fact, not all women do so, but there is social pressure to do so. People ridicule and gossip about middle aged women who act in ways that suggest active sexual interest (Vatuk, 1985). The presentation of self as a non-sexual person that occurs with age also appears among the hijras. The elderly ones may wear male clothing in public, dress more conservatively, wearing white rather than boldly colored saris, act in a less sexually suggestive manner, and take on household domestic roles that keep them indoors.

Although hijra elders are most vocal in expressing disapproval of hijra sexual relations, even younger hirjas who have husbands or practice prostitution admit that such behavior runs counter to hijra norms and lowers their status in the larger society. Hijra prostitutes say that prostitution is a necessary evil for them, the only way for them to earn a living. They attribute the frequency of hijra prostitution to the declining economic status of the hijras in India since the time of Independence. At that time the rajas and nawobs in the princely states, who are important patrons of hijra ritual performances, lost their offices. Hijras also argue that in modern India, declining family size and the spread of Western values, which undermine belief in their powers, also contributes to their lowered economic position, making prostitution necessary.

INDIA AS AN ACCOMMODATING SOCIETY

India is characteristically described as a sexually tolerant society (Bullough, 1976; Carrier, 1980). Indeed, the hijra role appears to be elastic enough to accommodate a wide variety of individual temperaments, identities, behaviors, and levels of commitment, and still function in a culturally accepted manner. This elasticity derives from the genius of Hinduism: although not every hijra lives up to the role at the highest level, the role nonetheless gives religious meaning to cross-gender behavior, that is despised,

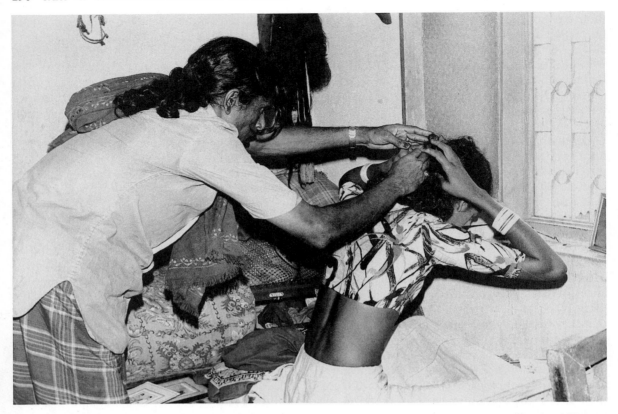

Ramachandra (left) is a hijra who has not yet fully adopted wearing women's clothing, as he works as a milkman, delivering milk on his bicycle. Here he is helping his chela, Kokila, get ready for a dance performance. Photo by Serena Nanda.

punished and pushed beyond the pale of the cultural system in other societies.

Several different aspects of Hindu thought explain both the ability of Indian society to absorb an institutionalized third gender role, as well as to provide several contexts within which to handle the tension between the ideal and real aspects of the role. Indian mythology contains numerous examples of androgynes (see O'Flaherty, 1980), impersonators of the opposite sex, and among both deities and humans individuals with sex changes. Myths are an important part of popular culture. Sivabhaktis (worshippers of Siva) give hijras special respect because one of the forms of Siva is Ardhanarisvara, ("the lord who is half woman"). Hijras also associate themselves with Vishnu, who transforms himself into Mohini, the most beautiful woman in the world, in order to take back the sacred nectar from the demons who have stolen it. Further, in the worship of Krishna, male devotees may imagine themselves to be female, and even dress in female clothing; direct identification with Krishna is forbidden, but the devotee may identify with him indirectly by identifying with Radha, that is, by taking a female form. Thousands of hijras identify themselves as Krishna's wives in a ritual performed in South India. These are only a few of the contexts within which the hijras link themselves to the Great Tradition of Hinduism and develop a positive definition for their feminine behavior.

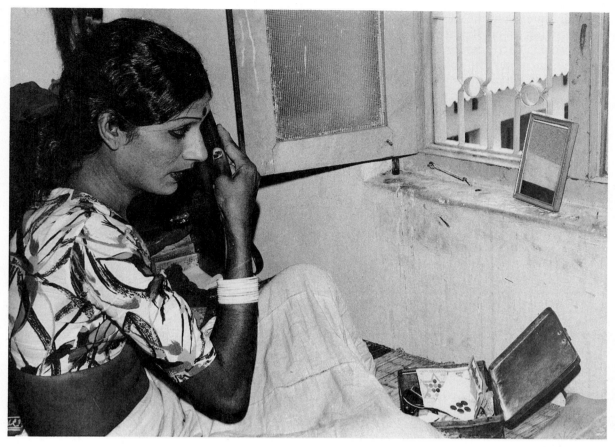

Kokila, a young hijra, gets ready for a dance performance. Photo by Serena Nanda.

In handling the conflict between the real and the ideal, hijras and other groups in the Indian population are confronted with the seemingly conflicting value which Hinduism places on both eroticism and procreation, on the one hand, and non-attachment and asceticism, on the other. Both Hinduism and Islam are what Bullough calls "sex-positive" religions (1976). Both allow for the tolerance of a wider range of sexual expression than exists in western culture with its restrictive Judeo-Christian, religious heritage. Hinduism explicitly recognizes that humans achieve their ultimate goals—salvation, bliss, knowledge and (sexual) pleasure—by following many different paths because humans differ in their special abilities and competencies. Thus, Hinduism allows a different ethic according to one's own nature and affords the individual temperament the widest latitude, from highly idealistic morality, through genial toleration, and, finally, to compulsive extremes (Lannoy, 1975).

Hindu thought attempts to reconcile the value conflict between sexuality and chastity through the concept of a life cycle with four stages. Each stage has its appropriate sexual behavior: In the first stage one should be a chaste student, in the second a married householder, in the third a forest dweller preparing for withdrawal from society, and in the final stage, a sannyasin, the ascetic who has renounced everything. Thus, the Hindu ideal is a fully integrated life in which each aspect of human nature, including sexuality, has its time. Hijras implicitly recognize these stages in their social organization through a hierarchy in which one begins as a chela and moves into the position of guru as one gets older, taking on chelas and becoming less sexually active.

Hindu mythology also provides some contexts within which the contradictions between the ascetic ideal and the sexual activity are legitimate: Siva himself is both the great erotic and the great ascetic. In myths he alternates between the two forms. In some mythic episodes Siva is unable to reconcile his two roles as ascetic and householder, and in others he is a hypocritical ascetic because of his sexual involvement with Parvati, his consort (O'Flaherty, 1973). Indian goddesses as sexual figures also exist in abundance and in some stories a god will take on a female form specifically to have sexual relations with a male deity.

Where Western culture feels uncomfortable with contradictions and makes strenuous attempts to resolve them, Hinduism allows opposites to confront each other without a resolution, "celebrating the idea that the universe is boundlessly various, and . . . that all possibilities may exist without excluding each other" (O'Flaherty, 1973, p. 318). It is this characteristically Indian ability to tolerate, and even embrace, contradictions at social, cultural and personality levels, that provides a context for hijras. Hijras express in their very bodies the confrontation of femaleness and maleness as polar opposites. In Indian society they are not only tolerated but also valued.

REFERENCES

ANDERSON, C. (1977). *Gay men in India.* Unpublished manuscript, University of Wisconsin.

BHIMBHAI, K. PAVAYAS. (1901). Gujarat population, Hindus. In J. M. Campbell (Compiler), *Gazetteer of the Bombay Presidency, 4,* part 1. Bombay: Government Central Press.

BRADFORD, N. J. (1983). Transgenderism and the cult of Yellamma: Heat, sex, and sickness in South Indian ritual. *Journal of Anthropological Research, 39,* 307–322.

BULLOUGH, V. L. (1976). *Sexual variance in society and history.* Chicago: University of Chicago Press.

CARRIER, J. (1980). Homosexual behavior in cross cultural perspective. In J. Marmor (Ed.), *Homosexual behavior: A modern reappraisal* (pp. 100–122). New York: Basic Books.

CARSTAIRS, G. M. (1957). *The twice born.* London: Hogarth Press.

FARIDI, F. L. (1899). Hijras. In J. M. Campbell (Compiler), *Gazetteer of the Bombay Presidency, 9,* part 2. Bombay: Government Central Press.

FREEMAN, J. M. (1979). *Untouchable: An Indian life history.* Stanford, CA: Stanford University Press.

HILTEBEITEL, A. (1980). Siva, the goddess, and the disguises of the Pandavas and Draupadi. *History of Religions, 20*(1/2), 147–174.

India Today. Fear is the key. (1982, September 15), pp. 84–85.

The Kama Sutra of Vatsyayana. (1964). (R. F. Burton, Trans.). New York: E. P. Dutton.

LANNOY, R. (1975). *The speaking tree.* New York: Oxford University Press.

LYNTON, H. S., & RAJAN, M. (1974). *Days of the beloved.* Berkeley: University of California Press.

MARK, M. E. (1981). *Falkland Road: Prostitutes of Bombay.* New York: Knopf.

MEHTA, S. (1945–1946). Eunuchs, pavaiyas and hijadas. *Gufarat ahitya Sabha,* Amdavad, Karyavahi, Part 2. Ahmedabad.

MONEY, J., & WIEDEKING, C. (1980). *Handbook of human sexuality* (pp. 270–284). B. B. Wolman & J. Money (Eds.), Englewood Cliffs, N.J.: Prentice-Hall.

NANDA, S. (1984). The hijras of India: A preliminary report. *Medicine and Law, 3,* 59–75.

NANDA, S. (in press). Dancers only? In Murray (Ed.), *Cultural diversity and homosexualities.* New York: Longman.

O'FLAHERTY, W. (1973). *Asceticism and eroticism in the mythology of Siva.* London: Oxford University Press.

O'FLAHERTY, W. (1980). *Women, androgynes, and other mythical beasts.* Chicago: University of Chicago Press.

OLDENBURG, V. (1984). *The making of colonial Lucknow.* Princeton, N. J.: Princeton University Press.

OPLER, M. (1960). The hijara (hermaphrodites) of India and Indian national character: A rejoinder, *American Anthropologist, 62,* 505–511.

RAJAGOPALACHARY, C. (1980). *Mahabharata.* Bombay: Bharatiya Vidya Bhavan.

ROLAND, A. (1982). Toward a psychoanalytical psychology of hierarchical relationships in Hindu India. *Ethos, 10*(3), 232–253.

SALUNKHE, G. (1976, August 8). The cult of the hijaras. *Illustrated Weekly,* pp. 16–21.

SHAH, A. M. (1961). A note on the hijaras of Gujerat. *American Anthropologist, 61,* 1325–1330.

SINHA, A. P. (1967). Procreation among the eunuchs. *Eastern Anthropologist, 20,* 168–176.

The Tribune, (1983, August 26). Five eunuchs in India, Pak. p. 2.

VATUK, S. (1985). South Asian cultural conceptions of sexuality. In J. K. Brown & V. Kerns (Eds.), *In her prime: A new view of middle-aged women* (pp. 137–152).

WIKAN, U. (1977). Man becomes woman: Transsexualism in Oman as a key to gender roles. *Man, 12,* 304–319.

VIII

CULTURE AND THE NATURE OF SEXUAL ORIENTATION

INTRODUCTION

Discussions of homosexuality abound in the literature of all the social and behavioral sciences today. There is simply too much variation in the literature to provide an adequate summary here.[1] Thus, we shall concentrate on a consideration of basic assumptions about sexual orientation.

We believe that many (perhaps most) discussions of sexual orientation are flawed at the outset by a single assumption. That is, they have taken the position that heterosexuality needs no explanation. It is seen as *completely* natural, the ran-

domly selected but natural result of evolution's design. This perspective commonly casts homosexuality as the polar opposite of heterosexuality. Offering no obvious direct reproductive advantages to individuals or groups, homosexual behaviors come to be seen as "abnormal." This problematic view of homosexuality as abnormal then takes on a life of its own, focusing attention on homosexuality as socially or psychologically deviant.

Along with Kinsey, we believe that sexual orientation is more accurately viewed as a continuum from the exclusively heterosexual orientation to the exclusively homosexual orientation. That perspective begins with the assumption that both of the extremes—and, perforce, the gradations

[1]For an excellent summary of anthropological approaches to the study of homosexuality, see Davis and Whitten (1987).

between them—are natural. In accordance with the readings in the first section of this book, we would suggest further that all sexuality as it is experienced is not only natural, but also always cultural.

Viewing sexual orientation on a continuum raises some interesting questions about culture. If we do not view the distinction between heterosexuality and homosexuality as reflective of absolute opposition, what is the role of culture in defining a homosexual or heterosexual identity? Obviously, a continuum view of sexual orientation requires that we distinguish between homosexual acts and identities. How are sexual orientations patterned to provide support for broader socio-cultural realms? That is, what is the interaction between the economy and sexual orientation, between religion and sexual orientation? How do historical sociocultural changes alter the established meanings attached to sexual orientation?

The readings in this section were chosen to address questions such as these. Although they cannot cover the range of literature available to the interested student, they seek to examine the interaction between culture and sexuality in ways we believe to be most productive for understanding issues of sexual orientation.

Gilbert H. Herdt writes about the Sambia of New Guinea, a horticultural group that defines homosexual contacts as normative during the first stages of a lengthy initiation into adulthood. During this time, heterosexual contacts are pervasively condemned. Later in the life course, heterosexual acts are defined as normative. Herdt argues that sexual interactions chart the power structure of Sambia society. Because semen is considered an object of exchange, all sexual acts—homosexual or heterosexual—can be seen as the creation or cancellation of social debt.

Evelyn Blackwood examines the prominent assumptions of anthropologists who study homosexual behaviors. She notes the lack of material on lesbian behaviors and argues that the focus on male behaviors in theory construction biases our understanding of same-sex interactions. She reviews the cross-cultural record on lesbian behaviors and suggests avenues for future research.

Judith Gay examines the cultural bases for a form of institutionalized friendship among young women in Lesotho. She draws interesting connections between the labor migratory system and this relationship between "mummy" and "baby." She notes that whereas sexual intimacy may be an important aspect of this relationship, the relationship primarily provides emotional support for women prior to marriage. She also shows how the changes caused by the structure of migratory labor and town life are evidenced in the unique social aspects of the mummy/baby relationship. Much of her data emphasize that homosexual bonds are not incompatible with heterosexual ones.

Philippe Ariès reviews the history of western Europe's interpretation of homosexuality. In the Middle Ages, the homosexual was seen as "perverted." The eighteenth and nineteenth centuries saw the continuation of that portrayal, but with the added imagery of the homosexual as "monster." In the late nineteenth and early twentieth centuries, homosexuals were portrayed as sufferers of illness. Today, Ariès believes that the scientific community is adopting a view of the homosexual as "normal." Ariès sees these changing views as reflections of broad social changes over the centuries, particularly the increasingly compartmentalized and specialized structures of society and their promotion of individualism.

SUGGESTED READINGS

BOLIN, ANNE. (1987). *In Search of Eve.* South Hadley, MA: Bergin & Garvey.

CARRIER, JOSEPH M. (1985). Mexican Male Bisexuality. *Journal of Homosexuality, 11*:1–2:75–85.

CARRIER, JOSEPH M. (1980). Homosexual Behavior in Cross-Cultural Perspective. In Judd Marmor (Ed.), *Homosexual Behavior: A Modern Reappraisal.* (pp. 100–122). New York: Basic Books.

DAVIS, D. L., AND R. G. WHITTEN. (1987). The Cross-Cultural Study of Human Sexuality. *Annual Review of Anthropology, 16*:69–98.

ENDLEMAN, ROBERT. (1986). Homosexuality in Tribal Societies. *Transcultural Psychiatric Research Review. 23*:187–218.

FRY, PETER. (1985). Male Homosexuality and Spirit Possession in Brazil. *Journal of Homosexuality, 11*:3/4:137–153.

GRAY, J. PATRICK, AND JANE E. ELLINGTON. (1984). Institutionalized Male Transvestism, the Couvade and Homosexual Behavior. *Ethos, 12*:54–63.

HERDT, GILBERT H. (ED.). (1984). *Ritualized Homosexuality in Melanesia.* Berkeley: University of California Press.

HERDT, GILBERT (ED.). (1992). *Gay Culture in America: Essays from the Field.* Boston: Beacon Press.

HUMPHREYS, LAUD. (1970). *Tea Room Trade: Impersonal Sex in Public Places.* Chicago: Aldine.

LEVAY, SIMON. (1991). A Difference in Hypothalamic Structure between Heterosexual and Homosexual Men. *Science,* Aug. 30:253:5023:1034–1037.

STEVENS, PATRICIA E., AND JOANNE M. HALL. (1991). A Critical Historical Analysis of the Medical Construction of Lesbianism. *International Journal of Health Services, 21*:2:291–307.

WHITAM, FREDERICK L. (1987). A Cross-Cultural Perspective on Homosexuality, Transvestism and Trans-Sexualism. In Glenn D. Wilson (Ed.), *Variant Sexuality: Research and Theory* (pp. 176–201). Baltimore: Johns Hopkins University Press.

23

SEMEN TRANSACTIONS IN SAMBIA CULTURE

GILBERT H. HERDT

INTRODUCTION

The theme of this study, semen transactions, may appear esoteric, not to mention vulgar: certainly the question of who gives and receives sperm is not one that much concerns Westerners today. Indeed, human fluids in general seem obvious and trivial, even embarrassingly natural, or unnatural, as the case may be. Seldom do we wonder how and why they are produced, or where and when they are consumed or discarded, or by whom. The perspective in certain

Melanesian societies, however, is contrary to our view, for semen, like other body fluids, is of considerable interest (and is neither obvious nor trifling but is vulgar) in the sense that semen as a scarce resource is among the everyday concerns of common folk. If we recognize and study these concerns in their own right and in their own symbolic environment, we are led to examine how and why they inform the structure and meaning of sexuality in general and institutionalized homosexual practices in particular. I want to analyze why, that is, peoples such as the Sambia of the Eastern Highlands have fetishized

SOURCE: From *Ritualized Homosexuality in Melanesia* by G. Herdt, pp. 167–210. Copyright © 1984 by University of California Press. Reprinted by permission.

semen, transforming it from an object into a subject, a living "commodity," with a personality and vital signs of its own.[1]

The more one thinks about this symbolic transformation, the more remarkable it seems. A simple bodily fluid, endowed with much significance, has become a sort of director of people—predicating their perceptions and interactions, molding their selves, marriages, families, and clans—thereby making them all objects valued against itself. In Western culture we have perhaps made money and sex into predicate subjects of this sort. In Melanesia, it seems, there are a few such subjects: pigs and shell valuables, women, spirits, blood, and semen. Access to or power over these things makes individuals and groups valued and powerful.

We have long known that some Melanesian cultures use the body (e.g., of humans, animals, spiritual beings) as a conceptual model of and for social action, speech, and thought (e.g., Leenhardt 1979; Malinowski 1929; Mead 1935; Newman 1964). Typically, though, the significance of these symbolic models has been obscured in anthropological preoccupations with individualism, group solidarity, and exchanges of wealth ("norms of reciprocity," i.e., "linear sequences basically concerned with discrete acts of giving and receiving" [Weiner 1980:71; see also M. Strathern 1979]). The meaningfulness of these cultural commodities, including how they are transformed from things into predicates of relationships between persons, as elements in cultural systems, is what concerns me.

If we take accord of the full value Sambia invest in fluids such as semen and breast milk, then

we can trace the systemic contours of the circulation of these valuable fluids in their culture. In this view, semen as a cultural idea and semen transactions may be understood as a special language, a kind of symbolic discourse for signifying the value and identities of persons, groups, and social and religious entities. Such a symbolic discourse may be trained on many objects (see Herdt 1982*b*; Weiner n.d.). But because of its centrality, semen as a commodity valuates and conditions basic Sambian cultural institutions—personhood, marriage, clanhood—as well as key social relationships in the family, village, and ritual cults, between men and women, humans and spirits.

Analytically, the value of semen may be understood at several conceptual levels that synergistically interact. For the Sambia we may ask: How do individuals valuate other persons, groups, or relationships (e.g., sexual, familial, kinship) as semen donors or recipients? Or we may ask: How do semen transactions underlying social relationships define who is related as kin or affines as well as what the nature of those social bonds is? Sambia men practice both homosexual and heterosexual activities. And since sexual intercourse may be defined by Sambia either as work or play, we may ask: Is it the mode of semen exchange or the type of sexual intercourse that registers the difference between, say, sex as work or sex as play? If semen is a scarce resource—a means of social reproduction of babies and hence, heirs, gardeners, and hunters, and females for marriage exchange for production, and warriors for group protection—who or what regulates this commodity in Sambia culture?

I will examine these perspectives in the following study of Sambia ritualized homosexual practices. My interest lies mainly in demonstrating the symbolic relationship between *ideas* about semen and all forms of sexual *transactions* in Sambia society. Thus, this account is primarily cultural and sociological in orientation; I am not concerned here with describing erotic acts or individual constructions of semen beliefs in

[1]Research among Sambia (1974–1976, 1979, 1981) has been supported by the following institutions, and I gratefully acknowledge their assistance: the Australian-American Education Foundation; the Australian National University, Research School of Pacific Studies; the National Institute of Mental Health; the Department of Psychiatry, Neuropsychiatric Institute, UCLA; the Department of Anthropology, Stanford University; the Stanford Center for the Study of Youth Development, Stanford University; and the Wenner-Gren Foundation for Anthropological Research. For their very helpful comments on this chapter, I wish to thank Michael Allen, Jan Van Baal, Nancy Lutkehaus, Fitz John Poole, Eric Schwimmer, Marilyn Strathern, and Donald Tuzin.

gender identity or psychosocial functioning, phenomena I have touched upon elsewhere (Herdt 1980, 1981; Stoller and Herdt 1982).

SAMBIA CULTURE

Sambia are a fringe-area Highlands people. They inhabit isolated ranges of the southern part of the Eastern Highlands near the Papuan border. Their high forest territory is vast, while the population (around 2,300) is small. Population density averages between 5 and 10 people per square mile throughout their territory. Historically, they migrated from the Papuan hinterland around Menyama during the last two centuries. Myth and legend relate that they fled after a great war. They share in cognate cultural traditions with other Anga tribes in the area, such as the Baruya (Godelier 1928a), with whom they also warred and traded. But Sambia have also been influenced by Eastern Highlands groups, especially the Fore (Lindenbaum 1979). So their society and culture embodies and reflects long-continued influences and transformations of imported patterns from both Papua and the Highlands.

Social organization and economy revolve around small sedentary hamlets built atop high mountain ridges for defense. Gardening and hunting are the main economic pursuits. Sweet potatoes and taro are the chief staples. Women do most garden work. Men do all hunting, primarily for possum, cassowary, birds, and eels. Pigs are few and are of little ceremonial importance. Descent is ideally organized on the basis of patriliny. Postmarital residence is patrivirilocal, so males grow up in their father's hamlet, inherit his land, and reside there. Marriage is by infant betrothal or sister exchange; bride-wealth was introduced only in the mid-1970s. Some men, especially senior leaders, have several wives. All marriage is arranged by elders, women being traded between exogamous clans, either within or between neighboring hamlets, though interhamlet marriage is the norm. Hamlets may have two or more constituent clans, which tend to be internally organized as an extended family. Inside hamlets, nuclear (or polygamous) families live together in small separate huts; but there is also one or two men's houses wherein all initiated, unmarried males live. The hamlet tends to function as a corporate group in matters of warfare, subsistence activities, marriage, ritual, and dispute settlements.

Sambia society is comprised of six different population clusters of hamlets in adjacent but separate river valleys. These population clusters are divided, in turn, into subgroups (phratries) believed related by ancestry, ritual, and common geographic origin. Each phratry has between two and six hamlets, situated on ridges often within sight of one another. These local hamlet groups, known as confederacies,* intermarry and engage in joint ritual initiations every three or four years. But they sometimes fight among themselves. Warfare has indeed been rife throughout the entire Highlands Anga area, taking two forms: intertribal war raids to kill and loot; and intratribal bow fights designed to bluster and get revenge for perceived wrongs. In other words, within the Sambia Valley, my fieldwork site, hamlets have intermarried, initiated, and fought—sociopolitical dynamics of the behavioral environment that are crucial for understanding social and sexual life.

Relationships between the sexes are highly polarized. One sees expressions of this polarization in virtually every social domain. A strict division of labor and ritual taboos forbid men and women from doing each other's tasks in hunting and gardening. Women are responsible for food preparation and child care. Authority rests in the hands of elders and war leaders. Men are in charge of public affairs, though women have interpersonal influence to some extent in domestic affairs. The hamlet itself is divided into male and female spaces and paths tabooed to the opposite sex after initiation. Men's rhetoric disparages older married women as oversexed or lecherous and

*Confederacies here marks the same social unit as "parish" and "subtribe" in other New Guineast typologies.

younger women as prudish or shy. Men fear being contaminated and sapped of their strength (*jerungdu*) by marriageable women.

Furthermore, male/female sexual relationships are generally antagonistic, and many marital histories reveal arguments, fights, jealousies, sorcery fears, some wifebeating, and even suicide attempts. Wives (much more than female kin) are stigmatized as inferior, as polluting and depleting to men, because of their menstrual and vaginal fluids. Sexual intercourse is supposed to be spaced to avoid depletion and premature aging or death. (Couples may have sex every three to five days, or as infrequently as once every two or three weeks, depending upon their ages, length of marriage, personalities, etc.) Prolonged postpartum taboos prohibit couples from engaging in coitus for up to two and a half years following the birth of a child. These generalizations indicate trends: Sambia heterosexual relationships are often extremely polarized compared even with other Highlands groups (Langness 1967; reviewed in Herdt and Poole 1982).

How do Sambia understand the nature and functioning of the sexes? Male is the socially preferred and valued sex. Female is perceived as inferior in every way, except reproductively. Infants are assigned either to the male or female sex, and sex-typing of behaviors and gender traits is rigid from childhood onward. Females, however, are believed to mature "naturally," without external aids, for their bodies contain a menstrual blood organ (*tingu*) which hastens physical and mental development, puberty, and eventually menarche, the key sign a woman is ready for marriage and procreation. (Menarche occurs late in New Guinea and is now between ages sixteen and nineteen for Sambia.) At menarche a woman is initiated in secret ceremonies in the menstrual hut forbidden to all males (cf. Godelier 1982a:74ff.). Males, by contrast, do not "naturally" mature as fast or as competently. Womb blood and maternal care not only hold them back but endanger their health. Males cannot attain puberty or other secondary sex-traits (e.g., facial hair, mature penis) without semen.

And their bodies, their semen organs (*keriku-keriku*), do not internally produce semen, Sambia believe. Therefore they require inseminations and magical ritual treatments of various kinds over many years to "catch up" with females and become strong, manly men (for details, see Herdt 1980, 1981, 1982a, 1982b).

Male development and masculinization after childhood are the responsibility of the men's secret cult and its initiation system. This cult is organized and perpetuated by the confederacy of hamlets. Boys are initiated at seven to ten years of age, when they are separated from their mothers, natal households, and younger siblings. Thereafter, they must avoid all females for many years while living in the men's house. Avoidance taboos are rigidly enforced with shaming, beatings, and ultimately death (the last used to keep boys from revealing ritual secrets). Males undergo six initiations in all over the next ten or fifteen years. First initiation (*moku*) graduates are called *choowinuku;* second-stage initiation (*imbutu*) occurs between ages eleven and thirteen; and third-stage initiation (*ipmangwi*), bachelorhood puberty rites, is for youths fourteen to sixteen years of age. These initiations are all done in sequence on large groups of boys who become age-mates. They are from neighboring hamlets, thus making them members of a regional cohort. Initiates also become members of a warriorhood, which has local units responsible for defending their own hamlets. Fourth-stage initiation (*nuposha*) may occur anytime afterward. It is a public marriage ceremony, associated with secret male rites and sexual teachings for individual youths, to whom a woman has been assigned for their marriage. Fifth-stage initiation (*taiketnyi*) occurs when a man's wife has her menarche. The bride then has her secret initiation in the menstrual hut. Afterward, the couple can engage in coitus. The final, sixth-stage initiation (*moondangu*), is held when a man's wife bears her first child. She then undergoes a final women's secret ceremony too. Two children bring full adult manhood (*aatmwunu*) and personhood for both sexes.

The men's secret cult is ideally organized as a social hierarchical system according to ritual rank. Initiates are lumped into ritual categories: *kuwatni'u* is a category term for first- and second-stage prepubescent initiates (who may also be referred to as *choowinuki* or *imbutnuku,* ritual-grade titles); *ipmangwi* (or *moongenyu,* "new bamboo") bachelors are third-stage initiates of higher adolescent status. Pubescent bachelors dominate prepubescent initiates; older youths and young married men dominate them; and elders are seen as politically and spiritually superordinate over everyone (Herdt 1982*b*). War leaders and shamans lead in fights and healing ceremonies, respectively. There is nothing unique about this kind of ritual system, for many similar forms can be found in Eastern Highlands (e.g., Read 1952), Papuan Gulf (e.g., Williams 1936*a*), and Telefomin (e.g., Barth 1975) societies. What is special, and what links Sambia and their Anga neighbors with Papuan lowland systems (e.g., Keraki, Kiwai Island, Marind-anim), is the widescale institutionalization of homosexual activities.

Sambia practice secret homosexual fellatio, which is taught and instituted in first-stage initiation. Boys learn to ingest semen from older youths through oral sexual contacts. First- and second-stage initiates may only serve as fellators; they are forbidden to reverse erotic roles with older partners. Third-stage pubescent bachelors and older youths thus act as fellates, inseminating prepubescent boys. All males pass through both erotic stages, being first fellators, then fellateds: there are no exceptions since all Sambia males are initiated and pressured to engage in homosexual fellatio.

The symbolism of the first homosexual teachings in initiation is elaborate and rich; the meaning of fellatio is related to secret bamboo flutes, and ritual equations are made between flutes, penis, and mother's breast, and between semen and breast milk (see Herdt 1982*a*, for a detailed analysis). Boys must drink semen to grow big and strong. At third-stage initiation, bachelors may experience personal difficulty in making the erotic switch in roles. Thereafter, they may continue having oral sex with boys until they father children. Essentially, youths pass from an exclusively homosexual behavioral period to a briefer bisexual period, during which they may have both homosexual and heterosexual contacts in secret, and finally to exclusive heterosexual relationships. Social and sexual failures in masculine personhood may be defined as the failure to achieve these transitions (Herdt 1980).

SUBJECT AND OBJECTS

For the Sambia, who ritualize obligatory homosexual practices on a broad scale, it may be said that two forms of sexual behavior characterize their culture and developmental experience. For males, first sexual contacts are secret, transitional, male/male oral sexual behaviors; for adult males and females, the parallel form is initial male/female oral (i.e., the woman is fellator) sex in marriage. Later, heterosexual genital contacts occur. To my knowledge, no other form of sexual behavior occurs, including masturbation to orgasm. The rules and norms surrounding these two sexual modes are, in certain respects, both similar and different; I shall describe them below. But in both cases, semen acquisition is an imperative organizing principle of people's social interactions and sexual behavior. Its magical power does things to people, changing and rearranging them, as if it were a generator. They, however, can do little to affect this semen principle: it does not reflect on them, but merely passes through them as an electrical current through a wire, winding its way into bodies as generator coils for temporary storage. Because it is instrumental to growth, reproduction, and regeneration, sperm (and its substitutes) is needed to spark and mature human life. Humans are its objects.

This view may seem upside-down to us, yet it is essential as a rational outcome of the Sambia point of view. By thus beginning with its novelty, we may hope to achieve a better understanding of the relative relationship between heterosexuality and homosexuality, subjects about which we Westerners assume so much. I will first examine cultural ideas about semen, and then study how these ideas influence sociological types of semen transactions, between males and males, and males and females. Taken together, these ideas and social transactions form a system of objects of the predicate semen. Though these two perspectives are conceptually distinct, their complementarity suggests how normative goals affect individual social action and the developmental cycle of the group. When we view all of the valuations based on this predicate, we are led to a systemic view of the structuring (but not the experience) of sexual interactions and eroticism in Sambia culture. It is essential to stress that semen predicates two different sorts of relationships: *direct sexual transactions* between semen donors and recipients, either on the individual or group level (in the latter sense, I am speaking normatively); and *indirect semen transactions* that affect changes in a third party via the semen recipient, who is believed to serve as a transformer of sperm (e.g., father to mother to baby). The concept "transformer" compares with Meigs's (1976) use of "transmitter," in which she argues that a person's body may store or deliver fluids (e.g., blood or semen) or essences to someone else. "Transformer" differs because of another dimension needed, transformation, that is, *changing* semen into something else, as medieval alchemists were thought to change lead into gold. I will later disentangle these levels of description and analysis.

CULTURAL IDEAS OF SEMEN VALUE

Sambia have five main cultural categories of semen valuation. These include erotic play, procreation, growth, strength, and spirituality, all of which are connected with sexual behavior. The metaphoric and analogical uses in rhetoric and imagination of these categories can be found in other domains, too (see Herdt 1981). Here, though, I shall explore their social significance

for insemination.[2] The study of these categories will involve us in understanding how persons (and in some ways, nonhuman entities) are represented as potential semen donors or recipients, transformers, or transmitters of semen value, in Sambia culture. This section is concerned with the cultural level of these concepts.[3]

There are two analytic senses in which I shall use the term *value*. First, the anthropological sense of conventional valuations in a culture: attributed or assumed meanings shared and assigned to persons, institutions, and substances. Thus we can speak of the cultural regard for semen and the social esteem with which it thus endows persons and relationships. (There is also a libidinal value, present in conscious and unconscious thought, which will not concern us.[4]) Second, there is the Marxist sense of the value of a commodity, such as gold, which "when impressed upon products, obtains fixity only by reason of their acting and reacting upon each other as quantities of value" (Marx 1977:248).[5]

[2]These cultural categories cross-cut various symbolic domains and social arenas, such as taboos (*kumaaku*), ritual (*pweiyu*), food sharing, myth, etc. One certainly could abstract from action and rhetoric the normative and metaphoric operations of these categories (cf. Wagner 1967, 1972). As I indicate below, sexual interaction is a conscious, although not always marked, frame for acting and speaking among Sambia, but I cannot here provide a complete description of all its manifestations.

[3]See Herdt 1981 for conceptual models. This essay considers mainly the male viewpoint, and it is not meant to be a complete cultural analysis, by any means.

[4]Sambia tend to treat and think of semen as an energy force in individuals and society which may be compared, by direct analogy, to Freud's concept of libido. The analogy is apt in several ways: this energy force circulates through others (e.g., as subjects) who may be taken in (e.g., as objects) via semen or its equivalents (mother's milk); and it can be dammed up or released—the imagery of the hydraulic model is apt (cf. Heider 1979:78–79, who thinks otherwise). We could also distinguish, following Federn (1952), between subject-libido (energy available to self qua subject) and object-libido (energy available for investment in objects). Technically, I think, semen as a symbol among Sambia is used narcissistically (object-libido invested in ego is narcissistic libido) in self/other interactions.

[5]My use of the terms *commodity* and *fetishization* are not meant to indicate a homology with Marx's usage, which was tied, of course, to the specific analysis of capitalist production, characterized by the production of commodities that emerge in a market economy. By analogy, though, these terms are useful for my analysis. Marx broadly argued that the results of human activity transform resources into items of use-value, which are assigned an exchange value by society (see my conclusion below); the worker's time is overshadowed by the

Hence, we can analyze semen as a scarce resource that can be consumed and produced, "conserved," "invested," or otherwise "spent." Persons and relationships may be valuated (as a means to an end) in regard to their status as donors or recipients of the commodity semen.

In Sambia sexuality, there are several tacit assumptions underlying the relation between semen and the categories examined below, and I begin with them. (1) Semen is the most precious human fluid. Because it is believed vital for procreation and growth and is in short supply, sperm is more precious than mother's milk, its closest cultural equivalent. But precious does not necessarily mean powerful: menstrual blood is the logical antithesis of semen, it is dangerous and, in some rituals, is equally as efficacious as semen (Herdt 1982b; cf. Faithorn 1975). (2) Sambia are by character prudish people (may I refer to them as "prudish lechers"? cf. Meggitt 1964). Semen, other fluids, and sexuality are sensitive subjects: the data and viewpoints described below took years to assimilate, even though the presentation makes my analysis seem easy. (3) Sexual pleasure is seen by Sambia only in relation to another person; that is, there is no equivalent to the Western narcissistic category "sex" (used in relation to masturbation, pornography, etc. as an indefinite noun, e.g., "sex is . . .

good, bad, fun, boring," etc.). Sex, in the Sambia sense, is only spoken of as: *duvuno* (pushing or penetrating into) a boy's mouth or a woman's vagina; or as the slackening of one's erect penis (lit., *laakelu mulu*, "penis fight") via "his bamboo orifice" (metaphor for boy's mouth) or "her thing down below" (euphemism for vagina). Again, the verb *duvuno* is not used for masturbation and only rarely for wet dreams in which the dream images concern copulating with persons (e.g., interpreted as spirits).[6] (4) When men refer to erotic desire (e.g., "I swallow my saliva [thinking about sex] with him/her") they tend to refer to their sexual outlets as if their alters' orifice (mouth or vagina) were fetishized objects like a commodity (i.e., they use "food" as a metaphor for their sexual needs). (5) All sexual intercourse may be defined as either work (*wumdu*) or play (*chermonyi*) or both. For example: it is *wumdu* to produce a baby by copulating with a woman many times; but it is *chemonyi* to promiscuously copulate with a boy once or twice knowing he will not procreate. Insemination is also an action that mediates (e.g., like ritual, *pweiyu*) between work and play, sacred and profane. Let us examine each category in turn.

EROTIC PLAY

When Sambia use *chemonyi* (play) as an adjective in relation to sexual intercourse, they normatively refer to sexual release as erotic pleasure.* Semen is expended and orgasm (*im-*

---

supreme importance attached to the commodity, a process through which the capitalist extracts surplus labor as profit. The Sambia, however, acknowledge semen to be a result of social relationships of production (e.g., as in marriage bonds), and they tend also to stress the importance of semen as a fluid that can transform resources into more useful reproductive items or characteristics (e.g., babies, warrior strength). Nonetheless, the way in which men fetishize semen as a circulating commodity has a mystifying effect upon these social relationships of production: they deny women's essential part in the reproductive process and claim final biological development in boys is achieved only through insemination. This mystification of the total reproductive process thus enables men to extract from others the resources needed to sustain and expand themselves and their clans, and to control the related scarce resources in relation to women. Finally, I do not mean to imply by use of these terms that other Melanesian groups, or even all (RH) societies, use semen as a key resource in the same way as Sambia, or that they fetishize it as a commodity in their systems of circulation in order to reproduce social entities. Elements or fluids such as semen and blood clearly have variable significance in Melanesian societies; our separable analyses of them must, in a certain sense, renegotiate their meaning in each cultural system.

[6]For instance, Sambia do not use *duvuno* in reference to masturbation, their term for which means "peeling away the glans from penis." Genital rubbing, in the limited sense (not necessarily erotic) of stimulation of the genitals, occurs; I have seen children do it, boys sometimes do it to bachelors (to produce erections for fellatio), and men sometimes report doing it to themselves in preparation for coitus with their wives. But what they *mean* is self-stimulation without ejaculation. This conceptual distinction is important and should not be misunderstood. Spilling one's own seed not only makes no sense to Sambia, it does not seem erotically exciting for them. Their fantasy life and erotic scripting have no place for it, an argument I will pursue elsewhere.

*There is no marked category for erotic play as such: it is signified in ideology and social intercourse by *chemonyi,* "orgasm," and several conditions of sexual excitement (e.g., erection). The term *sexual* has a wide range of connotations in English; *erotic,* however, refers specifi-

bimboogu) achieved. I begin with this category not because it is most crucial—Sambia themselves would rank procreation first (Herdt 1981)—but because it is essential for understanding semen valuations, and also because anthropologists often ignore erotic motivation as a native category.

The most general cultural attributes of erotic play may be sketched as follows. First, the factor of the sex of one's partner: erotic play symbolically typifies male/male sexual contacts more than male/female contacts. Male/male sexual contacts are culturally defined as behaviorally promiscuous. Male/female contacts, normative only in marriage, are viewed (unless adulterous) as steady transactions aimed toward procreation. Erotic play is of course an aspect of all male/female contacts, but it is not their most important one. *Exclusive* sexual access to a person seems inversely related to erotic play: a man's wife, as his sexual property, as Sambia see it, is less exciting than a boy or woman taken at first (i.e., as a virgin), or only once, on the sly. Age is a contributing factor here: sexual partners are perceived as having more "heat" and being more exciting the younger they are. A second factor is reciprocity: the more asymmetrical the sexual partners (youth/boy), the more erotic play seems to culturally define their contact. (By contrast, I have argued elsewhere that the husband/wife dyad is the most symmetrical relationship in Sambia culture; see Herdt 1982*b*.) Third, sexual constancy, that is, greater frequency of sexual contacts, generally transforms sexual contacts from erotic play into something else. Husband/wife contacts are the most constant in Sambia sexual life.

Erotic play may be defined also according to the social purpose of insemination. Erotic pleasure is attached to male/male and male/female sexual contacts, and to both oral and vaginal intercourse.* But only heterosexual genital contacts re-

sult in procreation; all other sexual contacts fulfill other quasi-reproductive functions (e.g., growth of spouse) or are for erotic play. Since homosexual fellatio cannot eventuate in reproduction (consummation of marriage), it becomes a demonstration of a fellated's psychosocial maturity, that is, of his power to masculinize a boy. But this valuation is of significance for *donors,* whereas boy-recipients highly value semen for "growth." What donors value also is the fellator's mouth as a sexual outlet: the social purpose is sexual release.

Erotic play may be defined, lastly, according to the flow of a scarce commodity. Semen is viewed as a very scarce resource by Sambia, for, in the reproductive process, it is believed instrumental from conception to adulthood. It takes many inseminations to procreate: large expenditures of time, energy, semen. From this viewpoint, all male/female contacts may be construed as benefiting procreation (see below). Homoerotic play unevenly fits this paradigm. It is, after all, play, not work: procreative work is defined as producing babies. So how do they benefit the donor? Essentially, homoerotic play is culturally defined as an unequal exchange of commodities: recipients acquire semen, donors get sexual services. This exchange is unequal because (as Sambia see it) a man's sperm is being depleted, but he gets only erotic pleasure in return ("which is insubstantial"). Homoerotic activity thus creates a dilemma for bachelors, which is perhaps why some engage in it less frequently as they approach marriage. Homoerotic play is, however, less depleting than heterosexual intercourse (work) which is, in part, why bachelors usually do not replenish the semen "lost" during their early homosexual activities.

PROCREATION

Procreation is defined as genital-to-genital heterosexual contacts that lead to the birth of offspring. Sambia regard vaginal intercourse as primarily focused on the production of babies. Oral

cally to that which stimulates sexual desire and psychophysiological arousal, so I prefer *erotic* in this usage. I shall not attempt to describe sexual excitement here, but see Stoller and Herdt (n.d.).

*All sexual contacts are symbolically defined against the norm of penetration and ejaculation into an insertee's mouth (initiate or woman) or vagina, insemination resulting from (the belief that) the full seminal

emission is ingested/absorbed by the recipient's body (mouth or vagina is entrance).

insemination prepares a wife's body for making babies by "strengthening" her, as well as by precipitating her menarche (if she has not already attained it). Fellatio also prepares her for lactation by semen being transformed into breast milk. Oral sexual contacts are not believed to make babies in anyone; only vaginal intercourse does that. All heterosexual genital intercourse contributes directly to procreation in one's own marriage, and *all* sexual contacts may be viewed as contributing directly to the recipients' procreative competence (wife or boy-fellator) or reproduction (wife).*

Procreation is jurally defined as resulting from genital-to-genital sexual contacts between formally married husband and wife. Since heterosexual contact is not morally or jurally allowed outside of marriage, privilege of sexual access to a woman's body is restricted by marriage; exclusive sexual rights belong to her husband. Likewise, exclusive access to a husband's body and semen, after birth of their first child, is his wife's right (which view is a key argument women use to resist polygyny). Traditionally, only infant betrothal and bride-service marriage (which was rare) required the transfer of goods or services to the donors bestowing a wife. Infant betrothal, though, required meat and small food prestations only, whereas bride-service required more wealth, in addition to the bridegroom's years'-long work for his prospective affines. Sister exchange requires no exchanges other than that of the women. Since infant betrothal is preferred, and sister exchange marriages far outnumber those of bride-service, marriage transactions are not much related to bride-wealth in its usual anthropological sense (cf. Collier and Rosaldo 1981). The "wealth" exchanged (e.g., meat prestations) is largely produced through the labors of hunting by the wife-receivers.

Genital-to-genital intercourse creates a fetus by successively injecting semen into a woman's womb. After initial oral sexual contacts, a woman's body is viewed as ready to procreate. One

instance of vaginal intercourse does not a fetus make: Sambia have no notion of conception in our Western scientific sense. The womb is the container and transformer of semen. It changes the sperm into fetal tissue: primarily bone and skin, but also muscle and internal organs. The semen coagulates inside the birth sac; this "biological" process is central to fetal development, and its imagery is important in social thought (Herdt 1981:167–172ff.). Womb and umbilical blood also become circulatory blood in the fetus; they do not produce any other parts of the child, which result only from semen. Social ideology thus defines procreation as productive work (not erotic play) in two senses: it is hard work to feed enough semen into a woman's womb to create a fetus; and it is hard work for the woman's body to change this sperm into a fetus, sapping her own blood, and carrying the child in her body for so long.

Blood and semen also differentially contribute to the sex of the offspring and his or her gender differentiation. First, both parents can magically influence the fetus's sex by ingesting various plants. They do this both because Sambia ideally prefer a boy as the firstborn and because they want to make the infant more attractive. Second, it takes more semen to create a girl than a boy. Two other beliefs explain why, and they pertain to the procreative/economic productive capacities of males versus females (i.e., in social reproduction). The most important is that females do more hard work (i.e., garden work) all the time; therefore, the female fetus "pulls" more semen from the mother to make itself. (A magical elaboration of this idea is that since females think about garden work constantly, their fetal thought anticipates and drains more "semen strength" in preparation.) The other belief is that a female fetus has a *tingu* (menstrual-blood organ), which makes the mother's vagina "hot," and therefore drains off more semen from the father during sexual contacts that create the fetus. During womb life, the sexes receive blood in differential amounts too. Essentially, girls have some of their mother's menstrual blood transmitted to their own menstrual-blood

---

*Oral heterosexual contacts indirectly help procreation; see below under section on "growth."

organs *in utero.* Later, during postnatal growth, this blood stimulates girls' psychobiological feminization (sexual and gender differentiation). Boys, by contrast, have no blood transmitted to their inactive tingus. Nor do they receive any of their father's semen for use in their own semen organs: father's semen in both sexes merely creates fetal tissue. (Mystical aspects of these fetal processes are described below.)

Marriage is fully consummated after the birth of a child. Procreation results in final but distinct initiation ceremonies for the husband-father and wife-mother alike. The new father and his clan bestow a meat prestation on the wife's cognatic kin, especially patrilateral female kin, and her ritual sponsor, in public village ceremonies. Because procreation defines full adulthood for men and women, childless adults are not perceived as full persons. Nonetheless, all childlessness in a marriage is attributed to barrenness in the woman or contraceptive sorcery by other men (usually thought to be envious fellow villagers who wanted the woman for themselves). Sambia men dogmatically deny the possibility of sterility in a husband (see also Read 1951); indeed, such is never discussed in social discourse, and the only category for sterility is "barren woman" (*kwoliku*). Childlessness is thus an acceptable reason for taking a second wife, but not for divorce. Once a marriage is consummated, it is contracted for life and cannot be broken: a woman is rarely taken back by the donor group; when warfare occurs, a woman's ties with her natal group (i.e., enemies) are severed; divorce is thus extremely rare and usually instigated by a husband over his wife's perceived adultery; their children become jural members of the father's clan; and so only death breaks the marital bond.

Growth

Sambia believe that biological growth in humans results from ingestion of semen and several equivalent substances (mother's milk, pandanus nuts). Sexual intercourse for growth is de-scribed as: *pinu pungooglumonjapi* ("pushing" to "grow" he/she, where *pinu* is an alternate verbal form of *duvuno*). This idiomatic form may be applied to both male/male and male/female sexual contacts.

The value of semen for human growth comes in successive stages which differ according to the mode of semen transmission and one's sex. Initial growth for every fetus occurs through semen accumulations in the mother's womb. Postnatal growth in babies results mainly from breast-feeding. A woman's body is again treated as a biological transformer of semen in this regard: a man's inseminations (especially oral) amass in and are transformed by his wife's breasts into mother's milk (*nu-tokeno,* breast food). Mother's milk is vital for the baby's growth. After breast-weaning, growth in early childhood is aided by eating pandanus nuts, which are seasonal but are treated as nearly equal nourishment to that of mother's milk. (The productive source of this nut food is one's father's trees and his "hard work" in tending and scaling them to procure the nuts.) Meat fed to children also contributes smaller increments to growth. Following weaning, though, girls continue to grow without further aids, whereas boys falter, staying weak and puny.

Male growth after weaning comes mostly from homosexual inseminations following initiation. This semen-nourishment form is male *monjapi'u,** which men liken to breast-feeding (Herdt 1981:234–236). Oral sexual contacts feed semen into a boy's body, distributing sperm to his maturing skin, bones, skull, and producing changes toward masculinization (i.e., eventuating in biological puberty). The bulk of externally ingested semen goes to the boy's semen organ, where it accumulates as a "pool." This pool is drawn on after puberty for two purposes: it produces pubescent secondary sex-traits, especially musculature, hairiness on the body, and the development of a mature penis; and it provides semen for later sexual contacts. (The first sign of

---

*Shortened by men from *pinu pungooglumonjapi.*

surplus semen in the body comes from seminal emissions in wet dreams.)

Girls require and are permitted no inseminations until marriage. Men believe that postmarital oral sexual contacts in cases of marriage before menarche provide a young wife's body with semen to stimulate the final "growth" changes necessary for childbearing. They also argue, as noted above, that women need semen to create breast milk. (Some women dispute these views and argue that a woman's body "naturally" creates breast milk; however, other women disagree with them on this matter.)

In sum, semen creates biological growth directly in initiates and wives through sexual contact, primarily fellatio, whereas it creates growth indirectly in fetus and newborn through being transformed by a woman's body into fetal tissue and milk. For the spouses, then, growth and procreation are concepts that refer to different aspects of the same sexual contacts. For the offspring, as third-party semen recipient, postnatal growth is vital after birth, and long postpartum taboos prohibit marital sexual intercourse for fear the infant will be harmed (be stunted or ugly, an outcome that would shame the parents, especially the father, who would be viewed as lacking sexual restraint). In homoerotic activity, men offer boys the normative goal that semen "grows" them. But from the donor's standpoint, although initiates' growth does provide vicarious (because of homosexual promiscuity) long-term confirmation of the fellated's manhood, a fellator's growth is not of direct importance to a bachelor's personhood. Rather, homoerotic play takes precedence as the fellated's motive; the boy's growth is a latent social function of the bachelor's behavior (and is, I think, largely a rationalization on the men's part).

STRENGTH

Strength (*jerungdu*) is a key concept in Sambia culture; we shall here examine only its implications for semen transmission and thereby human maturation.

Strength is absolutely derived from semen and its symbolic equivalents, mother's milk and pandanus nuts. But more than those latter substances, semen masculinizes a person's body; there is no substitute for it. Unlike procreation or growth valuations, strength can be obtained directly only through semen. In Sambia thought, there is a general tendency to play down strength and stress growth as characteristic of the breast-feeding relationship. Suckling milk definitely grows a baby, but it is much less associated with strengthening it. Sperm in the womb forms the skeletal fetus; nursing helps create the baby's teeth, the hardening of its skin and skull. But milk is more for growth. The "strong" results of milk, Sambia believe, are transformations of semen: mother ingests sperm, which her breasts convert into milk. The "strong" part of milk is also more crucial for male infants, but it alone will not masculinize them. Thus, in analytic terms, strength is not intrinsically produced but is rather derived from the mother/infant relationship, itself a product of marriage. In male Sambia terms, however, strength is a transactional product that makes use of the father's secret sexual acquisition of semen from other men, which he feeds to his wife, whose body, in turn, has a "natural" capacity to store the fluid and turn it into breast food that strengthens and matures the infant.

As with growth, a father can indirectly add small amounts of strength over the years following weaning by providing meat and pandanus nuts to children. Cassowary meat, too, which may be eaten only by males, has fat (*moo-nugu*) that sometimes is treated as a second-rate semen equivalent (Herdt 1981:110). (Other kinds of fat, e.g., from pigs or eels, are never likened to semen.) But these are small increments.

If one follows the semen cycle, we see a chain of links in which men strengthen persons: husband strengthens wife through initial fellatio; father strengthens baby through mother's milk; bachelor strengthens initiate through fellatio. Symbolically, homosexual fellatio provides the key ritualized strengthening of boys' postpartum bodies. As I have emphasized elsewhere (Herdt 1981, 1982*a*), fellatio insemination is chiefly seen as growing a boy, the perceived outcome of which is strength. Culturally, the act of feeding/inseminating is equivalent to the verbal category *monjapi'u*, male nursing, the social/perceptual outcome of which is the state of being *jerungdu*, as seen in both its physical and psychosocial manifestations: large size, attractiveness, valor, forceful speech, sexual potency, and many social achievements, including progeny.

There is another secret source of strength that is important in male thought and which concerns the nonhuman sources for the replenishment of semen expended in sexual intercourse. Analytically, this semen valuation might be treated as separate from the "strength" concept because of its ontogenetic status in the male life cycle (adults give semen away and then must replace it to stay strong). But Sambia do not think of the matter in this way, for this replenishment is seen simply as a further extension of strength-building. Yet, since this replenishment practice is learned later in ritual life, and comes from trees, not men, we shall here examine it as an auxiliary replacement process.

In semen transactions, one person's loss is someone else's gain: semen, which embodies strength, depletes the donor, whose strength therefore diminishes. Fear of semen depletion is an important theme in male ritual discourse and ideology. (It is registered, too, in individual gender aberrations; Herdt 1980.) Concern with too frequent semen loss is an inhibitor of initial homosexual contacts, bachelors being cautioned to go easy. (Here, again, fellateds and fellators are at odds.) Yet bachelors' fears are not great; and the early use of ritual mechanisms for semen replenishment in fellateds is played down. Among married men, the situation is quite different. A key pragmatic focus of fifth- and sixth-stage initiation ceremonies is teaching about secret ingestion of white milk-sap from trees, which is believed to replace semen "lost" to women. (Pandanus nuts are another semen replacement, though of lesser importance because

they not always available.) This milk-sap comes from a variety of wild forest trees and vines, and the sap is referred to as *iaamoonaalyu*, "tree mother's milk."

Trees are, in general, regarded as if they and their products were primarily of the female sex, e.g., as with pandanus trees. And myth also genderizes them this way (Herdt 1981). Thus, there seems little doubt that the imagery and symbolization of the adult man's semen replenishment is not, then, symbolic insemination, but rather that of symbolic breast-feeding. This interpretation is confirmed by their drinking of sap from long aerial roots of pandanus nut trees: the trees are ritually referred to as "females," and the roots are likened to "women's breasts." We see, therefore, that semen comes initially from homosexual fellatio, which can later be replaced by milk-sap (and, to a lesser extent, by pandanus nuts and cassowary fat); and semen, in turn, is transformed into breast milk and fetal tissue by women. At rock bottom, male ideology seems to postulate that these forest trees create *new* semen.

SPIRITUALITY

The final category of semen valuations I shall refer to as spirituality, though it is not a marked category in Sambia culture or language. Spirituality is, in our terms, an animistic composite of both natural and supernatural elements. These elements include most noticeably spirit familiars (*numelyu*) of various sorts, believed to be *transmitted* (not transformed) through semen for males (and through blood for females). The reproduction of spiritual elements in persons and groups is entirely a social outcome of sexual intercourse over which individuals have little control.

Before describing familiars, two other matters deserve mention. The first is the concept of soul (*koogu*), a spiritual aspect of personhood that is related to sexuality and parenting. There is no clearly formulated theory of the soul's origin in individual development. Some men attribute it only to the father's sperm. Others say it is a combination of semen and material in the mother's womb (they do not specify which parts of semen and/or blood). Though the womb is important, some people attribute the birth of a child's soul not to fetal life but to postnatal socialization. Men normatively relate the father's sperm to the child's soul in both sexes, especially in boys. This ambiguity is no doubt an expression of all persons' normative blood ties to mother and matrilateral kin. Yet, since the soul survives death and becomes a ghost, forest spirit (big men), or hamlet spirit (prominent women) haunting its clan's territory, its patrilineal origin and afterlife influence seem clear in sociopolitical organization. The skull and bones of the deceased also become powerful weapons in sorcery and are most efficacious when used by biological kinsmen, sons especially. In both cases—souls and bones—spiritual essences of semen are thought to survive death. The other concept is "thought" or *koontu,* which I gloss as personhood. "Thought" is the totality of one's experience, beliefs, and knowledge. Personhood is mainly a product of social training; its relation to body substance and biological inheritance is less certain. Socialization is its chief source, however, and this means that both mother and father influence personhood. (The ritual negation of maternal influences on boys' personhood is addressed by the process I have called "accountability"; Herdt n.d.)

Without question the most significant semen valuation for spirituality is the child's inheritance of spirit familiars. Transmission of familiars is ideologically clear and sex-linked. Boys inherit only their father's familiars via his semen. Girls inherit their mother's familiars through her blood. (Mother's milk, a semen derivative, is ignored in this domain.) Genealogical inheritance of clan familiars (i.e., totems) among males seems to derive from the semen that creates a son's body tissue. Later, males acquire other familiars attracted to them through ritual ceremonies: the nature of this attraction

again implies that father's semen is instrumental. Shamanic familiars, transmitted through semen from father to son in the mother's womb, is a clear case of necessary patrilineal inheritance required for legitimate performance of the shamanic role (Herdt 1977). Other familiars, both personal and clan-related, ensure longevity, spiritual protection, or strength. Male ideology generally denies women such blessings from their natal clan familiars. Men may have their familiars "stolen" unwittingly by male children, which leads to sickness or premature death. Homosexual inseminations do not transmit familiars to semen recipients (cf. Schieffelin 1976, 1977). Finally, men's ingestion of milk sap from trees is consistent with the perpetuation of their clan familiars (though this idea is not fully conscious in Sambia thought). We shall return to these points below.

SEMEN "VALUE" IN SOCIAL TRANSACTIONS

Who may and should have sexual intercourse with what categories of persons in Sambia society? What are the principles of these social transactions? In this section I examine social action in relation to the cultural ideas of semen valuation already described. The sociology of semen transactions involves two viewpoints. First, there are *direct* semen transactions between persons resulting from sexual intercourse. Second, there are *indirect* semen transactions with a third party believed to occur by the transformation of sperm into something else by a second party; whether the source of semen is human or nonhuman (i.e., trees), however, the semen transformers are always humans. A subcategory of indirect inseminations may be seen as *delayed exchanges* between social groups, semen being returned to donor groups via former recipients in the subsequent generation. I will study each of these types in turn.

DIRECT SEMEN TRANSACTIONS

All sexual contacts are restricted by exogamous taboos and social norms. Sexual contacts are permissible only between unrelated people; that is, those related through common cognatic links, especially agnates, are forbidden sexual partners. Marriage should be arranged between different clans, preferably of different villages. Statistically, though, up to 50 percent of all marriages are contracted within certain hamlets; FZD marriage is normatively permitted in delayed-exchange marriage contracts; and MBD marriage, though frowned upon, occurs rarely when no alternate wife can be found (Herdt 1981). Homosexual contacts are likewise prohibited between all clansmen, matrilateral kin, age-mates, and with ritual sponsors. (Homosexual infractions occur, however, as between matrilateral cross-cousins, or distant kin not normally encountered, though these are unusual.) Male initiates' ritual sponsors are called "mother's brother," a social title, since only some sponsors are actual or classifactory mother's brother. Nonetheless a boy's sponsor becomes, in effect, a pseudokinsman who combines both maternal and paternal attributes, making it very wrong for any sexual contact to occur between them. In general, all sexual contacts are highly regulated and tend to occur with people of other hamlets (who are potential or real enemies), so sexual contacts distinguish kin from nonkin, and friendly from hostile persons.

In direct sexual transactions, all the above cultural ideas of semen value come into play, but the domain of erotic play is especially important. Erotic play is a social motive and goal that applies mainly to adult men. Their motive for erotic play is sexual release, that is, orgasm. Boy-fellators never have orgasms in homoerotic play. And men deny, in general, that women experience orgasm, though they believe women are lascivious and that some enjoy sexual play.

Men's enjoyment of erotic play changes through the life cycle. Some older boy-fellators do experience vicarious erotic pleasure from homosexual fellatio, as indicated by their reports (near puberty) of their own erections while fellating a bachelor, or by certain feelings or body sensations during fellation. Bachelors (fellateds) engage in homoerotic play to (in local idiom) "straighten their penises," that is, to reduce sexual tension/frustration, or to "feel *ilaiyu*" (here meaning pleasure) from orgasm. Men get erotic pleasure from copulating with their wives, first through fellatio, and then in genital-to-genital intercourse, which most men favor over fellatio. To reiterate: male/female oral sexual contacts, like those with boys, are regarded more as erotic play.

Male social ideology defines both homoerotic and heteroerotic play as transactions in which the older male is *always* the inseminator. No role reversals are ever situationally permitted. The older male is viewed as the socially active party who should control the behavior interchanges that lead to the insemination. A man's control over sexual contacts is established by the social norms regulating the behavioral conditions of sexual intercourse. Men are physically bigger than boys and most women. During intercourse the man either stands over his fellator (who kneels) or lays on top of his wife (in the "missionary" position), methods that allow a man instant freedom to withdraw from body contact at will. Men are also usually years older than their insertees, either boys or women (even though men curiously regard younger wives as of like age and maturity; see Herdt 1981:177, 181). Again, these interactions are defined as asymmetrical: women and boys get semen, men get erotic pleasure. Most men are (consciously) uninterested in the erotic arousal of either boys or women, so direct sexual transactions emphasize the sexual excitement of the inserter.

In spite of the men's view, the concept erotic play admits of some social reciprocity between all sexual partners. Men grudgingly recognize that women have erotic interests; for instance, sexually experienced wives are rhetorically described as lascivious harlots consumed by insatiable erotic appetites (Herdt 1981:187). Perhaps this dogma is the men's response to knowing that women favor certain men over others as mates. Men also know that boys joke about fellatio among themselves and that initiates favor some bachelors over others in regard to the amount and taste of their semen.[7] Bachelors likewise favor certain boys over others: those who are more attractive to them are either more or less sexually aggressive and/or willing to perform fellatio. These reciprocal aspects thus underscore the frame of play, and they are not found in notions of sex for procreation, growth, strength, or spirituality, all of which are merely passive outcomes of insemination as a one-way street.

Since semen is highly valued as a means to valuable social ends—personal strength, marriage, offspring, personhood—it should be conserved and wisely spent. Men assume that women and boys *desire their semen* for those social ends; no other motive is searched for in understanding why insertees engage in sexual intercourse. (*We* know the situation is more complex: for instance, boys must at first be coerced into fellatio; but men also "know" this.) The seeming personal conflict on men's part, at least in homosexual contacts, is that *they get only sexual release in return for their sperm.* They recognize this in idioms that depict the penis as having a mind of its own: for example, "that no good man down there [penis] gets up and we follow its nose [euphemism for glans penis]." Meaning: men inseminate from sexual impulse, almost against their own will. Here, then, we may see a perceived conflict between private impulses and rational norms.

This psychosocial conflict is felt in two other ways. First, women are more prized as sexual outlets than are boys. Women are *owned:* this ownership is itself a contributing dynamic to the sexual excitement of Sambia men. Male/female relationships are, in general, filled with more power than are male/male contacts, for heterosexuality is more highly regulated. Sexually, women are also more powerful, for they can contaminate as well as deplete; and women deplete semen more than do boys. Moreover, sexual impulses leading to adultery are a tremendous social problem in Sambia society (see below). Second, when orgasm occurs it is treated as being beyond conscious control. Wet dreams are the best example.[8] For women, breast-feeding may also apply: some women report that they experience *imbimboogu,* which they liken to orgasm, when feeding, although it is not clear yet what this social labelling of their experience means (see Stoller and Herdt, n.d.). All these points support the conclusion that individual sexual impulses are stronger than the social need for semen constraint in heterosexual versus homosexual contacts. They also suggest that Sambia men are later motivated more toward heterosexual relationships.

What seems to underlie this conflict is the fact that sex for erotic play is the only sexual mode that produces no social advantage to the semen donor. Because all ejaculation is potentially debilitating, and semen is a male's most valuable resource, all sexual contacts are viewed as a "careful metering of semen" (Gell 1975:252). Seen this way, erotic play represents what Gell (1975) refers to as a "nemesis of reproductivity": it makes no personal sense in the scheme of things, even though it is personally pleasurable. All other categories of direct sexual transactions may be defined as work, not play, for this reason: like other forms of work (e.g.,

---

[7]Sambia have invented an art we could call *semenology:* they are fascinated with the forms, textures, and tastes of semen, which they discuss frequently, like wine tasters. Among boys, a fellated's penis size is not accorded much importance, whereas his seminal fluid, amount of flow, etc., is. (Privately and unconsciously, though, penis size is sometimes important.) Among women, the situation seems the reverse: a man's penis size (and sexual prowess) is important—women prefer men with big penises—whereas semenology is less significant, or so say men.

[8]Sexual behavior in the imagery of dreams is viewed as erotic play: wet dreams are pleasurable but wasteful erotic play with spirits, who may wish to harm the dreamer. Breast-feeding, even though women say they experience *imbimboogu,* is not ever conceived of as erotic play by women, as far as I know, though breast-feeding is apparently a common image and form of scripting for *men's* erotic daydreams (vis-à-vis fellatio performed upon them).

gardening), sex for procreation, growth, and so forth produces social products. One's semen is spent to reproduce heirs and perpetuate one's clan. With this view in mind I will now contrast other cultural ideas pertaining to heterosexual and homosexual contacts.

The idea of procreation applies only to male/female sexual contacts. In native theory all heterosexual contacts, oral or vaginal, contribute to a woman's reproductive competence. In practice, however, only early marital contacts are treated this way: oral sex is infrequent after a woman bears children. My impression is that both men and women in later years prefer genital-to-genital contact (and I think most women always prefer vaginal sex). Though homosexual transactions are not procreative (but cf. individual boys' fears of becoming pregnant [Herdt 1981] and similar beliefs about male pregnancy elsewhere [Meigs 1976; Williams 1936c]), semen in boys does assist in their overall attainment of reproductive competence as adults.

The concepts of growth and strength are applied to both homosexual and heterosexual transactions. In theory, boy-fellators as semen recipients "use" sexual contact first to grow and then to get strong. Until third-stage initiation this norm holds; youths are thereafter accorded biological maturity and may no longer serve as insertees. (By definition, a Sambia man who sought semen from another male would be terribly stigmatized as unmanly; and to do so with a boy—pederastic fellatio—would be morally unconscionable (Herdt 1980.) Growth and strength apply differentially to women as semen recipients. Essentially, all heterosexual fellatio grows and strengthens a woman until she is a mother. Later oral sex does not grow a woman, for she is viewed as biologically mature. It does replenish her strength, however; a sort of perpetual fountain-of-youth men must give up after bachelorhood. Indeed, men complain that women are healthier and outlive them because of this constant source of orally ingested strength. (In this sense, a wife is like a boy-fellator.) Vaginal sex is generally believed to contribute neither growth nor strength

to a woman: instead, indirectly, a man's sperm grows and strengthens fetus and infant.

Finally, the concept of spirituality applies unequally to direct sexual transactions. No transmission of spirit familiars occurs between males and females. None is imparted to one's wife: she is simply *one* source of the transmission of soul and familiars to one's offspring. Again, men believe that only sons inherit father's familiars (either indirectly, through sperm via mother, or directly, through cult ceremonies that call forth one's father's familiars after his death). A daughter's familiars come only from her mother; but her soul is linked (the notion is vague) to her father and his clan territory, though not irrevocably.[9] Moreover, there is absolutely no sense that a boy-fellator acquires his familiars from any bachelor-fellated; but the idea is neither here nor there, since Sambia never seem to consider the possibility.[10] Analytically, though, we should underline that their folk model of spiritual transmission keeps familiars discreetly in clans and firmly embedded in the genitor's procreative role. Here we see a firm separation between spirituality and sexuality, on the levels both of ideology and social action. The division between spiritual and material reproduction in marriage is especially notable (cf. Tuzin 1982).

There is one other notion, which we may define as spiritual, that involves direct homosexual transactions. *Kwolaalyuwaku:** a multivalent concept referring to masculine decorations and

---

[9]However, there is ambiguity here, since a woman who lives in another hamlet (her husband's) long enough, becomes after death a ghost or hamlet spirit who may haunt there, rather than returning to her natal hamlet or clan territory. Even so, the souls of females are not a subject in which men place much interest.

[10]Cf. the Great Papuan Plateau societies, especially Kaluli (Schieffelin 1976:127f.;1982), which have institutionalized such beliefs about homosexual insemination (see also Kelly 1976; Sørum 1982). On the individual level, Sambia boys evince fantasies and beliefs that make it clear that psychological introjection and projective identification are a part of their homoerotic experience, including, for instance, notions that incorporating a fellated's semen may bestow his personality traits.

*Kwol, marks male; aalyu, water; waku, a type of strong betel nut and a cover term for certain decorations. Sometimes the term is shortened to the secret name, Kweiwaku, which men use explicitly to refer to "the semen of all men."

ritual paraphernalia (as a category term) which is also a ritual secret pseudonym for semen. (It is also close to *kweiaalyu-waku,* which literally means "sun's white grease," an alternate for cassowary fat [*kaiouwugu moo-nugu*]). The semantic referent of the semen aspect is esoteric, yet clearly signifies a collective semen pool. This pool is perceived as the semen contained in the bodies of all men living within neighboring hamlets: it therefore reflects the ritual cult and the confederacy. The idea is that boys have access to this pool, which they can tap into through homosexual insemination, strengthening themselves. Symbolically, then, *kwolaalyuwaku* is a metaphor for the men's collective cult.

But on the individual level, the concept is bidirectional. For a long time I was skeptical of men's statements that it *strengthened themselves* to inseminate many boys. How could this be? Men argue that just as a boy draws strength from numerous men, who deposit their semen in his reserve for future use, so men are kept strong by having their sperm safely contained in many boys, who are likened to a sort of magical string of semen depositories for one's substance, spread throughout society. Should a man or any of his semen recipients get sick, other recipients remain strong and healthy. And since recipients harbor parts of one's sperm (strength) inside them, so, too, one is kept healthy (in sympathetic-contagious magical thought). A woman lacks this protection: she is not a cult initiate, and her semen comes from only one man, her husband. Nor is a man likewise protected by inseminating women or creating children: the concept is not extended beyond homosexual contacts. Thus, semen not only bestows but maintains strength, the only concrete evidence known to me that explains why homosexual insemination is less depleting than that of heterosexuality. In this ritual sense, homosexual practices are placed within a spiritual framework and are opposed to heterosexuality and marriage.

All the above sexual contacts concern normatively appropriate semen transactions between donors and recipients. *Illicit* heterosexual semen

transactions (adultery) reveal the social boundary of ideas about exclusive jural claims over a man's semen. All adultery is severely condemned; a man may use violence against a wife suspected of it. Therefore, it is hidden until discovered, when the spouses fight. If a husband is accused of adultery, or of wanting to take a second wife, the fight is called *kweikoonmulu,* literally "semen fight." Semen fights entail dreadful cursing and brawls. This adultery can be seen as "stealing another woman's semen," though it involves much more, of course. Accusations of a wife's adultery (which is rarer, for Sambia treat adulterous women harshly) also concern semen in two ways: fears that a husband's penis has been contaminated by intercourse with his wife's vagina after sex with another man (thought to bring him sickness); and questions about the wife's lover's semen contributions to a future child. In sum, adultery reveals that marriage bestows the right of exclusive spousal control over semen and insemination exchange as scarce resources.

What are the social effects of these direct sexual transactions on group relationships? Let me examine the most general latent and manifest functions of sexual contacts in the same generation. First, semen flow mirrors marriage transactions between groups. Semen may only be normatively transacted between persons of groups who can intermarry, that is, homosexual contact is forbidden with matrilineal kin and clansmen. The same clan that donates a wife thus has clansmen who are appropriate homosexual partners (cf. Kelly 1976). Affines of the same generation (e.g., brothers-in-law) are especially appropriate homosexual contacts. The paradigm of this affinal homoerotic bond would be a young man who marries a younger woman and who can inseminate her younger initiate brother, either consanguineal or classificatory WiB (cf. Serpenti, 1984 and Sørum, 1984). This man manifestly inseminates his wife to grow and strengthen her, and to procreate, and may (along with his fellow clansmen) inseminate her younger brother for erotic play, the effect of which is to grow and strengthen the boy. These sexual transactions would define a man and his clan as semen donors, while his wife and brother-in-law would be recipients. Yet ego's clan is also a wife recipient from his younger homosexual partner's donor clan. This set of social transactions is common in Sambia life.

Second, marital/sexual bonds tend to create closer political ties between unrelated groups. Sambia engage in marriage and homosexual contacts only with propinquitous groups in the same confederacy. One does not receive or give semen to true, intertribal enemies. Affinal ties, in particular, create closer political affiliations for mutual defense between and within hamlets. Affinal ties also establish marriage contractual obligations and sentimental bonds that persist in the next generation, influencing alignments among hamlets.

Third, semen metaphorically defines political power: inseminators are more powerful than recipients in virtually every sense. All male persons eventually serve as both direct semen donors and as recipients. All females are always direct recipients, or indirect donors, to their offspring whereas males constitute a category of both direct givers and takers. And their sexual status, of course, flip-flops during the male life cycle. Symbolically, I think, Sambia define the administration of semen as a masculine act, whereas the taking in of semen is a feminine act. One of the manifest functions of the secrecy of homosexual fellatio is to hide from women the shame men feel at having earlier performed in this feminine way (Herdt 1981:chap. 8). A latent function of homosexual secrecy is to rationalize and disguise men's use of boys as a sexual outlet. By the same token, the ritual secret of homosexual growth and strength unites all males as a category against all females. This social link, which also mystifies the nature of male/female relationships, politically reinforces male power and thereby perpetuates the men's ritual cult (Herdt 1982b).

INDIRECT SEMEN TRANSACTIONS

This mode of social transaction is based on the symbolic principle that sperm is transmitted to someone whose body transforms it into something else useful to a third party. The paradigm is the nuclear family triad: father → mother → child. The alternative form of indirect insemination views men as replenishing their semen from tree sap, which their bodies turn into semen: tree → man → semen recipient. Having already described direct sexual contacts, these semen transformations can be easily outlined.

We have seen that sexual intercourse between spouses involves all cultural ideas of semen value except spirituality. Now when we examine the effects of her husband's semen on the prospective infant, the woman's role as transformer is clarified at two developmental points. First, as we have seen, her orally ingested sperm is specifically transformed into breast milk. This milk is stored for the infant's nourishment after birth. Subsequent semen from vaginal intercourse is stored and transformed in the woman, converted by her womb into fetal tissue, as we saw. Both the intrauterine formation of the child, as well as its postnatal breast-feeding, are indirect products of the father's sperm.

In this type of indirect transaction, there is a subtle interplay of cultural beliefs being applied. Erotic play occurs between the spouses, leading to procreation; but the concept is not extended to the transformative outcome, since the father never has sexual intercourse with his offspring. Indeed the paradigm of sex as work suggests that woman, as wife/mother, is *the means of production* man needs to effect children's adult reproductive competence. Semen is indispensable for reproduction, yet so is a woman's body (breasts and womb). Moreover, no matter how much the men's ideology attempts to claim procreation as solely their production, a wife is vital for social reproduction: she not only gives birth but nourishes and cares for heirs, transforming semen into strength. She also transmits her husband's spirit familiars to sons, and her own to daughters. Both parents contribute to the child's personhood or thought; but men believe only they produce its soul. Following weaning, a girl is believed to mature on her own, but a boy needs more semen for growth and strength. Thus, a boy indirectly taps the semen pool of his father through homosexual contacts with other men who substitute, in his father's place, as ritual semen donors, motivated out of erotic play. The sexual cycle is completed when this son becomes an inseminator, and his sister is traded for his wife, sister and brother having reached sexual maturity.

The other form of indirect transaction consists in men ingesting the white tree saps. It may seem odd, here, to juxtapose this secret ritual practice with reproduction. But Sambia male ideology treats tree-sap ingestion as a part of the whole adult cycle of reproduction; and, in my experience, men directly associate tree-sap drinking as normal and regular links in a chain of psychosexual activities that are as much a part of everyday life as their own sexuality. Drinking tree sap is not actually taught until a man's last initiation, when he is a new father. Thereafter, men regularly ingest it at various times, but always in abundance after sexual intercourse with their wives. Men are thus preserving their biological maleness (semen) and restoring their strength. Neither erotic play, growth, nor procreation as cultural ideas are applied to contacts with trees. Drinking tree sap simply regenerates semen and preserves health against depletion. So this ritual practice may be considered a defensive tactic—and the more so because it is secret—yet it is also more than that.

Drinking tree sap also has a latent creative function: the creation of *new* semen that flows into the societal pool of sperm. Sambia men do *not* view it this way: to them, drinking tree sap merely replaces what they have personally lost. But, besides that, they see their society as a "closed system," its resources limited, for a variety of reasons I shall not here detail; suffice it to say that their religion is animistic and their ethos dominated by warrior values that recognize adulthood as a personal achievement which is, nevertheless, carefully structured through a strict ritual system of norms and customs that regulate people, marriage, sexuality, and semen.

This view is predicated on a cyclical model of time (cf. Leach 1961). Seasonal movements, ceremonies, and customary transactions repeat in regular cycles. They do not recognize that their population is now expanding or that the concomitant stress on their resources (means of production) may be increasing; nonetheless, men believe that they expend sperm and that they get more from trees. Let us now consider the implications of this view for their use of the concept spirituality.

The trees from which men acquire sap are on clan territory. The land itself is one's main material inheritance from previous generations; it is held in agnatic corporate estate, though men own specific tracts of it from which they exploit resources (game, pandanus nuts, milk-sap trees). Land is coveted and defended against other groups; it is central to a clan's residential and territorial organization. It is guarded also by clan spirits. Ritual practices, too, are a social heritage, customs valued in themselves and for group identity, having been handed down from previous generations. It seems obvious, therefore, that the social ideology of trees provisioning new semen through the bodies of clansmen is a latent function of the regeneration of patrilineality.

Patrifiliation thus provides land and trees, ritual practices, and the social personae needed to transform tree sap into sperm. Tree sap without an adult male body is just tree sap. The male body—the product of a long process of procreation with outside women and homosexual insemination from outside men, of magical ritual treatment making it fertile and procreatively potent—is the instrument that regenerates society. Tree sap maintains maleness and masculine personhood. It regenerates one's clan, its patriline and hamlet-based warriorhood, and thus the community itself. These social identities are conceptually placed, in time and space, through concentric social networks based on a magical notion of successive degrees of purest patrilineal substance. Hence, male ideology claims that father, son, and clansmen are of one semen substance, one common origin place, one residential location—all elements of genealogical ancestry that fan out to embrace a pool of spirit familiars, ancestral spirits, and the semen underlying all. Whether the trees are seen as beginning or finishing this process is beside the point: Sambia have a cyclic view of their system that makes tree sap pivotal in a greater chain of being. What is the nature of semen value in this whole system? This problem forms the last part of my chapter.

DELAYED EXCHANGE

The final category of indirect semen transactions concerns exchanges across generations between groups. This subject is very complex indeed, so I shall merely sketch contours of the system of intergroup relationships. What do groups give and receive? And do their exchanges of semen balance out across time?

The key principle of delayed exchange is that groups who exchange women also exchange semen through homosexual contacts. Group A takes a woman from group B. They become affines. Their initiated males of different cohort at different life cycle stages engage in homosexual intercourse both ways (giving and receiving semen). Children of groups A and B become matrilateral kin in the following generation. In delayed exchange (infant betrothal or bride-service) marriage, group A later returns a woman to group B. In direct exchange (sister exchange) they will not. Marriage between generation 2 of these groups is frowned upon, except in the case of delayed exchange infant betrothal to father's sister's daughter (FZD), that is, a daughter of group A goes back to group B. Yet actual FZD marriage (addressed as "sister" by her MBSo) is also disliked; more commonly FZD is traded for another woman from a different group. Homosexual contacts between generation 2 are also forbidden. In effect, generation 2 shares ties of blood and semen: boys of group A were formed from the blood of a woman of group B, and their body tissue came from their father, some of

whose own semen may have come from males of group B. These boys (of group A), must turn to a third, unrelated group, in order to take both a wife and semen.

What do groups A and B exchange? Group A gets a woman as garden producer and maker of babies. She reproduces heirs to perpetuate group A. Group B gets food gifts and a promise of a return woman (possibly her daughter) in the next generation. Boys of group A get semen from bachelors of group B, and vice versa. Homosexual insemination ensures masculinization and adult reproductive competence. Boys of groups A and B may receive ritual sponsors from each other's group (in purest form, MB). This man is the boy's guardian and teacher in sexual matters (remember they are forbidden to have sex). So each group provides boys of the other group with nurturance and sexual tutorship. In generation 1, a man may copulate with both his wife and her younger brother. The man gets a wife and another homoerotic transitional sexual outlet. His wife and her younger brother both receive semen: growth, strength. And the younger brother (or, if not himself, his sons or clansmen) will eventually receive a return wife, the brother-in-law's daughter, which the latter's sperm created and nourished.

What does intermarriage do to social relationships? First, marriage transforms groups from unrelated enemies to less hostile affines. Where homosexual contacts occur with groups who are politically hostile, and between which warfare and masculine competition are common, marriage places affines in a set of productive relationships where none existed before. Second, they exchange women as resources. It is in the wife-giver's best interests to ensure that the marriage is productive in every way, so that they receive a woman in return. Marital sex for procreation is productive social work; it outweighs erotic play in homosexual contacts and results in social sanctions against adultery and barrenness. Third, women and semen thus become circulating commodities. Unrelated groups exchange semen, on both sides, with the wife-donors getting a wife out of the bargain. The initiated boys of both groups require semen to complete their personhood, while the men need wives as sexual outlets and procreators to step out of the adolescent stage of homosexuality into the adult stage of marriage and family. Semen, therefore, although a crucial commodity, is secondary to women as a commodity: without wives men cannot attain full personhood. Even though semen is needed to attain manhood, and though it provides a village with the new warrior recruits it requires to protect and expand itself, this warriorhood goes for naught unless women are available for the group's economic and biological reproduction.

Finally, the value of semen as instigator of social reproduction at both the individual and group levels pits males against one another in symmetrical competition. This competition takes two forms, intragroup and intergroup transactions (Forge 1972). The one is intrahamlet individualized competition for homosexually procured semen in order "to grow" and have first pick of wives needed for reproduction later. Here, boys as age-mates try to outperform one another in a contest to achieve maturity first. (In fact, older brothers encourage their youngers toward this end.) The other competition is between hamlets, and, in a wider sense, between a confederacy of intramarrying hamlets vis-à-vis the other confederacies of Sambia society. Men aspire to make their confederacy outdo others in war and overall productivity. Hamlets also act together to find women for their bachelors so as to produce more children—potential warriors and females for the marriage trade— compared with other groups. A social race is on: its outcome is social reproduction. Social conflicts within hamlets do erupt over men competing with one another for wives and resources. Conflicts over women with peers in other hamlets also occur, sometimes precipitating warfare. But intrahamlet competition is overshadowed by the normative stress on achieving social maturity in concert with the best interests of one's own village group. Ultimately, social survival re-

quires competing neighbors too, for they provide women and semen, and are the best defense—strength in numbers—against attack from true enemies elsewhere.

CONCLUSION

In this chapter I have explored Sambia semen valuations from several different points of view: what seemed at first esoteric, vulgar, and trivial seems now complex and symbolically significant in understanding native concepts of sexual contacts and the structure of social relations and modes of production in Sambia culture. Ritualized homosexuality belongs to this symbolic field and cannot be understood, either subjectively or objectively, except in relation to the meaningfulness of this field seen over time.

Melanesianists have typically ignored ritualized homosexuality, especially in the construction of comparative models of social organization and culture. Even heterosexual activities have, in general, been scarcely studied as such; and the meaning of the temporal and symbolic structuring of heterosexuality has not been accorded much analytic value beyond the vague category "sexual antagonism," which has been implicitly used to support whatever explanatory model an author advanced (Herdt and Poole 1982). But what matters more, for my purposes, is that the fluids of sexual and reproductive acts—semen, blood, and milk—have been narrowly studies as entities and artifacts in exchange, or as parts of the growth process in reference only to individual development of societal functioning: they have not been seen as symbolic objects and commodities, expressed through concepts and social transactions, whereby the natives reproduce the identities of persons, social roles, clans, and intergroup relationships across generations.

Past analyses of semen and blood as culturally constructed concepts in New Guinea belief systems, for instance, reveal this structural-functional emphasis. These fluids have long been seen as important in native notions of sexual temperament and gender (e.g., Mead 1935). The great interest in procreation beliefs evinced in the 1920s, first raised by Malinowski (1913) among Aborigines, and then in Trobriand descent ideology (Malinowski 1929, 1954), illustrates this interest. Writers questioned whether natives were ignorant of procreation, and what this ignorance of conception meant (Ashley-Montague 1937; Róheim 1945; and see Bettelheim 1955; Leach 1966; Spiro 1968). We see now that denial of semen valuation in kinship and procreation belongs to a broader cultural ideology of social regeneration and reproduction (Weiner 1978, 1980). In Highlands studies, from Read's (1951, 1954) work onward, ethnographers have noted consistent concerns about the role of blood and semen in notions of the body, sex, and gender. Accounts of the norms of sexual contacts, dogmas about conception, sterility, and reproductive competence, and ideas about exchange of menstrual blood and semen between people as patrilineal kin and affines, all illustrate how ethnographers functionally related body fluids to sociosexual relationships and the positioning of persons in networks of social groups (e.g., see R. Berndt 1965; Glasse and Meggitt 1969; Langness 1967; Meggitt 1964; Newman 1964; Read 1959; A. Strathern 1972; M. Strathern 1972; Wagner 1967). Preoccupation with the exchange of sexual fluids between groups has, in particular, addressed Western concerns with "discrete acts of giving and receiving" (Weiner 1980:71; cf. for example, A. Strathern 1969a, 1972). More recent theorists have gone beyond exchange constructs, or structural models that view body treatment as "reflections" of society's divisions and boundaries (Douglas 1966), to conceptualize semen, blood, and other entities as the culturally valued materials out of which gender and reproductivity are symbolically constructed and perpetuated (Gell 1975; Herdt 1981; Lindenbaum 1972; Lipuma 1981; Meigs 1976; Panoff 1968; Poole 1981, 1982; M. Strathern 1978, 1980; Weiner 1980).

With the Sambia, and other societies reported upon in this book, we are dealing with peoples whose cultural systems use sexual relationships and fluids as objects and commodities to recreate social order in successive generations, for these are among the scarcest and most vital resources in this process. Weiner has stated this view succinctly.

> As these resources circulate through time, i.e., as they are embedded in others, they produce value in others because they embody a shared code that speaks directly to the processes through which identities such as clan, ancestors, kinship, or kingship, actively are transmitted through generations. Transmission, however, is not habitual, nor is it automatic. The work of reproduction is enacted with a counter awareness of the force of decay, rotting, and death. A cultural system is grounded in the very paradox of things running out. . . . The regenerating/degenerating paradox found in nature is no less understood as the very same paradox underlying the attachment of individuals to each other through time. *(Weiner n.d.:7–8)*

Semen and other fluids are not just things that *are:* they have a value beyond themselves for extending one's personhood—that is, existence—beyond the present. No doubt many experiences of these material things (e.g., fluids, sex, and others' bodies) entail this transcendent attitude. Sambia spiritual concepts speak to this issue directly,[11] just as the conflict between sex as work or sex as play addresses it indirectly. "Religion is an art of making sense out of experience, and like any other art, say, poetry, it must be taken symbolically, not literally," Firth (1981:596) recently said. His view is certainly germane to the ritual treatment of semen.

The social fact of semen for Sambia is that it is a scarce resource that circulates through time. Its material and phenomenological attributes make it usable as a commodity that can be consumed, stored, and given away. Its perceived use-value derives from the fact that (1) sperm can be "contained" indefinitely in bodies, and (2) then be

---

[11]One is tempted here to note similarities between Sambia male ideology and certain Hindu ideas, the latter of which couple semen retention with male spiritual prowess (see, for example, Eliade 1976).

seemingly passed, from person to person, without changing its essence or efficacy; (3) it represents an investment of labor (food, care, procreation of children), acquired through direct individual sexual transaction or indirect transformation (sperm into milk), that can be given or received; (4) in being transmitted semen extends its transformative value to make the recipient more reproductively and socially competent; (5) these recipients, in turn, will produce more wealth and future individuals who will fill productive roles and fill out social groups; and (6) by so doing, semen transactions recreate the social links between the living and the dead, the worldly and the spiritual realms, between ego and others, and between the divisions of society.

Semen extends its value as commodity through four types of transformations that underlie related modes of "biological" reproduction among Sambia. First, semen through oral sex strengthens and finishes the growth of wives. Second, it acts through wives' bodies to create fetuses, and becomes milk to feed babies after birth. Third, semen is "fed" through fellatio, ritually disguised as "male breast-feeding," to strengthen and grow homosexual partners. Last, sperm is produced in men by drinking certain tree saps, symbolically considered the "breast milk" of these trees, thus regenerating them and making more sperm available. In this last mode of production men, as biological transformers of tree sap into sperm, are recipients, not donors, but the semen cycle remains unchanged: men turn back to society as the dominant donors. Thus, semen as a commodity regulates and generates marriage and the family, clans and village units, and makes possible the ritual cult, which requires, in particular, secret homosexual intercourse.

In Sambia social reality, individuals are born and die, but semen flows through them (along with blood) to recreate society. Individuals pass on. Growth, as an aspect of these individuals, dies with them. But strength persists: in the form of bones and skin tissue in offspring; in spirit familiars; in ghosts and spirits; and in the de-ceased's bones, which after death may be used for sorcery. Erotic play passes on too, is useless, except insofar as it has effected growth, strength, and procreation. Sex as work is far more productive, if less exciting: family and heirs result. In this model, a woman's body as sexual-procreative property belongs to her husband, as much as his semen belongs only to her. Her blood, after marriage, belongs to his clan, through his offspring, which must be "paid for" in birth ceremonies. Both fluids are necessary for procreation, but it is semen that men "own" and control best. The "natural" fact that semen can be drunk (passed on) like any drinkable fluid sustains the view that it is a circulating, valuable, unchanging resource, which must be, nonetheless, internally transformed in certain ways by certain persons to achieve the desired ends.

The most powerful social fact of homosexual contacts is that they may only occur between potential enemies who may become affines (generation 1) and then kin (generation 2). Semen transactions not only define who is related and in what salient ways but homosexual contacts predicate the partners' relationship as prospective affines in their generation, which makes their children matrilateral kin in their own. Structurally, social ties based on blood and semen should not be mixed via sexual relationships: semen relates nonkin, who in turn, through women as links, have descendants sharing semen and blood. (A male ego may receive semen from his brother-in-law, whose children, that is, the ego's sister's children, possess her husband's semen and her blood.) Ties of semen, and blood (via women traded), flow in the same direction. The seeming exception is marriage to actual (not classificatory) FZD, a marriage Sambia frown upon. Such marriages are acceptable only when the FZD cannot be traded for a woman from another group. In these rare marriages, however, spouses share no blood, though they may indirectly share semen via their fathers' homosexual contacts with each others' groups. Thus, the cultural principle not to mix blood and semen is contravened, and people resist such marriages. In general, this cultural linkage (blood and semen) makes heterosexual relationships more socially important and multiplex than homosexual contacts. Both men and women, their bodies and fluids, are needed to achieve biological and social reproduction in this model (cf. Lévi-Strauss 1949; see Pettit 1977:70–72).

This view does not explain ritualized homosexuality among Sambia; it merely elucidates the phenomenon in broader terms. For to seek causes, not just of the sociocultural system of values, but of individual acts of homosexual behavior, we should have to examine its individual subjectivity and developmental context, according them an analytic role I have here ignored. Yet, Sambia do shed light on other, similar systems of social reproduction in Melanesia.

These systems should be seen as a continuum in relation to the value of semen. At one extreme, semen is regarded as rare and precious, so that it must be conserved and regulated, but not *replenished.* Here, we might see situated groups such as the Enga, Kuma, and Gahuku-Gama (Meggitt 1964; Read 1951, 1984). Sexual antagonism seems associated with the low social status of women here. At the other extreme would be societies in which semen is just another fluid, not regulated or conserved, so that it plays little or no role in descent ideology, such as among the matrilineal Trobriands (Malinowski 1929). Here, sex antagonism is weak and women's social status is high. A third type of system could be seen as one that highly values semen that comes from homosexual contacts first, flowing then into heterosexual contacts, as among Kaluli and Marind-anim (Van Baal 1966, 1984; Schieffelin 1982). Sambia, who also use semen replenishment techniques, would represent the extreme end of this valuation of semen. Among these groups, sex antagonism and women's social status is either ambiguous or, as among Sambia, high and low, respectively. The exact arrangement of such a typology is hinted at by Lindenbaum (1984).

What of the nature of the value accorded semen as a commodity in such Melanesian systems? Here, the gender researcher thinks immediately of the multiple facets of fetishism. We must distinguish between what Freud (1962) called erotic fetishization (a person or thing, e.g., shoe, breast, semen, creates sexual excitement as a representation of an unconscious object), and what Marx called fetishism in commodities. I have elsewhere considered erotic fetishization in relation to ritual flutes and Sambia homosexuality (Herdt 1982a). Though much remains to be said, I shall not pursue that discussion here. Yet it is clear that *because* the semen of most males *looks* the same, one can sustain the cultural illusion (Freud 1961) that the same substance is being circulated through time and space. Of semen as fetishized commodity, however, more can be said.

The value of semen does not merely derive from its economic "exchange value." Its significance stems from being necessary to socially and biologically reproduce the cultural identities described above. But because of its portable properties, and its relationship to sexuality, semen comes to take on the characteristics of a commodity in both male/male and male/female sexual contacts. What is the nature of this commodity? Godelier's (1977:155) comment on fetishism and magic is illuminating:

> The "exchange value" of a commodity is the value relationship established in exchanging the commodity for other commodities. This relationship does not create the "value" of the commodity because the value is born with the productive process of the commodity and not in the process of its circulation between producers. Circulation does not create value. The value *exists* before the commodity is circulated. Once commodities circulate or are exchanged, they enter into value relationships which may or may not correspond to their value. They may be sold, for example, for a price exceeding their value.

Semen may be "sold," to extend Godelier's metaphor, for homosexual access to a boy and marriage to his sister (Serpenti 1965:164ff.). But that mystified value of semen existed before the marriage exchange took place. For Sambia, again, it is the symbolic place of semen in the overall productive process of social relationships that compels actors to assign it use-value as a scarce resource. The point is that their cultural ideology bestows multivalent value on semen: the value is not intrinsic simply because sperm circulates or can be exchanged.

But we should not overlook the mystifying and rationalizing effects of this ideology for the politics of the men's secret cult. (We have, after all, been dealing with *male* ideology.) By positioning semen as a valued resource, men are placed firmly in control of *their part* of the means of sociobiological reproduction. And what is their part? It is the crucial role semen plays in every cultural domain described above; indeed, its biological role is unique in the generation of growth and strength in initiates (via homosexual contacts). Yet in regard to infants, growth and strength and procreation can occur only through the mother. Attitudes toward spiritual aspects of personhood reflect a tenuous hold, at best, on exclusive claims to patrifilial allegiance. Semen as commodity may thus exploit the rhetorical, paramount role of men in society. But the value relationships of semen are so caught up in the complementary requirement for women's procreative powers that the regeneration of social identities is conditional: affines and enemies live in close proximity with divided loyalties. Women's social status, interpersonally, not normatively, is probably higher and more consequential than men's rhetoric allows. Absolute control of sexual intercourse, through restriction of sexual access to women, female avoidance taboos for initiates, and obligatory homosexual activities, helps ensure the stability of the men's part in the social-reproductive process. The metering of sperm, so crucial for social development, keeps boys and women "in their place." Thus it is no mystery why Sambia severely sanction adultery, why childhood sexual experimentation is forbidden, or why men keep tree milk-sap drinking secret. If semen were free, easy, or readily at hand, its value would deflate. The traffic in women and, perhaps, the sexual activity with boys, would be undermined.

But only perhaps. This political economy perspective throws open the question of how semen valuations operate through time. Children become initiates and then men: at each life cycle stage they gain and lose certain social trappings of power and responsibility as their capital (e.g., semen) changes. Insemination in a boy is, in a sense, a gift to him, his reward for erotic play. Inseminating a wife is different: the value is on the "hard work" of making this investment pay off. Next to semen, a man's sisters are his most important capital in the marriage business (Van Baal 1970). Here, direct and delayed semen transactions become complex indeed.

> Until he has given in return, the receiver is *"obliged,"* expected to show his gratitude toward his benefactor, or, at least, to have regard for him, to refrain from using against him all the weapons he otherwise might, to pull his punches, lest he be accused of ingratitude and stand condemned by "what people say," which is what gives his actions their social meaning. *(Bourdieu 1977:6)*

Yes, the semen given in a homosexual act may not, after all, be free: it can be purchased at the expense of the boy's sister. If so, the two males are bound to refrain from direct conflict (e.g., see Allen 1967; Meggitt 1964). If not, the recipient is at least obliged to remember where some of his strength came from. At any rate, these two parties (semen donors and recipients), or their children, can become affines and then kin in time.

Understanding Sambia ritualized homosexuality depends upon this diachronic view. The inter*actors* live in the same small world: they are not going anywhere. Resources that flow out of one's group are destined to find their way back, if not in this generation, then in the next. Cyclical models of time have this reciprocal expectation built into them. Semen transactions, in homosexual and heterosexual contacts, imply this circularity; hence our use of *ritualized* as an adjective. It is not just the sex of one's partner, the social motives or outcomes, or the commodity value of semen that informs homosexual acts:

the *time* of ritualization counts, too, in their social meaning.

> Everything takes place as if the ritualization of interactions had the paradoxical effect of giving time its full social efficacy, never more potent than when nothing *but* time is going on. "Time," we say, "is on his side"; time can also work against one. In other words, time derives its efficacy from the state of the structure of relations within which it comes into play. . . . When the unfolding of action is heavily ritualized, as in the dialectic of offence and vengeance, there is still room for strategies which consist of playing on time, or rather the *tempo,* of the action, by delaying revenge so as to prolong the threat of revenge. To restore to practice its practical truth, we must therefore reintroduce time into the theoretical representation of a practice which, being temporally structured, is intrinsically defined by its *tempo. (Bourdieu 1977:7–8)*

The practice of homosexual behavior is embedded in a cyclical tradition of semen transactions that made one's mother and father, and will define one's own future relationships with boys and women. Identities follow from this semen flow. The tempo of such an ancient practice is to be found not only in this day's contacts or that's, but in the last generation and the next. The system sets rigid constraints, but individuals and groups follow strategies around broad time posts to maximize the value of themselves and their resources. Time does not forget who gave and who received semen.

REFERENCES

ALLEN, M. R.
  1964 The Nduindui: A study in the social structure of a New Hebridean community. Ph.D. dissertation, Australian National University.
  1967 *Male Cults and Secret Initiations in Melanesia.* Melbourne: Melbourne University Press.
  1968 The establishment of Christianity and cashcropping in a New Hebridean community. *J. of Pac. Hist.* 3:25–46.
  1969 Report on Aoba: Incidental papers on Nduindui District, Aoba Island. Edited by C. Leaney. Vila, New Hebrides. Mimeographed.
  1972 Rank and leadership in Nduindui, northern New Hebrides. *Mankind* 8:270–282.
  1981 Innovation, inversion and revolution as political tactics in West Aoba. In *Vanuatu: Politics, Economics and Ritual in Island Melanesia,* edited by M. R. Allen, pp. 105–134. Sydney: Academic Press.
  In press Elders, chiefs and big men: Authority legitimation and political evolution in Melanesia. *American Ethnologist.*
AMELSVOORT, V. F. P. M. VAN
  1964 *Culture, Stone Age and Modern Medicine.* Assen: Van Gorcum.
ASHLEY-MONTAGUE, M. F.
  1937 (–1938) The origin of subincision in Australia. *Oceania* 8:193–207.
ASHWORTH, A. E., AND W. M. WALKER
  1972 Social structure and homosexuality: A theoretical appraisal. *Brit. J. Sociol.* 23:146–158.

ATKINSON, J. J.
  1903 *Primal Law.* New York: Longmans, Green & Co.
AUGÉ, MARC
  1982 *Genie du Paganisme.* Paris: Gallimard.
BAAL, J. VAN
  1934 *Godsdienst en Samenleving in Nederlandsch-Zuid-Nieuw-Guinea.* Amsterdam: Noordhollandsche Uitgeversmaatschappy.
  1963 The cult of the bull-roarer in Australia and Southern New Guinea. *Bijdragen tot de Taal-, Land-, en Volkenkunde* 119:201–214.
  1966 *Dema, Description and Analysis of Marind-anim Culture.* The Hague: Martinus Nijhoff.
  1970 The part of women in the marriage trade: objects or behaving as objects? *Bijdragen tot de Taal-, Land-, en Volkenkunde* 126:289–308.
  1975 *Reciprocity and the Position of Women.* Assen: Van Gorcum.
  1981 *Man's Quest for Partnership.* Assen: Van Gorcum.
  1982 *Jan Verschueren's Description of Yéi-nan Culture.* The Hague: Martinus Nijhoff.
  1984 The dialectics of sex in Marind-anim culture. In *Ritualized Homosexuality in Melanesia,* edited by G. Herdt, pp. 128–166. Berkeley: University of California Press.
BAMLER, V. G.
  1911 Tami. In *Deutsch Neu-Guinea,* 3 vols. edited by R. Neubauss, pp. 489–566. Berlin: Verlag Dietrich Reimer/Ernst Vohsen.

BARKER, T. N.
1975 Some features of Ai'i society. Ph.D. dissertation, Dept. of Anthropology, Laval University.

BARTH, F.
1971 Tribes and intertribal relations in the Fly headwaters. *Oceania* 41:171–191.
1975 *Ritual and Knowledge Among the Baktaman of New Guinea.* New Haven: Yale University Press.

BATESON, G.
1932 Social structure of the Iatmul people of the Sepik. *Oceania* 2:245–291, 401–453.
1946 Arts of the South Seas. *Art Bulletin* 28:119–123.
1958 *Naven.* 2d edition. Stanford: Stanford University Press. (Orig. 1936).
1972 *Steps to an Ecology of Mind.* Scranton, Penn.: Chandler Publishing Company.
1978 Towards a theory of cultural coherence: Comment. *Anthropological Quarterly* 51:77–78.

BAUMANN, H. VAN
1955 *Das Doppelte Geschlecht. Ethnologische Studien zur Bisexualitat in Ritus und Mythos.* Berlin: Dietrich Reimer.

BERNDT, R. M.
1965 The Kamano, Usurfa, Jate and Fore of the Eastern Highlands. In *Gods, Ghosts and Men in Melanesia,* edited by P. Lawrence and M. J. Meggitt, pp. 78–104. Melbourne: Melbourne University Press.

BERNDT, R. M., AND C. H. BERNDT
1951 *Sexual Behavior in Western Arnhem Land.* New York: Viking Fund Publication no. 16.

BETTELHEIM, B.
1955 *Symbolic Wounds, Puberty Rites and the Envious Male.* New York: Collier Books.

BOURDIEU, P.
1977 *Outline of a Theory of Practice.* Trans. Richard Nice. Cambridge: Cambridge University Press.

COLLIER, J. F., AND M. Z. ROSALDO
1981 Politics and gender in simple societies. In *Sexual Meanings,* edited by S. B. Ortner and H. Whitehead, pp. 275–329. Cambridge: Cambridge University Press.

DOUGLAS, M.
1966 *Purity and Danger.* London: Routledge and Kegan Paul.

ELIADE, M.
1958 *Rites and Symbols of Initiation.* Trans. Williard R. Trask. New York: Harper Torchbooks.
1976 Spirit, light and seed. In *Occultism, Witchcraft, and Cultural Fashions,* by M. Eliade, pp. 93–119. Chicago: University of Chicago Press.

FAITHORN, E.
1975 The concept of pollution among the Kafe of Papua New Guinea. In *Toward an Anthropology of Women,* edited by R. R. Reiter, pp. 127–140. New York: Monthly Review Press.

FARQUHAR, J., AND D. C. GAJDUSEK
1981 *Kuru: Early Letters and Field-Notes from the Collection of D. Carleton Gajdusek.* New York: Raven Press.

FEDERN, P.
1952 *Ego Psychology and the Psychoses.* New York: Basic Books.

FIRTH, RAYMOND
1973 *Symbols Public and Private.* London: Allen and Unwin.
1981 Spiritual aroma: Religion and politics. Distinguished lecture for 1980. *American Anthropologist* 83:582–605.

FORGE, A.
1972 The Golden Fleece. *Man.* 7:527–540.

FREUD, S.
1961 The future of an illusion. In *The Standard Edition of the Complete Psychological Works of Sigmund Freud,* ed. and trans. J. Strachey, 21:3–57. London: Hogarth Press. (Orig. 1927).
1962 *Three Essays on the Theory of Sexuality.* Trans. J. Strachey. New York: Basic Books. (Orig. 1905).

GELL, A.
1975 *Metamorphosis of the Cassowaries.* London: The Athlone Press.

GLASSE, R. M., AND M. J. MEGGITT
1969 *Pigs, Pearlshells, and Women.* Englewood Cliffs, N.J.: Prentice-Hall, Inc.

GODELIER, M.
1969 Land tenure among the Baruya of New Guinea. *J. of the Papua New Guinea Soc.* 3:17–23.
1971 "Salt currency" and the circulation of commodities among the Baruya of New Guinea. In *Studies in Economic Anthropology,* pp. 53–73. Washington, D.C.: American Anthropological Association.
1976 Sex as the ultimate foundation and cosmic order of the New Guinea Baruya: Myth and reality. Godelier's translation of his paper in *Sexualité et Pouvoir,* edited by A. Verdiglione, pp. 268–306. Paris: Traces Payot.
1977 *Perspectives in Marxist Anthropology.* Trans. Robert Brain. Cambridge: Cambridge University Press.
1982a *La Production des Grands Hommes.* Paris: Fayard.

HEIDER, K. G.
1976 Dani sexuality: A low energy system. *Man* 11:188–201.
1979 *Grand Valley Dani: Peaceful Warriors.* New York: Holt, Rinehart and Winston.

HELD, G. T.
1957 *The Papuans of Waropen.* The Hague: Martinus Nijhoff.

HERDT, G. H.
1977 The shaman's "calling" among the Sambia of New Guinea. *J. Soc. Oceanistes* 56–57:153–167.
1980 Semen depletion and the sense of maleness. *Ethnopsy-chiatrica* 3:79–116.
1981 *Guardians of the Flutes: Idioms of Masculinity.* New York: McGraw-Hill.
1982a Fetish and fantasy in Sambia initiation. In *Rituals of Manhood: Male Initiation in Papua New Guinea,* edited by G. H. Herdt, pp. 44–98. Berkeley, Los Angeles, London: University of California Press.
1982b Sambia nose-bleeding rites and male proximity to women. *Ethos* 10:189–231.
n.d. The accountability of Sambia initiates. In *Anthropology in the High Valleys: Essays in Honor of K. E. Read,* edited by L. L. Langness and T. E. Hays.

HERDT, G. H., AND F. J. P. POOLE
1982 Sexual antagonism: The intellectual history of a concept in the anthropology of Melanesia. In *"Sexual Antagonism," Gender, and Social Change in Papua New Guinea,* edited by F. J. P. Poole and G. H. Herdt. *Social Analysis* (special issue) 12:3–28.

KELLY, R.
1976 Witchcraft and sexual relations: An exploration in the social and semantic implications of a structure of belief. In *Man and Woman in the New Guinea Highlands,* edited by P. Brown and G. Buchbinder, pp. 36–53. Washington, D.C.: American Anthropological Association.

LANGNESS, L. L.
1967 Sexual antagonism in the New Guinea Highlands: A Bena Bena example. *Oceania* 37:161–177.

LEACH, E.
1961 Two essays concerning the symbolic representation of time. In *Rethinking Anthropology,* by Edmund Leach, pp. 124–136. London: The Athlone Press.
1966 Virgin Birth. In *Proceedings of the Roy. Anth. Inst. of G.B. and N.I. for 1965,* pp. 39–50.

LEEDAN, A. C. VAN DER
1956 *Hoofdtrekken der Sociale Struktuur in het Westlijk Binnenland Van Sarmi.* Leiden: Ydo.

LEENHARDT, M.
1979 *Do Kamo.* Trans. Basia M. Gulati. Chicago: University of Chicago Press.

LEVINE, R. A.
1981 Foreward to *Guardian of the Flutes,* by G. H. Herdt, pp. xiii–xviii. New York: McGraw-Hill.

LÉVI-STRAUSS, C.
1949 *Les structures élémentaires de la parenté.* Paris: Presses Universitaires de France.

LINDENBAUM, S.
1972 Sorcerers, ghosts and polluting women: An analysis of religious belief and population control. *Ethnology* 11:241–253.
1979 *Kuru Sorcery.* Palo Alto: Mayfield Publishing Co.
n.d. The mystification of female labours. Paper presented to the Conference on Feminism and Kinship Theory, Bellagio, Italy.
1984 Variations on a sociosexual theme in Melanesia. In *Ritualized Homosexuality in Melanesia,* edited by G. Herdt, pp. 337–361. Berkeley: University of California Press.

LIPUMA, E.
1981 Cosmology and economy among the Maring of Highland New Guinea. *Oceania* 51:266–285.

MALINOWSKI, B.
1913 *The Family Among the Australian Aborigines.* London: University of London Press.
1927 *Sex and Repression in Savage Society.* Cleveland: Meridian Books.
1929 *The Sexual Life of Savages in North-Western Melanesia.* New York: Harcourt, Brace & World, Inc.
1954 *Magic, Science and Religion and Other Essays.* Garden City, N.Y.: Anchor Books.

MARX, K.
1977 The fetishism of commodities and the secret thereof. In *Symbolic Anthropology: A Reader in the Study of Symbols and Meanings,* edited by J. L. Dolgin et al., pp. 245–253. New York: Columbia University Press.

MEAD, M.
1935 *Sex and Temperament in Three Primitive Societies.* New York: Dutton.

MEGGITT, M.
1964 Male/female relationships in the Highlands of Australian New Guinea. *American Anthropologist* 66, Pt. 2:204–224.

MEIGS, A.
1976 Male pregnancy and the reduction of sexual opposition in a New Guinea Highlands society. *Ethnology* 25:393–407.

NEWMAN, PHILLIP
1964 Religious belief and ritual in a New Guinea Society. *American Anthropologist* 66, Pt. 2:257–272.

PANOFF, M.
1968 The notion of the double-self among the Maenge. *J. Poly. Soc.* 77:275–295.

PETTIT, P.
1977 *The Concept of Structuralism: A Critical*

Analysis. Berkeley, Los Angeles, London: University of California Press.

POOLE, F. J. P.

1981 Transforming, "natural" woman: Female ritual leaders and gender ideology among Bimin-Kuskusmin. In *Sexual Meanings,* edited by S. B. Ortner and H. Whitehead, pp. 116–165. Cambridge: Cambridge University Press.

1982 The ritual forging of identity: Aspects of person and self in Bimin-Kuskusmin male initiation. In *Rituals of Manhood: Male Initiation in Papua New Guinea,* edited by G. H. Herdt, pp. 100–154. Berkeley, Los Angeles, London: University of California Press.

READ, K. E.

1951 The Gahuku-Gama of the Central Highlands. *South Pacific* 5:154–164.

1952 Nama cult of the Central Highlands, New Guinea. *Oceania* 23:1–25.

1954 Cultures of the Central Highlands. *SWJA* 10:1–43.

1955 Morality and the concept of the person among the Gahuku-Gama. *Oceania* 25:233–282.

1959 Leadership and consensus in a New Guinea Society. *American Anthropologist* 61:425–436.

1965 *The High Valley.* London: George Allen and Unwin.

1980a *The High Valley.* Columbia: Columbia University Press. (New edition; orig. 1965.)

1980b *Other Voices.* Novato, Calif.: Chandler & Sharp.

1984 The *Nama* cult recalled. In *Ritualized Homosexuality in Melanesia,* edited by G. Herdt, pp. 221–247. Berkeley: University of California Press.

RÓHEIM, G.

1926 *Social Anthropology, a Psycho-analytic Study in Anthropology and a History of Australian Totemism.* New York: Boni and Liveright.

1929 Dying gods and puberty ceremonies. *JRAI* 59:181–197.

1932 Psycho-analysis of primitive cultural types. *Intl. J. of Psycho-Analysis* 13:1–224.

1945 *The Eternal Ones of the Dream.* New York: International University Press.

SCHIEFFELIN, E. L.

1976 *The Sorrow of the Lonely and the Burning of the Dancers.* New York: St. Martin's Press.

1977 The unseen influence: Tranced mediums as historical innovators. *J. Soc. Oceanistes* 56–57: 169–178.

1982 The Bau a ceremonial hunting lodge: An alternative to initiation. In *Rituals of Manhood: Male Initiation in Papua New Guinea,* edited by

G. H. Herdt, pp. 155–200. Berkeley, Los Angeles, London: University of California Press.

SERPENTI, L. M.

1965 *Cultivators in the Swamps: Social Structure and Horticulture in a New Guinea Society.* Assen: Van Gorcum.

1984 The ritual meaning of homosexuality and pedophelia among the Kimam-Papuans of South Irian Jaya. In *Ritualized Homosexuality in Melanesia,* edited by G. Herdt, pp. 292–317. Berkeley: University of California Press.

SØRUM, A.

1980 In search of the lost soul: Bedamini spirit seances and curing rites. *Oceania* 50:273–297.

1982 The seeds of power: Patterns in Bedamini male initiation. *Social Analysis* 10:42–62.

1984 Growth and decay: Bedamini notions of sexuality. In *Ritualized Homosexuality in Melanesia,* edited by G. Herdt, pp. 318–336. Berkeley: University of California Press.

SPIRO, M. E.

1968 Virgin birth, parthenogenesis and physiological paternity: An essay in cultural interpretation. *Man* 3:242–261.

STOLLER, R. J., AND G. H. HERDT

1982 The development of masculinity: A cross-cultural contribution. *J. Am. Psychoan. Assn.* 30: 29–59.

n.d. Intimate communications: Methodological aspects of clinical ethnography. Unpublished MS.

STRACHAN, J.

1888 *Explorations and Adventures in New Guinea.* London: S. Low, Marston, Searle and Rivington.

STRATHERN, A. J.

1969a Descent and alliance in the New Guinea Highlands: Some problems of comparison. *Proc. of the RAI for 1968,* pp. 37–52.

1969b Finance and production: Two strategies in New Guinea Highlands exchange systems. *Oceania* 40:42–67.

1970 Male initiation in the New Guinea Highland societies. *Ethnology* 9:373–379.

1972 *One Father, One Blood.* Canberra: A.N.U. Press.

1979 Gender, ideology and money in Mount Hagen. *Man* 14:530–548.

STRATHERN, M.

1972 *Women in Between.* London: Seminar Press.

1978 The achievement of sex: Paradoxes in Hagen gender-thinking. In *The Yearbook of Symbolic Anthropology,* edited by E. G. Schwimmer, pp. 171–202. London: C. Hurst.

1979 The self in self-decoration. *Oceania* 49:241–257.

1980 No nature, no culture: The Hagen case. In *Nature, Culture and Gender,* edited by C. P. Mac-Cormack and M. Strathern, pp. 174–222. Cambridge: Cambridge University Press.

TUZIN, D. F.

1976 *The Ilahita Arapesh.* Berkeley, Los Angeles, London: University of California Press.

1980 *The Voice of the Tamberan: Truth and Illusion in Ilahita Arapesh Religion.* Berkeley, Los Angeles, London: University of California Press.

1982 Ritual violence among the Ilahita Arapesh: The dynamics of moral and religious uncertainty. In *Rituals of Manhood: Male Initiation in Papua New Guinea,* edited by G. H. Herdt, pp. 321–355. Berkeley, Los Angeles, London: University of California Press.

WAGNER, R.

1967 *The Curse of Souw: Principles of Daribi Clan Definition and Alliance.* Chicago: University of Chicago Press.

1972 *Habu: The Innovation of Meaning in Daribi Religion.* Chicago: University of Chicago Press.

WEINER, A. B.

1976 *Women of Value, Men of Renown. New Perspectives in Trobriand Exchange.* Austin: University of Texas Press.

1978 The reproductive model in Trobriand society. In *Trade and Exchange in Oceania and Australia,* edited by J. Specht and P. White (special issue), *Mankind* 11:150–174.

1979 Trobriand kinship from another view: The reproductive power of women and men. *Man* 14:328–348.

1980 Reproduction: A replacement for reciprocity. *American Ethnologist* 7:71–85.

n.d. Transformations in gender constructs. Paper delivered at the American Anthropological Association Meetings, Los Angeles, December 4, 1981.

WILLIAMS, F. E.

1924 *The Natives of the Purari Delta.* Port Moresby: Government Printer.

1928 *Orokaiva Magic.* London: Oxford University Press.

1930 *Orokaiva Society.* London: Oxford University Press.

1936a *Bull Roarers of the Papuan Gulf.* Territory of Papua, Anthropology Report no. 17. Port Moresby: Walter A. Bock.

1936b Papuan dream interpretation. *Mankind* 2:29–39.

1936c *Papuans of the Trans-Fly.* Oxford: Oxford University Press.

24

Breaking the Mirror: The Construction of Lesbianism and the Anthropological Discourse on Homosexuality

Evelyn Blackwood

This essay reviews the anthropological discourse on homosexuality by examining the assumptions that have been used by anthropologists to explain homosexual behavior, and by identifying current theoretical approaches. The essay questions the emphasis on male homosexual behavior as the basis for theoretical analysis, and points to the importance of including female homosexual behavior in the study of homosexuality. Cross-cultural data on lesbian behavior are presented and the influence of gender divisions and social stratification on the development of patterns of lesbian behavior are broadly explored. The article outlines suggestions for examining the cultural context of lesbian behavior as well as the constraints exerted on women's sexual behavior in various cultures.

Recent years have seen a burgeoning of studies on homosexuality in the social sciences, much of it inspired by the feminist and Gay Rights movements of the 1970s. The focus of this new literature, particularly in sociology and history, concerns the historical and cultural influences on homosexual behavior. Plummer suggests that "specific ways of experiencing sexual attraction and gender behavior are bound up with specific historical and cultural milieux" (1981, p. 12). In a similar vein, historians looking at eroticism suggest that it is "subject to the forces of culture" (D'Emilio, 1983, p. 3), and thus accessible to historical analysis. The anthropological data on cross-cultural sexual variation provide much of the groundwork for such analyses; yet it has been one of the failings of anthropology that the field itself has developed no adequate theory regarding the cultural construction of homosexual behavior.

The author received her MA in anthropology from San Francisco State University in 1984. She was a research associate with the Center for Education and Research in Sexuality from 1984–85.

Source: From *The Many Faces of Homosexuality* by E. Blackwood. Copyright © 1986 by Harrington Park Press. Reprinted by permission.

To remedy this situation, the focus in this volume will be on homosexual behavior as it is organized both historically and culturally, with emphasis on the particular contexts in the cultures discussed that influence or shape homosexual behavior. The following essays show not only the wide variation in forms of female and male homosexuality, but also investigate the complex interaction of cultural and social factors affecting the expression of such behavior. The emphasis is on the cultural patterns or institutions rather than the individual who engages in same-sex behavior. In particular the articles diverge from the concept of homosexuality as a single cross-cultural institution. Instead they analyze homosexual behavior in terms of sexual patterns that are understandable only within the larger context of the culture that shapes it. Thus, it is hoped that this volume, by providing ethnographic and theoretical analyses of cross-cultural homosexual behavior, will advance the anthropological study of homosexuality and improve our understanding of the cultural construction of homosexual behavior.

This essay intends to place the following articles within the anthropological discourse on homosexuality by examining assumptions that have been used by anthropologists to explain homosexual behavior, and by identifying the current theoretical approaches. It also questions the continued emphasis on male homosexual behavior as a general model for theoretical analysis. It will bring women's sexual behavior within the purview of the current discussion on homosexuality by separating it from the historical construction of male homosexuality and by examining the particular cultural contexts of lesbian behavior. The terms *homosexuality* and *lesbianism,* as used in this essay, refer to sexual behavior between individuals of the same sex. Their use should not be construed as imposing the structure of Western sexual ideology on cross-cultural practices; in Western sexual systems, individuals who are identified by their sexual behavior form isolated subcultures. This pattern bears little resemblance

to the integral nature of homosexual practices in many tribal societies.

CROSS-CULTURAL THEORIES AND STUDIES

The anthropological study of homosexuality has been limited by serious methodological and theoretical problems. As Langness has aptly stated, "it is fair to say that we have no anthropological *theory* of homosexuality . . . " (Foreword to Read, 1980, p. vii). The reasons for this absence are numerous and have been discussed in detail by several anthropologists (Carrier, 1980; Fitzgerald, 1977; Read, 1980; Sonenschein, 1966). In particular, most anthropologists have been affected by or accepted the prejudices of Western society toward homosexual behavior, and consequently have not considered the study of homosexuality to be a legitimate pursuit. The data they have gathered are limited to brief reports of homosexual practices. According to Carrier, these reports "(are) . . . complicated by the prejudice of many observers who consider the behavior unnatural, dysfunctional, or associated with mental illness . . . " (1980, p. 101). Discussion of the topic has, in general, been restricted to statements regarding the presence or absence of certain types of sexual acts. Such cataloguing has resulted in a considerable amount of information about sexual variation, but has provided little understanding of the cultural contexts within which these behaviors occur.[1]

Certain basic assumptions have colored the brief discussion of homosexuality in the anthropological literature. The theoretical models used in the past to analyze homosexual data derived directly from western psychological concepts of

---

[1]Major works by non-anthropologists which make use of cross-cultural data are: Bullough, 1976; Burton, 1956; Ellis & Symonds, 1897/1975; Ford & Beach, 1951; Karsch-Haack, 1975; West, 1977; Westermarck, 1956; also Katz's (1976) chapter on Native Americans. The first anthropological cross-cultural survey by Opler (1965) strongly reflected Western biases on homosexuality.

sexuality. Most anthropologists based their evaluation of homosexual practices in other cultures on the deviance model of psychology and sociology, assuming that heterosexuality represented the norm for sexual behavior, and, therefore, homosexuality was abnormal or deviant behavior. Such evaluations were often in direct contrast to the meaning or value attached to homosexual behavior in the culture studied, since many groups accepted homosexual practices within their social system. For example, Berndt labelled the male homosexual practices of Australian aborigines as "sexual abnormalities" and "perversions" (1963). Other anthropologists, however, have shown that the aboriginal practices were acceptable and institutionalized in the form of "brother-in-law" exchange among aborigines (Layard, 1959; Roheim, 1950; Spencer & Gillen, 1927). Hill (1935) described the Navajo *nadle* (hermaphrodites) as unhappy and maladjusted individuals despite the fact that the *nadle* were (or had been) highly revered and respected by the Navajo (see Greenberg, this issue, on ridiculing berdache). In a classic example of the contrast between emic and etic categories, Metraux declared that "*abnormal* sexual relationships between women (were) tolerated and *accepted*" on Easter Island (1940, p. 108, emphasis mine).

Implicit in this approach has been the belief that sexual behavior belonged to the domain of the individual (see Padgug, 1979). As a private act, it has not been considered relevant to the larger functioning of the social group. For psychological anthropologists who studied sexual behavior, such behavior served as an indicator of the individual's adjustment to society. These anthropologists considered the homosexual individual to be a person unable to adjust to the prescribed gender role. As evidence, they cited the males among the Plains Indians who were thought to lack the temperament for a warrior, and so turned to the berdache role (see Benedict, 1939; Mead, 1935).

Another assumption in the anthropological discourse on homosexuality has been the belief in a "homosexual nature" underlying all expressions of homosexuality. This assumption was the basis of Kroeber's "homosexual niche" theory, which he used to explain the Native American berdache. He maintained that American Indian culture *accommodated* individuals who were homosexual by creating the berdache institution (Kroeber, 1925, 1940). He believed that individuals took on the berdache role as the result of psychological or congenital problems, and that these individuals were found in most tribes. His ideas reflected what is currently being called "essentialism," the argument for a common trans-historical substrate of behavior or desire in all cultures.[2] In the study of homosexual behavior, this view is expressed in the perception that a certain percentage of homosexual individuals will take on the role in their culture which allows the expression of a homosexual nature, such as the Native American berdache, the Tahitian mahu, or Chukchee shaman role (see Callender & Kochems, this issue, for other male roles).

Although their views were to some extent within this essentialist framework, certain anthropologists foreshadowed a later historical-cultural construction of sexuality through application of a learning theory model. Both Mead (1935) and Benedict (1934) referred to the great arc of human potential from which cultures chose particular traits. Yet they found that this "essential" core was less and less relevant to the social design of human behavior. Benedict proposed that human behavior takes the forms that societal institutions prescribe, while Mead also argued for the malleability of humans in learning cultural forms. In considering "the homosexual," the emphasis in both their works, as noted above, was on the failure of the individual to adjust; nevertheless, it was argued that cultural factors shaped the homosexual response. Mead (1961) later pointed out that various individual personality cues combine with the cultural interpretation of sexuality to shape an individual's

[2]For further discussion of this theory see Weeks, 1981, pp. 2–3; Whitehead, 1984; Rubin, 1984; De Cecco & Shively, 1983/1984; and Richardson, 1983/1984.

sex role. In contrast to the majority of anthropologists, both Mead and Benedict suggested that homosexual roles had certain valid cultural functions and were acceptable in some societies. Their suggestions opened the way for fuller analysis of the cultural context of homosexual behavior.

HISTORICAL-CULTURAL CONTEXT

Largely as a result of the feminist and gay movements of the late '60s and '70s, anthropologists began a new analysis of homosexual behavior. The feminist declaration that "the personal is political" underscored the realization, as Ross and Rapp point out, that "the seemingly most intimate details of private existence are actually structured by larger social relations" (1981, p. 51). Further prompted by the gay movement's rejection of the Western definition of homosexuality, anthropologists realized the need to understand sexuality from a perspective which took into account the importance of both the historical period and the cultural context. They joined other social scientists in the historical constructionist approach, or more appropriately for anthropology, the historical-cultural construction of sexuality.

Recent work on the historical-cultural construction of sexuality brings definition to the cultural factors which shape sexual behavior, and, in a sense, chips away at the essentialist core by establishing the importance of external, social factors. Ross and Rapp state that:

> Sexuality's biological base is always experienced culturally, through a translation. The bare biological facts of sexuality do not speak for themselves; they must be expressed socially. Sex feels individual, or at least private, but those feelings always incorporate the roles, definitions, symbols and meanings of the worlds in which they are constructed. (1981, p. 51)

Padgug has suggested the importance of the economic context in the construction of sexuality because "sexuality, class, and politics cannot easily be disengaged from one another" (1979, p. 5). Other areas that "condition, constrain and socially define" sexuality, as suggested by Ross and Rapp are: (1) kinship and family systems; (2) sexual regulations and definitions of communities; and (3) national and "world" systems (1981, p. 54). Patterns of homosexual behavior reflect the value system and social structure of the different societies in which they are found. The ideology regarding male and female roles, kinship and marriage regulations, and the sexual division of labor are all important in the construction of homosexual behavior. Thus, the historical-cultural factors affect and shape the expression of homosexuality.

Several recent works reflect this perspective to a greater or lesser degree. Levy (1971) suggested that the *mahu* of Tahiti, a traditional transvestite role for males (of which there was usually one in each village), functioned as a message to males regarding the non-male role which they should avoid. Others include Wolf's *The Lesbian Community* (1979), on the lesbian-feminist community in San Francisco, Read's *Other Voices* (1980), on the lifestyle in a male homosexual tavern in the U.S., Herdt's *Guardians of the Flutes* (1981) and *Ritualized Homosexuality in Melanesia* (1984), and Esther Newton's *Mother Camp: Female Impersonators in America* (1972). Carrier's (1980) cross-cultural survey established some basic correlations between socio-cultural context and the expression of homosexuality. He suggested that homosexual behavior correlated with the particular cultural ideology regarding sexuality and cross-gender behavior, as well as with the availability of sexual partners. Further, the articles in this volume examine the various cultural factors that shape the nature of homosexual behavior and, particularly for non-Western tribal societies, show how they are integrated within the social system.

MALE VS. FEMALE HOMOSEXUALITY

Until now the historical-cultural construction of homosexuality has been based predominantly on the theories of male homosexuality which have been applied to both male and female homosexual behavior or, even more abstractly, to a "trans-gender" homosexuality. In looking back at her classic article on the homosexual role, Mary McIntosh stated that "the assumption always is that we can use the same theories and concepts for female homosexuality and that, for simplicity, we can just talk about men and assume that it applies to women" (1981, p. 45). Because men's and women's roles are structured differently in all cultures, however, the structure of female homosexuality must be examined as well. A one-sided discourse on homosexuality does not adequately comprehend the complex interplay of factors which shape homosexual behavior, male or female. Frequently, the construction of homosexual behavior occurs at the level of gender systems, for example, in the context of gender redefinition (cross-gender or gender mixing roles) or gender antagonism (ritualized male homosexuality). Because of the importance of gender roles in homosexual behavior, no analysis can be complete without adequately evaluating both female and male gender roles. As Lindenbaum states, "gender is the mutual production of men and women acting in concert, whether it be in the form of cooperation or of opposition" (1984, p. 338).

Further, the different constraints placed on women and men demand a separate analysis of lesbian behavior in order to identify the contexts of women's roles that uniquely shape its expression. Past research on homosexuality reflects the implicit assumption that lesbian behavior is the mirror-image of male homosexuality. Yet, the act of having sex with a member of one's own sex may be culturally defined in rather divergent ways for women and men. The basic difference derives from the gender division which is imposed in all cultures and based on the physical differences between the two sexes. As Mead stated,

> all known human societies recognize the anatomic and functional differences between males and females in intricate and complex ways; through insistence on small nuances of behavior in posture, stance, gait, through language, ornamentation and dress, division of labor, legal social status . . . (1961, p. 1451)

The different constraints imposed on men and women affect the construction of homosexual roles, behaviors, and meanings. Therefore, the factors that are significant in male homosexuality may not be significant to the construction of female homosexuality. For example, the ritual homosexuality of New Guinea men was a result of the need to separate boys from the contaminating power of their mothers and of the belief that boys did not develop strength or masculinity naturally. Adult men helped them grow through ritual insemination (see Gray, this issue; also Herdt, 1981, 1984). Girls, on the other hand, were believed to have an inherent femininity and reproductive competence, possessing the female essence from birth (Herdt, 1981). Since it was not necessary for women to ritually implant femaleness in young girls, no ritual homosexuality analogous to male behavior existed for women. On the other hand, patterns of homosexual behavior may be similar for men and women, such as the cross-gender role among Native Americans, although still differentially affected by their separate roles and statuses. Consequently, the discourse on homosexuality must be informed by an analysis of the construction of lesbianism, which this next section will attempt to provide.

APPROACHES TO LESBIANISM

Despite the fact that no anthropological study other than Wolf's (1979) has focused on lesbianism, anthropologists and other social scientists have attempted to compare female and male homosexuality. Although their conclusions are questionable because of the lack of attention to the subject, they suggest that female homosexuality is less institutionalized, less well-developed, less important or less visible than male homosexuality (Carrier, 1980; Ford & Beach, 1951). The reasons given for the lack of female homosexual patterns frequently rely on the notion of biological constraints. Mead, for example, despite the prevalence of a learning theory model in most of her work, reverts to an essentialist position in her analysis of female homosexuality. She suggested that "female anatomy dictates no choices as to activity, passivity, asymmetry, or complementariness and seems to lend itself much less to institutionalization as a counter-mores activity" (1961, p. 1471). Whitehead (1981), in considering the Native American female cross-gender role, is also inclined to place the onus on the greater constraints of female biology as compared to male biology. Such arguments do not sufficiently take into account the cultural constraints and influences on women's roles, but rather fall back on the notion of biological determinism to explain women's activities and roles. Carrier is more to the point when he suggests that the "higher status accorded men than women in most societies" may account for the lower incidence of female homosexuality (1980, p. 103). Rather than explaining the data of lesbianism in terms of the prerequisites of physiology, patterns of lesbian behavior can be more accurately explained by the type of gender system and the autonomy of women in particular cultures.

ANTHROPOLOGICAL STUDY OF WOMEN

In looking at the anthropological data on women and lesbianism, a majority of ethnographies contain little or no data on lesbian behavior. There are several factors, other than the absence of lesbianism, that have contributed to this lack of information. Traditional anthropologists were concerned with the normative female role, studying women in activities that reflected the Western ideology of womanhood as supportive and nurturing of male concerns. Ethnographers focused on the role of women in domestic activities such as gathering, weaving, childrearing, and preparing food for their families, often to

the exclusion of women's activities outside this domestic sphere. They typically assumed that within the normative female role women engaged exclusively in heterosexual behavior. Consequently, they were unable to identify nonheterosexual behavior, or if they did, they failed to understand that in many instances it was acceptable, desirable, or easily accessible to a large number of women in non-Western cultures. For example, Firth concluded that Tikopia women did not engage in lesbianism because so many male partners were available to them (1936, p. 495). He was assuming a natural preference for heterosexuality over homosexuality.

To complicate the matter, anthropological fieldwork was done predominantly by males, talking to male informants about male activities. According to Reiter, the details of women's lives "[come] from questions asked of men about their wives, daughters, and sisters, rather than the women themselves . . . " (1975, p. 12). Male informants were frequently unqualified or unwilling to discuss women's business and their hesitance or lack of knowledge was particularly critical to the process of obtaining data on lesbian behavior. Evans-Pritchard (1970) reported that Azande women kept their lesbian relations as secret as possible even from their husbands. The data he gathered from his male informants on women's homosexual relations necessarily reflected male assumptions and feelings rather than the female experience.

On the other hand, though many ethnographies contain no reports of lesbian behavior, some anthropologists have had notable success eliciting such information from female informants. For instance Shostak's (1981) life-history of Nisa, a !Kung woman, reveals that homosexual relations among girls was an accepted adolescent phenomenon. Prior studies made no reference to lesbian behavior among the !Kung. Other data are muddled both by anthropologists' and informants' reticence on the subject. Mueller, who studied Lesotho "mummy-baby" relationships, did not obtain explicit information on the women's sexual activity because, as she admits, "I was not able to ask such personal questions, largely because of my own embarrassment" (1977, p. 167). Gay found that mummy-baby relationships are "regarded as very personal and are only discussed reticently with a stranger whose disapproval they fear" (this issue). In light of these discrepancies, references to the absence of homosexual behavior, whether female or male, may prove to be a poor basis for cross-cultural analysis.

Another problem with the anthropological data is that they have largely reflected the prevailing Western conception of lesbianism. From the late 1800s sexologists and social scientists identified masculine behavior in women as lesbianism; not surprisingly, women in "masculine" or cross-gender roles comprise nearly half of all the anthropological data on lesbianism (see Blackwood, 1984a). The remainder of the data simply reports the occurrence of sexual activity among adolescent girls or adult women. Anthropologists have ignored or overlooked other types of lesbian relations. Gay (this issue) candidly admitted that she was unaware of Lesotho girls' "mummy-baby" relationships, intimate girlfriend relationships, until a year after she had lived in her study area. She only then observed the relationship because her research assistant pointed it out. Thus, the anthropologist's knowledge or stereotype of Western lesbianism inhibits the collection of accurate data where relationships do not resemble the expected form.

The numerous problems with the data on lesbianism stem predominantly from the male biases and prejudices regarding lesbian behavior and women's roles. Although it is impossible to determine the universal prevalence of lesbianism, the small number of anthropological reports on the subject are more likely due to the limitation of the observers than to the condition of women's lives. Yet, even the perception that the amount of data is very small may be inaccurate. In Ford and Beach's (1951) cross-cultural survey of homosexual and lesbian behavior (the source most used in discussions of cross-cultural

variation in homosexuality), 17 out of 76 cultures surveyed in the Human Relations Area File reported female homosexuality. By comparison, a recent survey of lesbian behavior (Blackwood, 1984a) found 95 cultures where lesbian and female cross-gender behavior occurred (plus several more that hinted at a possible lesbian role). Although one-third of these were Native North American tribes, the amount of data nevertheless indicates the limitations of previous studies as well as the misconceptions they have fostered regarding the prevalence of female homosexuality.

THE CONSTRUCTION OF LESBIANISM

Systems of gender, kinship and economy (as suggested by Adam, in this issue) affect the construction of both female and male homosexuality. Yet, the differential experiences of gender provide the basis for divergent lesbian and male homosexual patterns. In order to understand the cultural factors significant to the construction of lesbian behavior, the focus in this section will be on the female role and the contexts within which lesbian behavior appears. In particular it will outline the influence of differing gender systems and different levels of social stratification on the development of patterns of lesbian behavior.[3]

Putting aside cross-gender behavior for the moment, the construction of lesbianism, where it occurs, takes place within the sphere of female activities and networks. Women in all cultures are expected to marry and bear children; in many they are betrothed and wed before or soon after puberty. Consequently, for the most part lesbian behavior locates within the structure of marriage relations, but within that system a variety of sexual relations are possible.

The range of lesbian behavior that appears

---

[3]Gender systems can be drawn to roughly parallel levels of social stratification, i.e., increased stratification, increased inequality of the sexes, though any particular society will need much greater analysis than can be provided here. The analysis here is suggestive rather than definitive.

cross-culturally varies from formal to informal relations. These patterns may be described as follows. Informal relations among women are those which do not extend beyond the immediate social context. Examples of such would be adolescent sex play and affairs among women in harems or polygynous households. Formal lesbian relations are part of a network or social structure extending beyond the pair or immediate love relationship, and occur within such social relationships as bond friendship, sisterhoods, initiation schools, the cross-gender role, or woman-marriage. An examination of social stratification suggests that, in societies where women have control over their productive activities and status, both formal and informal relations may occur. Where women lack power, particularly in class societies, they maintain only informal lesbian ties or build institutions outside the dominant culture.

NON-CLASS SOCIETIES

In non-class societies, depending on the degree of economic autonomy of women, several patterns of formal and informal lesbian relations occur. These patterns can be found in both highly stratified states, such as those of the Azande and Dahomey in Africa, and the more egalitarian !Kung of southern Africa and the Australian aborigines. The patterns in each group result from cultural factors such as kinship regulations, the marriage system, trade rights, and sexual customs. Among the Azande the husband's kin arranged marriage by paying a brideprice to the wife's kin. The brideprice gave them the right to claim the offspring of the wife for their lineage. Wealthier men married several wives and built a dwelling in the compound for each wife. Wives were given a plot of land to cultivate, and they controlled the profits made from the produce through trade. Women married shortly after puberty, but as they fulfilled their duties as a wife, certain rights accrued to them. Consequently, despite the demands of the marriage system, some Azande women established

formal lesbian relationships, often with their co-wives. According to Evans-Pritchard (1970, p. 1429), "All Azande I have known well enough to discuss this matter have asserted . . . that female homosexuality . . . was practiced in polygamous homes in the past and still [1930] is sometimes."

Azande women usually kept the sexual nature of their friendships secret from their husbands, who felt threatened by such activities, yet could not forbid them. Such relationships may have been fairly common for adult women in certain other African groups where marriage was polygynous, as among the Nupe (Nadel, 1942), the Haussa (Karsch-Haack, 1975), and the Nyakyusa (Wilson, 1963). A relationship between two Azande women could be formalized through a ritual that created a permanent bond (Evans-Pritchard, 1970). This bond secured the emotional and economic support of the partner, and may have served to widen the trade network of the woman and possibly enhance her position in the community.[4] Thus, both formal and informal relationships occurred within the context of marriage among women who were in daily contact through their domestic and trade activities. It indicated that male control of female activities did not extend to interactions and concerns between females.

In other non-class societies lesbian relations occurred in sex-segregated childhood and adolescent groups. Among the highly stratified Dahomeyans, adolescent girls prepared for marriage responsibilities by attending initiation schools, where, among other activities, they performed exercises in each other's presence to thicken their genitalia. It has been noted that they engaged in sexual activities on these occasions (Herskovits, 1967). Such activity was congruent with their school training and served to heighten awareness of their erotic responses. Among the egalitarian !Kung, girls engaged in sexual play with other girls before they did so with boys (Shostak, 1981). In another egalitarian

[4]Similar to men's blood-brotherhood, as described by Evans-Pritchard (1933).

group, the Australian aborigines, adolescent sex play was an acknowledged and integral part of the social system. It conformed to the kinship regulations for marriage partners (Roheim, 1933), occurring among girls who were cross-cousins. Thus, an Australian girl formed lesbian relations with her female cross-cousin, whose family would later give her their son to marry, the girlfriends thereby becoming sisters-in-law.

In comparing the highly stratified social structure of Dahomey or the Azande to the more egalitarian Australian aborigines, the different constraints on lesbian behavior stand out. Herskovits (1932) stated that the adolescent period for Dahomeyan women was an acceptable time for lesbian activity. Some adult women also engage in it, probably in the context of polygynous marriages, but this was secretly done. Azande women also maintained clandestine relationships. Roheim (1933) reported that married Australian women engaged in lesbian activities, one form of which was called *kityili-kityili,* tickling the clitoris with the finger. Although a woman's first marriage was controlled by her kin, she had the choice, following the death of her first husband, to engage in various marital and extramarital relations (Bell, 1980, 1981). While Dahomeyan women were forced to conceal their lesbian activities, the lesbian relationships of the Australian women were an acknowledged part of their sexual behavior and were included in ritual activities (Kaberry, 1939). Thus, different levels of social stratification and marriage systems shape different patterns of lesbian behavior in non-class societies.

CLASS SOCIETIES

The contrast in patterns of lesbian behavior is sharper between non-class and class societies. In those with rigid hierarchical gender systems women's sexual activities are strictly confined. Formal lesbian patterns do not exist unless they maintain a status marginal to the dominant culture. In such societies, with control of women's productive and reproductive rights vested in male kin, not only were women confined to heterosexual marriage, but also their sexual activities were restricted by law or custom to their marital partner. Islamic law called for imprisonment for homosexuality and death or divorce for a wife caught in adultery (Minai, 1981). In this context, lesbian behavior, if it occurred at all, was informal and private. Clandestine relationships developed among Near Eastern women in harems and within the Muslim institution of purdah. Wives of ruling class men rarely saw their husbands and therefore sought alternative sources of relationships. Some wealthy, educated Near Eastern women could choose to remain unmarried and found great satisfaction in lesbian relationships (Abbott, 1946; Bullough, 1976; Walther, 1981). Ultimately, the strict segregation of the sexes provided the only context for lesbian relations.

Conditions were similarly restrictive for Chinese women. The sisterhoods of Kwangtung province provide the only available evidence of lesbian relationships in China (Sankar, this issue). This institution of bond friendship necessarily arose outside the traditional marriage and kin structure. Although still guided by the cultural values of the dominant society, these women rejected the traditional gender role to form sisterhoods based on the traditions of girls' houses and celibacy vows. The availability of silk work in Kwangtung province gave them the economic independence to refuse marriage. Some women did not engage in heterosexual relationships because of cultural sanctions imposed on those who took non-marriage vows. Others formed lover relationships with a "sister" (Sankar, 1978). Thus, in the class societies of the Near East and China the construction of lesbian relations showed two opposing trends: First, an informal pattern resulting from the restrictions of male-dominant institutions and, second, a sisterhood existing outside the social relations of the dominant culture and dependent on the success of female bonding and the tolerance of the larger society. This second type applies as well to the lesbian subculture of Western society in the last 80 years.

A formal pattern of age-graded lesbian relations appears in cultures with a dual economic system, such as black South Africa and Carriacou in the Caribbean. In both areas males participate in a capitalist wage-labor system through migration to industrial areas, while women work the land and direct the affairs of the household. On Carriacou husbands are separated from their wives for most of the year and at home are unable to command the exclusive attention of their wives. Older married women secure the affections and assistance of younger, often single women whom they support with income from the absentee husband (Smith, 1962). This relationship provides both economic and emotional support and is a viable alternative to the domestic isolation of the women. A similar pattern exists in South Africa, the mummy-baby game. It maintains the same functions of emotional and economic support as in Carriacou but the age range between women is smaller (Blacking, 1978; Gay, this issue; Mueller, 1977). Despite the imposition of a capitalist wage-labor system on these groups, its effects are mitigated through female bonding in mutually beneficial relationships. In South Africa these relationships may have derived from a traditional pattern of affective relations between older and younger women (Gay, this issue).

Cross-Gender Role

The cross-gender role for women constitutes another formal pattern of lesbian relations, which appears in certain classless societies and, in particular, in egalitarian societies. This role was institutionalized mainly among western Native American tribes and integrated into the social structure of the larger society. Five western tribes in which the cross-gender role has been observed at some length include the Mohave, Maricopa, Cocopa, Kaska, and Klamath (Blackwood, 1984b). Depending on their interest and ability, some women in these tribes took on the male gender role, usually at puberty, and performed the duties associated with men, such as

hunting, trapping, and, for Cocopa *warrhameh*, fighting in battle. These women were not denied the right to marry and frequently took wives with whom they established a household and raised children. The significance of the female cross-gender role lay in the ability of women to take on a male role regardless of their biology. Further, it was possible for them to cross roles without threatening the definition of the male role because men and women had equal status and occupied complementary rather than antagonistic gender roles (Blackwood, 1984b).

In contrast to the flexibility of gender roles in egalitarian societies, class societies that have hierarchical gender systems define gender more rigidly. In such cultures the gender system is structured in a dichotomous fashion; neither sex participates in the behaviors nor activities of the other. In male-dominant cultures such as western Europe or the Near East, it is impossible for women to assume a cross-gender role because such behavior poses a threat to the gender system and the very definitions of maleness and femaleness. Those who did, such as the passing women of western Europe, risked grave repercussions; if discovered, they faced serious punishment or even death (Crompton, 1981; Faderman, 1981).

CONCLUSION

The construction of lesbianism shatters some basic assumptions about women which have been propounded in the discourse on homosexuality. The perception that men maintain universal hegemony over women's sexuality is contradicted by the data on alternative sexual relationships for women. Rubin (1975) theorized that women were forced, through marriage, to be heterosexual and that this condition prevailed in all cultures. Others have subscribed to the concept of "enforced heterosexuality"; for example, Adrienne Rich has suggested lesbianism "comprises both the breaking of a taboo and the rejection of a compulsory way of life . . . a direct or indirect attack on male right of access to women" (1980, p. 649). In contrast to this analysis, the history of sexual relations is not one of total heterosexual dominance. The construction of sexuality in many non-class societies validated variant sexual behavior for women. Women's lives were not wholly constrained by the dictates of marriage and child-bearing, nor did they live in total submission to men. Other types of sexual relations existed both before and after marriage. As the Azande example shows, various formal and informal lesbian relations co-existed with marriage, giving women several options and avenues for control of their lives and sexual activities. In many tribal societies lesbian relations were not considered deviant nor were the women "breaking taboos"; on the contrary, lesbian bonds were institutionalized and integrated into kinship and other social structures.

Social stratification and gender ideology may place serious restrictions on women's sexuality. The constraints of marriage and lack of property rights imposed on women in many societies apparently limits the development of non-marital homosexual behavior and institutions. These constraints, however, should not be construed to be the result of the "limitations" of the female's biological sex. Enforced heterosexuality is tied to women's lack of economic power and the restriction of female activity to the domestic sphere. Further, the embeddedness of sexuality with gender roles in Western societies proscribes homosexual activity and defines women as male sex objects.

The barriers to female power and sexuality in modern society reside in the male-dominant ideologies of gender and sexuality. Nevertheless, as the Chinese sisterhoods exemplify, even within strongly patriarchal societies women are capable of forming alternative institutions that circumvent male control. Similarly, lesbians in the United States are now building their own institutions and kin structures as well as creating sexual ideologies in opposition to the dominant society (Lockard, this issue).

Patterns of lesbian behavior develop from the particular conditions of the female gender role and the types of constraints which arise from the subordinate status women occupy in many societies. These constraints establish patterns which in many cases diverge from those for male homosexual behavior and yet are not less critical to a general understanding of homosexuality. Hopefully, future research will provide a more balanced approach to the study of the construction of both female and male homosexual behavior.

REFERENCES

ABBOTT, N. (1946). *Two Queens of Bagdad.* Chicago: University of Chicago Press.

ADAM, B. D. (1985). Age, structure, and sexuality: Reflections on the anthropological evidence on homosexual relations. *Journal of Homosexuality, 11* (3/4), 19–33.

BELL, D. (1980). Desert politics: Choices in the "marriage market." In M. Etienne & E. Leacock (Eds.), *Women and colonization* (pp. 239–269). New York: J. J. Bergin.

BELL, D. (1981). Women's business is hard work: Central Australian aboriginal women's love rituals. *Signs: Journal of Women in Culture and Society, 7,* 314–337.

BENEDICT, R. (1934). *Patterns of culture.* New York: Houghton Mifflin.

BENEDICT, R. (1939). Sex in primitive society. *American Journal of Orthopsychiatry, 9,* 570–573.

BERNDT, R. M. & BERNDT, C. H. (1963). *Sexual behavior in western Arnhem Land.* New York: Johnson Reprint.

BLACKING, J. (1978). Uses of the kinship idiom in friendships at some Venda and Zulu schools. In J. Argyle & E. Preston-Whyte (Eds.), *Social system and tradition in southern Africa* (pp. 101–117). Cape Town: Oxford University Press.

BLACKWOOD, E. (1984a). *Cross-cultural dimensions of lesbian relations.* Unpublished master's thesis. Department of Anthropology. San Francisco State University.

BLACKWOOD, E. (1984b). Sexuality and gender in certain Native American tribes: The case of cross-gender females. *Signs: Journal of Women in Culture and Society, 10,* 27–42.

BULLOUGH, V. L. (1976). *Sexual variance in society and history.* New York: John Wiley and Sons.

BURTON, R. F. (1956). Terminal essay. In D. W. Cory (Ed.), *Homosexuality, a cross-cultural approach* (pp. 207–224). New York: Julian Press (originally published 1886).

CALLENDER, C. & KOCHEMS, L. (1985). Men and not-men: Male gender mixing statuses and homosexuality. *Journal of Homosexuality, 11*(3/4), 165–178.

CARRIER, J. M. (1980). Homosexual behavior in cross-cultural perspective. In J. Marmor (Ed.), *Homosexual behavior: A modern reappraisal* (pp 100–122). New York: Basic Books.

CROMPTON, L. (1981). The myth of lesbian impunity: Capital laws from 1270 to 1791. *Journal of Homosexuality, 6*(1/2), 11–25.

DE CECCO, J. P. & SHIVELY, M. G. (1984). From sexual identities to sexual relationships: A contextual shift. *Journal of Homosexuality, 9*(2/3), 1–26.

D'EMILIO, J. (1983). *Sexual politics, sexual communities: The making of a homosexual minority in the U.S., 1940–1970.* Chicago: University of Chicago Press.

ELLIS, H. & SYMONDS, J. A. (1975). *Sexual inversion.* New York: Arno Press (reprint of Studies in the Psychology of Sex, Vol. I, 1897).

EVANS-PRITCHARD, E. E. (1933). Zande blood-brotherhood. *Africa, 6,* 369–401.

EVANS-PRITCHARD, E. E. (1970). Sexual inversion among the Azande. *American Anthropologist, 72,* 1428–1434.

FADERMAN, L. (1981). *Surpassing the love of men: Romantic friendship and love between women from the Renaissance to the present.* New York: William Morrow.

FIRTH, R. (1936). *We, the Tikopia.* New York: American Books.

FITZGERALD, T. K. (1977). A critique of anthropological research on homosexuality. *Journal of Homosexuality, 2,* 385–397.

FORD, C. S. & BEACH, F. A. (1951). *Patterns of sexual behavior.* New York: Harper and Brothers.

GAY, J. (1985). "Mummies and babies" and friends and lovers in Lesotho. *Journal of Homosexuality, 11*(3/4), 97–116.

GRAY, J. P. (1985). Growing yams and men: An interpretation of Kimam male ritualized homosexual behavior. *Journal of Homosexuality, 11*(3/4), 55–68.

HERDT, G. H. (1981). *Guardians of the flutes: Idioms of masculinity.* New York: McGraw-Hill.

HERDT, G. H. (1984). *Ritualized homosexuality in Melanesia.* Berkeley: University of California Press.

HERSKOVITS, M. J. (1932). Some aspects of Dahomeyan ethnology. *Africa, 5,* 266–296.

HERSHKOVITS, M. J. (1967). *Dahomey: An ancient West African kingdom* (2 vols.). Evanston: Northwestern University Press.

HILL, W. W. (1935). The status of the hermaphrodite and transvestite in Navaho culture. *American Anthropologist, 37,* 273–279.

KABERRY, P. M. (1939). *Aboriginal woman, sacred and profane.* London: George Routledge and Sons.

KARSCH-HAACK, F. (1975). *Das gleichgeschlechtliche leben der naturvolker.* [The homosexual life of primitive peoples.] New York: Arno Press (1st ed. Reinhardt 1911).

KATZ, J. (1976). *Gay American history: Lesbians and gay men in the U.S.A.* New York: Thomas Y. Crowell.

KROEBER, A. L. (1925). *Handbook of the Indians of California.* United States Bureau of American Ethnology. (Bulletin 78).

KROEBER, A. L. (1940). Psychosis or social sanction. *Character and Personality, 8,* 204–215.

LAYARD, J. (1959). Homo-eroticism in a primitive society as a function of the self. *Journal of Analytical Psychology, 4,* 101–115.

LEVY, R. I. (1971). The community function of Tahitian male transvestitism: A hypothesis. *Anthropological Quarterly, 44,* 12–21.

LINDENBAUM, S. (1984). Variations on a sociosexual theme in Melanesia. In G. H. Herdt (Ed.), *Ritualized homosexuality in Melanesia* (pp. 337–361). Berkeley: University of California Press.

LOCKARD, D. (1985). The lesbian community: An anthropological approach. *Journal of Homosexuality, 11*(3/4), 83–95.

MCINTOSH, M. (1981). The homosexual role, with postscript: The homosexual role revisited. In K. Plummer (Ed.), *The making of the modern homosexual* (pp. 30–49). Totowa, N.J.: Barnes and Noble.

MEAD, M. (1935). *Sex and temperament in three primitive societies* (3rd ed.). New York: William Morrow and Co.

MEAD, M. (1961). Cultural determinants of sexual behavior. In W. C. Young (Ed.), *Sex and internal secretions* (2 vols.) (pp. 1433–1479). Baltimore: Williams and Williams.

METRAUX, A. (1940). *Ethnology of Easter Island.* Honolulu: Bernice P. Bishop Museum.

MINAI, N. (1981). *Women in Islam.* New York: Seaview Books.

MUELLER, M. B. (1977). *Women and men in rural Lesotho: The periphery of the periphery.* Unpublished doctoral dissertation, Brandeis University.

NADEL, S. F. (1942). *A black Byzantium: The kingdom of Nupe in Nigeria.* London: Oxford University Press.

NEWTON, E. (1972). *Mother camp: Female imperson-ators in America.* Englewood Cliffs, NJ: Prentice-Hall.

OPLER, M. (1965). Anthropological and cross-cultural aspects of homosexuality. In J. Marmor (Ed.), *Sexual inversion: The multiple roots of homosexuality* (pp. 108–123). New York: Basic Books.

PADGUG, R. A. (1979). Sexual matters: On conceptualizing sexuality in history. *Radical History Review, 20,* 3–23.

PLUMMER, K. (1981). *The making of the modern homosexual.* Totowa, NJ: Barnes and Noble.

READ, K. E. (1980). *Other voices: The style of a male homosexual tavern.* Novato, CA: Chandler and Sharp.

REITER, R. R. (1975). *Towards an anthropology of women.* New York: Monthly Review Press.

RICH, A. (1980). Compulsory heterosexuality and lesbian existence. *Signs: Journal of Women in Culture and Society, 5,* 631–660.

RICHARDSON, D. (1984). The dilemma of essentiality in homosexual theory. *Journal of Homosexuality, 9*(2/3), 79–90.

ROHEIM, G. (1933). Women and their life in central Australia. *Journal of the Royal Anthropological Institute of Great Britain and Ireland, 63,* 207–265.

ROHEIM, G. (1950). *Psychoanalysis and anthropology.* New York: International Universities Press.

ROSS, E. & RAPP, R. (1981). Sex and society: A research note from social history and anthropology. *Comparative Studies in Society and History, 23,* 51–72.

RUBIN, G. (1975). The traffic in women: Notes on the "political economy" of sex. In R. R. Reiter (Ed.), *Towards an anthropology of women* (pp. 157–210). New York: Monthly Review Press.

RUBIN, G. (1984). Thinking sex: Notes for a radical theory of the politics of sexuality. In C. Vance (Ed.), *Pleasure and danger: Exploring female sexuality* (pp. 267–319). Boston: Routledge and Kegan Paul.

SANKAR, A. P. (1978). *The evolution of the spinsterhood in traditional Chinese society: From village girls' houses to chai t'angs in Hong Kong.* Unpublished doctoral dissertation. University of Michigan.

SANKAR, A. P. (1985). Sisters and brothers, lovers and enemies: Marriage resistance in southern Kwangtung. *Journal of Homosexuality, 11*(3/4), 69–81.

SHOSTAK, M. (1981). *Nisa, the life and words of a !Kung Woman.* Cambridge: Harvard University Press.

SMITH, M. G. (1962). *Kinship and community in Carriacou.* New Haven: Yale University Press.

SONENSCHEIN, D. (1966). Homosexuality as a subject of anthropological inquiry. *Anthropological Quarterly, 39*(2), 73–82.

SPENCER, B. SIR & GILLEN, E. J. (1927). *The Arunta* (2 vols.). London: Macmillan and Co.

WALTHER, W. (1981). *Women in Islam.* C. S. V. Salt, transl. Montclair, NJ: Abner Schram.

WEEKS, J. (1981). *Sex, politics, and society: The regulation of sexuality since 1800.* London: Longman.

WEST, D. J. (1977). *Homosexuality re-examined.* Minneapolis: University of Minnesota Press.

WESTERMARCK, E. (1956). Homosexual love. In D. W. Cory (Ed.), *Homosexuality, a cross-cultural approach* (pp. 101–136). New York: Julian Press.

WHITEHEAD, H. (1981). The bow and the burden strap: A new look at institutionalized homosexuality in native North America. In S. B. Ortner & H. Whitehead (Eds.), *Sexual meanings: The cultural construction of gender and sexuality* (pp. 80–115). Cambridge: Cambridge University Press.

WHITEHEAD, H. (1984). *Discussion of gender-crossing.* Paper presented at the 83rd Annual Meetings of the American Anthropological Association, Denver.

WILSON, M. (1963). *Good company: A study of Nyakyusa age-villages.* Boston: Beacon Press.

WOLF, D. G. (1979). *The lesbian community.* Berkeley: University of California Press.

25

"MUMMIES AND BABIES" AND FRIENDS AND LOVERS IN LESOTHO

JUDITH GAY

This paper examines an institutionalized friendship among adolescent girls and young women in southern Africa. Lesotho's economy is based on migrant male labor which leaves the women dependent on male earnings or subsistence from the land, and also creates unstable marital relations. Young girls in the modern schools develop close relationships, called "mummy-baby," with slightly older girls. Sexual intimacy is an important aspect of these relationships. Mummy-baby relationships not only provide emotional support prior to marriage, but also a network of support for married and unmarried women in new towns or schools, either replacing or accompanying heterosexual bonds.

This paper examines a type of institutionalized friendship in Lesotho[1], an independent migrant labor exporting country in southern Africa.

An earlier version of this article was published in *Cambridge Anthropology,* 1979, Vol. 5, No. 3, the "Issue on Sexuality." Data for this article were collected while doing field research concerning the impact of migrant labor on rural women in Lesotho during 1976 and 1977. The author acknowledges the Smuts Memorial Fund and Sir Bartle Frere's Memorial Fund at Cambridge University for financial assistance which helped to make this field work possible. Gratitude is also expressed to Dr. Susan Drucker-Brown for invaluable suggestions on the preliminary draft of this article, and to Judith Ennew and members of their seminar on Kinship and Structuring of Sexuality for their comments. The author may be contacted at the Episcopal Divinity School, 99 Brattle Street, Cambridge, MA 02138.

These friendships most often occur among adolescent Basotho girls, who refer to each other by the English terms *mummies* and *babies.* They are closely related to heterosexual courtship that becomes dominant in late adolescence. Few ethnographic accounts give details about social and emotional relationships during adolescence. During this critical period girls usually experience three of the most profound bodily changes of their lives: Puberty, loss of virginity, and first childbirth (Hastrup, 1978). Furthermore, few ethnographic accounts discuss "homosexual" physical and emotional relationships, nor the

SOURCE: From "Mummies and Babies" by J. Gay in *The Many Faces of Homosexuality* by E. Blackwood (Ed.). Copyright © 1986 by Harrington Park Press. Reprinted by permission.

adolescent shift from primary association with same-sex playmates and workmates to opposite-sex lovers and marital partners. Lionel Tiger (1969) argues in *Men in Groups* that women, in contrast to men, "do not form bonds. Dependent as most women are on the earnings and genes of men, they break ranks very soon" (p. 216). His argument is based on a lack of cross-cultural data concerning female friendships, which not only precede, but also exist alongside heterosexual relationships. It is my hope that this paper will contribute to the studies of female sexuality and the social roles of women, which are beginning to fill this ethnographic gap.

In such studies it is important to examine the nature of the sub-cultures girls create in adolescence, in order to see how they handle their physical maturation, emotional growth, and broadening social relationships. It is also necessary to break free from the ethnocentric polarization of homosexual and heterosexual relations that is such a marked feature of western culture, and take a fresh look at the neglected topic of affective relations among members of the same sex. Furthermore, any such inquiry into the structuring of sexual relations must be considered in light of the particular socio-economic conditions which dominate the lives of the individuals concerned.

SOCIAL AND ECONOMIC CONTEXT OF FEMALE FRIENDSHIPS IN LESOTHO

Lesotho is a country completely surrounded by the Republic of South Africa. The dominant feature of its socio-economic life is male migrant labor. About half of Lesotho's adult male labor force migrates to South Africa, leaving women in Lesotho for most of their lives as daughters without fathers, sisters without brothers, wives without husbands, and mothers without sons. In the rural lowlands village of 1,484 people where my fieldwork was conducted, 82% of the men between the ages of 20 and 39 were away as migrant workers for some portion of 1977.

Employment opportunities for women within Lesotho's towns are few and poorly paid, and most women are excluded by South Africa's "influx control" measures from living and working in The Republic. This forces them into increasing dependence on male earnings and on subsistence agriculture in impoverished rural areas. At the same time that the migrant labor system has increased female economic dependence, it makes marital relationships unstable. It prevents the establishment of close conjugal relations and encourages adultery, non-support, desertion and divorce. Marriage within a patrilineal family system remains the norm, but it is devalued in contrast to continuing close ties with mothers and siblings, who provide women with security in times of marital failure and economic distress.

Despite the importance of close ties with natal kin, fosterage arrangements are often made for children when marriages fail, extra-marital or pre-marital pregnancies occur, or mothers must seek employment. Many children are also separated from their mothers in order to attend school, or to provide help with child-care, house-work, or herding for relatives. Later, at the time of marriage, girls must leave their natal kin and move to their husband's homes. After just a few weeks of marriage they are often left with an unfamiliar mother-in-law and new neighbors when the husband goes off to his distant place of work. Young wives are eager to establish independent neo-local residence, but then they may spend the early years of marriage in lonely little homes waiting for the occasional visit of migrant husbands. Wives who are left alone in the rural areas, and unwed mothers and deserted wives who seek employment in towns, have to be self-reliant and independent in order to survive and to support their children.

Churches, schools, and a modern cash economy have undermined many social traditions. Sesotho initiation for girls is no longer practiced in most lowland villages, where about half of the nation's population lives. In the village I studied, there had been no girls' initiation conducted for twenty years; and only 10% of the women between the ages of 20 and 39 had been initiated. A western style education is highly valued, particularly for girls; 91.1 per cent of the girls and 65.7 per cent of the boys from ages 7 to 16 were attending school during 1977. Most aspects of the life of children, as well as of adults, are segregated by sex, but the common culture that develops in the co-educational schools provides a meeting ground for the sexes over which parents can exert little control. Traditional *rites de passage* and adult social control having declined in importance, modern youth culture plays an increasingly important role in socialization and regulation of adolescent interpersonal relations.

ORIGINS OF MUMMY-BABY RELATIONS

Basotho girls engage in three types of activities which they call *papali* (games), in which they act out different aspects of adult female roles. In playing house they pretend to cook and perform other domestic tasks without the drudgery of regular responsibility; in elaborate mock wedding festivities they celebrate marriages without husbands, in-laws or bridewealth; and in dyadic mummy-baby friendships they experience the nurturing aspects of mothering and being mothered, without the risks of childbirth or the responsibilities of child-care. This stands in contrast to the major role girls have in the care of younger children within their households.

In each of these activities young girls are gradually socialized into adult female roles and relationships by slightly older and more experienced girls. In Sesotho custom there is a strict prohibition against discussing sexual matters by a woman who has borne children with one who has not. Where such a barrier is created by discourse taboos, and where mothers advocate a sexual morality of marital fidelity which is at variance with their own conduct, it is unlikely that a girl can obtain sexual information and advice from her own mother. Thus, it is particularly significant that these mummy-baby relations have developed as a way in which a fictive mother can provide what a biological mother cannot.

John Blacking (1959) first pointed to the existence of fictive kinship relations among Venda girls 20 years ago. In a more recent article he described Venda and Zulu school-girl friendships as "part of a common Black South African culture . . . associated with modern school education," perhaps diffused from a single source or "invented more than once" (1978, p. 104). Martha Mueller (1977) reported similar relationships in two villages in Lesotho, and my own investigations have documented their presence in many parts of Lesotho, as well as in Johannesburg and Durban. Girls regard these relationships as very personal, however, and only discuss them reticently with a stranger whose disapproval they fear. Hence, my study is limited to observations and to interviews with 14 village women, who were willing to discuss their own relationships and those of other women in the village, the larger towns and in more distant boarding schools.

The origin and diffusion of these institutionalized friendships are not clear. In Lesotho, as in the areas Blacking discusses, these relationships seem strongest in the modern school culture, yet have their roots in traditional institutions and practices.

The dyads in Lesotho are almost invariably described by the English words mummies and babies, whether embedded in English or Sesotho sentences. The use of the English terms bears out the assertion of several of my informants that the mummy-baby game is relatively new, first occurring during the 1950s. It apparently spread rapidly through the secondary schools, which drew pupils from diverse parts of Lesotho, as well as from South Africa. Prior to South Africa's rigid apartheid laws, there was considerable movement of Basotho women and children in and out of South Africa, as well as circulation of the educated elite among mission schools and training institutions. Quite likely free movement between towns and schools of southern Africa was a mechanism for the development and diffusion of a common black southern African culture in which these relations are just one ingredient. However, it seems clear that there were features of traditional female society which provided basic models.

First, elderly informants told me that special affective and gift-exchange partnerships among girls and women existed in "the old days" of their youth. Informants said that these were known simply by the Sesotho terms: *ho ratana* (to like or love one another), *Lechako* (from the verb *ho chaka,* to visit) *sethaka* (a relationship between agemates, *lithaka* usually referred to girls who had been initiated together), and *mechaufa* (from *ho chaufa,* meaning to fall in love or to flatter). This last word is not in the standard Sesotho dictionary, but my two oldest informants said it refers particularly to a love affair between girls.

Secondly, there is the underlying influence of female initiation traditions, though none of my informants acknowledged a connection between the mummy-baby relations and the initiation-sponsor relationships that Blacking describes for the Venda (1959, 1978), and Krige for the Lovedu (1943, pp. 111–125). Certainly, wherever initiation is practiced, small groups of girls spend an intense period of time in the company of agemates and are prepared for adult sexual lives by female teachers who are not their own mothers. Modern female friendships, at the very least, help to fill a vacuum created by the decline of female initiation, even if, as Blacking believes, there is little evidence of direct cultural continuity (1978, p. 101).

An additional feature of traditional female sexuality in Lesotho, which may have an indirect relation to this institution, is the practice of lengthening the labia minora. This is still practiced by many girls, as a matter of female pride, and is believed to enhance sexual pleasure during intercourse (Longmore 1959, pp. 40–41). The process of lengthening is done alone or in small groups, but is not directly tied to initiation. The process is said to heighten *mocheso* (heat) and appears to provide opportunities for auto-eroticism and mutual stimulation between girls. This practice stands in sharp contrast to taboos against masturbation in our own society, and to the practice of clitoredectomy in other African societies. It is also true that girls are warned by adults to avoid eating eggs and the inside parts of sheep, for these are believed to heighten *mocheso* and to lead a girl prematurely to desire sexual relations with boys. Thus, in these two contradictory customs female sensuality is both encouraged and restrained, but it is never denied.

THE PARTICIPANTS IN MUMMY-BABY RELATIONS

Mummy-baby relations in the village I studied are most common among pre-adolescent and adolescent school girls, although pre-school girls occasionally form pairs in imitation of their older acquaintances. Older unmarried girls who have dropped out of school and remain in the village, and those who have gone to the towns to seek employment or to attend distant schools, often maintain old ties, and form new ones in the urban environment. One informant said that she thought these relationships were most common among *ma-hippi* (plural of the English term "hippy"), meaning smartly dressed, single students or young working women in the towns, who often live with other women in rented rooms apart from their families. But mummy-baby relationships are also important in the lives of many older women who have gone to the capital city to take up work as domestic servants. These women form their own urban community while living in tiny servant's quarters apart from kin and former friends. Within the village I studied and the villages in which Mueller worked, some young wives maintained old, and formed new intimate friendships. Some married women said that former "childish" types of relations had matured to become "real adult friendships." Informants stated that in villages that are near the main road and the South African border, most adult women are no longer involved in intimate female friendships. In these villages men often come home on leave and women appear to be more interested in adulterous male lovers than in women friends.

I only began asking about these relationships after living for a year in the village. I told my research assistant that I had never heard anybody mention them. She chided me by saying that if I observed, and listened to the way girls and women sometimes addressed each other, saw how they sat together in a concert or a beer hall, or seemed startled when we found them together when we arrived for an interview, such relationships would have been apparent. She was right, of course, but my oversight can be attributed to the privacy that is an essential aspect of these relations, and points out the women's fear of condemnation by an outsider.

A conversation on female friendships with three older women was interrupted by the arrival of a 24-year-old daughter-in-law, who gasped and clapped her hands in amazement when she heard the topic of our discussion. "Why are you clapping so?" asked the straightforward 97-year-old woman. "Haven't you ever fallen in love with another girl?"

INITIATION OF A RELATIONSHIP

Relationships are always initiated voluntarily by one girl who takes a liking to another and simply asks her to be her mummy or her baby, depending on their relative ages. Real kin are rarely chosen, except by very small girls whom older girls say "don't know what the game is all about and are only playing at it."[2] Girls sometimes ask a village acquaintance or a sister's friend, but often choose a newcomer to the village, a schoolmate from another village, or an attractive older girl or woman from the nearby town where most of the shops, churches, and schools are located. Thus, the initiation of such a relationship is a recognized means whereby a girl can extend the range of her social relations.

The most frequently given reason for initiating a particular relationship was that one girl felt attracted to the other by her looks, her clothes, or her actions. When I suggested that girls might approach an older girl or woman as a patron, thinking of the gifts or material help they can gain from the relationship, some informants expressed shock, saying that such an attitude would spoil the relationship, which should be based on sincere love, not on selfish calculation. Other informants admitted that some girls, particularly in the towns, do use the relationships as a calculated means to gain patrons, but they felt this practice debased the meaning of the bond.

The fictive kinship terminology used by the girls derives from the central mother-child bond of Basotho families, a bond that is often disrupted by fosterage and schooling. It is an accepted rule that a mummy may have several babies, but no baby may have more than one mummy at the same time. However, such rules do not prevent the formation of ties outside the village or school community, nor limit the number of relationships an individual may enter into as partners move away or marry. One of my informants reported having had six mummies between ages 12 and 18; and one of Mueller's cases, Clorina, was an unmarried mother still attending school, who had had nine mummies although never any fictive babies (see case 1). Some girls declined new relations because of previous commitments; Clorina's case was unusual. Other girls said they had not been particularly attracted to the person who proposed the relationship but they hadn't wanted to hurt her feelings by saying so. Others said they didn't know the other well, so they accepted the offer just to see how the relationship would develop.

THE NATURE OF A RELATIONSHIP: ENCOUNTERS AND EXCHANGES

Once two girls agree to be mummy and baby, the relationship develops through arranged encounters and by material, nurturant, and emotional exchanges which vary with relative age and marital status of the partners. Arrangements to meet somewhere or to do something together are almost always initiated by the older, dominant member of the dyad, and are generally arranged secretly so that others will not know of the arrangement or what they do when they meet. "You, as baby can't just go and visit your mummy," an informant explained, "for you respect her and would feel ashamed to do so. She must invite you." Thus, the deferential behavior appropriate towards older women is expected. A mummy may see her baby on the way to school and suggest that she come to visit and play cards on Saturday afternoon, knowing that her real mother will be away visiting that day. Or the mummy may hand the baby a letter suggesting that they meet at the football field, an evening concert, or that they go to collect firewood. Since letter writing is an essential means by which Basotho migrants keep in touch with their families and friends, it is not surprising that the exchange of letters is a feature of the mummy-baby game. Schoolteachers say that they often find "love letters" awkwardly scribbled by one school pupil to another. These children practice one of the principal uses to which literacy is put in Lesotho, and master the stock phrases used in such letters (see Blacking, 1959).

Gift-giving is an essential part of the mummy role. Mummies most often provide sweets, cosmetics, headties, or inexpensive items of clothing. One girl said that, whenever she is shopping and sees something nice, she will think of her baby and want to buy it for her. When one vil-

lage woman married and then delivered her first child, it was her former mummy of many years back who was the first village woman to visit and bring her gifts of soap and baby clothing. Babies will reciprocate if they can with a few peaches or vegetables from their homes, or any small thing they may have, although it is understood that they are normally on the receiving end of the transactions.

For those girls who go away to boarding schools, gift giving and other material help becomes much more important, as Blacking points out in this study, because of the regimented living conditions, limited recreation, and poor food (1978). Informants who had attended such schools in Lesotho not only had school girl mummies or babies, but mummies who were older married women from a nearby village who gave tinned biscuits, cooked food, clothing, soap, or creams and occasionally even loaned money to their babies. Some would invite the baby along with a few friends to a Sunday afternoon party in the village. Girls who had been unable to find dormitory accommodations were given rent-free housing by married women who became their mummies in the sense of an adult foster-mother rather than a partner in an adolescent friendship.

Other important help given by mummies was in the form of advice and protection concerning love-relationships with men. Among the Basotho, as among the Zulu whose youth culture is discussed in detail by Reader (1966), love-relations are not directed at first towards marriage but towards establishing one's personhood in society. Boys see sexual conquests as a mark of achieving manhood, and conquests are a dominant preoccupation of migrant men of all ages home on leave from the single-sex compounds where they live and work. Sexual relations are problematic for girls during adolescence when they realize the risks of premarital pregnancy. Yet they are anxious both to learn the rules of the heterosexual game and to have female support when they begin to play it in earnest.

A girl's own mother can rarely give realistic advice or protection because of traditional prohibitions on sexual discourse. Mothers advocate old-fashioned norms of premarital chastity and marital fidelity which few people follow, and the attitude that love between a boy and a girl should never be displayed in front of adults. But an adolescent mummy can provide advice on sex and protection from aggressively courting young men which a mother cannot give. For example, informants said that, when girls go to play netball, hold mock weddings, or participate in dancing and singing contests in other villages, their older mummies often go along for protection and to enjoy the fun of the inter-village female activities which they have outgrown.

The most important aspect of mummy-baby relations is the exchange of affection and sensual satisfaction. My informants talked openly about gifts, letters, visits, and advice, but were invariably reticent in discussing the emotional and sensual aspects of the relationships. Yet, when conversation became intimate, they said that, yes, this was what these relationships were really about and why they were different from ordinary friendships. One informant explained:

> Friends may visit, love each other, even give gifts now and then. But between mummies and babies it is like an affair, a romance, and being alone together to hug and kiss each other is always a part of it. (Field notes, 1976–77)

Every informant agreed that this aspect is essential, except in those cases where there is a great age differential which makes the relation more like that between a foster mother and her ward, or between very little girls who are really too young to "know what it is all about" and are just "playing at it."

Physical relations between females in Lesotho appear to fall into three distinct levels of intimacy. First, there is the common, public form of greeting when Basotho friends and relatives of either sex meet after a period of absence and kiss (*ho suna*) each other on the lips. At this level also friends or relatives of the same sex, who have lived all their lives with inadequate furniture in crowded households, often share a bed or sleep side-by-side in blanket rolls on the floor. The second form is distinguished from the public form as the way mummies and babies kiss and hug each other (*ho sunana* and *ho tsoarana,* with reciprocal verb endings) and rest together on the bed when they meet in private, or when one calls the other out in the dark at a concert or a dance to embrace. A third and more intense level of genital sexuality may exist between females. However, when I asked about "people of the same sex making love like a man and a woman," most women said they disapprove of it and regard it as quite distinct from the normal "hugging and kissing" of the mummy-baby game. Several informants said that the Bible forbids people of the same sex sleeping together and making love like a man and a woman, and cited sermons they had heard against homosexuality. Some said they had heard of men in mines who do such things, but they could not imagine how it could happen between women. But several younger unmarried informants said matter-of-factly that certainly it does happen, that some school girls learn to make love in that way, and that they personally see nothing wrong with it. My limited facility in the language, as well as my hesitance in asking, prevented clarification. The two types of responses may indicate that informants perceived my questions in quite different ways, in addition to affirming separate opinions about very subtle and personal matters.

It is the second level of physical contact which is the recognized norm in these fictive kinship relations. Although the informants were reticent in discussing their own present involvements, if they continued to have them, they were willing to discuss the relationships in general and their own past experiences. All expressed pleasure in remembering, and they insisted that they saw nothing wrong in such physical involvement with other girls. One girl said that at 15, when asked to be somebody's mummy, she had felt too shy to kiss although she realized that having accepted the senior role, she should have taken the initiative. The next year, an older girl became her mummy, and then, she said with a smile, "I was not too shy." Another informant told with pleasure of a church youth group outing where the bus had broken down in the night and couples rested together on their blankets, some girls with their boyfriends, and some with mummies or babies, while the teacher in charge and the bus driver were preoccupied with repairs. Although informants experienced these relationships as normal and enjoyable, and said their mothers usually permitted them if they knew, girls who had attended mission schools said that the nuns and matrons strongly disapproved and attempted to prevent them.

It is clear that these structured friendships provide opportunities for adolescent girls to discover and enjoy with other girls their own developing sexuality within a parentally tolerated relationship. They fill this need at an age when heterosexual relations are forbidden by adults and carry with them the risks of non-marital pregnancy and termination of schooling. Such mummy-baby relations also provide opportunities for girls to experience both dominant and receptive sexual roles, just as the experiences of real childbirth and childcare involve females first as dependent daughters and sisters and then as nurturing mothers. In courtship and marriage, on the other hand, it is always the Mosotho male who is expected to take the initiative in suggesting sexual encounters, in the act of sex, and in jural, ritual, and economic matters as head of the family. Within mummy-baby relations, as within mother-centered female society generally, a girl passes from junior to senior roles as relationships change. She may even be engaged in both at the same time, passing on to her baby by words and actions what she has learned of love-making, and nurture, from her older mummy.

The emotional appeal of these relations is not merely in the sensual intimacy. It is present equally in the drama of making, breaking, and re-creating relationships. This aspect appears in several recurrent themes in the accounts by informants. One theme is that girls take the initiative to propose love (*ho fereha*), an otherwise male prerogative and a dominant preoccupation of village men and boys. In heterosexual affairs, girls can only flirt and make themselves attractive (*ho iteka*) but in the mummy-baby game they can propose love with all its attendant excitement and anxiety. A second theme is secrecy, the idea that clandestine meetings must be arranged and that detection by critical adults, jealous age-mates, and prying youngsters should be avoided. Another is that of jealousy: hurt feelings when neglected, painful times of not speaking to one another and perhaps parting, or tender moments of apologizing and forgiving. Jealously among partners and potential partners is also common. One woman proudly said that, when she had moved as a new bride to the village, many young women had asked her to be mummy or baby to them. They had, however, troubled her a lot because they were so jealous of each other, so she used to beat her babies when they squabbled. Another woman, Malerato, said that, when she had gone away from home to attend high school, still unmarried at the age of 20, she had two babies who loved her very much but were jealous of each other, a problem she finally solved by "giving" one of them to become the baby of a friend (see case 2).

Thus, romantic dramas of attraction, proposal, jealousy, estrangement, reconciliation, and restructuring of relationships are features of this game. This is important to recognize as we try to relate these fictive kinship relations to real kinship and marriage: the mother-child dyad, and the husband-wife dyad.

Mother-child bonds are biologically determined and immutable. Although they can be shared through child-minding and fosterage arrangements, they cannot be fundamentally altered. The structure of husband-wife relations is also relatively unchangeable once it is established and sealed by bridewealth, the birth of children, and the economic interdependence of the family. But pre-marital and marital relations also have dramatic aspects in courtship, jealousy, infidelity, confession, reconciliation, wife beating, fighting and separation. These instabilities are deeply threatening to the conjugal bond which is vital for reproductive and economic security; but they are also foci of passion, and a dominant preoccupation of village life. Their centrality is expressed in the adulterous alliances in which most adult Basotho are involved. It is significant that in mummy-baby friendships, as well as in adulterous affairs and real mothering relationships, women are able to exercise a great degree of initiative and autonomous action. This stands in contrast to the formal rules of marriage, where women are constrained by both the male-dominated family system and by the modern male-dominated economic system.

ADULT HETEROSEXUALITY AND FEMALE FRIENDSHIP

In addition to the female-to-female interactions so far considered, mummy-baby relations provide a training situation through which older girls help to introduce their juniors into the world of heterosexual relationships. In order to discuss this aspect we must first consider the rules that govern these fictive kinship relations, the common extensions of simple mummy-baby dyads, and the interlocking of these fictive kinship relations with heterosexual relations.

It is accepted that a mummy may have several babies who are then like sisters who may argue or feel jealous if one thinks she is being unfairly treated. Such jealousy is considered perfectly normal among sisters, despite the problems it creates. Likewise, it is permissible to have multigenerational chains: A girl plays the mother role in one dyad and the baby role in another at the same time. In such cases the junior girl may call the oldest "grandmother," but such a second-order link does not involve any specific obligation since each dyad is uniquely created by affection and voluntary choice. What is distinctly not allowed is for a girl to have more than

one mummy; this only happens if done secretly, or in the case of consecutive relationships.

The rules of the game appear to be based on the biological nature of the uterine (mother and children) family group. However, the transactional aspects of the relation are equally important and suggest a parallel with conjugal as well as maternal bonds. Since a baby receives more in terms of gifts, help, advice and protection than she gives, and since long-term rearing reciprocities (see Goody, E. N., 1971) are not entailed, what she is expected to return is undivided loyalty and affection. Attempts to capitalize on the situation by accumulating many mummies are regarded as unfair because the loyalty with which a girl can reciprocate is thereby diluted. Should too many girls select the same wealthy or very attractive girl to be their mummy, they know that they must still give her their undivided loyalty even though they cannot expect undivided attention or a monopoly on gifts. Thus, the case of Malerato (case 2) is much more typical than that of Clorina (case 1).

The asymmetrical gift exchange, the dependency and loyalty of the junior to the senior, as well as the affective sensual relations between partners who are usually close in age, suggest a similarity to conjugal relations. In Lesotho, marriage is generally based on emotional attraction between peers. It is initiated by a dominant male who proposes to a receptive female, and involves economic ties and sexual relations initiated by the husband, to whom the wife is expected to be unfailingly loyal. This same loyalty is not expected from husbands. Women who do have other lovers must keep these affairs secret. Thus, there are enough similarities to conjugal relations to suggest that girls are learning the dynamics of the heterosexual relations within the mummy-baby game.

In fact the girls' game provides explicit opportunities for initiation into heterosexual relations. There are opportunities for older girls who have boyfriends to tell about their experiences to younger girls. Parents generally approve of the bonds between girls as a way of postponing heterosexual affairs, but distinctly disapprove of male participation in the game. However, the very same institution which helps to protect adolescent girls and to meet their emotional and physical needs also stimulates sexual interest and introduces girls into heterosexual affairs. This situation corresponds with the socialization pattern described as "transitional overlap" among the Xhosa youth groups (Mayer & Mayer, 1970), and also relates to the institutionalized Zulu courtship relations in which groups of girls advise, protect, and control their younger members in early heterosexual affairs (Hastrup, 1978; Krige, 1968; Reader, 1966).

In Lesotho, where education is now generally coeducational and girls normally engage in adolescent affairs with boyfriends, female friendships are always spoken of in mother-daughter, never in husband-wife terms. This arrangement is in contrast to situations Blacking (1978) describes in single-sex boarding schools in Natal, and Giallombardo (1966) describes in a female prison in America. In these cases affective relations between females are constructed as fictive marriages. In Lesotho it is biological males, not females in male roles, who introduce the heterosexual dynamic.

A girl may become involved with a boyfriend, become pregnant or even get married, while still a mummy to a younger girl. Sometimes an older girl may actually invite a girl to be her baby in order to assist a boy in arranging an affair. Occasionally boys participate in the game as "sonnys" or as "daddys." A girl may take a fancy to a younger boy and invite him to be her sonny. Usually such a sonny is simply an appealing little boy in town. Older girls may choose a schoolboy or even a single young man home from the mines. This differs from the West African "Godma" type of relation between a mature woman and a young boyfriend whom she finances (see the novel, *Jagua Nana,* Ekwensi, 1961). Most Basotho informants were shocked at the idea that sexual relations could exist between a fictive mother and son. But one informant said that a sonny might come to love another female baby

of their common mummy. This too is considered wrong since "they should be like brother and sister to each other"; they should observe family respect rules (incest taboo) since love between them would cause their mummy to be jealous. Another informant said that if a sonny is nearly the same age as the mummy he might "get a promotion" to the status of real boyfriend as he matures, apparently causing considerable confusion of role. Sonny relations were rare in the village and were considered to be a new and intrusive feature of the game.

The more common involvement of males occurs when the older mummy acquires a boyfriend. When this happens, he usually knows about the girl's female friendships and may give sweets now and then to the baby and be called daddy by her. The case of Makhotso shows how boyfriends of mummies may become involved in a girl's life (see case 3). When Makhotso was 13 and in the baby role, her mummy had a boyfriend who gave her sweets and was protective of her at school, and polite when he visited her at the mummy's home. She said that being with the couple had opened her eyes to what loving a boy is all about, something she had not learned in her own family because her mother had long been divorced from her migrant father. Not all daddys, however, were friendly and protective as this one was. They may use the game as a way of making sexual advances towards the younger girl and so destroy the female dyad. Because they are not actually part of the game, they are not bound by its incest rules. Makhotso's third mummy had a boyfriend who said he wanted to be the daddy to Makhotso, but in fact attempted to seduce her. She wanted to finish secondary school and so retreated from the relationship, engaging in a series of friendships with likeminded girls before she returned at a later age to heterosexual affairs.

Thus, although the mummy-baby game can postpone or replace relations with boys for a time, it can also introduce participants to heterosexuality. For most women, the game fades in importance or ceases as attention turns to the romantic dramas of adult life: to heterosexual courtship, marriage, childbirth, and the responsibilities of family life.

In many cases, however, the relations established with other girls are transformed, but do not cease altogether. Ties may be maintained by letters and visits and occasional gift exchanges. Such contacts can provide women with important assistance in finding work, new friends, or sleeping accommodations if one moves or travels to where the other lives. Thus, the game helps to maintain bridges across the geographical distance and status shifts which have brought its intense phase to an end. And if the pair remain resident in the same village, the relationship may become an adult friendship without romantic contact. Informants spoke of adult female friendships as more stable, dependable, and long-lasting than the mummy-baby relations, which some come to think of as childish and silly (Blacking, 1978). In such adult friendships, village women continue to exchange visits without the romantic uncertainties or the sensual exchanges. They discuss problems, give advice and consolation, and provide help and companionship in their domestic tasks.

In some cases, particularly for women in lonely, unfamiliar situations, the game itself may be continued and new relationships established. By finding new mummies or babies, the young bride in a strange village or the lonely domestic worker or clerk in the city can quickly become incorporated into a female social group where she finds emotional and material support. She can create a "family" which she selects for herself, no matter what strains may exist in her relations with male lovers, in-laws, co-workers or employers. These affective female relations also provide an important alternative to heterosexual affairs for married women who face possessive in-laws and jealous husbands. As one woman said, "if a husband comes home and finds you in bed with a woman, he won't mind. But if he finds you in bed with another man, he may kill someone."

Fictive kinship relations among females never replace the kinship relations with mothers and children, nor the heterosexual relations with lovers and husbands. However, they do provide important alternative bonds at critical moments in the women's lives.

SIGNIFICANCE OF MUMMY-BABY RELATIONS

Much more ethnographic data are needed to extend our understanding of the structure of female relations under variable socio-economic circumstances, and the nature of affective relations between members of the same sex. This paper, as well as the studies by Blacking and Mueller, suggests that certain features of the social and economic structure of southern Africa are significantly related to the form which female friendships take.

Segregation of the sexes in play and work, and the absence of the majority of adult men, encourage the development of close bonds among girls and women. Traditional female institutions have largely been destroyed, but new forms of female association have developed.

The mummy-baby game points to features of female sexuality and affective relations between same-sex partners which challenge some of our western assumptions. First, the compatibility of these intimate female relations with heterosexuality challenges our western insistence on polarizing homosexuality and heterosexuality. Both Blacking and Mueller insist that there is nothing essentially homosexual (Blacking, 1959, 1978) or lesbian (Mueller, 1977) about the relations they report, because they do not replace heterosexual relations with boyfriends and husbands. Schapera, on the other hand, discusses southern African groups in which homosexual relations among both men and women may have been "quite an ordinary occurrence" (1930, pp. 242–243). Rather than deny any homosexual aspects, I would argue that these relations point to the normality of adolescent homosexuality that is so rigidly censored in western societies. The fact that close physical and emotional relations between women often have a significant place, even after heterosexual relations have begun, suggests that the growing recognition of bisexuality in psycho-sexual studies may find support in studies of non-western societies. As one Mosotho woman said about the physical side of these relationships: "It's not wrong. It's just another part of life."

Second, there is a growing body of literature on the nature of female sexuality and the difference between male and female attitudes, again limited by the lack of non-western data. These female mummy-baby relations are structured differently from sexual relations among men in the enforced all-male living conditions of South African mine compounds. The reported male homosexuality of the mines seems to be solely for the purpose of obtaining sexual release when intercourse with women is not available. Younger male migrants who sell their favors are considered as "women of the compound" (*Another Blanket,* 1976), and there is no evidence that male sexual relations continue when migrants return to their women in Lesotho. The female relations, however, are compatible with heterosexuality and involve fictive kinship, not fictive marriage. They represent a broader kind of romantic-sensual relationship which has closer affinities to the physical and emotional pleasures of mother-child and perhaps sister-sister bonds, than to the genital pleasures of heterosexuality. In fact, girls do not consider genital contact essential to mummy-baby relationships. The contacts which may be involved in lengthening the labia minora are apparently not regarded as emotionally significant, whereas falling in love with a girl and simply caressing her is. One girl wondered if boys ever loved as seriously as girls, or if boys only wanted sexual satisfaction.

Recent research by women scholars is beginning to explore the broader concept of female sexuality. Smith-Rosenberg describes "emotional and sensual" same-sex relations which were accepted as normal for many 19th-century married American women, and were sometimes regarded as more emotionally satisfying than their stiff Victorian marriages (1975). Speaking specifically of female sexuality, Irigary argues that *touch,* rather than intercourse, is primordial for females (1977, p. 65). She makes particular reference to mother-daughter relations, arguing that most women in our western social system are "totally censored in the carnal relationships with their mothers and other women" and thus towards themselves. This situation leads to guilt and "narcissistic distress which the little girl suffers because of the devaluation of her relationship with her mother, and her own sex" (1977, p. 75). Perhaps the Basotho combination of warm, affectionate, early mothering, genital manipulation in childhood, and institutionalized female friendships which blend mother-daughter emotions with growing adolescent sexuality, are cultural features that spare Basotho women from some of the psychic distress of western women. Basotho women, however, experience more than their share of economic, social and psychic distress, because they live in one of the world's poorest countries as heads of households, workers or insecure dependents of underpaid migrants laboring in South Africa, one of the world's richest countries.

CASE STUDIES

In the following cases I have utilized a modified form of anthropological kinship diagram to show graphically the changing friendships of three adolescent girls. I have used circles to indicate females, triangles for males, lines for relationships, and levels for relative age and status. However, I have superimposed a series of circles representing "ego" in order to show successive relationships with female friends (single lines) and male friends (double lines). The age at the time of the particular relationship is written inside the relevant circle. Lines indicating mummy-baby relationships are crossed out with three bars if known to have been terminated; a question mark indicates uncertainty of the status of

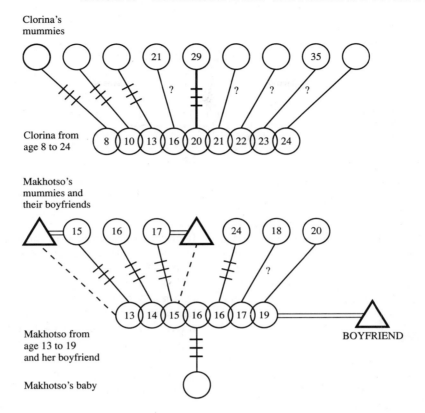

Clorina's mummies

Clorina from age 8 to 24

Makhotso's mummies and their boyfriends

Makhotso from age 13 to 19 and her boyfriend

BOYFRIEND

Makhotso's baby

the relationship. The dotted lines in case 3 indicate relationships between "ego" and the male friends of her mummies.

CASE 1—CLORINA

(My diagram and summary of a case reported in Mueller [1977, pp. 155–157].) Clorina is 25, unmarried, and has a year-old daughter. She was living at home and attending a nearby home economics school when interviewed by Mueller. She never had a fictive baby but had nine mummies most of whom live some distance from her home. Only two or three of these relationships have been maintained. Mueller's detailed account shows that five of the relationships since she was 16 were with married women 5 to 12 years her senior and primarily involved visits, letters, and gifts. Two of the bonds were established with close friends of Clorina's older sisters who lived away from home. Two mummies gave gifts to their "grandchild" when Clorina's own baby was born and one decided on the baby's name; thus as young married women they provided support for Clorina as an unmarried mother. The relationship established when she was 21 is the only one with a girl who also remained unmarried. In only this case were kissing and resting together said to be important aspects of the relationship.

CASE 2—MALERATO

Malerato is now 30 years old, married with three children. She states that she has not had time or interest in mummy-baby relations since her marriage at age 23. The first relationship lasted for three years, then faded out when the mummy

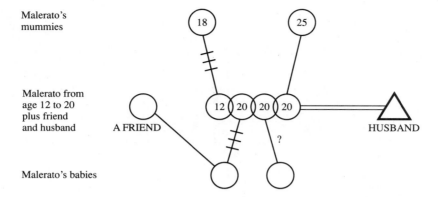

Malerato's mummies

Malerato from age 12 to 20 plus friend and husband

A FRIEND

HUSBAND

Malerato's babies

married. The second mummy has remained a friend whom she occasionally visits in the distant capital city. Malerato said the two babies loved her very much but were jealous of each other, so she gave one of them to a friend of hers.

CASE 3—MAKHOTSO

Makhotso is now 21, still unmarried and working far from her home and family. She is busy with her work, part-time studies, and boy-friends. She appreciates the companionship of female friends whom she no longer considers in terms of mummy-baby relations. The boyfriend of her first mummy was simply a friend and occasionally considered as her daddy but the relationship ended when the couple married and moved away. The boyfriend of the third mummy attempted to seduce her and the relationship with the couple ended abruptly. Her other relationships ended as she or the girls moved to different schools or jobs.

NOTES

1. Variants of the root word Sotho are as follows:
   Lesotho: The nation;
   Basotho: people of Lesotho;

   Mosotho: singular of Basotho;
   Sesotho: The language and culture.
2. Quotes are from the author's field notes (1976–77).

REFERENCES

BASOTHO THEOLOGICAL STUDENTS. (1976). *Another blanket.* Lesotho, Agency for Industrial Mission.

BLACKING, J. (1959). Fictitious kinship amongst girls of the Venda of the Northern Transvaal. *Man, 59,* 155–158.

BLACKING, J. (1978). Uses of the kinship idiom in friendships at some Venda and Zulu schools. In J. Argyle & E. Preston-Whyte (Eds.), *Social system and tradition in Southern Africa.* Cape Town: Oxford University Press.

BRAIN, R. (1976). *Friends and lovers.* London: Hart-Davis, Mac Gibbon.

EKWENSI, C. (1961). *Jagua Nana.* London: Hutchinson.

FRIDAY, N. (1978). *My mother, myself.* London: Fontana.

GIALLOMBARDO, R. (1966). *Society of women: A study of a women's prison.* London: John Wiley & Sons.

GOODY, E. N. (1971). Forms of pro-parenthood: The sharing and substitution of parental roles. In J. R. Goody (Ed.), *Kinship.* London: Penguin.

HASTRUP, K. (1978). The semantics of biology: Virginity. In S. Ardner (Ed.), *Defining females: The nature of women in society*. London: Croom Helm.

IRIGARY, L. (1977). Women's exile (C. Venn, Trans.). *Ideology & Consciousness, 1,* 62–76.

KRIGE, E. J. & KRIGE, J. D. (1943). *The realm of a Rain Queen*. London: Oxford University Press.

KRIGE, E. J. & KRIGE, J. D. (1968). Girls' puberty songs and their relationship to fertility, health, morals and religion among the Zulu. *Africa, 38,* 173–198.

LONGMORE, L. (1959). *The dispossessed*. London: Johnathan Cope.

MAYER, P. & MAYER, I. (1970). In P. Mayer (Ed.), *Socialization: The approach from social anthropology*. *ASA Monographs, 8,* London: Tavistock.

MUELLER, M. B. (1977). *Women and men in rural Lesotho: The periphery of the periphery*. (Doctoral dissertation, Brandeis University, Boston).

READER, D. H. (1966). *Zulu tribe in transition*. Manchester: Manchester University Press.

SCHAPERA, I. (1930). *The Khosian peoples of South Africa: Bushmen and Hottentots*. London: George Routledge and Sons.

SMITH-ROSENBERG, C. (1975). The female world of love and ritual: Relations between women in nineteenth-century America. *Signs, 1,* 1–29.

TIGER, L. (1969). *Men in groups*. London: Thomas Nelson and Sons.

26

THOUGHTS ON THE HISTORY OF HOMOSEXUALITY

PHILIPPE ARIÈS

As Michael Pollak has shown, one of the most striking features of contemporary western morality is the weakening of the ban on homosexuality. Today homosexuals form a compact group, still on the fringes of society but increasingly conscious of a group identity. It is a group which demands rights from dominant society which is not yet ready to accept it, and in fact in France penalizes it with laws that double the punishment for sexual offences committed by members of the same sex. The long held dogmas of society are, however, beginning to show cracks. Signs of toleration, and even concession,

unthinkable thirty years ago, are now appearing. Recently the newspapers reported a 'paramatrimonial' celebration in which a Protestant pastor (disavowed by his Church) tied two lesbians—not for life, of course, but for the longest time possible. The Pope has felt obliged to remind us of St Paul's denunciations of homosexuality, something which would hardly have been necessary were there not already signs of leniency within the Church itself. It is well known that in San Francisco the 'gays' have built up a formidable pressure group. In short, homosexuals are on the way to gaining recognition, and there are

SOURCE: From "Thoughts on the History of Homosexuality" by P. Ariès in *Western Sexuality: Practice and Precept in Past and Present Times* by P. Ariès and A. Béjin (Eds.). Copyright 1985 by B. Blackwell. Reprinted by permission.

plenty of diehard moralists who fume over their brashness and the feebleness of their opponents. Michael Pollak, however, has certain reservations. He feels that this situation may not last, may even be reversed, and Gabriel Matzneff echoes these thoughts in an article in *Le Monde* (5 January 1980) under the title of 'Le Paradis clandestin.' Paradise has been reached, but it is still clandestine. 'We shall see the return and triumph of moral order (don't worry: it won't be tomorrow!) and we shall need to conceal ourselves more than ever. The future lies in the shadows.'

There are still a few worries. There is certainly a kind of tightening up going on, at the moment more for the sake of national security than public morality.[1] A beginning? But the normalization of sexuality and homosexuality has gone too far to be forced to yield to pressure from the police and the courts. It has to be admitted that the positions gained—or won—by homosexuality are not just because of tolerance or indifference or 'Anything goes, nothing matters.' There is something more deeply interfused, structural and permanent, or at least likely to be long lasting. Henceforward society as a whole is tending, with some resistance here and there, more and more to adapt itself to the homosexual pattern. This was one of Michael Pollak's propositions that I found particularly striking, namely that models of society as a whole tend to approximate to portrayals of themselves by homosexuals, an approximation due to a distortion of images and roles.

Let us pursue this line of thought. The generally accepted model of a homosexual, beginning with the time when he first felt and recognized his peculiar character, usually as a disease or perversion, i.e. from the beginning of the eighteenth to the beginning of the nineteenth century, was an effeminate type, a transvestite with a very high pitched voice. In this we see the homosexual conforming to the prevailing pattern: the men he loved looked like women, and this, in a sense, was reassuring for society. He could also love children or young folk (pederasty), an ancient relationship that we can call classical, since it goes back to Greco-Roman antiquity and survives today in the Moslem world, in spite of Ayatollah Khomeini and the executioner. It was tied up with traditional forms of education or initiation which could become degraded and furtive, while special friendships bordered on homosexuality without being conscious or recognized as such.

According to Michael Pollak, today's homosexual credo often totally rejects these two earlier types, the effeminate and the pederast, and replaces them with a macho, athletic, super-virile type, though still with a slim and youthful figure, unlike the muscular toughs of Mexican and Soviet art of the twenties and thirties. It is the hell's angel type, with a tight-fitting leather jacket and an earring, copied by an entire age group, without distinction of sex, an adolescent model that even girls adopt, so that often one hardly knows with whom one is dealing—him or her?

Is not the obliteration, among adolescents, of the visible differences between men and women one of the most noteworthy and quite original features of our society, a *unisex society?* Roles are interchangeable, father and mother, husband and wife, lover and mistress. What is odd is the single idea of *virility*. Girls' figures start looking like boys'. They have lost that well-covered look so dear to painters from the sixteenth to the nineteenth century, still sought after in the Moslem world, perhaps because of the suggestion of potential maternity. Nobody today would make fun of a thin girl like this nineteenth-century poet who wrote:

> I do not mind your scragginess, my dear;
> A skinny bosom brings the heart more near.

Going back a little further in time one may find occasional hints of another faintly unisex society in fifteenth-century Italy, but without the ideal of virility and rather more androgynous.

The fact that the young everywhere aspire to an ideal physical type of obviously homosexual origin, perhaps explains their often sympathetic

[1]These lines were written during the years 1979 and 1980 in an atmosphere of moral restrictiveness and obsession about state security.

curiosity about homosexuality and their assumption of homosexual mannerisms at parties and pleasure spots generally. The 'homo' has indeed become a leading character in today's human comedy.

If my diagnosis is correct, the unisex fashion is a clear indication of a general change in society. Tolerance of homosexuality is the result of changes in the way the sexes present themselves to the world, in their actions, in their professional lives, in their families, but especially in their function as symbolic figures.

We have to make an effort to grasp what is going on before our eyes; but how can we get any idea of the moral postures of past ages except by studying the Church's interdictions? There a huge territory lies unexplored, and for the moment we have to content ourselves with a few impressions which could lead to avenues of research.

In the last few years books have appeared suggesting that homosexuality is an invention of the nineteenth century. In the discussion that followed his paper Michael Pollak expressed his doubts about this. Nevertheless the question is an interesting one. Obviously it does not mean that before then there were no homosexuals—an absurd idea. All we know is that there was homosexual behaviour, connected with certain periods of human life and special circumstances, which does not seem to have prevented those who indulged in it from behaving heterosexually at the same time. As Paul Veyne has pointed out, our knowledge of classical antiquity indicates not homosexuality on one side and heterosexuality on the other, but a bisexuality whose manifestations *seem* to have been dependent on chance encounters rather than biological determinism.

Of course the appearance of a rigorous code of sexual morals based on a world philosophy that Christianity has built up and preserved to this day has favoured a stricter definition of 'sodomy.' But this term, derived from the habits of the men of Sodom in the Bible, denoted not only a form of copulation that was against nature but

also men going to bed together, which was just as unnatural. Homosexuality was thus separated from heterosexuality, the only normal and permitted practice, but its rejection was so total that it was lumped in with every form of perversion. The *ars erotica* of the west is a catalogue of perversions that are all deadly sins. Hence arose a category of perverts, the so-called *luxuriosi,* from which it was hard for homosexuality to detach itself. The facts are, of course, a good deal more complex than this rather crude summary suggests. Later we shall see in Dante an example of this complexity turning into ambiguity. We have to admit that the homosexual of the Middle Ages and the *ancien régime* was a pervert.

By the end of the eighteenth and the beginning of the nineteenth century he has become a monster, a freak. This is an evolutionary process which incidentally makes one wonder about the link between the monster of the Middle Ages and the Renaissance and the biological sport of the age of the Enlightenment and the dawn of modern science (see J. Ceard). The freak, the dwarf, the old crone who gets suspected of witchcraft are affronts to God's creation and are accused of being creatures of the Devil. At the beginning of the nineteenth century the homosexual lived under this hereditary curse. He was at the same time a freak and a pervert. The Church was prepared to recognize the physical anomaly which made the homosexual a man-woman, an abnormal and always effeminate man; for we must not forget that this first stage towards the creation of an autonomous condition of homosexuality was under the label of effeminacy. The person who suffered from this anomaly certainly could not help it, but that did not save him from suspicion; for, being by his very nature more exposed to temptation, he was more liable to lead his neighbour astray. So he had to be shut up like a woman or watched over like a child, mistrusted by society. Merely by reason of his oddity he was suspected of becoming a pervert, a delinquent.

At the end of the eighteenth century the medical world adopted the Church's view of homosexuality, and it became an illness, or at least a disability, which could be diagnosed by clinical examination. Several recently published books have given us a recapitulation of these amazing doctors' views, which have caused much amusement. Within that murky world of prostitutes, wantons and debauchees a single *species* was emerging—consistent, homogeneous and with unique physical characteristics. The doctors had discovered how to track down the clandestine homosexual. Examination of anus and penis was enough to unmask them, for they displayed abnormalities, as did a circumcised Jew. They formed a sort of ethnic group, even though their characteristics had been acquired by use rather than inherited. Medical diagnosis was in fact caught between two forms of evidence. The physical evidence, the marks and blemishes of vice, could easily be found elsewhere among drunks and debauchees, whereas the moral evidence was an almost hereditary disposition for vice, which apparently threatened to corrupt their healthy-minded fellow beings. Faced with this wholesale denunciation as a race, homosexuals defended themselves, some by concealment, others by confessions. The latter were pathetic and pitiable, and occasionally cynical, but always displayed a distressing insistence, sometimes shamefaced, sometimes defiant, on their insurmountable separateness. Such confessions were not intended to be flaunted or made public, though one was sent to Zola, which so embarrassed him that he passed it on to someone else. These shamefaced avowals did not lead to special claims. Once the homosexual was declared as such, nothing was left for him but to retreat into the fringe society of perverts where he had languished till the doctors had brought him out to put him on show in their chamber of horrors. The anomaly condemned was one of sexual ambiguity, the effeminate man, the woman with male organs, the hermaphrodite.

In the next stage homosexuals threw off their clandestinity and the taint of perversion to claim their right to be openly what they were, and to assert their normality. As we have already seen, this change was accompanied by a change of pattern, with virility ousting effeminacy and boyishness. But this did not signify a return to the kind of classical bisexuality that still survived in college rags and school initiation ceremonies. The new type of homosexuality had no truck with heterosexuality, either from deliberate choice or through impotence. Now it was the homosexuals themselves—not the doctors and priests—who proclaimed their separateness, demanding, in the face of society, their own place in the sun.

I admit that Freud rejected the claim. 'Psycho-analysis absolutely refuses to admit that homosexuals constitute a group which has special characteristics distinguishable from those of other individuals.' In spite of this, the wider understanding of psycho-analysis has led not only to the emancipation of homosexuality, but also to its classification as a species, following in the path of the nineteenth-century doctors.

I have been tempted to argue that prior to the eighteenth century there was no such identifiable group as 'youth' or 'adolescence'—meaning an adolescence whose history might have been more or less the same (allowing for the difference in time-scale) as that of homosexuality: first the effeminate, Cherubino, then the virile, Siegfried. But, in contradiction, N. Z. Davis has rightly pointed to groups such as the *abbayes de la jeunesse* or the subculture of the London apprentices, which shows that there were social activities peculiar to adolescence and solidarity among young people.

All this is true. Youth did have its own status and functions, both in community life and in leisure activities, or in its working life and its relations with masters and mistresses. In other words there was a difference in status between unmarried adolescents and adults. *But this difference, even if it caused friction between them, did not divide them into two separate non-communicating worlds.* Although adolescents had their own special jobs to do, there was no separate category of adolescence, and so hardly any stereotype of adolescent. There were exceptions. For instance, in fifteenth-century Italy and in Elizabethan literature, adolescence does seem to be personified in a slim, elegant youthfulness, with a faintly ambivalent touch of homosexuality. In the eighteenth century, on the other hand, the male figure is virile, the female fecund. The seventeenth-century type is a youthful man, not a youth. It is the youthful man, and his wife, not the youth, who sit on the top of the age pyramid. Effeminacy, boyishness, even the slender youthfulness of the Quattrocento play no part in the dream fantasies of that age.

On the other hand, at the end of the eighteenth and especially in the nineteenth century, adolescence begins to acquire substance, though in contrast it gradually loses its status in society as a whole and ceases to be an organic part of it, becoming merely the threshold. This compartmentalization was restricted at the beginning of the nineteenth century (the Romantic period) to middle-class schoolboys. After the Second World War, for all manner of reasons, it was extended and generalized, so that now adolescence has swollen into a huge, unstructured age group that people enter early and leave, with some difficulty, rather late, after getting married. It has become a sort of dream state. It started by being a masculine affair, with girls continuing to share the life and activities of grown-up women. Later, when, as today, adolescence became unisex, girls and boys conformed to a common, rather masculine pattern.

It is interesting to compare the histories of the two myths—youth or adolescence and homosexuality. There are significant parallels.

The history of homosexuality raises another question linked with the history of sexuality in general. Up to the eighteenth century, and for long after, sex simply meant procreation and the functions of the sexual organs among the vast numbers of common folk in town and country. Poetry and high art bridged the gap between desire and love; but the world of feeling and the world of genesis were kept firmly apart. Popular songs and pictures and bawdy stories never strayed far from the genital. So there was a whole-heartedly sexy side facing a rather refined asexual side. Today, enlightened by Dostoevsky as well as Freud, and by our greater openmindedness, we know this is not a true picture. The people of the *ancien règime* and the Middle Ages were deceiving themselves. We know that the asexual was soaked in sex, though in a diffused and unconscious way. This was as true of the mystics as it was of Bernini and the Baroque. Not but what contemporaries were quite unconscious of the fact and, protected by their ignorance, walked serenely beside the abyss without losing their balance.

After the eighteenth century the two worlds overlapped, the sexual infiltrating the asexual. The recent popularization of psycho-analysis (an effect rather than a cause of this) has demolished the last barriers. We now think we can attach a label to all those desires and hidden urges which were once invisible and anonymous. We go too far, and splashing around in all directions we see sex in everything. Every cylinder is a phallus. Sex no longer sticks to its own domain; leaving the purely genital it has invaded man, the child, the whole of social life. We are in the habit of explaining the pansexuality of our age by the weakened hold of religious morality and the search for happiness derived from a defiance of social inhibitions. It is also a phenomenon of sensuous awareness, one of the strongest traits of modernity. The same eye can find beauty in a Gothic church, a Baroque palace and an African mask, whereas formerly appreciation of one would have excluded the others. Likewise, just as arts of very contrasting kinds may be invested with beauty, so sex, which has its own kind of beauty, suffuses every sector of life, of individuals and of societies, where earlier it had passed unnoticed. Now its image, once hidden or undeveloped, emerges from the unconscious like a photographic plate in developing fluid. This is not a totally new phenomenon; in fact it goes back to the days of de Sade, but in the last twenty years we have seen it frenziedly speeded up.

One of the most striking aspects of this pansexuality has been the awareness and recognition of homosexuality. I wonder if there is not some connection between the spread of a conventionalized form of homosexuality and the diminishing role of personal friendship in contemporary society. Friendship once bulked large in people's lives, as is shown by the evidence of wills, and curiously enough the word *amitié* was used in a wider sense than today, including love, or at least the love between engaged and married couples. It seems to me that a history of friendship would show its decline during the nineteenth and twentieth centuries among adults, in favour of close family ties, and a return to it among adolescents. It has become a trait of adolescence, disappearing later.

In recent decades friendship has carried sexual overtones that make it rather sheepishly equivocal or shamefaced. Society looks askance on friendship between men of widely different ages. Today Hemingway's Old Man returning with the boy from their trip to sea would arouse the suspicions of the vice squad and mothers of families. Advance of homosexuality, decline of friendship, prolongation of adolescence, now ensconced at the centre of today's society: such are the nodal characteristics of our time, and who can tell how or why they are interrelated?

Thirty years—that is a generation ago—thoughts on homosexuality would have devoted a lot of attention to the equivocal friendship, the love which attracted a man irresistibly towards another man, a woman towards another woman—tragic passions which sometimes ended in death or suicide. For archetypes we would have chosen Achilles and Patroclus (comrades in arms), Harmodius and Aristogeiton (man and *ephebos*), the epicene and mysterious friendships of Michelangelo, Shakespeare and Marlowe, and nearer our own times the officer in Julien Green's play *Sud*. We see nothing like this in Michael Pollak's analysis and his picture of homosexuality. Here we find a total rejection of the heart's emotion and romantic love, and nothing but exclusively sexual goods for sale in the market-place for orgasms.

In actual fact the homosexual society he de-

scribes is not totally devoid of sentiment, but this is deferred until after the rather brief period of sexual activity. Homosexuals, like contemporary heterosexuals, cannot endure prolonged attachments. Their love is not lifelong but lasts only for an unrepeatable moment that leaves no room for tender feelings. Sentiment is left to the veterans. Former lovers, Michael Pollak tells us, when they meet again, do so on a level of pure brotherly affection; anything else would be considered incestuous. This, of course, is after, not during the affair.

Earlier we spoke of pansexuality and its intrusion into every aspect of life today. That is only one aspect of it; another, which seems at first totally inconsistent, is the way it gets concentrated, canalized as it were. Sex now has nothing to do with procreation or love in the old sense, which in their turn were akin to friendship. It is quite uncontaminated by such sentimental considerations. It is a consummation of the deepest urges, allowing man and woman to experience total fulfillment during the moment, lived like an eternity, of the orgasm. The orgasm has in fact become an object of veneration. This is why homosexuality, having by its nature nothing to do with procreation, is independent, free to disregard tradition and the rules of society, and able to exploit to the utmost the sexual dichotomy involved in the orgasm. It becomes sexuality in its purest state, a sexuality that makes its own way.

In earlier communities sex was indulged in either for procreation, hence legitimately, or for perversion, which was condemned. Beyond these restrictions sentiment might find a place. Today sentiment has been taken over by the family, which earlier had no such monopoly. That is why friendship played such an important role. But sentiment between men went beyond friendship, even in its widest sense: it acted as a lubricant in many service relationships that today are governed by contracts. Social life was organized round personal ties, dependence, patronage, mutual help. Relations at work were man-to-man relationships which could evolve from friendship or mutual confidence into exploitation and hatred—a hatred that was close to love; but they never settled down into indifference or impersonality. To relationships with dependents were added those with clients, fellow citizens, clan members, one's own circle. One existed in the middle of a web of sentiment which was at once vague and haphazard, only partially arising from birth or locality, quickly affected by chance encounters or *coups de foudre*.

This sort of sentiment had nothing to do with the sexuality that later intruded on it. Nevertheless we may guess that sexual feelings were not entirely absent from the bands of young men in the Middle Ages described by Georges Duby, nor from the epic friendships of the *Gestes* and the *Romans,* all of which involved the very young. Were they *amitiès particulières*? This by the way was the title of a novel by Roger Peyrefitte—a masterpiece—in which the 'friendships' are shrouded in ambiguity, a vagueness which totally disappears in later works by the same author, where homosexuality is flaunted by quite unambiguous characters as a mode of behaviour with clear-cut outlines. I think that in certain cultures, e.g. the Italian Quattrocento and Elizabethan England, there developed, out of an apparently asexual form of sentiment, a particular kind of manly love that verged on homosexuality; but it was a homosexuality that was undeclared and unadmitted, that remained a mystery, less through fear of prohibition than from a distaste for labelling oneself in the eyes of contemporary society as non-sexual or sexual. One hovered in a mixed zone that belonged to neither.

It is not always easy to tell who was really homosexual and who was not, the criteria being mostly anachronistic (i.e. of our own time) or merely polemical, like Agrippa d'Aubigné's accusations against Henry III and his *mignons,* or else simply vague. The attitude of ancient communities towards homosexuality—about which we know very little and which we should study with fresh eyes and a disregard for the anachronisms of pyscho-analysis—seems more complex than the very strict and detailed codes of reli-

gious morality would lead us to believe. There were plenty of signs of vigorous repression. Take, for instance, the following extract from Barbier's *Journal,* dated 6 July 1750: 'Today, Monday the 6th, two workmen were publicly burnt at the stake in the Place de la Grève at 5 o'clock in the evening. They were a young carpenter and a pork butcher, aged 18 and 25, whom the watch had caught in the act of committing sodomy. It was felt that the judges had been a bit heavy-handed. Apparently a drop too much wine had led them to this degree of shamelessness' (meaning degree of unconcealment). If only they had been a bit more careful! But it was a period when the police were getting craftier, in order to catch more people by surprise, and punishments were heavier. 'I learnt on this occasion that a man dressed in dark clothes, who spies on what is going on in the streets without anyone suspecting him, walks ahead of the watch, and then calls it up.[2] The execution was to make an example, especially as this crime is said to be becoming very common, and there are many people being locked up for it in Bicêtre.' They preferred to shut 'public sinners' up in the General Hospital there.

So homosexuality seems to have been irrevocably damned. But when did this start? It is far from obvious. Perhaps in Barbier's time the guardians of public morality were tightening things up and sharpening their definition of the crimes they wanted to stamp on. We also have a view from much earlier times—the end of the thirteenth century—which we might expect to be much stricter, namely that of Dante. The way he classifies the damned, like the way St Paul classifies the sins, gives one an idea of how seriously or otherwise these sins were rated.

In St Paul the lustful come after homicides. Dante places them at the gates of Hell, just after Limbo, a 'noble castle' where 'on a green lawn'

[2] Philippe Rey, in a master's dissertation (supervised by Jean-Louis Flandrin) on homosexuality in the eighteenth century, did some detailed research among police dossiers. He moved on from listing homosexual acts to defining a 'breed' of homosexuals.

dwell in an attentuated form 'the great,' who suffer only from being deprived of God, having lived before Christ—Homer and Horace, Aristotle and Plato. The patriarchs of the Old Testament sojourned there until the risen Christ withdrew them. The others, pagans like Virgil, remained, staying in the first circle of Hell. The second circle is more sinister. Here Minos sits in judgement; but the punishments are still mild compared with those of the seven other circles. They are the storm, the storm of lusts which continually whirls around the souls of those who have yielded to them on earth—'a place deprived of every glimmer of light, which bellows like the sea battered in a gale by contrary winds'; 'I understand that into this torment carnal sinners were cast who abandoned reason to the onslaughts of lust.' Some are actual perverts, like Queen Semiramis: 'She was so broken to lascivious vice that she licensed lust by law in order to cover up her own guilt.' But these lascivious characters, lascivious even by our standards, were plucked, like Semiramis and Cleopatra, from the distant mists of antiquity. The confession of the beautiful Francesca da Rimini, Dante's own contemporary, is very different. Today, after de Musset and Tolstoy, we would never dare exclude her from the joy of God, so light was her fault, so poignant her suffering and so deep her love: 'Love, that inflames so soon a noble heart, seized him (her lover who is with her in Hell) for the lovely body that has been torn from me. . . . Love, that to no loving heart can refuse love, took me with such great joy of him that, as you see, he is still with me.' Make no mistake, Dante had to put the couple among the damned, but he feels like us today, and his soul revolts against it. Here one senses the tension between the priest-made law and the instinctive resistance even of the devout.

At the sound of the lamentation of the two damned lovers 'I swooned for pity, as if I were dying, and fell like a dead man.' There is nothing repellent about these two damned souls, and they are on the very border of the realms of punishment, only to be lightly punished. Yet, though Dante pities and sympathizes with these sad lovers, he places them alongside genuine perverts like Semiramis and Cleopatra.

The circle of the lustful does not include 'sodomites' whom St Paul associates with *adulteri, molles* (effeminate) and *fornicarii.* Dante moves them away, taking them from the company of sinners 'through incontinence,'[3] but far away among the *violent,* the sinners through *malizia* in the seventh circle. This is already fairly low, but not so low as the ninth, which harbours Cain and Judas, traitors and murderers, the very bottom of Hell where Satan lurks.

Let Dante himself explain (XI, 28) 'The Circle is full of violent men, but as they may have three kinds of victim it is divided into three rings. One may do violence to God, to oneself, to one's neighbour.'

1 Violence against one's neighbour: murder, robbery, banditry.
2 Violence against oneself and against one's own goods (note this association of being and having which seems an essential characteristic of the later Middle Ages): suicides and spendthrifts.
3 Violence against God, which is the most serious.

One can do violence to God by denying Him one's heart and blaspheming against Him. The first sort are not unbelievers or idolaters, but blasphemers. The second are the people of Sodom and Cahors, that is sodomites and userers. They are more or less on the same level: each has dishonoured God and nature, but the crime of the sodomites is considered to be less serious than that of the usurers.

Dante mingles with the sodomites without any feeling of disgust; moreover among them he meets his beloved teacher Brunetto Latini. He addresses him in terms of respect, gratitude and affection, which to us in the twentieth century

---

[3]Incontinence is a lesser offence against God and incurs less blame.

could not possibly be directed towards someone who had committed an awful crime, to which incidentally he makes no reference in the brief talk he has with him.[4] 'I still have with me engraved on my mind your dear and benign paternal image from the time when on earth you taught me how men may make themselves immortal; and as long as I live people shall learn from my words how deep is my gratitude.' That is how a man of the fourteenth century talked to an avowed sodomite: one, morever, among many, for the practice seems to have been widespread: 'Time is too short to mention the clerks and famous men of letters all defiled by the same taint on earth' says Master Brunetto. There were also husbands whose wives disgusted them: ' My shrewish wife certainly did me more wrong than anybody else.' Was that not an extenuating circumstance?

Dante does not feel the same outrage and scorn against the sodomites that he displays against the rest of the 'fraudulent,' and nothing remotely like the outbursts of Dr Ambroise Tardieu in the 1870s! Yet he is under no illusions about the seriousness of their offence, though the seriousness does not attach to its incontinence, or the act of *concubitus,* but to *malizia,* the crime against God through His creation, nature. This makes the offence more serious, more metaphysical. What is interesting about Dante's testimony is that it comes from someone who was at the same time a scholastic philosopher, a Latin writer who was imbued with twelfth-century cosmology and theology, and an ordinary man who shared the views of ordinary men of his time. 'The theologian condemns, the ordinary man admits to leniency.' Sodomy is the sin of the clerks, of educators, perhaps of young folk. Dante does not go into details, but through the mouth of Master Brunetto he makes it clear how frequent these nameless practices are.

We are told elsewhere how the prostitutes of the Latin Quarter used to solicit students in the street, and cursed them for sodomites if they rebuffed them.

The ecclesiastical authorities of the fifteenth and sixteenth centuries tried to take a hard line with college feasts that were just initiation ceremonies, rites of passage with lots of drinking and some fairly crude horseplay. No doubt whores would be present. But what the censorious objected to in general was a rather less obvious perversion than the resort to prostitutes, more likely a traditional bisexuality, which lasted some time among adolescents. This amorphous sexuality also figured in the great junketings that took place at the end of the year, between Christmas and Twelfth Night, a time of masks and fancy dress, of mirror games and Lords of Misrule, a sexual ambiguity. As François Laroque has said, 'In this misty world where the old merges into the new . . . doubts about sexual differences arise. But thanks to the festive magic of disguise the figure of Viola-Cesario is able to cross the frontier between the sexes at will: *bissexus* rather than *bifrons.*'

This is not real homosexuality, but only a ritualized, disturbing reversal of roles when annual feast days are an excuse for throwing social taboos to the winds, just for the moment. Relics of this ambiguity are still with us today in spite of the determined efforts of homosexuals to achieve a genuine identity. At least this is what is suggested by a remark of Laurent Dispot in *Le Matin* of 6 November 1979: 'Who says there are men who don't love each other? What about the scenes footballers make when someone has scored a goal? They certainly aren't homosexuals. Yet, if real homosexuals behaved like that in a crowded street, passers-by would be very shocked. Must we conclude from this that sports grounds and sport provide a safety valve for normal male homosexuality?'

[4]This has given rise to several suggestions that the text has been misinterpreted and that Brunetto Latini was there for reasons other than sodomy.

IX

CULTURE AND VARIETY IN SEXUAL PRACTICES

INTRODUCTION

Our notions of what is appropriate or normal are determined by our individual experiences, including our experience of enculturation, and different enculturation processes prevail in different societies. We already have seen this with regard to cultures such as those of the Trobrianders and the Sambia. Malinowski reports that sexual play, including intercourse, was encouraged as a normal part of adolescent life in the Trobriand Islands. And Herdt describes a culture in which every male is expected to engage in fellatio with other males as a normal part of growing up male.

Whereas these customs may seem strange and exotic to most North Americans, it should be apparent by now that there are few obvious universals related to human sexual behavior other than those determined by biology. We have chosen readings in this section that demonstrate additional variations in cultural patterns pertaining to sexual behaviors.

These readings explore what may be considered acceptable cross-culturally in the context of specific variations. Transvestism and cross-gender behaviors—as well as the cultural definition of what is sexually pleasurable—are discussed in these two articles.

Charles Callender and Lee M. Kochems provide a discussion of the status and role of individuals who assume cross-gender dress and behavior in indigenous North American cultures. They demonstrate variability in the specifics of the berdache, while noting its wide distribution. They conclude that the berdache was transformed into an intermediate gender status that cut across the boundaries between gender categories.

Donald E. Brown describes the use of the penis pin in Borneo. The penis pin is part of a Southeast Asian cultural complex that involves piercing the penis so that a pin can be worn in it. According to the men of Borneo, this device allegedly enhances female sexual pleasure during intercourse. However, Brown notes that there is no clear evidence to support this conclusion. The practice may have more to do with male machismo and male fantasies than with female sexuality.

SUGGESTED READINGS

ALLEN, DONALD M. (1980). Young Male Prostitutes: A Psychosocial Study. *Archives of Sexual Behavior, 9*:399–426.

ARNOLD, KATHERINE. (1978). The Introduction of Poses to a Peruvian Brothel and the Changing Images of Male and Female. In John Blacking (Ed.), *The Anthropology of the Body* (pp. 179–197). London: Academic Press.

DEVEREUX, GEORGE. (1948). Mohave Zoophilia. *Journal of the Indian Psychoanalytic Society, 2*:227–245.

NEWTON, ESTHER. (1972). *Mother Camp: Female Impersonators in America.* Englewood Cliffs, NJ: Prentice-Hall.

OTTERBEIN, KEITH F. (1979). A Cross-Cultural Study of Rape. *Aggressive Behavior, 5*:4:425–435.

SANDAY, PEGGY REEVES. (1981). The Socio-Cultural Context of Rape: A Cross-Cultural Study. *Journal of Social Issues, 37*:4:Fall:5–27.

SCHETKY, DIANE H. (1988). Child Sexual Abuse in Mythology, Religion, and History. In Diane H. Schetky and Arthur H. Green (Eds.), *Child Sexual Abuse: A Handbook for Health Care and Legal Professionals.* New York: Brunner/Mazel.

WEATHERFORD, JACK MCIVER. (1986). *Porn Row.* New York: Arbor House.

WILSON, GLENN D. (ED.). (1987). *Variant Sexuality: Research and Theory.* Baltimore: Johns Hopkins University Press.

27

The North American Berdache[1]

Charles Callender / Lee M. Kochems

The berdache among North American Indians

[1]We gratefully acknowledge the aid of Cynthia Beall, Ives Goddard, Italo Signorini, and Elisabeth Tooker, who provided information or made suggestions that are incorporated in this article.

may be roughly defined as a person, usually male, who was anatomically normal but assumed the dress, occupations, and behavior of the other sex to effect a change in gender status.

CHARLES CALLENDER was Associate Professor of Anthropology at Case Western Reserve University (Cleveland, Ohio 44106, U.S.A.). Born in 1928, he was educated at the University of Chicago (Ph.B., 1948; M.A., 1954; Ph.D., 1958). He had taught at the American University in Cairo (1961–63) and the University of Delaware (1963–65) and had done fieldwork among the Fox, Sauk, Potawatomi, and Kenuz. His research interests were social organization, gender relations, American Indians, and the Middle East. He published *Social Organization of the Central Algonkian Indians* (1963) and a number of articles about American Indians.

LEE M. KOCHEMS received his Ph.D. at the University of Chicago, Department of Anthropology. He was born in 1958 and received his B.A. and M.A. from Case Western Reserve University in 1980. His research interests are gender relations, the construction of the person, and East African pastoralists.

SOURCE: From "The North American Bedarche" by C. Callender and L. Kochems in *Current Anthropology 24 (4)*, 1987, pp. 443–456 and 467–470. Copyright © 1983 by The University of Chicago Press. Reprinted by permission.

This shift was not complete; rather, it was a movement toward a somewhat intermediate status that combined social attributes of males and females. The terminology for berdaches defined them as a distinct gender status, designated by special terms rather than by the words "man" or "woman." Literal translations of these terms often indicate its intermediate nature: halfman-halfwoman (Grinnell 1962, vol. 2:39), man-woman (Bowers 1965:167), would-be woman (Powers 1977:38).

The word "berdache" is used here as a generic term for this status throughout North America north of Mexico. The distinctions made by Martin and Voorhies (1975:95–100) seem unnecessary. While variation characterized the institution, it included a common core of traits. Although "berdache" originally designated a male, its etymology became irrelevant long ago, and it is used here for both sexes.

Although accounts of berdaches go back to the 16th century (Katz 1976:285–86), broad surveys of this status have appeared only in recent years. A few American anthropologists briefly summarized its features for North America generally or specifically for the Plains tribes (e.g., Benedict 1934:263; Linton 1936:480; Lowie 1924b:245–46). The most provocative early treatment, published in 1940 by Kroeber (1952:313–14), included a call for general syntheses. It drew almost no response. Except for a note by Angelino and Shedd (1955) centering on definitions of the status, anthropologists (e.g., Hoebel 1949:459; Mead 1949:129–30; 1961:1452) continued to limit their treatment to brief statements that differed little from earlier summaries. The recent large-scale examinations, beginning with Jacobs (1968), continued with Forgey's (1975) analysis of berdaches among the northern Plains tribes. Katz (1976:281–334) published a large collection of ethnographic data about homosexuality in general among American Indians, with comments from an explicitly gay standpoint. The new perspectives implicit in this recent work become very evident with Whitehead's (1981) analysis.

Broad syntheses appeared earlier among European anthropologists, who usually treated the berdache status as one aspect of a more widespread pattern of institutionalized transvestism (e.g., Baumann 1950, 1955; Bleibtrau-Ehrenberg 1970) and concentrated on phenomena outside North America. Signorini (1972), however, focuses explicitly upon berdaches.

Evidence for a cross-cultural examination of the berdache status is scanty, fragmentary, and often poor in quality. Still existing in a few societies, more or less covertly (Fire 1972:149–50; Forgey 1975:67), berdaches began to disappear soon after European or American control was established. Most accounts are retrospective, based on memory or tradition and describing phenomena no longer subject to observation. The waning of this status was a complex process in which the hostility of Western outsiders who were outraged by its open display and public acceptance was only one factor, if a very potent one. However, this cultural bias strongly skewed the gathering of information. Descriptions of berdaches sometimes contain much more denunciation than data (e.g., Dumont in Swanton 1911:100; Gatschet 1891:67; McCoy 1976). The extent to which bias determined what observers saw and reported is evident in accounts of 17th-century Illinois berdaches. Marquette (1900:129), a neutral observer, and Liette (1947:112–13), who was prejudiced, agree on little except transvestism. Sometimes the biases of editors or publishers came into play, excising data (e.g., in the London edition of James 1823) or coyly switching into Latin (e.g., Kroeber 1902:20; Lowie 1910:42), a form of evasion less destructive than Catlin's (1973, vol. 2:214–15) taking refuge in hopelessly garbled Sauk (Ives Goddard, personal communication). Indians who absorbed the biases of the dominant culture became reticent about berdaches or denied their former existence (cf. Gayton 1948:106; Lurie 1953).

The berdache status is occasionally confused with other conditions that partly resembled it. These include forcing female dress upon males who showed extreme cowardice in warfare; homosexuality; and hermaphroditism.

Observers sometimes interpreted berdaches as cowardly men upon whom transvestism was imposed as a sign of disgrace (Bradbury 1904: 64–65; Powers 1877:132). This practice did exist among some societies in the upper Midwest. Illinois men who deserted during military action had to dress like women but could rehabilitate themselves by demonstrating courage (Bossu 1962:82). Lurie (1953:71) describes the similar punishment of a Winnebago warrior who had compounded his offense by claiming war honors after his flight. Santee Dakota youths who had never joined a war party could be forced to wear dresses at social dances (Landes 1968:206–7; Pond 1889:245–46). This usage seems a more intense form of the widespread custom of shaming males who were reluctant to fight by calling them women (e.g., Wallace and Hoebel 1952: 273). Restricted to a few societies, in which berdaches also existed, it shared with the latter only the feature of transvestism. Forcibly imposed by human agents, this form of cross-dressing lacked the supernatural validation often attached to berdaches, was a mark of disgrace, and was temporary or potentially subject to change. The status it denoted was thus clearly distinct from that of the berdache.

Its frequent equation with homosexuality, even by explicitly gay writers (e.g., Russo 1981:218), distorts the sexual aspects of berdachehood. Certain interests were often believed to foreshadow the assumption of this status, but only one account (Gayton 1948:236) cites homosexual behavior. Rather than homosexuals' becoming berdaches, many berdaches, perhaps most of them, became homosexual; but their sexual partners were always nonberdaches. Evidence for homosexual activity unrelated to this status is abundant (Devereux 1937:498–500; Forde 1931:147; Holder 1889:625; Honigmann 1954:129–30; Jones 1907:141; Lowie 1910:223; Osgood 1958: 222–23). North American homosexuality transcended berdaches; though they were its most visible and—except for their spouses—its most consistent participants, their orientations could be bisexual or heterosexual.

Berdaches were often confounded with intersexual persons. Early observers who called them hermaphrodites sometimes assumed they were truly intersexual (Hennepin 1903:167–68; Membre 1922:131–59; Le Moyne du Morgues 1875:7–8; cf. Lafitau 1724:52). Morfi confessed his uncertainty on this point (Newcomb 1961:74). Font (1966:105) recorded his original impression that Yuma berdaches were intersexed and his later discovery of the error. Stevenson (1902:37) suggested that observers may have misunderstood such native terms as "halfman-halfwoman." One factor in the persistence of the hermaphrodite label may have been doubt about an alternative. Denig (1961:187–88) applied it to Crow berdaches even while pointing out that they were defined by their behavior rather than their anatomy.

The sharp distinction between berdaches and intersexes urged by Angelino and Shedd (1955: 124–25) is easily drawn at the conceptual level but harder to apply when examining the literature. Some cultures clearly separated the two statuses. Mead's (1961:1452) account of a boy who was classed as a berdache only after he was determined to be anatomically male indicates that the Omaha made such a distinction. Other cultures blurred the line by assigning berdaches and intersexes to the same status (Ray 1932:148; Spier and Sapir 1930:220–21; Steward 1941: 253; 1943:338; cf. Forgey 1975:2–3). The Navaho treated them as a single category but linguistically separated intersexes ("real *nadle*") from berdaches ("those who pretend to be *nadle*") and prescribed somewhat different rules of behavior for them (Hill 1935). Perhaps cultures that merged the two statuses generally separated them into different subclasses, but the evidence is no longer recoverable. While the data prevent drawing a clear and consistent distinction between berdaches and intersexes, most berdaches were anatomically normal and were culturally defined.

DISTRIBUTION

Scanty, fragmentary, and unsatisfactory as most of the data are, they provide reasonably good evidence for the berdache status among the 113 groups listed in Table 27-1. The evidence for its existence among another eight groups seems insufficient or ambiguous. One instance each was reported for the Coeur d'Alene (Ray 1932:18)

and Slave (Honigmann 1946:84), but descriptions of both persons as truly intersexual cloud the existence of a real berdache category in either culture. Bella Coola accounts of Haida women who dressed like men and hunted (McIlwraith 1948, vol. 2:95–96) are not confirmed by Haida sources. Tlingit statements combine denials that berdaches existed with an apparent assertion of their periodic reincarnation in a certain clan

TABLE 27-1 North American Cultures Recognizing the Berdache Status

1. Achumawi (Voegelin 1942: 134–35)
2. Acoma (Hammond 1882: 346)
3. Aleuts (Bancroft 1874, vol. 1: 92; Dall 1897: 402–3)
4. Arapaho (Kroeber 1902: 19–20)
5. Arikara (Holder 1889: 623)
6. Atsugewi (Voegelin 1942: 134–35)
7. Assiniboine (Lowie 1910: 42)
8. Bannock (Steward 1943: 385)
9. Bella Bella (McIlwraith 1948, vol. 1: 45–46)
10. Bella Coola (McIlwraith 1948, vol. 1: 45–46)
11. Blackfoot (Turney-High 1941: 128)
12. Caddo (Newcomb 1961: 301)
13. Carrier (McIlwraith 1948, vol. 1: 45–46)
14. Cheyenne (Grinnell 1962, vol. 2: 39–42; Hoebel 1960: 77)
15. Chilula (Driver 1939: 347)
16. Chiricahua Apache (Opler 1965: 111)
17. Choctaw (Bossu 1962: 169; Romans 1962: 82–83)
18. Chumash (Costanso 1910: 137; Harrington 1942: 32)
19. Coahuiltecans (Cabeza da Vaca in Katz 1976: 285)
20. Coast Salish (Barnett 1955: 149; Teit 1900: 321)
21. Cocopa (Drucker 1941: 163; Gifford 1933: 294)
22. Costanoan (Harrington 1942: 32)
23. Crow (Denig 1961: 187–88; Holder 1889; Lowie 1935: 48, 312–13; Simms 1903)
24. Eyak (Birket-Smith and de Laguna 1938: 206)
25. Flathead (Teit 1930: 384; Turney-High 1937: 85)
26. Fox (Michelson 1927: 257)
27. Gabrieleño (Harrington 1942: 32)
28. Gros Ventre (Holder 1889: 623)
29. Haisla (Olson 1940: 200)
30. Hidatsa (Bowers 1965: 166–68, 323–27)
31. Hopi (Beaglehole and Beaglehole 1935: 44; Fewkes 1892: 11)
32. Hupa (Driver 1939: 347)
33. Illinois (Liette 1947: 112–13; Marquette 1900: 129)
34. Ingalik (Osgood 1958: 219, 261–63)
35. Iowa (Lurie 1953: 711)
36. Ipai (Drucker 1937: 27)
37. Juaneño (Kroeber 1925: 647)
38. Kalekau (Essene 1942: 31, 65)
39. Kaniagmiut (Bancroft 1874, vol. 1: 82; Dall 1897: 402–3)
40. Kansa (Dorsey 1890: 386; Say in James 1823: 129)
41. Karankawa (Newcomb 1961: 74)
42. Kaska (Honigmann 1954: 129–30)
43. Kato (Driver 1939: 347; Essene 1942: 31)
44. Kitanemuk (Harrington 1942: 32)
45. Klamath (Spier 1930: 51–53; Voegelin 1942: 134–35)
46. Kutenai (Spier 1935: 26–27; Turney-High 1941: 128)
47. Laguna (Parsons 1923: 272; 1939: 53)
48. Lassik (Essene 1942: 31, 65)
49. Lillooet (Teit 1906: 267)
50. Lipan Apache (Gifford 1940: 66)
51. Luiseño (Boscana 1978: 54; White 1963: 146–47)
52. Mandan (Bowers 1950: 272, 296, 298)
53. Maricopa (Drucker 1941: 163; Spier 1933: 242–43)
54. Mattale (Driver 1939: 347)
55. Menomini (Skinner 1913: 34)
56. Miami (Trowbridge 1938: 68)
57. Miwok (Gifford 1926: 333)
58. Modoc (Ray 1963: 43)
59. Mohave (Devereux 1937; Kroeber 1925: 478–79; Drucker 1941: 173)
60. Natchez (Swanton 1911: 100)
61. Navaho (Hill 1935; Mathews 1897: 70)
62. Nez Perce (Holder 1889: 623)
63. Nisenan (Beals 1933: 376)
64. Northern Paiute (Gayton 1948: 174; Lowie 1924b: 283; Steward 1933: 238; Stewart 1941: 405)
65. Nootka (Drucker 1951: 333)
66. Nomlaki (Goldschmidt 1951: 387)
67. Ojibwa (Coues 1897: 163–65; Kinietz 1947: 155–57; McKenney 1827: 314–15)
68. Omaha (Fletcher and La Flesche 1911: 132–33; Dorsey 1890: 379)
69. Osage (Fletcher and La Flesche 1911: 132–33)
70. Oto (Irving 1888: 120–33; Whitman 1969: 50)
71. Papago (Drucker 1941: 163; Underhill 1969: 186–87)

72. Patwin (Kroeber 1925: 293; 1932: 272)
73. Pawnee (Dorsey and Murie 1940: 108)
74. Pima (Drucker 1941: 63; Hill 1938)
75. Plains Cree (Mandelbaum 1940: 256–57)
76. Pomo (Gifford 1926: 333)
77. Ponca (Dorsey 1890: 379; Howard 1965: 142–43)
78. Potawatomi (Landes 1970: 190–91, 195–96)
79. Quapaw (St. Cosme in Kellogg 1917: 360)
80. Quileute (Olson 1936: 99)
81. Quinault (Olson 1936: 99)
82. Rogue River (Barnett 1937: 185)
83. Salinan (Harrington 1942: 32; Mason 1912: 174; Hester 1978: 502)
84. Santa Ana Pueblo (Gifford 1940: 66, 168)
85. Santee Dakota (Landes 1968: 32, 57, 66, 112–13)
86. Sauk (Catlin 1973, vol. 2: 214–15; Keating 1825: 216)
87. Shasta (Holt 1946: 317; Voegelin 1942: 134–35)
88. Shoshoneans (Steward 1941: 252–53; 1943: 338)
89. Shoshoni (Shimkin 1947; Steward 1943: 271)
90. Sinkaietk (Cline 1938: 137, 149)
91. Sinkyou (Driver 1937: 347)
92. Siuslaw (Barnett 1937: 185)
93. Southern Paiute (Driver 1937: 90, 129; Drucker 1941: 173; Lowie 1924b: 282; Stewart 1944: 405)
94. Teton Dakota (Hassrick 1964: 122; Mirsky 1937: 416–17)
95. Thompson (Teit 1900: 321)
96. Timucua (Le Moyne du Morgues 1878: 7–8)
97. Tipai (Drucker 1941: 173)
98. Tolowa (Driver 1939: 347; Gould 1978: 131, 134)
99. Tubatulabal (Driver 1937: 90; Voegelin 1938: 47)
100. Ute (Gifford 1940: 55, 136; Lowie 1924b: 282–83; Stewart 1940: 298)
101. Washo (Steward 1941: 485)
102. Winnebago (Lurie 1953)
103. Wintu (Voegelin 1942: 134)
104. Western Apache (Gifford 1940: 66, 136, 168)
105. Wishram (Spier and Sapir 1930: 229–21)
106. Wiyot (Driver 1937: 347; Elsasser 1978: 159)
107. Yana (Sapir and Spier 1943: 275)
108. Yankton (Dorsey 1890: 467)
109. Yokuts (Gayton 1948: 66, 106, 236; Wallace 1978a: 455; 1978b: 466)
110. Yuki (Foster 1944: 183, 186; Powers 1877: 132–33)
111. Yuma (Forde 1931: 157; Gifford 1931: 56)
112. Yurok (Kroeber 1925: 46)
113. Zuni (Parsons 1916; Stevenson 1902: 37–38)

(de Laguna 1954:178). While Kardiner (1945:56–57, 88) said the Comanche prohibited transvestism, his reference to "effeminate" men who did the work of women suggests that berdaches may have existed in a covert form, as among the Pima (Hill 1938), but more information is needed to resolve this question. One possible instance from the Kinugmiut Eskimo (Ray 1975:89, 97) is inconclusive. Goddard (1978:231) cautiously notes indications of berdaches among the Delaware. Boyce (1978:283) raises the possibility that Tuscarora men who were poor hunters and followed other occupations might have been berdaches. Practice among the Creek is uncertain. Romans (1964:97) reported male homosexuality, but not berdaches; Underhill (1953:34) described the latter without citing a source; and Adair's (1966:25) reference to a woman rumored to be a hermaphrodite is not decisive.

Explicit denials that are not contradicted by other evidence have been reported for only nine groups: Cahuila (Drucker 1937:29, 49), Chimariko (Driver 1939:347, 465), Cochiti (Lange 1959:15), Karok (Driver 1939:347, 465), Maidu (Voegelin 1942:134, 228), Serrano (Drucker 1937:27), Walapai (Drucker 1941:218; McKennon in Kroeber 1935); Wappo (Driver 1936: 200), and Yavapai (Drucker 1941:163; Gifford 1936:296). Their significance is uncertain; similar denials are recorded for cultures known to have had berdaches. Driver is openly skeptical about the Chimariko and Karok statements; neither Drucker nor McKennon seems satisfied with the Walapai denials; and Drucker stresses the Cahuila and Serrano reluctance to discuss any sexual matters.

Direct evidence for the presence or absence of the berdache status does not seem available for other groups—a statement necessarily qualified by the possibility that we missed references. The significance of silence is hard to assess. It can stem from very diverse causes. For many of these cultures, destroyed very early and poorly known in every respect, the absence of references means very little. Other cultures in this group are well known, but those who described them may not have asked about berdaches; informants may have been reluctant to offer information; or the status may have been forgotten. That silence cannot automatically be interpreted as evidence that the status was absent is shown by the relatively well-described Winnebago, who would fall into this category except for Lurie's (1953) article. Yet to assume that it existed unless denials were recorded is equally dangerous. When specific references are lacking, our discussion of the distribution of the berdache status rests on three assumptions: First, a group whose neighbors were culturally similar and had berdaches probably had them; thus one may reasonably assume their probable presence among the Kickapoo, Missouri, and Yanktonai. Second, if detailed accounts of a culture by several observers over a period of time are consistently silent, berdaches probably did not exist. Third, if references are lacking for a large cluster of adjacent cultures that are fairly well known, the probability is that berdaches were not present.

The berdache status existed over a large area extending from California to the Mississippi Valley and upper Great Lakes, with scattered occurrences beyond it (Fig. 27-1). If probably distributed rather more widely than the maps indicate, it still seems to have been far from universal. In terms of culture areas, using Driver's (1969) classification, berdaches were ubiquitous in California and the Great Basin except for a few scattered groups that are poorly known or whose denials, as noted, are not entirely convincing. With similar exceptions they characterized the Plains and Prairies, except for the south. Their distribution in the Southwest and the Northwest Coast seems to have been decidedly less pervasive than in the four culture areas first noted. References are scantiest for the Arctic, Subarctic, Plateau, and East.

It might seem predictable that the berdache status should fade out toward the north, among band societies with a less complex level of sociocultural organization (cf. Opler 1965:111). This assumption may be unjustified. The distributional pattern in North America shows little cor-

relation between this status and the level of social organization. Almost universal among band societies of the Great Basin, even in the Subarctic it extended beyond the limits one might expect. Possibly its attenuation and disappearance in the north rested on the specific nature of Arctic and Subarctic subsistence economies, to which the contribution of males was too valuable to promote their transformation. A significant point, perhaps, is that the berdaches recorded for all Subarctic groups except the Ojibwa included females, who hunted, and only female berdaches are reported for the Kaska and Carrier.

The relative absence of berdaches among Plateau groups also seems predictable, perhaps deceptively so. Whatever the reasons, the extent to which this seems a Plateau characteristic is reflected in their concentration among marginal groups that adjoined other culture areas where the status was more common.

In the East, berdaches are documented for the lower Mississippi Valley among the Natchez, Caddo, Choctaw, and Quapaw; they also characterized the Timucua. References for other cultures, vague and uncertain at best, seem limited to the Creek, Delaware, and Tuscarora. The status might have been widespread in the past, disappearing soon after contact. It seems improbable, however, that reports as detailed as those for the Iroquois and covering so long a time period would never have mentioned berdaches if these had existed. Elisabeth Tooker (personal communication) interprets this silence as indicating their possible absence. We agree. The berdache status, then, seems to have been surprisingly absent, undeveloped, or very obscure throughout the East except for its southern fringe.

Another region, smaller in extent, in which references to berdaches are unexpectedly absent centers on the southern Plains with adjacent Prairie and Southwest cultures. The Comanche, as noted, as a debatable case, but their prohibition of transvestism, a cardinal trait of the status, seems to indicate hostility toward it. If berdaches were actually absent, the causes are

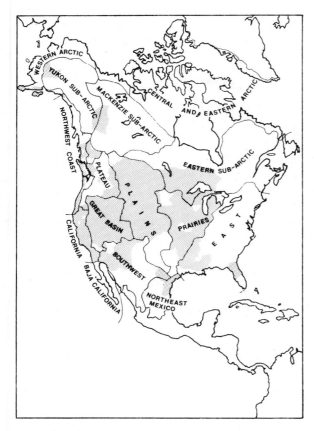

FIGURE 27-1. Distribution of berdaches, male and female (base map from Driver 1969).

obscure, particularly since they characterized most of the surrounding cultures and were prominent in the northern Plains.

Another distributional aspect is the limited occurrence of female berdaches, reported for only 30 groups: Achumawi, Atsugewi, Bella Coola, Carrier, Cocopa, Crow, Haisla, Ingalik, Kaska, Klamath, Kutenai, Lillouet, Maricopa, Mohave, Navaho, Nootka, Northern Paiute, Papago, Quinault, Shasta, Shoshoneans, Tipai, Ute, Washoe, Western Apache, Wintu, Wiyot, Yokuts, Yuki, and Yuma. They may also have characterized the Flathead and Haida. Male berdaches are not reported for the Carrier, Kaska, and Kutenai; the uncertain Haida reference mentions only women. Even more strongly than

the berdache status as a whole, its female variety tended to concentrate in western North America, restricted to the Subarctic, Northwest Coast, Plateau, Great Basin, California, and Southwest (Fig. 27-2). The only exception is a single instance reported for the Crow. Female berdaches tended to be more prevalent in less complex societies and those in which agriculture was absent or less important.

NUMBERS

Berdaches are usually described as rare or uncommon; numbers, if given, are few. Holder (1889:623) reported six among the Gros Ventre, five among the Teton Dakota, four for the Flathead, two for the Nez Perce, and one for the Shoshoni. Kroeber (1925:66) estimated that one Yurok man in a hundred assumed this status. Except among groups limiting the status to women, female berdaches tended to be much rarer than their male counterparts.

Early accounts that mention their frequency consistently describe berdaches as more numerous. Cabeza de Vaca (Katz 1976:285) reported many of them among the Coahuiltecans between 1528 and 1533. Le Moyne du Morgues (1875:7–8) said they were quite common among the Timucua in 1564. In 1769–70 Costanso (1910:137) reported them present in every Chumash village. Henry in 1799–1800 (Coues 1897:347–48) credited the Hidatsa with many berdaches, and Maximilian (1906:354) gave a similar account for the Crow around 1832. In 1822 Boscana (1978:54) reported a second-hand account that they were very numerous among the Yuma before a plague reduced their numbers. Perhaps these reports should be treated skeptically; yet when information is available for a specific group over time the number of berdaches dwindles rapidly. Maximilian's statement that in 1832 the Crow had many may be compared with Holder's reporting five in 1889 (1889:622–23), Simms's counting three in 1902 (1903:580–81), and Lowie's meeting only one (1924*b*:243–44).

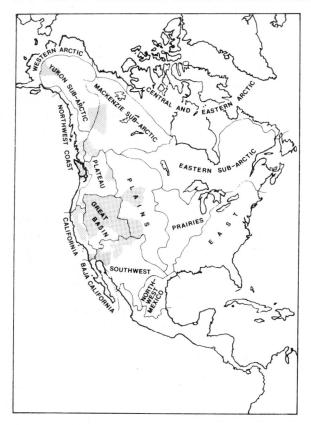

FIGURE 27-2 Distribution of female berdaches (base map from Driver 1969).

Hidatsa traditions held that their tribe once had as many as fifteen to twenty-five; Bowers's (1965:166–67) informants could remember only two in the generation before theirs. Grinnell (1962, vol. 2:39) said the Cheyenne had five, later dwindling to two, with the last one dying in 1879. Since overall population was also decreasing, the proportion of berdaches may have remained fairly constant, up to a point. Some early accounts suggest, however, that berdaches had a significant social role whose importance diminished as other factors combined to discourage the assumption of this status. Bowers (1965:168) attributes their disappearance among the Hidatsa to the disintegration of the religious system to which they were linked. While it seems

unlikely that berdaches were ever numerous, they were probably once more common than later accounts indicate.

TRANSVESTISM

Male berdaches usually adopted the dress and hairstyle of women. References to their imitating women's voices and using their forms of speech, if these differed from men's, are less common, but this may reflect gaps in reporting rather than actual frequency. Female berdaches usually dressed as men. Transvestism was one of the most widespread and significant features of the status, often marking the final stage of gender transformation (cf. Lurie 1953:708). Yet it was neither universal nor invariable.

Transvestism was prohibited by the Pima, whose male berdaches imitated the speech, behavior, and postures of women but wore men's dress (Hill 1938: 339), and by the Comanche (Kardiner 1945:56–57, 88), if they had berdaches. Female berdaches retained women's dress among the Achumawi, Atsugewi, Klamath, and Shasta (Spier 1930:51–53; Voegelin 1942:134–35), although no compulsion was reported and the male variety in these societies cross-dressed. The Crow female berdache carried weapons but dressed as a woman (Denig 1961:195–200). Grinnell's description of Cheyenne berdaches as dressing like elderly men (1962, vol. 2:39) was probably a misunderstanding (cf. Hoebel 1960:27). Accounts of male Shasta berdaches conflict, Voegelin (1942:134–35) describing transvestism but Holt (1946:317) denying it. Some societies permitted individual choice. While intersexual Navahos had to dress like women, unmarried berdaches of either sex dressed as they wished. Free choice is reported for male berdaches among the Northern and Southern Paiute (Gayton 1948: 174; Lowie 1924b:282; Stewart 1941:405), for the female variety among the Wintu (Voegelin 1942:134), and for all Shoshonean berdaches (Steward 1941:252–53; 1943:385).

Male berdaches sometimes assumed the dress proper to their anatomic sex in certain contexts. The Navaho required those who married to dress as men, whether their spouses were male or female (Hill 1935:273, 275–76). One condition that could evoke this shift was undertaking an action defined as specifically male. Miami and Osage berdaches who joined a war party intending to fight had to wear male clothing until they returned (Fletcher and La Flesche 1911:133; Trowbridge 1938:68). Among the Western Mono some alternated by occupation, dressing like women when gathering but changing to men's attire to hunt. Gayton's (1948:174) suggestion that this practice may have distinguished men who had undergone a partial transformation from those who had completed this and always dressed like women could perhaps be extended to other societies in which a berdache assumed this status gradually, with the complete adoption of women's clothing marking the end of the process. Landes (1970:198–202) describes a Potawatomi example. Such an assumption could reduce some of the variation evident in the data.

A further consideration bearing on the variability reported in dress is that most of the data were gathered after American control had been imposed. Some deviations from the general pattern of transvestism reflect attempts by officials to stamp out the institution by forcing male berdaches to dress as men (Bowers 1965:315; Simms 1903:580). American attitudes also promoted native hostility toward transvestism. Teit's (1930:384) statement that occasionally Flathead male berdaches briefly assumed male dress to please the men illustrates this pressure. The last Winnebago berdache wore a combination of male and female clothing because his brothers threatened to kill him if he completed the transformation (Lurie 1953:708). It seems, then, a valid generalization that in traditional North American societies and under ordinary circumstances a berdache usually cross-dressed. Yet some of the variability reported in the literature was a traditional attribute of the status.

OCCUPATIONS

Berdaches often followed the occupations of the gender whose dress they assumed. This was another particularly widespread feature of their status, one of the traits most often cited and, like transvestism, one of the most significant. A boy's interest in women's occupations and his propensity for engaging in these might be interpreted as signs that he would become a berdache and were sometimes advanced as the causal factors promoting change in gender status. Parsons (1939:38) said that a Pueblo male who did women's work beyond a point—the point not specified—had to become a berdache. Similar significance was seen in a girl's interest in work assigned to men.

Male berdaches are consistently described as exceptionally skilled in women's work, often as better than women. Among the Crow they had the largest and best-appointed lodges and were excellent sewers and the most efficient cooks (Simms 1903:581). This proficiency, noted by observers as well as informants, was another attribute of their status (Boscana 1978:54; Bowers 1965:167; Devereux 1937:513–14; Hassrick 1965:123; Hill 1935:275; Howard 1965:142–43; Kroeber 1952:313; Landes 1968:112–13; 1970:195–96; Linton 1936:480; Lowie 1935:48; Lurie 1953:708–10; Mathews 1897:215; Mirsky 1937:416–17; Parsons 1916:523; Underhill 1969:186). Accounts of their employment by local Whites or acculturated Indian families are also evidence to this point (Holder 1889:624; Landes 1970:198–202; Steward 1941:253). Admiration for their skill centered on crafts and housework rather than agriculture, although some references note their value as gatherers. Apparently female berdaches showed a similar pattern in excelling in male activities, with hunting most often cited (Devereux 1937:515; Honigmann 1954:129–30). Denig (1961:195–203) described Woman Chief as at least equal to any Crow man as a hunter; significantly, she was able to support four wives.

Further evidence that berdaches were considered exceptionally productive is the fact that households based on marriage between a man and a male berdache were exceptionally well-to-do, more prosperous than those founded on male/female unions (Bowers 1965:167; Devereux 1937:513–15; Stevenson 1902:38). So were extended families that included an unmarried berdache. The Navaho regarded such a family as particularly fortunate, since it was assured of wealth (Hill 1935:274). Even berdaches who constituted single-person households seem to have been well-off (Hassrick 1964:121–22; Landes 1968:324; Mirsky 1937:416–17).

Several observers attributed the productivity of male berdaches to their greater strength (Boscana 1978:45; Bowers 1965:167; Stevenson 1902:310–11; Underhill 1969:186–87). Cabeza da Vaca (Katz 1976:285) and Simms (1903:580–82) described them as unusually strong or robust even by comparison with other men. Stevenson (1902:310) called the berdache Wewha the strongest person at Zuni and perhaps the tallest. A Potawatomi berdache was said to be taller than most men (Landes 1970:200). Statements crediting berdaches with unusual size or strength are not frequent enough to provide evidence for a general tendency. That male berdaches were stronger than women seems reasonable, given their larger body size. This may have increased their productivity; but the crafts in which they were most often described as excelling did not require particular strength, nor does this explanation account for the hunting skill of female berdaches. Bowers's (1965:167) emphasis on their freedom from pregnancy and child care echoes Stevenson (1902:37), who estimated that a Zuni berdache could do almost twice as much work as a woman. This advantage again seems an insufficient explanation for excellent craftsmanship. Another possible factor in their productivity may have been industry, a trait often imputed to them (e.g., Devereux 1937:513–14; Stevenson 1902:38); perhaps berdaches had to try harder.

Perhaps this tendency to excel in the occupations assigned to their status also reflected belief in the supernatural powers often ascribed to this. Among the Dakota such supernatural beings as Double-Woman, who ordered men to become berdaches, were associated with proficiency in such activities as quillworking and could confer this talent upon women who experienced visions of them. Explicitly cited by Landes (1970:36–37, 41) and Mirsky (1937:416–17), the association of berdache skills with supernatural power can probably be extended to other cultures. Hassrick (1964:133) describes the items made by Teton Dakota berdaches as "highly desirable" and "eminently marketable." Whether these products were valued simply for their craftsmanship or whether their desirability rested in part on associations with the supernatural, their exchange provided income and was probably an important factor in the prosperity even of single berdaches.

Another important component of their economic role and a significant element in the prosperity often attributed to berdaches rested on the intermediate nature of their gender status, allowing them to combine activities proper to men and to women and maximize their economic opportunities. Mead (1961:1452) characterized the male berdache among the Navaho and Teton Dakota as "a totally self-sufficient 'household' capable of both male and female activities." Voegelin (1942:134–35) credits female berdaches among the Atsugewi, Shasta, and Wintu with this freedom; male berdaches had the same latitude among the Bannock (Steward 1943:385) and some Northern Paiute (Gayton 1948:174). Navaho berdaches of either sex could undertake men's and women's work (Hill 1935:275). Male berdaches are often described as hunting. While reporting that the Navaho forbade them this activity, Hill (1935:275) named it among their occupations; Gifford (1940:168) reported it for the western Navaho berdaches. The apparent contradiction between Mirsky's (1937:416–17) description of Teton Dakota berdaches as combining household work with hunting and Hassrick's (1964:121) argument that their inability to compete as hunters impelled them to adopt berdache status could be resolved by assuming that their hunting was limited and—if such a term is proper—noncompetitive; but we suspect that Hassrick assumed this inability from their status. Linton's (1936:480) statement that among the Plains tribes the husband of a male berdache was taunted for trying to obtain a wife who would hunt and keep house indicates that berdache status did not preclude hunting. Hunting is clearly implied in Cabeza da Vaca's report that Coahuiltecan berdaches, who also did the work of women, used bows (Katz 1976:285). While it seems improbable that one person could effectively carry on both kinds of work on a regular basis, a berdache's ability when necessary to alternate or combine the occupational roles associated with male and female genders would have increased his productivity.

A source of income limited to male berdaches involved specific duties tied to their status. They performed special services in a number of cultures. Accounts seldom specify compensation for these, but the examples described suggest that this practice was probably widespread. Teton berdaches received horses as payment for the secret names they were asked to give children (Fire 1972:217). Among the California cultures in which they were responsible for burial and mourning rituals they were paid for their services (Kroeber 1925:497, 500–501). Still another service peculiar to their status that may have required compensation was their use as go-betweens, facilitated by their ability to move freely between males and females (Mead 1932:189).

WARFARE

Berdache status is often described as a sanctuary for males who were unable or unwilling to accept the role of warrior (Benedict 1939:572; Hoebel 1949:459; Linton 1936:480; Marmor 1965:13; Mead 1961:1452; Mirsky 1937:416–17; Underhill 1969:186). Hassrick (1964:121–22) cast this interpretation in terms of what he called "sissies" and "mamma's boys" who could

not face the hardships of hunting and warfare. Fear of warfare is sometimes advanced as the primary reason for assuming the status (Underhill 1953:54; cf. Devereux 1937:517–18). Apparently formulated by anthropologists examining the Teton Dakota, this analysis of the male berdache does not really hold up when extended to North America generally. In our opinion the evidence, considered in its entirety, casts doubt upon this traditional view as valid even for the northern Plains.

No correlation is discernible between the existence of male berdaches and the prevalence or significance of warfare. Their status was as characteristic of the Hopi and Zuni as of the northern Plains tribes, and, granting that the Western Pueblos were less peaceful than they have sometimes been described, they differed qualitatively in this respect from the Teton. Very warlike societies, such as the Iroquois, could lack berdaches, who were at best obscure and perhaps altogether absent in the southern Plains.

Men who feared war did not have to assume berdache status. Information about this group is slight, but its existence is indicated by several sources, including Linton's (1936:480) comment that berdaches had higher status than the men who failed as warriors. Further evidence is provided by the measures to shame them, described in the first section of this article, superficially resembling the cross-dressing feature of the berdache status but sharply distinguished from it in concept. Also relevant here, we think, is Catlin's account of the young Mandan men he called "dandies," whom the warriors despised. Whatever their sexual orientation may have been— and we doubt that his reference to them as "gay and tinselled bucks" (1973, vol. 1:112–14) should be taken in the contemporary sense— they were obviously not berdaches.

Berdache status, usually assumed at adolescence or foreshadowed earlier, was occasionally embraced by an established warrior. Tixier (1940: 234) describes such an event among the Osage; Irving (1888:120–22) gives an Oto example. De Smet (1904:1017) met such a man among the

Crow. A similar interpretation may apply to the Osage berdache described below, except that he continued warrior activity. These incidents seem to have been rare, but so were berdaches.

The frequent exclusion of male berdaches from warfare seems to us best analyzed as part of a widespread but variable prohibition against their engaging in certain actions defined as specifically male. Sometimes this prohibition was a cultural rule, sometimes it was individual practice. It was neither universal nor absolute. Illinois berdaches fought but were forbidden to use bows, symbolic of maleness (Marquette 1900:129). As we have seen, the Miami required them to dress as males when going to war (Trowbridge 1938:68), and a similar practice may be inferred for the Osage on the basis of the account of a young man who, returning as leader of a successful raid, was supernaturally revealed to be a berdache and accepted this status, although he continued to act as a war leader and in this capacity dressed as a man (Fletcher and La Flesche 1911:133). The Crow berdache Lowie knew had fought (1935:8). Henry (Coues 1897:163–65) described a berdache who acted as rear guard for a group of Ojibwa, fighting off a Dakota war party while his companions retreated. This was the Yellow Head, whose "disgusting advances" later outraged John Tanner (1956:89–91) and whom Whitehead (1981:108) cites as an example of an unsuccessful berdache. When the leader of a Hidatsa war party that came upon three Dakota women decided to count coup upon them, one "woman" revealed himself as a berdache and drove off the warriors with a digging stick, his threats aided by their leader's arrow's failing to penetrate his robe (Bowers 1965: 256). It is also clear that berdache status did not ensure safety from enemy attack (cf. Kurz 1937:211).

In contexts outside warfare, berdaches were capable of violent behavior contradicting naive assumptions that they were necessarily gentle by nature (cf. Underhill 1953:54). The Yellow Head, whom Henry described as troublesome when drunk, lost an eye in a fight (Coues 1897:53). Mohave berdaches might assault unfaithful husbands or men who ridiculed them (Devereux 1937:510–14). The berdache Wewha was imprisoned for a year for attacking three policemen trying to make an arrest at Zuni (Parsons 1939:65).

In some societies, berdaches fought. In others, although not fighting, they had significant roles in the war complex. They accompanied warriors to carry supplies among the Natchez and Timucua (Dumont in Swanton 1911:110; Le Moyne du Morgues 1878:7–8), to herd the horses taken from the Spanish among the Karankawa (Newcomb 1961:74). Cheyenne war parties often invited berdaches to accompany them (Grinnell 1962, vol. 2:40–41); besides treating the wounded, they had custody of scalps, carried these into camp, and ran the dance that followed the raiders' return. The Teton Dakota consulted berdaches to divine their success in projected battles (Grinnell 1956:237–38; Hyde 1937:147).

Rather than a group of males who feared warfare, berdaches were closely tied to the war complex in a number of societies and perhaps even a crucial part of it. Admitting that direct evidence for his argument is lacking, Hoebel (1960:77) suggests that the Cheyenne attributed the success of a war party to its inclusion of a berdache, whose stored-up unexpended virility was essential for this end. We do not entirely accept Hoebel's precise argument, although we agree that by rejecting the kinds of power normally accessible to males berdaches might be regarded as acquiring special and potent kinds of power that could affect military actions, among other activities. We do think that Hoebel has discerned much more of the actual relationship between berdaches and warfare than those who formulated or accept the traditional analysis. Further evidence for such an association is provided by Bowers (1965:108, 327), who points out that Hidatsa men became berdaches through visions sent by the Holy Women, supernatural beings closely associated with warfare and aiding young warriors; and he attributes their disappearance to the end of warfare and the collapse of the ceremonial structure associated with it.

Female berdaches did not emulate male behavior by becoming warriors. Gifford's (1933:5) report that this was one of their attributes among the Cocopa, not confirmed by accounts of other River Yuman groups, is explicitly denied by the Mohave (Devereux 1937:518–19). The female Kutenai berdache fought (Spier 1935:26–27), and Woman Chief achieved high rank as a Crow warrior (Denig 1961:195–200), but their activity in the war complex was exceptional for their status and differed only in scale from that of occasional nonberdache woman warriors.

SEXUALITY

Sexual behavior is the aspect of the berdache status in which the reticence of informants most often combines with the prudery of observers to obscure actual practice and in which suppositions have been most frequent. Early European observers, when aware that berdaches were not intersexual, tended to assume that men who dressed and acted like women were necessarily homosexual (cf. Lafitau 1724:52). That this belief, reflected in their use of the word "berdache," was sometimes only an assumption is shown by Dumont's 18th-century account of the Natchez (Swanton 1911:100): "as among these people [the Natchez], who live almost without religion and without law, libertinism is carried to the greatest excess, I will not answer that these barbarians do not abuse this pretended chief of the women [berdache] and make him serve their brutal passions." Most later observers continued to hold this view, at least implicitly. Yet if often accurate, the assumption that berdaches were homosexual is oversimplified. Like their other attributes, sexual behavior was variable and very complex.

Questioning whether homosexuality was an integral feature of berdache status, Kroeber (1952:313) pointed out that informants emphasized its social aspects—transvestism and occupations—rather than sexual behavior. This emphasis, prominent in the literature, could reflect reluctance to offend Western sensibilities rather than indicating the native view. Most accounts of Crow berdaches stress social behavior, yet Holder (1889) obtained explicit data about sexual practices. Mohave informants gave Devereux (1937) detailed descriptions of homosexual activity. The Yellow Head's intentions toward Tanner (1956:89–91) were very clear. Homosexual exploits were an important attribute of berdaches among the Santee, who claimed these were too lewd to describe to Landes (1968:112–13). Noting this Santee contrast with the Potawatomi emphasis on berdaches' concern with "proper" female behavior, she interprets this as a cultural difference (1970:198–202). While reticence cannot be ignored as a factor potentially skewing anthropologists' perceptions of the native view of berdaches, it seems possible that if some cultures considered homosexual activity a significant aspect of this status, others did not.

Most descriptions of berdache sexual behavior stress homosexuality. This involved intercourse with persons of the same anatomical sex, but not with other berdaches, and entailed relations ranging in form from casual promiscuity to stable marriages. Information is, as usual, unsatisfactory. Many sources are silent. Most of them specify little more than that berdaches lived with persons of the same sex or say they never married without describing other relationships. Even statements about marriage seldom note its nature or frequency. Enough data are available for a few societies to discern or infer certain recurring patterns. Promiscuity apparently characterized Santee and Teton Dakota berdaches, who were not allowed to marry men or even to establish relatively long-term sexual relationships (Hassrick 1964:121–22; Landes 1968:32; Mirsky 1937:416–17). Catlin's Sauk account (1973, vol. 2:214–15), also implying promiscuity, suggests that their sexual partners were young men, perhaps not yet married, although it seems likely a berdache's lovers also included married men. We think this was one common pattern. Both casual relations and marriage are reported for some societies. Holder (1889:624) implies that Crow berdaches seldom married, but apparently it was not forbidden; the female berdache in this tribe married women. Papago berdaches, who could marry, often lived alone and received male lovers (Underhill 1969:186–87). Among the Navaho they were free to pursue any kind of relationship, including marriage (Hill 1935). Brittle, unstable marriages are described for Mohave berdaches (Devereux 1937:157) and may be inferred for the Ojibwa (Tanner 1956:89–91). Stable unions, reported for the Yuma (Forde 1931:157), also characterized the Hidatsa, whose berdaches usually married older men, childless, who had difficulty keeping wives, and if the husband also had female wives insisted upon a separate lodge (Bowers 1965:166–68). A Hidatsa berdache could develop a complete family by adopting children, either village orphans or war captives taken by his relatives, of whom he was considered the mother. Among the Cheyenne (Hoebel 1960:77) and Luiseño (Boscana 1978:54), berdaches could only be auxiliary wives.

Although direct evidence for this conclusion is scanty, we suspect that homosexual relations with berdaches were generally accepted as long as they did not obstruct "normal" marriages or, in some cultures, take the form of these. Concern with preventing any interference with the child-producing male/female unions necessary to perpetuate a society would center most intensely upon marriage and could explain those cultures that prohibited formal unions with berdaches. Bowers's description of the husbands of Hidatsa berdaches, cited above, is suggestive, even when marriage was strongly encouraged, the husbands were relative failures maritally or already had female wives. Moreover, the relatively few indications that sexual relations with berdaches drew disapproval usually focus on marriage rather than casual affairs. This emphasis seems clear in Linton's (1936:480) account of the ridicule directed at the husband of a Plains berdache. Devereux (1937:513–18) attributes the instability of Mohave berdache marriages to the derision their spouses experienced; affairs with them did not draw this response.

This analysis might also explain the anomalously vehement denunciations of sexual rela-

tions with berdaches attributed to the Teton Dakota. Mirsky (1937:416–17), describing berdaches as "passive" homosexual males, reported that the Teton ostracized their "active" counterparts. If the latter terms designate the sexual partners of berdaches, their ostracism seems improbable; Forgey (1975:3–4) argues that berdaches served the needs of "active" homosexuals. Perhaps Mirsky meant nonberdache males who were exclusively homosexual and refused to marry. Hassrick (1964:122) cites a man's warning to his son that relations with a berdache will draw punishment in the afterlife. Since his informant simultaneously described homosexual intercourse as the culminating step in their transformation, berdaches obviously found sexual partners. Unless such warnings were an empty form, it seems probable that they were actually directed against long-term relationships rather than intercourse or, if really addressed to young boys, as Lame Deer (Fire 1972:149) seems to imply, were meant to discourage close associations with berdaches that might lead to assuming the same status.

Accounts of the modes of intercourse practiced by male berdaches in the homosexual context are very rare. Kroeber (1902:19–20) describes anal intercourse performed upon Arapaho berdaches. Holder (1889:625) notes its practice by the Crow without indicating whether the context was heterosexual or homosexual and nonberdache; he insists that berdaches limited themselves to fellation of their partners. Devereux (1937:511–15), who credits Mohave berdaches with both practices—which also characterized heterosexual intercourse in their culture—is the main authority on the forms of intercourse for female berdaches. Among the Mohave these were limited to digital manipulation of the sexual partner and to various techniques producing vulvic contact. He denies the practice of cunnilingus, to which Mohave men were extremely averse; while women might not share this aversion, female berdaches imitated male behavior. Vulvic contact, perhaps common among other groups, is implied by Jones's

(1907:141) account of a sexual encounter between two nonberdache women. The Kutenai female berdache is said to have used an artificial phallus to convince her wife she was actually a man (Schaeffer 1976:294).

If homosexuality is the orientation most often described or assumed for berdaches, it is not the only one recorded or implied. Kroeber (1952: 312) suggested that some of them may have found transvestism—including general social behavior—satisfying in itself. Benedict (1934: 263) held that the status included some men who were impotent or had a weak sexual drive. Both suggestions draw some support from the ethnographic evidence. Osgood (1958:261–62) concluded that his information about Ingalik berdaches suggested asexuality. Teit's (1930:38) denial that Flathead berdaches were homosexual, corroborated by Turney-High's (1937:85) later study, may also have held for their Nootka counterparts (Drucker 1951:331). The Pima prohibited homosexuality (Hill 1938:339). None of these accounts describe heterosexual behavior. Descriptions of individual berdaches among the Plains Cree (Mandelbaum 1940:256–57), Chiricahua Apache (Opler 1965:111), and Bella Coola (McIlwraith 1948, vol. 1:45–46) include denials of any overt sexual activity. Fletcher and La Flesche's (1911:182) statement that Omaha berdaches "must sometimes become subject to gross actions" hint at homosexuality but implies that only some of them engaged in this. We conclude, then, that the berdache category included some essentially asexual persons; perhaps certain cultures even defined this orientation as proper.

Other accounts ascribe heterosexual behavior to berdaches, either exclusively or as part of a general bisexual orientation. Olson (1940:288) described those of the Haisla as entirely heterosexual, male berdaches marrying women and female berdaches men. The sexual partners of one male Quinault berdache were elderly women (Olson 1935:99). McIlwraith (1948, vol. 2:45–46) reported that some male Bella Bella and Bella Coola berdaches married women. One

male Osage berdache had a wife (Fletcher and La Flesche 1911:133). Although Navaho intersexes were restricted to male sexual partners, their berdaches were essentially bisexual, engaging in sexual relations with males and females (Hill 1935:276). So were Illinois berdaches, whom Liette (1947:112–13) described as homosexuals who also had intercourse with women. Informants said a Crow berdache occasionally had sex with women, although he denied it (Holder 1889:624). Spier (1930:50–53) described a bisexual female Klamath berdache. If the Mohave account of a woman who turned heterosexual after her rape by the husband of a woman she was courting sounds rather too much like a male fantasy, reports of her earlier earnings as a prostitute suggest a bisexual capacity (Devereux 1961:416–25). One of Steward's Shoshonean informants said his great-grandfather had been a berdache (Steward 1941:253); so was the grandfather of a Navaho berdache (Hill 1935:273).

Besides reports of open heterosexual behavior that was culturally approved or at least viewed neutrally, some accounts describe berdaches as engaging in this surreptitiously. Discounting a Yurok suggestion that transvestism afforded males sexual access to women without rousing suspicion, Kroeber (1952:314) accepted this as an occasional possibility. Miami berdaches may have taken similar advantage of their status (Trowbridge 1938:68). Stevenson (1902:37–38) recorded a parallel belief among the Zuni. To her statement that Zuni berdaches never married women she added the qualification that they seldom had sexual relations with them; and while discounting rumors that the berdache Wewha had fathered several children she believed one child to be his. Tixier (1940:23) noted rumors that an Osage berdache was the lover of the chief's wife.

Evaluating this scattered information about heterosexual behavior presents special problems. Some of it is obviously hearsay, of uncertain reliability. Another factor complicating an assessment of its significance is uncertainty about the time in an individual's life when heterosexual behavior occurred. A berdache usually entered this status at adolescence but could do so as an adult and after marriage; or, rarely, might move from it back into a normal gender status. The female Kutenai berdache had a husband before her transformation and later marriages to women (Spier 1935:26–27). Some Mohave women became berdaches after experiencing difficult deliveries (Devereux 1937:507–8). Spier (1930:51–53) describes two Klamath men who withdrew from the berdache status but says nothing about their sexual activity while in it. Yet, even with these reservations, it seems necessary to conclude that a number of berdaches were bisexual while they held this gender status. At first sight, indeed, the extent of their bisexuality seems surprising, but, here again, the intermediate nature of the status could well have been expressed sexually as it was in occupations and dress.

ONTOGENY

Most accounts of the processes by which individuals became berdaches center around two themes. One view, relatively secular and matter-of-fact, describes them as entering this status in childhood by showing interest in the work of the other gender and by associating with its members. This behavior led their parents to dress and treat them as berdaches and their societies to accept them as such. The second and more widespread view is that the status required supernatural validation, usually in the form of a vision and generally occurring at adolescence or later, resulting in a public transformation of gender status.

Still other modes of recruitment are reported for a few groups. Several accounts describe berdaches as chosen, in infancy or very early childhood, and trained for their role. Kaska couples who wanted a daughter to become a hunter dressed her as a boy and gave her masculine work (Honigmann 1954:129–30). The Luiseño, who valued berdaches as auxiliary wives for their chiefs, selected certain male infants for this purpose (Boscana 1978:54). Bancroft (1874, vol. 1:82), citing Langsdorff and Sauer as sources, said Kaniagmiut women chose their handsomest and most promising sons for this status, which provided wives for wealthy men. The most divergent account, Hammond's (1882) report that each Pueblo feminized one of its most virile adult males through a combination of continuous horseback riding and incessant masturbation, seems best interpreted as a misunderstanding, perhaps stimulated by too enthusiastic a search for parallels with the Scythians.

Statements that male war captives were forced to become berdaches seem mostly an anthropological myth. Extrapolating from Iroquois reports, Carr (n.d.:18–19, 33) explained berdaches as captives assigned to agricultural work. Angelino and Shedd (1955) based their argument that berdaches included feminized captives on the rhetoric used by Iroquois orators to describe their political relations with the Delaware (cf. Goddard 1978:223), interpreting this imagery literally and transferring it to an entirely different context. Apart from flaws in method, both hypotheses are handicapped by the complete lack of evidence for Iroquois berdaches. A Tlingit account suggesting an attempt to force homosexual relations upon a captive male did not involve berdache status (de Laguna 1960:155). The references in Hill's novel *Hanta yo* (1979) to sodomizing male enemies are entirely fictional, according to Powers (1979:825), who explains these as an invention based upon Hill's misunderstanding of Dakota. Evidence for this method of recruitment consists of a single Winnebago instance, which Lurie's (1953:710) informants apparently regarded as exceptional.

The distribution of the two major processes is indicated in Table 27-2. A few groups appear in both lists because sources disagree. Emphasis on childhood behavior may also be inferred for cultures requiring a formal test to determine whether a boy who liked women's work was really destined for berdachehood. The Papago placed such a child in a brush windbreak containing basketry material as well as a bow and arrow and set fire to the enclosure; choosing the basketry as he fled ensured his future as a berdache (Underhill 1969:186–87). Similar tests involving objects symbolizing male and female work are reported for the Pima (Hill 1938:339–40), some Ute (Stewart 1944:298), and one Shoshonean group (Steward 1941:253). A Klamath incident rather similar in form occurred in adolescence and coincided with a vision experience (Spier 1930:51–53).

Belief in visions may also be inferred when not explicitly reported. Pawnee and Yankton berdaches (Dorsey 1890:67; Dorsey and Murie 1940:108) were influenced by the moon, a frequent source of transformation visions among neighboring cultures. Marquette's Illinois account (1900:129), silent about such visions, strongly implies them.

Descriptions of transformation visions, mostly

TABLE 27-2   Main Factors Leading to Berdache Status

Culture	Childhood Interests	Vision Experience
Achumawi (Voegelin 1942: 134–35)	. . .	x
Arapaho (Kroeber 1902: 19–20)	. . .	x
Assiniboine (Lowie 1910: 42)	. . .	x
Bella Bella (McIlwraith 1948, vol. 1: 45–46)	x	. . .
Bella Coola (McIlwraith 1948, vol. 1: 45–46)	x	. . .
Cocopa (Drucker 1941: 163; Gifford 1933: 294)	x	x
Crow (Denig 1961: 187–88; Simms 1903: 580–81)	x	. . .
Flathead (Teit 1930: 384)	. . .	x
Hidatsa (Jackson 1962: 531; Bowers 1965: 105–6)	x	x
Illinois (Liette 1947: 112–13)	x	. . .
Ingalik (Osgood 1958: 262–63)	x	. . .
Iowa (Lurie 1953: 711)	. . .	x
Kansa (Say in James 1823: 129)	. . .	x
Mandan (Bowers 1950: 272, 296)	. . .	x
Maricopa (Drucker 1941: 163; Spier 1933: 242–43)	. . .	x
Miami (Trowbridge 1938: 68)	. . .	x
Mohave (Devereux 1937: 501–3; Drucker 1941: 173; Kroeber 1925: 478)	x	x
Ojibwa (Kinietz 1947: 155–56; McKenney 1827: 314–15)	. . .	x
Omaha (Dorsey 1890: 379; Fletcher and La Flesche 1911: 132)	. . .	x
Osage (Fletcher and La Flesche 1911: 132–33)	. . .	x
Oto (Irving 1888: 120–22)	. . .	x
Ponca (Dorsey 1890: 379; Howard 1965: 142–43)	x	x
Potawatomi (Landes 1970: 190–91)	. . .	x
Santee Dakota (Landes 1968: 57)	. . .	x
Sauk (Keating 1825, vol. 1: 216)	. . .	x
Teton Dakota (Hassrick 1964: 122; Powers 1977: 58–59)	. . .	x
Ute (Stewart 1940: 298)	. . .	x
Winnebago (Lurie 1953: 70)	. . .	x
Yokuts (Gayton 1948: 236)	x	. . .
Yuma (Forde 1931: 157)	. . .	x
Zuni (Parsons 1916: 526–27)	x	. . .

obtained from Prairie and Plains tribes, usually involve female supernaturals. The most widespread was the moon, reported for the Omaha, Sauk, and Winnebago, implied for the Yankton and Pawnee, and inferable for the Iowa, Kansa, Osage, Oto, and Ponca, whose term for berdache, *mixuga,* is glossed as "instructed by the moon" (Fletcher and La Flesche 1911:132). The female deity associated with Miami berdaches may also have been the moon, given their use of the term "white face" for the status (Trowbridge 1938:68). The moon, then, had a paramount role in berdache visions among the Dhegiha and Chiwere Siouans, the Pawnee, and some Algonquian tribes. In Omaha accounts, the most detailed, it held a burden strap in one hand and a bow and arrow in the other; and when the dreamer reached for the bow, quickly crossed its arms and tried to force the burden strap on him, sealing his status as a berdache (Fletcher and La Flesche 1911: 132–33).

Double-Woman, similarly important for Santee and Teton Dakota berdaches, was particularly skilled in women's work. Women who had visions of her became, like berdaches, expert in this, or, alternatively, could become seducers of men (Lowie 1916:118–19; Wissler 1916:92). Like the moon among the Omaha, Double-Woman offered Teton men a choice between male and female implements, the latter making them berdaches. Hidatsa berdaches dreamed of Village-Old-Woman or deities that she created, Woman Above and the Holy Women, or of a loop of sweetgrass (Bowers 1965:166–67, 323–30). Women who dreamed of them entered the Holy Women society, which also included the berdaches. Among the Mandan, transformation dreams came from Old Woman Above or other holy women; later, the dreamer picked up porcupine quills or a rope in the forest (Bowers 1950:272, 298).

Supernatural elements in gender transformation were probably more important than the accounts emphasizing childhood interests suggest. Reporting that Hidatsa boys who showed any signs of effeminacy were classed with girls and brought up as such, Biddle (Jackson 1962:537)

completely missed this aspect of the process. While the Hidatsa thought boys who showed inordinate interest in women's occupations were more likely to dream of the deities who ordered males to become berdaches, this behavior was discouraged, even forbidden; the transformation occurred among young men and required repeated visions (Bowers 1965:105–6, 115, 130). Omitting the supernatural aspects of Illinois berdaches and describing their status as one automatically assigned to boys interested in women's vocations, Liette (1947:112–13) greatly distorted their social role. Supernatural validation could be rather covert, and informants could view the transformation process very differently. Like some of his Mohave informants, Devereux (1937:501–3) emphasized the secular view, concentrating on children's behavior. Yet Drucker (1941:173) and Kroeber (1925:7–8) reported that dreams preceded this behavior and were believed to produce it. Some of Devereux's informants described a supernatural experience in the form of dreams coming to the embryo in the womb. The Mohave transformation came in later childhood, when the family of an incipient berdache secretly prepared an initiation ceremony which, if accepted by the child, certified its status.

In societies lacking visions, mythological sanctions may have substituted for them, although the figures involved were usually hermaphrodites rather than berdaches. The Bella Coola regarded Sxints, a supernatural hermaphrodite, as the prototype of the berdaches, who were somehow affected by him (McIlwraith 1948, vol. 1:45–46). The Navaho closely associated the berdache/intersex category with the hermaphrodite twins born to First Man and First Woman, important mythical figures who invented pottery and other artifacts associated with women (Hill 1935:273–74; Mathews 1897:70, 217; Reichard 1950, vol. 4:140). The transvestite-hermaphrodite had a prominent role in Zuni myths and ceremonies (Cushing 1896:401; Parsons 1916:524–25; Stevenson 1902:37) and figures in rituals at Acoma (Parsons 1939:540, 765) and among the Hopi (Titiev 1972:153, 214–15). One Tipai culture hero was a transvestite (Gifford 1931:12, 56). Transvestite episodes involving the culture hero as trickster were widespread in North America (e.g., Jones 1907:315–31). The Sinkaietk cited one of these as the precedent for their berdaches (Cline 1938:149). That mythical sanction could be significant seems demonstrated by the Oto, who described Elk as the first transvestite and whose berdaches came from the Elk clan (Whitman 1969:50).

Another indication that berdache status, even when described as attained by entirely secular processes that did not involve vision experience, still included important supernatural aspects centers on the skills typically associated with it. In North American cultures, exceptional ability itself usually signified supernatural power. The Navaho belief that their berdaches were predestined to be wealthy and control wealth illustrates this point. Despite Devereux's secular emphasis, he notes that Mohave berdaches, especially females, were exceptionally powerful shamans and points out parallels in the processes leading to the two statuses (1937:516).

The secular and supernatural views of the processes leading to berdachehood are inherently neither contradictory nor mutually exclusive. Incipient berdaches might well have shown interests foreshadowing their future transformation, but we doubt that cultures automatically assigned such children to the berdache category. Evidence that parents might discourage this prefiguring behavior (Bowers 1965:105–6; Denig 1961:187–88; Simms 1903:580–88) or be reluctant to admit its implications (Devereux 1937: 508) suggests there must have been some point at which the transformation had to be accepted and made formal. From this point of view, perhaps, a vision was equivalent to the brushwood test or the Mohave initiation ceremony as an event that fixed a berdache's destiny beyond doubt. Yet to assume that a vision simply sanctioned or validated a disposition that had already shown itself (e.g., Meyer 1977:75) seems

an extreme oversimplification. Transformation visions could come unexpectedly. Omaha men sometimes tried to conceal them, unsuccessfully, or even killed themselves to escape their destiny (Dorsey 1890:379; Fletcher and La Flesche 1911:132–33). As noted earlier, men who had achieved warrior status sometimes had visions directing their transformation. Berdache-type visions often offered the dreamer a choice between alternatives, with his selection determining his future; yet the significance of his choice might be clear only in retrospect. Osage accounts credit the supernaturals with surprising trickery and deceit (Fletcher and La Flesche 1911:133). One youth, offered his choice of weapons, selected a battle-axe as the most manly of these, only to find that near his village it became a hoe. The meaning of the bow-or-burden-strap choice offered Omaha men by the moon was obvious, but dreamers did not choose the strap; it was forced upon them as they tried to seize the bow.

A neglected aspect of the selection process involves statements that only members of certain social groups could become berdaches. While all Hidatsa boys were discouraged from showing behavior predisposing them toward receiving visions from female deities, in fact berdache status was potentially open not to all males, but only to those whose fathers or brothers owned ceremonial rights to bundles associated with these (Bowers 1965:168). Mandan practice was similar (Bowers 1950:502). One of Devereux's informants claimed that generally only members of prominent Mohave families could acquire the status (1937:502). If the Tlingit did have berdaches, they had to belong to a particular clan (de Laguna 1954:178), as among the Oto (Whitman 1969:50). Other societies may have had similar restrictions even if these were not general.

SOCIAL POSITION

The attitudes toward berdaches reported for North American cultures varied from awe and reverence through indifference to scorn and contempt. We attribute this diversity to declining esteem, influenced by Western views. Some early accounts (e.g., Le Moyne du Morgues 1878:7–8) describing the status as scorned seem explicable as expressions of the European reaction rather than actual native views. Attitudes toward berdaches may have varied in the past. Certainly their absence could be interpreted as evidence of hostility toward the status. The ambivalent Mohave views reported by Devereux (1937) could represent disapproval of the claims of anatomical transformation made by their berdaches, rather than contamination by the Western outlook. With these reservations, we hold that statements ascribing low status to berdaches generally represent shifts away from older and very different views.

Statements that the status carried high prestige use remarkably similar terms for societies widely separated in space and time. Thus, the Navaho regarded berdaches as holy and sacred (Hill 1935:297), the Hidatsa as mysterious and holy (Bowers 1965:326–27). Lowie's description of Assiniboin berdaches as *wakan* (1910:42) corresponds almost precisely with Marquette's assertion over two centuries earlier that their Illinois counterparts passed for *manitus* (1900:129). Ascriptions of low status seem less convincing. References to them as unproductive or lazy (Birket-Smith and de Laguna 1938:206; Gifford 1940:136, 138) conflict sharply with the productivity usually stressed as one of their main attributes. A southern Ute claim that berdaches "were kept hard at work at tasks reserved for women" (Opler 1940:147) seems a pejorative reinterpretation of this attribute and of the standard occupational aspect of their status. Such statements, resembling the Western bias evident in Stephen's (1936:276) reference to berdaches as "abominable," seem to be a reappraisal of the status, in retrospect, under its influence. Lurie (1953:708) wrote on this point, "Most informants felt that the berdache was at one time a highly honored and respected person, but that the Winnebago had become ashamed of

the custom because the white people thought it was amusing or evil." (Hill 1935:274) found this shift occurring among the Navaho. In traditional Indian societies, berdaches were respected, perhaps feared, because their condition manifested power given them by the supernatural. Perhaps strongest in societies where visions sanctioned their status, this attitude also characterized other groups such as the Navaho.

The supernatural power of berdaches apparently manifested itself in the gender-mixing attributes of their status rather than in distinctive public roles apart from these. They did not hold formal offices. Occasional suggestions of a close association with chieftainship (Boscana 1978:54; Tixier 1940:34), perhaps most explicit in Marquette's (1900:129) report that Illinois councils decided nothing without their advice, resemble early accounts of transvestites from the Circum-Caribbean area (Guerra 1971:48–49, 55) but are too fragmentary to indicate a general pattern. A few accounts note distinctive ritual functions. Berdaches conducted burials among several California tribes (Gayton 1948:46, 236; Kroeber 1925:497–501; Voegelin 1942:134–35) and the Timucua (Le Moyne du Morgues 1878:7–8). In Zuni ceremonies they took the role of the transvestite/hermaphrodite (Parsons 1916:325; Stevenson 1902:37–38). Some cultures assigned them ritual duties as part of the war complex (Grinnell 1962, vol. 2:37–38; Underhill 1969:186–87). Most reports emphasize the intensity and extent of their ritual participation rather than any distinctive features. Navaho male berdaches were very active in ritual, but their activities did not differ in kind from those of other men (Hill 1935:275)—another indication of their ability to mix gender-related behavior. They were the most active Hidatsa ritual group, taking part in every ceremony, but shared these activities with the postmenopausal women who also belonged to the Holy Women society except that, being stronger, berdaches were responsible for certain duties such as selecting and raising the poles for the Sun Dance (Bowers 1965:167, 326). Berdaches might be shamans, although this was usually an individual attribute rather than a property of their gender status. Even when characteristic of all berdaches, as among the Mohave and Yurok, shamanism was not limited to them (Devereux 1937:516; Kroeber 1925:46).

The importance or significance of their power for the societies to which berdaches belonged apparently lay in beliefs that this could extend beyond the individuals belonging to this status to affect others. Intimations of this attitude in Landes's (1970:195–202) discussion of the Potawatomi are somewhat more pronounced in Hoebel's (1960:77) analysis of Cheyenne beliefs and are explicit in Navaho statements that their prosperity and even their existence as a people depended upon berdaches (Hill 1938:274).

CONCLUSIONS

The transformation of a berdache was not a complete shift from his or her biological gender to the opposite one, but rather an approximation of the latter in some of its social aspects, effecting an intermediate gender status that cut across the boundaries between gender categories. A male berdache, who might be referred to as "she," could be called a man (Stevenson 1902:87) but not a woman. Usage here resembled the current Western practice of using "she" for a male performing in drag but not labeling him a woman. In noting this parallel we are not equating the two statuses and would reject their identification except insofar as berdache status could be called a performance. The native view here seems illustrated by the Zuni, who buried male berdaches in women's dress but men's trousers on the men's side of the graveyard (Parsons 1916:528).

Transformation was anatomically circumscribed. No matter how successfully a male berdache imitated the social behavior of a woman, he could not become one physiologically, lacking her reproductive capacities, unable to menstruate or conceive. Nor could a female berdache impregnate women. Indian societies sharply rejected claims that berdaches had transcended their anatomical sex in any sense other than the social. The acceptable limits of transformation were represented by Hidatsa berdaches, who became mothers by adopting children. The female Kutenai berdache's pretense that she had physiologically become a male was exposed by her brother (Schaeffer 1976:296).

The Mohave openly ridiculed their male berdaches for insisting that female terms be used for their sexual organs and for their simulations of menstruation, pregnancy, and childbirth and taunted female berdaches for lacking penises (Devereux 1937:510–13). The only possible exception to limiting transformation was the apparent belief among the Mohave and other River Yuman cultures that female berdaches did not menstruate or did so only sporadically. Yet assuming at least a partial lack of the female reproductive process, while perhaps facilitating their practice as shamans, did not define them as men. A Mohave man who had intercourse with a pregnant woman could become her child's father and give it membership in his clan. The same assertion by a female berdache who acquired a pregnant wife was rejected; the child belonged to the clan of its biological father (Devereux 1937:514). Her male counterpart who claimed he had given birth to a stillborn infant had to bury the supposed corpse privately; public cremation, implying acceptance of his pretense, was not permitted.

Berdaches who observed the anatomical limits bounding their gender status gained acceptance and respect. Yet in another sense these restrictions expanded social opportunities for male berdaches—who, as nonwomen, free of menstrual pollution, enjoyed the status advantages of women who had passed menopause and could take nonmale roles in ritual contexts—and were probably an important factor in the mixing of gender features in their social behavior.

The berdache status allowed men to combine roles assigned to male and female genders, mixing aspects of these categories. Cross-dressing, perhaps their most consistently observed gender feature, was not universal and was assumed voluntarily. Regulations forcing them to wear men's clothing for specifically male activities are a significant indication of their potential ability to cross and recross the social boundaries between the two main gender categories. The occupations associated with berdache status, perhaps its most important attribute, also crosscut these boundaries. They permitted a combination of male and female work which, given their freedom from child care, let them achieve exceptional productivity. This gender mixing may have given them credit for supernatural power that translated into their outstanding craft skills. Certainly it facilitated their role as go-betweens, which rested on their freedom to mingle with both sexes. A potential for gender mixing in activities relating to warfare is not surprising. Individual nonberdache women often crossed gender boundaries in this area. The role of male berdaches in the war complex sometimes approximated that of male or female warriors but sometimes resembled that of noncombatant women without being identical to it. Their sexual behavior again mixed aspects of gender categories and in a sense transcended their limits. Conventionally taking the role of women in intercourse with men, many also had sex with women. Their privileged sexual status was most explicitly described for the Navaho, who permitted them any form of sexual intercourse with either sex (Hill 1935:276). Finally, their ritual activity, often associated with the vision-based power on which their transformation frequently rested, also depended on their definition as nonwomen. Hill's (1935:276) conclusion that Navaho berdaches "enjoy more opportunities for personal and material gratification than the ordinary individual" can be extended to other North American cultures even if, as he points out, not all berdaches took advantage of these. Opportunities for female berdaches, except perhaps among the Navaho, seem to have been fewer.

A berdache thus transcended the boundaries of a gender category that was biologically and culturally defined to attain an intermediate gender status biologically the same but culturally redefined. Crossing the boundary between these gender categories was not a single process or a one-directional movement. Berdache status included a continuing crossing of this boundary, in both directions, to such an extent that we prefer to characterize the status as gender mixing rather than gender crossing. Like the opportunities open to those who adopted this status, these gender-mixing features seem much more pronounced among male berdaches. Among the Navaho, at least, they also sharply distinguished the status of berdaches from that of intersexes, who were not allowed to cross back.

In examining the berdache status and its attributes we have not directly addressed the reasons for its existence. This issue involves two closely interwoven problems: why persons became berdaches and why North American cultures gave this mixed gender status formal recognition. Most explanations offered by American anthropologists cluster around two hypotheses, neither of them satisfactory.

One hypothesis describes berdachehood as a status instituted specifically for homosexuals. Implicitly held by those who class it as a form of institutionalized homosexuality, this position has also been adopted by some gay writers. It was presented most explicitly and in greatest detail by Devereux (1937) in his study of the Mohave. Devereux equated berdaches with homosexuals, using the terms interchangeably. He specified homosexual inclination as the factor impelling Mohave individuals to become berdaches. To answer the second problem, he argued that formal recognition of the berdache status had advantages for Mohave society. Publicly identifying homosexuals and making them an institution gave them a protected status. At the same time, it forced them into the open and robbed homosexuality of its glamour as something secret and forbidden. Requiring homosexuals to dress like the other gender prevented their misrepresenting themselves to seduce and recruit unsuspecting heterosexuals. It also allowed heterosexuals to satisfy impulses toward sexual experiment without jeopardizing their normal status. Anyone who had sexual relations with a berdache was only a temporary bisexual, apparently even someone who spent most of his life having sex with berdaches. These practices, according to Devereux, promoted overall social health by localizing the homosexual "disorder."

This hypothesis, in all its forms, embodies an archaic view of homosexuality as equivalent to defective gender and defines it in terms of transvestism and occupation rather than sexual activity. The homosexual bent that Devereux ascribed to incipient male berdaches manifested itself as intense interest in women's activities, not as the homosexual behavior occasionally characterizing other Mohave boys. Throughout their range, berdaches had intercourse only with nonberdaches. Nonberdache males could have intercourse with women, with berdaches, and with each other. Sexual partners for nonberdache women similarly included men, female berdaches, and one another. Perhaps only berdaches, free of pressures to marry heterosexually, could be exclusively and permanently homosexual, but their status did not preclude heterosexual behavior. Our position, stated earlier, is that homosexuality was a secondary phenomenon following from assuming berdache status rather than precipitating this decision. We agree with Whitehead (1981:97) that North American Indian definitions of gender generally reversed the criteria used in Western societies: they emphasized occupational pursuits and social behavior rather than choice of sexual object, which in itself was not sufficient to change gender status.

The second hypothesis explains berdaches as men who were unable to meet the demands of the warrior role or strongly averse to the aggressive male role in general (e.g., Driver 1969:441; Hoebel 1949:459; Linton 1936:480). A variant blaming berdaches on overprotective mothers, suggested for the Teton Dakota by Hassrick (1964:121–22), was extended to the northern Plains by Forgey (1975:12) and attributed to the Mohave in a novel by McNichols (1967:170–71). Proponents of these arguments apparently share the implicit assumption—explicit in Forgey (1975:3–4)—that North American societies recognized two sharply distinct gender categories, male and female, and automatically assigned to the female category those males who did not show the features of social behavior defining their own gender category. Earlier we rejected the view that men who feared war became berdaches as incompatible with the evidence. Some berdaches fought; some nonberdache males did not; nor, for that matter, did most female berdaches. Berdache status was not a complete rejection of the male role; gender mixing was one of its essential features. Formulated for societies that lacked female berdaches, this hypothesis attempts to account for only the male variety. Even if inverted to explain the women entering this status as "too aggressive for feminine pursuits" (Whitehead 1981:98), we doubt that this characterization fits them unless one accepts hunting as a form of aggression. We doubt the assumed dichotomy between aggressive males and nonaggressive females. Aggressive Blackfoot women may have been called manly-hearted (Lewis 1941) but were clearly defined as women.

European anthropologists, on the other hand, have approached the berdache status from a very different perspective, as part of a much more widespread pattern of institutionalized transvestism that they examine as a primary religious phenomenon. Their approach often emphasizes its androgynous aspects' uniting such oppositions as male and female and, by so doing, attaining completion or "totality" and acquiring power (Signorini 1972:159–60). They also stress links between this status and deities who are themselves bisexual or androgynous. Eliade (1965:116), referring to Siberian shamanism, suggests that ritual homosexuality "is believed to be at once a sign of spirituality, of commerce with gods and spirits, and a source of sacred power." As this example suggests, these analyses are often drawn from other parts of the world and applied to the berdache institution. Similarly, Baumann's (1950, 1955) extended discussion of such phenomena generally concentrates on areas outside North America. Signorini (1972:159), coming from this intellectual tradition but directly examining berdaches, holds that the sexual ambiguity attached to their status drew respect because they were believed to possess qualities superior to those of a normal individual or at least particular qualities their societies needed for their own ends.

Granting that gender mixing seems closely related to sexual ambiguity, we would further concede that a general disposition to ignore this European tradition and concentrate on individual psychological motivations has been a major analytical weakness in discussions of the berdache status by American anthropologists. Yet we have some reservations about this approach. Particularly, we doubt that the European analysis can be transferred to North America without distorting the berdache status. Some ethnographic accounts describe berdache as an essentially secular phenomenon. We agree with Signorini (1972:156) that this secular emphasis may reflect the fieldworker's interpretation or, for that matter, informants' lack of knowledge. Yet in some cultures berdaches may have been secular. Religious concepts consonant with those stressed by the European school of thought are scattered throughout American Indian cultures but seem much less systematized. Perhaps this effect reflects the fragmentary nature of the data and more research would uncover far-reaching connections. Thus, Signorini points out (p. 159) how well the berdache status fits the Earth-female/Sky-male dualism that suffused Omaha culture. It also seems to us that the general North American concepts of individual relations with the supernatural allowed many persons to obtain various kinds of superior qualities, of which the attributes of berdaches were a very important variety but not necessarily superior to other kinds. The status was usually separated from shamanism or from a priesthood,

where this existed, and it had very important economic implications. Nevertheless, the similarities between our views and Signorini's seem very strong, including his emphasis (p. 160) on the ability of berdaches to move between male and female occupations with economic advantage and their function as talismans.

Whitehead's (1981) recent and provocative reanalysis of the berdache status differs significantly from earlier studies and represents still a fourth hypothesis. We agree with important parts of her argument, including her stress on occupation and prestige, and with her analysis of the criteria used for defining gender in North America. Emphasizing the social and cultural context of berdachehood seems a more productive approach than analyses based on speculation about individual motivation, usually phrased in psychosexual terms that are embedded in Western cultural attitudes. Certainly the status itself must be understood before one can comprehend the reasons individuals adopted it. Our major disagreements with Whitehead center on her specific hypotheses explaining the relative infrequency of female berdaches and the social approval extended to the male berdache status.

Pointing out that while occupational gender crossing by men led to their transformation into berdaches, Whitehead notes (pp. 90–91) that women who crossed social gender boundaries to engage in such male activities as hunting and warfare were not defined as berdaches. She argues that transformation was more difficult for females. The biological component of gender had greater significance for women, whose reproductive capacity in the form of menstrual and parturient blood threatened males, their activities, and supernatural power in general. She holds that almost all reports of female berdaches come from the Southwest, where gender crossing included "a mystique of anatomical change" (p. 92). River Yuman groups, believing that women who became berdaches did not menstruate, therefore assumed they lacked the female reproductive process. Without the physiological factor that inhibited the assumption of berdache status by women elsewhere, the occupational component in definitions of gender could promote their transformation.

Women's reproductive capacity may have inhibited the incidence of female berdaches; certainly some factor did. But, if rare, they occurred more widely than Whitehead assumes and were not concentrated in the Southwest. The anatomical-change mystique that accompanied berdache status, for both sexes, among River Yuman cultures seems to have been a local elaboration without wider significance, viewed with at least partial disapproval on its home ground and strongly repressed elsewhere. We agree with Whitehead that hunting and warring by women represented a crossing of social gender boundaries (or, in our terms, a mixing of gender aspects) but see a significant difference between these two activities as they related to berdachehood. In some cultures hunting did not redefine the gender status of women; in others, we suspect, this activity promoted their transformation. Female berdaches typically hunted, but participation in warfare was not an attribute of their status and apparently did not affect gender definitions for women. Among the Mohave, where hunting was an important occupation for female berdaches, it was nonberdache women who took part in warfare, accompanying their husbands or brothers in the same manner Grinnell (1962, vol. 2:44–47) described for the Cheyenne. Women who gained honor and prestige through warfare were usually not the women who became berdaches when this status was open to them. Given Whitehead's emphasis on occupational prestige, could it not be argued that women who engaged in high-prestige male activities like warfare but remained within their gender category had higher status in their societies than women who became berdaches, and that this difference in prestige might explain the infrequency of transformations among women?

Examining social approval of the male berdache status, Whitehead argues (pp. 101–9) that the "permissiveness" of North American cultures in accepting individual variations in behavior for which supernatural sanction was claimed actually centered upon occupations that were relevant to prestige and closely associated with gender. The regular economic activities of women included the production of important durable goods that figured in gift exchange and in trade. Women who made these articles and circulated or exchanged them could acquire wealth and social prestige in their own right, particularly if age and marital status gave them control over the services of other women. Except for male fear of female blood, the boundary between male and female occupations was not strongly "defended," and occasional crossings of this line were acceptable. Extending Lewis's (1941) description of the wealthy and powerful Piegan women called "manly-hearted" to the entire northern Plains, Whitehead concludes that very successful women approached successful males in prestige and surpassed unsuccessful men. A boy who could not aspire to success in the male occupational sphere could seek another form of success through women's occupations. She writes (pp. 108–9):

> Stated broadly, the culturally dominant American Indian male was confronted with a substantial female elite not perceivable as simply dependents of powerful men. Within such a context, the response to feminine transgressions into the traditional male sphere (hunting, warfare) was amazingly dispassionate. A woman who could succeed at doing the things men did was honored as a man would be. . . . What seems to have been more disturbing to the culture—which means, for all intents and purposes, to the men—was the possibility that women, within their own department, might be onto a good thing. It was into this unsettling breach that the berdache institution was hurled. . . . Through him, ordinary men might reckon that they still held the advantage that was anatomically given and unalterable.

We agree that the individual abilities or powers acquired through the vision quest or sanctioned by more diffuse beliefs were not entirely random and tended to emphasize skills that may broadly be called occupational. The relation of occupations to systems of prestige and to definitions of gender in North America seems beyond argument. Yet these personal abilities were not equal any more than visions were. The ideology enveloping berdaches, seen in their frequent description as holy, transcended a simple confirmation of their right to engage in high-prestige occupations that involved crossing gender boundaries, just as their status itself transcended gender categories. Perhaps crossing these boundaries required unusually strong endowment with power; perhaps, as we hold, the primary locus of their holiness and power was the gender mixing that characterized their status.

Concurring with Whitehead that North American women acquired prestige in their own right and that the female elite did not derive its position from men, we do not agree that their status was generally based on the production of durable prestige goods. Apparently this activity was the foundation for their position among northern Plains cultures. The early incorporation of eastern Prairie tribes into the fur trade and the consequent influx of European goods crippled the native production of these items; yet a female elite persisted. It was also evident among the Iroquois, where its status rested on control of agricultural production and the distribution of food (Brown 1975). We suspect that an examination of other areas in North America would uncover still other bases for women's position. This objection may seem minor but has significant implications. Perhaps men of the Plains and western Prairie cultures did promote the male berdache status to assert their superiority over women in an occupational sphere defined as female and associated with prestige. The absence of berdaches in their culture suggests that Iroquois men did not use this strategy—or that Iroquois women did not permit it. This last suggestion, entirely speculative, raises an issue we consider important: Could berdaches have been successful in this occupational sphere without the consent and cooperation of women?

The literature suggests that women reacted favorably to male berdaches and found them helpful. Tanner's outraged reaction to the Yellow Head's pursuit only amused his Ojibwa hostess, who welcomed the berdache, "very expert in the various employments of the women" (1956:89–91) and obviously a much more valuable asset to the household than Tanner—perhaps even a better hunter. Women's approval could exceed that of men. When a Zuni male decided to become a berdache, it was the men of his lineage who were unhappy; its women were favorable because he would remain a resident of their household and increase its work force (Stevenson 1902:31). Perhaps women encouraged and promoted the status of male berdache, while "defending" their side of the occupational boundary by insisting that men who crossed it had to go through a transformation.

This speculation raises our fundamental disagreement with Whitehead's position that men were considered superior in worth to women throughout North America and that men determined cultural practices. Systems of prestige existed for men and for women, with the male system the more visible, the more public, and the more often described. Outsiders often overlooked the female system (Brown 1975:239–40). The greater visibility of the male system does not mean it was actually dominant or alone determined policy. Grinnell (1962, vol. 1:103, 128), who characterized Cheyenne women as masterful, described them as the rulers of the camp. Black Hawk (1955:107–8) thought it important that women of his Sauk band supported his actions.

The male and female systems of prestige sometimes intermeshed, with a husband and wife working together to enhance their joint status. At certain points either gender could move into the other's prestige system: women by going to war, men by doing women's work. As far as berdache status carried prestige, this aspect was usually much stronger among its male members. The gender-mixing activities of male berdaches, as noted earlier, seem much less prominent among the female variety. In both aspects, the female counterparts of male berdaches were not female berdaches, but women who behaved in some respects like men without changing their gender status. Rather than interpreting this as a restriction imposed upon such women by their reproductive capacity, we view it as a privilege confined to women and suggest that it was at

their insistence that men who entered their occupational sphere had to shift to an intermediate gender status, accomplished by the mixing of attributes of the two gender categories within their culture.

REFERENCES

ADAIR, JAMES. 1966. *History of the American Indians.* Edited by Samuel Cole Williams. New York: Argonaut Press.

ANGELINO, HENRY, AND CHARLES L. SHEDD. 1955. A note on berdache. *American Anthropologist* 57:121–26.

BANCROFT, HUBERT HOWE. 1874. *The native races of the Pacific states of North America.* Vol. 1. New York: D. Appleton.

BAUMANN, HERMANN. 1950. *Der kultische Geschlechtswandel bei Naturvolkern.* Zeitschrift fur Sexualforschung (Frankfurt/M.) 1.

——— 1955. *Das doppelte Geschlecht.* Berlin.

BENEDICT, RUTH. 1934. Anthropology and the abnormal. *Journal of General Psychology* 10:59–82.

——— 1939. Sex in primitive society. *American Journal of Orthopsychiatry* 9:570–75.

BIRKET-SMITH, KAJ, AND FREDERICA DE LAGUNA. 1937. *The Eyak Indians of the Copper River delta, Alaska.* København: Levin and Munksgaard.

BLACK HAWK. 1955. *Ma-ka-tai-me-she-kio-kiak, Black Hawk: An autobiography.* Edited by Donald Jackson. Urbana: University of Illinois Press.

BLEIBTREU-EHRENBERG, GISELA. 1970. Homosexualität und Transvestition im Schamanismus. *Anthropos* 65:189–228.

BOSCANA, GERONIMO. 1978. *Chinigchinich.* Banning, Calif.: Malki Museum Press.

BOSSU, JEAN-BERNARD. 1962. *Jean-Bernard Bossu's travels in the interior of North America 1751–1762.* Translated and edited by Seymour Feiler. Norman: University of Oklahoma Press.

BOWERS, ALFRED. 1950. *Mandan social and ceremonial organization.* Chicago: University of Chicago Press.

——— 1965. *Hidatsa social and ceremonial organization.* Bureau of American Ethnology Bulletin 194.

BOYCE, DOUGLAS W. 1978. "Iroquoian tribes of the Virginia–North Carolina coastal plain," in *Handbook of North American Indians,* vol. 15. Edited by Bruce G. Trigger, pp. 282–89. Washington, D.C.: Smithsonian Institution.

BRADBURY, JOHN. 1904. *Travels in the interior of America in the years 1809, 1810, and 1811. (Early*

western travels, edited by Reuben G. Thwaites, vol. 14). Cleveland: Arthur H. Clark.

BROWN, JUDITH K. 1975. "Iroquois women: An ethnohistorical note," in *Toward an anthropology of women.* Edited by Rayna R. Reiter, pp. 235–51. New York: Monthly Review Press.

CARR, LUCIEN. n.d. The mounds of the Mississippi Valley, historically considered. Reprinted from *Memoirs of the Kentucky Geological Survey* 2.

CATLIN, GEORGE. 1973. *Letters and notes on the manners, customs, and conditions of the North American Indians.* 2 vols. New York: Dover.

CLINE, WALTER. 1938. "Religion and world view," in *The Sinkaietk or southern Okanogan.* Edited by Leslie Spier, pp. 131–49. (General Series in Anthropology 6.) Menasha, Wis.: George Banta.

COSTANSO, MIGUEL. 1910. *The narrative of the Portola expedition of 1769–1770.* Edited by Adolph Van Hemeri-Engert and Frederick J. Teggard. (Publications of the Academy of Pacific Coast History 1[4].) Berkeley: University of California Press.

COUES, ELLIOTT. 1897. *New light on the early history of the greater Northwest: The manuscript journals of Alexander Henry and of David Thompson, 1799–1814.* New York: Francis P. Harper.

CUSHING, FRANK HAMILTON. 1896. *Outlines of Zuni creation myths.* Bureau of American Ethnology Annual Report 13.

DE LAGUNA, FREDERICA. 1954. Tlingit ideas about the Indian. *Southwestern Journal of Anthropology* 10:172–79.

——— 1960. *The story of a Tlingit community: A problem with relationships between archaeological, ethnological, and historical methods.* Bureau of American Ethnology Bulletin 172.

DENIG, EDWIN T. 1961. *Five Indian tribes of the upper Missouri.* Edited by John C. Ewers. Norman: University of Oklahoma Press.

DE SMET, PIERRE JEAN. 1904. *Life, letters, and travels of Father de Smet among the North American Indians.* Edited by Hiram Martin Chittendon and Alfred Talbot Richardson. Vol. 3. New York: Francis P. Harper.

DEVEREUX, GEORGE. 1937. Institutionalized homosexuality of the Mohave Indians. *Human Biology* 9:498–527.

———— 1961. *Mohave ethnopsychiatry: The psychic disturbances of an Indian tribe.* Washington, D.C.: Smithsonian Institution.

DORSEY, GEORGE A., AND JAMES R. MURIE. 1940. *Notes on the Skidi Pawnee society.* Field Museum of Natural History Anthropological Series 27(2).

DORSEY, J. OWEN. 1890. *A study of Siouan cults.* Bureau of American Ethnology Annual Report 11.

DRIVER, HAROLD E. 1936. *Wappo ethnography.* University of California Publications in American Archaeology and Ethnology 36(3).

———— 1939. *Culture element distributions 10: Northwest California.* University of California Anthropological Records 1(6).

———— 1969. *Indians of North America.* Chicago: University of Chicago Press.

DRUCKER, PHILIP. 1937. *Culture element distributions 5: Southern California.* University of California Anthropological Records 1(1).

———— 1941. *Culture element distributions 12: Yuman-Piman.* University of California Anthropological Records 6(3).

———— 1951. *The northern and central Nootkan tribes.* Bureau of American Ethnology Bulletin 144.

ELIADE, MIRCEA. 1965. *Mephistopheles and the Androgyne: Studies in religious myth and symbol.* Translated by J. J. Cohen. New York: Sheed and Ward.

FIRE, JOHN, WITH RICHARD ERDOES. 1972. *Lame Deer, seeker of visions.* New York: Simon and Shuster.

FLETCHER, ALICE C., AND FRANCIS LA FLESCHE. 1911. *The Omaha tribe.* Bureau of American Ethnology Annual Report 27.

FONT, PEDRO. 1966. *Font's complete diary of the second Anza expedition.* Translated from the original Spanish manuscript and edited by Herbert Eugene Bolton (*Anza's California expeditions,* edited by H. E. Bolton, vol. 14) New York: Russell and Russell.

FORDE, C. DARYLL. 1931. *Ethnography of the Yuma Indians.* University of California Publications in American Archaeology and Ethnology 28(4).

FORGEY, DONALD G. 1975. The institution of berdache among the North American Plains Indians. *Journal of Sex Research* 11:1–15.

GATSCHET, ALBERT B. 1891. *The Karankawa Indians, the coast people of Texas.* Archaeological and Ethnological Papers of the Peabody Museum 1(2).

GAYTON, ANNA H. 1948. *Yokuts and Western Mono ethnography.* University of California Anthropological Records 10(1–2).

GIFFORD, EDWARD WINSLOW. 1931. *The Kamia of Imperial Valley.* Bureau of American Ethnology Bulletin 97.

———— 1933. *The Cocopa.* University of California Publications in American Ethnology and Archaeology 31(5).

———— 1936. *Northeastern and western Yavapai.* University of California Publications in American Archaeology and Ethnology 34(4).

———— 1940. *Culture element distributions 12: Apache-Pueblo.* University of California Anthropological Records 4(1).

GODDARD, IVES. 1978. "Delaware," in *Handbook of North American Indians,* vol. 15. Edited by Bruce G. Trigger, pp. 213–39. Washington, D.C.: Smithsonian Institution.

GRINNELL, GEORGE B. 1956. *The fighting Cheyennes.* Norman: University of Oklahoma Press.

———— 1962. *The Cheyenne Indians.* 2 vols. New York: Cooper Square.

GUERRA, FRANCISCO. 1971. *The pre-Columbian mind.* London: Seminar.

HAMMOND, WILLIAM A. 1882. The disease of the Scythians (Morbus Feminarum) and certain analogous conditions. *American Journal of Neurology and Psychiatry* 1:339–55.

HASSRICK, ROYAL B. 1964. *The Sioux.* Norman: University of Oklahoma Press.

HENNEPIN, LOUIS. 1903. *A new discovery of a vast country in America.* Edited by Reuben G. Thwaites. Chicago: A. C. McClurg.

HILL, RUTH BEEBE. 1979. *Hanta yo: An American saga.* New York: Doubleday.

HILL, WILLARD WILLIAMS. 1935. The status of the hermaphrodite and transvestite in Navaho culture. *American Anthropologist* 37:273–79.

———— 1938. Note on the Pima berdache. *American Anthropologist* 40:338–40.

HOEBEL, E. ADAMSON. 1949. *Man in the primitive world: An introduction to anthropology.* New York: McGraw-Hill.

———— 1960. *The Cheyennes: Indians of the Great Plains.* New York: Holt, Rinehart and Winston.

HOLDER, A. B. 1889. The bote: Description of a peculiar sexual perversion found among North American Indians. *New York Medical Journal* 50:623–25.

HOLT, CATHERINE. 1946. *Shasta ethnography.* University of California Anthropological Records 3(4).

HONIGMANN, JOHN H. 1946. *Ethnography and acculturation of the Fort Nelson Slave.* Yale University Publications in Anthropology 33.

———— 1954. *The Kaska Indians: An ethnographic reconstruction.* Yale University Publications in Anthropology 51.

HOWARD, JAMES H. 1965. *The Ponca tribe.* Bureau of American Ethnology Bulletin 195.

HYDE, GEORGE E. 1937. *Red Cloud's folk.* Norman: University of Oklahoma Press.

IRVING, JOHN TREAT. 1888. *Indian sketches taken dur-*

ing a U.S. expedition to make treaties with the Pawnee and other tribes of Indians in 1833. New York: Putnam.

JACKSON, DONALD. Editor. 1962. *Letters of the Lewis and Clark Expedition, with related documents 1783–1854.* Urbana: University of Illinois Press.

JACOBS, SUE-ELLEN. 1968. Berdache: A brief review of the literature. *Colorado Anthropologist* 1:25–40.

JAMES, EDWIN. 1823. *Account of an expedition from Pittsburgh to the Rocky Mountains in the years 1819 and '20, by order of the Hon. J. C. Calhoun, Sec'y of War: under the command of Major Stephen H. Long.* Philadelphia: H. C. Carey and I. Lea.

JONES, WILLIAM. 1907. *Fox texts.* Publications of the American Ethnological Society 1.

KARDINER, ABRAM. 1945. *The psychological frontiers of society.* New York: Columbia University Press.

KATZ, JONATHAN. 1976. *Gay American history: Lesbians and gay men in the U.S.A.* New York: Crowell.

KROEBER, ALFRED L. 1902. *The Arapaho.* American Museum of Natural History Bulletin 18.

——— 1925. *Handbook of the Indians of California.* Bureau of American Ethnology Bulletin 78.

——— 1935. Editor. *Walapai ethnography.* Memoirs of the American Anthropological Association 2.

——— 1952. *The nature of culture.* Chicago: University of Chicago Press.

KURZ, RUDOLPH F. 1937. *Journal of Rudolph Friedrich Kurz: An account of his experiences among fur traders and American Indians on the Mississippi and Missouri rivers during the years 1846 to 1852.* Edited by J. N. B. Hewitt. Bureau of American Ethnology Bulletin 115.

LAFITAU, JOSEPH FRANÇOIS. 1724. *Moeurs des sauvages ameriquains, comparées aux moeurs des premiers temps.* Vol. 1. Paris: Saugrain l'aine.

LANDES, RUTH. 1968. *The Mystic Lake Sioux.* Madison: University of Wisconsin Press.

——— 1970. *The Prairie Potawatomi.* Madison: University of Wisconsin Press.

LANGE, CHARLES R. 1959. *Cochiti, a New Mexico pueblo, past and present.* Austin: University of Texas Press.

LE MOYNE DU MORGUES, JACQUES. 1875. *Narrative of Le Moyne, an artist who accompanied the French expedition to Florida under Laudonniere, 1564.* Translated by Fredrick B. Perkins. Boston: James R. Osgood.

LEWIS, OSCAR. 1941. The manly-hearted woman among the North Piegan. *American Anthropologist* 43:173–87.

LIETTE, PIERRE. 1947. "Memoir of Pierre Liette on the Illinois country," in *The western country in the 17th century.* Edited by Milo Milton Quaife. Chicago: Lakeside Press.

LINTON, RALPH. 1936. *The study of man.* New York: D. Appleton-Century.

LOWIE, ROBERT H. 1910. *The Assiniboine.* Anthropological Papers of the American Museum of Natural History 4, pt. 1.

——— 1916. *Dance associations of the Eastern Dakota.* Anthropological Papers of the American Museum of Natural History 11, pt. 2.

——— 1924b. *Primitive religion.* New York: Liveright.

——— 1935. *The Crow Indians.* New York: Farrar and Rinehart.

LURIE, NANCY O. 1953. Winnebago berdache. *American Anthropologist* 55:708–12.

McCOY, ISAAC. 1976. "His presence was so disgusting," in *Gay American history.* Edited by Jonathan Katz, p. 300. New York: Crowell.

McILWRAITH, T. F. 1948. *The Bella Coola Indians.* 2 vols. Toronto: University of Toronto Press.

McNICHOLS, CHARLES L. 1967. *Crazy weather.* Lincoln: University of Nebraska Press.

MANDELBAUM, DAVID G. 1940. *The Plains Cree.* Anthropological Papers of the American Museum of Natural History 37(2).

MARMOR, JUDD. 1965. "Introduction," in *Sexual inversion.* Edited by Judd Marmor, pp. 1–24. New York: Basic Books.

MARQUETTE, JACQUES. 1900(1674). "Of the first voyage made by Father Marquette toward New Mexico, and how the idea thereof was conceived," in *The Jesuit Relations and allied documents,* vol. 59. Edited by Reuben T. Thwaites. Cleveland: Burrows.

MARTIN, M. KAY, AND BARBARA VOORHIES. 1975. *Female of the species.* New York: Columbia University Press.

MATHEWS, WASHINGTON. 1897. *Navaho legends.* Memoirs of the American Folklore Society 5.

MAXIMILIAN, ALEXANDER P. 1906. "Travels in the interior of North America," in *Early western travels,* vol. 22. Edited by Reuben G. Thwaites. Cleveland: Arthur H. Clark.

MEAD, MARGARET. 1932. *The changing culture of an Indian tribe.* New York: Columbia University Press.

——— 1949. *Male and female: A study of the sexes in a changing world.* New York: William Morrow.

——— 1961. "Cultural determinism of sexual behavior," in *Sex and internal secretions.* Edited by William C. Young, vol. 2, pp. 1433–79. Baltimore: Williams and Wilkins.

MEMBRE, ZENOBIUS. 1922. "Narrative of LaSalle's voyage down the Mississippi, by Father Zenobius Membre, Recollect," in *The journeys of Rene Robert Cavelier Sieur de la Salle.* Edited by Isaac Joslin Cox, pp. 131–59. New York: Allerton.

MEYER, ROY W. 1977. *The village Indians of the upper Missouri.* Lincoln: University of Nebraska Press.

MIRSKY, JEANNETTE. 1937. "The Dakota," in *Cooperation and competition among primitive peoples.* Edited by Margaret Mead, pp. 382–427. New York: McGraw-Hill.

NEWCOMB, W. W., JR. 1961. *The Indians of Texas from prehistoric to modern times.* Austin: University of Texas Press.

OLSON, RONALD L. 1936. *The Quinault Indians.* University of Washington Publications in Anthropology 6(1).

———— 1940. *Social organization of the Haisla of British Columbia.* University of California Anthropological Records 2(5).

OPLER, MARVIN K. 1940. "The Southern Ute of Colorado," in *Acculturation in seven American Indian tribes.* Edited by Ralph Linton. New York: D. Appleton-Century.

———— 1965. "Anthropological and cross-cultural aspects of homosexuality," in *Sexual inversion.* Edited by Judd Marmor, pp. 108–23. New York: Basic Books.

OSGOOD, CORNELIUS. 1958. *Ingalik social culture.* Yale University Publications in Anthropology 53.

PARSONS, ELSIE CLEWS. 1916. The Zuni la'mana. *American Anthropologist* 18:521–28.

———— 1939. *Pueblo Indian religion.* Chicago: University of Chicago Press.

POND, GIDEON H. 1889. Dakota superstitions. *Minnesota Historical Society Collections* 2:215–55.

POWERS, STEPHEN. 1877. *Tribes of California.* U.S. Geographical and Geological Survey of the Rocky Mountain Region. Contributions to North American Ethnology 3.

POWERS, WILLIAM K. 1977. *Oglala religion.* Lincoln: University of Nebraska Press.

———— 1979. The archaic illusion. *American Indian Art* 5:68–71.

RAY, DOROTHY JEAN. 1975. *The Eskimos of Bering Strait, 1650–1898.* Seattle: University of Washington Press.

RAY, VERNE F. 1932. *The Sanpoil and Nespelen.* University of Washington Publications in Anthropology 5.

REICHARD, GLADYS A. 1950. *Navaho religion: A study of symbolism.* New York: Bollingen Foundation.

ROMANS, BERNARD. 1962. *A concise natural history of East and West Florida.* Gainesville: University of Florida Press.

RUSSO, VITO. 1981. *The celluloid closet: Homosexuality in the movies.* New York: Harper and Row.

SCHAEFFER, CLAUDE E. 1976. "The Kutenai female berdache," in *Gay American history.* Edited by Jonathan Katz, pp. 293–98. New York: Crowell.

SIGNORINI, ITALO. 1972. "Transvestitism and institutionalized homosexuality in North America." *Atti del XL Congresso Internazionale degli Americanisti,* vol. 2. Genova: Tilgher.

SIMMS, S. C. 1903. Crow Indian hermaphrodites. *American Anthropologist* 5:580–88.

SPIER, LESLIE. 1930. *Klamath ethnography.* University of California Publications in American Archaeology and Ethnology 30.

———— 1935. *The Prophet Dance of the Northwest and its derivatives: The source of the Ghost Dance.* (General Series in Anthropology 1.) Menasha, Wis.: George Banta.

SPIER, LESLIE, AND EDWARD SAPIR. 1930. *Wishram ethnography.* University of Washington Publications in Anthropology 3, pt. 3.

STEPHEN, ALEXANDER. 1936. *The Hopi journals of Alexander M. Stephen.* Edited by Elsie Clews Parsons. Vol. 1. New York: Columbia University Press.

STEVENSON, MATILDA G. 1902. *The Zuni Indians: Their mythology, esoteric societies, and ceremonies.* Bureau of American Ethnology Annual Report 23.

STEWARD, JULIAN H. 1933. *Ethnography of the Owens Valley Paiute.* University of California Publications in American Archaeology and Ethnology 33, pt. 3.

———— 1941. *Culture element distributions 13: Nevada Shoshone.* University of California Anthropological Records 4(2).

———— 1943. *Culture element distributions 23: Northern and Gosiute Shoshoni.* University of California Anthropological Records 8(3).

STEWART, OMER C. 1941. *Culture element distributions 1: Northern Paiute.* University of California Anthropological Records 4(3).

———— 1944. *Culture element distributions 28: Ute-Southern Paiute.* University of California Anthropological Records 6(4).

SWANTON, JOHN R. 1911. *Indian tribes of the Lower Mississippi Valley and adjacent coast of the Gulf of Mexico.* Bureau of American Ethnology Bulletin 43.

TANNER, JOHN. 1956. *A narrative of the captivity and adventures of John Tanner.* Edited by Edwin James. Minneapolis: Ross and Haines.

TEIT, JAMES. 1900. *The Thompson Indians of British Columbia.* American Museum of Natural History Memoir 2, pt. 4.

———— 1930. *The Salishan tribes of the western plateau.* Bureau of American Ethnology Annual Report 5.

TITIEV, MISCHA. 1972. *The Hopi Indians of Old Oraibi.* Ann Arbor: University of Michigan Press.

TIXIER, VICTOR. 1940. *Tixier's travels on the Osage*

prairies. Edited by John Francis McDermott. Norman: University of Oklahoma Press.

TROWBRIDGE, CHARLES C. 1938. *Meearmeear traditions.* Edited by Vernon Kinietz. Occasional Contributions from the Museum of Anthropology at the University of Michigan 7.

TURNEY-HIGH, HARRY HOLBERT. 1937. *The Flathead Indians of Montana.* American Anthropological Association Memoir 8.

UNDERHILL, RUTH M. 1953. *Red man's America.* Chicago: University of Chicago Press.

———— 1969. *Social organization of the Papago Indians.* Columbia University Contributions to Anthropology 30.

VOEGELIN, ERMINIE W. 1938. *Tubatulabal ethnography.* University of California Anthropological Records 2(1).

———— 1942. *Culture element distributions 20: North-* *west California.* University of California Anthropological Records 7(2).

WALLACE, ERNEST, AND E. ADAMSON HOEBEL. 1952. *The Comanches: Lords of the south Plains.* Norman: University of Oklahoma Press.

WHITEHEAD, HARRIET. 1981. "The bow and the burden strap: A new look at institutionalized homosexuality in native North America," in *Sexual meanings: The cultural construction of gender and sexuality.* Edited by Sherry B. Ortner and Harriet Whitehead, pp. 80–115. New York: Cambridge University Press.

WHITMAN, WILLIAM. 1969. *The Oto.* Columbia University Contributions to Anthropology 28.

WISSLER, CLARK. 1916. *Societies and ceremonial associations in the Oglala division of the Teton-Dakota.* Anthropological Papers of the American Museum of Natural History 11.

28

The Penis Pin: An Unsolved Problem in the Relations Between the Sexes in Borneo

Donald E. Brown

Although little is known about human sexuality in Borneo, one aspect of Bornean sexuality has been the subject of scholarly writing in every decade since the 1830s: the use of the penis pin. In spite of this long period of scholarly attention, we still don't really know what the penis pin is all about; that is, we don't know what motivates the practice. Let us begin with a summary of what *is* known about Bornean penis pins.

The penis pin is part of a Southeast Asian cultural complex that in its commonest form involves surgery to the penis to install a device that allegedly enhances female sexual pleasure. This complex may have had its origin in India, and portions of the complex have diffused to peoples far outside Southeast Asia (Brown n.d., Brown *et al.* 1988; Vale and Juno 1989).

In Borneo the surgery involves piercing the penis—much as one might pierce an earlobe—so that a pin can be worn in it.[1] Sometimes the

[1] There is a single report of an alternative form of surgery to the penis in Borneo: after presenting a conventional account of Bornean penis pins, Hansen (1988) also states that "Bahau River villagers" scarify the upper surface of the glans penis by making incisions into which ash is rubbed. As a modern variant, men go to a government dispen-

Source: From "The Penis Pin" by D. Brown in *Female and Male in Borneo: Contributions and Challenges to Gender Studies* by V. Sutlive (Ed.), pp. 435–454. Copyright © 1990 by The Borneo Research Council, Inc. Reprinted by permission.

pins are simply straight rods with rounded ends. More typically, the pins have protuberances at each end, at least in part to keep the pins from falling out. In the simplest of these forms, the pins look like little barbells; in more complex variants, the protuberances have a considerable variety of shapes and textures. Sometimes a tube is inserted into the pierced hole in the penis to serve as a sleeve within which the pin can rotate (Friesen and Schuman 1964, Kleiweg de Zwaan 1920). One recent account (Macdonald 1982) says that the Berawan of Long Terawan use the various sizes of shear pins of outboard motor propellers as penis pins. (For published sketches or photos of penis pins see Appell 1968, Barclay 1980, Friesen and Schuman 1964, Harrisson 1964 and 1966, Kleiweg de Zwaan 1920, Miklucho-Maclay 1876a, Miller 1942, Moll 1912.)

Palang, which in Malay or Iban means cross or crossbar, is probably the commonest name for the penis pin in the literature. But the Kayan term, *uttang,* is also widely reported. Less frequent are the Kenyah term, *aja,* and a term used in southeast Borneo, *kaleng* or *kaling.* (For discussions of these terms and many of the terms for parts of the penis pin and the devices used to install them, see especially Barth 1910, De Waal 1855, Gaffron 1859, Mayer 1877.)

The shafts of the penis pins are made from a variety of materials, including bone, bamboo, wood, and metal; brass is particularly common. The materials employed to construct the protuberances show even greater variation—including, for example, gemstone, glass, seeds, feathers, and pig's bristles (Bock 1887, Dalton 1837, Griffith 1955, Hardeland 1859, Harrisson 1959 and 1964, Hose and McDougal 1912, Mayer 1877, Miklucho-Maclay 1876b, Nieuwenhuis 1904–07, Richards 1981, St. John 1863, Veth 1854). The diameters of the pins vary from about 2 to 4 mm; lengths vary from 21 mm to more than 5 cm (Appell 1968, Burns 1849, De Waal 1855, Gaffron 1859, Juynboll 1909,

sary, where the operation is performed with an anesthetic and the incisions are sutured so as to leave 3 to 5 parallel ridges.

Macdonald 1982, Richards 1981). One source (Richards 1981) says that the pin should be as long as the middle phalange of one's finger, while another source (De Waal 1855) says as long as the distance between the teeth (assuming that distance between the teeth means between the upper and lower incisors when the mouth is held wide open, these two measures are both about the same).

The pins always or nearly always pierce the glans penis, and probably most commonly are placed in a horizontal position above the urethra (Bock 1887, Burns 1849, Dalton 1837, De Waal 1855, Griffith 1955, Hose and McDougal 1912, Kleiweg de Zwaan 1920, Kuhlewein 1930, Moll 1912, Nieuwenhuis 1900, Richards 1981, Tillema 1934–35). But sometimes the piercing deliberately transects the urethra (Griffith 1955, Kuhlewein 1930, Richards 1981), and sometimes the piercing is vertical or at an angle (Barclay 1980, De Waal 1855, Nieuwenhuis 1900). As many as five pins may be worn at once (Richards 1981), but a single pin is probably commonest. Most pins appear to be easily removable (Appell 1968, Friesen and Schuman 1964, Griffith 1955, Kuhlewein 1930, Mayer 1877, Nieuwenhuis 1900 and 1904–07, Veth 1854).

A clamp made of wood or bamboo is usually placed on the penis prior to the piercing operation in order to drive blood from the penis at the point where it will be pierced. This desensitizes the penis and reduces bleeding. The man who is about to be pierced may achieve further desensitizing by standing in water. A pointed shaft is then driven through the penis, guided by holes in the clamp. After the penis is pierced and the clamp has been removed, a temporary pin or wire may be employed to keep the piercing open during healing (Appell 1968, Harrisson 1959 and 1966, Juynboll 1909, Kleiweg de Zwaan 1920, Kuhlewein 1930, Low 1892, Miklucho-Maclay 1876b, Nieuwenhuis 1900 and 1904–07, Richards 1981).

There is little consensus on the extent of pain and risk of medical complications that penis pins entail for either men or women (Bock 1887,

Dalton 1837, Gaffron 1859, Griffith 1955, Low 1892, Mayer 1877, Nieuwenhuis 1900, St. John 1863). Kuhlewein (1930) looked into the matter most carefully—examining the genitals of 2500 Bornean men—and reports only that he found no evidence of lesser fertility among those native groups with the higher percentages of men who had penis pins. Friesen and Schuman (1964) give the only specific evidence of a medical problem: a penis pin that had been left inserted for a lengthy period acquired calcium deposits and thus had to be removed surgically.

Penis pins are normally installed at puberty or later (Burns 1849, Dalton 1837, Friesen and Schuman 1964, Kuhlewein 1930, Nieuwenhuis 1900 and 1904–07, Veth 1854). Sometimes specialists perform the operation (Dalton 1837, Hansen 1988, Harrisson 1959, Richards 1981). There appears to be little ritual or supernatural belief associated with the practice, though the piercing operation is conducted in secret among the Iban (Richards 1981). For some peoples there are reports of certain qualifications that must be met before one can wear the pin (De Waal 1855, Mayer 1877, Nieuwenhuis 1904–07). For example, a man may have to have been on a headhunt or have taken a head before he can wear the pin. Sometimes rank is indicated by the quality of the material of a man's penis pin or by such ornamentation as accompanies it (Dalton 1837, Low 1892, Nieuwenhuis 1900, Veth 1854).

There is considerable variation in the proportion of men who wear penis pins. For example, among some groups in south central Borneo virtually all men had pins; among Iban in recent times about one third of the men wore them (Dalton 1837, Kuhlewein 1930, Richards 1981).

Although penis pins are either absent or rare among the coastal Malays of Borneo, the pins are widely reported among the pagans in all areas (Bock 1887, Burns 1849, De Waal 1855, Friesen and Schuman 1964, Gaffron 1859, Griffith 1955, Haddon 1936, Hardeland 1859, Harrisson 1959, Hose and McDougal 1912, Juynboll 1909, Kleiweg de Zwaan 1920, Kuhlewein 1930, Le Bar 1972, Low 1892, Macdonald 1982, Moll 1912, Nieuwenhuis 1900, Richards 1981, Schneebaum 1979, Tillema 1934–35, Walchren 1907) except north-central and northwest Borneo (Appell 1968, Walchren 1907). The most frequent reports seem to be from the south or southeast. The Kayan are the only group credited with the invention and dissemination of the practice within Borneo—allegedly having introduced it to the Iban, Kenyah, and some Punan groups (Burns 1849, Harrisson 1959, Low 1892, Veth 1854, Walchren 1907).

Among some peoples penis pins are very much a part of public culture. The Iban, for example, commonly depicted penis pins on fabrics (see, e.g., Haddon and Start 1936), and an Iban or Berawan man may tatoo himself in a way that advertises that he is equipped with a penis pin (Richards 1981, Macdonald 1982). Derek and Monica Freeman found the penis pin in a sketch by a young Iban boy, which implies that the use of the pins was common knowledge from an early age (D. Freeman, personal communication). In central Borneo, statues designed to ward off spirits are equipped with ostentatious penis pins (Nieuwenhuis 1904–07).

Finally, we know that one explanation for the use of penis pins is very widely reported, but that other explanations are given too. By far the commonest explanation is that the penis pin enhances the sexual pleasure of women (Barclay 1980, Dalton 1837, De Waal 1855, Friesen and Schuman 1964, Gaffron 1859, Griffith 1955, Harrisson 1959, Kleiweg de Zwaan 1920, Low 1892, Mayer 1877, Miklucho-Maclay 1876b, Richards 1981). This point is embroidered in a number of ways. For example, it is said that women may request their husbands to get pierced, or that women will divorce husbands who won't be pierced (Gaffron 1859), or that once habituated to it women cannot go without the pin (Miklucho-Maclay 1876). Women are alleged to say that the penis pin is to sex what salt is to rice (Gaffron 1859, Mayer 1877). On the other hand, it is also said that it is older women in particular (and so presumably not just women

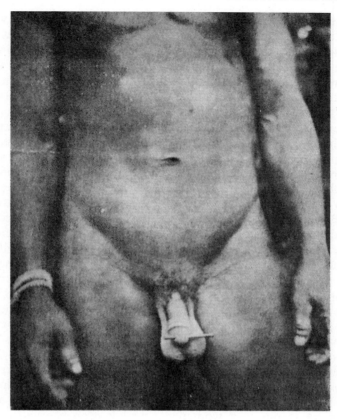

in general) who want their husbands to have the penis pin (De Waal 1855, Kleiweg de Zwaan 1920, Mayer 1877).

Among the alternative explanations, two that appear in the primary sources referring to Borneo require only brief comment. First, Miller (1942) says that the purpose of penis pins is to infibulate, i.e., to ensure celibacy. But there is little reason to trust his testimony—which runs counter to all other evidence—for he was merely a traveller in Borneo and he did not speak the local languages. Second, it is sometimes alleged—and the allegation may be indigenous to Borneo—that penis pins have been inspired by the *palang*-like protuberances on the penis of the Bornean rhinoceros (Harrisson 1956, Macdonald 1982, Richards 1981). However, even if this allegation is correct, it is not an alternative ex-

planation of the purpose of the penis pin, of *why* the rhinoceros was imitated.

Three other explanations are found in the secondary or non-Bornean literature. One is that the penis pin is a precautionary measure against a folk illness, called *koro,* that is found in China and parts of Southeast Asia (Wulfften Palthe 1936). It is believed that the penis of a man afflicted with this disease shrinks into his body; when it shrinks all the way in, the man dies. The penis pin, according to this explanation, prevents the penis from shrinking all the way, or gives one something to hold on to should this fate seem imminent. There is no indication, however, that this explanation is known in Borneo. Another explanation from secondary sources is that the penis pin is an antidote or weapon against the vagina *dentata,* the vagina with teeth gman 1975). A belief that the vagina has teeth is widespread, and the penis pin might conceivably be a response to this male fear. Again, however, there is no evidence that this is a Bornean explanation. Yet another explanation is that penis piercing, like other forms of body piercing, results from the idea that such practices magically strengthen the body, or at least the part of the body that is pierced (Kleiweg de Zwaan 1920). Judging by published materials on penis inserts elsewhere in Southeast Asia (Brown *et al.* 1988), this explanation may have merit, but it is an idea that has not been pursued in the literature on Bornean penis pins. Since none of these three explanations has so far been put to the test by persons with experience in Borneo, their relevance to Bornean peoples is uncertain.

The only explanation of the penis pin that is found in the literature and that commands attention as a serious alternative to the woman-pleaser explanation is that the penis pin is a product of male machismo (bravado). This explanation is discussed in later sections of this paper.

· · ·

The claim that the penis pin is a woman pleaser, even though it appears to be a widespread indigenous explanation, poses some real and very interesting problems—problems that lead away from what is known into areas of uncertainty. A few considerations about the woman-pleaser explanation are particularly important:

First, there is all too little evidence that it is *women* who say the penis pin gives them pleasure. Only a single published source gives unequivocal evidence that a woman was interviewed to obtain this explanation in Borneo, but what she is reported as actually saying is not a ringing endorsement of penis pins. When asked "how she enjoyed" her husband's three penis pins, she replied that "she preferred to make love when he only had one" (Barclay 1980:96). Moreover, this woman was interviewed by a man, in a bantering manner, in mixed company, and through two interpreters—so the result car-

ries little weight anyway. While two anthropologists and a linguist (James Peter Brosius, B. J. L. Sellato, and Patricia Whittier, personal communications) report that at least one woman told each of them that the penis pin gave them pleasure, the questioning was not private and was not pursued in depth.

Second, the neurology, physiology, and anatomy of the female genitalia provide little or no clear evidence that the penis pin could bring pleasure to women. According to Kinsey and his associates (1953:580), the inner walls of the vagina are generally insensitive (a partial exception will be discussed below). This suggests that once intromission is achieved, the penis pin should give a woman neither pleasure nor pain (unless the pressure of the penis pin were transmitted through the insensitive vaginal walls to sensitive tissue that lies beyond).

Third, the subjective reports of women in the West provide little support for the woman-pleasing explanation of penis pins. Comfort (1972: 174) reports that women in the West show little interest in "French ticklers," which are the non-surgically-attached functional equivalents of penis pins. In the literature on piercers in the West, which is strongly oriented to a male—and particularly a male homosexual—audience, there are only a few statements by women who report enjoying sex with pierced men, along with a few who report not enjoying it, and a few noticing no difference (Brown n.d.; Buhrich 1983; Vale and Juno 1989).

Fourth, the shapes and sizes of some of the penis pins seem more likely to do damage in sexual intercourse than to give pleasure. Kuhlewein (1930:94) describes some of the penis pins as "monstrous" and "sharp"; Harrisson (1959) says some are elaborated with broken glass. Women that I have spoken to in the U.S. not only express skepticism that penis pins would enhance their sexual pleasure, they sometimes indicate that the very thought of some of the penis pins is painful and repugnant.

Thus there is no solid evidence from Bornean women that penis pins enhance their sexual pleasure, and there is little in the way of non-Bornean evidence to suggest that the pins really should or normally do give pleasure. What other evidence bears on the matter, and what are we to make of these reports that Bornean women find pleasure in the penis pin?

A potentially relevant piece of evidence is that traditional pagan Bornean societies were among the most sexually egalitarian societies known to ethnography (see, e.g., Freeman 1981; Ward 1963). Given the high level of female autonomy that this entails, perhaps it makes sense that Bornean men should go to unusual lengths to try to please Bornean women.

Another consideration is that under certain circumstances perhaps penis pins *could* give pleasure, or at least cause no harm. For example, if the pin had smooth ends and did not protrude too far it might cause no harm. If the pin caused no physical harm, the psychological effect of a man wearing a penis pin might be beneficial for a number of reasons (for example, Jerome Rousseau has suggested to me that a woman might derive an indirect pleasure from knowing how much her man was willing to endure in order to try to please her—the "thought" counting more than the actual "gift" to her). Or, since recent literature on what is called the "Grafenberg spot" (see, e.g., Jayne 1984) suggests that there may be a region in the vaginal wall that *is* pleasurably sensitive, perhaps the penis pin rubs this spot. In most cases, however, this does not seem likely: the Grafenberg spot—if indeed it exists—is on the upper surface of the vagina, while most penis pins protrude on the sides. Another possibility, mentioned above, is that the penis pin is felt through the vaginal walls, causing pleasurable sensations elsewhere (e.g., in the perineum, which, according to Kinsey *et al.* [1953:385; see also Masters and Johnson 1966], probably is pleasurably stimulated in some forms of deep vaginal penetration). Finally, since some individuals in the West find pleasure in pain, perhaps what is rare here might be commoner elsewhere (assuming that the penis pin could be felt at all).

But in contradistinction to these conditions that might make the woman-pleaser explanation plausible, consider the following questions:

If the idea is to give women greater sexual pleasure, why attach the device surgically? Why not just wrap something around the penis? Non-surgically attached penis augmentations for sexual intercourse (like the "French ticklers" mentioned above) are widely reported in Southeast Asia; among Bornean peoples they were already known in the nineteenth century, at least to the Iban (Low 1892). Surgical attachment must have some rationale that has no obvious connection with pleasing women (unless there are the indirect psychological benefits mentioned above).

If the penis pin is a woman-pleaser, why is it often associated with rank, prestige, or achievement? The association between rank and surgically installed penis augmentations of one sort or another is widespread in Southeast Asia (Brown, Edwards, and Moore 1988)—probably in part because rank-consciousness spills over into many facets of Southeast Asian societies (Brown 1976). Whatever the reason may be for this association, it suggests some factor or factors with no clear connection to providing sexual pleasure for women.

If the penis pin is a woman-pleaser, why is it associated with weapons? There are at least three indications in the literature that Bornean peoples saw the penis pin as a sort of sexual weapon:

One is that in an upland Kenyah account of the introduction of the penis pin the first woman on whom it was used died as a consequence; this would have ended the practice, according to Harrisson, "had counterbalancing impulses not been so strong" (1959:61). I take this to mean that although the Kenyah were willing to risk the danger of the penis pin for the pleasure that it allegedly afforded, they knew that the penis pin was lethally dangerous—and thus like a weapon.

Another indication is that the Mendalam Kayans erected large warrior-like figures to ward off disease-causing spirits. The figures had

osed outsize genitals with penis pins (Nieu-
venhuis 1904–07). Since neither the Kayans nor
other Borneans normally expose their genitals,
and since such phallic displays are widely regarded as threats (Eibl-Eibesfeldt 1979:17),
there is reason to think that the inclusion of the
penis pin is part of the figures' threatening aspect. Surely it makes little sense to prominently
place an object designed to give pleasure on a
figure that is designed to frighten.

Yet another indication of the equation of the
penis pin with weapons is found in the taunts
from women that an Iban man is reported to
endure if he does not wear a penis pin: that he is
"unarmed" or is "with spear unsharpened"
(Richards 1981:245). The latter taunt implies
that the penis itself is seen as a weapon—as it
sometimes is elsewhere.

In addition to the troubling questions I have
just posed, there are a few indications of a skeptical attitude toward the woman-pleaser explanation from scholars well informed about Borneo.
One of the most important is found in the report
of an extensive medical study of men who wore
penis pins (Kuhlewein 1930). As noted above, the
medical personnel who conducted this study in
1929 examined the genitals of some 2500 adult
males, representing several ethnic groups dwelling in the upper Mahakam region of Kalimantan.
Kuhlewein thought that the "one sex will rather
inculpate the other" for the perpetuation of the
practice (1930:95). If I understand him correctly,
Kuhlewein was suggesting that although men
gave him the usual reason for wearing penis
pins—that "the wives will it so" (1930:95)—he
somehow formed the impression that women
told a different story, i.e., that men wore the pins
for their own (unstated) reasons.

Even Harrisson, who clearly accepts the woman-pleaser explanation (1959), notes that masculine ideals—the ability and willingness to endure
the pain and danger of piercing—is part of the
story (1966). Derek and Monica Freeman, who
studied the Iban, concluded that male bravado
was even more important than Harrisson thought
(D. Freeman, personal communication).

The Freemans were able to discuss the penis
pin with a few Iban women, who denied that it
gave them pleasure and who viewed the penis
pin as a "potentially, if not actually, injurious
and injury-inflicting device." The women saw
the use of penis pins as "a peculiar male conceit." The Freemans concluded that among the
Iban the penis pin is an ornament that men wear
for essentially male reasons: wearing the penis
pin is a male "conceit or affectation," and the
claim that it pleases women is "a male rationalization and projection" (D. Freeman, personal
correspondence). If the Freemans are correct,
the sexual pleasure of women may be a very
small part of the explanation of penis pins.

. . .

What the evidence suggests, then, is a widespread Bornean folk conception that men wear
penis pins in order to enhance the sexual pleasure of women—but with no clear evidence that
this conception adequately captures the real rea-
son(s) why Bornean men wear penis pins. The
most glaring problem is that the validity of this
conception is not supported by the most relevant kind of evidence: reliable female testimony
to the effect that they do enjoy penis pins—or
even that they allow their men to have intercourse with them while wearing the pins. Clearly
we need a Bornean women's perspective on this
matter, and those who are presently in a position
to throw light on it—women's health care professionals, for example—could be of real assistance in providing this obviously important evidence (use of the "monstrous" and "sharp"
penis pins would presumably leave telltale signs
for the gynecologist or obstetrician, and surely
even women from the more backward populations in Borneo occasionally see these specialists). If it should turn out that Bornean women
do find pleasure in penis pins, it would then be
of some interest to know why and how (in the
anatomical or physiological sense).

But if it should turn out that Bornean women
are not so pleased by penis pins as the reported
folk belief would have it, the next question is:

why is the practice nonetheless perpetuated? Two answers can be suggested, both having more to do with the male psyche than with female sexuality. One, already mentioned, is male machismo. Since machismo manifests itself in painful and dangerous mutilations of the male body among many peoples throughout the world, it is entirely reasonable to assume that penis piercing is a Bornean variant of the phenomenon, i.e., that machismo is at least a substantial component in the explanation of penis pins. Another component, I will argue, is the possibility of some Bornean cultural *mis*conceptions.

One of the striking ways in which cultural conceptions and reality can and often do diverge is in each sex's conceptions of the other sex's sexuality (Symons 1979). Male conceptions of female sexuality in the West are heavily influenced not merely by ignorance but by wishful thinking and the projection of male attitudes onto females. Marcus (1966) coined the term "pornotopia" to refer to certain aspects of the fantasy world of pornography. The penis pin is perhaps an element in a Bornean pornotopia, a reflection less of Bornean female sexuality than of the Bornean male's image of female sexuality. Now, given the autonomy of Bornean women, as noted earlier, it is understandable that Bornean men might be particularly preoccupied with how to win and keep their women—and so long as men imagined that penis pins would give them greater sexual access to women, the incentive to wear the pin might be substantial.

One of the few Bornean accounts of the origin of the penis pin clearly expresses this concern for men to please women *and,* in all probability, provides a glimpse of pornotopia. In a Kayan version of the invention of the penis pin, a woman who masturbates with a rolled up leaf tells her lover that he is no better than the leaf. So he invents and installs the penis pin, which she does find better (Harrisson 1964). There are some clear messages in this story—that the man wanted to please a woman, that he didn't think he could do it with nature's equipment alone,

that the penis pin seemed like a reasonable solution to his problem, and that it worked.

But in spite of the concern for womanhood that this story expresses, there is reason to think that it isn't a woman's story: it assumes that vaginal penetration is a normal or even necessary part of female masturbation. This assumption, according to the findings of Kinsey *et al.* among American women, is another male "conceit" (1953:162; see also Masters and Johnson 1966). Few women in the West masturbate in a manner that involves anything more than superficial penetration of the vagina (since that is all that is required to stimulate the clitoris). Like so many origin stories, then, this one may be, as Freeman suggests, a rationalization rather than an explanation.

· · ·

In sum, the most widely reported explanation of the penis pin in Borneo—an explanation that focuses on female sexuality and that derives from or is compatible with Bornean cultural conceptions—may have little or no validity. The true explanation may lie more with males than with females, more with male machismo and male fantasies than with female sexuality. At present we simply do not know which motives—conscious or unconscious—are the principal ones that lie behind the use of the penis pin.

The state of our ignorance is of course partly the result of the privacy or secrecy that surrounds the sexual act itself and often much else that relates to sexuality, in Borneo as everywhere else. But part of the problem is that many of those who have written about the penis pin probably did not realize that there even was a problem: the thought that Bornean women crave the stimulation of an augmented penis, even a dangerously augmented one, is a thought as much at home in Western pornotopia as it appears to be in Bornean. Until the pioneering research of Kinsey and his associates, and of Masters and Johnson—all of whom *did* get female perspectives on sexuality—most men simply lacked a reason for thinking that female sexuality might be other than what they imagined it to be. In readily accepting the woman-pleaser explanation of the penis pin, as many Western observers did, they may have been content to perpetuate a myth rather than identify it as such.

A careful attempt to find out what the penis pin *is* all about would not only give us a much better understanding of the traditional peculiarities of sexuality, of images of sexuality, and of the rela-

tions between the sexes in Borneo, but might well throw light on these topics nearly everywhere. For what may be fundamental components of the Bornean penis pin complex—male and female sexualities, machismo, and pornotopia—may also be fundamental components in the relations between the sexes among many if not all peoples, differing only in the local ways in which they are combined and expressed.

REFERENCES

APPELL, G. N. 1968 The Penis Pin at Peabody Museum, Harvard University. Journal of the Malaysian Branch, Royal Asiatic Society 41:203–205.

BARCLAY, JAMES 1980 A Stroll Through Borneo. London: Hodder and Stoughton. (See pp. 90, 94, 96, and photo.)

BARTH, J. P. J. 1910 Boesangsch-Nederlandsch Woordenboek. Batavia: Landsdrukkerij. (See p. 174.)

BOCK, CARL ALFRED 1887 Reise in Oost-en Zuid-Borneo van Koetei naar Bandjarmassim . . . in 1879 en 1880. 's-Gravenhage: Martinus Nijhoff. (See p. 98.)

BROWN, DONALD E. 1976 Principles of Social Structure: Southeast Asia. London: Duckworth.

n.d. Piercers in America. Unpublished typescript.

BROWN, DONALD E., JAMES W. EDWARDS, AND RUTH MOORE 1988 The Penis Inserts of Southeast Asia: An Annotated Bibliography with an Overview and Comparative Perspectives. Occasional Paper No. 15, Center for South and Southeast Asian Studies, University of California, Berkeley.

BUHRICH, NEIL 1983 The Association of Erotic Piercing with Homosexuality, Sadomasochism, Bondage, Fetishism, and Tattoos. Archives of Sexual Behavior 12:167–71.

BURNS, ROBERT 1849 The Kayans of the North-West of Borneo. Journal of the Indian Archipelago and Eastern Asia 3:140–52. (Reprinted in the Sarawak Museum Journal 3:477–489; see p. 486.)

COMFORT, ALEX, ed. 1972 The Joy of Sex: A Gourmet Guide to Love Making. New York: Simon and Schuster.

DALTON, JOHN 1837 [1831] Mr. Dalton's Essay on the Diaks of Borneo. *In* Notices of the Indian Archipelago, and Adjacent Countries. Ed. by J. H. Moor. Singapore. Pp. 41–54. (See p. 53.)

DE WALL, H. VON 1855 Aanteekeningen omtrent de Nordoostkust van Borneo. Tijdschrift voor Indische Taal-, Land- en Volkenkunde 4:423–458. (See pp. 457–58.)

EIBL-EIBESFELDT, IRANAUS 1979 Human Ethology: Concepts and Implications for the Sciences of Man. The Behavioral and Brain Sciences 2:1–57.

FREEMAN, DEREK 1981 Some Reflections on the Nature of Iban Society. An Occasional Paper of the Department of Anthropology, Research School of Pacific Studies, The Australian National University, Canberra.

FRIESEN, STANLEY R. AND NORVID D. SCHUMAN 1964 Medicine in Sarawak: The Medical Missionary Program at Work. The Journal of the Kansas Medical Society 65:125–131. (See pp. 128, 129.)

GAFFRON, VON 1859 Over Menschen met Staarten op Borneo. Natuurkundig Tijdschrift voor Nederlandsch-Indie 20:227–232. (See pp. 231–32.)

GALVIN, A. D. [1967] [Kenyah Vocabulary]. Ms. [Miri, Sarawak]. (See p. 2.)

GRIFFITH, G. T. 1955 Health and Disease in Young Sea Dayak Men. Sarawak Museum Journal 6:322–327. (See p. 327.)

HADDON, ALFRED C. AND LAURA START 1936 Iban or Sea Dayak Fabrics and Their Patterns. Cambridge: The University Press. (See pp. 42, 44.)

HANSEN, ERIC 1988 Stranger in the Forest: On Foot Across Borneo. London: Century. (See pp. 224–29.)

HARDELAND, AUGUST 1859 Dajacksch-Deutsches Worterbuch. Amsterdam: Frederik Muller. (This source anomalously describes the *palang* as a ring worn on the male genitals. See p. 400.)

HARRISSON, TOM 1956 Rhinoceros in Borneo: and Traded to China. Sarawak Museum Journal 7:263–74.

1959 World Within: A Borneo Story. London: The Cresset Press. (See pp. 59, 61–62.)

1964 The "Palang," Its History and Proto-History in West Borneo and the Philippines. Journal of the Malaysian Branch, Royal Asiatic Society 37:162–174. (Note that the Povedano MS 1578, which is quoted, has been shown to be a forgery by William Henry Scott.)

1966 The "Palang": II. Three Further Notes. Journal of the Malaysian Branch, Royal Asiatic Society 39:172–74.

HOSE, CHARLES AND WILLIAM McDOUGAL 1912 The Pagan Tribes of Borneo: A Description of their Physical, Moral and Intellectual Condition with Some Discussion of their Ethnic Relations. Vol II. London: Macmillan. (Reprinted 1966 by Barnes and Noble.) (See p. 170.)

JAYNE, CYNTHIA 1984 Freud, Grafenberg, and the Neglected Vagina: Thoughts Concerning an Historical Omission in Sexology. Journal of Sex Research 20:212–15.

JUYNBOLL, H. H. 1909 Katalog des Ethnographischen Reichsmuseums. Band I: Borneo. Leiden: E. J. Brill. (See p. 60.)

KINSEY, ALFRED C. et al. 1953 Sexual Behavior in the Human Female. Philadelphia: W. B. Saunders Company.

KLEIWEG DE ZWAAN, J. P. 1920 Over de Penis-staafjes der Inlanders van den Indischen Archipel. Nederlandsch Tijdschrift voor Genesskunde II (A):289–293.

KUHLEWEIN, M. VON 1930 Report of a Journey to Upper Mahakam (Borneo), February–May 1929. Mededeelingen van den Dienst der Volksgezondheid in Nederlandsche-Indie, Foreign-Edition 19:66–152. (See pp. 83, 92, 94–95, 112. This article appeared simultaneously in a Dutch-language version of the same journal.)

LE BAR, FRANK M., ed. 1972 Ethnic Groups of Insular Southeast Asia. Vol. I. New Haven: HRAF Press. (See p. 188.)

LEGMAN, G. 1975 No Laughing Matter: An Analysis of Sexual Humor. Bloomington: Indiana University Press. (See p. 431.)

LOW, BROOKE 1892 The Natives of Borneo. Ed. from the Papers of the Late Brooke Low, Esq., by H. Ling Roth. Journal of the Anthropological Institute 22:22–64. (See p. 45.)

MACDONALD, DAVID 1982 Expedition to Borneo: The Search for Proboscis Monkeys and Other Creatures. London: J. M. Dent & Sons. (See pp. 166–67.)

MARCUS, STEVEN 1966 The Other Victorians: A Study of Sexuality and Pornography in Mid-Nineteenth-Century England. New York: Basic Books.

MASTERS, W. H. AND V. E. JOHNSON 1966 Human Sexual Response: Boston: Little, Brown and Company.

MAYER, A. B. 1877 Ueber die Perforation des Penis bei den Malayan. Mittheilungen der Anthropologischen Gesellschaft in Wien 7:242–244.

MIKLUCHO-MACLAY, N. V. 1876a Ueber die kunstlich Perforatio Penis bei den Dayaks auf Borneo. Verhandelingen der Berliner Gesellschaft fur Anthropologie, Ethnologie und Urgeschichte 22–24. 1876b Perforatio glandis penis bei den Dajaks auf Borneo und analoge sitten auf Celebes und auf Java. Verhandelingen der Berliner Gesellschaft fur Anthropologie, Ethnologie und Urgeschichte 24–26 (and addendum).

MILLER, CHARLES C. 1942 Black Borneo. New York: Modern Age Books. (See photo opp. p. 199.)

MOLL, ALBERT 1912 Handbuch der Sexualwissenschaften, vol. I. Leipzig: F. C. W. Vogel. (See p. 240.)

NIEUWENHUIS, A. W. 1900 In Centraal Borneo: Reis van Pontianak naar Samarinda. Leiden: E. J. Brill. (See pp. 68–69, 118.) 1904–07 Quer durch Borneo: Ergebnisse seiner Reisen in den Jahren 1894, 1896–97, und 1898–1900. Leiden: E. J. Brill. (See Vol. I, pp. 78–79, 223; Vol. II, p. 369 and plate opp. p. 390.)

O'HANLON, REDMOND 1984 Into the Heart of Borneo. New York: Random House. (See pp. 8–9, 17, 82–83.)

PERELAER, M. T. H. 1870 Ethnographische Beschrijving der Dajaks. Zalt-Bommel: Joh. Noman & Zoon. (See pp. 60–61 for the only doubts in a primary source that penis pins even exist.)

RICHARDS, ANTHONY 1981 An Iban-English Dictionary. Oxford: Clarendon Press. (See pp. 245–46.)

SCHNEEBAUM, TOBIAS 1979 Wild Man. New York: The Viking Press. (See p. 124.)

SCHWANER, C. A. L. M. 1853 Borneo, Beschrijving van het Stroomgebied van den Barito. Vol. I. Amsterdam: P. N. van Kampen. (See p. 127.)

ST. JOHN, SPENSER 1863 Life in the Forests of the Far East; or Travels in Northern Borneo. Second ed., revised. Vol. I. London: Smith, Elder and Company. (See pp. 122–23.)

SYMONS, DONALD 1979 The Evolution of Human Sexuality. New York: Oxford University Press.

TILLEMA, H. F. 1934–35 Poenans (Apo-Kajan en Tidoengsche landen). Tropisch Nederland 7:2–11, 18–24, 43–48. (See p. 24.)

VALE, V. AND ANDREA JUNO 1989 Modern Primitives: An Investigation of Contemporary Adornment and Ritual. Re/Search #12. San Francisco: Re/Search Publications.

VETH, P. J. 1854 Borneo's Wester-afdeeling, geographisch, statistisch, historisch, voorafgegaan door eene algemeene schets des ganschen eilands. Vol. I. Zaltbommel: Noman. (See p. 177–78.)

WALCHREN, E. W. F. VAN 1907 Eene reis naar de bovenstreken van Boeloengan (Midden-Borneo), 12 Nov. 1905–11 April 1906. Tijdschrift van het

Nederlandsch Aardrijkundig Genootschap 24:755–844. (See pp. 822, 823.)

WARD, BARBARA 1963 Men, Women and Change: An Essay in Understanding Social Roles in South and South-East Asia. *In* Women in the New Asia: The Changing Social Roles of Men and Women in South and South-East Asia. Ed. by B. E. Ward. UNESCO. Pp. 25–99.

WULFFTEN PALTHE, P. M. VON 1936 Psychiatry and Neurology in the Tropics. *In* A Clinical Textbook of Tropical Medicine, ed. by C. D. de Langen and A. Liechtenstein. Batavia: G. Kolff & Co. Pp. 525–47. (See pp. 536–38.)

X

CULTURE AND DISEASES RELATED TO SEXUALITY

INTRODUCTION

Have you ever wondered why we classify educational programs about sexually transmitted diseases (STDs) as "Social Hygiene"? One might suggest that it reflects our society's position that STDs are social problems first and biomedical problems second. Allan Brandt (1985) has suggested that this is part of the reason that we have not found effective biomedical controls for STDs. One certainly can get treatment for syphilis and gonorrhea in the form of penicillin and tetracycline; but, as a means of control, those drugs have had a greater impact on the morbidity associated with these STDs than they have had on the incidence of the diseases.

Both remain among the three most common communicable diseases in America. Perhaps, as Brandt suggests, this is because we have unrealistically demanded that people change their behavior, rather than demanding that our government adequately fund biomedical research. Yet, as Brandt notes, there is more to it than that.

For example, Judith Ross has examined the social response to AIDS. Beginning with the notion that the "newness" of the disease requires us to find a way to conceptualize it, she proceeds to discuss the metaphorical ways in which AIDS is presented. She points out that in many ways, the metaphors are constructed so as to blame the victims. Echoing Brandt's (1985) conclusions, she notes that "HIV does not flourish because it finds itself in homosexual relationships, in multiple sexual partnerships, in IV drug users, or in illegal activities. It is simply a virus doing its job." (Ross 1988:85).

However, we continue to believe that STDs are the problems of the immoral, of the deviants, of the "other." Thus, the diseases come to be seen as symbolic of corrupt or perverse sexuality. This is unfortunate; only one sexual contact is usually enough to acquire an STD. Promiscuity certainly increases one's chances of contracting an STD, yet the victims of STDs need not have been "promiscuous"—once is enough.

The relationship between sociocultural beliefs and behaviors and the transmission or the conceptualization of STDs has become a topic of growing importance in anthropology, particularly since the advent of AIDS. Two articles in this section consider a few of the approaches and perspectives common to this body of research.

Brenda J. Baker and George J. Armelagos review the literature on the origin of syphilis. There have been several approaches to explaining its origin in the past. Some have suggested that it was confused with leprosy prior to the sixteenth century, thus implying an Old World origin for the disease. Others have suggested that it was present in both the Old World and the New World prior to Columbus's voyage. When Columbus's crew returned, a hybrid of the two forms, more virulent than either of the original strains, resulted in the modern form of the disease. Still others suggest that it originated in the New World and was transmitted to Europe through the return of Columbus's crew. This last idea—a New World origin—is the explanation that Baker and Armelagos believe best fits the facts.

Benedicte Ingstad discusses the importance of examining the impact of AIDS in Botswana not only from a biomedical point of view, but also from the perspective of Tswana "traditional" healers. She describes how the disease is incorporated into the traditional understanding of disease etiology and nosology. She also considers the implications for the future prevention of AIDS in that nation.

There are other connections between disease and sexuality. One of the more interesting is the way in which culture-bound syndromes emerge as a result of socio-sexual mores and ideals. Culture-bound syndromes are illnesses that are experienced wholly or mostly by the members of a particular cultural group. Typically, they represent physical expressions of problematic individual adjustment to the demands of a society, although they may represent particular dietary deficiencies associated with particular environments.

The final two essays in this section both explore culture-bound syndromes of relevance to studies of sexuality. Pow Meng Yap discusses an illness of Southeast Asia. Male patients suffering from *koro* believe that their penises are withdrawing slowly into their bodies, a condition that they believe will eventually result in death if not successfully treated. Yap attributes *koro* to severe anxiety over sexual excesses in a society that idealizes sexual control.

Michael P. Levine looks at two culture-bound syndromes of American society that are classed as eating disorders—anorexia nervosa and bulimia. Levine explains the problems inherent in simply attributing causation to culture without considering other predisposing factors. He suggests that research over the past decade shows clearly that the "cultural glorification of thinness" associated with ideal female body image and standards of feminine beauty contribute strongly to the increased incidence of these disorders in our society.

REFERENCES

BRANDT, ALLAN. (1985). *No Magic Bullet: A Social History of Venereal Diseases in the United States Since 1880.* New York: Oxford University Press.
ROSS, JUDITH WILSON. (1988). An Ethics of Compassion, A Language of Division: Working Out the AIDS Metaphors. In Inge B. Corliss and Mary Pittman-Lindeman (Eds.), *AIDS: Principles, Practices, and Politics* (pp. 81–95). New York: Hemisphere Publishing.

SUGGESTED READINGS

BOLTON, RALPH (Ed.). (1989). *The AIDS Pandemic: A Global Emergency.* New York: Gordon and Breach.

FELDMAN, DOUGLAS A. (Ed.). (1990). *Culture and AIDS.* New York: Praeger.

HERDT, GILBERT, WILLIAM LEAP, AND MELANIE SOVINE (Eds.). (1991). Anthropology, Sexuality and AIDS. *Journal of Sex Research, 28*:2:[Special Issue].

MARSHALL, PATRICIA A., AND LINDA A. BENNETT (Eds.). (1990). Culture and Behavior in the AIDS Epidemic. *Medical Anthropology Quarterly 4*:1:[Special Issue].

MILLER, MARCIA INHORN. (1987). Genital Chlamydial Infection: A Role for Social Scientists. *Social Science and Medicine, 25*:12:1289–1299.

PARKER, RICHARD G. (1987). Acquired Immunodeficiency Syndrome in Urban Brazil. *Medical Anthropology Quarterly, 1*:2:155–175.

SHANNON, GARY W., GERALD F. PYLE, AND RASHID L. BASHSHUR. (1991). *The Geography of AIDS: Origins and Course of an Epidemic.* New York: The Guilford Press.

TIEFER, LEONORE. (1986). In Search of the Perfect Penis. *American Behavioral Sciences, 29*:579–599.

29

THE ORIGIN AND ANTIQUITY OF SYPHILIS: PALEOPATHOLOGICAL DIAGNOSIS AND INTERPRETATION

BRENDA J. BAKER / GEORGE J. ARMELAGOS

A review of the literature regarding the origin of syphilis in the light of paleopathological diagnosis and interpretation strongly suggests a New World origin. Whereas the evidence for pre-Columbian treponematosis in the Old World is documentary and equivocal, abundant skeletal evidence indicates the presence of a nonvenereal form of treponemal infection in the Americas before Columbus.

BRENDA J. BAKER is a Ph.D. candidate in anthropology at the University of Massachusetts (Amherst, Mass. 01003, U.S.A.). Born in 1959, she received her B.A. from Northwestern University in 1981. She has done archaeological fieldwork in Illinois, Arizona, New England, and Egypt. Her research interests are nutrition and disease in prehistory and settlement patterns and demography; her current work involves analysis of bone collagen from human skeletal remains from the Wadi Halfa area of Sudanese Nubia.

GEORGE J. ARMELAGOS is Professor of Anthropology at the University of Massachusetts. He was born in 1936 and educated at the University of Michigan (B.A., 1958) and the University of Colorado (M.A., 1963; Ph.D., 1968). He taught at the University of Utah in 1965–67, before joining the faculty at Massachusetts, and at the University of Colorado in the summers of 1983–87. He has done extensive research with human skeletal remains on diet, disease, and demography in prehistoric populations from Dickson Mounds, Illinois, and from the Wadi Halfa area of Nubia. His publications include, with Alan C. Swedlund, *Demographic Anthropology* (Dubuque: W. C. Brown, 1987); with Peter Farb, *Consuming Passions: The Anthropology of Eating* (Boston: Houghton Mifflin, 1980); and, with coeditor M. N. Cohen, *Paleopathology at the Origins of Agriculture* (Orlando: Academic Press, 1984).

SOURCE: From "The Origin and Antiquity of Syphilis" by G. Armelagos and B. Baker in *Current Anthropology, 29 (5),* 1988, pp. 732–737. Copyright © 1988 by The University of Chicago Press. Reprinted by permission.

Despite Thomas Gann's 1901 publication of "Recent Discoveries in Central America Proving the Pre-Columbian Existence of Syphilis in the New World," the controversy concerning the origin and antiquity of syphilis remains. As the Columbian quincentenary draws near, it is appropriate to reassess the documentary and skeletal evidence regarding the origin of syphilis and its dispersion throughout the world in the light of paleopathological diagnosis and interpretation. A review of the literature strongly suggests a New World origin of the treponemal infections. Whereas the evidence for pre-Columbian treponematosis in the Old World is documentary and equivocal, there is a vast array of skeletal evidence indicating the presence of a nonvenereal form of treponemal infection in the Americas prior to Columbus's arrival.

HYPOTHESES ON THE ORIGIN OF SYPHILIS

Three hypotheses have been advanced to explain the origin and subsequent spread of venereal syphilis throughout the world.

The Columbian hypothesis, proposed by Crosby (1969), Dennie (1962), Goff (1967), Harrison (1959), and others, is that syphilis originated in the Americas and was carried to Europe by Columbus's crew in 1493. Subsequently, a syphilis epidemic occurred in Europe about 1500. The rapid spread of syphilis throughout Europe at that time suggests the introduction of a virulent disease into a population that had not previously been exposed to it and had no immunity to it.

Proponents of the diametrically opposed pre-Columbian hypothesis (e.g., Hackett 1963, 1967; Holcomb 1934, 1935) assert that venereal syphilis was present in Europe prior to Columbus's voyage but was not distinguished from "leprosy." The alleged epidemic resulted from the recognition of syphilis as a separate disease in the 1490s. Cockburn (1961; 1963:153–59) provides an evolutionary framework for the pre-

Columbian origin of syphilis in which geographical isolation led to speciation of *Treponema.* Throughout most of human history, treponemal infection (i.e., pinta, yaws, endemic syphilis, and venereal syphilis) was mild and chronic because populations were small. As population size increased, more acute infections were selected for and spread by direct skin-to-skin contact among children. By 1492, European living standards had improved to the point of differentially affecting the transmission of *Treponema* species. Those dependent upon skin contact were disadvantaged and replaced by a hardier strain that was sexually transmitted (Cockburn 1961:226). Thus in Cockburn's view the discovery of America and the appearance of venereal syphilis are not cause and effect; rather, both resulted from other social and economic events.

A third, unitarian hypothesis is that the agent of syphilis has evolved with human populations and was present in both the Old and the New World at the time of Columbus's discovery. Hudson (1963a, b, 1965a, b, 1968) maintains that pinta, yaws, endemic (nonvenereal) syphilis, and venereal syphilis are four syndromes of treponematosis, a single disease caused by *Treponema pallidum,* which evolved simultaneously with humans. The syndromes form a biological gradient in which various social and environmental factors produce different manifestations of treponematosis (Hudson 1965a). Although Hudson and Cockburn agree on the role of improved hygiene in the appearance of venereal syphilis, they disagree on several aspects of its etiology and epidemiology.

According to Hudson (1963a, 1965a), treponematosis originated during the Paleolithic period as a childhood disease (yaws) transmitted by skin-to-skin contact in the hot, humid climate of sub-Saharan Africa. The infection accompanied gatherer-hunters in their migrations throughout the world. As groups moved into drier zones bordering the tropics, the focus of treponemal activity retreated to the moist areas of the body (mouth, armpits, and crotch), as in endemic syphilis (Hudson 1965a:891). Treponematosis in the form of endemic syphilis was carried into the New World by the earliest migrants from the Old World. As the tropical zones of the Americas were populated, the climatic change caused the shift back to yaws (p. 893). The appearance of villages in the Neolithic period did not alter the nonvenereal nature of the infection; crowded, unsanitary conditions and increased frequency of child-to-child contact in village settings facilitated its spread (1963a:1042–43; 1965a:892–93).

Urbanization, beginning in Mesopotamia and Egypt by 4000 B.C., was accompanied by an improvement in personal and community hygiene (Hudson 1963a:1043). Although it seems counterintuitive for sanitation to have improved in cities, Hudson (1965a:895) points out that "hygienic barriers do not have to be very high to prevent the spread of touch-contact syphilis." Availability of water, washing and bathing with soap, separate sleeping quarters, and the like became adequate barriers to the proliferation of treponematosis by casual contact among children. As a result, individuals reached sexual maturity without prior exposure to it. Hence, "coitus . . . became the only personal contact of sufficient intimacy to permit transmission of treponemas," and adults disseminated the disease in a society in which there was "promiscuity and prostitution" (p. 895).

Hudson (1965b:738) indicates that both venereal and nonvenereal forms of treponematosis may be present within a narrow geographical area, for example, where a city characterized by venereal syphilis is surrounded by a rural area characterized by yaws. Despite identical climates, the higher hygienic level and different social customs in the city promote venereal transmission. Dissolution of urban life would result in a shift from venereal to nonvenereal forms of treponematosis (either endemic syphilis or yaws, depending upon the climate).

SYPHILIS AND LEPROSY

Because the pre-Columbian and unitarian hypotheses suggest that diseases such as yaws,

endemic syphilis, venereal syphilis, and leprosy were confused from ancient times and grouped under the term "leprosy" (Holcomb 1935:277; 1940:177; Hudson 1965a:896), before examining the evidence it is necessary to discuss the differential diagnosis of these diseases.

Venereal syphilis has an incubation period of 10–90 days before the primary lesion appears in the anogenital region (Olansky 1981:299). Secondary lesions usually develop on the skin and mucous membranes. Prior to the advent of penicillin treatment, the prevalence of syphilis was about 5% in mostly urban adult populations (Steinbock 1976:110). Steinbock's survey of the clinical literature predating penicillin use indicates skeletal involvement in 10–20% of cases (cf. Hackett 1976:108, who cites a single study in which osseous lesions developed in only 1% of untreated patients). Since asymptomatic bone lesions often go undetected in early syphilis, skeletal involvement may be underestimated (Hansen et al. 1984; Steinbock 1976:109). Following Steinbock's (p. 110) arithmetic, however, one obtains a frequency of osseous involvement in 1 of every 100–200 individuals in a skeletal series representing an adult urban population (a prevalence of 0.5–1% in skeletal populations). Hackett (1976:108, 114) indicates that only 1 in 1,000 adults would develop syphilitic bone lesions.

Skeletal involvement in venereal syphilis most often affects the cranial vault, the nasal area, and the tibia. Together, these three locations comprise 70% of all tertiary syphilitic bone lesions (Ortner and Putschar 1985:182). The major diagnostic criterion of skeletal syphilis is the caries sicca sequence, described in detail by Hackett (1976:30–49), which results in the "worm-eaten" appearance of the outer table of the cranial vault, characterized by the formation of stellate scars. Caries sicca is usually accompanied by naso-palatine destruction. This destruction, more extensive and rapid than in leprosy, usually involves the nasal bones and is accompanied by healing and sclerosis (Hackett 1976:63–65; Ortner and Putschar 1985:192, 197; Steinbock 1976:145, 208). Where there is gross destruction of the naso-palatine region, there is often maxillary alveolar damage as well (Hackett 1976:65).

Postcranially, formation of subperiosteal bone begins in the metaphyses of the long bones, with the tibiae being most often involved. Inflammation of the entire periosteum initiates a subperiosteal response resulting in thickening and possible bone deformation (Steinbock 1976:115). Hackett (1976:79–90) proposes a sequence for nongummatous periostitis that ranges from finely striated nodes and expansions to grossly rugose expansions, which he tentatively considers diagnostic criteria of syphilis. Gummatous lesions—nodes/expansion with superficial cavitation—he regards as certainly diagnostic (pp. 93–97). Gumma formation may occur periosteally or in the medullary cavity, resulting in both proliferative and degenerative changes. Syphilis lacks the smooth cloacae and the sequestrum and involucrum formation of pyogenic osteomyelitis (Hackett 1976:95; Steinbock 1976:137). Generally, the affected bone appears roughened and irregular because of thickening and increased density. The medullary cavity, particularly in the tibia, is greatly narrowed by cortical thickening (Steinbock 1976:117, 123). Hands and feet are rarely affected.

Pinta, yaws, endemic (nonvenereal) syphilis, and venereal syphilis have been thought to be caused by different species of *Treponema* (respectively, *T. carateum, T. pertenue,* and two subspecies of *T. pallidum*). The causative organisms of each disease, however, cannot be distinguished from each other by any known test. In electron microscope studies, the "species" of *Treponema* are morphologically identical (Hovind-Hougen 1983:5). Their antigenic structures differ only quantitatively (Hudson 1965a:886). DNA sequence homology analysis indicates that *T. pertenue* and the subspecies of *T. pallidum* are identical and "might be regarded as a single species" (Fieldsteel 1983:50). Partial cross-immunity exists between the treponemal syndromes (Cannefax, Norins, and Gillespie 1967:473–74). Clinically, yaws and endemic

and venereal syphilis closely resemble each other in the prolonged course of the disease, with early and late manifestations. Primary yaws is similar to primary syphilis; secondary yaws resembles secondary syphilis, although the skin lesions of the former are often larger and more exuberant; the lesions of tertiary yaws, characterized by gummatous lesions of the skin, soft tissue, bones, and naso-palatine area, are indistinguishable from those of tertiary syphilis (Musher and Knox 1983:114–15). Where (as in all forms except pinta) bone lesions result from the treponemal syndromes, they are also indistinguishable from each other (Hackett 1976:113). Except for the dental stigmata and osteochondritis found only in congenital syphilis, the bone lesions found in one disease are identical to those found in the others (Steinbock 1976:139, 143). Steinbock stresses that the differences in skeletal involvement are merely quantitative. For example, in endemic syphilis and yaws, the cranial vault is infrequently affected in comparison with venereal syphilis, whereas tibial lesions are much more common.

Skeletal series in areas in which either endemic syphilis or yaws occurs are expected to reveal bone lesions in approximately 1–5% of the entire series (Steinbock 1976:139, 143).

Leprosy (now known as Hansen's disease) is a chronic infectious disease caused by the bacillus *Mycobacterium leprae.* The incubation period averages at least three to five years (World Health Organization 1980:16). A prevalence of about 0.5% (4.6 per 1,000) is found in modern Africa, where leprosy is endemic (p. 10). In clinical studies, skeletal manifestations occur in 15–68% of leprosarium patients (Chamberlain, Wayson, and Garland 1931, Esguerra-Gómez and Acosta 1948, Faget and Mayoral 1944, Murdock and Hutter 1932, Paterson 1961). Although leprosy is best known as a skin disease, its effects on the nervous and skeletal systems are well known. Skin changes usually consist of rough, dry macules, in which hypopigmentation may occur (Drutz 1981, World Health Organization 1980).

Skeletal manifestations of leprosy have been described in detail by Møller-Christensen (1967), Møller-Christensen and Faber (1952), Møller-Christensen and Inkster (1965), and Paterson (1959). The most reliable diagnostic criterion of leprosy is the occurrence of facies leprosa in the skull. This condition is characterized by atrophy of the anterior nasal spine, atrophy of the maxillary alveolar margin, mainly in the incisor region, and inflammatory changes of the superior surface of the hard palate. Facies leprosa has been identified in 60–82% of modern leprosy patients (Steinbock 1976:201). Postcranial changes accompanying facies leprosa include atrophy and resorption of the phalanges in the hands, beginning distally, and at the metatarsophalangeal joints in the feet. At a medieval Danish leper cemetery (St. George's Hospital, Naestved), 71.3% of 185 adequately preserved skeletons exhibited both facies leprosa and changes in the hands and feet (Weiss and Møller-Christensen 1971:262–63). Changes affecting only the hands and feet occurred in 26.5% and changes in the skull alone in 2.2% (Weiss and Møller-Christensen 1971:262–63). Examination of the hands and feet is therefore important in differentiating other diseases, such as syphilis, from leprosy. Subperiosteal bone deposits occur occasionally in the tibia and fibula in leprosy, but other long bones remain uninvolved. In contrast to the situation in syphilis, where extensive bone destruction is always accompanied by reactive new bone formation (Møller-Christensen 1953:106–7), bone resorption is not accompanied by proliferation.

DOCUMENTARY EVIDENCE

In the absence of extensive skeletal evidence for syphilis, medical historians have turned to ancient and medieval documents in an effort to establish the antiquity of syphilis in the Old World (Baker 1985). Supporters of the pre-Columbian and unitarian hypotheses argue that syphilis was confused with leprosy in the ancient literature and have sought passages purported to delineate the venereal communication of the disease. Columbianists discount such descriptions and point to accounts of a new disease of foreign origin at the close of the 15th century.

BIBLICAL REFERENCES TO "LEPROSY"

The Old Testament (written between the 8th and 2d centuries B.C.) is the most frequently cited text in reference to leprosy. The Hebrew word *tsara'at,* which is translated into Greek as *lepra,* "scaly," denotes ritual uncleanliness and probably refers to a wide range of diseases with dermatological manifestations (Cochrane 1959:viii; Hulse 1975; Møller-Christensen 1967:304–5). Lepromatous leprosy, originally described by the Alexandrian medical school about 300 B.C., is referred to as elephantiasis because of the thickening and corrugation of the skin (Dols 1979:315). As a result of inexact translation, the biblical term "leprosy" could, therefore, refer to syphilis.

Biblical passages suggesting syphilis have been reviewed at length by Willcox (1949; see also Hudson 1961:552–54 and Rosebury 1971: 98–104). Moses describes punishment for disobedience as manifesting "emerods," scabs, itches that cannot be healed, madness, and blindness (Deuteronomy 28:27–28). Job (Job 16, 19, 30) suffered from a genital lesion, and boils covered his body; iritis is suspected from his failing sight and mucous patches from his corrupt breath. David's illness (Psalms 38:1–11) is also cited as a case of pre-Columbian syphilis masquerading as "leprosy." David suffered from shooting pains and odoriferous lesions, and his "loins are filled with a loathsome disease." Like Job, he had failing vision and recovered from his illness. David believed his condition to have resulted from sleeping with Bathsheba, who was "unclean" at the time (2 Samuel 2–5).

Leviticus 13 and 22:4 and Numbers 5:2 are among passages discussing the skin lesions of "leprosy" and the restrictions placed upon the "unclean" in great detail (see Brody 1974:108–14 for further explication of biblical references to leprosy). Depigmentation and discoloration characterize the lesions reported. The lengthy description in Leviticus is actually a list used by priests to differentiate among diseases that may or may not result in ritual impurity (Hulse 1975; Sussman 1967:211).

If the foregoing passages are references to venereal syphilis, one would also expect biblical descriptions of congenital syphilis. In Jeremiah 31:29, where "the fathers have eaten sour grapes and the children's teeth are set on edge," the dental condition is suggestive of Hutchinson's teeth, a sign of congenital syphilis (Willcox 1949:32). Willcox also points to Exodus 20:5, where "the iniquity of the fathers" is visited "upon the children to the third and fourth generation." Although syphilis can be inherited only by the second generation, Brown et al. (1970:2) find this passage significant because "syphilis is one of the few known communicable diseases that can be passed from one generation to another."

Miriam's "leprosy" is described in Numbers (12:9–15). A possible macerated syphilitic fetus is suggested by Aaron's statement, "Let her not be as one dead, of whom the flesh is half consumed when he cometh out of his mother's womb." Leviticus (21:16–20) states that "he who hath a flat nose," perhaps indicative of congenital saddle nose, was ostracized. Similarly, in 2 Samuel 12 it is said that the child conceived from the adulterous and unclean union of David and Bathsheba died seven days after birth. If David's subsequent disease was syphilis, the baby may also have been afflicted.

OTHER ANCIENT REFERENCES SUGGESTIVE OF SYPHILIS

Several Greek and Roman physicians and historians including Hippocrates, Martial, Pliny, and Celsus described genital lesions following sexual activity (Brown et al. 1970:3; Hudson 1961; 1963b:646; Kampmeier 1984:22–23;

Rosebury 1971:105–7). During the 1st century A.D., Celsus described hard and soft genital sores, reporting that the latter exuded a malodorous discharge (Hudson 1961:555). Galen (born in A.D. 131) differentiated dry ulcers from moist ulcerating tubercles analogous to mucous patches (Kampmeier 1984:22). Such lesions were described by both Greeks and Romans as resembling mulberries or figs, which Hudson (1961) and others (see Kampmeier 1984:22) interpret as genital condylomata diagnostic of syphilis. Martial and Pliny (1st century A.D.) refer to *mentagra,* a term derived from the Latin *mentum,* "chin," from which *mentule,* "little chin," also originated. Hudson (1961:554–55; 1963b:646) points out that the latter term was euphemistic for the pubic area and concludes that the lesions and contagious nature of *mentagra* were venereal. Byzantine physicians of the 3d through 7th centuries documented several types of genital lesions that have been attributed to gonorrhea and syphilis (Kampmeier 1984:23). Finally Hudson (1961:551), in his thorough etymological treatise, links the term *bubas* to Greek and Latin terms denoting "serpent." Diaz de Isla employed this term to describe syphilis in 1539, noting that it was previously used in Spain to describe "leprosy" and the Roman's *mentagra.*

The ancient literatures of India and China have also been cited as containing "unmistakable proofs" that genital lesions were associated with sexual activity (Hyde 1891:117). Kampmeier (1984:22) indicates that the Sanskrit Veda contains several references to genital disease, which some have interpreted as syphilis. Lu and Needham (1967) mention no disease resembling syphilis in ancient China, and Crosby (1969:219) quotes Wong and Wu (1936:218) as saying that no Chinese writer "has ever described syphilis as being mentioned in ancient literature." Wong and Wu, however, assert in the following sentence that these writers "did not know the connection between chancres and syphilides, for the former were mentioned as early as the 7th century A.D." As to whether these chancres are syphilitic, they indicate (p. 219) that "the original texts are too brief to enable us to form any definite conclusion." Clinical descriptions of leprosy in China and India from as early as 600 B.C. are, in contrast, quite clear (Browne 1970: 641; Lu and Needham 1967:226, 236–37; Steinbock 1976:192).

MEDIEVAL "LEPROSY"

Medieval texts have also been studied for evidence that syphilis was included with other diseases under the term "leprosy." True leprosy was apparently unknown in the Mediterranean region prior to 300 B.C. Andersen (1969:123) has proposed an introduction from India after Alexander the Great's campaign in 327–326 B.C. Celsus, Pliny the Elder, Galen, and Aretaeus were the first to describe the disease, which they called elephantiasis, in the first two centuries A.D. (Dols 1979:315; see also Patrick 1967:245). The generic term *lepra* was not applied to true leprosy until the 8th century A.D. (Steinbock 1976:192–93) in the translation of Arab medical texts into Latin (Richards 1977:9). Thus, a previously distinct and well-defined disease of no religious significance was blended with the biblical concept of impurity and acquired the stigma still attached to the word "leper" (Richards 1977:9–10). As a result, the medieval diagnosis of leprosy may have incorporated several afflictions, including true leprosy and syphilis.

The mode of transmission of medieval leprosy is confused. Bartholomeus Anglicus (ca. 1230–50) wrote that leprosy was caused by "intercourse with a woman after she had been with a leprous man, heredity, and feeding a child with the milk of a leprous nurse" (Rubin 1974:153; see also Gordon 1959:493–94). Theodoric of Cervia (1205–98) provides one of the more detailed descriptions of the disease within the prevailing humoral theory (7 of his 12 common signs of leprosy correspond to those found by modern diagnosticians), but he also insists that those "lying with a woman with whom a leper has lain" will be infected (Brody 1974:34–41).

Numerous medieval scholars refer to "venereal leprosy," "hereditary leprosy," and "leper whore" and describe genital lesions (Brody 1974:54–56; Holcomb 1935:297–303; Hudson 1961:548; 1972:150–51; Kampmeier 1984:23–24). Leprosy is neither hereditary nor sexually transmitted. It does show a strong family incidence (4.4–12% of household contacts of lepromatous leprosy patients show signs of the disease within five years [World Health Organization 1980]), but both husband and wife are affected in less than 5% of couples (Richards 1977:xvi).

Leper hospitals were established throughout Europe prior to the Crusades (A.D. 1096–1221) in an effort to separate lepers from society. "Leprosy" reached its peak prevalence in Europe in the 11th through 13th centuries (Rubin 1974:151), coinciding with the Crusades. Hudson (1963b) has outlined the importance of concurrent pilgrimage to the Middle East in disseminating disease, which he contends included treponemal infection disguised as "leprosy." As supporting evidence he cites the use of "Saracen ointment," which contained mercury, by the returning lepers (1961:548; 1963b:648; see also Hackett 1967:163–64). Mercury has no effect on true leprosy but was the mainstay in treating syphilis until the early 20th century (Steinbock 1976:88).

Perhaps the most explicit description of medieval "leprosy" is found in Robert Henryson's poem "The Testament of Cresseid." Written in Scotland prior to 1492, the poem has been variously claimed as a delineation of venereal syphilis (Hudson 1972) and as a sensitive portrayal of an individual afflicted with leprosy (Richards 1977:6–8). The poem, a contemporary version of the myth of the Trojan lovers, Troilus and Cressida, depicts a fallen woman who acquired an "incurable disease" and died "a leper" (Hudson 1972:146). Cresseid's face became "o'erspread with black boils," her "clear voice" became "hoarse," "rough and raucous" (quoted in Richards 1977:6–7). Cresseid's condition resulted from her lustful life. She was confined to a leper house to prevent the spread of her infection to others. Her life as a leper is detailed, including the last will and testament required for entrance into the leper hospital, her wandering with cup and clapper, and her diet of "mouldy bread, perry, and cider sour" (quoted in Richards 1977:6–8). Henryson called Cresseid's disease leprosy, but Hudson (1972:149) suggests that because it is associated with immorality and sex it is venereal syphilis. Richards (1977:6) finds Henryson so compassionate in his portrayal of the "leper" that he must have had firsthand knowledge of leprosy and "of lives broken by it."

THE EPIDEMIC OF 1500

By 1500, a "new" disease, which we know as syphilis, was being described in Europe (see Crosby 1969, Dennie 1962, Holcomb 1934, Williams, Rice, and Renato Lacayo 1927). As syphilis became widely recognized and described, "leprosy" became less common. Historical events unrelated to the return of Columbus may explain this trend. For example, the invention of the printing press in the mid-15th century led to rapid diffusion of information. By 1566, 58 books had been published on the subject of syphilis. Kampmeier (1984:24) argues that the proliferation of such publications led to the widespread recognition of the disease at this time, making it appear as if it were a new disease of epidemic proportions. This dissemination of knowledge was accompanied by historical events that caused the displacement of people throughout Europe.

Papal proclamations in 1490 and 1505 abolished all leper houses (Holcomb 1935:282), allowing the dispersal of thousands with "leprosy." Holcomb notes (p. 278) that Matthew Paris, an English monk who died in 1259, records "in somewhat ambiguous terms" the existence of 19,000 leper houses in Europe. While this figure may be exaggerated, Gordon (1959:493) indicates that "France and Germany alone had nearly 10,000 leprosaria" in 1400, and Richards (1977:11) notes approximately 200 leper hospitals "in their thirteenth- and fourteenth-century heyday" in Britain. It should be cautioned, however, that most leper hospitals were ecclesiastical foundations that accommodated only about ten lepers and at least as many chaplains and sisters (Richards 1977:11). Richards (see also Creighton 1965 [1894]:86–100) concludes that the number of hospitals is not a reliable estimate of the number of lepers because of the propensity of the church to establish the institutions to garner perpetual charity. Whatever the motive for establishing the hospitals, they did house thousands throughout Europe. If the diseases were confused, it is possible that some of the inhabitants were syphilitic and therefore that when the hospitals were closed syphilis was dispersed.

Hudson (1964; 1968:11) claims that treponemal infection existed in venereal and nonvenereal forms in pre-Columbian Spain and Portugal because of the Moorish occupation and the importation of slaves from sub-Saharan Africa. When an estimated 160,000 to 400,000 Jews were expelled from Spain in 1492, they allegedly carried syphilis throughout Europe (Holcomb 1935:284). The expulsion of Jews and lepers coincided with the discovery of America and the apparent epidemic of syphilis.

In late 1494, Charles VIII of France conducted a campaign against Naples. The city fell in February of 1495 as a plague broke out among the mercenary troops. They subsequently disbanded, carrying their disease throughout Europe (Brown et al. 1970:5; Williams, Rice, and Renato Lacayo 1927:683). It is generally agreed that this disease was syphilis; the controversy concerns the time of arrival of Spanish troops purported to have contracted the disease from Columbian contacts and the issue of several edicts regarding the disease elsewhere in Europe. Holcomb (1934:419; see also Hudson 1968:5–6; 1972:152) claims that Charles's army left Naples on May 20, 1495, and the Spaniards did not arrive until June. Although Charles did not reach France until October 27, 1495, an edict had been issued by the Diet of Worms more than two months earlier (August 7, 1495), indicating that syphilis was already widespread in Germany (Gordon 1959:536; Holcomb 1935:289, 427; see also Harrison 1959:4). While this would seem to vindicate Charles VIII, Waugh (1982: 92) has pointed to problems in dating events of the time due to the variety of calendars in use (e.g., Gregorian vs. French).

Further confusion in the dates of early edicts on syphilis has resulted from modern errors. Holcomb (1935:293) laments the penchant of some writers (Columbianists) for accepting ideas "without first assuring themselves of the correctness of the historical data that they introduce." Reliance upon Sudhoff's archival work, however, has led to wide acceptance of the 1495 date of the aforementioned edict of the Diet of Worms. Sudhoff later amended the date to August 8, 1496, and subsequent research by Haustein revealed that the text was actually drafted by the Diet of Lindau on January 12, 1497 (cited in Temkin 1966:32–33). Thus, it is possible that the passage regarding syphilis was a response to its dissemination by soldiers returning from Italy.

Holcomb's pre-Columbian thesis hinges largely upon an edict issued in Paris that bars those with *grosse verole* (syphilis) from the city. Holcomb (1934:416, 421; 1935:293) dates this edict to March 25, 1493, or ten days after Columbus returned to Spain from his first voyage. This would render it impossible for the disease to have been imported from America. In an attempt to verify this date, Harrison (1959:4–6) followed a series of errors in later compilations of ancient French laws (one of which was cited by Holcomb) and discovered that the ordinance with the text in question was actually issued on June 25, 1498 (verified by Haustein's research, cited in Temkin 1966:33). A thorough search of the French archives revealed that the earliest Parisian reference to the disease was contained in an edict promulgated by the Paris parliament on March 6, 1497 (Harrison 1959:4–6, see also Creighton 1965:[1894]:436), nearly four years after Columbus's crew returned from the first voyage. Holcomb (1934:428) misdates this edict

as well, stating that it was issued on March 16, 1496.

Several edicts ostracizing people infected with syphilis were issued elsewhere in Europe beginning in 1496. In that year, 12 such ordinances were passed at Nuremberg and syphilitics were barred from the baths of Zurich and other municipalities throughout Switzerland and Germany (Holcomb 1934:428; Kampmeier 1984:24–25). Ten persons with "the Neapolitan disease" were expelled from Besançon, France, in April of 1496, while an edict at Lyon, dated August 12, 1497, required those with the disease to report within ten days or be apprehended (Harrison 1959:4, 6). Early references to syphilis in Britain is from an ordinance of Aberdeen dated April 21, 1497, in which it is stated that "the infirmity came out of France" (Creighton 1965 [1894]:417). A proclamation issued in Edinburgh by James IV on September 22, 1497, requires those with "Grandgor" (syphilis) to go to the island of Inch Keith in the Firth of Forth, "there to remain until God provide for their health" (Creighton 1965 [1894]:417–18). Hospitals for the syphilitic such as St. Jobsgasthuis, founded in Utrecht in 1504 (Fuldauer, Bracht, and Perizonius 1984), were established throughout Europe by the beginning of the 16th century.

It would appear from the dates of European edicts that a new disease swept the continent within three or four years of the return of the first Columbian voyagers. The concurrence of these events has been challenged, however, by those who point out that edicts after 1493 closely resemble those previously issued to isolate lepers. For example, a Parisian edict of 1488 is directed against *les lepreux,* while those following the papal proclamation of 1490 refer to syphilis (Creighton 1965 [1894]:73; Holcomb 1934:416; 1935:282). Creighton questions the sudden reappearance of leprosy in the late 15th century, especially since the Paris edict is so close in date to those concerning syphilis. Thus, one is left to wonder whether these ordinances were issued as a consequence of the importation of syphilis or if the discovery of America was merely coincidental with the recognition and re-naming of the disease as it was differentiated from "leprosy."

Late 15th- and Early 16th-Century Treatises on Syphilis

Treatises on syphilis proliferated in the late 1490s and early 1500s (for reviews see, e.g., Crosby 1969, Dennie 1962, Holcomb 1934, Hudson 1961). Williams, Rice, and Renato Lacayo (1927) provide translations of large portions of early Spanish works, the most important of which is Ruy Diaz de Isla's "Treatise on the Serpentine Malady, Which in Spain is Commonly Called Bubas, which was drawn up in the Hospital of All Saints in Lisbon," first printed in 1539. In it, he claims that the serpentine disease (syphilis) appeared in Barcelona in 1493, originated on the island of Española (Haiti), and was brought to Europe by Columbus's crew (p. 693). He goes on to say that in the following year Charles VIII entered Italy with "many Spaniards infected with this disease." Not knowing what it was, "the French called it the disease of Naples," and the Italians, "as they had never had acquaintance with a like disease, called it the French disease." This portion of Diaz de Isla's account is confirmed by Gonzalo Fernández Oviedo y Valdés (1478–1557): "Many times in Italy I did laugh, hearing the Italians say the French disease and the French calling it the disease of Naples; and in truth both would have hit on the right name if they had called it the disease from the Indies." Oviedo also verifies that among Charles VIII's army were Spaniards, "touched with this disease," but he indicates that they did not join the French until 1496 (see Williams et al. 1927:687–89 and Crosby 1969:222). Much has been made of this discrepancy in dates (e.g., Holcomb [1935:292] uses it to dismiss Oviedo's entire account); Waugh's (1982:92) caution regarding the difficulty in dating such events must be borne in mind.

Critics of the 16th-century treatises, such as

Holcomb (1934, 1935), point out that no mention is made of an American origin of syphilis for more than 30 years after the discovery of the New World. Earlier texts attribute the disease to divine wrath visited upon a sinful populace, astrologic convergences, and the weather; Oviedo's work is among the first to mention an American origin. His "Summaria of the Natural History of the Indies" was published in 1526 and is purported to have been written from memory. His larger work, "General and Natural History of the Indies," was first printed in 1535 (Holcomb 1934:406–7; Williams et al. 1927:687). In it he says that, while he is writing from memory, he is referring to "notes which were written at the time when the things described in them happened." Holcomb (1934:407) points out that taking such notes is not the usual activity of a teenager (Oviedo was only 15 when Columbus returned from his first voyage). Crosby (1969:222) maintains that Oviedo was quite friendly with the explorer's sons and cites a passage in which Oviedo asked several of his friends sailing with Columbus in 1493 (second voyage) to provide him with detailed reports (his affiliation with several crew members is also recorded in the translation by Williams et al. 1927:688).

The original manuscript of Diaz de Isla's account is dedicated to King Manuel of Portugal, who died in 1521 (Williams et al. 1927:695). In a paragraph omitted from the printed versions, he writes of an island "discovered and found by the Admiral Dom Cristoual Colon at present holding intercourse and communication with the Indies" (Williams et al. 1927:695). Since Columbus's last voyage culminated in his death in the New World in 1506, it seems that the manuscript must have been written prior to that event. Furthermore, Diaz de Isla states that "in the year 1504 there were given me in writing all the remedies that the Indians used for this disease," indicating that his belief in its American origin dated to within 11 years of its alleged importation. Thus, the manuscript, usually ascribed to the period 1510–20, would appear more likely to have been written in 1505 or 1506. Holcomb (1934:412–13), however, asserts that Diaz de Isla "frequently states he had 40 years' experience in the treatment of the disease" and therefore acceptance of such dates would place his treatment well before the discovery of America. Holcomb's observation is not apparent in the translation provided by Williams et al. (1927:694), in which Diaz de Isla writes only that he has had "long experience." It seems that a decade or more would qualify as such.

Several 16th-century tracts written by European scholars in the New World document the lifeways, languages, and mythologies of various native groups and refer to a disease much like syphilis among them. These documents have been employed to support the Columbian hypothesis in publications of the past century (e.g., Brühl 1890, Crosby 1969, Williams et al. 1927), while others (e.g., Holcomb 1934:417–18) attribute such references to the introduction of the disease by Europeans. The biography of Christopher Columbus, by his son Ferdinand, includes a 1495 manuscript by Fray Roman Pane recording an Arawak myth in which the hero, Guagagiona, "saw a woman . . . from whom he had great pleasure, and immediately he sought many lotions to cleanse himself, on account of being plagued with the disease that we call French," and afterwards went to a secluded place "where he recovered from his ulcers" (Williams et al. 1927:687; see also Brühl 1890:276 and Crosby 1969:221–22). Crosby, reminding the reader that folklore is very slow to change, finds it unlikely that the Arawaks would have altered their legend to give the hero a new disease, thus implying that the malady was extant among the natives long before the Europeans arrived. This is corroborated by Bartolomé de las Casas, who questioned the natives as to the origin of the disease and was told they had had it from time immemorial (Crosby 1969:222; Williams et al. 1927:690). Further examples of "syphilis" in native mythology, as well as differential burial treatment of those afflicted, were documented by Bernardino de Sahagún, who lived in Mexico from 1529 to 1590 (Brühl 1890:275–76; Williams et al. 1927:690–91).

Linguistic evidence compiled by Montejo y Robledo from 16th- and 17th-century dictionaries of native Mexican and Central and South American languages reveals indigenous terms for *bubas* and related European expressions (Williams et al. 1927:685–86). Brühl (1890:278–80) counters the view that these terms were invented after the arrival of Europeans by reviewing the ways in which names were assigned to previously unknown things—adopting the European word with little or no change or deriving the name from a conspicuous feature of the object. While the terms for previously unknown diseases described a prominent symptom, the words synonymous with European appellations for syphilis were "formed at the development of the respective languages" and, in many cases, associated with chieftains and gods (Brühl 1890:279).

SKELETAL EVIDENCE

The preceding review of ancient and medieval documentary sources reveals many ambiguities in disease description and the dating of events. The ensuing interpretations of these passages remain controversial. Skeletal evidence of pre-Columbian syphilis is subject to similar disagreement. As Williams (1932:780) states, "one must have proof that a bone is ancient and that it is syphilitic. It is owing to a difference of opinion as to what constitutes proof that the controversy continues." Unfortunately, many of the remains thought to be syphilitic (primarily those recovered prior to Williams's review) lack archaeological provenience and cannot, therefore, be assumed pre-Columbian. Further difficulties arise in interpreting many late 19th- and early 20th-century descriptions of syphilitic specimens. These reports often present descriptions of an isolated skeletal element. Since skeletal lesions resulting from yaws, endemic syphilis, and venereal syphilis are identical, speculation regarding the mode of transmission of the treponeme in a single individual is impossible (i.e., an isolated case of treponematosis cannot be assumed to have resulted from venereal transmission). Reliable conclusions regarding the prehistoric distribution of treponemal disease may, however, be drawn from skeletal evidence. The pattern of treponemal infection discerned in entire skeletal series, viewed in conjunction with social and climatological factors, may permit epidemiological inferences.

Old World Remains

Although numerous cases of alleged pre-Columbian Old World syphilis have been described in the literature of the past century, few have withstood reexamination. Once Parrot (1879) had aroused European interest in the paleopathological identification of syphilis, nearly every French anthropologist discovered syphilitic specimens (Sigerist 1951:56). Parrot, however, confused the manifestations of congenital syphilis and rickets, delineating a "rachitic period" of congenital syphilis for which "swelling . . . of the articular ends of the bones" and "cranial osteophytes" resulting in "the form of a cross" on the skull vault were diagnostic (1879:697–98). Thus he reported syphilis in prehistoric Ecuador, Peru, and France solely on the basis of cranial vaults exhibiting circumscribed areas of bone deposition (i.e., cranial bossing) that were more likely due to rickets, iron deficiency anemia, or congenital anemia (Steinbock 1976:101). Reliance on Parrot's diagnostic criteria underlies Wright's (1971) contention that syphilis is evident in Neanderthal remains in the form of cranial bossing, thinning and pitting of the occipital and parietals, and "the relative depression of the bridge of the nose" in both children and adults. Worn taurodont molars are suggested to resemble the mulberry molars of congenital syphilis. Bowing of the femur is attributed to syphilitic osteitis, also hypothesized to "account for Neanderthal long bone being so short and stout." Many of the lesions Wright describes are diagnostic of rickets, while the general skeletal variations he attributes to syphilis are the consequence of genetic and biomechanical differences between Neanderthal and modern populations.

The alleged skeletal evidence of pre-Columbian syphilis was thoroughly reviewed by Williams in 1932. Prior to investigating archaeological specimens, he examined the bones of over 500 modern individuals known to be syphilitic in order to establish diagnostic criteria. Various specimens described in the early literature as syphilitic had apparently been lost by the time of his research, and others were too incomplete for diagnosis to be attempted. In many of the remaining cases, the supposedly syphilitic lesions could be attributed to other causes. For example, several Egyptian cases had actually suffered postmortem damage by rodents or insects (pp. 802–3), and the lesions on Parrot's (1879:698) Peruvian crania were attributable to porotic hyperostosis (Williams 1929:852; 1932:971). Williams considered five cases of reputed Old World syphilis "suspicious." In the case of the tibia and fibula from Japanese shell middens, said to be more than 2,500 years old, he thought trauma or healed osteomyelitis with periostitis the cause of the lesions described (p. 802) and judged the antiquity of the remains questionable in any event (p. 974). For a Nubian femur and tibia dated to 1000 B.C., insofar as his examination of the published illustrations permitted, he found the diagnosis of syphilis plausible, although "other causes of periostitis would be equally probable" (pp. 803, 975). For the remaining "suspicious" instances, all from France—a tibia from Solutré, a humerus and ulna from the Marne Valley, and an ulna, femur, and femur fragment from the museum at Saint-Germain (pp. 805–9, 975)—he found the diagnosis of syphilis equivocal. The few possible instances of pre-Columbian syphilis consist of isolated long bones with inadequate archaeological provenience (Sigerist 1951:56; Williams 1932:974). Jeanselme, Pales, and others concur that the Old World evidence presented prior to 1930 is inconclusive or negative (Williams 1932:975–76; see also Sigerist 1951:56 and Steinbock 1976:97).

Possible skeletal evidence accumulated since 1930 is sparse. Steinbock (1976:97) regards Siberian material consisting of several tibiae, a radius, and an ulna dated 1000–800 B.C. as the earliest indication of possible Old World syphilis. In addition, two tibiae dated 500–200 B.C. and three crania dated A.D. 100–700 are reported to show syphilitic lesions (cf. Hackett 1976: 18, who indicates that the dates may be unacceptable). Evidence of pre-Columbian syphilis reported since 1930 in Europe is tantalizing but inconclusive. The skull of an adult female from Spitalfields Market in London presents the diagnostic stellate scars of caries sicca (Brothwell 1961:324–25; Morant and Hoadley 1931:222, pl. 3; Steinbock 1976:97). Historical records indicate that the site was part of the cemetery at the church of St. Mary Spittle, used A.D. 1197–1537 (Morant and Hoadley 1931:202). Brothwell (1961:324–25) finds it a "remarkable coincidence" that the woman succumbed to syphilis within 35 years of its supposed appearance in London, but the possibility cannot be dismissed. Similarly, excavations at the Helgeandsholmen cemetery in Stockholm, used from A.D. 1300 to 1531, have yielded syphilitic remains (Madrid 1986).

Hudson (1961:547–48) contends that "syphilitic skulls and other bones have been found in 'leper cemeteries' and doubtless many a European 'leper' lost his nose and his voice, or was covered with purulent crusts, as a result of treponemal infection." If he is correct, then excavations of cemeteries associated with medieval leprosaria should reveal skeletons of syphilitics in addition to lepers (his citations are to publications of 1868 and 1891, prior to the establishment of diagnostic criteria for syphilis and leprosy). Excavations at Danish leper hospitals and medieval churchyards and extensive examination of European skeletal collections reveal no evidence of pre-Columbian treponemal disease (e.g., Møller-Christensen 1952, 1967; Møller-Christensen and Faber 1952; Weiss and Møller-Christensen 1971).

Yaws and/or endemic syphilis have occasionally been reported in skeletal material from the Old World. An isolated skull from Iraq, dated prior to A.D. 500, exhibits a large crater-like depression on the mid-frontal and a smaller, slightly depressed area on the right side of the frontal bone that have been attributed to treponematosis (Guthe and Willcox 1954:fig. 2; Steinbock 1976:141). An elliptical area of porosity on the occipital of an eight-year-old child (INM 196) from the Chalcolithic site of Inamgaon in western India (dated 1000–700 B.C.) is interpreted as evidence of yaws (Lukacs and Walimbe 1984: 123–24, fig. 7). This attribution is tenuous, however, since there is no other skeletal involvement and treponemal lesions are infrequent on the occipital.

Australia and the Pacific islands have yielded many examples of treponematosis in skeletal remains. Hackett (1976:109, 114) found treponemal changes in 1% of the 4,500 Australian Aboriginal crania he examined and argues that treponemal infection has probably existed in Australia "for some thousands of years." Unfortunately, no information regarding the antiquity of these remains is furnished, and it is uncertain if they predate European contact (see Steinbock 1976:141, 158). Two subadults from Tinian, in the Mariana Islands, display treponemal lesions thought to result from yaws (Stewart and Spoehr 1967[1952]). Pathological changes consist of a crater-like depression surrounded by an irregular zone of porosity on the frontal bone of one individual and similar lesions on the parietals. Parts of a femur, humerus, and radius from the same individual exhibit periostitis with cavitation. The incomplete tibia from the second subadult shows prominent thickening of the cortex along the anterior aspect (saber shin) accompanied by pitting and cavitation (Stewart and Spoehr 1967[1952]: 311–17; see also Steinbock 1976:153, 158). The site is radiocarbon-dated to A.D. 854 ± 145, thus predating European contact by a considerable margin (Stewart and Spoehr 1967[1952]:311). Yaws has also been described in a precontact skeletal series from Tonga (Steinbock 1976:159).

New World Remains

Interest in prehistoric skeletal evidence of syphilis developed in America at about the same time as in Europe. The earliest discussion is usually attributed to Jones (1876), although Williams (1932:931) cites an 1875 account, by R. J. Farquharson, of syphilitic lesions in skeletal remains from mounds near Davenport, Iowa. Jones's (1876:49, 65–67, 71–72, 85) detailed descriptions of skeletal lesions in ancient inhabitants of Tennessee and Kentucky support his conclusion that syphilis (i.e., a treponemal infection) was the cause of pathology observed in several individuals. Jones remarks (p. 66) that the tibiae are, in many cases, "thoroughly diseased, enlarged, and thickened, with the medullary cavity completely obliterated by the effects of inflammatory action, and with the surface eroded in many places." Skeletal involvement was not confined to the tibial shafts but included the cranium, clavicle, sternum, and other long bones. Significantly, Jones notes the symmetrical distribution of the skeletal lesions. The crania are described (p. 66) as exhibiting lesions "in which a network of periosteal deposit had been formed, and which had been perforated by ulcers, subsequently forming and assuming the annular type." Williams (1932:966) examined some of the skulls in the Jones collection and verified the presence of stellate scars in one specimen that he also attributed to syphilis. Soon after Jones's disclosure, claims of pre-Columbian syphilis in the Americas proliferated (e.g., Gann 1901, Lamb 1898, Langdon 1881, Orton 1905, Parrot 1879), although much of the purported evidence was deemed inconclusive by others (e.g., Hyde 1891; Putnam 1878:305; Whitney 1883). As with the European material, difficulty in differentiating disease processes, incomplete skeletons, and absence of archaeological context precluded reliable diagnoses in most cases. Even the most conservative, however, described skeletal lesions in ancient American remains that they admitted might have been due to syphilis (e.g., Hyde 1891:128; Whitney 1883:

366). Williams (1932:976–77) considered reported cases of syphilis from several areas of North and South America "as nearly free from suspicion as any that can be found."

In the Southeastern United States, reported evidence of pre-Columbian treponematosis abounds. Following Jones's (1876) report, Lamb (1898) described syphilitic lesions in a skeleton excavated by Clarence B. Moore at Lighthouse Mound, in northeastern Florida. Moore (quoted in Bullen 1972:157) found the percentage of pathological specimens and degree of skeletal involvement in the 74 individuals recovered remarkable and indicated that "cranial nodes" were apparent. The skeleton examined by Lamb (1898:63–64) was not accompanied by the skull but exhibited "lesions of osteoperiostitis, both hyperostotic and ulcerative," on the shafts of the long bones. Williams (1932:968) also examined this individual and agreed that the lesions "were in all probability syphilitic."

Bullen's (1972) survey of prehistoric skeletal material from Florida reveals considerable evidence suggestive of treponematosis. Enlarged long bones exhibiting encroachment upon the medullary cavity have been recovered from the Tick Island Archaic site, radiocarbon-dated to 3300 B.C. (p. 166). Burial 352 from Palmer Mound (FSM 97527) presents the most convincing case of pre-Columbian treponemal infection in Florida (pp. 138–50). The site belongs to the Weeden Island period and dates to A.D. 850. The nearly complete skeleton of an adult female displays cranial caries sicca (see also Hackett 1976: 110) and lesions on several long bones. The right humerus shows focal areas of destruction surrounded by diffuse osteitis and dense reparative bone, the radii and left fibula are slightly thickened with some periosteal new bone formation, and the left tibia is expanded and irregular. A radiograph of the left tibia reveals multiple lytic areas surrounded by sclerotic bone that Hackett (1976:110) has identified as superficial cavitation of nodes—diagnostic of syphilis. Additional remains from Palmer and several other prehistoric sites (mostly Weeden Island, A.D. 850–1350) exhibit treponemal lesions (Brothwell and Burleigh 1975:394; Bullen 1972:150–62; Iscan and Miller-Shaivitz 1985), indicating that the Palmer burial is by no means an isolated case.

Treponematosis has also been identified in a prehistoric skeletal series from Georgia. The remains of 265 individuals from Irene Mound (A.D. 1200–1450), near Savannah, reveal widespread inflammatory response with marked diaphyseal expansion in the lower legs and arms (Powell 1988c). Few cranial and naso-palatine lesions are noted, but in some cases focal lytic lesions of the skull vault are apparent. The demographic and anatomical patterning of skeletal lesions suggests endemicity rather than venereal transmission.

Syphilis is proposed as the cause of bone pathology in several specimens from northern Alabama, including a cranium in which the palate has been almost completely eroded and only the remodeled edges remain (Rabkin 1942:220–21, fig. 6). No specific provenience is provided for the syphilitic remains, but the sample includes material from as late as A.D. 1400–1600 (p. 218). Prehistoric pathological remains suggestive of syphilis at Moundville, Alabama, were first noted by Moore (1907:339–40). One skull that has received considerable attention in the literature (e.g., Bullen 1972:163–64; Hackett 1976: 109–10; Haltom and Shands 1938; Williams 1936:785–86) displays extensive erosion and new bone formation on the frontal, resulting in the stellate scars characteristic of caries sicca. Hackett (1976:110) indicates that although the changes in this skull are not typical caries sicca, "in which the nodules are smaller and of more regular size," the diagnosis of treponematosis is "fully supported by the presence of similar changes in [crania found in] European medical museums and in Australian anthropological collections." Two tibiae from another individual present thickening due to osteoperiostitis, probably a result of treponemal infection (Williams 1936:786).

In an examination of over 500 individuals at Moundville, Powell (1988a) observed a "high prevalence of subperiosteal apposition on lower limb long bone shafts and moderate prevalence on cranial stellate lesions." Periostitis of major long bones is reported in 207 cases, of which 72% appear minor in extent and well-healed at death (Powell 1988b). The absence of the dental stigmata associated with congenital syphilis and the frequency of healed tibial lesions have led Powell (1988a,b) to attribute the observed pathology to a nonvenereal treponemal syndrome (yaws or endemic syphilis).

A possible case of treponematosis from the Late Woodland Hardin side in the North Carolina piedmont has been described by Reichs (1987). The skeleton exhibits destructive and proliferative changes resulting in node formation, expansion and cortical thickening of long bone shafts, medullary encroachment, and pathological fracture, with both cranial and postcranial involvement. Although the lesions are suggestive of treponematosis, Reichs recognizes that the overall pattern of pathology in this individual may be due to the synergistic effects of multiple diseases.

An apparent case of congenital syphilis in a six-to-seven-year-old child (U.S. National Museum of Natural History, Smithsonian Institution collection [hereafter NMNH], No. 379177) from Virginia dates prior to A.D. 1400 (Ortner and Putschar 1985:207–10). Abnormal reactive bone is evident in a frontal lesion, and the surface of the nasal aperture displays thickened, porous, periosteal bone. The extant deciduous incisors have hypoplastic defects so severe that, in three, the superior portion of the crown had broken off before death. The deciduous and first permanent molars are unaffected, as is an observable unerupted permanent incisor. Postcranial skeletal involvement is extensive. The shafts of both tibiae are thickened, with periosteal expansion occurring primarily on the anterior aspect. The other long bones also exhibit periosteal apposition and diaphyseal expansion, although to a lesser degree. A similar process is apparent in several metacarpals and metatarsals. Dactylitis is more common in yaws than in syphilis (Steinbock 1976:143); however, a congenital disease is indicated by the development of hypoplastic dental defects at about the seventh fetal month (Ortner and Putschar 1985:210). Thus, a pattern in which the bones with minimal overlying tissue are most severely affected, as is commonly observed in treponematosis, accompanied by congenital dental defects suggestive of Hutchinson's teeth is strong evidence of congenital syphilis. Although such dental stigmata are not pathognomonic of congenital syphilis, they are associated with characteristic bone lesions in about 50% of all cases, and the diagnosis in such instances is "very reliable" (Steinbock 1976:106).

The skeleton of a 25–35-year-old male (NMNH 385788) from a site radiocarbon-dated to A.D. 925 provides additional evidence of treponematosis in prehistoric Virginia (Ortner 1986). Remains from tidewater and piedmont sites in Delaware, Maryland, and Virginia that exhibit inflammatory lesions on the frontal and associated long bones are in some cases suggestive of syphilis (Stewart and Quade 1969). Hackett (1976:110) indicates that the skull from Accokeek, Maryland (NMNH 378196 [Stewart and Quade 1969:pl. 1-*C*]), exhibits serpiginous cavitation (diagnostic of treponematosis). Although the piedmont sites are late prehistoric, the tidewater sites discussed by Stewart and Quade (1969:92–93), including Accokeek, date from A.D. 1200–1600; it is therefore uncertain if the remains are pre-Columbian.

A possible case of pre-Columbian treponematosis from the Veddar site (Cnj 43-2, also known as the Palatine Bridge site) in the Mohawk Valley of New York is the only evidence reported in northeastern North America (Elting and Starna 1984). The remains in question are thought to date to the Early Woodland component of the site (500 B.C.) and are undoubtedly pre-Columbian. The tibiae and fibulae of one individual exhibit diffuse periosteal inflammation and new bone formation with narrowing of the medullary canals. Coarse striations and nodes with superficial cavitation are described, and the latter is noted to be one of Hackett's (1976) diagnostic criteria. The changes evident from the photographs (Elting and Starna 1984:270–71, figs. 2 and 3) may more closely correspond to Hackett's (1976:82–83) coarsely striated and pitted expansions, only tentatively considered diagnostic. The absence of sequestrum and cloaca formation, however, rules out osteomyelitis, and the changes apparent in the medullary canals indicate that "a diagnosis of treponematosis is reasonably secure" (Elting and Starna 1984:272).

Syphilis was reported in remains from the Ohio Valley as early as 1881 (Landgon 1881: 254–56). William C. Mills's excavations at several Ohio sites in the early 1900s revealed a large number of burials, many of which were pathological. For example, of 127 individuals from the Baum site (A.D. 950–1250), 21 were diseased and at least 12 were deemed syphilitic by Orton (Mills 1906:126–35; Orton 1905). Williams (1932:954–62) examined much of the prehistoric skeletal material from the Ohio State Museum and found long bones with possible syphilitic lesions in 15 individuals (at least one of which had been previously described by Means [1925]). In 9 cases, three different roentgenologists agreed that the proliferative bone changes resulted from syphilis. Six tibiae from 4 different individuals are depicted and described in detail. In general, they display thickening of the anterior aspect, with a slightly nodular surface perforated by small openings. Where both tibiae are presented, the involvement is bilateral. Hackett (1976:109) indicates that these specimens do not exhibit diagnostic criteria of treponematosis. Williams (1932:955), however, states that the bones he described were "only a portion of the ancient diseased, probably syphilitic, bones that have been disclosed by the investigations of the Ohio State Museum."

Nine individuals from May's Lick, Kentucky, radiocarbon-dated to A.D. 1325 (580 ± 108 B.P.), show cranial vault changes suggestive of treponematosis (Brothwell and Burleigh 1975:394). At least two skeletons from Indian Knoll, Kentucky (radiocarbon-dated ca. 3350 B.C.), exhibit such lesions (Brothwell and Burleigh 1975:393; Steinbock 1976:96), thus extending the evidence in the Ohio Valley region to the Archaic period. Cassidy (1980:136–138; 1984:325, 330–32) has identified a "syndrome of disseminated periosteal reactions," distinct from localized inflammatory lesions, in skeletal series from Indian Knoll and the late Fort Ancient–period Hadin Village (ca A.D. 1525–1675). This syndrome is characterized by thickening of the long bones, particularly those of the legs; development of "stripes of smooth billowed material or patches of rough porous material on the surfaces; and some diminution of the medullary canals in severe cases" (Cassidy 1980:136–37). Such lesions are indicative of a nonvenereal treponematosis that affected 2.4% of the Indian Knoll population and 31.4% of the Hardin Village series, where eight individuals display severe manifestations (Cassidy 1984:325, 330). The increase in incidence of this syndrome in the post-Columbian group is postulated to be a result of increased population size and sedentism (Cassidy 1980:137).

A considerable amount of purported treponematosis has been discovered in Woodland and Mississippian remains in Illinois. The material is from the lower Illinois River valley, in the west-central portion of the state. A high incidence of cranial lesions (attributed to various causes) in a skeletal series from the Jersey County Bluff mounds (A.D. 400–1400) is noted by Stewart and Quade (1969:95–96). Of 122 relatively complete skeletons, 4 (3.3%) exhibit both frontal and long bone lesions. Hackett (1976:110) indicates that one skull (NMNH 380044 [Stewart and Quade 1969:pl. 1-*A*]) from this series exhibits serpiginous cavitation and another (NMNH 379875 [Stewart and Quade 1969:pl. 2-*C*]) "a rather atypical caries sicca." The cranium and left tibia of an individual from the Middle Woodland (ca. 100 B.C.–A.D. 400) component of the Carter Mound Group (Burial 7, Mound 1) in adjacent Greene County illustrates the pathology usually reported in the literature as "syphilis" (Buikstra 1979:233). A 40-year-old Middle Woodland male

from the Klunk site (C40, Burial 21) in Calhoun County also exhibits cranial and long bone lesions suggestive of treponematosis (Morse 1978: 136–37, pl. 15 *A–C*).

Additional cases have been reported somewhat farther up the Illinois River in Schuyler and Fulton Counties. The skeleton of a 30–40-year-old male from the Rose Mound Group (Middle Mississippian, A.D. 1200–1400) in Schuyler County displays cranial and postcranial pathology suggestive of treponematosis (Morse 1967:48–52; 1978:53–55, 166–69, pls. 30 *A* and *B*, 31 *A–E*). The naso-palatine destruction is extensive, including the alveolar area, intranasal structures, and nasal bones. The maxillary incisors have been lost antemortem. Some healing is evident along the perimeter of the nasal cavity. There is slight involvement of the frontal bone. The anterior portions of both tibiae show periostitis and osteitis with cavitation, as do the distal portions of the humeri, the upper third of the right ulna, and the left clavicle. Hackett (1976:97) categorizes the long bone lesions as nodes/expansions with superficial cavitation and therefore diagnostic of treponematosis. A case described by Morse (1967:52–58, 1978:55–57, 166–69, pls. 30 *C–E*, 31 *W–Z*) in Fulton County consists of the fairly complete skeleton (T-6) of a 35-year-old male. The remains are from the Thompson site and date to the Early Mississippian period, approximately A.D. 1000. The anterior portion of the frontal displays subperiosteal thickening with cavitation of the outer table surrounded by slight erosion. Postcranial lesions are evident on the right tibia, radius, ulna, and humerus, both femora, and the right clavicle. Generally, they exhibit cortical thickening and sclerosis, with some focal destruction (pitting and sinus formation) and encroachment on the medullary cavity. Lesions on the sacrum and greater trochanter of the right femur are of a different nature and are attributed to bed sores. The skeleton of a Middle Woodland resident of Fulton County (originally described by Denninger) exhibits osteoperiostitis that Williams (1936:787) diagnoses as syphilis. Both tibiae and fibulae present bone proliferation of periosteal origin with some narrowing of the medullary cavity. Hackett (1976:97) notes the similarity of the "pronounced periostitis" on the anterior surfaces of the femora, tibiae, and fibulae in a Late Archaic Red Ocher burial (1500–1000 B.C.) from Fulton County to that in yaws patients in Uganda and in Australian Aboriginal bones. The skeleton of this 22-year-old female from the Morse site (F772, Burial 12) is described and illustrated by Morse (1978:17, 132–33, pl. 13 *A* and *B*). According to Hackett (1976:97), the long bones depicted exemplify the diagnostic nodes/ expansions with superficial cavitation.

In an epidemiological study of Illinois Woodland populations, Cook (1976, 1984) observes a pattern of osteitis and periostitis suggestive of treponematosis. In the Late Archaic Klunk skeletal series, 31 of 123 individuals (25%) exhibit treponemal lesions, whereas Middle and Late Woodland populations show an overall prevalence of approximately 50% (Cook 1984:259). The Mississippian Schild site reveals a prevalence similar to that of the Woodland groups. The prevalence of the treponemal disease and absence of indicators of congenital infection, while atypical of venereal syphilis, are characteristic of nonvenereal treponematosis (Cook 1976, 1984). Thus, yaws or endemic syphilis seems to have existed in Illinois for nearly 3,000 years.

In Arkansas, the incomplete skeleton of an adult female (NMNH 258778) discovered during Moore's excavations on the St. Francis, White, and Black Rivers in the early part of the century includes several pathological bones (Ortner and Putschar 1985:210–14, figs. 329– 32). The external table of the skull vault exhibits an "irregular lumpy appearance" with "typical gummatous lesions characterized by a mixture of bone formation and destruction" (Ortner and Putschar 1985:212). There is some involvement of the inner table. The proximal metaphysis of the left ulna and the proximal shaft of the left femur show expansion of the cortex. The entire shaft of the right femur and the left proximal tibia exhibit cortical enlargement with porosity.

The anterior surfaces consist of raised plaques and spicules. The remains are thought to be pre-Columbian.

Remains from the Late Mississippian Nodena culture (ca. A.D. 1400–1700 [D. F. Morse 1973: 83]) are reported to display evidence of treponematosis. Typical lesions are described in six skeletons and additional isolated bones from the "vicinity" of the mounds in Crittenden and Mississippi Counties in northeastern Arkansas (Wakefield, Dellinger, and Camp 1937). The tibial shaft is most often affected, and in some cases "the sharp anterior crest was replaced by a rounded surface and this thickening gave the shaft the appearance of having been bowed anteriorly" (p. 491, fig. 4). Fibulae, radii, ulnae, and clavicles show a similar "deforming osteitis." Erosion of the palate and nasal bones is evident in one skull. Extensive cranial and postcranial involvement in one skeleton (pp. 491–92, fig. 3) provides a convincing case. The cranial vault of this individual (No. 6) has a nodular surface typical of caries sicca, and the long bone X-rays reveal cortical thickening with encroachment upon the medullary canals. Although no European trade items were found with these burials, their apparent Nodena affiliation indicates that they may postdate 1492.

Morse (1973:50–52, 54–55) has also described Nodena material from Mississippi County with lesions suggestive of treponematosis. HM 916, an isolated skull of a 26-year-old female, displays "an area of sclerotic periosteal reaction with pitting over almost the entire left half of the frontal bone," substantial involvement occurring above the left orbit (fig. 27a). Steinbock (1976:96) agrees that this "closely resembles syphilis." An X-ray (Morse 1973:fig. 27b), however, reveals the presence of a mud-dauber nest inside the skull. In our opinion, the lesions are not diagnostic of treponematosis and are far more likely to have resulted from destruction by the wasps. HM 900 consists of the skull of a female aged 22 and exhibits cicatrization of the nasal aperture, with loss of the anterior nasal spine and nasal septum and involvement of the nasal bones. The entire palate is eroded, with healed sclerotic borders remaining. The maxillary sinuses have large eroded openings, and the involvement extends to the ethmoid and orbits. Morse (1973:54) attributes the observed pathology to a malignant tumor but does not rule out the possibility of treponematosis or leprosy. The lack of alveolar involvement would eliminate leprosy, and healing is not found in neoplasm (Hackett 1976:65). The absence of frontal pathology does not preclude the possibility of a treponemal lesion similar to the gangosa of yaws. Hackett (1976:63; see also Ortner and Putschar 1985:192, figs. 274–79, and Steinbock 1976:145, 151) indicates that such naso-palatine destruction is characterized by "an empty nasal cavity . . . presenting a smooth, 'bored out' tunnel-like passageway" and may be accompanied by opening of the ethmoid sinuses and partial or complete destruction of the palate and maxillary alveolus. Thus, "when extensive and healed," this type of naso-palatine destruction "is a *diagnostic criterion of syphilis*" (p. 65).

Despite excavation of nearly 2,000 Nodena burials, few complete skeletons are extant. Early excavators did not consistently save skeletal material, and the majority of the collection consists of crania and pathological specimens. Thus, of 43 relatively complete individuals from the Upper Nodena site, 37 (86%) display inflammatory lesions, as do 9 of 16 such individuals (56.3%) from the Middle Nodena site (Powell 1988*d*). Powell reports that the lower long bones show "localized patches of mild to moderate periostitis, well-healed at death, most typically affecting the anterior crests and lateral aspects of . . . tibia shafts." Several tibiae are noted to display "saber shin." Five of the individuals with mild to moderate tibial periostitis exhibit remodeled cranial lesions. Six isolated crania (one identified as HM 900) also present focal lytic lesions, in one case described as "lesions of the distinctive 'stellate' configuration associated with the gummateous skin ulcers of treponemal infection" (Alabama Museum of Natural History, Nod 432 [Powell 1988*d*:pl. 1]). The lesions evident in the photograph correspond to Hackett's

(1976:36) confluent clustered pits, diagnostic of treponematosis when accompanied by healing. From the evidence Powell concludes that an endemic treponematosis was present in the Nodena population. A high frequency of generalized periostitis, noted by several investigators (see Rose et al. 1984:414–15), is evident in skeletal series from Baytown (A.D. 300–700), Coles Creek (A.D. 700–1200), and Mississippian (A.D. 1200–1680) sites in eastern Arkansas and Louisiana, providing support for the long-standing occurrence of treponematosis in the lower Mississippi Valley.

Stewart and Quade (1969:91) describe frontal lesions in a Hopewellian skull (NMNH 379109) found near Kansas City, Missouri, as possibly due to treponematosis. The skull has three depressed scars on the middle of the frontal and similar scars around each parietal boss. At the precontact Morris site in southeastern Oklahoma, over a third of the adults exhibit "osteitis with tremendous swelling," primarily in the tibiae (Brues 1966:108–9). Brues describes a sequence of long bone lesions very similar to Hackett's (1976), culminating in the formation of pits. Cranial lesions similar to those illustrating syphilis are also noted. Two precontact skulls with "gnarled and pitted" surfaces are described by Goldstein (1957:302, pl. 1 *b–d*) as suggestive of syphilis. One skull (Cat. No. 411, Sanders Site, Lamar County) is accompanied by pathological tibiae, fibulae, and a femur (Goldstein 1957:pl. 1 *c* and *d*). The other (Cat. No. 660B, Willison Farm, Bell County) does not appear to be accompanied by postcranial remains. In South Dakota, several bones from the 14th-century Crow Creek site (39BF11) display varying degrees of periostitis, with considerable new bone formation and narrowing of the medullary cavity in some tibiae, resulting in a saber-shin appearance (Gregg, Allison, and Zimmerman 1981).

Osseous lesions from a possible syphilitic aortic aneurysm provide the only evidence of treponemal disease in a gatherer-hunter group from the northern Plains. The remains are from one of five individuals interred in the Bracken Cairn (DhOb-3) in southwestern Saskatchewan (Walker 1983:499). The site, radiocarbon-dated to 515 B.C., is affiliated with the Pelican Lake phase of the Late Archaic period. Resorptive lesions appear on the right margin of the manubrium, the sternal end of the right clavicle, and the left side of the centra of the second and third thoracic vertebrae of a 36–46-year-old male. Walker suggests (pp. 501–2) that the erosion is due to pulsation of an aneurysm. Clinical descriptions indicate that syphilitic aneurysms typically occur on the ascending aorta and cause pulsation of the right sternoclavicular joint. In contrast, aneurysms due to atherosclerosis are very rare in the aortic arch and in the age-group of this individual.

Evidence of pre-Columbian treponematosis is lacking in northwestern North America. Syphilitic skeletal material abounds, however, in 18th- and 19th-century Alaskan material (see Cook 1985; Holcomb 1940; Meer 1985; Ortner and Putschar 1985:214–18, figs. 333–40), where venereal syphilis was apparently introduced after Russian contact. In California, nine individuals exhibiting periostitis suggestive of treponematosis were recovered from a Middle Horizon (500–200 B.C.) site in Sonoma County (Son 299; Roney 1966:101–2). A Late Horizon specimen (Scr.I.83.4434) has been radiocarbon-dated to A.D. 1105 (Brothwell and Burleigh 1975:394). Tenney's (1986) survey of osteological material in the Lowie Museum of Anthropology disclosed many individuals with generalized skeletal lesions like those expected in treponematosis. Nasal destruction, palatal perforation, cranial sclerotic new bone formation, and fusiform tibial lesions without cloacae are noted.

In the Southwestern United States, additional evidence of pre-Columbian treponematosis has accumulated. Hyde (1891:119–20, 124–28, fig. 6) reported two pathological tibiae from a prehistoric (Basket-maker?) burial found near the Animas River, about 45 miles from Durango, Colorado. The tibiae are enlarged, and the surfaces of both shafts are roughened and porous,

with apparent striations and "superficial erosions" resulting from a "chronic inflammatory process." The left tibia appears bowed. While syphilis is not ruled out as the cause of this "chronic rarefying and formative osteitis, with osteomyelitis and chronic formative periostitis," it is indicated that such a diagnosis may not be justified (pp. 127–28). At Mesa Verde National Park, the remains of a 24-year-old male from the Pueblo III (A.D. 1100–1300) Mug House exhibits bilateral symmetrical enlargement and bowing of the tibiae in the anterior-posterior plane (Miles 1966:96; 1975:28, fig. 33). Although treponematosis is possible, the smooth periosteal surface does not support such a diagnosis (Miles 1975:28).

The skull and right femur of an adult female (Case 60455) from Pecos Pueblo, New Mexico, excavated by Kidder and originally described by Hooton (1930), show caries sicca on the frontal and parietals, partial destruction of the nasal bones, with subsequent healing, and dense periosteal bone apposition on the femur (Williams 1932:932–34). Hackett (1976:109) concurs with Williams's diagnosis of syphilis in this individual. Two other crania from Pecos Pueblo (Cases 59864 and 59814) exhibit cicatrization of the nasal and palatal areas (Williams 1932:934–37) similar to that described in the Arkansas HM 900 skull. Ceramics associated with these remains indicate that they date to the Pueblo IV period (A.D. 1300–1540). Case 59814 dates to the latter portion of this period and may not be pre-Columbian. Elsewhere in New Mexico, an isolated tibia (SM 56A) recovered from Smokey Bear Ruin exhibits periostitis and deformation due to considerable subperiosteal bone apposition (El-Najjar 1979:604, fig. 3*b* and *c*). Sequestra and cloacae are absent. Ceramics indicate that the site was used around A.D. 1250–1350.

Scattered sites in Arizona have yielded further evidence of treponematosis. Williams (1936: 786–87) reports that a skeleton from the Basketmaker period (ca. 200 B.C.–A.D. 700) exhibits lesions in four long bones accompanied by a stellate scar on the skull, which he attributes to syphilis. Of some 400 burials from Tuzigoot Ruin, near Clarkdale (south of Flagstaff), one skull shows extensive destruction of the frontal and nasal bones and perforation of the palate (Denninger 1938). Tuzigoot was inhabited from about A.D. 1000–1350. A 20–25-year-old female (CdC No. 2) from a Pueblo II (A.D. 900–1100) site at Canyon de Chelly displays gummatous destruction and bone necrosis producing a "worm-eaten" appearance of the cranial vault (El-Najjar 1979:604–5, fig. 4 *a* and *b*). The photographs are illustrative of Hackett's (1976:43–45) diagnostic criteria of serpiginous and nodular cavitation. South of Canyon de Chelly, near Fort Apache, 2 of 57 individuals excavated at Kinishba and Vandal Cave are suspected of suffering from treponematosis. Tree-ring dates at Kinishba range from A.D. 1233 to 1306, while the Basketmaker II and Pueblo III occupations at Vandal Cave date from A.D. 608 to 683 and prior to A.D. 1300 respectively (Cole et al. 1955: 231). Pronounced fusiform expansion and focal pitting of the cortex of the right tibia shaft accompany periosteal bone proliferation in the skull of A-17-0-17 from Kinishba (pp. 232–35, figs. 1–3). An isolated right tibia from Vandal Cave (VI-B-5) has a saber-shin appearance caused by deposition of new periosteal bone on the anterior aspect of the shaft (pp. 235–36, fig. 4). In the Salt River Valley, near Phoenix, excavations conducted at Los Muertos in the late 1890s revealed several skeletons that suggest the possibility of treponematosis. Matthews, Wortman, and Billings (1893:172) describe one individual with "irregular nodular hypertrophy" of the shafts of both tibiae, both ulnae, and the distal right fibula and other individuals with involvement of the tibial shafts alone. Los Muertos is a Classic Hohokam site, dating between A.D. 1100 and 1450 (Gumerman and Haury 1979).

Mexican remains also provide evidence of pre-Columbian treponematosis. Goff (1963; 1967:289–91, figs. 2–6, 9–11) attributes pathological changes in 20 skulls and several long bones from Cueva de la Candelaria, Coahuila,

northeastern Mexico, to treponemal infection. The skulls exhibit osteitis and periostitis resulting in a nodular appearance. In one case (1967:fig. 3), an active lesion surrounded by serpiginous and nodular cavitation is apparent. The long bones illustrated (figs. 9–11) present fusiform expansion of the shafts. Dating of the site does not seem well established and ranges from the 6th to the 16th century (p. 289). Williams (1936:784–85, fig. 1) reports that a pre-Hispanic Aztec skull from Santiago Tlaltelolco (near Mexico City) exhibits two lesions, one of which has destroyed nearly half of the frontal. This defect is accompanied by reactive bone formation at the perimeter, resulting in "the characteristic worm-eaten appearance seen on some syphilitic skulls," and resembles the active lesion described in the Candelaria skull. The skull of an adult male, dated to 300 B.C., from the Tehuacán Valley in Puebla exhibits similar destruction of the cranial vault (Anderson 1965).

Mayan remains from Central America also include individuals with apparent treponemal disease. Goff (1967:288–89, fig. 7) refers to two crania from Zaculeu, Guatemala (A.D. 900–1000), as syphilitic. One shows apparent caries sicca on the frontal, while the other displays a large parietal defect with no evident healing and periostitis on the frontal. Inflammatory lesions in ten individuals (15.9% of adults) buried at Altar de Sacrificios, Guatemala, before A.D. 950 exhibit osteitis suggestive of treponematosis (Saul 1972). Cranial lesions alone are evident in two individuals (table 8). Burial No. 96 (fig. 10) exhibits periostitis, which is not diagnostic. Cranial lesions of Burial No. 129 (p. 42, fig. 7) may actually be due to postmortem insect damage. Six individuals show only postcranial involvement, while two have both cranial and postcranial lesions (table 8). Postcranial lesions consist of cortical thickening and enlargement of the long bone shafts, resulting in the saber-shin tibia evident in Burial No. 112 (figs. 22–24). In Belize, a Mayan tomb revealed the remains of an adult male with enlarged tibiae presenting a surface "covered with a number of small nodular outgrowths, between which were small pits or depressions" (Gann 1901:969). With this skeleton were three clay figures of men performing an operation with a pointed implement on the head of the disproportionately large penis and "a natural-sized model of the human penis in a state of semi-erection" on which "three longitudinal incisions" were made on the glans (p. 969). Gann takes this as evidence that the buried individual suffered from a venereal disease and that this disease, as indicated by osseous involvement of the tibiae, was syphilis.

South American evidence of pre-Columbian treponematosis comes primarily from Peru. At Paracas, two individuals from tombs excavated by Julio Tello in 1929 are considered by Williams (1932:937–46) to be syphilitic. The remains are affiliated with the early Nazca culture, approximately 200 B.C. (Lanning 1967:25–27, 122; Williams 1932:938). The first individual displays stellate scars (caries sicca) over much of the cranium. The accompanying long bones (both femurs and the left tibia, humerus, and ulna) show marked periosteal bone apposition with some encroachment upon the medullary canal and present nodular surfaces with small openings. The second, mummified individual suffered from a large ulcer on the roof of the mouth that had perforated the hard palate. The lower portion of the body was poorly preserved. Hackett (1976:109), referring to the photographs of the Paracas crania, indicates that the diagnosis of syphilis in both cases "may not be acceptable." Although his caution is justified, the photographs and description do lend credence to a diagnosis of treponemal infection in the first case.

A burial excavated by Kroeber in the Cañete Valley, Peru, dated about A.D. 500, is also described as syphilitic (Williams 1932:948–54). Although the skull is normal, a chronic inflammatory osteoperiostitis produced "dense, ivory-like bone" over the entire shaft of the left femur and both tibiae, with some encroachment upon the medullary canal. The left fibula is involved to a lesser extent. The lateral view of the right tibia indicates considerable bone apposition on the anterior aspect. Hackett (1976:109) states that these long bones do not exhibit lesions diagnostic of treponemal disease, but according to Williams (1932:948) "the absence of sequestrums and of deep sinuses tends to exclude non-syphilitic periostitis and osteomyelitis."

An eight-year-old child from Machu Picchu (Peabody Museum, New Haven, No. 51–9210) dated ca. A.D. 1100–1200 allegedly exhibits congenital syphilis (Goff 1967:293, fig. 12; Williams 1932:972). Lesions are evident on the frontal and are accompanied by saber-shin tibiae. No reference is made to the dentition. Other tibiae in this series exhibit similar enlargement (Williams 1932:972). MacCurdy (1932:264, pls. 38, 41) reports three cases of possible syphilis at sites in the Urubamba Valley near Cuzco. The cranium of a six-year-old from Paucarcancha (Cat. No. 51) exhibits considerable necrosis of the left parietal and frontal. At Patallacta, the left parietal of an eight-year-old child (Cat. No. 938) has a circular area of necrosis 4.2 cm in diameter, and the cranium of a 26-year-old male (Cat. No. 635) displays an area of necrosis nearly 5 cm in diameter that has a large perforation at its center. In none of these cases is reactive new bone formation apparent; therefore treponematosis is probably not the cause. Williams (1932:972) agrees with this assessment in the first two cases but considers the adult male a possible example of syphilis. The apparent Inca affiliation of these sites indicates that they may be post-Columbian.

At Aguazuque, a preceramic site in central Colombia, 13 of 40 individuals (32.5%) demonstrate lesions associated with treponematosis, particularly in the tibia, in some resulting in a saber-shin deformity (Correal Urrego 1987). Three of these individuals also display caries sicca. A skeleton with both cranial and postcranial lesions is radiocarbon-dated to 2080 B.C. (4030 ± 80 B.P.). Correal Urrego suggests that since yaws is rare in this part of modern Colombia the pathology stems from venereal syphilis.

In Argentina, a pre-Columbian skull from Río Negro is regarded as above suspicion by

Williams (1932:946–48, 976) although he did not personally examine it. It had previously been described as exhibiting "little elevations and depressions that were like scars" and pronounced syphilitic by Broca and other European authorities. From the Chubut River valley, a probably pre-Columbian skull shows gummatous lesions (p. 973). Another skull, from Calchaqui, exhibits a mass of smooth-edged scars, with thickening of adjacent areas and nasal destruction accompanied by healing (pp. 973–74).

DISCUSSION

Review of the documentary and skeletal evidence for pre-Columbian syphilis reveals many ambiguities in dates and differential diagnosis. What, then, can be determined from the evidence?

Is it possible that syphilis and leprosy were confused before the 1490s? Ancient and medieval texts portray leprosy as a highly contagious disease with a short incubation period, associated with immorality, sexually and congenitally transmitted, and responding to mercury treatment (Holcomb 1935:297–303; Hudson 1972:149). Leprosy has none of these characteristics. Syphilis, however, is not the only disease that manifests such features. It is just as likely that such descriptions refer to other venereal or skin diseases. Drawing diagnostic conclusions from these accounts is "unconscionable," as one is "faced with a spectrum of dermatologic diseases, exanthems, leprosy, tuberculosis, and epidemics in the Middle Ages of louse-borne typhus, bubonic plague, and widespread ergotism" (Kampmeier 1984:28).

Many authorities (e.g., Brown et al. 1970:82; Harrison 1986:51; Kampmeier 1984:19, 21, 28; Sussman 1967:214; see also Rosebury 1971:20–21) attribute biblical and other ancient disease descriptions such as those previously summarized to gonorrhea rather than syphilis. Galen, in the 2d century A.D., invented the term "gonorrhea" (seed flow) to describe the discharge as-

sociated with the disease (Brown et al. 1970:82; Kampmeier 1984:28). The hard and soft genital sores described by Galen and Celsus may have been not syphilitic condylomata but evidence of chancroid, genital herpes, venereal warts, granuloma inguinale of leishmaniasis, or other nonvenereal skin diseases (Kampmeier 1984:26–27). Along with cutaneous lesions and granuloma inguinale, leishmaniasis may also cause destruction of the nasopharynx (Steinbock 1976:151). In addition to syphilis, several other diseases causing skin lesions can cross the placenta to infect the fetus. Among these are rubella (German measles), measles, smallpox (variola), chickenpox and shingles (varicella-zoster virus), genital herpes, and gonorrhea (Rosebury 1971:55–56). All of these are highly contagious diseases with short incubation periods, and the latter two are acquired through sexual intercourse.

Mercury treatment has been cited by proponents of the pre-Columbian hypothesis as proof that ancient "leprosy" was syphilis. Mercury, however, was commonly prescribed for many disorders. In his medical treatise of 1546, Fracastor advocates rubbing mercurial ointment on the inner arms to cure a severe headache (Rosebury 1971:47). Although application of mercury is known to have an effect on syphilis, it also results in a rapid reduction in gonorrheal discharge and probably relieved symptoms of several other diseases (Harrison 1959:6–7; cf. Hudson 1961:548–49).

Did an epidemic of syphilis begin in the late 1490s? The documentary evidence regarding the appearance of a new disease is ambiguous in terms of symptoms described, but the numerous ordinances passed throughout Europe in the late 1490s in an effort to control the disease and the proliferation of publications regarding it indicate that a highly contagious infection that caused genital and cutaneous lesions was raging at that time.

Was this epidemic the result of differentiation of syphilis and its widespread recognition as a disease distinct from "leprosy"? In support of the pre-Columbian hypothesis, it has been noted that leprosy declined at this time and that edicts regarding the new disease were quite similar to those previously issued to isolate lepers. The characteristic hard chancre of syphilis was first described in 1514 by de Vigo, and syphilitic and nonsyphilitic condylomata were differentiated in 1563 (Brown et al. 1970:82; Kampmeier 1984:26–27). It is possible, however, that these lesions were not described prior to 1500 because they did not previously exist in the Old World. Holcomb (1934, 1935) has explained the decline in "leprosy" as a transference of the symptoms associated with that disease to syphilis. If the two diseases were differentiated by the late 1490s, why do 16th-century descriptions continue to apply the term "leprosy" to syphilis? Paracelsus (1493–1541), for example, thought that "leprosy and venereal bubas" (quoted by Brody [1974:56–57]) were the first stage of syphilis. His description is usually explained as confusion of syphilis with gonorrhea (Brown et al. 1970:82; Kampmeier 1984:26). Similar diagnostic difficulties plagued scholars of the 16th through 19th centuries until syphilis and gonorrhea were finally differentiated (Brown et al. 1970:82–83; Hackett 1963:29; Kampmeier 1984:26–28; Rosebury 1971:181). By the end of the 15th century "leprosy" had become identified with syphilis to the extent that Job, once the patron saint of lepers, became the patron saint of syphilitics (Brody 1974:56–58, 191–92; Creighton 1965 [1894]:102). Although the symptoms were being transferred from one disease to another, it appears that syphilis was being grouped with ailments having similar symptoms rather than being differentiated from them. This would seem to indicate that syphilis was a new disease.

Was the epidemic of venereal syphilis due to increasing urbanization and improved hygiene in late 15th-century Europe? The decline in the incidence of leprosy actually began in the 14th century and has been attributed to improved living conditions (Clay 1966 [1909]:41–43; Rubin 1974:151–53). The incidence of nonvenereal treponematosis, if it had been present in Europe, would also have decreased with such improve-

ments. Hudson (1961:548; 1965a:897) postulates that endemic syphilis was present in Europe from Roman times and retreated to rural areas in the Balkans, Russia, and Scandinavia as standards of living rose during the Middle Ages. In the meantime, the treponeme was increasingly being transmitted sexually in the more advanced areas, culminating in the identification of syphilis at the end of the 15th century. Endemic syphilis, associated with poor hygiene and primitive living conditions, did exist in Europe until the mid-1800s—as sibbens in Scotland, button scurvy in Ireland, *radesyge* in Norway, *saltfluss* in Sweden, and *spirocolon* in Greece and Russia—but was not recognized until the middle of the 17th century (Morton 1967:374; Steinbock 1976:138). In Scotland, the introduction of endemic syphilis was blamed on Cromwell's army in 1650 (Morton 1967:374–75). In contrast, edicts concerning venereal syphilis were issued in Aberdeen and Edinburgh in 1497. Thus, while the cities and towns were ravaged by a venereal disease, treponemal infection seems to have spread slowly to the countryside, where social conditions allowed nonvenereal transmission to prevail. The epidemiological aspects of the unitarian hypothesis are supported. However, if syphilis was recognized as a distinct disease at the end of the 15th century, documentary evidence indicates that the venereal form of treponematosis was the first to appear, followed by reversion to an endemic form in rural areas. Again, rather than supporting the pre-Columbian existence of treponematosis, a case can be made for the appearance of a new disease which was subsequently included in a category of maladies manifesting similar lesions.

As Hudson (1968:6) indicates, "by selecting the 'right' witnesses and dates and discarding the rest, it is possible to build a case for either view, depending on the credibility of the witnesses and the credulity of the reader." On the basis of the documentary evidence prior to 1492, syphilis cannot be excluded from the list of diseases that may have been grouped under the term "leprosy." The lack of syphilitic skeletal material in

European leper cemeteries, combined with the dearth of Old World remains that have even been suggested to exhibit treponemal lesions, however, precludes this possibility. If treponematosis evolved with *Homo,* as postulated in the unitarian hypothesis, and was among the diseases described in biblical, Greek, Roman, and medieval texts, then skeletal evidence suggestive of treponematosis should be abundant in the materials recovered from Old World sites. The case for pre-Columbian syphilis in the Old World rests solely on vague and ambiguous disease descriptions and must, therefore, be rejected.

Was syphilis present in the New World before 1492? A substantial amount of documentary evidence from the early 16th century indicates that it was. These documents, as previously discussed, present ambiguous descriptions and inconsistencies in dates. Williams and coworkers (1927:686) find the Native American linguistic evidence tenuous because of possible confusion of syphilis and yaws. The absence of the dental stigmata associated with congenital syphilis (with the possible exception of the child from Virginia) has been cited as proof that venereal syphilis did not exist in the New World. The etiological unity of the treponemal syndromes, however, renders such objections moot.

Despite Williams's (1932:977) assertion that the amount of New World skeletal evidence of treponematosis is "almost embarrassing" in comparison with the Old World data, Hackett (1976:111) is alarmed that few pre-Columbian American bones (about 1 in 500) exhibit the diagnostic criteria of treponematosis. It must be reiterated that bone lesions are expected in only 1–5% of individuals in skeletal series from areas in which yaws or endemic syphilis occurred. Furthermore, a considerable amount of material has come to light since Hackett's review. Investigations in the Midwestern and Southeastern United States (e.g., Cassidy 1980, 1984; Cook 1976, 1984; Powell 1988*a, b*) reveal treponemal infections involving up to half of the population. While these reports differentiate localized inflammatory lesions from the syndrome of diffuse periostitis suggestive of treponematosis, the reported frequencies are so high that attribution to a single infectious disease may be questionable. Hill (1986) cautions that "postcranial marrow hypertrophy associated with acute and chronic anemia in children is virtually indistinguishable from generalized periostitis indicative of infection" and that "postcranial periosteal lesions associated with cranial porotic hyperostosis have been treated as a separate entity, i.e., infection." While the synergism of infection and nutritional deficiencies (such as iron deficiency anemia) cannot be overlooked, the appearance of diagnostic changes in some individuals from these skeletal populations indicates that a treponemal infection was undoubtedly present in the eastern half of the United States from Late Archaic times (as early as 3000 B.C.) and contributed to the generalized periosteal involvement evident in these remains.

The nature of the skeletal evidence found in North and South America is explained by treponemal epidemiology. The apparent absence of congenital syphilis is not surprising, considering that most of the populations in pre-Columbian times were gatherer-hunters or horticulturalists residing in small camps or villages rather than large cities. The prevailing hygienic conditions would be insufficient to prohibit transmission of the treponeme by casual contact among children. Such a pattern probably characterized more populous areas prior to European contact as well. The high frequency of treponemal lesions reported in some skeletal series may reflect population nucleation, particularly where sociopolitical organization allowed for widespread exchange of material goods and infectious diseases, as among Middle Woodland and Mississippian groups (cf. Buikstra 1984:229–30; Cassidy 1980:137; 1984:334–35; Cook 1984:261–62; Larsen 1984:379–80; Perzigian, Tench, and Braun 1984:356–58; Rose et al. 1984:415–18). Skeletal series in the pre-Columbian New World would therefore be expected to display a pattern of pathological involvement more typical of nonvenereal than of venereal syphilis—a situation encountered in several large skeletal series from the eastern half of the United States. As Buikstra (1979:232) has indicated, "it appears that certain forms of intercourse are less important in explaining the archaeological record than previously suggested."

The absence of skeletal evidence of treponematosis in the Old World and the abundance of such evidence in the New necessitates revision of Hudson's thesis that treponematosis originated in Africa and was subsequently carried throughout the world in the course of human migrations. It appears, instead, that treponematosis is a relatively new disease that originated in the tropical or temperate zone of the Americas and was spread by casual contact. This nonvenereal infection is the disease that was initially contracted by Columbus's crew, but social and environmental conditions in Europe at that time were conducive to its venereal dissemination in urban areas. The transition of one treponemal syndrome to another under differing environmental and social circumstances has been frequently documented in modern populations (e.g., Grin 1961; Hudson 1965a:889; 1965b: 743–44; Willcox 1974:174).

This contention will undoubtedly meet with much dissent. Although there is universal agreement that Native American populations were decimated by diseases introduced by Europeans to which they had no immunity, the possibility of a parallel introduction of American diseases into Europe is rejected. Nearly 30 years ago, Harrison (1959:7) suggested that "if one could test mummies for antibodies to *T. pallidum* . . . one might perhaps settle this eternal question of the birth-place of syphilis." He thought his suggestion far-fetched, but immunological tests have recently been attempted on skeletal materials. An effort to inoculate rabbits with an extract from a pathological Crow Creek specimen to produce an antibody titre indicative of the presence of treponematosis ended with the animals' death (due to *Clostridium* contamination) before any results could be obtained (Gregg et al. 1981). A method developed in Czechoslovakia

has proved capable of determining the presence of *Treponema* in a recent case of yaws from an Australian bone sample and in European cases of syphilis from the 16th and 19th centuries (Smrcka 1985). The most recent and significant immunological test has demonstrated the presence of treponemal antigen in the remains of a Pleistocene bear from Indiana radiocarbon-dated to 11,500 ± 520 B.P. (Rothschild and Turnbull 1987). Skeletal lesions include gumma formation and periosteal reaction in the mandible, humeri, radii, and ulna and in three thoracic vertebrae. Immunofluorescence analysis of histological sections revealed the presence of treponemal antigens, while tests for *Neisseria gonorrhea, Streptococcus,* and *Legionella pneumophilia* were negative. The pursuit of similar immunological analyses in pre-Columbian remains with skeletal lesions suggestive of treponemal infection should eventually resolve the controversy.

CONCLUSION

Current attention is focused on the epidemic of AIDS, which is similar in some respects to the epidemic of syphilis nearly 500 years ago. Because of disease synergism and the numerous complications that may finally cause the death of an AIDS patient, the question arises how long AIDS was present in human populations before it was recognized as a distinct disease. The AIDS virus has been recently discovered in tissue saved after the puzzling death of a St. Louis teenager in 1969, a decade before AIDS was recognized elsewhere in the United States (Associated Press 1987). As with syphilis, it could be argued that the "epidemic" of AIDS is a result of its differentiation from an array of complications with which it was previously confused. Arguments as to its point of origin (e.g., African green monkeys, Haitians, homosexual males, etc.) have ensued.

Recent research reveals that a positive serological test for syphilis in men, a history of syphilis in men, and a history of genital warts in women are significantly associated with seropositivity for human immunodeficiency virus (HIV), which causes AIDS (Quinn et al. 1988). Thus, sexually transmitted diseases which disrupt epithelial surfaces (particularly syphilis) may increase the efficiency of HIV transmission (Quinn et al. 1988: 201–2). In light of these findings and the recent report that syphilis is at its highest level in the United States since 1950 (NBC News, January 28, 1988), it is apparent that the attention accorded syphilis in the past is likely to be renewed.

This review of the documentary and skeletal evidence of treponematosis supports the Columbian hypothesis. The abundance of New World human skeletal material exhibiting lesions suggestive of treponemal infection, particularly when encountered in large skeletal populations, and the discovery of treponemal antigens in the remains of a Pleistocene bear from the Midwestern United States clearly demonstrate the presence of the disease prior to 1492. The paucity of possible treponemal lesions in the vast collections of pre-Columbian Old World skeletal remains is a telling contrast to the New World situation. Newly developed immunological analysis should finally lay the controversy regarding the origin of syphilis to rest.

REFERENCES

ANDERSEN, J. G. 1969. Studies in the mediaeval diagnosis of leprosy in Denmark. *Danish Medical Bulletin* 16(suppl. 9):1–142.

ANDERSON, JAMES E. 1965. Human skeletons of Tehuacan. *Science* 148:496–97.

ASSOCIATED PRESS. 1987. Report says AIDS surfaced in 1969. *Boston Globe,* October 25, p. 21.

BAKER, BRENDA J. 1985. Use of written documentation in diagnoses of pre-Columbian syphilis. Paper presented at the 12th annual meeting of the Paleopathology Association, Knoxville, Tenn.

BRODY, SAUL N. 1974. *The disease of the soul: Leprosy in medieval literature.* Ithaca: Cornell University Press.

BROTHWELL, DON. 1961. The palaeopathology of early British man: An essay on the problems of diagnosis and analysis. *Journal of the Royal Anthropological Institute* 91:318–44.

BROTHWELL, DON, AND RICHARD BURLEIGH. 1975. Radiocarbon dates and the history of treponematoses in man. *Journal of Archaeological Sciences* 2:393–96.

BROWN, WILLIAM J., JAMES F. DONOHUE, NORMAN W. AXNICK, JOSEPH H. BLOUNT, NEAL H. EWEN, AND OSCAR G. JONES. 1970. *Syphilis and other venereal diseases.* Cambridge: Harvard University Press.

BROWNE, S. G. 1970. How old is leprosy? *British Medical Journal* 3:640–41.

BRUES, ALICE M. 1966. "Discussion," in *Human palaeopathology.* Edited by Saul Jarcho, pp. 107–12. New Haven: Yale University Press.

BRÜHL, G. 1890. Pre-Columbian syphilis in the Western Hemisphere. *Cincinnati Lancet-Clinic* 63:275–80.

BUIKSTRA, JANE E. 1979. "Contribution of physical anthropologists to the concept of Hopewell: A historical perspective," in *Hopewell archaeology.* Edited by David S. Brose and N'omi Greber, pp. 220–33. Kent: Kent State University Press.

——— 1984. "The lower Illinois River region: A prehistoric context for the study of ancient diet and health," in *Paleopathology at the origins of agriculture.* Edited by Mark N. Cohen and George J. Armelagos, pp. 215–34. Orlando: Academic Press.

BULLEN, ADELAIDE K. 1972. Paleoepidemiology and distribution of prehistoric treponemiasis (syphilis) in Florida. *Florida Anthropologist* 25:133–74.

CANNEFAX, GEORGE R., LESLIE C. NORINS, AND EUGENE J. GILLESPIE. 1967. Immunology of syphilis. *Annual Review of Medicine* 18:471–82.

CASSIDY, CLAIRE MONOD. 1980. "Nutrition and health in agriculturalists and hunter-gatherers," in *Nutritional anthropology.* Edited by Norge W. Jerome, Randy F. Kandel, and Gretel H. Pelto, pp. 117–45. Pleasantville: Redgrave.

——— 1984. "Skeletal evidence for prehistoric subsistence adaptation in the central Ohio River valley," in *Paleopathology at the origins of agriculture.* Edited by Mark N. Cohen and George J. Armelagos, pp. 307–45. Orlando: Academic Press.

CHAMBERLAIN, W. E., N. E. WAYSON, AND L. H. GARLAND. 1931. The bone and joint changes of leprosy: A roentgenologic study. *Radiology* 17:930–39.

CLAY, ROTHA MARY. 1966 (1909). 2d edition. *The me-*

diaeval hospitals of England. New York: Barnes and Noble.

COCHRANE, R. G. Editor. 1959. *Leprosy in theory and practice.* Bristol: John Wright.

COCKBURN, T. A. 1961. The origin of the treponematoses. *Bulletin of the World Health Organization* 24: 221–28.

———. 1963. *The evolution and eradication of infectious diseases.* Baltimore: Johns Hopkins Press.

COLE, HAROLD N., JAMES C. HARKIN, BERTRAM S. KRAUS, AND ALAN R. MORITZ. 1955. Pre-Columbian osseous syphilis. *Archives of Dermatology* 71:231–38.

COOK, DELLA COLLINS. 1976. Pathologic states and disease process in Illinois Woodland populations: An epidemiologic approach. Ph.D. diss., University of Chicago, Chicago, Ill.

———. 1984. "Subsistence and health in the lower Illinois Valley: Osteological evidence," in *Paleopathology at the origins of agriculture.* Edited by Mark N. Cohen and George J. Armelagos, pp. 235–69. Orlando: Academic Press.

———. 1985. Treponematosis in the Chirikof Island population. Paper presented at the 54th annual meeting of the American Association of Physical Anthropologists, Knoxville, Tenn. (Abstracted in *American Journal of Physical Anthropology* 66: 158.)

CORREAL URREGO, GONZALO. 1987. Paleopathology in preceramic bones from Colombia: Examples of syphilitic lesions from the site of Aguazuque, Soacha. Paper presented at the 14th annual meeting of the Paleopathology Association, New York, N.Y.

CREIGHTON, CHARLES. 1965 (1894). 2d edition. *A history of epidemics in Britain.* Vol. 1. *From A.D. 664 to the Great Plague.* New York: Barnes and Noble.

CROSBY, ALFRED W., JR. 1969. The early history of syphilis: A reappraisal. *American Anthropologist* 71:218–27.

———. 1972. *The Columbian exchange: Biological and cultural consequences of 1492.* Westport: Greenwood Press. [RS]

DENNIE, CHARLES C. 1962. *A history of syphilis.* Springfield: Thomas.

DENNINGER, HENRI S. 1938. Syphilis of Pueblo skulls before 1350. *Archives of Pathology* 26:724–27.

DOLS, MICHAEL W. 1979. Leprosy in medieval Arabic medicine. *Journal of the History of Medicine and Allied Sciences* 314–33.

DRUTZ, DAVID J. 1981. "Leprosy," in *The science and practice of clinical medicine,* vol. 8, *Infectious diseases.* Edited by Jay P. Sanford and James P. Luby, pp. 298–305. New York: Grune and Stratton.

EL-NAJJAR, MAHMOUD Y. 1979. Human treponematosis and tuberculosis: Evidence from the New World. *American Journal of Physical Anthropology* 51:599–618.

ELTING, JAMES J., AND WILLIAM A. STARNA. 1984. A possible case of pre-Columbian treponematosis from New York State. *American Journal of Physical Anthropology* 65:267–73.

ESGUERRA-GÓMEZ, GONZALO, AND EMILIO ACOSTA. 1948. Bone and joint lesions in leprosy. *Radiology* 50:619–31.

FAGET, G. H., AND A. MAYORAL. 1944. Bone changes in leprosy: A clinical and roentgenologic study of 505 cases. *Radiology* 42:1–13.

FIELDSTEEL, A. HOWARD. 1983. "Genetics of *Treponema,*" in *Pathogenesis and immunology of treponemal infection.* (Immunology Series 20.) Edited by Ronald F. Schell and Daniel M. Musher, pp. 39–55. New York: Marcel Dekker.

FULDAUER, A., A. H. BRACHT, AND W. R. K. PERIZONIUS. 1984. Difficulties in scoring syphilis: The limits of systematic diachronic paleopathology. Paper presented at the 5th European Members' Meeting of the Paleopathology Association, Siena, Italy.

GANN, THOMAS. 1901. Recent discoveries in Central America proving the pre-Columbian syphilis in the New World. *Lancet* 2:968–70.

GOFF, CHARLES W. 1963. New evidence of syphilis(?), yaws(?) from Cueva de la Candelaria, Mexico. (Abstract.) *American Journal of Physical Anthropology* 21:402.

———. 1967. "Syphilis," in *Diseases in antiquity.* Edited by Don Brothwell and A. T. Sandison, pp. 279–93. Springfield: Thomas.

GOLDSTEIN, MARCUS S. 1957. Skeletal pathology of early Indians in Texas. *American Journal of Physical Anthropology* 15:299–311.

GORDON, BENJAMIN L. 1959 *Medieval and Renaissance medicine.* New York: Philosophical Library.

GREGG, JOHN B., MARVIN J. ALLISON, AND LARRY J. ZIMMERMAN. 1981. Possible treponematosis in fourteenth-century Dakota Territory: A progress report. *Paleopathology Newsletter,* no. 34, pp. 5–6.

GRIN, E. J. 1956. Endemic syphilis and yaws. *Bulletin of the World Health Organization* 15:959–73. [MLP]

———. 1961. Endemic treponematoses in the Sudan. *Bulletin of the World Health Organization* 24: 229–38.

GUMERMAN, GEORGE J., AND EMIL W. HAURY. 1979. "Prehistory: Hohokam," in *Handbook of North American Indians,* vol. 9, *Southwest,* Edited by Alfonso Ortiz. Washington, D.C.: Smithsonian Institution.

GUTHE, T., AND R. R. WILLCOX. 1954. Treponematoses: A world problem. *Chronicle of the World Health Organization* 8:37–113.

HACKETT, C. J. 1951. *Bone lesions of yaws in Uganda.* Oxford: Blackwell Scientific Publications.

——— 1963. On the origin of the human treponematoses. *Bulletin of the World Health Organization* 29:7–41.

——— 1967. "The human treponematoses," in *Diseases in antiquity,* Edited by Don Brothwell and A. T. Sandison, pp. 152–69. Springfield: Thomas.

——— 1976. *Diagnostic criteria of syphilis, yaws, and treponarid (treponematoses) and of some other diseases in dry bones.* Berlin: Springer-Verlag.

HALTOM, W. L., AND A. R. SHANDS, JR. 1938. Evidences of syphilis in Mound Builders' bones. *Archives of Pathology* 25:228–42.

HANSEN, KLAUS, KELD HVID-JACOBSEN, HELLE LINDEWALD, PER SOELBERG SORENSEN, AND KAARE WEISMANN. 1984. Bone lesions in early syphilis detected by bone scintigraphy. *British Journal of Venereal Diseases* 60:265–68.

HARRISON, L. W. 1959. The origin of syphilis. *British Journal of Venereal Diseases* 60:265–68.

HARRISON, WILLIAM O. 1986. "Gonorrhea," in *Sexually transmitted diseases.* Edited by Yehudi M. Felman, pp. 51–63. New York: Churchill Livingstone.

HILL, M. CASSANDRA. 1986. Postcranial periostitis: A problematic in the differential diagnosis of porotic hyperostosis and infection. Paper presented at the 55th annual meeting of the American Association of Physical Anthropologists, Albuquerque, N.M. (Abstracted in *American Journal of Physical Anthropology* 69:214.)

HOLCOMB, RICHMOND C. 1934. Christopher Columbus and the American origin of syphilis. *United States Naval Medical Bulletin* 32:401–30.

——— 1935. The antiquity of syphilis. *Medical Life* 42:275–325.

——— 1940. Syphilis of the skull among Aleuts and the Asian and North American Eskimo about Bering and Arctic Seas. *United States Naval Medical Bulletin* 38:177–92.

HOOTON, EARNEST A. 1930. *The Indians of Pecos Pueblo.* New Haven: Yale University Press.

HOVIND-HOUGEN, KARI. 1983. "Morphology," in *Pathogenesis and immunology of treponemal infection.* (Immunology Series 20.) Edited by Ronald F. Schell and Daniel M. Musher, pp. 3–28. New York: Marcel Dekker.

HUDSON, ELLIS HERNDON. 1961. Historical approach to the terminology of syphilis. *Archives of Dermatology* 84:545–62.

——— 1963a. Treponematosis and anthropology. *Annals of Internal Medicine* 58:1037–49.

——— 1963b. Treponematosis and pilgrimage. *American Journal of the Medical Sciences* 246:645–56.

——— 1964. Treponematosis and African slavery. *British Journal of Venereal Diseases* 40:43–52.

——— 1965a. Treponematosis and man's social evolution. *American Anthropologist* 67:885–901.

——— 1965b. Treponematosis in perspective. *Bulletin of the World Health Organization* 32:735–48.

——— 1968. Christopher Columbus and the history of syphilis. *Acta Tropica* 25:1–16.

——— 1972. Diagnosing a case of venereal disease in fifteenth-century Scotland. *British Journal of Venereal Disease* 48:146–53.

HULSE, E. V. 1975. The nature of biblical "leprosy" and the use of alternative medical terms in modern translations of the Bible. *Palestine Exploration Quarterly* 107:87–105.

HYDE, JAMES N. 1891. A contribution to the study of pre-Columbian syphilis in America. *American Journal of the Medical Sciences* 102:117–31.

ISCAN, M. YASAR, AND PATRICIA MILLER-SHAIVITZ. 1985. Prehistoric syphilis in Florida. *Journal of the Florida Medical Association* 72:109–13.

JONES, JOSEPH. 1876. Explorations of the aboriginal remains of Tennessee. *Smithsonian Contributions to Knowledge* 22(259):1–171.

KAMPMEIER, RUDOLPH H. 1984. "Early development of knowledge of sexually transmitted diseases," in *Sexually transmitted diseases.* Edited by King K. Holmes, Pers-Anders Mardh, P. Frederic Sparling, and Paul J. Weisner, pp. 19–29. New York: McGraw-Hill.

LAMB, D. S. 1898. Pre-Columbian syphilis. *Proceedings of the Association of American Anatomists* 10:63–69.

LANGDON, F. W. 1881. The Madisonville prehistoric cemetery: Anthropological notes. *Journal of the Cincinnati Society of Natural History* 4:237–57.

LANNING, EDWARD P. 1967. *Peru before the Incas.* Englewood Cliffs: Prentice-Hall.

LARSEN, CLARK SPENCER. 1984. "Health and disease in prehistoric Georgia: The transition to agriculture," in *Paleopathology at the origins of agriculture.* Edited by Mark N. Cohen and George J. Armelagos, pp. 367–92. Orlando: Academic Press.

LU, GWEI-DJEN, AND JOSEPH NEEDHAM. 1967. "Records of diseases in ancient China," in *Diseases in antiquity.* Edited by Don Brothwell and A. T. Sandison, pp. 222–37. Springfield: Thomas.

LUKACS, JOHN R., AND SUBHASH R. WALIMBE. 1984. "Paleodemography at Inamgaon: An early farming village in western India," in *The people of South Asia: The biological anthropology of India, Pakistan, and Nepal.* Edited by John R. Lukacs, pp. 105–32. New York: Plenum Press.

MACCURDY, GEORGE G. 1923. Human skeletal remains from the highlands of Peru. *American Journal of Physical Anthropology* 6:217–329.

MADRID, ALFONSO. 1986. Work in historical osteology at the National Museum of Antiquities in Sweden. *Museum* 38(3):155–57.

MATTHEWS, WASHINGTON, J. L. WORTMAN, AND JOHN S. BILLINGS. 1893. Human bones of the Hemenway collection in the United States Army Medical Museum. *Memoirs of the National Academy of Sciences* 6:141–286.

MEANS, H. J. 1925. A roentgenological study of the skeletal remains of the prehistoric Mound Builder Indians of Ohio. *American Journal of Roentgenology* 13:359–67.

MEER, R. M. 1985. Health and disease in protohistoric Alaska. Paper presented at the 84th annual meeting of the American Anthropological Association, Washington, D.C.

MILES, JAMES S. 1966. "Diseases encountered at Mesa Verde, Colorado. II: Evidences of disease," in *Human palaeopathology*. Edited by Saul Jarcho, pp. 91–97. New Haven: Yale University Press.

——— 1975. Orthopedic problems of the Wetherill Mesa populations. Mesa Verde National Park, Colorado. National Park Service Publications in Archeology 7G.

MILLS, WILLIAM C. 1906. Baum prehistoric village. *Ohio Archaeological and Historical Publications* 15: 45–136.

MØLLER-CHRISTENSEN, VILHELM. 1952. Case of leprosy from the Middle Ages of Denmark. *Acta Medica Scandinavica* 142 (suppl. 266):101–8.

——— 1967 "Evidence of leprosy in earlier peoples," in *Diseases in antiquity*. Edited by Don Brothwell and A.T. Sandison, pp.295–306. Springfield: Thomas.

MØLLER-CHRISTENSEN, VILHELM, AND BORGE FABER. 1952. Leprous changes in a material of mediaeval skeletons from the St. George's Court, Naestved. *Acta Radiologica* 37:308–17.

MØLLER-CHRISTENSEN, VILHELM, AND R. G. INKSTER. 1965. Cases of leprosy and syphilis in the osteological collection of the Department of Anatomy, University of Edinburgh. *Danish Medical Bulletin* 12: 11–18.

MOORE, CLARENCE B. 1907. Moundville revisited. *Journal of the Academy of Natural Sciences of Philadelphia* 13:337–405.

MORANT, G. M., AND M. F. HOADLEY. 1931. A study of the recently excavated Spitalfields crania. *Biometrika* 23:191–248.

MORSE, DAN. 1967. "Two cases of possible treponema infection in prehistoric America," in *Miscellaneous papers in paleopathology,* vol. 1. Edited by William D. Wade, pp. 48–60. Museum, of Northern Arizona, Technical Series 7.

——— 1973. "Pathology and abnormalities of the Hampson skeletal collection," in *Nodena: An account of 75 years of archeological investigation in southeast Mississippi County, Arkansas.* Edited by Dan F. Morse, pp. 41–60. Arkansas Archeological Survey Research Series 4.

——— 1978. 2d revised edition. *Ancient disease in the Midwest.* Illinois State Museum Reports of Investigations 15.

MORSE, DAN F. 1973. "The Nodena phase," in *Nodena: An account of 75 years of archeological investigation in southeast Mississippi County, Arkansas.* Edited by Dan F. Morse, pp. 65–85. Arkansas Archeological Survey Research Series 4.

MORTON, R. S. 1967. The sibbens of Scotland. *Medical History* 11:374–80.

MURDOCK, J. R., AND H. J. HUTTER. 1932. Leprosy: A roentgenological survey. *American Journal of Roentgenology* 28:598–621.

MUSHER, DANIEL M., AND JOHN M. KNOX. 1983. "Syphilis and yaws," in *Pathogenesis and immunology of treponemal infection.* (Immunology Series 20.) Edited by Ronald F. Schell and Daniel M. Musher, pp. 101–20. New York: Marcel Dekker.

OLANSKY, SYDNEY. 1981. "Treponematosis," in *The science and practice of clinical medicine,* vol. 8, *Infectious diseases.* Edited by Jay P. Sanford and James P. Luby, pp. 298–305. New York: Grune and Stratton.

ORTNER, DONALD J. 1986. Skeletal evidence of pre-Columbian treponemal disease in North America. Paper presented at the 6th European Members' Meeting of the Paleopathology Association, Madrid.

ORTNER, DONALD J., AND WALTER G. J. PUTSCHAR. 1985. Reprint edition. *Identification of pathological conditions in human skeletal remains.* Washington, D.C.: Smithsonian Institution Press.

ORTON, S. T. 1905. A study of the pathological changes in some Mound Builder's bones from the Ohio Valley, with especial reference to syphilis. *University of Pennsylvania Medical Bulletin* 18:36–44.

PARROT, M. J. 1879. The osseous lesions of hereditary syphilis. *Lancet* 1:696–98.

PATERSON, D. E. 1959. "Radiographic appearances and bone changes in leprosy: Their cause, treatment, and practical application," in *Leprosy in theory and practice.* Edited by R. G. Cochrane, pp. 243–64. Bristol: John Wright.

——— 1961. Bone changes in leprosy: Their incidence, progress, prevention, and arrest. *International Journal of Leprosy* 29: 393–422.

PATRICK, ADAM. 1967. "Disease in antiquity: Ancient Greece and Rome," in *Disease in antiquity.* Edited by Don Brothwell and A. T. Sandison, pp. 238–46. Springfield: Thomas.

PERZIGIAN, ANTHONY J., PATRICIA A. TENCH, AND DONNA J. BRAUN. 1984. "Prehistoric health in the Ohio River valley," in *Paleopathology at the origins of agriculture.* Edited by Mark N. Cohen and George J. Armelagos, pp. 347–66. Orlando: Academic Press.

POWELL, MARY LUCAS. 1988*a. Status and health in prehistory: A case study of the Moundville chiefdom.* Washington: Smithsonian Institution Press.

—— 1988*b.* Endemic treponematosis and tuberculosis in the prehistoric southeastern United States: The biological costs of chronic endemic disease. Paper presented at the 12th International Congress of Anthropological and Ethnological Sciences, Zagreb, Yugoslavia.

—— 1988*c.* "On the eve of the conquest: Life and death at Irene Mound, Georgia," in *Postcontact biocultural adaption of Native American populations on St. Catherines Island, Georgia.* Edited by David Hurst Thomas and Clark Spencer Larsen. New York: American Museum of Natural History. In preparation.

—— 1988*d.* "Health and disease at Nodena, a Late Mississippian community in northeast Arkansas," in *Towns and temples along the Mississippi.* Edited by David Dye. Birmingham: University of Alabama Press. In press.

PUTNAM, FREDERIC W. 1878. Archaeological explorations in Tennessee. *Report of the Peabody Museum* 2:305–60.

QUINN, THOMAS C., DAVID GLASSER, ROBERT O. CANNON, DIANE L. MATUSZAK, RICHARD W. DUNNING, RICHARD L. KLINE, CARL H. CAMPBELL, EBENEZER ISRAEL, ANTHONY S. FAUGI, AND EDWARD W. HOOK III. 1988. Human immunodeficiency virus infection among patients attending clinics for sexually transmitted diseases. *New England Journal of Medicine* 318:197–203.

RABKIN, SAMUEL. 1942. Dental conditions among prehistoric Indians of northern Alabama. *Journal of Dental Research* 21:211–22.

REICHS, KATHLEEN J. 1987. Treponematosis: A possible case from the Late Woodland of North Carolina. Paper presented at the 14th annual meeting of the Paleopathology Association, New York, N.Y.

RICHARDS, PETER. 1977. *The medieval leper.* Cambridge: D. S. Brewer.

RONEY, JAMES G., JR. 1966. "Palaeoepidemiology: An example from California," in *Human palaeopathology.* Edited by Saul Jarcho, pp. 99–107. New Haven: Yale University Press.

ROSE, JEROME C., BARBARA A. BURNETT, MARK W. BLAEUER, AND MICHAEL S. NASSANEY. 1984. "Paleopathology and the origins of maize agriculture in the Lower Mississippi Valley and Caddoan culture areas," in *Paleopathology at the origins of agriculture.* Edited by Mark N. Cohen and George J. Armelagos, pp. 393–424. Orlando: Academic Press.

ROSEBURY, THEODOR, 1971. *Microbes and morals.* New York: Viking.

ROTHSCHILD, BRUCE M., AND WILLIAM TURNBULL. 1987. Treponemal infection in a Pleistocene bear. *Nature* 329: 61–62.

RUBIN, STANLEY. 1974. *Medieval English medicine.* New York: Barnes and Noble.

SAUL, FRANK P. 1972. *The human skeletal remains of Altar de Sacrificios.* Papers of the Peabody Museum of Archaeology and Ethnology, Harvard University, 63(2).

SIGERIST, HENRY E. 1923. L'origine della sifilide. *Archivio di Storia della Scienza* 4:163–70. [AD]

—— 1951. *A history of medicine.* Vol. 1. *Primitive and archaic medicine.* New York: Oxford University Press.

SMRCKA, VACLAV. 1985. Treponematosis. *Paleopathology Newsletter,* no. 50, p. 9.

STEINBOCK, R. TED. 1976. *Paleopathological diagnosis and interpretation.* Springfield: Thomas.

STEWART, T. D., AND LAWRENCE G. QUADE. 1969. Lesions of the frontal bone in American Indians. *American Journal of Physical Anthropology* 30:89–110.

STEWART, T. D., AND ALEXANDER SPOEHR. 1967 (1952). "Evidence on the palaeopathology of yaws," in *Diseases in antiquity.* Edited by Don Brothwell and A. T. Sandison, pp. 307–19. Springfield: Thomas.

SUSSMAN, MAX. 1967. "Diseases in the Bible and the Talmud," in *Diseases in antiquity.* Edited by Don Brothwell and A. T. Sandison, pp. 209–21. Springfield: Thomas.

TEMKIN, OWSEI. 1966. "Discussion, " in *Human palaeopathology,* Edited by Saul Jarcho, pp. 30–35. New Haven: Yale University Press.

TENNEY, J. 1986. Possible treponemal bone lesions among early native Californians. Paper presented at the 6th European Members' Meeting of the Paleopathology Association, Madrid.

WAKEFIELD, E. G, SAMUEL C. DELLINGER, AND JOHN D. CAMP. 1937. A study of the osseous remains of the "mound builders" of eastern Arkansas. *American Journal of the Medical Sciences* 193:488–95.

WALKER, ERNEST G. 1983. Evidence for prehistoric cardiovascular disease of syphilitic origin on the northern Plains. *American Journal of Physical Anthropology* 60:499–503.

WAUGH, M. A. 1982. Role played by Italy in the history of syphilis. *British Journal of Venereal Diseases* 58:92–95.

WEISS, D. L., AND V. MØLLER-CHRISTENSEN. 1971. Leprosy, echinococcosis, and amulets: A study of a medieval Danish inhumation. *Medical History* 15:260–67.

WHITNEY, WILLIAM F. 1883. On the existence of syphilis in America before the discovery by Columbus. *Boston Medical and Surgical Journal* 108:365–66.

WILLCOX, R. R. 1949. Venereal disease in the Bible. *British Journal of Venereal Diseases* 25:28–33.

——— 1974. Changing patterns of treponemal disease. *British Journal of Venereal Diseases* 50:169–78.

WILLIAMS, HERBERT U. 1929. Human paleopathology with some original observations on symmetrical osteoporosis of the skull. *Archives of Pathology* 7:839–902.

——— 1932. The origin and antiquity of syphilis: The evidence from diseased bones, a review, with some new material from America. *Archives of Pathology* 13:799–814, 931–83.

——— 1936. The origin of syphilis: Evidence from diseased bones, a supplementary report. *Archives of Dermatology and Syphilology* 33:783–87.

WILLIAMS, HERBERT U., JOHN P. RICE, AND JOSEPH RENATO LACAYO. 1927. The American origin of syphilis, with citations from early Spanish authors collected by Dr. Montejo y Robledo. *Archives of Dermatology and Syphilology* 16:683–96.

WONG, K. CHIMIN, AND WU LIEN-TEH. 1936. 2d edition. *History of Chinese medicine.* Shanghai: National Quarantine Service.

WORLD HEALTH ORGANIZATION. 1980. *A guide to leprosy.* Geneva: WHO.

WRIGHT, D. J. M. 1971. Syphilis and Neanderthal man. *Nature* 229:409.

30

THE CULTURAL CONSTRUCTION OF AIDS AND ITS CONSEQUENCES FOR PREVENTION IN BOTSWANA

BENEDICTE INGSTAD

In this article I describe how traditional Tswana healers perceive AIDS and classify it as either a "Tswana disease" or a "modern disease." I also discuss the consequences that these categorizations may have for preventing the spread of HIV, as well as the possible role that healers can play in this important effort.

Traditional healers in Botswana are perhaps the most important carriers of Tswana medical tradition.[1] Yet their views and practices are not static but are under constant influence from religious and cosmopolitan medical sources (Ingstad 1989a). The way healers perceive information about AIDS, how they integrate that information into their way of thinking, and how they reflect it in their preventive and curative practices may have major consequences for the spread or curtailment of this disease in their country. In this light, I shall describe the beliefs

and practices of Tswana healers regarding AIDS and HIV infection.

My main data on traditional practices and Tswana illness beliefs were gathered in Kweneng district during 1984–85, before AIDS had become an issue in Botswana.[2] At the time it had been mentioned only very briefly in the newspapers as "something happening in far away countries." The striking similarities of some Tswana medical beliefs, which will be discussed in this article, to the biomedical explanation of the spread of HIV is therefore purely coincidental

SOURCE: From "The Cultural Construction of AIDS and Its Consequences for Prevention in Botswana" by B. Ingstad in *Medical Anthropology Quarterly* 4:1, 1988, pp. 28–40. Copyright © 1988 by The American Anthropological Association. Reprinted by permission. Not for further reproduction.

and not the result of influence from modern health information.[3] A total of 28 traditional healers were interviewed during this fieldwork, and seven were followed very closely during the entire two-year period of my research.

In addition, valuable information was gathered during monthly meetings between a different set of about 60 traditional healers and modern health personnel of the United Health Committee.[4] Differences in concepts of sickness and cure, as well as ways of possible future cooperation, were the ongoing topics of these meetings.[5] On short return visits since 1985, I have had the opportunity to observe the newly launched AIDS campaign (1987), to reinterview my seven key informants (1989), and to attend a United Health Committee meeting in which prevention of AIDS was the main topic (1989).

AIDS IN BOTSWANA

So far, the AIDS epidemic has not reached the dimensions in Botswana that have been reported from several other African countries. This is most probably because the country is landlocked and is peripherally located in relation to the most severely stricken countries of the continent. Even Zambia,[6] rumored to have a high incidence of infected persons, is not a country with which most Batswana seem to have frequent contact. The main contact routes abroad (excluding air routes) are between Botswana and South Africa, which claims to be among the less affected countries on the continent.[7]

The first AIDS case was reported in Botswana in December 1985, and screening for HIV started in November 1986 at the central hospital (Botswana Ministry of Health 1987; Botswana National Health Laboratory 1988; Maganu 1988; Osei & Maholane 1985). By March 1989, the World Health Organization (WHO) reported 49 diagnosed AIDS cases in Botswana (World Health Organization Weekly Epidemiological Record 1989). A well functioning reporting system for infectious diseases for a population of only 1.2 million gives reason to believe that these figures are fairly accurate. In addition to cases of disease, by November 1987 a total of 107 HIV-positive cases had been detected (Maganu 1988). No official number of HIV-positive cases has been given, but unofficial sources state that the proportion found among blood donors is 1–1.5%.

No major screening for HIV has been conducted in the total population. A health status survey conducted in 1984 among the rural population found no HIV-positive cases (Owuor-Omondi et al. 1986). A screening of inhabitants of areas remote from population centers (mainly people of San origin), which was conducted in Kweneng district in 1986–87, found no HIV-positive cases (Johnsen, Johnsen, and van Dorp 1987). While transmission in the first diagnosed cases of AIDS could be traced to sources outside the country (Dr. Osei, personal communication 1987), a recently conducted study from the Gaborone area found that all HIV-positive cases had reported contacts from within Botswana only, thus indicating that HIV is by now endemic (Dr. H. Haukeland, personal communication 1989). As in other African countries, the main pattern of transmission in Botswana is through heterosexual intercourse. Intravenous drug use and homosexuality are believed to be uncommon. Although only two cases of babies infected through their mothers had been reported by 1988 (Maganu 1988), this mode of transmission is expected to be seen more frequently in the future.

A campaign for public education, awareness, and prevention of AIDS was launched by the Ministry of Health in March 1987 with the support of WHO. The radio and press were used extensively.[8] Pamphlets, T-shirts, and bumper stickers with slogans like "AIDS Kills," "Use Condoms," and "Stick To One Partner" were distributed, and similar posters were placed on the walls of health-care facilities and other public offices. Public meetings were held, both in the *kgotla* (traditional court) and elsewhere. Because Botswana has already had many years of experience with health education in general, this type of campaign seems to have been implemented quite easily.[9] On my first return visit in 1987, I had the strong impression of an active, ongoing effort, while in 1989 some of the early "fighting spirit" seemed to have worn off, and people talked ironically about AIDS as the "radio disease," meaning it had been widely publicized on the radio but had not been experienced by most people.

In a study of the effect of the AIDS education campaign in June–July 1987, Ahmed and Brunborg (1988) found that 80% of the respondents in a national survey had heard about AIDS, a figure which has been interpreted as showing that the campaign has been successful in reaching most of the population. Actual knowledge, however, varied considerably, and almost one-fifth of those who had heard about AIDS knew nothing about it. Respondents in Gaborone were better informed, however, than those in small and remote villages. Another survey on knowledge and attitudes among students at the University of Botswana showed that knowledge of AIDS and its transmission and prevention was quite high—as good and sometimes better, according to the authors, than the knowledge of a U.S. population sample who were interviewed using some of the same questions. Despite their awareness only 45% reported having changed their sexual habits because of their knowledge about AIDS, and only 27% thought that other students had done the same. 5.6% had abstained from sexual relationships as a preventive measure against AIDS. (The proportion of the sample who were celibate before AIDS appeared and remained so is, unfortunately, not reported.) As many as 65% of the students believed that traditional medicine could cure AIDS.

A public opinion poll conducted in urban and semiurban areas after the AIDS education campaign had been launched showed that fewer than 50% of those surveyed ($N = 74$) identified viruses as the agent responsible for AIDS (Botswana Ministry of Health 1987). 40% thought that sexual transmission was the sole mode of spread, 66% believed that it was safe to use condoms, 93% were aware that healthy people could be carriers, and 82% believed that one faithful partner could reduce the spread of AIDS. 75% of the respondents had obtained their information about AIDS from the radio, and 25% from the newspapers. It is interesting to note that in this fairly small sample, 15% admitted to having had homosexual experiences, a fact which seems to undermine the common belief that homosexuality is a rare occurrence among African people. The study does not mention whether the respondents had homosexual experiences in Botswana or while in the mines of South Africa.

It is difficult to make any predictions about the future development of the AIDS epidemic in Botswana. A well developed primary health-care system, routines for reporting and following up on patients with infectious diseases, as well as experience in giving and receiving health education, give some reasons for optimism. On the other hand, patterns of sexual relations with frequent changes of partner and fairly high incidences of other sexually transmitted diseases also give ample reason for concern. Furthermore, although knowledge about AIDS seems to be surprisingly high in the population, the extent to which this information has influenced people's sexual behavior is still uncertain. I have had informants tell me that they have gone for voluntary testing together with their partner or have refrained from accepting a scholarship to a Central African country for fear of catching AIDS, but these were people who had more education and health awareness than the average Batswana. Recently, however, a survey found that 45% of students interviewed reported having changed their sexual habits, while the equivalent figures were 58% for other literate informants, and 38% for illiterates (Ahmed and Shastri 1989).

It seems clear that in the present situation, with no cure or vaccine for HIV, the most important preventive strategy is to advocate behavioral change ("Stick To One Partner") and, perhaps more realistically, to promote the use of condoms. Traditional healers may play an important role in this effort; therefore, knowledge about their position in society and their medical practices and beliefs is pertinent for predicting its success.

TSWANA HEALERS

The type of healer most frequently found in Botswana today is the *ngaka ya diatola* ("doctor of the bones"), who combines divination by a set of carved bones with the knowledge and use of herbs. A less common type is the *ngaka ya dishotswa* ("doctor of herbs"), who sometimes specializes in one or a limited number of illness conditions. Because of the many similarities between these two kinds of healers and the common cultural tradition from which they have emerged, no distinction will be made between them in the following discussion, and they will be referred to simply as *ngaka ya Setswana* (Tswana doctor) or *ngaka* (plural, *dingaka*) for short.

Another type of healer that has increased considerably in numbers and influence during the last 10 to 15 years is the "prophet" (*profiti;* plural: *baprofiti*) of the Independent African Churches that are related to the Zionist movement (Comaroff 1985). Prophets combine the role of church leader with that of healer. Their concepts of disease are much the same as the *dingaka* in deriving from general Tswana culture, but emphasize spiritual power and evil in their etiological ideas. It thus makes sense to classify them among traditional healers, although their role is of more recent origin. Most prophets, however, reject the use of herbs, which they associate with witchcraft, and instead use "holy water" rituals and prayer for all healing purposes. An exception here is the *sangoma*[10] (plural: *disangoma*), who uses herbs as well as

factory made "traditional medicines." Thus, the *sangoma* role in Botswana may be said to represent a strategic choice, combining elements of the *ngaka*-role as well as the typical role of a prophet. (For further discussion of these differences and similarities, see Ingstad 1989a).

While a *ngaka* has been through a period of training, sometimes over several years and often involving extensive travel, to learn the secrets of others in order to become a "strong" healer, most prophets and usually the *disangoma* have received their calling more or less overnight, often in a dream and/or through a period of critical illness. Thus, the prophets have less knowledge of Tswana medical traditions than the *dingaka* and place less emphasis on "diagnosis" of symptoms, since they treat most illnesses in the same way (Ingstad 1989a).

In the old days, the *dingaka* had a close relationship with tribal leaders at different levels. The chief knew every *ngaka* within his region and would call upon them for various purposes—as healers, advisors, religious specialists, and assistants for throwing the bones to find the guilty party in cases of witchcraft accusations. The *dingaka* were also seen as intermediaries between the living and the ancestral spirits *(badimo)*. Today ties between the chiefs and the *dingaka* have weakened, partly as a result of the Witchcraft Act (1927), the introduction of Christianity, and changes in the role of the chief through the introduction of a modern system of governmental administration (Ingstad 1989a). However, both chiefs and healers of various kinds still retain much influence locally. For instance, in the Kweneng district the chief on various occasions has called upon the healers to discuss matters of common concern.[11]

The *ngaka* role is not static but constantly adapts to socioeconomic, religious, and perhaps most important, medical changes in society. Still, the core of their medical beliefs remains remarkably intact, with only minor variation throughout the country (Alver 1984; Anderson and Staugård 1987; Comaroff 1981, 1985; Fako

1978; Haram 1988; Ingstad 1989a; Karlsen 1986; Staugård 1985; Ulin 1979).

TSWANA CONCEPTS OF DISEASE

Tswana medical beliefs focus on the origin of the medical condition but also incorporate other types of misfortune within the conceptual system. Etiology concerns two levels of causality: the *origin* and the *immediate cause* (Foster 1976). At the level of origin, there are three main causes of sickness and other types of misfortune: witchcraft, ancestors' anger, and pollution through breaking of taboos. These causes are mutually exclusive explanations of symptoms and may be divined by the *ngaka* through using bones.

The immediate cause of sickness is most often explained by properties of the blood. Blood is seen as one of the most important essences of life, and various disturbances such as "high blood," "dirty blood," and "too much" or "too little" blood are believed to cause a variety of symptoms in the body. The blood is also seen as going to the head or heart or as coagulating in lumps to cause pain in certain places. Accidents may also be seen as an immediate cause which is often ascribed to an origin beyond the individual herself, most often to witchcraft.

Seen from the point of view of a *ngaka ya Setswana,* the type of treatment recommended to the patient depends on the origin of the condition. If it is a "Tswana disease," one that may be explained by the Tswana conceptual model, the *dingaka* see themselves as superior to modern doctors. Tswana diseases have specific Setswana names, and healers classify them according to their causal history (witchcraft, a breach of taboo, etc.). Thus, the healers use an alternative classification system to the biomedical system. Oracle bones also may tell the healer that a disease is "modern" (i.e., one that arrived after contact with the Europeans) or that it "just happened" (i.e., implying an absence of discernible

social or moral causality). In such cases the healer may refer the patient to the hospital or a nearby clinic. Failure to cure a suspected Tswana disease through traditional treatment may lead to a revision of the diagnosis. Lack of a cure is usually attributed to "the will of God," and the patient must then resign himself to his destiny (Ingstad 1989b).

There is a considerable degree of consensus among healers about classifications of disease and the main symptoms by which they classify "Tswana diseases," though symptoms are not in fact of prime importance for diagnosis. Patients who have been diagnosed by healers as having the same Tswana disease may differ considerably in their illness presentations, and similar symptoms may lead to quite different diagnoses depending on the social circumstances surrounding the illness episode. Similar symptoms that consistently are given the same Tswana diagnosis are very often also identified as a disease in the biomedical system of classification. For example, *tibamo* is recognized as a discrete Tswana illness, with severe coughing as the main symptom. It is generally diagnosed biomedically as tuberculosis of the lungs, though Batswana attribute the disease to a woman's uterus having become polluted through an abnormal delivery (e.g., a child born facing the "wrong" way). (The uterus is said to have become "dangerous as the poison of a snake.") This pollution may be passed to a man through sexual intercourse, and from him to other sexual partners.

As a result of Tswana patterns of diagnosis, I am reluctant to call their disease names culture-bound *syndromes.* They do constitute culture-bound *categories.* However, more research is needed before saying anything definitive on this matter. Patients' explanatory models of specific episodes of illness (Kleinman 1980, 1987) tend to contain elements of both traditional and modern medical knowledge and to be less confined within the Tswana classification system than the explanatory models of healers (Ingstad 1989a).

THE CULTURAL CONSTRUCTION OF AIDS

IDEAS OF DISEASE TRANSMISSION: VIOLATION OF SEXUAL TABOOS

In order to understand how AIDS may be culturally constructed to fit into the Tswana medical explanatory system, it is necessary to examine the concept of disease transmission in Tswana thought. Concepts of transmission have mainly been connected with concepts of pollution that originate in the female body. This type of pollution may be transmitted to men via sexual intercourse that takes place within culturally proscribed periods after birth, abortion, etc., and before ritual purification has taken place. The man, through sexual intercourse, may then transmit the pollution to other women. Pollution that is caused by such violation of sexual taboos is called *meila*. The pollution is believed to originate in the blood of a woman in connection with various bodily processes (menstruation, parturition, etc.), and is particularly dangerous when associated with something abnormal (e.g., abortion, a child born in an unusual position). Blood and semen are seen as the basic vehicles for transmission of the pollution, and it is interesting to note that these two bodily fluids are called by the same word in Setswana, *madi,* which illustrates their symbolic connection. (*Madi* also means wealth or money, an association which may reflect the value placed on children as future providers of wealth for the family.)

An example of a Tswana disease caused by *meila* is *mopakwane,* which may afflict very small children with general weakness, apathy, and eventually mental retardation or death. In this case the father is believed to have had intercourse with the mother before the three-month period of abstinence after the birth is over and after having had intercourse with another (presumably polluted) woman without having had a healer perform the necessary rituals of purification.

According to my present understanding, the only Tswana disease in which *melia* is seen to originate equally in the male and female body is *boswagadi*. When a man or a woman becomes a widow *(moswagadi)* a state of pollution occurs which requires one year of sexual abstinence, followed by ritual purification before sexual relations can be resumed. (Some healers claim, however, that if extra money is paid, very strong herbs may be found that can shorten the period of abstinence to six or even three months—but only for men.) Various healers describe the symptoms of *boswagadi* as aching legs and general pain in the body, urinary incontinence, diarrhea, and pain in the stomach. Healers generally agree that *boswagadi* will lead to death if not treated at an early stage of development.

AIDS AND MEILA

There is a striking similarity between ideas of disease transmission and *meila* in the Tswana medical system and notions of AIDS transmission in biomedicine. In both conceptual systems sexual intercourse, blood, and transmission from mothers to their babies play a role. Also in both systems disease or AIDS is strongly associated with violation of the sexual rules of society.[12] An interesting question, therefore, is whether healers will define AIDS—which so far few, if any, of them have seen—as a "Tswana disease" or a "modern disease," and what consequences such a choice will have for their future cooperation with modern health care.

Various ways of thinking about AIDS are illustrated by four of the healers whom I reinterviewed in 1989. These healers also exemplify different trends of opinion that were clearly expressed in the larger group of healers attending a United Health Committee meeting about AIDS.

> *Healer A, a "conservative" ngaka:*
> AIDS is nothing new. It is a Tswana disease, and we have known it always. It may be any type of *melia*, but I think it is *boswagadi*. . . . Of course I can cure it. I use herbs to boil with water and give [it to] the patient to drink or inhale.

Healer B, a "modern" ngaka:

AIDS is not a Tswana disease. It is something new that we never had before. It is like the airplane; nobody knows where it comes from and nobody knows where it goes. I am not able to cure it.

Healer C, the entrepreneur:

AIDS is new in a way. It occurs when white and black people have sex together, because their blood *(madi)* does not mix well. Before, we did not used to have it, since the blacks and the whites were kept apart from each other. Now they mix sexually quite often. When AIDS has occurred in this way, they can also spread it further within their own group by whites having sex with whites and blacks with blacks. . . . Some people say that AIDS comes from homosexuality, but it is not so. We have always had some homosexuality among the workers in the mines, but that did not make AIDS occur. . . . No, it is definitely the mix of black and white blood that causes it. . . . I can cure AIDS, but it is difficult because I have to try many different herbs. I had a patient that was sent to me by the doctor at the clinic. She had been tested [HIV] positive, but I cured her and she even got a baby.[13]

Healer D, the sangoma:

AIDS is *boswagadi,* the widow disease. I can cure it by using "holy water," prayers, and herbs.

In order to get a full understanding of how and why these healers chose the explanations that they did, it is necessary to know more about their backgrounds, both as individuals and as representatives of different types of healing. Healers A and B are both *ngaka ya Setswana* of the old school, using bones for divination as well as herbs and rituals for healing and prevention. They differ markedly, however, in their approaches to the modern health care system. A represents the group of healers (probably the largest) who rarely or never attend the United Health Committee meetings where modern and traditional health workers meet and discuss common issues. He has an affluent practice, but some people fear him, saying that he also practices witchcraft. He has been trained by his father and is now training one of his sons to take over after him.

B, on the other hand, is the deputy chairman of the United Health Committee and one of its most faithful promoters. He has been trained by a healer who is today an old man and, like A, rejects all contact with the biomedical profession. Interestingly, B's own medical beliefs and practices have not been markedly influenced by modern medicine. Thus his defining AIDS as a "modern" disease is as much within the Tswana conceptual model (dividing the familiar from the unfamiliar) as it would be to define AIDS as *meila.* However, B sees cooperation as essential for securing legal and economic status for healers, as well as for gaining recognition for Tswana medical traditions. In this way, he represents a growing number of healers who are taking up the challenge of cooperation which the government has launched as part of its "Health For All By Year 2000" efforts. Through his attendance at United Health Committee meetings over several years, he has gained greater access to modern health information than have healers of type A. He has also become more aware of distinguishing between what he himself can cure and what he should refer for biomedical treatment.

Healer C, the entrepreneur, does not have his roots in Botswana. Like several other healers, he came from a neighboring country but carries with him a medical heritage that is closely related to that of the Batswana. He has traveled extensively and has had teachers in different countries. C found a niche with a practice near the capital in which he combines traditional remedies and means of divination with the use of mail-order herbs from India and China and factory-made "traditional medicines" from South Africa. He also offers his patients the use of modern devices, including an enormous electric vibrating chair.

Healer D, the *sangoma,* is a bishop in one of the Independent African Churches. The parish members gather several times a week for sermons in which healing and purification rituals play an important part. He was trained by his late mother, who was the daughter of a famous *ngaka ya Setswana* and very influential and "strong" *sangoma* herself. Healer D used to attend United Health Committee meetings regularly with his mother, since she was the group's chairperson for many years. While she was much in favor of co-operating with modern medicine, he has attended hardly any meetings since her death.

DISCUSSION

We see from the material presented above that the choice of classifying AIDS as a "modern" or a Tswana disease can hardly be said to be coincidental. On the contrary, it is a strategic choice that must be understood against the background of the healers themselves. It is important, however, to keep in mind that although these choices may represent different types of adjustment to biomedical influences, the Tswana classification system itself provides for both interpretations.

Tswana traditional healers, in spite of the explanatory model that they share, do not form one unified category but represent several different types of healing and may vary considerably in their approach to actual cases of illness. Their construction of AIDS, which they have been acquainted with so far mainly through health information, reflects in part their cultural inheritance. In part, too, it reflects their individual orientations to a situation in which modern medicine may be seen either as undesired competition or as an opportunity for consolidating their own strength by receiving legal recognition. Thus the fact that healer A (and others) calls AIDS a Tswana disease, implying that he can cure it, is quite predictable knowing his background and general attitude toward modern medicine. To choose differently would be, from his point of view, to undermine his own competence and influence. Similarly, healer B has found it more advantageous to leave AIDS out of his healing repertoire. He realizes through the health information he has received that his chances of working a successful cure are slight. He also sees his interests as better served by continuing to be a bridge builder between traditional and modern medicine.

Healer C is somewhat special in that his explanatory model may be interpreted as a new invention within the traditional framework. It is not uncommon, however, for healers of the entrepreneurial type to do exactly this (Barth 1963). In order to build up an image of themselves as having especially strong "medicines" and healing power, they choose approaches and explanations that are easily understood by their patients but at the same time are different from those of both the *dingaka* and the biomedical doctors. Healers of this type usually are very confident in themselves and would be reluctant to admit that there are diseases they cannot cure. Healer C's interpretation of AIDS can also be seen as reflecting the commonly heard statement in Botswana that AIDS has been brought by white tourists—in a way a countermyth to the biomedical statements that AIDS originated in Africa. It is also interesting to note that, in contrast to biomedical knowledge that homosexual practices *spread* AIDS, healer C is considering whether such practices *generate* the disease. This concern is in line with the focus on origin in Tswana medical diagnosis.

Healer D represents the "prophets" of the Independent African Churches. As a *sangoma,* he is in many ways closer to *dingaka* in his practices than to faith healers who reject the use of herbs. Thus his explanation of AIDS may be seen partly as a reflection of this general orientation, as well as his recent withdrawal from the United Health Committee. The reactions of faith healers to the AIDS issue is on the whole difficult to predict. Many of them claim that faith, prayers, and "holy water" can cure anything, regardless of the severity of the condition, and that their patients should go only to them and never to the *ngaka* or the hospital. Others do not mind referring patients to the hospital but reject all forms of cooperation with the *dingaka.* Thus in some districts like Kweneng most faith healers will hardly be seen at meetings together with *dingaka,* while in other areas (like Kgatleng and South East District) they meet quite freely. Usually faith healers are less concerned about classifying sickness as either "modern" or "traditional," which partly reflects their lack of traditional training and partly their use of the same cure for all conditions.

Statements by the four healers about their ability to cure AIDS before they have been confronted with patients actually suffering from symptoms of the disease becomes understandable in light of the Tswana medical model which emphasizes curing the origin of a disease as much as the symptoms themselves. Defining the disease as "traditional" also explains statements occasionally made in African newspapers that healers know how to cure AIDS, remarks which are usually met with an overbearing smile by the biomedical profession. The choice of the widows' disease, *boswagadi*, as the Tswana category into which to assign AIDS is probably because it is one of the few adult conditions which people agree leads to death. Later, as more newborns come to be affected, we may also expect the category of *mopakwane* to be used for this purpose.

Although from a biomedical point of view healers probably cannot cure AIDS nor influence the course of the disease, their beliefs and practices still have important consequences for prevention. In July 1988, the chief of the Bakwena called a meeting of local traditional healers to inform them about AIDS and to encourage them to advocate the use of condoms. One of his arguments was that by using condoms men could avoid catching and spreading *meila* of all kinds and thus have sex with their women without having to worry about culturally prescribed periods of abstinence or ritual purification. Consequently, the risks involved in having intercourse with women who have unknown medical histories would also be diminished (Dr. P. Stensland, personal communication 1989). Several of the healers reported this speech to have been quite a revelation for them.

While the chief chose to approach healers by using explanations befitting their explanatory models, biomedical doctors have chosen a different approach. In several districts the District Medical Officers (DMOs) have given healers stocks of condoms to sell. Their profit is minimal, but it still gives healers some extra incentive. Healers consider themselves extremely important in this distribution, because, as they say, "we see more patients than the DMO." However, they complain that so far, their main customers have been secondary school boys who are afraid of being kicked out of school if they make a girl pregnant. As the healers see it, to make other villagers use condoms on a regular basis would be a very long process.

How AIDS is categorized—as a Tswana disease or a modern disease—may have important consequences for prevention. Advocating condoms as a way to prevent *meila* probably carries more incentive than advocating them to prevent pregnancy or other sexually transmitted diseases. Once a condition is perceived as a Tswana disease, it implies that it can be cured by traditional healing methods. Thus, as we have seen with healer C, an HIV-positive patient without symptoms (or an AIDS patient with mild symptoms that decrease occasionally), may easily come to trust a promise of cure and end up transmitting the virus to their children or sexual partners before the mistake became evident. Therefore, from a biomedical standpoint, it is probably useful for healers to distribute condoms along with advice that is understandable to people. Yet most biomedical doctors see using traditional beliefs for preventive purposes, while simultaneously advocating a biomedical explanation, as an ethical dilemma (for further discussion of this see Ingstad 1989a). Nevertheless, it seems only reasonable to influence healers to refer AIDS patients to biomedical doctors for counseling and treatment. In addition, such treatments as ritual scarification and sucking of blood, used by some *dingaka* and even some faith healers, need to be reconsidered and if possible, dropped in order to reduce the risk of transmitting HIV.

It is difficult to make predictions. However, it seems likely that as time goes by, more AIDS patients will be seen, healers will fail to save their lives, and more health information will lead more healers to redefine AIDS as a "modern disease." This process happened with *tibamo* following considerable pressure on healers to refer patients to biomedical doctors as part of a nationwide fight against tuberculosis. To quote healer B, "Before we thought that TB was *tibamo,* and we killed many patients by treating them ourselves, but now we know better." Healer C put it differently, in a way that preserves the validity of the old model: "When the cough is light, it is *tibamo,* but if it goes untreated [by Tswana medicine] for long, it becomes TB and must be referred to the hospital."

CONCLUSION

Faced with the task of preventing such a contagious fatal disease as AIDS, health officials should enlist the Tswana medical system as an important resource. Cooperating with traditional healers brings to bear on the problem their considerable knowledge about villagers, as well as their influence over villagers' health-seeking behavior.

It is important, however, not to consider healers as a homogeneous group, but to be aware of their differences in practice and motivation. While some are eager to cooperate and quite receptive to modern health information, others are skeptical, prefer to keep a distance, and may promote behavior that is counterproductive to prevention. Considering the seriousness of the AIDS epidemic and the likelihood that the incidence of the disease will increase in Botswana in the near future, it is important that healers be made to feel that they have a role to play in the prevention of this disease.

NOTES

Acknowledgments. The fieldwork on which this article is based was made possible by grants from the following sources: The Royal Norwegian Ministry of Development Cooperation, the World Health Organization, Carl Lumholtz Fund, The Scandinavian Institute of African Studies in Uppsala, and the University of Oslo.

Jeanine Stenhjem has given valuable comments. Special acknowledgement is given by my Batswana assistant Patricia Ntonge, without whose help and enthusiasm I would hardly have been able to establish the good rapport with healers that I eventually achieved.

Correspondence may be addressed to the author at the Institute of Social Medicine, University of Oslo, Rikshospitalet 0027, Oslo 1, Norway.

1. In this article I follow Setsuana orthographic conventions: Botswana refers to the country/nation; Batswana, the people of Botswana; and Setswana, the language. Tswana, the term most commonly used in the anthropological literature for both the people and the culture, omits all prefixes. Bakwena refers to people of the Kwena tribe of Batswana; Kweneng is the district in which they reside.

2. The main Kweneng data were supplemented by a few interviews with healers in Gaborone and Kgatleng district.

3. Most of the healers interviewed during this fieldwork were illiterate, and only few of them had a functioning radio.

4. The Government of Botswana has encouraged the formation of United Health Committees (UHC) in all Health Districts as part of the WHO "Health for all by the year 2000" strategy, which encourages cooperation between modern and traditional health workers. During the UHC meetings cosmopolitan and traditional health workers would meet and discuss topics of common concern. In Kweneng district the healers would most often take the lead and present their views, but the District Medical Officer would also use this opportunity to give health information.

5. The fact that I was the wife of the District Medical Officer, in addition to being a researcher, was a valuable asset in allowing me to attend and be accepted at these meetings. Because of these meetings, I met a total of about 60 healers in the district and heard their spontaneous accounts (and sometimes disagreements) about their illness beliefs and healing practices.

6. By May 1, 1989, Zambia was reported by WHO as having 1,892 registered AIDS cases (World Health Organization 1989). By most people familiar with the situation this figure is believed to be a massive underreporting.

7. By the end of June 1989 there were 231 reported

AIDS cases in South Africa, but the possibility of major underreporting cannot be ruled out (World Health Organization 1989).

8. There is no TV station in Botswana.

9. On a mission to neighboring Zimbabwe in November 1988, I observed an incipient AIDS campaign which was launched by the Government with more mixed feelings than had been the case in Botswana (Robinson 1989).

10. *Sangoma* is not an original Tswana term but is also found in several other Bantu groups and was introduced to Botswana through the Zionist churches.

11. For instance stressing that patients with symptoms of severe cough (TB) must be referred by the healers to the hospital, that all healers should attend the United Health Committee meetings, and

asking their assistance in campaigns to heighten awareness and prevent AIDS.

12. I am grateful to an anonymous reviewer of this article for reminding me of this point.

13. I later had a chance to check this account with the doctor who was supposed to have referred the patient. She had tested HIV positive during a screening for venereal disease among patients at a particular clinic. The doctor had been approached by the young woman's mother, who asked for consent to take her to a traditional healer. The young woman was without any symptoms of AIDS. She did not return to the clinic for additional testing after she had been to the healer. (She may of course have gone elsewhere.)

REFERENCES

AHMED, GHYASUDDIN, AND HELGE BRUNBORG. 1988. Knowledge, Attitudes, Prevalence and Prospects of AIDS in Botswana. Paper read at the Annual Meeting of the Population Association of America, New Orleans.

AHMED, GHYASUDDIN, AND G. H. SHASTRI. 1989. People's Fear of Catching AIDS in Botswana: What Are They Doing to Prevent It in the Society? Paper read at the Annual Conference of the International Union for the Scientific Study of Population, New Delhi.

ALVER, BENTE. 1984. Botswana *ngaka*. Tradisjon 4:3–24.

ANDERSON, SANDRA, AND FRANTS STAUGÅRD. 1987. Traditional Midwives. Gaborone: Ipelegeng Publishers.

BARTH, FREDRIK, ed. 1963. The Role of the Entrepreneur in Social Change in Northern Norway. Bergen: Universitetsforlaget.

BOTSWANA MINISTRY OF HEALTH. 1987. AIDS Update 1. Gaborone.

BOTSWANA NATIONAL HEALTH LABORATORY. 1988. HIV Screening in Botswana. Paper read at the First National Workshop on AIDS, Francistown.

COMAROFF, JEAN. 1981. Healing and Cultural Transformation: The Tswana of Southern Africa. Social Science and Medicine 15B(3):357–378.

——— 1985. Body of Power, Spirit of Resistance. Chicago: University of Chicago Press.

FAKO, THABO. 1978. Traditional Medicine and Organizational Issues in Botswana. Gaborone: National Institute of Development and Cultural Research.

FOSTER, GEORGE M. 1976. Disease Etiologies in Non-Western Medical Systems. American Anthropologist 78(4):773–782.

HARAM, LIV. 1988. The Batswana Encountered by Western Medicine: Cooperation or Confrontation? Cand. Polit. thesis, Department of Anthropology, University of Bergen.

INGSTAD, BENEDICTE. 1989a. Healer, Witch, Prophet or Modern Health Worker?: The Changing Role of *Ngaka ya Setswana. In* Culture, Experience and Pluralism: Essays on African Ideas of Illness and Healing. Anita Jacobson-Widding and David Westerlund, eds. Stockholm: Almqvist & Wiksell International.

——— 1989b. The Myth of the Hidden Disabled: Sociocultural Factors in Community-based Rehabilitation. A Study from Kweneng District, Botswana. (Manuscript, files of author).

JOHNSEN, NILS, HELGA JOHNSEN, AND GERHARDT VAN DORP. 1987. Health Survey among Remote Area Dwellers (RADs) in the Central Kalahari Game Reserve (CKGR) and Northern Kweneng. (Manuscript: files of author).

KARLSEN, MARIT. 1986. Helseforestillinger i endring. Om kvinners forhold til helse og sykdom etter innføringen av moderne helsetjeneste i Botswana. Institute of Sociology, University of Oslo.

KLEINMAN, ARTHUR. 1980. Patients and Healers in the Context of Culture: An Exploration of the Borderland between Anthropology, Medicine, and Psychiatry. Berkeley: University of California Press.

——— 1987. Illness Narratives: Suffering, Healing and the Human Condition. New York: Basic Books.

MAGANU, E. T. 1988. AIDS in Botswana. Paper read at the First National Workshop on AIDS, Francistown.

OSEI, W. D. AND L. D. MAHLOANE. 1985. AIDS in Botswana: Nonsexual, Heterosexual or Multifactoral. Botswana Epidemiological Bulletin 6(4):276–281.

OWOUR-OMONDI, ET AL. 1986. National Health Status Evaluation Survey. Botswana Ministry of Health, Gaborone.

ROBINSON, PETER, ED. 1989. Zimbabwe Country Study: Final Draft. The Royal Norwegian Ministry of Development Cooperation/HIFAB/ZIMCON-SULT, Oslo.

STAUGÅRD, FRANTS. 1985. Traditional Medicine in Botswana. Gaborone: Ipelegeng Publishers.

ULIN, P. R. 1979. The Traditional Healer of Botswana in a Changing Society. *In* African Therapeutic Systems. Z. A. Ademuwagun et al., eds. Pp. 243–246. Waltham, MA: Crossroads Press.

WORLD HEALTH ORGANIZATION (WHO). 1989. Weekly Epidemiological Record, No. 31. Geneva.

31

Koro—A Culture-Bound Depersonalization Syndrome

P. M. Yap

The term "koro" refers to an unfamiliar state of acute anxiety with partial depersonalization leading to the conviction of penile shrinkage and to fears of dissolution. Among the South Chinese (Cantonese) koro is known as *suk-yeong*. Van Brero in 1897 first discussed the psychopathology of this syndrome on the basis of cases described in South Celebes. He thought it was a peculiar manifestation of obsessional-compulsive illness. After

P. M. Yap. M. A., F.R.C.P.Ed., D.P.M., *Senior Specialist in Psychiatry, Hong Kong Government, and Head of the Division of Psychiatry, Department of Medicine, Hong Kong University.*

many years the syndrome again received attention from Van Wulfften Palthe (1934), who concluded that it was an unusual form of anxiety neurosis. Slot in the same year also gave an account of it in the Dutch literature. Van Wulfften Palthe (1936, 1937) further mentioned the existence of corresponding female cases who complained of shrinking of the vulval labia and the breasts. He made a distinction between a real anxiety state and an imaginary organic illness based on folk belief, comparable for example to the popular notion in Southern Europe that urinating against the wind

SOURCE: From "Koro—A Culture-bound Depersonalization Syndrome" by P. Yap in *British Journal of Psychiatry, 111,* 1965, pp. 43–50. Copyright © 1965 by The Royal College of Psychiatrists. Reprinted by permission.

would cause a person to "catch a cold" in the metaphorical sense of getting gonorrhoea.

Kobler (1948) gave a psychoanalytic account of the condition, but was able to report only on one case seen in South China. He preferred to label it simply as an "acute castration fear." Devereux (1954) published an erudite psychoanalytic discussion of koro and related neurotic phantasies of genital mutilation, and pointed to parallels between these and certain widely distributed beliefs and customary practices. He gave examples of koro phantasies in western patients. Linton (1956) in a systematic survey of the influence of culture on mental disorder dwelt on the psychotic-like loss of touch with reality in koro cases. Baasher (1963) stated that the syndrome was encountered among Sudanese. At the joint Japanese-American Psychiatric Conference in Tokyo in 1963 the subject was discussed by Yap and by Rin (1963), the latter attempting a psychoanalytic interpretation of the syndrome.

Cases identical with, or similar to, koro among westerners have been reported by Kraepelin (1921), Schilder (1950) and Bychowski (1952)—see under "Aetiology" below.

CASE MATERIAL

Over the last 15 years in Hong Kong I have been able to gather 19 cases of koro for study. Apart from these 19 typical cases composing the sample there were 6 others who presented features of the syndrome against a schizophrenic background, and one each against the background of general paresis and of a sub-delirious state due to heroin withdrawal. The characteristics of the 19 sample cases are analysed below.

The ages of the patients ranged from 16 to 45 years, the median being 32 years. The marital status of the cases were as follows: Married, 9 cases; Single, 8; Separated, 1; Widowed, 1. The occupational distribution of the patients revealed that with one exception, a bookkeeper, they were all from the working class. Two patients were without any schooling at all; fourteen had been to primary school for a varying number of years; one had gone two years beyond primary school, another was a secondary school graduate, and a third (a bookkeeper) had had post-secondary education.

None of the patients had a family history of psychosis or psycho-neurosis, although the mother of one had suffered from a febrile delirious state. As regards past medical history, one patient had passed through what might have been a brief psychotic illness at the age of 14, the nature of which could not be determined, and a second had had attacks of depression and mania. One patient had undergone a recent operation for phimosis, and two had suffered from veneral disease.

For practical purposes of communication the personality types encountered could be categorized using the scheme found in the Diagnostic and Statistical Manual of the American Psychiatric Association: Passive-dependent, 11 cases; Compulsive, 4; Emotionally unstable, 3; and Passive-aggressive, 1. The general impression was one of a preponderance of traits indicating a slow, shy, self-effacing and nervous temperament, not endowed with much intelligence. There were 4 among the passive-dependent who were also inept and lacking in stamina and at the same time free from noticeable tension. The passive-aggressive man with a post-secondary education was vain, socially active and inclined to be haughty, but with an underlying sense of insecurity.

The decided immaturity of many of our cases was revealed in a striking manner in their behaviour. One, aged 22, was the butt of much teasing by girls because of his shyness; he insisted on following his mother about when he was taken ill and caused the latter much exasperation, although she was very loving towards him. His father had died three years previously. Another, stupid, ignorant, and also aged 22, was obedient and filial to the extent that he never left the house without asking his father's permission. A third man, aged 32, had all along been greatly dependent on his mother and to the same degree distant from his father. He was the only surviving boy in the family, the other two having died in infancy. During his attacks of koro he would seek urgent help from his mother first rather than from his wife. It is of interest to note that the first patient mentioned above was an only child, and the second an only son. Still another patient aged 26, whose only surviving relative was his father, rushed out to seek him during the attack in a tearful, agitated and possibly clouded state.

The sexual history of our cases told an unusual story of conflict and maladjustment. Thirteen patients were troubled by sexual deprivation, because they were either single, excessively shy, fearful of venereal disease, or too poor to resort to prostitutes; the married patients suffered because of lack of co-operation from (or the death of) their wives, separation, or fear of having further children. All these patients resorted to masturbation. One who had been abandoned by his wife and who was much afraid of venereal disease masturbated nightly in order to get to sleep; another, with a frigid wife who insisted on *coitus interruptus*, also indulged in this habit nightly with the same intention. Two of these men were impotent and achieved orgasm only through masturbation; one of them had never consummated his marriage. A third man had a poor sperm count and was childless. At least four patients who masturbated habitually also visited prostitutes; one of them could not afford to remarry although he would have liked to do so. Two patients were much interested in pornography. There were two patients who gave a history of excessive sexual activity. One of these used to masturbate three or four times a week, and although married, was promiscuous; before his illness he indulged in coitus every night and sometimes even twice a night. The second masturbated once or twice a week and might sometimes have coitus three times a night with his wife. Both these patients complained of occasional nocturnal emission (but this condition also afflicted at least half our sample cases).

In contrast to the two men with hypersexual

proclivities, there were two patients in their mid-twenties who in addition to being immature, dependent and unintelligent had never developed any contacts even of an ordinary social kind with girls; one of them had indulged half-heartedly in masturbation with some guilt. The first of these, an only child, was plunged into a psychogenic psychosis with koro symptomatology after having fallen in love with a female colleague who showed no interest in him. The second, the only boy in a humble family with two children, was afraid of marriage, but having been forced into it by his parents, became panic-stricken and confused on his wedding night, and complained of koro.

There were two married patients whose history did not reveal sexual difficulties. One, however, was very nervous by nature, with chronic palmar sweating and easily excited and upset. He was much afraid of venereal disease. The second was a borderline feeble-minded fisherman who had become rather preoccupied with his sexual functioning because he was unable to father a son, although he had four girls. Following business worries he became rather anxious and developed a hysterical wry-neck along with his koro symptom.

It may be concluded that all our patients were gravely worried over what they imagined in varying ways to be sexual excess. Most of them were of immature personality, lacking confidence in their sexual capacity, and in a broader sense, their virility. Some were plunged into a whirlpool of sexual anxiety because of sex-deprivation, and others, the minority, because of constitutionally determined hypereroticism. Compulsive sexual activity was not encountered in our series.

Not all our patients were seen in their first attack. As far as the age of this is concerned it ranged from 16 to 42, the median being 29 years. The cases were distributed as follows: under 21, 3 patients; 21–30, 7; 31–40, 8; 41–50, 1. In our series, 10 patients were seen on the occasion of their first attack, 3 during their third attack and 6 after they had had many more than three attacks.

SYMPTOMATOLOGY

Each episode usually lasted several hours; at the shortest it was half an hour and the longest two days. Nearly all our patients were of a nervous temperament, and in 14 cases there were long-established symptoms of anxiety, weakness, irritability and hypochondriacal concern, particularly over nocturnal emissions and sexual inadequacy. A clear exception was the 16-year-old boy, who suffered merely from a brief attack after mounting worry over masturbation for three months. In our sample there was also one case of phthisis, one with the ulcer syndrome, and one with signs of avitaminosis B.

Most of the episodes occurred at night, as might be expected, when thoughts are apt to stray on to sexual interests. Nevertheless, it is remarkable how varied were the precipitating causes of individual attacks. Four patients had their attacks after masturbation, one of them also sometimes after urination and coitus. Three patients had their attacks precipitated by coitus, in one case *coitus interruptus*. In three patients attacks were precipitated by ordinary sexual arousal, and one of them ascribed his attacks on one occasion to involuntary mechanical stimulation on a moving bus. Three patients started to have their attacks after hearing of people allegedly dying from koro, or after listening to koro being discussed. In one case the attack occurred during a cold bath, in a second after a cold bath, and in a third when a wintry wind blew on him during micturition. Two others ascribed their attacks to a cold wind, but this could have been simply a retrospective assumption. Another patient, who said his attack has come on after a cold bath, also incriminated thoughts of koro, as well as physical exertion. There was still another patient, a hairdresser, who found that attacks were produced by physical exertion and also by sexual arousal when he handled women's hair during his work. One patient had attacks brought on whenever he was frightened, e.g. when his mother fainted, or when a cat suddenly jumped down near him; he also fell prey to attacks when he exposed his genitals to the cold in winter either while urinating or during coitus. The last three cases described were of severe degree.

The actual attack was accompanied in the more serious cases by symptoms of acute anxiety and even panic, with faintness and clouding of the sensorium in 4 cases, and additionally a feeling of impending death in 3 cases. Most complained of palpitation, sometimes coming on suddenly, a cold sweat, breathlessness, precordial discomfort, trembling, belching and, in one case, diarrhoea. Four patients experienced paraesthesia in the genital area. So convinced were some of the patients that their penis was disappearing that they held on to it all the time.

Among our 19 sample cases of the syndrome, one had become predominantly depressed because of environmental pressure bearing upon an inadequate, anxious personality, and two were considered to be examples of psychogenic psychosis. Of the latter, the first was a very unintelligent, retiring single man of 26, without any kind of heterosexual contacts at all, and living alone by himself. He was depressed because he could not go to Canada, and was also in conflict with his employer. After a cold bath one night he became agitated, tearful and disorientated, and ran out saying his penis was shrinking. On examination he had paranoid ideas of being made ill by his employer, but recovered in 3 weeks with psychotherapy and modified insulin. The second patient (already referred to earlier) was a shy and quiet man of 31, living away from his wife, who under pressure from her mother was about to come back to him. He had made advances to a woman who, however, rejected him. Following this he passed a restless night, and the next morning developed florid delusions that this woman as well as his wife and her mother had poisoned him to give him koro. This led to an attempt at suicide. With conservative drug and psychotherapeutic treatment he recovered in two weeks.

TREATMENT AND FOLLOW-UP

The patients were treated with psychotherapy distributed according to symptoms and to aetiologically significant points in the history, tranquillizing and hypnotic drugs, and in three cases with modified insulin and/or electroplexy. The two cases of psychogenic psychosis were treated as in-patients, along with five others, but the rest were day-patients or out-patients.

A follow-up of the sample was undertaken, the period between initial contact with the patients and the follow-up examination ranging from 1 year and 9 months to 9 years (median, 2 years and 9 months). It was possible to recall 9 cases for re-examination. Of these, 3 had recovered completely, 4 had ceased to have further attacks but were still subject to anxiety at different times, one had had rather fewer attacks, and one had shown no improvement at all. As might be expected, the prognosis appeared to be better with a good previous personality, a short history, infrequency of attacks and a relatively uncomplicated sexual life; but our cases are too few to justify confident generalization.

AETIOLOGY

Among the Chinese, koro is confined to South China and the lower Yang-tse valley. Bingham Dai (personal communication) did not encounter it in Peking. It is also to be found among oversea Chinese in S.E. Asia, especially Malaysia and Indonesia, and, less frequently, among the Malay and Indian inhabitants of these countries too.*

*Undoubtedly the koro phenomenon must have spread from China to Indonesia and adjoining lands with Chinese migration. "Koro" in Malay means the head of a turtle (or tortoise). The Chinese until the Ming Dynasty used the turtle as an artistic and literary symbol for longevity and the vital forces, but later the symbol acquired scatlogical connotations. There is an obvious similarity between the head of this long-lived

Inquiries made of a number of psychiatrists from S. Asia and the Near East, including Israel, did not reveal the occurrence of this illness there. Baasher (1963) however has reported the syndrome in a few Sudanese. My informants from the Philippines denied that it was found there, although they suspected it might be encountered in the south. It is not known in Japan and Korea.

Sporadic cases of an exactly similar kind have been reported in countries where the syndrome is not "endemic." Dr. M. R. Chaudhry of Lahore has informed me of the case of a law student with acute anxiety and worries over potency who complained of a retracting penis. Bychowski (1952, p. 109) reported the case of a depressed middle-aged American struggling against forbidden sex impulses, who suffered from "estrangement" of his genitals, so that in typical koro fashion he had to seize hold of his organ in order to be sure that it was there. Schilder (1950, pp. 127, 164) in his well-known monograph on pathological distortion of the body-image mentioned two cases of what was in fact the koro syndrome. The first patient reported diverse emotions being experienced in his penis, which was felt to be shrinking in. The second patient was a young man who complained of insomnia, nocturnal leakage, poor memory, coldness in his extremities, frequent erections at the sight of the feet of either sex, and much worry over masturbation while asleep. Like one of our cases, his attention had been drawn to his penis by a hydrocele, and he was greatly perturbed by the feeling that the member was shrinking. It is also relevant to recall that Kraepelin (1921, p. 92) in his classic textbook on manic-depressive insanity mentioned shrink-

creature and the *glans penis* (see R.H. Van Gulik, 1961, pp. 225 f.). A passage is quoted on p. 279 from a Ming treatise on the art of attaining longevity through *coitus reservatus,* wherein the retraction of a tortoise's head is used as a simile. This learned book by the well-known sinologist gives a fully documented account of traditional Chinese sex beliefs and practices, and emphasizes the importance that was given to sexual hygiene and adequate sexual performance in the interest of maintaining the classical polygamic household.

ing of the penis among the hypochondriacal delusions to be found in depressive states.

Clearly the koro symptoms can occur anywhere, and the fear of collapse and perhaps death during acute anxiety is universal; but the fact that the syndrome is to be seen among certain large sections of the Chinese populace must be accounted for. The reason is to be sought in traditional ideas of sex physiology (or pathology). These ideas are founded on a theory of humours, the harmonious equilibrium of male (*yang*) and female (*yin*) principles, elaborated first by Chu Chen Hang, who is recognized as the founder of one of the schools of medicine in the Chin-Yuan period some 700 years ago (cf. Lee *et al.,* 1962).* In some form or other the belief appears to be obscurely held that during normal coitus a healthy exchange of *yang* and *yin* humours take place. With masturbation and nocturnal emission however this cannot occur, and the unbalanced loss of the *yang* humour produces koro. The Chinese term for koro, *sukyeong,* means literally "shrinking of the penis," and it denotes a possibly mortal illness presenting with such a symptom. The traditional medicine also recognized a neurasthenic state (*sunk'uai*) associated with sexual excess, and the symptoms of this condition were thought to be giddiness, debility both physical and mental, as well as aching in the loins and excessive shivering at the end of micturition. We can see from this the importance of the factor of cultural expectation in the genesis of koro. Banal fears of nocturnal emission, impotence and of general debility associated with it are widespread, and by themselves are neither peculiar nor clearly abnormal (see, e.g. Carstairs, 1956). Without the koro and related beliefs, however, only a small proportion of persons so troubled will present themselves to the doctor. Thus the belief is not simply pathoplastic but actually pathogenic in effect, much in the way that a belief in hell-fire can help to bring about depressive states of clinical severity under certain circumstances. This finding is of some import in view of the denial by Berne (1960), supported by insubstantial evidence, of the pertinence of cultural factors in the aetiology of mental illness.

NOSOLOGY AND DIAGNOSIS

The pathological intensity of the belief in penile shrinking is due to an underlying perceptual distortion of proprioceptive perception, a distortion of a part of the body image; it is not a question of delusion without sensory basis. Patients have been observed urgently touching and visually inspecting their penis in order to check its size, especially when their statement about retraction has been challenged. Because of guilt and fear over sexual impulses, there occurs a dissociation from the Ego of the kinaesthetic and tactile sensory components of the amalgam of perceptions, images and feelings normally associated with sexuality. A comparison with hysterical anaesthesia or micropsia suggests itself. The dissociation can take place centrally, for genital somaesthesia does have a central locus; Money (1961) has shown that erotic arousal and orgasm occur even with extensive surgical resection of the penis. Certain workers have related depersonalization to dissociation of consciousness (Hermann and Strömgren, 1944; Roth and Harper, 1962). Others, following Pötzl and Schilder, have studied partial depersonalization in terms of body-image pathology and stressed the importance of the affective element in asomatognosia. The genital portion of the total body-image is likely to be weakly structured and therefore more liable to catathymic distortion because the organ is toneless, beyond voluntary control, and its outlines dependent upon episodic emotional arousal.

The koro patient has not lost touch with reality as far as the conviction of penile retraction goes,

*It is interesting to compare this ancient humoral theory of sexual dysfunction with that prevalent in medieval Europe based on demonological concepts. Trethowan (1963) has discussed the illusion of penile deprivation that was regarded as evidence of witchcraft causing impotence.

because this is based on partial depersonalization. This conviction, rather than being delusional, is reinforced by the existence of a folk belief in the reality of a possible dangerous koro illness. Not only does the belief condition the patient's insight into his own abnormality, it also arouses acute anxiety which may disorganize him psychologically. Koro in this way differs from ordinary depersonalization states which are usually associated with full insight and a deadening of emotional responses (Ackner, 1954). In view of its psychogenic basis, it is important to note that koro even in its mildest form cannot be accompanied by secondary gain. This is unlike some other psychogenic disorders—e.g. possession states (Yap, 1960)—where the patient may seek to exploit his condition, so that his abnormality has then to be decided largely on the degree of dissociation involved and the extravagance of the symptomatology.

The complaint of penile shrinking may rarely occur as a secondary embellishment of disparate illnesses like confusional states from epilepsy, heroin withdrawal, cerebral syphilis, and schizophrenia and mania; but this should not prevent us from recognizing that a pure, reversible psychogenic syndrome exists. This is psychogenic in the sense that remote as well as recent experiential factors are necessary and even sufficient causes of it; and further it has a psychopathological coherence of its own, "understandable" in the Jaspersian sense. Its coherence is essentially dependent on the patient's learning a certain cluster of beliefs, the existence of which not only moulds the form of the illness but also determines its occurrence. The fact that isolated cases may be seen in widely separated cultures does not invalidate this conclusion, since it is still necessary to account for the consistent and relatively frequent occurrence of cases within a particular culture area which allows a modal syndrome to be distinguished. This does not mean that koro cases cannot present over a wide range of severity, from cases best described simply as anxiety states with koro preoccupations and

fears to states of ego-disorganization involving dissociative mechanisms and presenting with disorientation, dysmnesia, and paranoid misinterpretations in addition to depersonalization.

Because of the close connection with its cultural background koro may be regarded nosologically as a "culture-bound psychogenic disorder"; or if we use the word "psychosis" in a sense denoting loss of touch with reality, "culture-bound psychogenic psychosis." Not only is the condition psychogenic, it is clearly atypical and uncommon when compared with psychoneurotic and psychotic illnesses even within its own culture area. I have elsewhere proposed that the term "atypical culture-bound psychogenic psychosis" should replace the antique appellation "exotic psychosis" (Yap, 1962, 1964). The former is from the nosological point of view relatively precise (cf. Faergeman, 1963), and with refinement is capable of integration into widely accepted systems of disease classification.

From a strictly clinical point of view, koro has to be distinguished from vasovagal attacks, various kinds of syncope, angina pectoris, coronary thrombosis, spontaneous hypoglycaemia, and epileptoid states with localized body distortion. (It is likely that the popular notion of the deadliness of koro has arisen partly because of confusion with some of these possibly mortal conditions.) Roth and Harper (1962) and Harper and Roth (1962) have recently delineated the "phobic-anxiety depersonalization syndrome," a mixed psychoneurotic illness to be distinguished from temporal lobe epilepsy and showing symptoms of panic, fear of death, syncope, visual illusions and depersonalization. Our cases have features comparable to Roth's; in both conditions the subjects are immature, dependent and over-sensitive, but our patients are not precipitated into illness by acute stress, nor are they young women with phobic anxiety. What emerges from the comparison is the important fact that while depersonalization following stress is a universal phenomenon, such depersonalization can be specially structured and brought into being by particular cultural beliefs and expectations.

SUMMARY

An exhaustive survey is made of the scanty literature on koro (which is called *suk-yeong* among the Southern Chinese). A series of 19 typical cases, collected over 15 years and some of them followed up, are analysed. Reference is also made to sporadic cases of a comparable kind reported in the West and elsewhere outside S.E. Asia.

The syndrome is usually to be found among young men of poor education and immature, dependent personality who lack confidence in their own virility and are in conflict over the expression of genital impulses, although some may show hypersexual tendencies. The presenting complaint of penile shrinkage is shown to be in fact a depersonalization of that organ, occurring in the context of acute anxiety with fears of dissolution.

This is a unique example of a depersonalization syndrome whose form and content, and indeed occurrence and distribution, are determined by a combination of social and cultural factors acting on predisposed personalities. The depersonalization is seen as a dissociative mechanism affecting the integrity of the body-image. Unlike ordinary states of depersonalization, the koro patient has insight into his own condition only in a restricted sense, and moreover does not suffer a general disturbance of affective responsiveness.

The need to recognize a class of "atypical culture-bound, psychogenic disorder (or psychosis)" is stressed, and koro is held to belong to this group.

REFERENCES

ACKNER, B. (1954). "Depersonalization. I. Aetiology and phenomenology: II. Clinical syndromes." *J. Ment. Sci.,* 100, 838–872.

BAASHER, T. A. (1963). "The influence of culture on psychiatric manifestations." *Transcultural psychiat. Res.,* No. 15, 51–52.

BERNE, E. (1960). "The cultural problem: psychopathology in Tahiti." *Amer. J. Psychiat.,* 116, 1076–1081.

BRERO, P. C. J. VAN (1897). "Koro, eine eigenthümliche Zwangsvorstellung." *Allg. Z. Psychiat.,* 53, 569.

BYCHOWSKI, G. (1952). *Psychotherapy of the Psychoses.* New York.

CARSTAIRS, G. M. (1956). "Hinjra and Jiryan: two derivatives of Hindu attitudes to sexuality." *Brit. J. med. Psychol.,* 29, 128–138.

DEVEREUX, G. (1954). "Primitive genital mutilations in a neurotic's dream." *J. Amer. psychoanal. Ass.,* 2, 484–492.

FAERGEMAN, P. (1963). *Psychogenic Psychoses.* London.

GULIK, R. H. VAN (1961). *Sexual Life in Ancient China.* Leiden.

HARPER, M., AND ROTH, M. (1962). "Temporal lobe epilepsy and the phobic anxiety-depression syndrome. Part I." *Comprehen. Psychiat.,* 3, 129–151.

HERMANN, K., AND STRÖMGREN, E. (1944). "Paroxysmal disturbances of consciousness in verified localized brain affections." *Acta psychiat. scand.,* 19, 175–194.

KOBLER, F. (1948). "Description of an acute castration fear, based on superstition," *Psychoanal. Rev.,* 35, 285–289.

KRAEPELIN, E. (1921). *Manic-Depression Insanity and Paranoia* (trans. Barclay). Edinburgh.

LEE, T., CH'ENG., C. F., AND CHANG, C. S. (1962). "Some early records of nervous and mental diseases in traditional Chinese medicine." *Chin. med. J.,* 81, 55–59.

LINTON, R. (1956). *Culture and Mental Disorders.* Springfield, Ill.

MONEY, J. (1961). "Components of eroticism in man. II: The orgasm and genital somesthesia." *J. nerv. ment. Dis.,* 132, 289–297.

RIN, H. (1963). "Koro: a consideration on Chinese concepts of illness and case illustrations." *Transcultural psychiat. Res.,* No. 15, 23–30.

ROTH, M., AND HARPER, M. (1962). "Temporal lobe epilepsy and the phobic anxiety-depression syndrome. Part II." *Comprehen. Psychiat.,* 3, 215–226.

SCHILDER, P. (1950). *The Image and Appearance of the Human Body.* New York.

SLOT, J. A. (1934). "Koro in central Celebes." *Geneesk. Tijdschr. Ned.-Ind.,* 75, 811.

TRETHOWAN, W. H. (1963). "The demonopathology of impotence," *Brit. J. Psychiat.,* 109, 341–347.

WULFTTEN PALTHE, P. M. VAN (1934). "Koro, a peculiar anxiety neurosis." *Geneesk. Tijdschr. Ned.-Ind.,* 74, 1713.

—— (1935). "Addendum." *Ibid.,* 75, 836–837.

—— (1936). Chapter on Neuro-psychiatry in *A Clinical Textbook of Tropical Medicine* (ed. A. Lichtenstein). Batavia.

—— (1937). "Il significato forense del 'Koro' ". *Arch. Anthrop. Crimin. Psichi. Med. leg.,* 57, 173–182.

YAP, P. M. (1960). "The possession syndrome: a comparison of Hong Kong and French findings." *J. Ment. Sci.,* 106, 114–137.

—— (1962). "Words and things in comparative psychiatry with special reference to the exotic psychoses." *Acta psychiat. scand.,* 38, 163–169.

—— (1964). Review of P. Faergeman's *Psychogenic Psychoses. Acta psychiat. scand.* In the press.

32

THE ROLE OF CULTURE IN THE CAUSE OF EATING DISORDERS

MICHAEL P. LEVINE

Dr. CraigJohnson is a co-director of the Eating Disorders Program at Northwestern University's Institute of Psychiatry in Chicago. He has treated hundreds of bulimics and anorexics, most of whom are female. During his initial consultation with a bulimic, he usually asks whether she would relinquish the binge-purge cycles in exchange for a weight gain of 10 pounds. Although nearly three-quarters of these women are of low or normal weight, they regard his proposal with caustic dismay. Most flatly state that "they'd rather be *dead* than gain 10 pounds" (7).

What is responsible for this destructive equation of thinness with happiness and hope? How has fat, still a sign of prosperity and health in poorer countries, come to represent helplessness, ugliness, and immorality? What role do these equations play in the development of eating disorders? There are no simple answers to these questions, because research and clinical experience confirm that anorexia nervosa and bulimia must be understood as multidimensional outcomes of a transaction between biological

ED. NOTE: References in this article to particular chapters are referring to the original source of this article.

SOURCE: From "The Role of Culture in the Cause of Eating Disorders" by M. Levine in *How Schools Can Help Combat Student Eating Disorders: Anorexia Nervosa and Bulimia* by M. Levine (Ed.). Copyright © 1987 by the National Educational Association. Reprinted by permission.

constitution, family dynamics, personality, life circumstances, and culture (12, 19; and see Chapters 8 and 9).

Culture as a factor in eating disorders is a particularly important topic for all school employees interested in preventing eating disorders (13, 21, 22, 23). When we conceive of anorexia nervosa and bulimia solely in terms of "mental illness" or "oral fixations" or "enmeshed families," there is a strong temptation to distance ourselves from them as "interesting" phenomena in the realm of psychiatry. If our society is somehow encouraging eating disorders, however, then teachers, staff, and students have the opportunity, if not the responsibility, to shift from inadvertent participation in a negative process to active elimination of pernicious attitudes, expectations, and practices.

BOUNDARIES OF A CULTURAL MODEL

It is easy to speculate about the influence of culture. The fact that 95 percent of the people with eating disorders are young women strongly suggests that the meaning of femininity in modern Western society has something to do with the development of anorexia nervosa and bulimia. The association between eating disorders and socio-economic privilege also points directly to the operation of social forces. From a historical perspective our society's obsession with thinness evokes numerous examples—Chinese footbinding, suffocating corsets with steel stays, pornography—of the culturally sanctioned oppression of women's bodies and minds (3, 12).

Our present lack of methodological sophistication and the scarcity of actual data make it possible to theorize about these and other cultural factors with little fear of contradiction. Thus, before considering the available research it is necessary to clarify the limits of a sociocultural theory of eating disorders.

Culture is but one of a number of interrelated influences. Consequently, culture cannot cause anything because it is manifested only through an interaction among differentially receptive individuals, their families, and their particular life circumstances (see Chapters 8 and 9). A cultural perspective begins with the simple but important fact that not all people exposed to the same set of overt cultural factors develop eating disorders. A substantial percentage of the women born between 1950 and 1960 have no "disorders," whereas large numbers suffer from other disabling problems such as depression and agoraphobia (29). We must also keep in mind that anorexia nervosa predates the industrial revolution; an excellent description of it dates from the seventeenth century (Morton, 1694, reproduced by Andersen [1]).

Another limitation is a significant degree of uncertainty about exactly what we are trying to explain. Is there one set of cultural factors for anorexia nervosa and a different set for bulimia? The answer depends on the relationship between the two disorders, and it is not known for certain if they are separate afflictions or different expressions of the same psychopathology.

This chapter assumes that anorexia nervosa and bulimia are not completely separate afflictions. Severe caloric restriction and binge-eating are frequently associated, and the transition between anorexia nervosa and bulimia can take place in either direction (35; and see Chapter 1). In addition, anorexics and bulimics share many characteristics (1; and see Chapters 8 and 9). The sufferers of both disorders are predominantly white females from the upper social classes. With both disorders there is an increased prevalence of depression, eating disorders, and weight problems in the immediate families. Finally, anorexics and bulimics share a drive for thinness, an intense fear of becoming fat, and a distorted body image.

The final constraint on efforts to specify the role of culture is the sheer number and variability of people with eating disorders (see Chapter 6). The extent to which a disorder affects a large number and wide variety of people is inversely proportional to the likelihood of a simple explanation of the ways in which culture or any factor influences that disorder. Coronary-prone (Type A) behavior is a constellation of time urgency, runaway ambition, and cynical hostility that appears to characterize 40 to 60 percent of the white urban male population (28). Repeated failures to discover consistencies in the personalities, life stressors, and familial circumstances of Type A males have taught us that generalizations about widespread problems are necessarily elusive.

The stereotyping of bulimics and anorexics is misleading and imparts a false confidence about the direct role of cultural factors. But beyond this, the oversimplifications contained in the deluge of magazine articles, books, and films about eating disorders may themselves be a cultural contribution to the apparent upsurge during the past 10 years. Trumpeting phrases like "The Best Little Girl in the World" and "the golden girl syndrome," or reveling in the tale of Jane Fonda's battle against bulimia, the media inadvertently or sometimes purposely strengthen the association between eating disorders and culturally valued characteristics such as social status, intelligence, perfectionism, and self-control (16). In effect, a range of books, television dramas, and magazine articles have glamorized eating disorders, much as some Victorian observers came to associate a tubercular appearance or malady with artistic genius (12, 16).

THE GLORIFICATION OF THINNESS
Can a Woman Be Too Thin?

The study of sociocultural factors in the development of eating disorders has been shaped in large part by Drs. Paul Garfinkel and David Garner of the University of Toronto (12, 14, 16). Their research makes it clear that the increase in eating disorders over the past 15 years coincides with a cultural glorification of thinness that has placed "intense pressure on women to diet in order to conform to an unrealistic standard for feminine beauty" (16, p. 515).

The Duchess of Windsor is reputed to have said that "No woman can be too rich or too thin." Before dismissing this cliché with a smile, consider that each year the many thousands of visitors to Madame Tussaud's wax museum in London are asked to state their choice for the most beautiful woman in the world. In 1970 their favorite was the curvaceous Elizabeth Taylor. In 1974 a young model named Lesley Armstrong made the top five. At age 17 she stood 5'7" and weighed 97 pounds. By 1976, Lesley Armstrong, better known as "Twiggy," was number one (4, 31).

A variety of studies conducted since 1970 confirm that women perceive slenderness to be the most important aspect of physical attractiveness (16). Most teenage girls when asked about this issue will state that "guys like thin girls." This belief and its connection with body dissatisfaction were examined in a recent study at the University of Pennsylvania (10). A large number of male and female college students were shown two scales consisting of masculine and feminine outlines in gradations from thin to portly. The students then selected the points along these dimensions that best represented their current figure, their ideal, the figure most attractive to the opposite sex, and the shape of the opposite sex they found most attractive.

The results reveal just how deeply the worship of thinness has been implanted into women's minds. For males, the current, ideal, and attractive figures were nearly identical, and each was significantly more rounded than the average male figure preferred by women. That is, in general men misperceive the shape that appeals to women in a manner that reconciles it with their perception of their current shape and their ideal shape for themselves. It is very plausible that this "distortion" serves to maintain self-esteem (24).

For females, the pattern of ratings was very different. Roughly 65 percent felt themselves to be too heavy relative to their ideal and to the shape they believe men to prefer. This level of discontent is very similar to that reported by the 33,000 women who returned *Glamour Magazine's* body image survey (11). On the average, the female physique preferred by a college man is indeed significantly thinner than a college woman's perception of her current physique. What a college woman thinks is attractive to men, however, is actually significantly thinner than the shape preferred by those men. Most important is the sad fact that the woman's ideal shape is even thinner than her misperception of the shape ideally attractive to men—in other words, it is the thinnest of all the ratings. This study leaves little doubt that, for college women at least, there is a significant internal need to become thinner, and that slenderness is much more than an issue of attractiveness to the opposite sex.

Intrigued by the shift in standards of beauty from Elizabeth Taylor to Lesley Armstrong, Garner and Garfinkel analyzed the measurements of *Playboy* magazine centerfolds and Miss America contestants from 1959 to 1978 (12). For the centerfolds there were statistically significant decreases in average bust and hip size accompanied by an increase in waist size. This trend toward a more tabular, Twiggy-like shape was also seen in Miss America contestants. The correlation between year and their percent of average weight for height was an astounding +0.83, a degree of relatedness that would occur by chance less than 1 time in 10,000. Further, since 1970 the winners of the pageant have weighed significantly less than the other contestants.

These data do not constitute regret over the abandonment of Elizabeth Taylor as an ideal of feminine beauty. In fact, I am reluctant to discuss body measurements at all, because there is a strong possibility that the sexual objectification of women in any form contributes to the identity diffusion, body dissatisfaction, obsession with dieting, and misplaced anger manifest in many people with eating disorders (3, 27, 39). Nevertheless, the research just reviewed clearly supports the contention that over the past 20 years or so important segments of our culture have come to glorify thinness (3, 12). Even though correlation does not imply causality, it is at least thought-provoking that the emergence of Lesley Armstrong as a standard of beauty has paralleled both an absolute *increase* of approximately five pounds in the average weight of women under 30 and the emergence of eating disorders as a major health problem (12).

THE MEDIA

How is the obsession with slenderness transmitted? Scanning through any popular magazine or watching TV for a few hours, it is easy to develop the conviction that the media assault us with outrageously thin models and preposterous advertisements whose claims for the restorative power of worthless or dangerous diets rival the cant of any "snake oil" salesperson (13). And the propaganda is by no means always so primitive. For example, in a recent series of articles about sociocultural factors in the development of eating disorders, the Cleveland *Plain Dealer* (October 6–8, 1985) included "10 Weight Loss Tips That Really Work," thereby undoing its own criticism of prejudice against obesity.

Despite my impressions and those of many experts (such as Bruch [6]), there has been surprisingly little systematic investigation of the media's contribution to the glorification of thinness. I came across only one study of television, which found that a mere 2 percent of the actresses on prime time were plump or overweight, and that thinness in actresses was positively correlated with a likable personality (Kurman, cited in Garner and others [14]). I admit that further research is necessary to convert impressions into facts, but I still find myself very concerned about the role of the media when—

1. I see pictures of Mary Decker Slaney and other athletes who are extremely thin and extremely successful.
2. I see my first grader's cartoons interrupted by commercials for a product aimed at elementary school girls called "Get in Shape, Girl."

3. I stop by the newsstand at the supermarket and find *Slimmer: America's Fitness Magazine.*
4. I see the romanticizing of anorexic-like ballet dancers in the Cleveland *Plain Dealer* (August 2, 1985): "Moore, a painfully thin young dancer who looked at though she might float away at any moment, was perfectly cast as the ghostly Giselle. With her fragile body, huge eyes, pale face, and fluid arms, she created a touchingly poetic character who danced weightlessly and ultimately wafted into the wings like a zephyr" ("Friday Magazine," p. 4).

Women's magazines such as *Vogue* and *Seventeen* may be particularly influential in the glorification of thinness, although *Sports Illustrated's* "Swimsuit Issue" certainly contributes to the objectification of women and to the reigning misbelief that to be fit is to be thin and vice versa (16). In a survey of five popular women's magazines, Garfinkel and Garner found that from 1970 to 1978 the number of feature articles on dieting was double that published in the previous decade (12). Anyone interested in eating disorders should find it disquieting that invariably these magazines offer an "anorexic" mix of thin models, articles about dieting and exercising, recipes for sweets, and numerous photographs of mouthwatering food in binge proportions.

THE PURSUIT OF THINNESS

The worship of thinness can also be seen in attitudes toward overweight and the extent of people's involvement in weight control. If our culture is somehow setting the stage for eating disorders, we would expect that (1) negative attitudes about overweight people would be common, (2) there would be widespread dissatisfaction with body weight and shape, (3) a large number of people would be intensely involved in dieting and weight control, and (4) the attitudes and practices of "normal dieters" would be similar to those of people with eating disorders. Before going any further, readers might

carefully examine their immediate, "gut-level" answer to the following question: "Assuming I could make your choice magically come true, would you rather become more loving in your personal life, or would you rather lose 20 pounds from wherever you wish and keep it off?"

PREJUDICE AND OVERWEIGHT

One night a skinny actress appearing on "The Tonight Show" said pointblank that fat people pollute the esthetic environment (36). This is prejudice, impure and simple.

Drs. Susan and O. Wayne Wooley, the directors of the Eating Disorders Clinic at the University of Cincinnati Medical Center, have reviewed a great deal of research that suggests that hostile attitudes toward overweight are widespread and deep-rooted (16, 36, 37, 38). Prospective parents rate a picture of a chubby child as less friendly, lazier, stupider, dirtier, and otherwise less desirable than pictures of a medium or thin child. Preschoolers prefer to play with a thin rag doll rather than a fat one, even though they cannot say why. By the second grade many children of both sexes and all weights are following in the footsteps of their parents; even the overweight children describe the silhouette of a fat child as "dirty," "lazy," "sloppy," "ugly," and "stupid."

The research with prospective parents makes it clear that most people do not outgrow this vicious stereotype. College students recommend a thin or medium person for a job over a fat one, even though all the applicants' performance of a task on videotape is identical. I am also ashamed to say that, in the late 1960s at least, psychologists, physicians, and medical students did not differ significantly from elementary school children in judging fat people to be "slow," "unsuccessful," "weak," "passive (lazy)," "not nice," and "ugly" (16, 36).

The prejudice and ostracism that surround the overweight child undoubtedly influence later perceptions of self and others, particularly when they are reinforced by our cultural overemphasis on a woman's appearance (37, p. 82):

> The child whose build is socially "deviant" comes, early in life, to be regarded by others as responsible for his/her "condition," and deserving of social disapproval, and, sooner or later, is subjected to pressures to restrict food intake in order to "correct" his/her condition. Failure to do so is seen as "weakness," "wanting to be fat," or even as a masochistic desire for rejection.

Can there be any doubt that fat children internalize this hatred and rejection, and that children who are not fat learn to dread the prospect and significance of being overweight (37)? Hatred, rejection, ostracism—strong words, but words that clearly capture the emotional basis for arguing that in our culture the management of weight and shape is much more than a cosmetic or medical concern. In our culture avoiding fat is a moral issue (21, 39).

At this point many readers will find themselves resisting the implication that there is absolutely nothing wrong with being overweight. This is understandable. For at least two decades the medical and psychological communities have, with great authority, proclaimed that not only is being overweight a health hazard, it is a stigma of emotional disturbance. These beliefs are so ingrained in our cultural heritage that it seems foolhardy to challenge them. Nevertheless, they are false, and their perpetuation must be considered a way in which the helping professions, in collaboration with insurance companies and organizations such as the American Heart Association, contribute to eating disorders (2, 16, 37). Extreme obesity is potentially unhealthy, but mild-to-moderate obesity simply does not matter (except for the stress created by the reactions of the individual or others). Epidemiological research indicates that within an 80-lb range—for example, 115–195 pounds for women 5'3" to 5'6"—there is no association between obesity and mortality. In fact, some studies have shown that, for certain ages, obesity is inversely related to mortality. Further, although 95 percent of those with eating disorders are

women, the mortality rate for women is significantly less than that for men in all under- and overweight categories (2, 16, 37).

The contention that being overweight is a sign of psychological dysfunction is also contradicted by the preponderance of evidence. Garner notes that "most controlled studies do not find the obese to be more neurotic, sexually inadequate, or emotionally disturbed than individuals of normal weight. In fact some studies have found obese individuals to be less anxious, less depressed, and less prone to suicide than those of normal weight" (16, p. 522). It is true that many people characteristically overeat in response to stress, loneliness, or boredom (11). More and more evidence is accumulating, however, that this coping style is not the cause of obesity (16).

In summary, the physical risks and the psychological significance of being overweight have been greatly exaggerated. There are indeed problems associated with being overweight in our society, but these problems derive from the prejudice against obesity and the pressure on overweight people to diet (16, 36). Restrictive dieting is an ineffective long-term method of weight control, and it places one at risk for anorexia nervosa and bulimia (see Chapters 8 and 9).

BODY DISSATISFACTION AND DIETING

Consider the following recollection:

> One night, I gave myself permission to really splurge . . . I mixed it all: grease, cheese, and salt . . . I was sure I had gained. The next morning I could feel it as I rolled out of bed. When I looked in the mirror my hip bones had vanished . . . I was terrified. The whale that I had once been was looming. I inched onto the scale with dread and horror. With one eye shut, barely breathing, I looked down. Three numbers stared up at me— 102; I had not gained an ounce! . . . I was overcome with joy and relief, and when I looked in the mirror again, my hip bones had reappeared. (36, p. 65)

Although this sounds like the diary of someone with an eating disorder, it is a selection from a best-selling diet book. Its publication marks "the first time an eating disorder—anorexia nervosa—has been marketed as a cure for obesity" (36, p. 57).

Every year numerous popular weight-loss regimens capitalize on our prejudice against obesity as they pander the thin body to otherwise intelligent readers seeking a magical solution to life's problems (13, 36). According to Wooley and Wooley, some of these programs are particularly pernicious because they glamorize dieting while blithely encouraging readers to plan binges and compensations—fasts, days restricted to eating only one food, foods designed to induce diarrhea, and manipulations of water retention instead of body fat (36). The popularity of the weight-loss genre is a tragic testament to the willingness of millions of Americans to reject themselves and embrace the primitive but seductive equations that constitute the foundation of the diet-exercise industry: dieting = slenderness = goodness; eating normally = fat = badness. The popularity of some diet regimens only serves to increase the risk of eating disorders by perpetuating "the prevailing belief . . . that nothing is worse than being fat; that no price is too high for thinness, including health" (36, p. 65).

In 1978 a Nielsen survey revealed that 55 to 60 percent of all women ages 24 to 54 diet, and of that group three-quarters acknowledge doing so in order to look better rather than to feel better (30). Similarly, 42 percent of the 33,000 women who completed *Glamour Magazine*'s body image survey said losing weight would make them happier than "success at work," or "a date with a man you admire" (11). Moreover, a full three-quarters of these respondents considered themselves too fat, including 45 percent of those who were underweight. The pressure these women feel to diet is captured succinctly by the startling fact that two-thirds of the *underweight* women "often want to diet because they feel fat."

Studies conducted during the 1960s revealed that 50 to 80 percent of high school girls in the United States, England, and Sweden had dieted at some time because they considered themselves overweight, even though only half of them were too heavy according to standardized measures (14, 20). To update this research John Kelly and Sonia Patten of the University of Minnesota recently surveyed nearly 2,000 boys and girls from 12 suburban high schools serving predominantly white and middle- to upper-middle-class students (20). This investigation focused on the attitudes and weight management practices of the 85 percent who were considered neither too thin nor too fat because their weight "fell between the 85th and 114th percent of standard weight for height and age" (p. 194).

Kelly and Patten found that a large percentage of normal-weight teenagers, particularly girls, were dissatisfied with their weight and/or concerned about being overweight. Around 40 percent of the boys and girls wanted to lose weight, but a closer analysis indicates that this parity is illusory. In general the boys *wanted* to reduce so that they could be more successful in competitive sports, but they were unlikely to translate their desire into either dieting or exercising with the intention of losing weight.

On the other hand, the figure of 40 percent probably underestimates the percentage of girls who were concerned about their weight and trying to lose weight. A majority of the girls—none of whom was technically overweight—were "frequently" or "constantly" concerned about being overweight (69 percent), wanted to be "very thin" (59 percent), liked losing weight (68 percent), and got angry with themselves after overeating (69 percent). Just under half of these girls were currently dieting with the express intent of losing weight and increasing their attractiveness, which they see as less than that of their female peers. The extent to which the glorification of thinness has influenced today's teenage girls is seen in the fact that not a single one whose actual weight was between 95 to 115 percent of the standard of her height and age endorsed the item "I feel more attractive than most other people."

Kelly and Patten's research suggests that, at any given time, at least 40 percent of all white, middle-class, *normal-weight* girls attending sub-urban high schools are actively engaged in losing weight in order to become very thin. Of equal importance is the finding that for girls, but not boys, slenderness was positively correlated with higher grades, more friends, and a greater interest in dating. This raises the disturbing possibility that, as a result of cultural messages equating thinness with beauty and virtue, slenderness is actually becoming a significant characteristic in the development of feminine self-concept and self-esteem (20, 39).

If slenderness has indeed moved from the category of a magical solution to a real asset, then there exists a double jeopardy that is bound to place more and more young girls at risk for eating disorders (20). On the one hand, girls who do not wish to be thin or who are genetically incapable of it will be actively discouraged from feeling good about their bodies and themselves. On the other hand, the vast majority of those who buy into this new "American dream"—slenderness—will be continually fighting the dictates of their biological constitution, the abundance of both nutritious and non-nutritious food, and the cleverness of professionals who earn a lot of money advertising pizza, beer, hamburgers, and candy. The dieter who sees no choice but to reduce may or may not become and remain thin (and the odds are very much against both), but either way the cost of rigorous dieting will be very high—a perpetual hunger for food and unconditional positive regard, indulgence in dangerous weight-control practices, an unstable self-image, a constant war with the self and others over the issue of control, and disillusionment upon discovering that in the long run self-denial is no more a solution to life's complexities than indulgence (16, 20).

EATING DISORDERS AND NORMAL WEIGHT CONTROL

The fact that weight anxiety, body dissatisfaction, dieting, and dangerous weight-control practices (see Chapter 6) occur with great frequency among high school and college students raises the possibility that anorexia nervosa and bulimia lie at the extreme end of a culturally supported continuum of maladaptive beliefs and behaviors. To test this hypothesis Garner devised the Eating Disorders Inventory or EDI (14, 15). The 64 items on this questionnaire cluster into eight behaviors and attitudes present in most cases of anorexia nervosa and bulimia. These are a drive for thinness, engagement in binge-eating and self-induced vomiting, body dissatisfaction, perfectionism, a sense of personal ineffectiveness, interpersonal distrust, disturbances of interoceptive awareness (see Chapter 2, pp. 43–44), and fears of maturity.

Garner and his associates administered the EDI to anorexic patients and to a large group of female undergraduates. Based on their responses, the students were grouped into those who were weight-preoccupied and those who were not. As dictated by the EDI's standardization, the anorexics' scores on all eight subscales were significantly greater than those of the non-weight-preoccupied students. The weight-preoccupied students, however, were very comparable to the anorexics in their high levels of drive for thinness, body dissatisfaction, and perfectionism. Anorexics appear to have some unique psychological problems (such as mistrust and maturity fears), but the fact that they share several salient features of their disorder with normal female undergraduates provides support for the role of culture in the development of this form of psychopathology (14, 34).

THE RELENTLESS PURSUIT OF THINNESS

During one of my all-too-rare visits to the college athletic complex for an afternoon workout, I happened across two sheets of paper in an empty locker. These pages from *The Runner* magazine (25) invited me to rate my "running commitment" on a scale adapted from a popular book, *In Pursuit of Excellence.* As a sedentary psychologist interested in eating disorders, I read all the questions, but replaced each "running" or "excelling" with "losing weight" or "staying thin."

I was disturbed by the fit between these substitutions and the attitudes manifested in anorexia nervosa and bulimia. People with eating disorders are extremely "willing to sacrifice other things to excel in [staying thin]." They "never let up or give up in a race [to lose weight]." They also "push hard even when it hurts." Further, they "feel more committed to improvement in [losing weight or staying thin] than anything else" and "they feel more successful or gain more recognition in [losing weight or staying thin] than anything else."

I believe that the glorification of fanatical self-control increases the danger inherent in our culture's idealization of thinness. Many dieters, dedicated to the pursuit of thinness despite their genetic heritage and in the face of constant temptation, see their bodies as the "enemy" (11, 34). As demonstrated previously, quite often the goal of this battle with biology is self-control, not improved health or even heightened sexual attractiveness. For centuries, fasting in the presence of plenty has signified a distinctive purification of the soul (9, 14). The goal of many of today's dieters is to be similarly virtuous and special through the exercise of fanatical self-denial (see Chapter 3). Now that the standard of living in Western culture is higher for all classes, body fat is no longer a sign of wealth or power. On the contrary, being thin has become a symbol of uncommon beauty and goodness, as well as a sign of youth in culture that does not respect the elderly (3, 39). The negative correlation between obesity and social class highlights all too clearly the positive correlation between eating disorders and socioeconomic privilege (14).

Many people will angrily resist the implication that there is anything wrong with sacrificing "everything" in order to be the best. Competitive ambition and perfectionism are highly valued commodities in our male-dominated, achievement-oriented society (28). Moreover, in a culture such as ours, where external restraints on behavior are lessened or at least muddled, there is often open admiration for those who struggle against great odds to blend self-control and achievement (14).

A striking example is our reverence of triathletes. In one sense these men and women are highly skilled athletes dedicated to peak physical and mental conditioning. The successful triathlete, however, is often a person who sacrifices relationships and a multidimensional life in order to achieve recognition and, in some cases, riches through an "all-consuming" devotion to exercising, eating huge quantities of food, and obsessing about diets, appearance, and competition. To an impressionable youngster the positive significance of the triathlon may be superseded by a more primitive message that supports both an egocentric desire for uniqueness and the seductive suggestion that one can eat huge quantities of food as long as one balances it out with fanatical exercise.

To investigate the dangers posed by a combination of fanaticism, competition, and pressures for a thin body, Garfinkel and Garner administered the Eating Attitudes Test (EAT) to female students at three different professional ballet schools, a professional modeling school, a Canadian university, and a music conservatory (12). The music students were evaluated because their training is intensely competitive, but they are under no apparent pressure to be thin as they perform. The EAT is similar in structure to the EDI, but focuses more on specific aspects of anorexia nervosa such as extremely restrictive dieting, food preoccupation, and internal versus external control of eating (12).

The results of this study clearly demonstrate that circumstances emphasizing dedication, competition, and pressure for thinness foster anorexia nervosa and anorexic attitudes. Twelve of the 183 (6.5 percent) professional dance students met the *DSM-III* criteria for anorexia nervosa (see Chapter 6, Table 6–1). Another 26

(14 percent) of the dancers were not technically "anorexic," but they did report a "drive for thinness" and a "morbid fear of weight gain" equivalent to those of hospitalized anorexics. In addition, this subgroup reported frequent use of self-induced vomiting and laxatives to control their weight. In general, the dance and modeling students had significantly higher scores on the EAT than the female undergraduates and professional music students, and the dancers from more competitive programs had the highest scores. This correlation and the low scores of the music students indicate that dedication and competition do not cause eating disorders. They become sinister only when coupled with explicit pressures to remain thin.

EATING DISORDERS AND THE PSYCHOLOGY OF WOMEN

The observation that 1 to 5 percent of bulimics and anorexics are male means that it is a serious mistake for school staff, students, and professionals to classify eating disorders as a "women's issue" (1; and see Chapter 6). Nonetheless, the fact remains that 95 percent of those who admit to having an eating disorder or present themselves for treatment are female. At present the relationship between eating disorders and feminine biology or sex-role identity remains unclear; anorexia nervosa and bulimia have been variously associated with a rejection of femininity (9), a confused acceptance of femininity (4), and a rebellious redefinition of femininity (27). These discrepancies in theory should not, however, obscure the obvious: the extreme sex difference in the prevalence of eating disorders means that the nature of femininity in our culture is a significant risk factor in the development of anorexia nervosa and bulimia. (See Streigel-Moore, Silberstein, and Rodin [33] for an extensive discussion of the relationship between eating disorders and many issues in the psychology of femininity—for example, the con-

nections among physical attractiveness, pleasing and serving others, and self-esteem.)

The astute, as well as the cynical, observer will note that the emergence of eating disorders as a widespread problem coincides with the expansion of the feminist movement (18, 31). This in no way means that feminism "causes" eating disorders; Lincoln's emancipation proclamation is certainly not to blame for the economic plight of millions of poor Blacks in the United States. Rather, the association between the feminist movement and eating disorders may indicate that "if one lives in a culture where the roles of women are complex, conflicting, and in change, and if these pressures exist in a milieu which emphasizes a high positive value on slimness and negative value on obesity, one is at greater risk for anorexia [and bulimia]" (31, p. 87).

In their book, *Bulimarexia: The Binge/Purge Cycle* (4), Marlene Boskind-White and her husband William describe their therapeutic work with female bulimics from Cornell University and other colleges around the country. In general, these young women are bright, energetic, talented, interesting, and privileged. But this potential only seems to contribute to a strong feeling of being trapped between a dedication to traditional feminine values and an overpowering sense that they *must* compete with men and women in developing a successful career. Janice Cauwels, author of another highly recommended book, *Bulimia: The Binge-Purge Compulsion* (7), is convinced that these women and our society in general have misperceived the feminist emphasis on opportunity and choices for women as an obligation to achieve professional success at an early age.

In my opinion many men and women are extremely threatened by attempts to expand the gender identities of both sexes in the direction of greater depth and freedom. Consequently, to maintain the balance of power in favor of men or some vague conception of the status quo, this resistant majority has perverted the feminist demands for equality of opportunity into an unrealistic insistence that women reconcile the traditional and contradictory masculine and feminine roles into a "super" identity (3, 7). This identity retains many features of the established feminine role—for example, an obsession with the body, sensitivity to others, and dependence on male approval—but redefines the substance and style of femininity to emphasize thinness, youth, ambition, self-control, and self-sufficiency (3). Ironically, radical feminists may be adding to this diffused identity by rejecting those women who *choose* to delay or even eschew a career in favor of the traditional homemaker role.

It is likely that rejection of the stereotypical feminine role with its images of a soft, rounded, and self-effacing mother contributes in some way to our cultural obsession with thinness (14). The other side of this new coin may be the need to look younger and more masculine—that is, thinner—in order to compete and gain respect in the essentially masculine world of business. Or both motives can be condensed into a single need—to compete with other women over who is the thinnest and most virtuous at the dinner table (7). A cigarette continually reminds women that they have "come a long way, *baby*" (italics added) in their quest for social and economic autonomy. This cigarette is not called "Virginia Fats." The painful irony here is that the commercialization of thinness is actually a means of "cashing in on women's gullibility, self-consciousness, uncertainty, and anxiety" (3, p. 123). The new, slender style is not a true symbol of liberation, but simply a newer badge of subjugation, this time to a god of thinness that is much more dangerous than whalebone corsets or stiletto heels (3, 13).

Arguing from a historical and a clinical perspective, Boskind-White and the Wooleys make a convincing case that the relentless pursuit of thinness is embedded within a broader and very complex cultural issue, the expansion and diffusion of the feminine sex role (3, 39). This hypothesis was examined in a recent study by Dr. Catherine Steiner-Adair of the Children's Hospital Medical Center in Boston (32). The

subjects of her research were 32 girls attending a private high school—a group at risk for eating disorders (see Chapter 6). Steiner-Adair found that all the girls were quite aware of the "superwoman" ideal. Each was able to describe her as *thin*, attractive, smart, active, independent, autonomous and dominant within relationships, and somehow *perfectly* successful in establishing a career, being an exciting wife, and raising a family. Nineteen (60 percent) of the girls seemed to understand that pursuing this myth would jeopardize the sense of interpersonal connectedness around which girls, as opposed to boys, tend to build their identities (17). The remaining 13 girls (40 percent) wholeheartedly embraced this contradictory vision of interdependent autonomy, seeing no internal inconsistencies and no dissonance between the intense pressure to be separate versus their socialization to value relationship above complete individuation. Of the girls who saw through the superwoman myth and rejected it, not one had an EAT score in the eating disorder range. Of the girls who identified with the superwoman, 11 (85 percent) had scores in the eating disorder range and another was borderline.

It may well be that the bulimic college women who participate in Dr. Boskind-White's therapy groups are at a later stage of the doomed struggle to become superwomen. The ambiguous and conflicting pressures created by separation from men and reliance on their approval leave these women feeling "empty" (= hungry?), out of control, and angry (4). In this regard, dieting, bingeing, and purging can be construed as counterbalanced and culturally legitimate means of aspiring to the ideal of thinness while combating such disruptive feelings.

The work of Boskind-White and Steiner-Adair provides strong support for the belief that complex transformations in the feminine role constitute a sociocultural factor in the proliferation of eating disorders. The key feature here is change itself; it is a serious mistake, as well as a great injustice to women and men, to interpret the research on sex roles as suggesting that girls would be better off if only they would accept the traditional feminine characteristics. The ability of the fashion and diet industries to inculcate the goal of thinness is based squarely on the traditional feminine identification of self-esteem with personal appearance (3, 39). Moreover, research conducted in the 1970s demonstrated that male and female psychologists listed the same ideal characteristics for a healthy "person" and a healthy "male," whereas their conception of a mature female was antithetical to their description of a healthy "person" (5)! We certainly do not need to return to a lopsided feminine sex role whose actualization moves one in the direction of psychological disturbance (8).

A recent survey of women attending Miami University in Ohio suggests that changes in both the feminine sex role and the ideal body shape form a cultural backdrop for the proliferation of eating disorders (Debs and others, cited in Wooley and Wooley [39]). Although most of the women believed their mothers to be generally approving of them, only 43 percent felt the mother's attitude toward the daughter's body was at least "mostly positive." More important, the degree of this perceived negativity was highly correlated with all but one of the EDI subscales. Body dissatisfaction was the strongest predictor of bulimic behavior, but the next strongest was the daughter's perception that her mother was very critical of the daughter's body. This is very interesting in light of two findings of the *Glamour Magazine* survey (11). First, very few of today's women feel that their mothers like their own bodies. Second, a woman's negative attitude toward her own body is highly correlated with the perception that both mother and father are or were critical of her body shape.

Assembling these correlations into a dynamic portrait of familial interactions is difficult, but the Wooleys offer a thought-provoking and plausible interpretation (39). They note that the mothers of today's teenage girls are the first cohort of women to experience generalized dissatisfaction with their weight and themselves as a result of fashion propaganda, the changing roles of women, and our culture's increasing emphasis on

youth (see also Boskind-White [3]). It is hard to see how this lack of respect for body and self would not color the development of their daughters in some important ways. When these girls reach puberty, or even before, their body shape may become a projective surface for the mother's unfulfilled wishes and uncertainties and for the daughter's needs to act like a woman (mother) while becoming her own, "better" woman (not mother). In this emotionally charged interaction, "dieting may serve simultaneously as identification, differentiation, revenge, and penance" (39, p. 392). The pain of this conflict and confusion is great, but not as great as that involved in rejecting the female role. Perhaps the hostile purification of the anorexic and the uncontrollable gorging and purging of the bulimic represent a culturally supported lack of respect for the normal female body and a need to escape the choices posed by the dilemma of maternal versus paternal identification (39).

The role of hostility, expressed outwardly as anger and inwardly as self-loathing, in the development and expression of eating disorders is deserving of more research. The proliferation of eating disorders has coincided, not only with feminism and increasing pressures for thinness, but also with an explosion of violence against women in the streets, in the home, on film, and in "literature." Surely such denigration does nothing to help girls and women learn to respect their bodies and themselves. In addition, women are socialized to deny anger or keep it to themselves (3, 17). Both these factors increase the likelihood that eating disorders are in part self-directed expressions of rage that also serve to mock the very same dependency, objectification, and idealization of thinness that many anorexics and bulimics cannot refrain from embodying.

HISTORY, CULTURE, AND PSYCHOPATHOLOGY

Sociocultural theories of psychopathology maintain that culture shapes the nature of anxiety and the means by which people cope with inner turmoil. The classic illustration of this principle is the conversion hysteria that afflicted a number of middle- and upper-class women in England and Western Europe at the close of the Victorian era (26, 31). In response to overwhelming life stress these women unconsciously converted deep-rooted conflicts between internal urges (such as sexuality and anger) and external proprieties (being "feminine") into an apparent physical disorder (hysterical paralysis). This strategy protected the person and others from the power and significance of the emotional conflict. However, the conversion also permitted some satisfaction of the urges (through attention, massage, and passive aggression), while enabling the individual to retain the feminine qualities of helplessness and dependency (she "couldn't stand on her own two feet").

Eating disorders may well be the conversion disorders of our times (31). As our culture has changed, so have our anxieties, proprieties, and coping strategies. But now many vulnerable people—young women—convert powerful new conflicts between internal needs (to "be in control" and to "be someone") and external proprieties ("being thin" and "feminine") into eating disorders. Anorexia nervosa and bulimia reconcile both these pressures before they devolve into a dangerous parody of each.

CONCLUSIONS AND IMPLICATIONS
THE ROLE OF CULTURE

CONCLUSION.   It is difficult to establish the influence of culture on psychopathology. Nevertheless, the evidence reviewed in this chapter leaves little doubt that sociocultural factors are encouraging the development of eating disorders. Of special significance in this respect is the finding that a large number of people in our culture, particularly teenage girls, manifest many of the psychological characteristics and weight control practices that form the basis of anorexia nervosa and bulimia.

IMPLICATION.   All school employees who wish to transform the school into a positive force in the prevention of eating disorders must acknowledge that people with eating disorders are not "crazies" who fall prey to an incomprehensible "mental illness." Rather, they are people— our students, our children, our colleagues, and our friends—struggling with insecurities and pressures that we as members of our culture have helped create or sustain.

THE GLORIFICATION OF THINNESS AND RIGID SELF-CONTROL

CONCLUSION.   The increase in the prevalence of eating disorders is in part attributable to the emergence of thinness as an ideal of feminine beauty and as a concrete expression of virtuous self-control. A drive for thinness is arguably the most important feature of both anorexia nervosa and bulimia. This motive is reinforced by a host of cultural messages: the ultra-thin models of a high-class fashion magazine like *Vogue,* a coach's misguided advice to "come back after you've lost some weight," a cigarette called "More" that features a thin woman clad in an expensive outfit. The dark side of this culturally supported drive for thinness is widespread prejudice toward overweight individuals, particularly women. In this context weight loss and slenderness have become standards of beauty and goodness. There is little evidence that the health of Americans has benefited from these values, but there is substantial evidence of widespread dissatisfaction with natural body shapes and of intense pressure to challenge normal weight by restrictive dieting. For certain vulnerable individuals, the long-term outcome of this anxious self-rejection is an eating disorder (see Chapters 8 and 9).

IMPLICATIONS.   The glorification of thinness and fanatical self-control illuminates the many obstacles faced by school staff interested in the prevention of eating disorders. First, there is the challenge of examining one's own beliefs and behaviors for evidence of a psychological investment in slenderness and/or prejudice against overweight. At the very least educators should try to eliminate negative statements about overweight people from their language and other educational tools. Second, the fusion of slenderness with beauty and virtue means that body weight, body shape, and attractiveness will be very sensitive issues for discussion within a mixed-sex group that probably includes several overweight students and numerous dieters (21). And third, examination of the totally unwarranted prejudice against overweight and even normal-weight people will likely conclude with sound but controversial contentions—for example, most people should not eat less than 2,000 well-balanced calories per day (see Chapter 9) and the definition of healthy body weight should depend on the person's function and fitness, not on a table of heights and weights that overlooks vast individual differences in "natural" body weight (16).

This list of challenges is not meant to discourage consideration of sociocultural factors in the development of eating disorders. Far from it. My intent is rather to encourage careful preparation for discussion of some of the most important factors in the cause of anorexia nervosa and bulimia: prejudice, the media, fashions, competitive ambitiousness, sex differences, the biological regulation of eating and weight, and the normalization of excessive dieting (see Chapter 10). This rich variety of topics makes the influence of sociocultural factors a fertile ground for teachers of social studies, history, speech, home economics, health science, and biology (21).

Eating Disorders and the Changing Feminine Sex Role

Conclusion. Three facts clearly connect eating disorders with changes in the feminine sex role. First, the upsurge of eating disorders coincides with the increased impact of the feminist movement and the resultant expansion of the feminine sex role to include contradictory demands for autonomous and interdependent behaviors. Second, most anorexics and bulimics are females who develop their eating disorders during adolescence, a time of life in which the issues of identity and intimacy are paramount in personal development. Third, the research by Steiner-Adair demonstrates a correlation between identification with the "super-thin superwoman" ideal and anorexic-like attitudes and behaviors. At present we do not know how these confusing and oppressive changes in the feminine sex role combine with the traditional feminine investment in personal appearance to set the stage for eating disorders. It is very likely, however, that the relentless pursuit of thinness reflects numerous themes, including identification with current ideals of youthful beauty, rejection of traditional feminine shapes and limitations, and the struggle for control of something concrete—weight and shape—in a world of abstract ambiguities (6, 27, 39).

Implications. As noted earlier, educators interested in eating disorders must deal carefully and sensitively with the emotional topics of body weight, body shape, and body image. Self-conscious teenagers, in particular, find it difficult to discuss openly these fundamental aspects of what is often an imcomplete self-concept. This challenge to teachers is intensified by the fact that these topics have a different meaning for girls and boys. The entire notion of a sex role is tricky, because it blurs individual differences, emphasizes constraints on personal freedom, and points to gender inequities. Nevertheless, consideration of cultural expectations for males and females is necessary if two crucial questions are to be addressed: Why do people diet? (see Levine [21]) and Why do more girls than boys diet? Given the emotional nature of these questions, they might be best addressed initially through nonthreatening assignments such as the collection and analysis of boys (men) and girls (women) as portrayed in a variety of advertisements.

A Sociocultural Approach to Prevention

CONCLUSION.   The multidimensional nature of eating disorders, as well as their history of at least 300 years, suggests that even radical changes in Western culture are not likely to eliminate anorexia nervosa and bulimia completely. Nonetheless, if culture shapes the nature of our fears and our strategies for coping with them, then the school as an influential representative of society can play an important role in combating many of the constituents of eating disorders, such as the inflexible need to be thin, the normalization of dieting, and the glorification of competitive self-control.

IMPLICATION.   The role of the school in socialization is controversial, but one of the bases of this book is my conviction that, through education and personal example, teachers can promote a healthy acceptance of self and others by actively resisting cultural pressures to equate thinness with fulfillment, perfectionism with virtue, and opportunity with obligation. Not all teachers will have the inclination or time to become involved in the prevention of eating disorders. Those who choose to must join with counselors and other school staff, parents, and students in resisting the strong temptation to dissociate themselves from eating disorders by marveling at their bizarre signs and symptoms, giving them impressive psychiatric labels, and then turning over all responsibility for comprehending, identifying, and preventing them to experts (21, 22).

REFERENCES

1. Andersen, A. E. *Practical Comprehensive Treatment of Anorexia Nervosa and Bulimia.* Baltimore: Johns Hopkins University Press, 1985.
2. Bennett, W. G., and Gurin, J. *The Dieter's Dilemma: Eating Less and Weighing More.* New York: Basic Books, 1982.
3. Boskind-White, M. "Bulimarexia: A Sociocultural Perspective." In *Throey and Treatment of Anorexia Nervosa and Bulimia: Biomedical, Sociocultural, and Psychological Perspectives,* edited by S. W. Emmett, pp. 113–26. New York: Brunner/Mazel, 1985.
4. Boskind-White, M., and White, W. C., Jr. *Bulimarexia: The Binge/Purge Cycle.* New York: W. W. Norton, 1983.
5. Broverman, I., and others. "Sex-Role Stereotypes: A Current Appraisal." *Journal of Social Issues* 28 (1972): 59–78.
6. Bruch, H. *The Golden Cage: The Enigma of Anorexia Nervosa.* Cambridge: Harvard University Press, 1978.
7. Cauwels, J. M. *Bulimia: The Binge-Purge Compulsion.* New York: Doubleday, 1983.
8. Chesler, P. *Women and Madness.* New York: Avon Books, 1973.
9. Crisp, A. H. *Anorexia Nervosa: Let Me Be.* London: Academic Press, 1980.
10. Fallon, A. E., and Rozin, P. "Sex Differences in Perception of Desirable Body Shape." *Journal of Abnormal Psychology* 94 (1985): 102–5.
11. "Feeling Fat in a Thin Society." *Glamour Magazine* (February 1984): 198–201, 251–52.
12. Garfinkel, P. E., and Garner, D. M. *Anorexia Nervosa: A Multidimensional Perspective.* New York: Brunner/Mazel, 1982.
13. Garner, D. M. "Sociocultural Issues in the Development of Eating Disorders." Paper presented at Fourth National Conference on Eating Disorders of National Anorexic Aid Society, Columbus, Ohio, October 1985.
14. Garner, D. M.; Garfinkel, P. E.; and Olmsted, M. P. "An Overview of Sociocultural Factors in the Development of Anorexia Nervosa." In *Anorexia Nervosa: Recent Developments in Research,* edited by P. L. Darby and others, pp. 65–82. New York: A. R. Liss, 1983.
15. Garner, D. M.; Olmsted, M. P.; and Polivy, J. "The Eating Disorders Inventory: A Measure of Cognitive-Behavioral Dimensions of Anorexia Nervosa and Bulimia." In *Anorexia Nervosa: Recent Developments in Research,* edited by P. L.

Darby and others, pp. 173–84. New York: A. R. Liss, 1983.

16. Garner, D. M., and others. "Psychoeducational Principles in the Treatment of Bulimia and Anorexia Nervosa." In *Handbook of Psychotherapy for Anorexia Nervosa and Bulimia,* edited by D. M. Garner and P. E. Garfinkel, pp. 513–72. New York: Guilford Press, 1985.

17. Gilligan, C. *In a Different Voice: Psychological Theory and Women's Development.* Cambridge: Harvard University Press, 1982.

18. Johnson, C. "Biopsychosocial Model of Etiology for Bulimia." Paper presented at Third National Conference on Eating Disorders of National Anorexic Aid Society, Columbus, Ohio, October 1984.

19. Johnson, C., and Maddi, K. L. "The Etiology of Bulimia: Bio-Psycho-Social Perspectives." *Annals of Adolescent Psychiatry* 13 (1986): 253–73.

20. Kelly, J. T., and Patten, S. E. "Adolescent Behaviors and Attitudes Toward Weight and Eating." In *Anorexia Nervosa and Bulimia: Diagnosis and Treatment,* edited by J. E. Mitchell, pp. 191–204. Minneapolis: University of Minnesota Press, 1985.

21. Levine, M. P. *The Psychology of Eating Disorders: A Lesson Plan for Grades 7–12.* Edited by A. B. Enright, N. Kayne, and C. Tootell. Columbus, Ohio: National Anorexic Aid Society (NAAS), 1983. Available from NAAS, 5796 Karl Road, Columbus, OH 43229 (614-436-1112).

22. ———. "The Role of Culture in the Cause of Eating Disorders." *Kenyon College Alumni Magazine* 9 (Winter 1985): 8–13. Available from Michael Levine, Psychology Department, Kenyon College, Gambier, OH 43022 (614-427-2244).

23. ———. "Whatever Happened to Lesley Armstrong? The Role of Culture in the Cause and Prevention of Eating Disorders." Workshop presented at Fourth National Conference on Eating Disorders of National Anorexic Aid Society, Columbus, Ohio, October 1985.

24. Lewinsohn, P. M., and others. "Social Competence and Depression: The Role of Illusory Self-Perceptions." *Journal of Abnormal Psychology* 89 (1980): 203–12.

25. Lynch, J. "Commitment: What You Give Is What You Get (Better Running)." *Runner* (December 1984): 20–21.

26. Monte, C. *Beneath the Mask: An Introduction to Theories of Personality.* 2d ed. New York: Holt, Rinehart and Winston, 1980.

27. Orbach, S. "Visibility/Invisibility: Social Consideration in Anorexia Nervosa—A Feminist Perspective." In *Theory and Treatment of Anorexia Nervosa and Bulimia: Biomedical Sociocultural, and Psychological Perspectives,* edited by S. W. Emmett, pp. 127–38. New York: Brunner/Mazel, 1985.

28. Price, V. A. *Type A Behavior Pattern: A Model for Research and Practice.* New York: Academic Press, 1982.

29. Rosenhan, D. L., and Seligman, M. E. P. *Abnormal Psychology.* New York: W. W. Norton, 1984.

30. Schwartz, D. M.; Thompson, M. G.; and Johnson, C. "Anorexia Nervosa and Bulimia: The Sociocultural Context." *International Journal of Eating Disorders* 1 (1982): 20–36.

31. Schwartz, D. M.; Thompson, M. G.; and Johnson, C. "Eating Disorders and the Culture." In *Anorexia Nervosa: Recent Developments in Research,* edited by P. L. Darby and others, pp. 83–94. New York: A. R. Liss, 1983.

32. Steiner-Adair, C. "The Body Politic: Normal Female Adolescent Development and the Development of Eating Disorders." Paper presented at Fourth National Conference on Eating Disorders of National Anorexic Aid Society, Columbus, Ohio, October 1985.

33. Streigel-Moore, R. H.; Silberstein, L. R.; and Rodin, J. "Toward an Understanding of Risk Factors for Bulimia." *American Psychologist* 41 (1986): 246–63.

34. Thompson, M. G., and Schwartz, D. M. "Life Adjustment of Women with Anorexia Nervosa and Anorexic-Like Behavior." *International Journal of Eating Disorders* 2 (1981): 47–60.

35. Vandereycken, W., and Meermann, R. *Anorexia Nervosa: A Clinician's Guide to Treatment.* New York: Walter de Gruyter, 1984.

36. Wooley, O. W., and Wooley, S. C. "The Beverly Hills Eating Disorder: The Mass Marketing of Anorexia Nervosa" (editorial). *International Journal of Eating Disorders* 1 (1982): 57–69.

37. Wooley, O. W.; Wooley, S. C.; and Dyrenforth, S. R. "Obesity and Women—II. A Neglected Feminist Topic." *Women's Studies International Quarterly* 2 (1979): 81–92.

38. Wooley, S. C., and Wooley, O. W. "Obesity and Women—I. A Closer Look at the Facts." *Women's Studies International Quarterly* 2 (1979): 69–79.

39. Wooley, S. C., and Wooley, O. W. "Intensive Outpatient and Residential Treatment for Bulimia." In *Handbook of Psychotherapy for Anorexia Nervosa and Bulimia,* edited by D. M. Garner and P. E. Garfinkel, pp. 391–430. New York: Guilford Press, 1985.

XI

CONCLUSION

33

A Critical Appraisal of Sexual Studies in Anthropology: Toward a Nomothetic Anthropology of Sexuality

David N. Suggs / Andrew W. Miracle

THE EVOLUTION OF ANTHROPOLOGICAL THEORY

The evolution of anthropological approaches to the study of sexuality has roughly followed the broader development of general anthropological theory. Therefore, in order to appreciate the former, we must situate it within the context of the latter. Moreover, it is important to note that anthropology is a very young discipline as compared with most sciences. Though people everywhere have shown some interest in "the other" throughout recorded history, it was only in the late nineteenth and early twentieth centuries that

anthropology took on an academic standing. At that time, there were several intellectual trends that, when viewed from today's perspective, serve as a backdrop against which we can understand the development of anthropological theory.

EARLY PERSPECTIVES ON HUMAN DIFFERENCES

Up to the mid-nineteenth century, most European social thought was focused on the biblical record. Differences between peoples were seen as "essential," inherent in the Judeo-Christian god's act of creation. The Catholic universe was believed to have a largely static and ordained hierarchical structure in the realm of the sacred, one that was mirrored by a similarly hierarchical and ordained social structure in the secular world. That is, in the realm of the sacred, there was a hierarchy of God, archangels, angels, and the saved; on Earth there was a hierarchy of the Pope, cardinals, bishops, priests, and the laity; in Hell the hierarchy was Satan, archangels of Hell, angels of Hell, and the damned. In a basically static structure such as this, differences between the various peoples of Earth came to be seen as part of a "great chain of Being," in which western Europeans were deemed to be at the top of the hierarchy and all others were ranked below them. Similarly, the animals were ranked below all humanity, and plant life was ranked below all animal life.

Yet, in the mid-nineteenth century, work by geologists such as Charles Lyell and by naturalists such as Charles Darwin brought us a view of the world that was anything but static in character. Lyell's principles of geological succession and gradualism combined with Darwin's theory of natural selection to produce a conception of a changing and evolving world. Developments in the system of Linnaean taxonomy brought us closer to understanding the relationship between the various forms of life on Earth, and Darwin's ideas gave us an inkling of how these relationships were produced in response to competition for natural resources.

Those developments in turn impacted the social thought of the time in significant ways. If the world was not to be understood as something created *as we see it today*, then how were we to account for the differences between peoples and societies? Clearly, one of the formative questions of the nineteenth century for both anthropology and sociology was, "How is it that we [western Europeans] are 'modern' (that is, different from those who are more 'primitive'), and how did humanity's evolution produce these differences?"

EVOLUTION AND CULTURAL THEORY

Just as this question clearly reflected the evolutionary thought in the physical and natural sciences at the time, so too did the other central question of the time reflect the taxonomic developments in these disciplines. That is, the other definitional concern of nineteenth-century social science was the question of how, given a natural order produced via evolution, we might build a taxonomy of peoples and cultures against which to view and understand their many differences.

All of the seminal thinkers in social science at this time—among them Emile Durkheim, Max Weber, and Karl Marx—were concerned primarily with answering one or both of these questions. However, most important for the anthropology of this period was the dominance of a school of thought referred to today as unilineal evolutionism. L. H. Morgan, E. B. Tylor, Herbert Spencer, and others of this school argued that human culture evolved in a single line of development, with western European culture representing the endpoint of that evolutionary trajectory and the other cultures of Earth representing less progressive forms. In short, other cultures came to be seen as representative of Europe's past, and Europe's present was seen as representative of other cultures' future.

The mechanism underlying this evolution was a point of debate. For Morgan, it was technological development; for Tylor, increasing rationality; for Spencer, increasing social structural complexity. However, the implication for all of them was that other cultures were inferior, backwards, and less evolved than European cultures. Whether the mechanism was political-economic, social-structural, or bioracist, it gave to the Western world a carte blanche for dominating other peoples.

It was Franz Boas, at the turn of the century, who would reorient anthropology from this position. Boas, in opposition to the racism and Eurocentrism of his time, suggested that every culture was the product of a *particular* historical development; and Boas argued that there were no reliable data on which to base a suggestion that all cultures evolved in a single line of development. He showed that if one lived among other peoples, one would discover that no culture is any more or less rational, any more or less advanced, any better than any others. As the product of unique historical circumstance, each culture could be understood only on its own terms. No longer could anthropology rely on the questionable accounts of travelers and missionaries. Similarities between cultures, he suggested, were better explained by contact and diffusion than by any spurious notion of a unilineal evolution. This school of thought, known now as historical particularism, would dominate American anthropology well into and beyond the first half of the twentieth century.

The legacy of historical particularist studies of sexuality is most significant. Specifically, they gave to us the realization that our sexual behavior is less the result of innate biological drives than it is the product of individual learning. In short, our culture patterns our sexuality. It defines our society's sexual norms and it structures our sexual behavior. It provides a system of meaning by which we understand sexuality. Historical particularist ethnographies—works such as Mead's, Marshall's, and Messenger's in this volume—give us an idea of the variety of ways in which culture does these things, and they impress upon us the cultural diversity of a set of behaviors previously believed to be primarily or wholly "natural."

The weight of these contributions has led William Davenport (1987:189) to claim that the "signal contribution [of] the anthropological study of sex [is] the demonstration that human culture . . . shape[s], structure[s], and control[s] all manifestations of sexuality." In short, he notes that anthropology has concerned itself primarily with the elucidation of the diversity in the "culture of sex." To date, this is an accurate assessment of the discipline. Anthropology has focused on the ways in which history has shaped particular cultural constructions of sexual "normalcy" and on the ways in which those constructions are consistent with a people's worldview. As a result, most research has focused on the symbolic and structural dimensions of sexuality.

Although this has been as important for the study of sexuality as Boasian-styled anthropological contributions have been in other areas of study, it is no longer sufficient for an anthropology of sexuality in the 1990s. Historically particular studies, while always significant, must by their design be atomistic. Ultimately, focusing solely on historical particularism will yield no understanding of the sexuality of humans *qua* humans. It can lead us only to the chaotic "shreds and patches" position adopted by Davenport: that there *is no such thing as* human *sexuality*.[1] That is, particularist studies will inform us about the sexual practices *of the Samoans*, about the sexual morality *of the Irish*, about sexual beliefs *in Polynesia*. Yet, beyond what are merely descriptive statements of the universality or near universality of a handful of traits, particular descriptions (in and of themselves) cannot yield a general explanation of *human* practices, beliefs, and moral structures. Data alone describe much but explain very little. Explanation derives from theory, and the Boasians were simply unrealistically inductive in their approach to general explanations.

For this reason, we reject the position taken by Davenport that the ethnology of sex is simply "the means by which we learn the extent of cultural variation" (Davenport 1987:198). Although we would certainly agree that this is *one* benefit of ethnology, we hold that it must be more than just descriptive of humankind's diversity. It must be explanatory in its approach to human variation as well. From Davenport's position, "sexual customs isolated from their cultural contexts are either meaningless in themselves or subject to gross misinterpretation when not seen in their cultural contexts" (1987:198–199). From our perspective, we cannot speak of human sexuality at all without utilizing a theoretical perspective that asks us to look beyond the particular cultural context. For Davenport, the goal of an anthropological study of sex is to describe the emics[2] of particular sexuality for a particular culture. Although we share this goal, we also reach for more. For us, an anthropology of sexuality should also look to the etics[3] of sexual beliefs and behaviors. Again, only through a theory that intends to generalize can one do so in a meaningful sense.

Given that Davenport begins from the positions just noted, his conclusion regarding the "meaningless" character of sexual practices outside of their cultural environment is logical. The question of meaning, however, must be more closely examined. If we limit the meaning of a practice to the emic logic of cultural actors, then indeed such acts are meaningless outside of their context. But, if we begin with a position on how, *in general*, human beings are most likely to construct meanings, then we can examine sexual practices in that light and find an etic meaning. And, even more interestingly, we can examine not only the emics of sexuality and the etics of sexuality, but also—and, perhaps most importantly—the relationships between them. But, we are getting ahead of ourselves.

FUNCTIONALISM

In the years surrounding the world wars, another influential school of anthropological thought arose that began with the quest for a *general* understanding of human culture. Its chief architects were Bronislaw Malinowski and A. R. Radcliffe-Brown. Although there are important differences between these two thinkers, both began with the assumption that human cultural beliefs, structures, and behaviors all function to benefit humanity. As did the Boasians, these functionalist anthropologists believed that no culture was more rational or more advanced than any other. Yet, in contrast to the Boasians, they attempted to understand particular beliefs and behaviors in a general format. For Malinowski, the function of any cultural trait was to provide for individual human needs. For Radcliffe-Brown, the function of any cultural trait was its role in the maintenance of that culture as a whole.

Functionalist comparisons, then, attempted to be more than merely descriptive statements of particular and universal cultural traits. They attempted to compare the ways in which seemingly different particular beliefs and behaviors served the same function or, conversely, how seemingly similar traits actually served quite different functions. Also, whereas the functionalists focused heavily on the symbolic aspects of culture, they differed from the Boasians in that they devoted considerable time to the study of the social structure. Works in this volume by Malinowski and Schapera are clear representatives of this approach in the anthropology of sex.

Functionalist theory, however, also suffers from some serious limitations. Perhaps the greatest problem is the almost strictly synchronic approach that it adopted. That is, functionalists might tell us that functional similarities existed but, by ignoring questions of change over time, they could offer little in the way of explaining *why* differences in particular settings emerged. To know the function of a trait is not necessarily to know the functional *origin* of that trait.

For example, we know the function of legs: legs are one type of adaptation that allows land-dwellers to move in a nonaquatic environment. Yet, as J. D. Romer (1960; cited in Kottak, 1991:241–242) has pointed out, legs did not evolve so that creatures might live terrestrial existences. On the contrary, they evolved in areas where small pools frequently dried up, and therefore where a creature who could move to another pool could *maintain* an aquatic existence. That adaptation for stability then allowed for subsequent changes that gave the Earth land-dwellers. So, the point is that the function today is not strictly equivalent with the original function. Surely, this is the case for cultural traits, as well as for biological ones.

Anthropology has come to understand the need for diachronic studies, and in doing so has returned to us the ability to talk about the evolution of cultures. These approaches differ from the nineteenth-century evolutionists in that (1) they have abandoned the idea of a unilineal evolution, and (2) they maintain a commitment to the methodological utility of cultural relativity. Contemporary evolutionary approaches continue to focus on the importance of firsthand data collection for understanding internal meanings of beliefs and behaviors. However, they also attempt to produce a system for understanding—from a scientific perspective—why such traits evolved.

For cultural ecologists, cultural traits are presumed to be particular adaptations to particular environments. They assume that similar environments will demand similar adaptations, even if particular cultures attribute different meanings to the traits in question. Cultural materialists assume that all human cultures must first concern themselves with material adaptation to the environment. That is, given a particular environment, the technological means by which people acquire food and exchange it, as well as the way they organize themselves in space to do so, is likely to determine much of their social structure and beliefs.

There are other approaches that attempt to explain the development to human culture (for example, structural Marxism and historical materialism). Still, this is not the place to review them for the simple reason that, as Davenport noted, such approaches have not yet made lasting and significant contributions to the anthropology of sexuality. We believe that the need for such studies in the area of sexuality is crucial to the further development of the field.

The following, then, is a first attempt to systematize a future for the discipline's studies of human sexuality. It is meant to make the reader think about larger questions, to see the potential in a broader anthropology of sexuality, and to suggest avenues of fruitful research in the future.

CONTEMPORARY ANTHROPOLOGICAL STUDIES OF SEXUALITY

Sexuality is of intrinsic interest to most, if not all, humans. For that reason, it is surprising that, on the surface, anthropology has not devoted more effort to studies of sexuality *qua* sexuality.

Beneath the surface, the explanation is not so surprising: few anthropologists have felt comfortable asking other people questions of an explicitly sexual nature because of their own cultural biases against sex as a "proper" subject of study. At the same time, issues of political and economic culture seem to us to be more relevant concerns in a world that has practical problems. Furthermore, those who make decisions in granting agencies may view proposals of sexual studies as prurient. Finally, sexuality seems to many (as individuals) to be in the realm of the purely biological; it's about the "birds and the bees" and "doin' what comes naturally." Whatever the various other reasons we might offer, the anthropological literature on sexuality, even though more substantial than it was 50 years ago, remains relatively undeveloped. This is an unfortunate state of affairs, for to be human is to be sexual and, like all things human, the sexual *is* the cultural.

IDEOGRAPHIC STUDIES OF HUMAN SEXUALITY

In the nineteenth century, Morgan, Bachofen, and others imagined a human *urkultur* in which sexual access was naturally unregulated. A century of anthropological research has left little basis for such a belief. Primate studies show clearly that even among our nonspeaking relatives, social control mechanisms *structure* sexual interactions. Sexuality is at once both a potential force for effective social bonding and a potential source of disruptive social conflict. The social organization of primates, based largely on age and sex, promotes social bonding and limits social conflicts.

Sarah Hrdy suggests that female primates (in general) are socially organized around the quest for food. Males, she says, are more clearly organized around the quest for sexual access to females. Regardless of whether one accepts Hrdy's sociobiological reasoning, most anthropologists would agree that evolution progressively has selected for those better adapted to their environment and better able to reproduce. The result for apes and humans has been the evolution of a structured society and, therefore, of structured sexuality.

What separates apes and humans, then, is not the presence of a structured, orderly sexual life; rather, it is the symbolic meaning in such structure and its elaboration through symbols of such structure. It is not, as Morgan and Bachofen thought, that evolution has brought us from "unregulated" to "regulated" sexual relations. Rather, it is that evolution has brought us from the primarily *physical* regulation of sexuality to the primarily *symbolic* regulation of sexuality.

Symbolic regulation is effective within boundaries of shared meaning—that is, within a culture. Moreover, symbolic regulation is likely to be well integrated with the physical *significata* of sexuality. For example, consider the evolutionary result of sexual dimorphism. Male and female *Homo sapiens* have distinct physical characteristics that may have once predisposed some complementary role specialization (see Symons, 1989; see also Hrdy, 1988 for precautionary statements regarding this idea). Culture has reinforced or in most cases extended such gender role specialization, with increasingly distinct meanings given to male and female roles.

It has been argued that cultural evolution has taken advantage of the physical parameters of sexual specialization as an adaptation to local environments, rather than attempting to counter these parameters by establishing their symbolic as opposed to their biological characteristics (Symons, 1989). Of course, any shared meanings that develop become part of the total environment affecting subsequent physical and cultural evolution. In that light, Hrdy (1988) suggests that culture has been responsible for defining generalized (rather than contextual) male social dominance that is well out of proportion to primate males' dominance in practice.

Clifford Geertz (1980:4) has remarked that sexuality is a "cultural activity sustaining a biological process." Clearly, whereas the biology of human reproduction is a "given," it is equally given for humans to bestow symbolic meaning upon the natural. In short, it is our nature to be cultured. Geertz's quote reminds us that, although we can study human sexual behaviors from the point of view of the ethologist—as behavior that is literally *specific*—no human being fully experiences sexuality in this fashion. We understand the behavior according to the complex whole of knowledge, beliefs, arts, morals, and customs that we acquire through our society as it interacts with our individual psychological makeup. That is, we experience sex as a *meaningful* interaction.

Even when the purpose of sexual interaction is procreation, we do not reproduce as individuals because of an innate need to replicate the species. We do so because of *culturally* specific desires associated with reproduction: here it may be in response to a charge from God ("Be fruitful and multiply"); there it may be to validate one's own status as an adult; elsewhere, it may be a response to wider affective desires or even economic interests. In all places and at all times, our sexuality has meaning: *culturally informed* and distinct from, even if limited by, our animalian, evolutionary heritage.

It is because of this that anthropology traditionally has valued studies of sexuality that are ideographic and culturally specific. Such studies of sexual life are historically particular in character. They literally vary with the number of cultures on Earth. Ideographic studies of sexual life allow us to understand the behaviors of others that, from our own cultural vantage point, may seem bizarre, quixotic, or irrational. As with other thought and meaning systems, those of sexuality are generally consistent with the larger worldview of a society. That is, sexual meanings reflect and are reflected by the larger cultural milieu. In that sense, understanding others' sexual behavior requires that we contextualize that behavior the same way that they do; it requires an emic perspective.

Ideographic studies of sexual life impress upon

us the ingenuity of the human will to make sense out of things. Undertaken without ethnocentrism, such studies show that people everywhere have systematically logical beliefs and behaviors. What one society condones as proper another condemns as perverse. What one considers sexually natural is considered unnatural by others. One goal of anthropological studies of sexuality should be to make the "other" become the "familiar"—to discover the ways that people construct meaningful sex. Much of the sexual ethnography of the first half of this century was devoted to the ideographics of sexual life. Malinowski on courtship in the Trobriands, Mead on Samoan sleep-crawling, Schapera on Kgatla theories of procreation—such anthropologists sought to contextualize the beliefs and behaviors of others. They sought to discover the rules for culturally appropriate sexual expression and to show the logical consistency of such rules within the larger worldview of those under study.

Still, the last 50 years of anthropology has witnessed a willingness not only to understand the particular but also to explain the universal and the generalizable. It is not enough simply to document the curiosities of sexual behaviors and beliefs and to point out that they are not so curious in the total cultural context of a specific society. Beneath all of the variation of cultural life lies a less variant set of problems to which humans (as biological beings) everywhere must respond.

Carole S. Vance (1991) has taken an analogous position in arguing against the dominant anthropological approach to sexuality, which she labels the cultural influence model. According to Vance, most anthropologists have viewed sexuality "as the basic material—a kind of universal Play Doh—on which culture works" (1991:878).

Commenting on Sumner's famous line that the "mores can make anything right," Robert Murphy notes that mores have a harder time making some things right than others. (Murphy, 1979). In that vein, even though the historically particular meanings of sexuality are indicative of the richness of human variation and ingenuity, sex is nevertheless the vehicle by which individuals, societies, and cultures are perpetuated. In short, sexual beliefs and practices can be seen as varying solutions to relatively invariant problems of human life.

People everywhere must find food in sufficient quantities to maintain the health and reproduction of the group. People everywhere must solve relational problems, to control conflict. People everywhere need positive emotional affect. The various materialist and ecological approaches in anthropology all have sought to explain the ways that cultures solve these and other problems as adaptations to their environments. Whether one begins with Harris' biopsychological constants (Harris, 1979) or Malinowski's list of basic needs (Malinowski, 1939), anthropologists must more fully explore the question of how sexual beliefs, behaviors, and structures contribute to the adaptive genius of a culture. Studying the systematic and adaptive potential apparent in sexual beliefs and behaviors would yield an understanding of human sexuality that is generalizable to the entire species. This would constitute a nomothetic study of human sexual life.

TOWARD A NOMOTHETIC ANTHROPOLOGY OF HUMAN SEXUALITY

The goal of a nomothetic anthropology of sexual life would be the elucidation not only of the factors that shape sexual beliefs and behaviors, but also of the larger processes that shape cultural systems in general. Ideally, a nomothetic study of sexuality should draw our attention to the similarities in adaptive demands that are made upon a diverse humanity. Its value is based on an etic understanding of culture, one in which meanings are relevant not only to the particular culture, but also to the general human context. What we propose is a holistic examination of the full range of human sexuality and its implications. This would include, for example, procreation, gender roles, and beliefs about sexuality for the individual, the society, and the species, as well as how these change over time.

A nomothetic anthropology of sexuality must begin with a consideration of the biology of sexual life, and there remains a great deal to learn about the biological parameters of human sexuality. Through the work of researchers such as Masters and Johnson (1966) we now understand a great deal about the physiology of sexual response. However, we know little about the effects of genetic variation on sexual behavior. For example, we still have little more than conjecture to suggest the existence of any biological bases for behavioral differences between males and females. It may be that there are no biological bases of any real significance. Certainly, this has been the anthropological consensus to date. Yet, however limited the significance of our biological parameters in human sexuality, it is clear that cultural patterns have developed on top of species-specific capacities and limitations. Thus, it is essential that we push forward the understanding of these biological bases.

In the search for the generalizable biological bases of sexuality, care must be taken to appreciate the wide range of individual variability. With so numerous a population as that of *Homo sapiens*, the potential variability of individual members of the species is great. Given the interaction between personal psychology and cultural patterning of behaviors, a nomothetic anthropology of sexuality will certainly be more probabilistic than absolute in character.

All societies attempt to control individuals' sexuality. Although this has benefits for the society, as well as for at least some of its individual members, it does compromise individual freedom. And, even though we would suggest that sexual beliefs and behaviors will reflect and support the society's mode of production, it is important to note that in sexuality, societal procreation and individual pleasure are inextricably integrated. Whereas the pleasures of sexuality may have served to ensure that individuals would achieve their procreational potential, *Homo sapiens* can find pleasure in sexuality apart from its procreational aspect. This fact undoubtedly has had great consequences for both physical (especially neurophysiological) and cultural evolution.

We realize that pleasurability may lead to individual behaviors within populations that are maladaptive for the group. Thus, we would suggest that it is unlikely that a society could or would bear the cost of promoting such behaviors for an extended period of time. In the long run, institutionalized sexual beliefs and behaviors are likely to support a society's technoeconomic adaptations to the environment.

Analyzing cultural change has proven extremely difficult, owing to both the complexity of life as a laboratory and to the general lack of necessary data, especially from the past. For example, although we posit that cultures are generally adaptive to local environments, we are also aware that even when environmental changes occur, cultures may not respond immediately. The structural and psychological costs of a specific cultural change may be so great as to negate the potential benefits of immediately modifying the culture. Still, the sexual meanings that a society constructs are likely to be consistent with (to support and promote) the modes of production and reproduction upon which the existence of its people depends.

Consider the case of Mormon polygyny. Polygyny had been a useful means of increasing family size (and, therefore, productive potential in agriculture) during the years of the great westward migration. Even though polygyny may have lost its demographic and productive utility after the Mormon settlers had established themselves in the Utah territory, the practice was maintained. It was not until the United States Congress demanded that polygyny be dropped as a condition for statehood that the practice was officially abandoned. Even so, there are an estimated 50,000 people who continue to live in polygynous households today, mostly in Utah and Arizona (Johnson, 1991).

Societies may attempt to meet perceived environmental needs through any of several mechanisms, such as controlling population growth or specifying gender roles. Usually this is done either through the belief structure or through systems of positive or negative sanctions. For example, religion is commonly used to prescribe or proscribe particular sexual attitudes and practices to enhance or to limit population growth. On the other hand, some societies have taken a more direct approach, utilizing taxes to encourage or discourage births. (China's practices in this regard have received much publicity in recent years.)

CONCLUSION

The anthropology of sexuality has been decidedly particularistic in orientation, aimed at interpreting the logic in the sexual beliefs and behaviors of specific peoples. This has given us a broad appreciation for the malleability of sexuality. Indeed, as Geertz has said, sex *is* experienced as a cultural activity, even if it sustains a biologically necessary process. The readings in this volume can only emphasize this fact.

Yet, Davenport's assertion to the effect that there is no such thing as *human* sexuality is premature. We would suggest that his conclusion is better understood as an artifact of a methodology that can produce no meaningful generalizations. To date, only the sociobiologists have made a serious effort toward producing a conception of panhuman sexuality. Yet, most of that work suffers from an impoverished understanding of the cultural nature of human sexual experience. We need not reduce all of culture to the realm of the biological when a century of anthropological research has shown it to be largely in the realm of the metabiological (see Sahlins, 1976).

Just as the readings in this volume argue eloquently for understanding the ways that particular cultures structure people's sexuality, so are they also an implicit call for a broader method in anthropological research. We need more work on sexuality from those research strategies that are specifically oriented toward seeking an explanation of "Culture"—as opposed to "cultures." We need cultural ecological studies to determine to what extent similar environments in the world yield similarly structured sexuality as an adaptive response. We need cultural materialist studies that examine how variations in societal modes of production and reproduction condition human sexual behavior and belief in general. We need historical materialist research to study how, given the broad structural and ideological changes that accompanied both the Neolithic and the Industrial Revolutions, food production and mechanization have led to adjustments in our sexuality.[5]

The past 50 years of anthropological research have given us a significant understanding of how human political systems develop. We have come a long way in explaining how human family forms adjust to changes in technoeconomic adaptations. Now it is time for anthropology to begin the research that will yield such an understanding of human sexuality as well.

NOTES

1. Most anthropologists are very wary of making statements to the effect that culture accounts for *all* behavior, or that there is no universal experience of humanity. Christopher Lasch, a sociologist, also warns against that view of the "overdetermination" of culture.
2. *Emics* refers to those explanations that are meaningful to the people under study.
3. *Etics* refers to explanations that—regardless of the meanings attributed to things by the people under study—are based in anthropological theory and are therefore meaningful to the scientist conducting the study.
4. We would point out to the reader that there is a danger here in oversimplifying the relationship between conflict and solidarity. That is, historical Marxists would remind us that *conflict and its resolution*, when seen as a single event, is productive of

solidarity. Thus, conflict and solidarity are not necessarily opposite states when viewed as a singular social process.

5. Historians have begun this sort of analysis most profitably. Estelle Friedman and John D'Emilio's *Intimate Matters: A History of Sexuality in America* (1988) is a superb work that links changing sexual morals and behaviors to periods of major economic transition.

REFERENCES

DAVENPORT, WILLIAM H. (1987). An Anthropological Approach. In James H. Geer and William T. O'Donohue (Eds.), *Theories of Human Sexuality.* New York: Plenum Press.

FREIDMAN, ESTELLE, AND JOHN D'EMILIO. (1988). *Intimate Matters: A History of Sexuality in America.* New York: Harper & Row.

GEERTZ, CLIFFORD. (1980). Sociosexology. *New York Review of Books,* January 24:3–4.

HARRIS, MARVIN. (1979). *Cultural Materialism: The Struggle for a Science of Culture.* New York: Random House.

HRDY, SARAH BLAFFER. (1981). *The Woman That Never Evolved.* Cambridge: Harvard University Press.

JOHNSON, DIRK. (1991). Polygamists Emerge from Secrecy, Seeking Not Just Peace but Respect. *New York Times,* April 9.

KOTTAK, CONRAD PHILLIP. (1991). *Anthropology: The Exploration of Human Diversity* (5th ed.). New York: McGraw-Hill.

LASCH, CHRISTOPHER. (1978). *The Culture of Narcissism: American Life in an Age of Diminishing Returns.* New York: Norton.

MALINOWSKI, BRONISLAW. (1939). The Group and the Individual in Functional Analysis. *American Journal of Sociology, 44*: 938–964.

MASTERS, WILLIAM, AND VIRGINIA JOHNSON. (1966). *Human Sexual Response.* Boston: Little, Brown.

MURPHY, ROBERT. (1979). *An Overture to Social Anthropology.* Englewood Cliffs, NJ: Prentice-Hall.

ROMER, ALFRED S. (1960). *Man and the Vertebrates: Vol. 1* (3rd ed.). Harmondsworth, England: Penguin. (Cited in Kottak 1991.)

SAHLINS, MARSHALL. (1976). *The Use and Abuse of Biology.* Ann Arbor: University of Michigan Press.

SYMONS, DONALD. (1979). *The Evolution of Human Sexuality.* New York: Oxford University Press.

VANCE, CAROLE S. (1991). Anthropology Rediscovers Sexuality: A Theoretical Comment. *Social Science & Medicine, 33*:8:875–884.

INDEX